ART LAW

ART LAW

The Guide for Collectors, Investors, Dealers, and Artists

RALPH E. LERNER
JUDITH BRESLER

Date of Publication: October 1989

SIXTH PRINTING

G1-1010
Practising Law Institute
New York City

pli

Library of Congress Catalog Card Number: 89-63038

ISBN 0-87224-000-2

To our own works of art—Alix and Ella

About the Authors

RALPH E. LERNER is an attorney at law and a partner in the law firm of Sidley & Austin in its New York City office. He earned a B.S. degree from Bucknell University, a J.D. degree from Boston University School of Law, and an LL.M. (Taxation) degree from New York University School of Law. Ralph specializes in art law and in individual tax, financial, and estate planning. He has published and lectured extensively on the tax aspects of art law and has chaired the art law seminar for the Practising Law Institute since 1974. He is married to Judith Bresler and lives in Scarsdale, New York.

JUDITH BRESLER is an attorney at law in private practice in Scarsdale. She earned a B.A. degree from the University of Pennsylvania and a J.D. degree from New York Law School, where she was on the Law Review. Judith specializes in art and entertainment law and was formerly a Vice President of Business Affairs with MGM/UA Corporation. Prior to that she was a General Attorney with the American Broadcasting Companies, Inc. She has published and lectured in the art and entertainment law fields. She is married to Ralph E. Lerner and lives in Scarsdale, New York.

Table of Chapters

Table of Contents

II *Artwork Transactions*

IV *Collectors*

V *Tax and Estate Planning*

Foreword

When I began my career in the art business more than fifteen years ago, almost every transaction was casual. Large deals were negotiated through an informal telephone conversation and consummated with a handshake. Now it seems that even simple purchases and sales are often accompanied by pages of legal documents. The escalation in the price of artworks coupled with a world made smaller by technologies has given rise to an array of art transactions demanding ever more sophisticated legal protections. To avoid the profusion of liabilities inherent in such transactions, it has now become essential for dealers, collectors, artists, and other art professionals to have a precise and up-to-date knowledge of art law. In fact, I have learned that even the most basic art business arrangements can be full of legal pitfalls that could have been easily avoided with the proper legal advice.

I have long hoped to find a concise, readable book that could provide the art world with guidance and solutions to the plethora of legal issues relating to the creation of art and to the art market. I am very happy to report that there is now just such a book. *Art Law* by Ralph E. Lerner and Judith Bresler succeeds remarkably well in presenting an in-depth, up-to-the-minute treatment of a broad variety of legal issues affecting art and the business of art. Additionally, this book contains a variety of model forms addressing specific business transactions, which should be extremely useful to the reader, along with source references should additional information be required.

Ralph and Judith are among the most knowledgeable people in the field and I strongly urge everyone who creates, appraises, buys, sells, invests in, or advises on art to take advantage of the authors' practical experience and avoid future problems by obtaining a copy of this book. It is a most welcome addition to the art world.

JEFFREY DEITCH

Jeffrey Deitch operates an Art Advisory Service in New York City. Prior to opening his own business in 1988, he was a Vice President of Citibank, where he was instrumental in the development of the bank's art advisory and art finance activities.

Preface

As the prices paid for works of art have spiraled ever higher, the need for a legal and general guidebook providing individuals with the nuts and bolts of Art Law has become increasingly crucial. In 1970 very little had been written on the topic of Art Law. At that time, Ralph E. Lerner published an article entitled "Estate Planning for the Art Collector" in Prentice Hall's *Successful Estate Planning Ideas*. This was followed by the first Art Law seminar run by the Practising Law Institute in 1974, which was chaired by Ralph E. Lerner. Following this, a number of texts have pioneered in the field of art law. These include Feldman & Weil, *Art Works: Law, Policy, Practice* (1974), revised as the two-volume Feldman, Weil & Biederman, *Art Law: Rights and Liabilities of Creators and Collectors* (1986); Duffy, *Art Law: Representing Artists, Dealers and Collectors* (1977); DuBoff, *The Deskbook of Art Law* (1977 & Supp. 1984); Merryman & Elsen, *Law Ethics and the Visual Arts* (2d ed. 1987); and Crawford, *Legal Guide for the Visual Artist* (1987). These publications are informative, and have served to stimulate interest in the field of Art Law. We gratefully acknowledge the background and assistance provided by those authors in the foregoing texts.

We felt, however, that there still did not exist a practical one-volume book that would extract the law and provide the requisite guidance to investors, collectors, dealers, artists, appraisers, and museum directors, as well as to practicing attorneys and others involved in the art world. Our book provides such guidance in what we hope is a concise and easy-to-understand manner.

We are grateful for the encouragement and support of William C. Cubberley of the Practising Law Institute, who envisioned this book and kept after us to ensure its completion. We also wish to acknowledge the dedicated staff of the Practising Law Institute—particularly its editors Karen P. Clancy and Henry W. Enberg. We are deeply appreciative of the guidance and suggestions proffered with such alacrity by our outside editor, Joan Welsh. We also wish to acknowledge the kind contributions of Constance Lowenthal, Victor Wiener, David Lowden, Jeffrey Haber, Warren P. Weitman, Karen Carolan, Stephen S. Lash, Peter O'Conor, and the Copyright Office of the Library of Congress. This book would not have been possible without the generous support of many people at Sidley & Austin in New York. This includes Ralph Lerner's secretary, Cathy Miller; his legal assistant, Joe Leptak; and the word processing department headed by Migna Huertas. In particular, Gene Philley, who did the bulk of the typing, deserves special thanks. We also wish to thank Mary Ann Porubic and Marianne De Santo, who helped with the typing, and the Sidley & Austin library staff headed by Sharon Nickerson and Margo Alleyne; the proofreaders, including David Garrick and Jim Shaffer; the Sidley & Austin duplicating department headed by Muhammed Habib; and our many other friends who offered patience, support, and understanding to make this book possible.

Introduction

On May 9, 1989, seventy-seven works of art sold at Sotheby's for $204.8 million dollars. The next night, ninety-three works of art sold at Christie's for $172.7 million dollars. Total sales for the fiscal year ending June 30, 1989, of just those two auction houses are expected to exceed $3 billion. Sales through other auction houses and private dealers will probably total another $3 billion. Obviously, art is big business and big money is involved.

Although most of us cannot afford to spend in excess of $1 million on a work of art, almost everyone has artwork hanging on a wall in his or her home or office. Any purchaser of a work of art should be generally familiar with what is now generically referred to as "art law." Art law encompasses all the legal ramifications involved in the creation, purchase, sale, or transfer of a work of art. Much like entertainment law, art law traverses a variety of legal disciplines, such as first amendment law, copyright law, commercial law, tax law, contract law, and torts.

This book addresses the topic of art law from five broad perspectives:

- The artist/dealer relationship
- The commercial aspects of buying and selling artwork either through a dealer or at auction
- The rights of the artist
- The tax and financial aspects of being either a collector, an investor, or a dealer in artwork
- The tax and estate planning problems for collectors and artists

DEALERS

Ordinarily, the legal relationship between artist and dealer, where the artist delivers works of art to the dealer for sale, is one of consignment. In such a case, the dealer becomes the artist's agent and the law of agency, with the applicable fiduciary duties attendant thereto, applies. Much of the time, the artist-dealer relationship is not memorialized in writing. This can work to the detriment of the dealer as where, in *O'Keeffe v. Bry*,[1] the failure of Doris Bry, the longtime agent of the artist Georgia O'Keeffe, to formalize the relationship in writing caused her to sustain considerable financial loss as well as the loss of Ms. O'Keeffe as a client. Lack of a formal agreement can also harm the artist by presenting problems of proof as to the parties' accord regarding various aspects of the agreement, such as the degree of artistic control retained by the artist concerning any exhibition of his or her works. A well-written agreement, on the other hand, serves to protect both parties: it can provide assurances to the artist that the works of art will be sold at prices acceptable to the artist and that there will be a proper and timely distribution of the sales proceeds. Moreover, such an agreement can protect the dealer who invests considerable time and money in the promotion of an artist against sudden desertion by the latter.

This book enumerates issues that should be addressed in the agreement memorializing the relationship between artist and dealer and provides a model of such an agreement at the close of the first chapter.

ARTWORK TRANSACTIONS

After art leaves the artist's studio, it enters the stream of commerce known as the art market.

Chapter 2 addresses in depth the spectrum of issues associated with the private sale of art through dealers or among individual collectors. Such issues include the incidence of theft and forgery that plagues the art market, along with resources available for the recovery of artwork; chain-of-title questions; compliance with particular provisions of the Uniform Commercial Code, including express and implied warranties and the attendant disclaimers; and statute-of-limitations questions. A model collector-dealer consignment agreement is found at the close of the chapter.

Some recent art purchases that have made headlines include the $53.9 million paid for Vincent Van Gogh's *Irises* in November 1987 and the $47.85 million paid for Picasso's 1901 self-portrait, *Yo Picasso*, on May 9, 1989. Both purchases—events that excited the art-buying public—took place on auction. Chapter 3 delves into the intricacies of the auction process.

An increasing number of state and government agencies have devoted portions of their public funds to the purchase and installation of works of art. These so-called public commissions are discussed in chapter 4, which also addresses the problems encountered by Richard Serra in the installation and ultimate removal of his sculpture, *Tilted Arc*, from the Federal Plaza in New York City.

Certain situations may propel the art collector into the role of plaintiff in a lawsuit: namely events casting doubt on a work's uniqueness, reputation, or physical condition. Chapter 5 ranges over this territory in its discussion of infringement, fair use, duplication by artists of prior themes, duty of care with respect to loans of art to museums and other institutions, and liability that may be incurred by experts for the rendering of an opinion on an artwork's authenticity or value. That last issue was the subject of a recent case,[2] treated in chapter 5, in which an art appraiser, placing a value of $50 on an original oil painting worth some thousands by J.F. Cropsey, a noted American artist of the Hudson River Valley School, was found liable for negligent misrepresentation.

Finally, chapter 6 addresses the international dimension to art transactions in focusing on the preservation of cultural property and its (illicit) transportation out of a country. Poorer nations are often looted of their cultural heritage by unscrupulous individuals willing to transport cultural property out of one country for the purpose of sale to collectors living in a more affluent nation. Legal restrictions exist and are mandated for the preservation of a sovereign nation's national heritage.

ARTISTS' RIGHTS

Some rights of the artist apply with particular force to the artist's person. Other rights attach primarily to the artistic creation.

Chapters 7 and 8 are in the first category. Chapter 7, which deals with first amendment rights, raises the question of whether the creation, exhibition, and placement of a work of art is a protected form of speech.

The distinctions among pure speech, conduct, and such visual speech as art are discussed, along with satire, public art, and the American and state flags as vehicles of protest. Limitations on freedom of expression, including obscenity, the right of privacy, and the right of publicity, are also examined.

Chapter 8 considers copyright issues specifically applicable to the visual artist. Material elements of the United States Copyright Acts of both 1976 and 1909 are discussed. Additionally noted is the Berne Convention Implementation Act, which became effective March 1, 1989, and how that amendment of the Copyright Act of 1976 affects the visual artist.

Chapters 9 and 10, in the second category, discuss rights that attach primarily to the artistic creation. Chapter 9 addresses an artist's moral rights:

- The right to determine when and how to make a work of art public
- The right to withdraw a work from publication
- The right to be recognized as the author of a work or, conversely, to disclaim authorship from distorted editions of a work
- The right, even after title to a work is transferred, to affirmatively prevent any tampering with the work

Chapter 10 focuses on the resale rights of the artist, raising the issue of whether an artist is entitled to a royalty on each resale of his or her work of art, much in the same way an author receives royalties from a book. Federal legislation is expected to be introduced in the next Congress that may affect both moral and resale rights, and various states have also introduced legislation addressing such rights.

COLLECTORS

As the price of art continues to escalate, the question of an individual's status as a collector, an investor, or a dealer becomes increasingly important. As a collector, an individual's expenses incurred in maintaining possession of a collection will, most likely, not be tax deductible. As an investor or a dealer, expenses incurred would be tax deductible. Chapter 11 discusses the current state of the law in drawing the line of demarcation between a collector and an investor, and sets forth the applicable rules for each category. The chapter also examines the differences between an investor and a dealer.

TAX AND ESTATE PLANNING FOR ARTISTS AND COLLECTORS

Finally, tax and estate planning for collectors (chapter 12) and artists (chapter 13) is a crucial topic that has not received the salient attention it demands. Chapters 12 and 13 discuss the tax and estate planning aspects of charitable contributions, the drafting of wills, the transfer of works of art from generation to generation, pitfalls to avoid, and other relevant legal matters affecting collectors and artists. The Internal Revenue Code is marked by frequent amendments and new rulings: this chapter includes a description of those provisions, including both the Tax Reform Act of 1986 and the Technical and Miscellaneous Revenue Act of 1988.

NOTES TO INTRODUCTION

1. O'Keeffe v. Bry, 456 F. Supp. 822 (S.D.N.Y. 1978).

2. Estate of Querbach v. A & B Appraisal Serv., No. L-089362-85 (N.J. Super. Ct. 1987).

I

Dealers

Artist / Dealer Relations

1

An art dealer is anyone who buys, sells, and trades in works of art, and the term "dealer" covers a spectrum of commercial entities: a dealer may be an individual proprietor dealing in a small stock and perhaps operating from home, a dealer may be the common one-branch commercial gallery, a dealer may be a gallery with numerous branches or franchised outlets, or a dealer may be part of a conglomerate. Although not all dealers are galleries, a great many are; therefore this chapter, except where specifically indicated to the contrary, uses the terms "dealer" and "gallery" interchangeably.

The dealer's role as seller is covered at length in chapter 2, and the technical definition for tax purposes of who is a dealer, as opposed to an investor or a collector, is dealt with in chapter 12. This chapter addresses the transaction between dealer and artist and the resultant rights and obligations of each of the two parties.

On rare occasions, such as when a dealer secures a commission to be executed by an artist, each aspect of the artist-dealer relationship must be negotiated and embodied in an agreement unique to the particular circumstances. However, the legal relationship between artist and dealer usually takes one of two basic forms: outright sale and, most frequently, consignment.

OUTRIGHT SALE

Generally

A dealer may buy works from the artist outright for purposes of resale. Unless a portion of the purchase price remains to be paid or unless the artist has reserved rights through the use of a contract of sale, the relationship between artist and dealer ends at the time of sale. Although traditionally quite common in Europe, outright purchase is rare in the United States. Many dealers do not have sufficient capital to buy works outright; even when they do have the capital, dealers are usually reluctant to use large amounts of their capital while assuming the risk of being unable to resell a purchased work at a reasonable profit.

The Outright Sale Contract

On those rare occasions when an outright sale between artist and dealer takes place, it should be evidenced by a written document. The dealer may require the artist to make written warranties with respect to the creation and ownership of the work. Moreover, the dealer should insist on a written document if any reproduction rights or other portion of the copyright is to be licensed, sold, or otherwise transferred. Under the Copyright Revision Act of 1976, unlike the rule at common law,[1] ownership of a copyright is distinct from ownership of the material object in which the copyright is embodied.[2] In other words, if an artist sells a painting, the copyright in the work is not transferred. If the buyer wishes to own the copyright in the work, he or she must obtain a specific written transfer of the copyright.[3]

The artist, too, should insist on a written contract for an outright sale. Aside from the memorialization of the sales price and the keeping of good records for tax purposes, any other rights that the artist is able to retain in the artwork beyond its sale to the dealer, such as the right to collect royalties on any subsequent sale of the work or the right to "borrow back" the work for various exhibitions, are rights that should be retained through the use of a written contract. It is the dealer, not the artist, who will have privity of contract with the next purchaser, and it is the dealer to whom the artist would look for recourse if agreements reached at the time of the original sale are not fulfilled. A written sales contract could require the gallery to include rights that inure to the benefit of the artist in any subsequent resale contract.

CONSIGNMENT

In General

Under the usual arrangement in the United States, the dealer accepts works from the artist on consignment. That arrangement permits the dealer, usually operating a gallery, to increase activity without tying up large amounts of capital.

Upon accepting works from an artist on consignment, the dealer becomes the artist's agent and the law of agency applies.[4] That is, in the hands of the dealer, the artwork becomes trust property, and the proceeds of sale become trust funds. A fiduciary duty is imposed on the dealer with respect to each work of art consigned,[5] and that fiduciary duty continues until the completion of the delivery of the sales proceeds to the artist.[6]

Fiduciary Duties

When a dealer accepts an artist's work on consignment and thereby becomes the artist's agent, the dealer is also considered to be a fiduciary.[7] As a fiduciary, the dealer is bound to the artist by an array of obligations:

- To care for and manage the consigned property prudently;[8]
- To deal fairly and honestly with the artist;[9]
- To account periodically to the artist as to dispositions of the property;[10] and

- To disclose to the artist all information relevant to the subject matter of the agency.[11]

What about the dealer who wishes to handle the works of two artists from the same "school"? If the artists are in competition, the dealer arguably should not handle them both, in view of the general rule that an agent should not act for two or more competing principals.[12] Although common industry practices fly in the face of that general rule, the prudent dealer should require the artist to acknowledge in writing that the dealer handles works by other artists who may occupy a competitive position.

Additionally, as a fiduciary, a dealer should not buy work outright from the artist unless the dealer has disclosed all the circumstances relating to the purchase, and the artist fully consents.[13] An example of a breach of fiduciary duty would be the dealer who purchases a work of art outright from the artist for, say $50,000 without divulging to the artist that he or she had secured an agreement to resell the work to a third party for, say, $250,000.

A dealer who breaches any fiduciary duties is liable to the artist for damages resulting from the breach.[14] If fraud or criminal intent can be proved under applicable criminal statutes, a dealer may be criminally liable for the wrongful conduct. In New York, for example, misappropriation by the dealer of either the artwork itself or the proceeds from sales may subject the dealer to liability on a theory of larceny.[15]

Exclusivity

Under section 2-306 of the Uniform Commercial Code (UCC) a dealer who has the exclusive right to handle an artist's works is obligated to use best efforts to promote sales. Correspondingly, the artist must use best efforts to supply works that he or she agreed to consign. The parties, however, may alter those obligations by contract.[16]

Borrowing from the analogous field of real estate brokerage, note that the dealer may have: (1) an exclusive agency or (2) an exclusive power to sell.[17] If the dealer is merely the exclusive agent, the artist can sell works directly without incurring any liability to the exclusive dealer.[18] On the other hand, if the dealer has an "exclusive power to sell," the artist is responsible for the commission if he or she effects a sale without involving the dealer.[19] Many dealers erroneously believe, however, that a mere exclusive agency entitles them to a commission on any direct sale by the artist. Although that belief is contrary to the legal principles that apply, many an artist, dependent on a dealer to promote reputation and sales, prefers to pay a dealer a commission, even when, strictly speaking, there is no legal obligation to do so, rather than risk angering the dealer.

The situation is similar with barter arrangements: many dealers with some form of exclusivity *vis-à-vis* an artist's work feel entitled to compensation after the artist exchanges artwork for, say, a sailboat, medical services, the use of a summer house, or even the work of another artist. Whether a barter transaction violates a dealer's exclusivity depends on the intention of the artist and the dealer. In any event, it is clearly difficult, if not impossible, for a dealer with an exclusive power to sell to monitor the barter transactions of an artist. It is equally clear that barter transactions, when engaged in by the artist to any great extent, may actually divert a significant portion of the artist's salable production from the dealer.

Contractual Rights

Historically, an arrangement between artist and dealer for exhibition and sale of the artist's work was cemented by a handshake. Artists in general and many dealers believed that to memorialize their agreements in writing would constitute an insult to the uniqueness of the artist-dealer relationship. Although an oral agreement may indeed be as valid as a written one, varying state laws impose particular restrictions limiting the scope of oral agreements enforceable in a court of law. In New York, for example, an oral contract that cannot be performed within one year is unenforceable,[20] and the term of such an oral agreement may be difficult to establish. Consequently, with increasing awareness of their rights, many artists today insist on a written contract defining the artist-dealer relationship.

Necessity of a Written Contract: *O'Keeffe v. Bry*

If an artist and a dealer envision a relationship beyond the most casual and transient, the advisability of a written contract cannot be overstated. However long-standing the relationship, failure to formalize it in writing can give rise to tragic results for both the dealer and the artist. The suit Georgia O'Keeffe brought against her longtime agent, Doris Bry,[21] illustrates the kind of loss a dealer may suffer in the absence of a written contract.

For many years O'Keeffe employed Bry as a commissioned sales agent authorized to sell not only the full array of O'Keeffe's art, but the photographic works of Alfred Stieglitz, O'Keeffe's late husband, as well. At some point O'Keeffe and Bry had a falling-out that ended the agency and gave rise to the suit by O'Keeffe for the return of the art and the photographs and an accounting from Bry for any money due on the sales. Once the artwork was transferred to a safe place, Bry filed various counterclaims, including several for breach of contract. In one counterclaim Bry alleged that in return for agreeing to act as exclusive agent, market-maker, publicist, and in-house curator for O'Keeffe's art during O'Keeffe's life, O'Keeffe agreed to make Bry the exclusive agent and market-maker during O'Keeffe's lifetime. In another counterclaim, Bry alleged that in return for the above-stated services to O'Keeffe during O'Keeffe's life and to her estate, O'Keeffe had agreed to name Bry the executor of the O'Keeffe estate and to empower Bry to act as sales agent after O'Keeffe's death. O'Keeffe sought dismissal of those counterclaims, alleging that they were barred by the statute of frauds. Bry argued that the process of discovery might yield documents containing writings satisfying the statute of frauds requirement.

Discovery unearthed a number of O'Keeffe's wills and trusts, as well as a document known as the Harvard Agreement, which provided that O'Keeffe would leave a gift of her works to Harvard University. The document also stated that O'Keeffe expected Bry to supervise the disposition of all or most of O'Keeffe's paintings at the time of her death and that to the extent Bry did not do so, Harvard was responsible for disposing of them, and that O'Keeffe wished, but did not direct, that Harvard employ Bry for the sale of the paintings.

The United States district court reviewed those documents, determined that New York law applied, and then examined Bry's first counterclaim—that O'Keeffe promised her a lifetime exclusive agency—in light of the relevant provision of New York's Statute of Frauds,[22] which requires a writing when an agreement, like the Harvard Agreement, cannot be fully performed before the conclusion of a lifetime (in this instance, O'Keeffe's). The court found no written evidence in the Harvard document or anywhere else of a grant of a lifetime exclusive agency to Bry by O'Keeffe. The court found the Harvard Agreement language to be merely precatory, not language to constitute a binding commitment. Moreover, the court found that the Agreement was concerned not with Bry's lifetime agency, but rather with the distribution of O'Keeffe's work after her death.

Bry had also argued that, under New York case law, a "confluence of memoranda,"[23] that is, the Harvard Agreement and other documents, when pieced together, satisfied the statute of frauds. The court, however, held that a "confluence of memoranda" may satisfy the statute of frauds only when at least one document already exists establishing the underlying contractual commitment. The court further reasoned that additional memoranda could be looked to only to supply essential terms of an alleged agreement and only when the additional memoranda specifically referred to the transaction covered by the core document.[24] Since the court found no core document evidencing a lifetime, exclusive agency, Bry's counterclaim was dismissed.

Another of Bry's counterclaims—that in return for her professional services to O'Keeffe during O'Keeffe's life and to her estate after O'Keeffe's death, O'Keeffe promised to name Bry executor and to empower Bry to act as a sales agent after O'Keeffe's death—was based on alleged oral promises, which were found to be unenforceable.[25] Bry's promises to render professional services during O'Keeffe's lifetime and, thereafter, to O'Keeffe's estate came within the statute of frauds, since her performance could not be completed during O'Keeffe's lifetime. O'Keeffe's alleged promises were promises to make a testamentary disposition, and, as such, were governed by section 13-2.1 of the New York Estates, Powers and Trusts Law. Because the promises were not evidenced in the Harvard Agreement, the wills, or any other document, they were held to be unenforceable, and that counterclaim was dismissed.[26] Bry would have been able to protect herself if there had been a written contract along the lines of the model agreements included at the end of this chapter.

Limitations on a Contract

The previous section stressed the importance of a written contract to memorialize the artist-dealer relationship. Equally significant is the need to draft the contract, whether of consignment or of outright sale, with an eye to averting any dire consequences that may arise as a result of its existence. For example, a contract should be specific in defining its intent; otherwise, it runs the risk of being recharacterized by the courts. In one instance, a contract between an artist's widow and a dealer provided that the widow "sell" her late husband's work to the dealer, and the dealer contracted to use his best efforts to sell the work and pay the widow one-half of the sale proceeds. The Surrogate Court found that the contract had elements of both a sale and a consignment, and, therefore, considered extrinsic evidence with respect to the parties' intent. The Appellate Division upheld the Surrogate's conclusion that the agreement was properly treated as one of consignment.[27]

Like any other commercial agreement, the artist-dealer contract may be subject to attack as being "unconscionable" under the UCC[28] and may also be vulnerable to challenge as a breach of fiduciary obligations.[29] In New York, where artist-dealer consignment relationships are governed by statute,[30] any provision of a contract in which the consignor (the artist) waives any provision of that article is void, except for the provision that treats sale proceeds of fine art as trust funds for the benefit of the artist. That provision alone under particular circumstances and within limits may be waived.[31] Even broader nonwaiver provisions *vis-à-vis* the consignor currently exist in the counterpart artist-dealer statutes of a number of other states.[32]

The Consignment Contract

As noted earlier, the legal relationship between artist and dealer is generally either that of seller to buyer or that of consignor to consignee, most often the latter. A number of artist-dealer consignment contract forms are currently in use. Some of those forms, such as those developed by the various volunteer lawyer organizations throughout the country and the form developed by Artists Equity Association, Inc., are geared to reflect the interests of the artist. Other contract forms, such as those prepared and used by the major galleries, reflect the interests of the dealer.

The following checklist of issues that most frequently arise between artist and gallery is by no means exhaustive, nor do all of the issues arise in every instance of negotiation. Many of the points are of mutual concern, some of the issues speak mainly to the artist, and others address largely the gallery. Negotiation, compromise, and an insightful view as to where problems may arise play pivotal roles in the successful conclusion of an agreement between artist and dealer.

1. *Contracting Parties.* An agency to deal in an artist's work normally terminates upon the artist's death.[33] If the gallery is to have any right to deal in the artist's work after his or her death, that right should be provided in the contract, and the applicable law should be checked to ensure that the covenant is enforceable. If the artist creates works of art through a corporation, a specific provision as to when the agency terminates must be included, since the artist's corporation does not automatically terminate upon the death of the artist. Additionally, the legal entity of the gallery should be specified.
2. *Limited (Exclusive) Agency.* There should be a provision that establishes the principal-agent relationship between artist and gallery, with the artist being the principal and the gallery the agent. This provision calls forth the fiduciary responsibility of the gallery to the artist within the context of their relationship; the gallery has a legal obligation to act only in the artist's interest and to forgo all personal advantage aside from the agreed-upon compensation for its services as agent.

   The contract should address the manner and the extent of exclusivity, if any, that the gallery has in dealing in the artist's work. If the gallery has no exclusivity, the contract should address what priority, if any, *vis-à-vis* other parties, the gallery has in making selections from the artist's work.

   If the gallery does have exclusivity, the issue must be addressed territorially; perhaps the gallery's exclusive right is limited to a particular geographic area. The exclusivity must also be addressed in terms of the type of work consigned; on occasion, an artist may wish to appoint one gallery his agent for his sculpture and another gallery his agent for his drawings or paintings and still a third for his graphics. The exclusivity must be addressed in terms of its nature: Does the gallery have merely an exclusive agency, or does it have an exclusive power to sell? (See pages 6-7.) Whichever is the case, the personal relationship between artist and dealer makes it advisable to anticipate and address in the contract these further issues:

- The extent of studio sales, if any, permitted by the artist;
- Whether the gallery should be paid a commission on studio sales and, if so, whether it should be at a lower rate, since the work was not subject to the gallery's effort and overhead expense;
- Whether studio sales not exceeding a specified maximum amount should be exempt from gallery commissions;
- Whether sales of particular types of works or sales to family and friends should likewise be exempt from or, at least, subject to a lower gallery commission;
- The extent of barter transactions, if any, to be permitted the artist and whether barter transactions shall be exempt from or subject to full or lower gallery commissions;
- The extent, if any, of charitable and other gifts permitted by the artist and whether those transactions shall be exempt from or subject to full or lower gallery commissions;
- Whether the gallery is entitled to a full or lower commission, if any, if a gallery customer or a party unrelated to the gallery directly commissions the artist to create a work.

Moreover, regardless of whether a gallery has any exclusivity to deal in an artist's work, the contract may address the question of whether the gallery should receive a courtesy credit on loans of the artist's work.

3. *Duration*. The length of the term of consignment should be specified. The term may end on a date certain, or it may be contingent on, for example, the number or dollar value of sales made by the gallery or on the artist's productivity. If there are any options to extend the term, those, too, should be included in the contract.

   The artist should give serious consideration to the duration of his or her initial term of consignment. A new artist may find it detrimental to be tied too long to a single gallery. On the other hand, the gallery needs the association with the artist to be lengthy enough to provide it with the proper incentive to promote the artist's works and to benefit from the artist's (it is hoped) increased reputation over the years. Most galleries want to retain the artist at least through two exhibitions of his or her work.
4. *Scope and Description of Work*. The works consigned should be described as specifically as possible. That includes listing the media of all works and addressing the issue of availability of the artist's past and future work for sale by the gallery. The gallery may wish to include a provision that continuation of the contract or, say, regular monthly payments to the artist be conditioned on the artist's creating and providing the gallery with a "reasonable number" of new works throughout the term.
5. *Territory of Consignment*. Just as the territory of exclusivity should be delineated, so, too, should the territory of representation be specified. An artist, for example, may engage a gallery in New York to represent his or her works throughout the eastern portion of the United States and may simultaneously engage a gallery in Los Angeles to represent such works throughout the western United States.
6. *Selling Prices*. The contract should make provision for the initial setting of prices, which are generally jointly established by artist and gallery. In addition, the contract

should provide for a periodic review of prices in light of changes in the artist's reputation and the condition of the art market.

Also to be considered is the matter of discounts. It is customary for galleries to give discounts to certain classes of purchasers, such as museums, architects, interior decorators, and, at times, other artists, certain collectors, and other galleries. Discounts to such purchasers are beneficial to both the artist and the gallery, as they encourage the sale of the artist's work to buyers in a position to promote the work's exposure. The agreement should specifically identify those classes of purchasers entitled to a discount and the percentage of discount those purchasers shall receive. Alternatively, the agreement may specify the maximum amount of any discount the gallery may give without consulting the artist, or the agreement may require the gallery to consult the artist before any discount is given. A discount of 10 percent to 20 percent is customary, but the gallery may request authority in the contract to grant greater discounts to certain preferred buyers.

A gallery may also seek the right to make outright purchases from the artist at a discount. In that case, the artist should seek to keep the discount at a minimum or to limit the number of outright purchases permitted the gallery during the agreement term; after all, the artist stands to gain little from any increase in value in the works sold outright to the gallery and stands to lose much if the gallery, as seller, is positioned as a direct competitor. The artist also wants to keep the gallery from selecting what may be the artist's best work to inventory against a time when that work has increased in value.

The contract should also make provision for negotiation of the price of works, if any, commissioned directly by the gallery or by a customer of the gallery. And, the contract may address the issue of the right, if any, of the gallery to rent a work of art in lieu of or in addition to the right to sell it. As a practical matter in a consignment arrangement, however, the right to rent a work does not exist unless it is specifically provided for, since the dealer is under a fiduciary duty to sell the works of art.

7. *Gallery Commission.* This is one of the key provisions of the contract, as it sets forth how much of the purchase price is retained by the gallery and how much goes to the artist. Gallery commissions can range from 25 percent to 60 percent, with commissions averaging between 33⅓ percent and 50 percent. The agreement should specify the percentage of the gallery commission, and can even provide that it is subject to periodic review by both parties. Generally, the better-known galleries obtain higher commissions. An artist with a well-established reputation, however, whose works have a known market and command high prices, can usually negotiate a favorable, that is, lower commission rate. In any event, an artist should consider, among other factors, how aggressively a gallery will promote his or her work when endeavoring to arrive at a fair commission.
8. *Computation of Gallery Commission: Net Price Method.* Under this arrangement, the artist, with respect to each work, designates the price that must be paid net to the artist, and the gallery retains any sales proceeds in excess of that figure. Provision should be made for an accelerated review of the net prices set by the artist in the event of a rapidly changing market. Moreover, here, as in the method described below, the effect of discounts and returns must be considered in describing the manner of computing commissions.
9. *Computation of Gallery Commission: Percentage of Sales Price.* Under this more common method of computation, the gallery, with respect to each sale of the artist's

work, receives a commission in an amount equal to an agreed-upon percentage of the sale proceeds. If the production of the works has been of significant expense to the artist, as in the cases of sculpture involving costly materials or foundry work and graphics involving printer's expenses, the commission is generally computed solely on the amounts in excess of the artist's direct costs. Under that arrangement, the artist supplies the gallery with a statement of direct costs for each work of art before a price is set and the work is placed on sale.

10. *Payments to Artist.* An artist is customarily paid by the gallery on either a monthly or a quarterly basis. The interval and the time within which payments must be made should be specified, as well as the amount of the payments and the currency in which the payments will be made. Special provision may be made for the timing of payments when an installment sale to a customer is involved.

    The artist may wish to be paid an advance on commissions upon entering into the contract. If that arrangement is agreed to, it should be included in the contract, along with the amount of the advance. The contract should then also address the following issues: the effect of money due the artist from sales on the amounts to be advanced; when, if at all, the advance is repayable to the gallery if a sufficient number of works are not sold; whether the advance is repayable by the artist with work and, if so, how and when the work is selected and the process of its valuation for purposes of repayment.

    If the artist intends to use a royalty reservation agreement—that is, a contract in which the artist retains certain residual rights to the artwork sold—he or she should require the gallery to obtain the purchaser's execution of such an agreement. (See discussion of resale rights on pages 477-500.) Also, when such an agreement is used or when state law provides for the payment of royalties to artists on resale of their works, the contract should provide that the gallery furnish the artist with the names and addresses of purchasers of the works so that the artist can monitor subsequent resales. That provision may disturb the gallery, however, since it could place the artist in the role of direct competitor.

A related question arising from the use of the royalty agreement or from the existence of royalty legislation, one that should be addressed by both parties, is whether the gallery is contractually entitled to receive any portion of any royalty payments accruing to the artist from subsequent sales of the artwork. Actually, from the artist's stance and regardless of whether he or she uses a royalty reservation agreement, it is always a good idea to require the gallery to furnish the name, address, and telephone number of each purchaser. Doing so enables the artist to verify with the purchaser the price actually paid for a work of art and enables the artist to keep a mailing list of purchasers, should his or her relationship with the gallery terminate.

11. *Crating and Shipping.* The contract should designate which party assumes the costs for crating and shipping the artist's work to and from the gallery and the artist's studio or storage facility. On some occasions the parties share the costs. Some factors to consider in determining responsibility for the costs are the location of the studio or storage facility in relation to the gallery, whether the works must be crated and shipped from other locations, and the scale of the works to be crated and shipped. For example, the shipping of a Henry Moore or David Smith sculpture can be a major expense because of the sculpture's size and weight.
12. *Storage.* If the works require storage during the time of the consignment, the party responsible for paying the

storage fees should be designated, as should the location of the storage facility. Moreover, the extent of access to the facility by the artist should be agreed on.

13. *Insurance.* Customarily, a gallery insures works consigned to it under an all-risk "floater" policy, putting on a "binder" each time new works come in. Generally, galleries insure works at between 40 percent and 70 percent of the sales price. Although it is ideal for the artist to be named on the policy as the beneficiary in case of a claim, that is not always possible. When work is consigned by an artist to a gallery, the work is still owned by the artist. Therefore, the consignment agreement should specify who is entitled to the insurance proceeds. The gallery insures the work for only a percentage of the sales price because it owes the artist only a percentage of the sales price (fair market value) of the work. The contract should set forth the amount of coverage by the gallery.

    The artist may also want the contract to specify where the works are insured—for example, are the works insured while in transit to and from the gallery's place of business, and are they insured while on loan to locations outside the gallery's place of business? The artist should attempt to have the gallery insure the works from the moment they leave the artist's studio to the moment they are returned or sold. The artist should secure his or her own coverage for those situations in which the works are not covered by the gallery's policy.

14. *Framing.* If applicable, the contract may address the following matters: which of the parties shall bear the initial burden of framing expense, with, perhaps, a cap on such expenditure; the amount of artwork to be framed; the specifications of the framing; the treatment of the framing expense on works sold; and the ownership, at the end of the term, of the frames of unsold works.

15. *Promotion.* The parties may want the contract to specify

the degree of marketing activity and promotion expected of the gallery in connection with exhibitions of an artist's work. That activity includes the production and preparation of catalogs, photographs of the artist and his or her work, biographical material, and other advertising and promotional matter.

The contract may clarify the number and the type of promotional items, such as catalogs and photographs, to be produced for each exhibition and specify which party shall assume the expense of production. Ownership and control of each promotional item must also be made clear. In addition, the gallery may want the right to use and publish the name, likeness, and biography of the artist for promotional purposes. The artist may want the right to review all such material.

16. *Artistic Control.* The artist may want the contract to indicate the degree of control, if any, held by the artist in connection with the inclusion of his or her consigned work in gallery group exhibitions and in other exhibitions. That control is important, as it permits the artist to withdraw works from an exhibition that is not appropriate for displaying the work. In addition, the artist may want to require the gallery to consult with the artist before hanging any exhibition. Further, if the artist is concerned that the work may fall into "inappropriate" or ill-meaning hands, he or she may want a contractual grant of a veto over purchasers of his work.
17. *Gallery Exhibitions.* The contract should clearly indicate the number of solo and group exhibitions (perhaps pending the artist's consent) to be required of the gallery. As to each exhibition, the parties may wish to address the issues of the date, duration, space allocated to the artist's work, and selection of works to be shown. The contract may also deal with the following matters as needed:

- Control over installation;
- Expenses of partitions and pedestals;
- Scope and the expense of "opening night" events;
- The artist's availability for those opening events;
- Benefit exhibitions and the artist's availability;
- Scope and expense of announcements of exhibitions and other mailings;
- Disposition of the proceeds from the sale of exhibition catalogs.

18. *Sales Tax.* The parties should designate who is responsible for collection and payment of any applicable sales tax. The artist should require the gallery to collect and pay the taxes and to indemnify the artist against any liability for the taxes.
19. *Damage to or Loss or Deterioration of Consigned Works.* The contract should state who is responsible for loss or deterioration or damage to the consigned works and when that responsibility begins. The contract may further address, in the event of damage or deterioration: selection of the restorer, the expense of outside restoration, compensation for any restoration performed by the artist, the artist's right to inspect the restoration, and the financial treatment of total or partial losses.
20. *Reproduction Rights.* The contract may address copyright notice. Copyright notice may be placed on the back of a painting or may be placed on other works in such a manner so as not to interfere aesthetically with the appearance or the appreciation of the work itself. (See discussion of copyright in chapter 8.) Alternatively or in addition, the contract may, as appropriate, require the gallery to affix a copyright notice on any reproduction or

image of the consigned work, such as a promotional brochure prepared by the gallery. The purpose of affixing a copyright notice is to help keep a work from unintentionally falling into the public domain or, put another way, to benefit the rights holder of the artwork by preserving the reproduction rights and other rights of copyright in and to the work.

The contract may also address the following issues: who has control over the right to reproduce the image of the consigned work before sale; what reproduction rights, if any, will be retained by the rights holder upon the transfer or sale of the artwork; and what portion, if any, of the copyright will be transferred upon the sale or transfer of the artwork itself.

21. *Loans and Displays.* The artist may wish to require the dealer to impose certain exhibition obligations on the purchaser, such as making the works available for display in museum shows. The artist may require the dealer to limit the purchaser in the number of times a piece of art can be loaned and the duration of each loan. In addition, the artist may wish to exercise some censorship over the occasions on which the work is exhibited. As a practical matter, however, such rights are of limited application and may have a negative effect on the fair market value of the work.
22. *Warranties of the Artist.* The gallery may want the artist to warrant that the works are original creations and that they do not impinge on any personal or property rights of third parties. Clearly, a gallery does not want to be involved in litigation brought by a third party because of an alleged invasion of privacy or copyright infringement resulting from the exhibition or sale of a work. Because of the gallery's potentially great liability to a purchaser in the event that the gallery is not in a position to convey good title to a purchaser, the gallery may want the artist

to warrant that he or she has good and unencumbered title to the consigned works.

23. *Artist's Right of Accounting.* It is in the artist's interest to designate in the contract the frequency with which he or she will be entitled to a full accounting of money paid and money due from the gallery. The contract should specify the degree of completeness required in the accounting and, in addition, should afford the artist or the artist's designated representative the right to inspect all books and records of the gallery relating to the sale of the artist's works.

    In addition, the artist may require the gallery to deliver a complete statement of inventory at regular periodic intervals, including all or some of the following information: enumeration of the particular artworks sold and the dates, amounts, and terms of each sale, that is, whether cash, barter, exchange, credit, or partial payment; a listing of all unsold artworks, their locations, and whether, if in the possession of the gallery, those works are currently being displayed and, if so, for what length of time.

24. *Billing and Terms of Sale.* In the event sales on an installment basis seem likely, the contract may address the following issues: allocation of payments between the artist and the gallery, allocation of interest payments between the artist and the gallery, qualified installment sales for tax purposes, and the gallery's responsibility to file a financing statement under the UCC. (See pages 27-28.)

    With respect to any purchases, installment or not, the contract may name the party responsible for determining the creditworthiness of any potential purchaser and which party shall bear the risk of loss in the event the purchaser defaults.

    For those occasions when a buyer may purchase artwork from a gallery using, as currency, works by other artists accepted by the gallery, the contract may address the issues of the valuation of those works, the procedure whereby exchanges ("trading up") can occur, and returns.

The contract may make provision for duplicate statements to be sent to the artist and the gallery with respect to framing, packing, shipping, and other charges.

25. *Status of Consigned Artworks and Sales Proceeds.* The contract may confirm that ownership of the works is vested in the artist, pending sale. In those states where artist-art dealer consignment statutes have not been adopted, consigned works may be subject to claims of the dealer's creditors. Accordingly, in the absence of statutory protection, the artist may wish to require the gallery to take the steps necessary to prevent the subjection of the consigned works to such claims. The contract may also highlight the fiduciary nature of the relationship between the artist and the art dealer and designate the proceeds from the sale of the consigned work as trust funds for the benefit of the artist. Further, where an artist-art dealer consignment statute is in effect, the contract may address any waiver by the artist of his or her rights to the extent permitted by that statute.

The gallery may wish to reserve the right to purchase the consigned works for the minimum designated sales price or, in the case of a "net price" arrangement, for the "net price." If so, that right should be specifically provided for in the contract.[34] Even if the artist grants such a right to the gallery, in a number of states, including New York, artist-dealer consignment law requires the dealer fully to disclose relevant information concerning the purchase to the artist,[35] and the artist's waiver, where permitted,[36] and consent should be obtained at the time of the gallery's purchase.

A gallery may wish to reserve a lien on the consigned works for any amounts, such as advances, storage charges, or freight costs, for which the artist may be contractually responsible.[37]

26. *Artist's Retention of Works.* The artist may reserve the right to retain such work as the artist shall determine.
27. *Arbitration.* If a reasonable arbitration arrangement can be agreed to by the parties, the gallery and the artist may wish to include an arbitration provision in the event of future disputes. The American Arbitration Association now has art experts on whom it can draw if so required.
28. *Assignment.* Because the relationship between artist and gallery is often very personal, the artist may want the contract to provide that the gallery may not transfer its responsibilities or rights under the agreement to a third party, at least not without the artist's prior written consent.
29. *Termination.* The contract should have a clause citing the circumstances under which the agreement can be terminated. The clause should refer to any other termination provisions in the agreement and may include death, disablement, involuntary bankruptcy, and dissolution. In the event that one party wishes to be released from the agreement before the normal termination date, language could be used permitting each party to terminate the agreement on, for example, sixty days' written notice to the other, allowing for an orderly termination of the relationship on fairly short notice.

    In addition, the contract may make provision, in the event of termination, for the gallery within a certain time to conclude its sale of the artist's works; settle the artist's account; transfer to the artist the balance of the money due; return all of the artist's works in the gallery's possession; and allow the artist access to all photographs, transparencies, catalogs, and other materials relating to the artist or the artwork.

STATE STATUTES ON CONSIGNMENT

To date, at least twenty-nine states have enacted legislation governing consignment of artwork for exhibition or sale.[38] Passage of those laws was fueled by concern about the inadequacy of then-existing civil and criminal law remedies for misappropriation of sale proceeds or consigned property and about certain abusive practices.

For example, some dealers attempt to undermine the principal-agent relationship between artist and dealer and the fiduciary obligations inherent in that relationship by means of disguised purchase agreements and contractual waivers. Under those circumstances, the relationship on its face resembles that of debtor and creditor, with the artist's only remedy often being a civil action for contractual amounts due if the dealer refuses to pay the artist. If the artist is reluctant to sue, the dishonest dealer may be in a position wrongfully to retain artwork or the artist's share of sale proceeds.

It was that sort of victimization of the artist in New York City during the early 1960s that gave rise to the passage of artist-dealer consignment legislation in New York in 1966. By clarifying the fiduciary nature of the consignment arrangement in the artist-dealer relationship, the New York statute lay the foundation for the application of criminal sanctions for misappropriation of the artist-consignor's property. Within the following twenty years, at least twenty-eight other states have followed suit, to enact art consignment legislation, many using New York's statute as a model.

Consignment Statutes in General

At the core of most artist-dealer consignment statutes is the delineation of the fiduciary nature of the relationship. Most of the statutes are based on the following premises: unless a work has been delivered to a dealer pursuant to an outright sale or the artist has received full compensation for the work, it is a delivery on consignment, and upon delivery of a consigned work, the dealer is the agent of the artist, the work delivered is trust property, and the sale proceeds are trust funds held for the benefit of the artist-consignor. Since many artists do not bother with a written consignment agreement, the statutes serve to protect the artist. A few statutes—Michigan's and Connecticut's, for example—extend to the nonartist consignor the benefits of the same fiduciary relationship with the dealer as is enjoyed by the artist delivering to the dealer a work of his or her own.

Consignment Statutes and the UCC

Most consignment statutes, including those of New York and of California,[39] provide that the rules of the consignment statute will prevail over any conflicting provision of the UCC. One case in which conflict ordinarily arises involves the gallery's creditors. In the absence of a consignment statute, a consigned artwork or the proceeds of its sale may be subject to the claims of creditors of the consignee-gallery. That is because the law ordinarily governing that issue is section 2-326(3) of the UCC, which provides that consigned goods are subject to the claims of creditors of the consignee, even when title is reserved, unless the consignor (1) complies with the applicable sign-posting law, (2) files a financing statement under the UCC as in effect in the state governing the transaction, or (3) can show that the consignee is "generally known by his creditors to be substantially engaged in selling the goods of others." Where they exist, the consignment statutes in a majority of the states either reverse or exempt the artist-dealer relationship from the effects of UCC section 2-326(3) or the state equivalent, thereby making it entirely clear that a gallery's creditors may lay no claim to consigned artworks.

In those states having no artist-art dealer consignment legislation, the consignor-artist should comply with the filing provisions of Article 9 of the UCC[40] and give written notification of the filing to any prior secured parties of the consignee-gallery.[41] A form of consignment sale reserving security interest is found at the end of this chapter.

Risk of Loss or Damage

The UCC may also come into play with respect to the issue of which party, the artist or the dealer, bears the risk of loss for works damaged or stolen while in the dealer's possession. Under the general rule of liability established in section 2-327(2)(b) of the UCC, the return of the goods is at the buyer's (the dealer's) risk. Although California's statute,[42] as well as the statutes of several other states,[43] is consistent with that section of the UCC—that is, a burden is placed on the dealer either through negligence or strict liability—other state statutes, such as that of New York,[44] are silent on the matter. In the instance of a silent statute, it is questionable as to which of the two parties, the consignor or the dealer, bears the risk of loss of or damage to the consigned work, that is, whether the UCC or the usual laws of principal and agency govern. In the latter case, the risk of loss is on the consignor unless the dealer was grossly negligent.[45]

As to who between dealer and prospective buyer bears the risk of loss of a work of art, section 2-327(1) of the UCC allocates the risk to the dealer (the seller), when the sale is on approval, until the time of acceptance of the artwork by the buyer.[46]

Reclamation by Artist

If a dealer sells a consigned work to a bona fide purchaser but fails to pay the artist, and the artist has not filed a financing statement, the artist-consignor cannot reclaim the work. That is because section 9-307 of the UCC provides that a buyer of consumer goods takes free of a security interest even though perfected if he buys without knowledge of the security interest unless prior to the purchase the secured party has filed a financing statement covering such goods. State consignment statutes do not change that result.[47]

The Artist's Waiver

A question frequently arises as to whether the artist is permitted, in states having consignment statutes, to waive statutory rights by contract. Although a number of states, including California,[48] permit no waiver of rights by the artist, others do permit limited waivers on behalf of the artist. New York's legislation, for example, permits a limited, written waiver of that portion of the statute that provides that sales proceeds are trust funds for the benefit of the artist,[49] excluding from the waiver the first $2,500 of proceeds received in any twelve-month period, commencing with the date of the waiver. Therefore, in New York a dealer may use a waiver to share with the artist in proceeds of installment purchases, rather than pass along all first payments to the artist and wait for his share.

COOPERATIVE GALLERIES

Unlike the typical dealer-operated gallery, cooperative galleries are run by artists, usually as joint ventures for the purposes of exhibiting their works and offering them for sale. Generally, cooperative galleries are formed by artists who are experiencing difficulty obtaining exposure for their works in local commercial galleries. Although some such galleries have endeavored to function as tax-exempt entities as a way to reduce overhead costs, as a practical matter, tax-exempt status is unavailable if some part of the sales proceeds goes to the benefit of the individual artists.[50] Moreover, in most cases tax-exempt status is not necessary, since the cooperative gallery rarely operates at a profit. Cooperative galleries are not always successful, since the artists' lack of business acumen, when coupled with an artistic temperament, can interfere with effective merchandising techniques. Moreover, the better artists of a cooperative, when recognized, often resent supporting their less fortunate colleagues and move on, leaving the cooperative in the hands of unappreciated and unsuccessful artists. That there are, nevertheless, so many cooperative galleries in operation today attests to the hardships that many artists experience in securing commercial representation.

In any event, those artists who do form cooperatives are advised to formalize the arrangement by written agreement to avoid future misunderstandings. Among the topics that should be covered are:

- Liability for rent and other expenses
- Admission of new members
- Staffing of the gallery
- Types of exhibitions
- Frequency and dates of exhibitions
- Extent of promotional activity
- Sales commissions of the gallery
- Insurance of works
- Public liability insurance
- Monthly dues or fees and
- Withdrawal from the venture

Member artists should be aware that their liability to third parties is joint and several. If the artists consider the potential liability (other than liabilities that can be protected against through insurance) to be substantial, they may wish to incorporate the gallery. If the corporation is adequately capitalized and corporate formalities are observed, the members should be shielded from personal liability for the obligations of the corporation.

THE DEALER AND POTENTIAL TORT LIABILITY

As noted earlier, the relationship between artist and dealer is unique because of its often personal nature. Because it is a personal relationship, it is often fraught with complexities that, to the unwary dealer, can all too readily become liabilities.

The dealer should be aware that there is an inherent conflict of interest if he or she also serves as an artist's business adviser, and the dealer can be held liable for negligence in rendering such advice.[51] If a dealer signs a contract with an artist who is already under contract to another dealer, the second dealer may be subject to liability for inducing a breach of contract.[52] Even in the absence of an agreement between an artist and a dealer, a dealer who actively solicits an artist from another dealer may be subject to a suit for interference with advantageous business relations.[53] Moreover, under applicable criminal statutes, a dealer can be held jointly liable with the artist for exhibiting work that is obscene,[54] that constitutes a public nuisance,[55] or that defames the United States flag[56] or displays other protected symbols or emblems.[57] Further, if a work invades the privacy of another[58] or constitutes a defamation,[59] the dealer can be held civilly liable to the injured party or parties. (If works in an exhibit represent recognizable persons or contain their names, the dealer should consider obtaining releases from those persons.) In displaying a work, a dealer may also be civilly or criminally liable with the artist for infringement of copyright.[60]

NOTES
to Chapter 1

1. *See, e.g.*, Pushman v. New York Graphic Soc'y, Inc., 287 N.Y. 302, 42 N.E.2d 249 (1942).

2. 17 U.S.C. § 202 (1989). *See also* discussion of copyright, *infra* chapter 8.

3. 17 U.S.C. § 204 (1989).

4. RESTATEMENT (SECOND) OF AGENCY § 1 (1958).

5. *Id.* at § 13; *see also* Britton v. Ferrin, 171 N.Y. 235, 63 N.E. 954 (1902).

6. *Id.*

7. *Id.*

8. RESTATEMENT, *supra* note 4, at § 379.

9. *Id.* at §§ 13, 379.

10. *Id.* at § 382.

11. *Id.* at § 381.

12. *Id.* at § 394.

13. *Id.* at §§ 387, 388, 390, 393.

14. *Id.* at § 399, 407; *see also*, Estate of Mark Rothko, 84 Misc. 2d 830, 379 N.Y.S.2d 923 (1975), *modified and aff'd*, 56 A.D.2d 499, 392 N.Y.S.2d 870 (lst Dept.), *aff'd*, 43 N.Y.2d 305, 401 N.Y.S.2d 449 (1977), *on remand* 95 Misc. 2d 492, 407 N.Y.S.2d 954 (1978). The case is discussed at pp. 688-89.

15. N.Y. PENAL LAW § 155.05 (McKinney 1975 & Supp. 1989).

16. UCC § 2-306(2). All states in the United States except for Louisiana have adopted Article 2 of the UCC. In addition, Article 2 has been adopted by the District of Columbia, Guam, and the Virgin lslands.

17. *See* E. BISKIND & C. BARASCH, THE LAW OF REAL ESTATE BROKERS § 67.03 (1969 & Supp. 1983).

18. *Id.*

19. *Id.*

20. *See* N.Y. Gen. Oblig. Law § 5-701 (McKinney 1989) for an enumeration of those types of contracts requiring a writing.

21. O'Keeffe v. Bry, 456 F. Supp. 822 (S.D.N.Y. 1978). For another case illustrating the importance of finalizing art arrangements in written form, see Gordon v. Herstand & Co., N.Y.L.J., Oct. 14, 1986, at 6, cols. 4–6 (Sup. Ct. 1986); N.Y.L.J., Apr. 29, 1987, at 7, cols. 2–3 (Sup. Ct. 1987), between an art consultant and a gallery owner.

22. N.Y. Gen. Oblig. Law § 5-701(a)(1) (McKinney 1989).

23. *O'Keeffe v. Bry* cited Crabtree v. Elizabeth Arden Sales Corp., 305 N.Y. 48, 110 N.E. 551 (1953), in support of her argument. Conversely, the court noted that *Crabtree*, 305 N.Y. at 55, as well as every other case cited by *Bry*, permitted the use of a "confluence of memoranda" so long as at least one document existed establishing the basic, underlying contractual commitment. That continues to remain the law in New York. *See* Manala v. Milford Management Corp., 559 F. Supp. 1000 (S.D.N.Y. 1983).

24. O'Keeffe v. Bry, *supra* note 21, at 829.

25. *Id.* at 830.

26. *Id.*

27. *In re* Friedman, 91 Misc. 2d 201, 397 N.Y.S.2d 561, *aff'd*, 64 A.D.2d 70, 407 N.Y.S.2d 999 (2d Dept. 1978).

28. *Id.*

29. *See* Rothko, *supra* note 14.

30. N.Y. Arts & Cult. Aff. Law § 12.0l (McKinney 1984 & Supp. 1989).

31. *Id.* at § 12.0l(1)(b).

32. Among the states that have adopted a consignor-art dealer statute that contains a nonwaiver provision broader than that of New York are Arizona, Arkansas, California, Colorado, Connecticut, Florida, Illinois, Kentucky, Massachusetts, Ohio, and Wisconsin. Iowa's statute contains a nonwaiver provision vis-à-vis the art dealer. For citations of those and consignor-art dealer statutes from other states, *see* note 38.

33. *See* Estate of Franz Kline, N.Y.L.J., Mar. 31, 1964, at 14, cols. 6-7 (Sur. Ct. 1964).

34. *See* Estate of Franz Kline, *supra* note 33.

35. N.Y. Arts & Cult. Aff. Law § 12.0l, *supra* note 30.

36. As indicated *supra* in note 32, a number of states have enacted consignor-art dealer statutes containing broad nonwaiver provisions.

37. *See* Sidney Janis Ltd. v. de Kooning, 33 A.D.2d 555, 304 N.Y.S.2d 826 (lst Dept.), *aff'd*, 26 N.Y.2d 910, 258 N.E.2d 396, 310 N.Y.S.2d 97 (1970), in

which the court held that a statutory factor's lien did not give a dealer a lien on an artist's works for advances made to the artist in the absence of a contractual provision to that effect.

38. ALASKA STAT. § 45.0.326 (Supp. 1986); ARIZ. REV. STAT. ANN. §§ 44-1771 to -1778 (Supp. 1988); ARK. STAT. ANN. §§ 68-1806 to -1811 (Supp. 1985); CAL. CIV. CODE §§ 1738, 1738.5-.9 (1988); COLO. REV. STAT. §§ 6-15-101 to -104 (Supp. 1986); CONN. GEN. STAT. ANN. §§ 42-116k to -116m (West Supp. 1987); FLA. STAT. ANN. §§ 686.501 to .503 (West 1989); IDAHO CODE §§ 28-11-101 to -106 (Supp. 1988); ILL. REV. STAT. ch. 121½, ¶¶ 1401–1407 (West Supp. 1988); IOWA CODE ANN. §§ 556D.1 to .5 (West 1989); KY. REV. STAT. ANN. § 365.850-.990 (Michie Co. 1987); LA. REV. STAT. § 51:2151 (1987); MD. COM. LAW CODE ANN. § 11-8A-01 to -04 (1983), 11-8A-03 (Supp. 1986); MASS. ANN. LAWS ch. 104A, §§ 1-6 (Law. Co-op. Supp. 1987); MICH. COMP. LAWS ANN. §§ 442.311-.315 (West Supp. 1987); MINN. STAT. ANN. §§ 324.01-.10 (West Supp. 1987); MO. REV. STAT. §§ 407.900-.910 (Vernon Supp. 1987); MONT. CODE ANN. tit. 22, §§ 2-50l to -505 (1985); N.J. STAT. ANN. 12A:2-230, 2-331 (Supp. 1989); N.M. STAT. ANN. §§ 56-11-1 to -3 (Supp. 1987); N.Y. ARTS & CULT. AFF. LAW art. 12 (McKinney Supp. 1989); N.C. GEN. STAT. §§ 25C-1 to -5 (Supp. 1986); OHIO REV. CODE ANN. §§ 1339.71-.78 (Page Supp. 1986); OR. REV. STAT. §§ 359.200-.240 (1985); PA. STAT. ANN. tit. 73 §§ 2121 *et seq.* (Purdon Supp. 1987); TENN. CODE ANN. §§ 47-25-1001 to -1007 (1986); TEX. OCC. & BUS. CODE ANN. art. 9018 (Vernon Supp. 1987); WASH. REV. CODE ANN. §§ 18.110.010-.905 (Supp. 1987); WIS. STAT. ANN. §§ 129.01-.08 (West Supp. 1986).

39. N.Y. ARTS & CULT. AFF. LAW, *supra* note 30, at § 12.01; CAL. CIV. CODE, *supra* note 38.

40. U.C.C. § 2-326(3).

41. U.C.C. § 9-408 permits a financing statement to be filed that uses the terms "consignor" and "consignee," rather than "secured party" and "debtor."

42. CAL. CIV. CODE, *supra* note 38.

43. See, for example, the consignment statutes for the states of Arkansas, Colorado, Connecticut, Massachusetts, Missouri, Minnesota, Montana, Oregon, Washington, and Wisconsin, *supra* note 38.

44. N.Y. ARTS & CULT. AFF. LAW, *supra* note 30, at § 12.01.

45. RESTATEMENT, *supra* note 4, at ch. 13. Under the general law of bailment, which can govern certain situations, such as the loaning of artwork to museums and other institutions, the risk of loss in many cases is borne by the bailor (lender). See the summary of the *Colburn* and *Gardini* cases and the general discussion of bailment at pp. 263-68.

46. U.C.C. § 2-326. Goods delivered primarily for use constitute a "sale on approval," whereas goods delivered primarily for resale constitute a "sale or return."

47. See the general discussion on secured transactions at pp. 103-111. If the consignor-artist *does* file a financing statement, he or she may be able to reclaim the work.

48. See, for example, the consignment statutes for the states of Arizona, Arkansas, California, Colorado, Connecticut, Ohio, Massachusetts, and Wisconsin, *supra* note 38.

49. N.Y. Arts & Cult. Aff. Law, *supra* note 30, at § 12.01.

50. Rev. Rul. 71-395, 1971-2 C.B. 228. To support its view, the IRS cited Treas. Reg. § 1.501(c)(3)-1(d)(1)(ii). The IRS subsequently affirmed and clarified its position in Rev. Rul. 76-152, 1976-1 C.B.152.

51. *See* W. Keeton, R. Keeton, D. Dobbs & D. Owen, Prosser and Keeton on the Law of Torts § 32, at 185 (5th ed. 1984).

52. *Id.* § 129, at 979.

53. *Id.* § 129, at 981.

54. *See* discussion of obscenity at pp. 333-41.

55. *See* discussion of artwork and public nuisance at pp. 331-33.

56. *See* discussion of artwork and the United States flag at pp. 327-39.

57. *See* discussion of emblems and insignia at pp. 329-31.

58. *See* discussion of invasion of privacy at pp. 342-43.

59. *See* discussions of defamation at pp. 333 and 342-43.

60. *See* discussion of copyright infringement at pp. 243-46.

FORMS

FORM

MODEL ARTIST-GALLERY AGREEMENT

AGREEMENT made as of the ___ day of ___, 198___, between ______, residing at __________, __________ (hereinafter referred to as the "Artist"), and ________________________, a ____________ Corporation having an office at __________, ________________ (hereinafter referred to as the "Gallery").

W I T N E S S E T H:

WHEREAS, the Artist is in the business of creating works of art and the Gallery is in the business of selling works of art; and

WHEREAS, the parties hereto wish to enter into a business relationship for the sale by Gallery of works of art created by Artist.

NOW, THEREFORE, in consideration of the premises, and of the mutual promises and undertakings set forth below, the parties hereto agree as follows:

1. *Exclusive Agent.* Artist hereby appoints Gallery, and Gallery hereby accepts such appointment, to serve as the sole and exclusive agent and representative of Artist with respect to works of art created by Artist (hereinafter sometimes referred to as the "Artist's Works"). The term "Artist's Works" shall include paintings, drawings, collages, assemblages, sculptures, theatrical sets and installations, and all other artistic creations, but exclude prints and the production and distribution of prints.

2. *Territory.* The representation covered by this Agreement shall be worldwide.

3. *Term.* This Agreement shall commence on   and terminate on   . Unless notice to the contrary is given by either party to the other sixty (60) days prior to   , this Agreement will automatically be renewed for two (2) additional years. Notice shall be given by certified mail by any party to the other at the addresses shown above.

4. *Sales Prices.* The sales prices of the Artist's Works ("Sales Prices") shall be set by the Gallery in a written schedule and be subject to approval by the Artist by her signing such schedule, which approval shall not be unreasonably withheld.

5. *Commission to Gallery.* The Gallery shall be entitled to receive a commission for the sale of any of the Artist's Works in an amount equal to fifty percent (50%) of the Gallery's receipts from such sale in excess of the Artist's Direct Costs for the work of art sold. The term "Direct Costs" shall mean the Artist's direct out-of-pocket costs in creating a particular work of art, including, without limitation, cost of materials,

fabrication, and labor (other than that of the Artist). The Artist agrees to supply the Gallery with a statement in reasonable detail of such Direct Costs for each work of art prior to the time that the work of art is placed on sale with the Gallery and the price thereof set by the Gallery. The commission referred to in this paragraph shall be considered earned by the Gallery only when such Direct Costs have been credited to Artist's Sales Account as described in paragraph 6 below and when the sales proceeds are actually received by the Gallery. The remaining fifty percent (50%) of the sales proceeds in excess of the Artist's Direct Costs shall be credited to the Artist's Sales Account as described in paragraph 6 below.

6. *Artist's Sales Account.* The Gallery shall maintain an Artist's Sales Account in order to keep a record of monies due the Artist from the Gallery. Upon the sale by the Gallery of any of the Artist's Works, the Gallery shall first credit the Artist's Sales Account with the Direct Costs for the work of art sold. The Gallery shall then credit the Artist's Sales Account with fifty percent (50%) of the Gallery's receipts from such sale over such Direct Costs. The Artist, Artist's attorney, and Artist's accountant shall have the right to inspect the Artist's Sales Account and other books and records of the Gallery relating to the sale of the Artist's Works from time to time during normal business hours upon the Artist's giving the Gallery three (3) days written notice. The Artist, Artist's attorney, and Artist's accountant shall maintain in strict confidence all information relating to the Gallery obtained in the course of such inspection.

7. *Payments to Artist.* The Gallery shall at the end of each calendar month pay to the Artist any balance in the Artist's Sales Account.

8. *Expenses of Sales.* The Gallery shall pay all crating and shipping expenses of the Artist's Works from the Artist's studio or storage facility to the Gallery and from the Gallery to the Artist's studio or storage facility.

The Gallery shall keep the Artist's Works insured up to an amount not less than that required to pay the Artist the amount she would be entitled to receive if the Artist's Works had been sold at the Sales Prices under the terms of this Agreement. The Gallery shall pay for such insurance from the time such Artist's Works leave the Artist's studio or storage facility for delivery to the Gallery until they are returned to the Artist's studio facility or until they are sold and leave the Gallery's possession.

The Gallery shall pay all of the Gallery's costs and expenses in connection with the sale of the Artist's Works, including without limitation all costs and expenses for all catalogs, photographs, advertising, preview, promotion and openings, such expenditures to be within the sole discretion of the Gallery.

In order to promote sales, and for the purpose of advertisement and promotion, the Gallery shall have the right to use and publish the name, likeness, and biography of the Artist and to reproduce and distribute material incorporating photographs of the Artist's Works. The Gallery shall have the right to sell and retain the proceeds from the sale of catalogs produced by it, but shall not sell any other items referred to in this paragraph without the prior written approval of the Artist. The artist shall cooperate with the Gallery in such advertising and promotional efforts.

The Gallery agrees that no amount expended by it under this paragraph shall be deducted from the amount due the Artist pursuant to the Artist's Sales Account.

9. *Gifts and Exchanges.* The Artist may, from time to time, make a reasonable number of gifts of the Artist's Works to anyone of the Artist's choice. The Artist may also make a reasonable number of exchanges of the Artist's Works for services or with other artists. The Artist shall promptly notify the Gallery about any such gift or exchange and provide sufficient information to permit the Gallery to keep accurate records of the Artist's Works.

10. *Shows.* During any two-year period of this Agreement, the Gallery shall arrange for at least one exhibition and show of the Artist's Works at the Gallery's office in New York City. In connection with such exhibition and show the Gallery shall produce at its expense an appropriate catalog of the Artist's Works. The Gallery, with the approval of the Artist, may arrange for other exhibitions and shows at other locations of the Artist's Works, so long as any such exhibition or show is on a financial basis no less favorable to the Artist than the terms and conditions set forth in this Agreement.

11. *New Works of Art.* During the term of this Agreement, the Artist shall create and provide the Gallery with new Artist's Works for sale by the Gallery, it being understood however that the Gallery may also offer for sale any Artist's Works heretofore produced by the Artist (and the Artist shall cooperate with the Gallery in this regard). In the event the Artist fails to create and provide the Gallery with a "reasonable number" of new Artist's Works of reasonable size during any consecutive six-month period, the Gallery may terminate this Agreement.

The Artist agrees to use her best efforts to create and provide the Gallery with new Artist's Works sufficient to have at least one exhibition and show of such works in the Gallery's main gallery no later than the eighteenth month during the two-year term of this Agreement.

12. *Sales by Artist.* The Artist shall not exhibit or sell any works of art created by the Artist, whether from the Artist's studio or otherwise, to clients, private or public, without the prior consent of the Gallery. Such sales, if allowed, will be fully commissionable to the Gallery at the time of payment for such sale unless specifically excepted in writing signed by the Gallery.

13. *Purchase by Gallery.* The Gallery, with the written consent of the Artist, which consent shall not unreasonably be withheld, may from time to time purchase for cash (or by credit to the Artist's Sales Account if there is at the time a deficit in such Account) any of the Artist's Works for its own account at fifty percent (50%) of the Sales Price in excess of the Direct Costs plus the Direct Costs for such Artist's Works. In the case of sales by the Artist to the Gallery under this paragraph, the Gallery shall receive no commission and the total proceeds of such purchase by the Gallery shall be credited to the Artist's Sales Account.

14. *Artist's Works Retained by Artist.* Any other provision of this Agreement to the contrary notwithstanding, the Artist shall have the right to retain for herself such of the Artist's Works as she in her sole discretion shall determine.

15. *Installations.* The Artist shall have the right to create "installations" for exhibition from time to time in her sole discretion and at her sole expense, provided, however, that she has consulted with the Gallery.

16. *Copyright.* The Gallery shall take all steps necessary to ensure that the Artist's copyright to the Artist's Works is protected and shall inform all purchasers of the Artist's Works that the Artist has retained the copyright and the copyright is not being transferred.

17. *Termination.* This Agreement may be terminated by the Gallery in accordance with paragraph 11 of this Agreement or otherwise as expressly provided in this Agreement, may be terminated by the Artist or the Gallery in accordance with paragraph 3 of this Agreement, or shall terminate upon the death of the Artist.

Upon any event of termination, the Gallery shall have ninety (90) days to sell the Artist's Works and to settle and transfer to the Artist the balance due the Artist in the Artist's Sales Account. During such ninety-day (90-day) period following an event of termination, the Artist agrees to make no sales of the Artist's Works either by herself or through another dealer.

Upon any event of termination, the Gallery, at its sole expense, shall within ninety (90) days return to the Artist's studio or storage facility all of the Artist's Works within the possession of the Gallery.

Upon any event of termination, the Gallery shall allow the Artist access to all photographs, transparencies, catalogs, and other materials pertaining in any way to the Artist or the Artist's Works. Such access shall be allowed in such manner to allow the Artist to duplicate any such materials at the Artist's expense. The Artist shall have access to such materials for as long as the Gallery remains in business and the Gallery agrees not to dispose of such materials without first offering them to the Artist.

18. *Arbitration.* Any controversy or claim arising out of or relating to this Agreement, or the breach thereof, shall be settled by arbitration in accordance with the Commercial Arbitration Rules of the American Arbitration Association, and judgment upon the award rendered by the arbitrators may be entered in any court having jurisdiction thereof.

19. *Entire Understanding.* This Agreement contains the entire understanding of the parties with respect to the subject matter hereof; it may not be changed or amended except in writing signed by the parties; and it shall be construed and governed in accordance with the laws of the State of New York.

20. *Binding Effect.* This Agreement shall inure to the benefit of, and shall be binding upon, the successors, heirs, executors, and administrators of the parties.

This Agreement is not assignable by the Artist or the Gallery.

IN WITNESS WHEREOF, the parties have hereunto set their hands and seals as of the date first above written.

GALLERY, INC.

By:______________________________

President

____

Artist

FORM

ARTIST CONSIGNMENT WITH SECURITY AGREEMENT

[DATE]

ABC Galleries, Inc.
1234 Madison Avenue
New York, NY 10000

You hereby acknowledge receipt of the following oil painting created by me (the "Painting"):

Title:
Medium:
Size:
Signature:
Date:

The purchase price of the Painting less your commission of _______ percent shall be delivered by you to me within ten (10) days from and after the date on which delivery shall be made by you under any sale or contract of sale. Title to, and a security interest in, the Painting (and any proceeds thereof) is reserved in me until sale of the Painting by you, whereupon the proceeds of such sale shall be held for me and delivered (except for such commission set forth above) to me as herein provided. You shall have no right to sell the Painting until the Form UCC-1 is signed by you and returned to me for recording.

In the event of any default by you, I shall have all of the rights of a secured party under the Uniform Commercial Code.

You agree to hold the Painting for sale at a price of $ ____________. You agree that you will not sell the Painting for a price less than $ ____________ without permission from me.

You agree specifically to inform any purchaser of the Painting from you of the existence of my security interest as stated herein. I agree to sign and file a Form UCC-3 termination statement once I have approved the terms of the sale of the Painting.

Notwithstanding the foregoing, at any time prior to any sale of the Painting by you, at my request you will deliver the Painting to me immediately upon receipt of any instruction from me.

____

Artist

The foregoing is confirmed and
agreed to: ABC Galleries, Inc.

By:________________________________

II

Artwork Transactions

Private Sales 2

In many ways the purchase and sale of fine art is unique among commercial transactions. First, the property involved is often singular and irreplaceable. Second, since the market value of a work of art is largely dependent on the artist's reputation at the time of the sale, and given that reputation is a matter of public whim, the value of the artwork may fluctuate widely. Third, art is often purchased on impulse by a shockingly uninformed buyer. All too often, the buyer fails to secure a written purchase contract (let alone have it reviewed by legal counsel), neglects to have the property physically inspected or appraised by a professional or to have its title searched, and, when the work is prepared in editions, neglects even to inquire about the technique of production.

Defects abound in artwork as frequently as in other property. Accordingly, the art buyer should observe the same precautions ordinarily used by the prudent buyer in other commercial transactions of like value. Those precautions are addressed at length throughout this chapter.

As a further spur to prudence, the prospective buyer should be aware that the escalation in the value of artwork and the traditionally casual commercial practices in the industry have caused numerous art transactions to flourish in a climate of abuse. Among the most serious concerns from the buyer's perspective are the circulation of stolen artworks, fakes, and forgeries. Another widespread abuse is the sale of fine art multiples of prints and sculpture without furnishing the buyer with adequate information as to their nature or uniqueness, thereby misleading the buyer. To protect the consumer against shoddy production practices, a number of states have enacted disclosure legislation regulating the selling of prints. Disclosure legislation covering reproduction of sculpture has also been proposed in at least one state. See the discussion of such legislation at pages 94-96.

ART THEFT

The International Foundation for Art Research (IFAR) estimates that there are billions of dollars worth of stolen and smuggled art currently in circulation. Recent sensational thefts include:

- A Vermeer, a Goya, and nine other paintings stolen in May 1986 from a collector's mansion in Russborough, Ireland. The total value of that theft is estimated at $30 to $45 million.[1]
- Two paintings by Fra Angelico and twenty-six other paintings and drawings by old Dutch and Italian masters were stolen from a commercial gallery in February 1988. That $6 million theft is the largest single art theft reported to date in New York City.[2]

Art theft is one of the fastest growing crimes both in the United States and around the world; statistics indicate that art theft increased at a disturbing rate in the past decade alone. Although the art buyer must be aware of this sobering trend and its effects on subsequently acquired title,[3] the resources currently available for both investigation of title to artwork and recovery of stolen art should give some comfort.[4]

Resources for Recovery and Investigation of Title

Among the principal organizations focusing on art theft throughout the world are the Art Dealers Association of America

(ADAA), IFAR, and the Art Program of INTERPOL. Both ADAA and IFAR are located in New York City.

ADAA has maintained an extensive archive of stolen fine art since 1971 and accepts reports of art theft from private persons, art dealers, museums, and institutions. The organization publishes a monthly notice containing descriptions and photographs of stolen artwork and distributes it to art dealers, museums, auction houses, associations, publications, and law enforcement personnel throughout the world.

IFAR was established in 1968 by a group of attorneys, art historians, and scientists to study and combat fraudulent art practices. Since 1975, IFAR has maintained an archive, computerized since 1983, of art thefts from domestic and foreign dealers, private collections, and museums. IFAR responds to inquiries from any interested persons. In addition, IFAR publishes and distributes its magazine *IFARreports* ten times each year. The magazine contains a "Stolen Art Alert," compiled in cooperation with the art community, insurance companies, police, the FBI, and INTERPOL, which lists entries on stolen art objects, and includes an "Index of Stolen Art" as part of its year-end issue.

The Art Program of INTERPOL (the International Criminal Police Organization, a group of police agencies in 134 countries[5]) is primarily involved with dissemination of information about stolen or forged art believed to have been smuggled across international borders. The United States, a member nation since 1938, transmits to IFAR, ADAA, the FBI, customs officials, and other select agencies monthly stolen-property notices received from INTERPOL's headquarters in France. In addition, INTERPOL publishes and distributes to appropriate agencies in all member nations a biannual poster of stolen objects, compiled from the monthly notices.

Since May 1979, the FBI has maintained a National Stolen Art File in Washington, D.C., for artwork valued at $2,000 or more. Reports of art thefts are forwarded from either local police or regional FBI offices to FBI headquarters in Washington, D.C.

Only law enforcement agencies may request to search the stolen art file, however, and the request must be prompted by suspected criminal activity.

FORGERIES

Diverse forces operate to encourage art forgery today:

- Demand exceeds the supply of quality authentic work, driving prices up and creating an incentive for fraud;
- American and European modern art can be imitated with relative ease and is currently popular (older paintings are frequently more difficult to imitate, since the Old Masters usually primed their own canvases and ground and mixed their own pigments, resulting in more individuality of material and workmanship);
- Valuable works with provenance deranged by war have occasionally been found in unusual places;
- Purchasers often fail to seek expert assistance;
- Serious collectors who have been defrauded may perpetuate the deceit, desiring to avoid publicity lest public awareness of the deception impair their credibility as connoisseurs;
- Dealers, in an effort to protect their sources, frequently fail to provide purchasers with accurate documentation of provenance; and
- Because of difficulty in obtaining recognition, artists are tempted to make forgeries.

Ancient Forgeries

People have forged art objects for centuries. The Romans often created copies of Greek sculptures. Albrecht Durer, the renowned German printmaker of the late fifteenth and early sixteenth centuries, was often victimized by forgeries of his prints and ended a series of his woodcuts with the curse: "Woe to you! You thieves and imitators of other people's labor and talents. Beware of laying your audacious hand on this art work."

Modern Forgeries

We have colorful art forgers in our own time. One is David Stein, a former art dealer who can paint in the style of Picasso, Chagall, Matisse, Miro, Braque, Klee, and other great artists. After producing forty-one paintings in the styles of such noted artists, forging their signatures to the paintings and selling them, he was convicted in the United States in 1967, on a plea of guilty to six counts of counterfeiting artwork and grand larceny. After serving his jail sentence, he was deported to France, where he was subsequently convicted and imprisoned for selling art forgeries there. While confined, Stein was allowed to continue painting "in the style of" famous artists, so long as the works bore his own signature, rather than those of the masters he copied. The paintings Stein executed in prison were exhibited and sold in 1969 in London by an affiliate of the Wright Hepburn Webster Gallery of New York. In 1970 the New York gallery advertised the exhibition of almost seventy Stein paintings by placing in its window a notice that read, "Forgeries by Stein." The show drew large numbers of people willing to pay high prices, and the New York Attorney General sought to enjoin the exhibition and sale on the grounds of its being a public nuisance, contending that Stein's name could easily be removed from the master look-alikes, and that the paintings would eventually flood the market as original Chagalls, Picassos, etc.[6] The court rejected that argument, holding that the paintings could not constitute a public nuisance on the mere possibility of the future commission of a crime.[7]

Modern forgeries abound. During the 1950s and 1960s, thousands of forged Utrillos flooded the market, significantly devaluing a number of genuine works not having the benefit of unblemished provenance. In 1977 thousands of forged De Chiricos, along with materials used to manufacture sophisticated false authentications were discovered in a forgery factory and a warehouse in Milan.

Still more recent is the prevalence of fraud in the Dali print market, which has caused consumers in a number of states to be swindled out of millions of dollars,[8] resulting in a number of criminal prosecutions. In Hawaii in January 1989, for example, a federal grand jury returned a ninety-three-count indictment on charges of mail fraud, wire fraud, and securities fraud against Center Art Galleries-Hawaii, Inc. and its officers. Since the late 1970s, Center Art has sold large numbers of so-called Dali lithographs at prices ranging from $1,000 to $20,000 each that, the indictment alleges, were mere photomechanical reproductions of little value. The indictment alleges, among other charges, that the gallery represented to buyers that Dali had personally participated in the creation of the original lithograph when there was no participation by Dali, and that the gallery sold these Dali reproductions on "presigned" paper that was never even seen by Dali. A trial is not expected before late spring.[9]

In other instances, the Federal Trade Commission (FTC), in bringing suit against an Arizona art gallery[10] and an Illinois art gallery[11] for unfair and deceptive trade practices in selling artworks purportedly by Dali, Picasso, Miro, and others, obtained, as of this writing, a permanent injunction and an order that it provide redress to customers in the amount of $4.6 million as to the Arizona gallery and a preliminary injunction as to the Illinois gallery.

The exploits of other well-known forgers—such as Hans van Meegeren, Alceo Dossena, the Spanish Forger, and Elymr de Hory—highlight the ease with which works of art can be faked, as well as the degree of success attainable by the forgers.

Before the end of World War II, Hans van Meegeren, a Dutch forger of art, had masterfully faked a number of paintings by Jan Vermeer of Delft and Pieter de Hoogh. Alceo Dossena, an Italian "King of Forgers," who lived from 1878 to 1937, was able to recreate a wide range of styles and periods, ranging from ancient

Greek to Renaissance. The Spanish Forger, who lived around the turn of the century, probably in Paris, created "original" Medieval and Renaissance manuscripts and paintings inspired by the Masters. He worked with ancient wood or parchment and caused the finished works to be passed off as newly discovered creations of the Masters. Between 1961 and 1967, Elymr de Hory imitated an estimated $60 million worth of paintings and drawings of such contemporary artists as Picasso, Derain, Dufy, and Modigliani that were sold to collectors, art dealers, and museums.

When forgeries are well done, they can confound the experts and wreak havoc at auction houses. One recent example embodied in a lawsuit now settled (also discussed in chapter 3) concerned the purchase of a Fabergé egg by an Iranian businessman living in New York. In 1977 the businessman bought the egg from Christie's in Geneva for $250,000 upon representations that it had belonged to the Russian Imperial family, but later he doubted its authenticity and refused to pay for it. Christie's sued and presented an expert who pronounced the egg an authentic "Imperial," whereupon the purchaser ultimately paid $400,000 for it (including $150,000 in legal fees). In 1985, however, when the same purchaser consigned the egg for auction to Christie's in New York, that same expert revised his opinion and stated that, although he believed the egg to be undoubtedly by Fabergé, it had been elaborately doctored. Christie's then canceled the sale. As an Imperial, the egg was worth about $1.75 million; otherwise it was worth about $50,000. The Iranian businessman sued Christie's for $37 million. Christie's, taking the position that it had acted in good faith in both instances, filed a motion to dismiss the suit on technical grounds.[12] Upon settlement of the case the court file was sealed.

Forgeries of Sculpture and Antiquities

Because there is less of a market for sculpture and because it is more difficult and costly to fake, forged sculpture is not so common as forged paintings and fine prints. Unauthorized posthumous castings and recastings of artworks, however, are prevalent and pose a significant peril to the art-buying public.[13] Antiquities and artifacts, too, may be faked—and the experts confounded. In one notable instance, after a six-year probe the New York Metropolitan Museum of Art in 1967 consigned to storage a once-revered Greek statue, the Etruscan Horse. A Metropolitan Museum expert contended that the bronze, formerly believed to be 2,400 years old, had been cast in sand, a method not developed until the fourteenth century. The very next year, a panel of art scholars found that the first expert's determination was erroneous. Further thermoluminescent study of the statue's ceramic core prompted the panel to decide that the horse was "an irrefutably genuine work of antiquity,"[14] and the museum restored the horse to its place of honor.

Methods of Art Forgery

There are five basic ways to forge artwork:

1. Copy a specific original work of art.
2. Forge an artist's signature to a work and to supporting documentation.
3. Use another artist's style to create a work otherwise original in subject matter.
4. Complete an unfinished work by an artist.
5. Combine diverse compositional elements from original paintings to produce new compositions attributed to a specific artist (sometimes called "pastiche").

Gauging Authenticity

Artwork is generally authenticated by (a) stylistic inquiry, (b) documentation, and (c) scientific verification. (Documentation of the history of ownership and public exposure of a work of art is sometimes unavailable, inasmuch as documentation itself is, on occasion, either forged or missing entirely.)

Stylistic inquiry is subjective: an expert examines the work and on the basis of his or her knowledge, experience, and intuition determines its authenticity. Unfortunately, the results of stylistic inquiry may vary from expert to expert. Moreover, experts are often reluctant to render opinions for fear of incurring tort liability.[15] Nevertheless, stylistic inquiry remains a viable test of authenticity, particularly for contemporary works, since even the most gifted copyist cannot totally repress his or her personality during the execution of a forgery.

Scientific verification, frequently used in conjunction with stylistic inquiry, employs objective procedures, thereby permitting the accuracy of the results to be tested by other scientists. Because it is objective, and because technological analysis is usually the only means of securing information relating to the age and composition of a work of art, scientific verification may be the primary method of challenging authenticity and attribution. Some of the better-known scientific techniques available for the authentication of artwork include radiocarbon dating,[16] thermoluminescent analysis,[17] X-ray photography,[18] comparative analysis,[19] and chemical analysis.[20]

ASSURANCE OF AUTHENTICITY AND PROVENANCE

Failed Attempts

Recent years have seen a number of attempts to establish a method whereby an expert, through the use of various technologies and working in conjunction with a computer databank, can guarantee the authenticity and provenance of a work of art. For example, a bill introduced by a New York congressman more than twenty years ago envisioned a federal art archive administered by the Smithsonian Institution. The archive's functions would have included photographs of the works of living artists, recordation of certificates of authenticity filed by the artists, and an owners' index. A second example was a three-year project initiated by the Mellon Institute in 1968 to study and perfect the process of atomic fingerprinting of paintings by the Old Masters. The failure of those attempts to date can be attributed in part to the secretive nature of both dealers and collectors with respect to their art holdings.

Assurance of authenticity, however, through state legislative attempts has proved to be more successful. In the late 1960s the New York legislature enacted art legislation providing that, absent a clear and conspicuous disclaimer, any certificate of authenticity or other written instrument that, in a sale by an art merchant to a nonmerchant, identifies the work as the product of a specific artist is deemed to be an express warranty of genuineness.[21] Other states enacted similar legislation over the next twenty years.[22]

In light of the prevalence of art thefts and forgeries, the remainder of this chapter focuses on issues an informed buyer should be aware of when considering the purchase of a work of art. Ordinarily, a buyer purchases works of art from a dealer or from a collector. The discussion here, therefore, focuses on sales by dealers, sales by collectors, and the differences between the two.

Sales by Dealers

Art sales—whether the dealer be a private dealer, a one-branch commercial gallery, or a gallery with numerous branches or franchised outlets—are governed by principles of contract and tort law, by federal and state penal statutes, and in certain jurisdictions by specific legislation regulating sales of art. The most important commercial statute, the Uniform Commercial Code (UCC), applies to most of the issues arising from the sale of artwork, including assurance of authenticity. It is here, therefore, that the discussion begins.

Express Warranties

Art's unique characteristics argue against total applicability of the UCC to all art transactions. That is, the UCC deals with transactions of tangible personal property, and not all art is personal property. Art can also take the form of real property, such as buildings, earthworks, and such temporary installation pieces as Christo's "Stacked Oil Drums." However, to keep this discussion manageable, whenever artworks are referred to in this chapter, we are referring to those traditionally regarded as personal property. Moreover, art that is tangible personal property embodies significant intangible rights that are more or less ignored by the UCC. Further still, many states, including New York, doubting the sufficiency of the UCC alone to safeguard art buyers, have enacted legislation that in some cases overrides the UCC. Nevertheless, the UCC governs an array of issues arising in art transactions.

Under common law, the buyer of goods generally labored under the rule of caveat emptor, absolving the seller from all responsibility for the quality of the goods sold unless the quality was expressly guaranteed. As the law evolved, the courts turned a compassionate ear to the purchaser, whereupon the rule of caveat emptor was relaxed and the doctrine of express warranty emerged, that is, an express warranty was created without the use of particular words of guarantee as long as the buyer could reasonably have understood that the seller was affirming essential qualities of the goods and the buyer relied on such affirmation in good faith.[23]

The foundation of the express warranty provision as codified in the UCC[24] is twofold: it rests, first, on the core description of goods to be sold[25] and, second, on those statements of the seller that become "part of the basis of the bargain."[26] Express warranties may arise regardless of a seller's intention; good faith is no defense to the falsity of an assertion.[27] They may arise in documents other than a sales contract; affirmations in catalogs,[28] brochures,[29] or advertisements,[30] for example, may give rise to express warranties if the buyer knows of and relies on the affirmation. Further, an advertisement need not necessarily set forth the precise warranty asserted by the buyer as long as it conveys the "essential idea" underlying the claimed warranty.[31] Express warranties may arise from assertions made before, after, and during a sale.[32] Finally, express warranties may arise from oral representations made by the seller; the UCC does not require that all material terms of an agreement be included in a written contract.[33]

Warranty by Affirmation of Fact or Promise: The UCC provides that an express warranty arises upon

> any affirmation of fact or promise made by the seller to the buyer which relates to the goods and becomes part of the basis of the bargain. . . .[34]

If the goods do not conform to the affirmation or promise made, the warranty is breached, and an action will lie, regardless of the seller's good-faith or malicious intentions in making the false statement. It has been suggested that if the documentation alone to a work of art has been forged, that, too, should constitute a breach of warranty[35] as the authorship of the work would have been rendered questionable. In such a case it has been recommended[36] that the seller reimburse the buyer for any diminution in value caused by the lack of certification, or compensate the buyer for expenses reasonably incurred in resolving the question of attribution through scientific analysis or expert opinion, and that punitive damages be allowable if the seller acted in bad faith.

Warranty by Description: A warranty may also arise from the seller's description of the goods,[37] provided the description becomes part of the basis of the bargain. The UCC places no limits on what may be considered a description: included are blueprints and technical specifications[38] and, for a work of art, the results of a scientific analysis or an expert examination of the stylistic evidence.[39] Therefore, assertions made by an art merchant about a work's authenticity (whether that it is by a specific artist, by a specific school, or created during a particular period of time) and statements asserting a work's provenance are deemed to give rise to express warranties.

Statements of Opinion: Both warranties by description and warranties by affirmation of fact must be distinguished from a seller's expression of opinion, which does not necessarily give rise to a warranty.[40] A seller's opinion, for example, concerning the aesthetics or the value of a work of art is viewed as mere "puffing,"[41] whereas the seller's opinion as to a work's authenticity or provenance may well give rise to an express warranty *if he or she is an art merchant.* Since art is customarily valued on the basis of expert opinion, experts—including art merchants—are deemed to bear the commercial responsibility for rendering such opinions. Thus, it has been held that when the party making the representations has superior knowledge regarding the subject of those representations, and the other party's level of expertise is such that that party may reasonably rely on such supposedly superior knowledge, representations may be considered as facts and not as mere opinions.[42]

Exclusion of Warranty—Examination of Goods: In the absence of suspicious circumstances, a buyer need not examine the purchased goods to affirm the accuracy of the seller's representations; it is enough that the buyer believes in and relies on them. If, however, a buyer elects to inspect the purchased goods, the UCC does not provide an unqualified answer as to whether that inspection nullifies the UCC's express warranties. Rather, the UCC indicates that various factors surrounding the transaction must be weighed.[43] A buyer with experience in the goods being sold may be able to discover defects not discernable by an inexperienced purchaser. On the other hand, when a defect is obvious, even an unsophisticated purchaser may be held to have relied on his or her inspection, rather than on the seller's warranty.[44]

When the buyer is aware of the falsity of a seller's representation, that representation cannot be relied on, does not become part of the basis of the bargain, and, therefore, does not give rise to an express warranty.[45] Sales of artwork consummated for prices below market value do not in themselves necessarily constitute notice sufficient to deny buyers relief for claimed breaches of warranty.[46] If, however, a buyer and a seller have approximately the same level of sophistication about the type of goods purchased or if there is an absence of documented pedigree, those facts, when coupled with a low price, could be sufficient to present a factual determination for a jury.[47]

Exclusion of Warranty—Disclaimer: Generally, disclaimers of warranties are viewed as contradicting the warranties and are therefore disfavored by the courts. When possible, disclaimer language is construed as being consistent with the express warranty;[48] when that is not possible, the disclaimer language is found to be inoperative.[49] Reconciliation of the warranty and the disclaimer depends on the language used. In certain jurisdictions today, such as New York[50] and Michigan,[51] enactment of state statutes has clearly delineated the circumstances under which disclaimers are given effect. Other jurisdictions must rely on case law; although disclaimers in certain instances have been upheld when found to be clear, conspicuous, and adverting to the attribute or attributes being disclaimed with sufficient particularity to apprise the buyer of the risk,[52] such judicial precedent is not unanimous. The *Weiscz* cases described below, for example, illustrate how two different courts examined the issue of a disclaimer's effects.

Weiscz v. Parke-Bernet Galleries, Inc.:[53] At a Parke-Bernet auction in 1962, the plaintiff Weiscz purchased a painting listed in the auction catalog as the work of Raoul Dufy. In 1964 plaintiff Schwartz likewise purchased at auction a work listed in the catalog as a painting by Raoul Dufy. Subsequent to a criminal investigation, Weiscz and Schwartz (the plaintiffs) learned that their Dufys were forgeries and commenced lawsuits against Parke-Bernet. The cases were tried jointly, and the court found that, at the time of the auctions, Parke-Bernet also believed the paintings ascribed to Dufy in the catalogs to be his work. Parke-Bernet defended on the grounds that in both cases the sales were "as is" and subject to the various disclaimers contained in the "Conditions of Sale" set forth in the auction catalogs.

The court found that plaintiff Weiscz did not know of the Conditions of Sale and could not, therefore, be charged with knowledge of its contents. The court found that plaintiff Schwartz was chargeable with knowledge of the Conditions of Sale. Consequently, the court had to determine whether the language of the disclaimer set forth in the Conditions of Sale in the Schwartz auction catalog was effective to immunize Parke-Bernet from the legal consequences flowing from the sale.

The court concluded that the disclaimer was inoperative. It found, instead, that Parke-Bernet intended and expected that its bidders at auctions would rely on the accuracy of its descriptions, that the Parke-Bernet gallery was vested in the mind of the public with an aura of expertise and reliability, that the wording of its auction catalog and its organization were designed to emphasize the genuineness of the works to be offered, and that the disclaimer was worded in a highly technical manner that the average reader would not interpret as affecting his or her understanding that he or she was buying authentic works of art.[54]

Weiscz was appealed, and in a brief per curiam opinion the appellate court reversed the judgments and dismissed the complaints of both Weiscz and Schwartz. It held that at the time of each of the plaintiffs' purchases neither the applicable statutory law nor decisional law recognized the seller's expressed opinion or judgment as giving rise to any implied warranty of authenticity of authorship and that the disclaimer in the defendant's auction-sale catalog gave "prominent place . . . to a clear, unequivocal disclaimer of any express or implied warranty or representation of genuineness of any paintings as products of the ascribed artist."[55] Were the UCC, rather than the former Uniform Sales Act, applied to the *Weiscz* transactions and were *Weiscz* appealed today, the disposition of the appellate court would probably remain unchanged. Even though under the UCC the catalog description by Parke-Bernet would more likely be deemed to create an express warranty, the court's reasoning as to the disclaimer's effect would still govern, provided the catalog disclaimer was found to be sufficient to inform a purchaser in the plaintiff's position as to the risk of title, since the disclaimer specifically repudiated a representation of genuineness with respect to the items sold.

Parol Evidence Rule: The effectiveness of a disclaimer also depends on the UCC's parol evidence rule—that is, terms of a writing intended as the final expression of the parties' agreement may not be contradicted by evidence of prior or contemporaneous oral agreements.[56] Given, therefore, an oral disclaimer with a written warranty, the parol evidence rule excludes evidence of the disclaimer. Given, however, an oral warranty with a written disclaimer, evidence of the warranty is excluded. The rule does, however, permit parol evidence of usage of trade or the parties' course of dealing or course of performance when that evidence explains or supplements the contract terms.[57] Moreover, evidence of consistent additional terms is admissible "unless the court finds the writing to have been intended also as a complete and exclusive statement of the terms of the agreement."[58]

Implied Warranties

After the evolution in common law of express warranties, the early nineteenth century witnessed the development of two distinct implied warranties for the quality of goods sold: (a) that of merchantability and (b) that of fitness for purpose. Today there is a somewhat Procrustean fit between commercial transactions in artworks and the law of implied warranties as embodied in the UCC.[59] From its language and the examples used in the comments, it appears that the primary thrust of the warranty of merchantability is directed at the sale of goods more fungible than artworks. Nevertheless, it is entirely possible to envision those warranties affording redress to the consumer in the context of art forgery. Only in the future, however, will we discover the extent of judicial application of those warranties to the unwitting purchase of forged works.

Warranty of Merchantability: The implied warranty of merchantability, as it evolved, has come to mean that goods must be capable of passing under the description specified in the agreement of sale and be reasonably fit for the *ordinary* uses to which such goods are put. Unless disclaimed, that warranty is implied in a contract for the sale of goods by a "merchant seller."[60] The warranty's scope limits liability to a "merchant with respect to goods of that kind," and, unlike the seller in an action for fraud, wherein it is generally necessary to prove that the seller knew that his or her representation was false, the merchant will incur liability regardless of his or her knowledge of the existence of any defect in the goods sold.[61] Under the UCC, "merchant," in part, means "a person who deals in goods of the kind or otherwise by his occupation holds himself out as having knowledge or skill peculiar to the practices or goods involved in the transaction."[62] Thus, as it relates to dealing in art, "merchant" includes a commercial art gallery, an art auctioneer, and a private art dealer[63] and excludes a collector whose occupation is not related to art and who sells items from his or her art collection only occasionally.[64] Reliance by the buyer on the seller's skill and judgment is not required under this warranty.[65]

Section 2-314(2) of the UCC defines "merchantability" with particularity. In order for goods to be merchantable, they must be at least such as:[66]

a. Pass without objection in the trade under the contract description;
b. In the case of fungible goods, are of fair average quality within the description;
c. Are fit for the ordinary purposes for which such goods are used;

d. Run, within the variations permitted by the agreement, of even kind, quality, and quantity within each unit and among all units involved;
e. Are adequately contained, packaged, and labeled as the agreement may require; *and*
f. Conform to the promises or affirmations of fact made on the container or label, if any. Note that all the requirements must be met. In addition, UCC section 2-314(2) comment 6 states that subsection (2) "does not purport to exhaust the meaning of 'merchantable.'"

As to works of art, the most relevant tests of merchantability are found in subsections (a), (c), and (f).

As to *subsection (a)*, whether goods would pass without objection is determined with reference to the standards of the particular line of trade. Accordingly, merchantability of artwork would be interpreted by reference to dealer recognition, categorization, and evaluation of specific artists, periods of art, and specific works relating to those artists and periods. An original, documented work of art, therefore, would pass without objection in the trade and, consequently, be merchantable. Similarly, a poorly rendered fake or an item of significant worth without adequate documentation of provenance would not pass without objection in the trade and, accordingly, would not be merchantable.[67]

A different situation is posed by the skillfully rendered fake, say a Turner, complete with documentation, that has passed unnoticed for 150 years. Even though it passed without objection in the trade for years, discovery of the defect would render the work unmerchantable, and the buyer would have redress under the UCC. The art industry has tried to minimize the possibility of that situation's arising by creating a standard classification as to the degrees of certainty in attributions of works of art. For example, the following Glossary of attributions is reproduced from a February 1989 catalog of the auction house Christie's New York.

Glossary

For Pictures, Drawings, Prints and Miniatures

Terms used in this Catalogue have the meanings
scribed to them below. Please note that all statements
n this catalogue as to Authorship are made subject to
he provisions of the CONDITIONS OF SALE,
IMITED WARRANTY and ABSENCE OF
THER WARRANTIES.

1. PABLO PICASSO (The artist's first name or names and last names)	In our opinion a work by the artist.
2. Attributed to FRANCESCO GUARDI*	In our qualified opinion a work of the period of the artist which may be in whole or part the work of the artist.
3. Circle of FRANCESCO GUARDI*	In our qualified opinion a work of the period of the artist and closely related to his style.
4. Studio of; Workshop of FRANCESCO GUARDI*	In our qualified opinion a work possibly executed under the supervision of the artist.
5. School of FRANCESCO GUARDI*	In our qualified opinion a work by a pupil or follower of the artist.
6. Manner of FRANCESCO GUARDI*	In our qualified opinion a work in the style of the artist, possibly of a later period.
7. After FRANCESCO GUARDI*	In our qualified opinion a copy of the work of the artist.
8. 'signed'	Has a signature which in our qualified opinion is the signature of the artist.
9. 'bears signature'	Has a signature which in our qualified opinion might be the signature of the artist.
0. 'dated'	Is so dated and in our qualified opinion was executed at about that date.
1. 'bears date'	Is so dated and in our qualified opinion may have been executed at about that date.

This term and its definition in this glossary is a
ualified statement as to Authorship. While the use of
is term is based upon careful study and represents the
pinion of experts, Christie's and the Seller assume no
sk, liability or responsibility for the authenticity of
uthorship of any lot in this catalogue described by this
rm.

As to *subsection (c)*, even if a work of art passes without objection in the trade, it is subject to another test of merchantability—that is, its fitness "for the ordinary purposes for which such goods are used." A UCC comment[68] elaborates on that by explaining that merchantable goods must be "honestly resalable in the normal course of business because they are what they purport to be." The purchase of a forgery defeats the purpose of buying an original and is certainly not "honestly resalable" as an original.

Still another test of merchantability for artwork is posed by *subsection (f)*, whereby, to be merchantable, goods must "conform to the promises or affirmations of fact made on the container or label if any." Paintings and sculpture are often sold with wooden or brass plaques attached to the frame or the base of the piece. Such plaques bear the title of the work and its attribution. If plaques are regarded as labels and if a work of art and its plaque are inconsistent, it could be argued that a breach of the implied warranty of merchantability may arise. Such a breach would also arise from an artist's forged signature and, in fact, if a signature is fraudulently added to an original painting to improve its salability, the buyer might be able to recover for any difference in value between an unsigned work and a signed original under this subsection.

Warranty of Fitness for a Particular Use: Goods may be merchantable and yet still be unfit for a particular use. The warranty of fitness for a particular use arises if three requirements are met:[69]

1. The seller must know of the buyer's particular purpose; an explicit statement of purpose is unnecessary if the circumstances are such that the seller should realize the purpose.
2. The seller must have actual or constructive knowledge that the buyer is relying on his or her skill.
3. The buyer must actually rely on the seller.

A seller's intention to create this warranty is immaterial,[70] and a seller's good faith is no defense in a suit for its breach. Moreover, the fact that a defect is difficult to find does not eliminate the warranty if it is otherwise created. Although the usual fact situation involves a merchant-seller, when the circumstances are appropriate, the warranty of fitness can arise as to a nonmerchant-seller.[71]

Exclusion of Implied Warranties

Examination of Goods: In certain circumstances the implied warranties of merchantability and fitness may be excluded by a buyer's examination of the goods bought or by the buyer's refusal to examine them.[72] If, for example, prior to purchase a buyer of artwork refuses the seller's demand that the buyer examine it, the implied warranties are excluded as to any defects "an examination ought in the circumstances to have revealed."[73] That results because the demand constitutes notice to the buyer that he or she is assuming the risks of any defects that the examination would reveal. If, on the other hand, a seller's offer of examination is accompanied by statements relating to the quality or the characteristics of a work of art and the buyer indicates that he or she is relying on those statements, rather than on the examination, the seller will likely be deemed to have given an express warranty.[74]

Whether the buyer's examination of the goods results in the exclusion of the warranties depends on the buyer's sophistication, the normal method of examining goods in the circumstances, and the obviousness of the defect.[75] If a flaw is discernible on visible inspection before purchase, the implied warranties are excluded. If, on the other hand, a defect in forged artwork can be detected only by scientific investigation or extensive research, a buyer's inspection should not ordinarily result in an exclusion of the implied warranties.[76]

Disclaimer: The UCC permits sellers to disclaim implied warranties under circumscribed conditions.[77] The warranty of merchantability may be disclaimed either orally or in writing.[78] If written, the disclaimer must be conspicuous.[79] The disclaimer language must specifically include the word "merchantability."[80]

Alternatively, the language may be general, provided it informs the buyer that no warranties are attendant to the transaction and that the buyer assumes the risk of the quality of goods purchased. Examples of such general language are "as is," "as they stand," and "with all faults."[81] See discussion of *Weiscz v. Parke-Bernet* at pages 62-64.

The warranty of fitness for a particular use may be disclaimed only in writing,[82] and the disclaimer must be conspicuous.[83] The disclaimer language may be general, such as, "there are no warranties which extend beyond the description on the face hereof."[84] Alternatively, the disclaimer language may include such phrases as "with all faults," "as they stand," and "as is."[85]

In addition, both implied warranties may be disclaimed through a course of dealing between the parties, a course of performance by the parties, or usage of trade.[86]

With all that said, however, the courts have significantly limited the ability of the seller of artwork to disclaim implied warranties. Courts have strictly construed the warranty disclaimer language,[87] or determined that the disclaimer was not sufficiently "conspicuous,"[88] or found the disclaimer to be unconscionable.[89] Moreover, legislation in a number of states[90] has significantly impeded the ability of a seller to disclaim implied warranties of merchantability or fitness with respect to "consumer goods,"[91] within which category artwork falls.

Implied Warranties and Privity

Privity is that connection or relationship existing between two or more contracting parties, such as the relationship between a seller and a purchaser. The UCC takes no position with respect to the seller's liability to a subpurchaser.[92] The trend as developed by case law is away from privity and toward foreseeability as a criterion for liability.[93] Moreover, it has been held that, if advertising is involved, that provides another argument for dispensing with privity.[94] It has been asserted that, in an action for the transfer of fake art, the ultimate purchaser should be able to dispense with privity on the basis of advertisements and that, even in the absence of advertising, lack of privity should not preclude recovery by the ultimate purchaser against the remote seller if it is reasonably foreseeable that breach of an implied warranty will cause that ultimate purchaser economic loss.[95]

Warranty of Title: At common law under the doctrine of caveat emptor, the buyer bore the risk of poor title. Today the buyer is afforded substantial protection by the UCC, which provides that unless specifically excluded or modified, a warranty of title by the seller exists in every sales contract.[96] The statutorily imposed warranty of title includes the following assertions:

1. That the title to the work or works being conveyed is good.[97]
2. That the seller has the right to transfer title.[98]
3. That the works are delivered free from any security interest or other lien or encumbrance of which the buyer at the time of contract has no knowledge.[99]

In addition, when the sellers are merchants, there is an implied warranty on the part of the seller that the goods will be delivered free of any third-party claim of infringement of a patent or trademark.[100]

Exclusion of Warranty of Title

Disclaimer: Warranty of title may be excluded or modified only by specific language[101] or by circumstances that give the buyer "reason to know" that the seller does not claim title in himself or that he is purporting to sell only such rights in the goods as he or a third person may have.[102] Since the UCC's objective is to prevent surprise, general disclaimer language that merely negates all warranties will not nullify the warranty of title, because it does not give the buyer reason to know of any risk of title failure. Thus, language in a bill of sale to the effect that the seller "does hereby sell . . . any right, title and interest seller may have" was not sufficient to constitute a disclaimer of the warranty of title.[103]

More than mere constructive notice imported by public recordation or filing is required to give a buyer reason to know that the seller does not claim to have full title.[104] Circumstances sufficient to put the buyer on notice would include an announcement at an art auction that the seller does not claim title in itself or that the seller is purporting to sell only such title as third persons may have.[105] Other circumstances in which a buyer should be aware that a warranty of title is not present are judicial sales and foreclosure sales.[106]

If, where there is no exclusion of warranty, a buyer can establish that the goods are subject to a security interest that was not known to the buyer or that the seller had neither the right nor the power to deliver good title, the buyer can surrender the property and recover damages.[107] If the rightful property owner brings an action against the buyer to recover the property, the buyer may implead the seller and require the seller to defend the action.

Warranty of Title and Measure of Damages: Menzel v. List[108]

In 1932 the plaintiffs Menzel bought a painting by Marc Chagall at auction in Brussels for approximately $150. In 1940 the Germans invaded Belgium and the Menzels fled, leaving the Chagall painting in their residence. Six years later the Menzels returned to find that their painting had been removed and that a receipt for the painting had been left. The Germans had, in fact, removed the painting as degenerate art in 1941, and its whereabouts remained unknown until 1955, when it was purchased for $2,800 from a Parisian art gallery by Klaus Perl and his wife, proprietors of a New York gallery. Later that same year the Perls, who knew nothing of the painting's previous history and made no inquiries concerning it, sold it to Albert List for $4,000. In 1962 Mrs. Menzel noticed a reproduction of the Chagall in an art book along with a statement that the painting was in Albert List's possession.

Upon List's refusal to surrender the painting to Mrs. Menzel on demand, she instituted a replevin action against him, and List, in turn, impleaded the Perls, alleging that they were liable to him for breach of the warranty of title. Expert testimony was introduced to establish the painting's fair market value at the time of the trial. The court charged the jury that, if it found for Mrs. Menzel against List, it was to assess the present value of the painting. The jury did find for Mrs. Menzel, requiring that List either return the painting to her or pay her its then fair market value ($22,500). In addition, the jury found for List as against the Perls in the amount of $22,500, plus the legal costs incurred by List.

List returned the painting to Menzel and the Perls appealed on the issue of damages. The appellate court reduced the amount awarded to List to $4,000 (the price he paid for the painting), plus interest from the date of the purchase. The court also held that Mrs. Menzel's action was not barred by the statutes of limitation of either New York or Belgium, since her cause of action for replevin and conversion arose not upon the taking of the painting, but upon List's refusal to return the painting on demand.

List and the Perls each appealed the appellate court's modification order, and the New York Court of Appeals reversed the order, finding that the modification order would not have fully compensated List for his loss, since he would have been deprived of the benefit—that is, the appreciated value—of his bargain. In the court's reasoning:

> Clearly, List can only be put in the same position he would have occupied if the contract had been kept by the Perls if he recovers the value of the painting at the time when, by the judgment in the main action, he was required to surrender the painting to Mrs. Menzel or pay her the present value of the painting. Had the warranty been fulfilled, i.e., had title been as warranted by the Perls, List would still have possession of a painting currently worth $22,500 and he could have realized that price at an auction or private sale. If List recovers only the purchase price plus interest, the effect is to put him in the same position he would have occupied *if the sale had never been made.* Manifestly, an injured buyer is not compensated when he recovers only so much as placed him in

> *status quo ante* since such a recovery implicitly denies that he had suffered any damage.[109]

Thus, in *Menzel v. List* the plaintiff recovered her painting, List was awarded a sum of money equal to the painting's then fair market value, and the Perls were left to seek recourse from a foreign defendant, the Parisian art dealer.[110] The court's refusal to impose mere rescission on List as a "remedy" indicates judicial awareness that works of art, unlike most other chattel, sometimes appreciate in value after an initial sale. More to the point was the court's relatively high-handed treatment of the Perls. In dismissing their objection to the court's measure of damages, the court noted that a seller is in a position to ascertain a work's provenance before acquiring it for resale—and that if the seller has any doubts about its provenance, the seller can secure protection on resale of the work by employing suitable disclaimers of warranties.[111] The court, however, ignores the reality that should the seller seek the protection of such disclaimers, he or she may well have trouble selling the work.

Warranty of Title and Measure of Damages—The UCC: Menzel was decided under the Uniform Sales Act, as enacted in New York, which predated the UCC. In *Menzel* the New York Court of Appeals, in upholding the trial court's award of damages, concluded that the proper damages in breach of warranty cases involving at least those commodities that appreciate in value were those that would place the injured party in the position the party would have occupied had the warranty not been breached. Thus, the buyer List was awarded damages based on the then-market value of the painting. While the UCC provides that the

> measure of damages for breach of warranty is the difference at the time and place of acceptance between the value of the goods accepted and the value they would have had if they had been as warranted, unless special circumstances show proximate damages of a different amount,[112]

the *Menzel* measure of "benefit of the bargain" (which requires damages, in cases involving appreciating commodities, to acknowledge the appreciation in value) was reinforced, despite the UCC provision, in the recent case discussed below.

In *Koerner v. Davis*,[113] plaintiff Henry Koerner, a Viennese artist living in Pennsylvania, brought one of his paintings, "The Family," to New York City in 1964 for framing. While running an errand in the city, he left the painting in a taxi and told the driver to wait. When he returned from his errand, the taxi was gone. Koerner reported the loss to the police department as well as to his insurer, who paid him the insured value of the painting: $1,000.

In June 1983 the painting surfaced on the market for sale at the William Doyle Galleries, and was sold that month at auction to defendant David J. Davis for $1,200. At the time of the sale, the painting's provenance was unknown. In September 1983, following a search by Davis, Davis learned that Koerner was the artist and Koerner learned that Davis had his painting. Koerner demanded the return of the painting, whereupon Davis refused and instead placed it for sale with the Gertrude Stein Gallery. In March 1984 Koerner demanded of both Davis and the Stein Gallery that the painting be returned. The Gallery responded by returning the work to Davis, who did not return it to Koerner, whereupon Koerner brought suit against Davis and the Gallery to recover the work of art or its fair market value. In the face of the action, Davis delivered the work to an antiques dealer, who then died. The painting has disappeared once again.

In holding for the plaintiff, the court noted that since the painting was originally stolen from the plaintiff, no title to the property could be conveyed, and that, moreover, both Davis and the Gallery were converters: Davis, when he refused Koerner's demand to return the painting in March 1984 and the Gallery, when it disposed of Koerner's property by returning it to Davis with full knowledge of competing claims to it. The court further noted that plaintiff's insurance proceeds did not cover the full value of the stolen property, he was not divested of all interest in the painting, and he was therefore a proper party plaintiff.

Finally, as to damages, the court was satisfied with the evidence that Koerner's work had appreciated in value and that his painting, "The Family," would command a price in the 1984 market of $30,000. Accordingly, the court applied the "benefit of the bargain" measure propounded in *Menzel* and awarded damages to the plaintiff in the amount of $30,000.

Warranties and Notice of Breach[114]

If, after accepting delivery of a work of art, a buyer discovers that the seller has breached a warranty, the buyer must notify the seller, either orally or in writing,[115] of that breach within a reasonable time after its discovery or risk losing whatever remedy the buyer has against the seller.[116] What constitutes "reasonable" time of notification varies with the facts; a more stringent test may be applied to a merchant buyer than to a consumer buyer.[117]

In the event that the buyer is sued by a third party, the buyer should notify the seller in writing of the litigation. The notice should include all relevant information pertaining to the litigation, as well as a demand that the seller defend the action or else be bound by any determination of fact in the litigation.[118]

Statute of Frauds

Section 2-201 of the UCC provides that a contract for the sale of goods costing $500 or more is unenforceable unless documented by a writing indicating that such a contract between the parties has been made. The document must be signed by the party against whom enforcement is sought or by that party's authorized agent or broker. In the absence of other statutory provisions, one who promises to purchase a work of art costing $500 or more has to have signed a memorandum in order to be bound to consummate the purchase.

When both the buyer and the seller are merchants, a written confirmation of the sale by either party correctly stating all material terms of the agreement and received within a reasonable time by the other party, when he or she should know its contents, is binding against that party unless he or she objects in writing to the confirmation within ten days after its receipt.[119]

A contract not yet put into writing but otherwise valid may be enforceable if goods are to be specially manufactured, if the person against whom enforcement is sought admits the contract in court, or if the contract is for goods for which payment has been made and accepted or that have been received and accepted.[120] An interesting question is whether the commission of any artwork is one for the sale of services or for the sale of goods. In *National Historic Shrines*[121] it was held that the commission was a contract for the sale of services, and therefore not addressed by the sale-of-goods provision of the statute of frauds. See chapter 13 at pages 679-80, which discusses the sale of services versus the sale of goods from a tax perspective vis-à-vis the artist.

The Unconscionable Contract

The UCC provides that a court may refuse to enforce any contract or any portion of a contract that it finds as a matter of law to have been unconscionable at the time it was made.[122] Unconscionability alone may not support a claim for damages; it merely gives the court the right to refuse to enforce the contract.[123] Whether a contract or any clause of a contract is unconscionable is a matter for a court to decide against the background of the contract's commercial setting, purpose, and effect.[124] Although the statute has no guidelines as to the determination of unconscionability,[125] the thrust of the provision is to prevent oppression and unfair surprise to the contracting parties, not to disturb the allocation of risks to a party merely because the other party has superior bargaining power.[126]

An example of unconscionability is found in the case of *Vom Lehn v. Astor Art Galleries, Ltd.*[127] There, the plaintiff-buyers of twenty Oriental jade carvings for the sum of $67,000 brought an action against the sellers, alleging conspiracy to fraudulently induce them to buy the carvings by misrepresenting their true value and by fraudulently misrepresenting them as being Ming Dynasty jade. In the course of the tranasaction, which included drinks at the prospective buyers' house and going out to dinner, the sellers allegedly told a tale of woe as to their personal circumstances, and the prospective buyers ultimately made a down payment of $19,000 on the merchandise and issued four postdated checks totaling $48,000 for the balance. Upon subsequently discovering that the carvings were not Ming Dynasty jade as represented, the buyers brought suit against the sellers. While the New York Supreme Court, among other findings, noted that no conspiracy or fraud was proven, it did find that the purchase price was unconscionable, and therefore would not enforce the contract requiring the buyers to pay the balance of the purchase price.[128]

Voidable Title

It has long been settled law that one who acquires goods from a thief has no title in and to the goods and, therefore, cannot pass ownership of the goods to successive transferees.[129] Distinguishable from that situation is one with voidable title. The UCC provides that a person with voidable title has power to transfer a good title to a good-faith purchaser for value.[130] Key to the concept of voidable title is this: the original transferor voluntarily relinquishes possession of the goods and intends to pass title. The original transferor may be defrauded, the check that the transferor received may have bounced, or the transferor may have intended to sell to *Y*, rather than to *Z*; nevertheless, the transferor intended to pass title. In such cases, the transferor may void the sale, but the transferee can pass good title.[131]

The Buyer in the Ordinary Course of Business

When goods are entrusted to a merchant who deals in goods of that kind, that merchant under the UCC[132] is empowered to transfer all rights of the entruster to a buyer in the ordinary course of business. A buyer in the ordinary course of business means

> a person who in good faith and without knowledge that the sale to him is in violation of the ownership rights or security interest of a third party in the goods buys in ordinary course from a person in the business of selling goods of that kind. . . .[133]

But what is good faith? In the case of a merchant, the UCC defines it as "honesty in fact and the observance of reasonable commercial standards of fair dealing in the trade."[134] Good faith cannot include indifference on the part of the merchant buyer as to the provenance or history of ownership of the artwork purchased by the buyer.

Thus, when an owner of a Utrillo painting sought to recover its possession from the Richard Feigen art gallery, which had sold the painting to a buyer out of the country, the court held in favor of the plaintiff-owner.[135] In that case, plaintiff Samuel Porter, an art collector, had had a number of dealings with Harold Von Maker. Von Maker used the name Peter Wertz (Wertz was an acquaintance of Von Maker's) and was known as Peter Wertz to Porter. In the spring of 1973 Porter permitted Von Maker to take Porter's Utrillo home temporarily, pending Von Maker's decision whether to buy the painting. In July 1973 Porter discovered that Von Maker had purchased another of Porter's paintings with bad notes. After an investigation, Porter learned that he had not been dealing with Peter Wertz, but with a man named Von Maker, who had an arrest record for theft-related crimes. Although Von Maker subsequently assured Porter that he would either return the Utrillo or pay $30,000, he had already disposed of the painting by using the real Peter Wertz to effect its sale to the Feigen art gallery for $20,000.

Peter Wertz was a delicatessen employee, not an art merchant, and the Feigen art gallery seemed aware of this fact. Feigen found a buyer for the Utrillo and collected a commission. The buyer in turn sold the painting, resulting in its shipment to Venezuela. On ruling in favor of Porter and against the Richard Feigen art gallery, the court noted that Feigen was not a buyer in the ordinary course of business, since (1) the gallery did not purchase the Utrillo from an art dealer and (2) by departing from normal commercial standards in failing to inquire into the provenance of the Utrillo and the status of the party who sold it to the gallery, the gallery was not acting in good faith.[136]

The Duty of Inquiry into Title: If an art dealer, on buying works of art, fails to inquire into the nature of the seller's authority to sell that artwork, the dealer is not deemed to be a buyer in the ordinary course of business and, accordingly, is no better than a converter.[137] Similarly, a purchaser of art who is not a dealer must meet the test of being a buyer in the ordinary course of business; however, the test for the nonmerchant is less stringent.[138]

In *Taborsky v. Maroney*[139] a federal court of appeals affirmed a district court's holding that the suspicious circumstances surrounding the purchase and sale of a Grant Wood drawing between two art merchants imposed on the buying merchant a duty to inquire as to the selling merchant's authority. Citing Wisconsin law, the court noted that a merchant dealing in goods and entrusted with the possession of goods of that kind can transfer all rights of the entruster to a buyer in the ordinary course of business.[140] The court further addressed the more stringent standard pertaining to buyers who are also merchants, and noted that a merchant buyer must (1) be honest in fact, (2) not have knowledge that a sale would be in violation of the ownership rights of a third party, and (3) observe reasonable commercial standards of fair dealing in the trade and be charged with the knowledge or skill of a merchant.[141] That higher level of knowledge attributed to a merchant means that actual knowledge of certain information concerning unusual circumstances surrounding a transaction can prevent a merchant from becoming a buyer in the ordinary course of business, even though the buyer does not have actual knowledge that the sale is in violation of the ownership rights of a third party.[142] If, as in *Taborsky*, a merchant buyer fails to inquire into the propriety of the transaction when suspicious circumstances arise, the merchant buyer has failed to conform to the reasonable commercial practices of fair dealing in the trade and, therefore, cannot qualify as a buyer in the ordinary course of business.[143]

The Merchant's Duty of Disclosure

Recent case law has indicated that the dealer as seller must disclose information relating to possible title problems in the works it offers for sale. In *Van Rijn v. Wildenstein*[144] a Dutch art dealer contracted with the Wildenstein dealership to buy two paintings, one by El Greco and one by Boticelli. Van Rijn in turn agreed to sell the two works to a Tokyo art dealership. However, the Tokyo dealership canceled its contract with Van Rijn upon discovering that the government of Romania had a claim of ownership in and to the El Greco work. Van Rijn brought suit against Wildenstein for breach of warranties and fraud, claiming Wildenstein falsely and fraudulently represented the title of the two paintings as being free of all claims. The trial, in the United States District Court for the Southern District of New York, took place in October and November of 1987, and resulted in a jury verdict against the defendant for $450,000 and a finding of breach of warranty of merchantability. (There was, however, no finding of fraud or breach of warranty of title.) The parties later reached a settlement, the terms of which are confidential.

Risk of Loss

As the UCC makes clear,[145] the risk of loss for goods, including artwork, that are damaged or stolen while consigned is borne by the consignee, usually an art dealer. Even so, the consignor, usually a collector, is wise to insist that the consignee maintain insurance covering artwork delivered to it for consignment so that the consignor will be paid in full in the event of any loss. When artwork is purchased from a nonmerchant seller, the risk of loss of the goods passes to the buyer on the buyer's receipt of notification necessary to enable the buyer to take the delivery.[146] On the other hand, when artwork is purchased from a merchant, the risk of loss of the goods passes to the buyer only on actual receipt of the goods.[147]

The Statute of Limitations

The rising incidence of art theft has caused a flow into legitimate channels of commerce of numerous artworks in connection with which good title cannot pass. Since neither a thief nor any purchaser through a thief can take good title,[148] the rightful owner may either reclaim the artwork at any point, primarily through an action in replevin,[149] or may seek damages for unlawful dominion and control of the artwork through an action in conversion,[150] provided the suit is brought within the statute of limitations period. Since all civil actions are subject to a limitations statute,[151] plaintiffs are on occasion barred by time from obtaining recovery.

The statute's foreclosing potentials, however, are counterbalanced by its policies and objectives: first, it encourages a party to sue promptly, on the premise that those having valid claims will not delay in asserting them.[152] Second, it protects the defendant after a substantial period of repose from having to defend a claim with evidence lost or destroyed by the passage of time.[153] Finally, it promotes the free trade of goods by ensuring that those who have dealt in good faith with property will enjoy secure possession and peace after a certain period of time.[154]

Concept of Accrual

The typical statute of limitations provides that the time during which a cause of action may be brought begins to run from the time the cause of action accrues.[155] Because accrual in most states has been left to judicial interpretation,[156] several theories of accrual pertinent to art theft victims have arisen over the years, only to be subsequently rejected by a majority of states[157] for reasons of innate injustice. One theory is accrual by adverse possession,[158] a method of transferring title to property without the owner's consent.[159] To effect a transfer under that doctrine, the property-holder must have had hostile, actual, open and notorious, exclusive, and continuous possession of the property for the duration of the limitations period.[160] One major drawback of that theory is that the existence of each of the above-stated elements of possession must be proved with clear and convincing evidence[161] by the defendant-possessor before the limitations period can begin to run,[162] and the very character of possession of most artwork—that is, exclusive residential display—does not satisfy the requirement of "open and notorious" possession.[163] Accordingly, the adverse possession theory could delay the possessor's right of repose indefinitely, in contradiction of an objective of the limitations statutes.[164]

In the vast majority of states today, both an action to recover stolen property from a good-faith purchaser and an action for conversion accrue when the good-faith purchaser acquires the stolen property.[165] Accrual of the cause of action in those states depends upon neither the rightful owner's discovery of the sale[166] nor the owner's discovery of the purchaser's identity.[167]

A notable exception occurs in New York, where, in order for a cause of action to accrue in a suit for either conversion[168] or replevin,[169] the plaintiff must demand the return of the goods and the defendant must refuse to comply. Like the adverse possession theory, the requirement of demand and refusal proposed in *Menzel v. List*[170] (the first case to rule directly on the statute of limitations issue in a claim to recover stolen art[171]) indefinitely postpones accrual of a cause of action, thereby putting off the time when a good-faith possessor can get good title and repose.

On the other hand, and perhaps unfairly, no demand for the goods is necessary against a bad-faith possessor. Therefore, the statute starts running immediately in favor of the bad-faith possessor, possibly barring a suit against a thief or converter at a time when a suit against a good-faith purchaser could still be brought.[172]

Mitigating that potential unfairness, New York subsequently modified the demand-and-refusal requirement to hold that, when demand and refusal are necessary to start a limitations period, once the possessor of stolen property is identified, the rightful owner's demand may not be unreasonably delayed.[173]

Recently, in *DeWeerth v. Baldinger*,[174] discussed below, the rule was modified yet again. Today, to postpone the running of the statute of limitations against a good-faith purchaser, three factors must coalesce: (a) there must be a demand by the rightful owner and a refusal of the return of the property; (b) the demand must be made without unreasonable delay; and (c) the demand must include an obligation to use due diligence to locate the stolen property.[175]

DeWeerth v. Baldinger

The plaintiff, Gerda DeWeerth, a West German citizen, inherited a painting by Claude Monet in 1922 from her father, who had owned a substantial art collection. The current estimated worth of the Monet is in excess of $500,000.[176] Except for a two-year period (1927-1929) when the painting was in the possession of her mother, the plaintiff kept the Monet in her home in West Germany from 1922 until August 1943, when she forwarded the painting and other valuables to her sister's home in southern Germany for safekeeping during World War II. At the war's end in 1945 the sister, who had quartered American soldiers, noticed upon their departure that the painting was missing. She told her sister in the fall of 1945.

DeWeerth contacted several authorities about the lost Monet. In 1946 she filed a report with the military government administering the Bonn-Cologne area after the war; in 1948, in a letter to her lawyer regarding insurance claims on lost property, she inquired whether something could be done about the lost Monet, whereupon, without initiating an investigation, her lawyer told her that the Monet would not be covered by insurance; in 1955 she issued a photograph of the painting to a former art professor, asking him to investigate the painting's whereabouts, whereupon he responded that the photo was insufficient evidence on which to begin a search; finally, in 1957 DeWeerth sent a list of artwork she had lost during the war to the West German federal bureau of investigation. None of her efforts to locate the Monet was fruitful, and she gave up.

Meanwhile, the Monet surfaced in the art market in December 1956, when it was acquired on consignment by the New York gallery of Wildenstein & Co. from an art dealer in Switzerland. From December 1956 until June 1957 the painting was in the possession of the New York gallery. In June 1957 the painting was sold for $30,900 to defendant Edith Baldinger, a good-faith purchaser. Baldinger had kept the Monet in her New York City apartment since 1957 except for two brief public exhibitions.

In 1981 the plaintiff's nephew, Peter von der Heydt, learned through a cousin that his aunt had owned a Monet that had disappeared during the war. Shortly thereafter, von der Heydt identified the painting in a *catalogue raisonné* of Monet's works located in a museum less than twenty miles from where DeWeerth had been living since 1957. Through the *catalogue raisonné*, von der Heydt traced the painting to the Wildenstein gallery, and in 1982 DeWeerth brought an action to compel Wildenstein to disclose the identity of the current owner. Wildenstein was compelled to identify Baldinger, whereupon in December 1982 DeWeerth by letter demanded the return of the Monet, and by letter in February 1983 Baldinger refused. Later that month, DeWeerth initiated an action to recover her painting. The United States District Court for the Southern District of New York ruled that DeWeerth owned the painting and ordered Baldinger to return it, finding that the action was timely, since DeWeerth had exercised reasonable diligence in searching for the painting. Baldinger appealed the judgment, and the Second Circuit reversed, disagreeing that DeWeerth exercised the requisite diligence.

In holding that New York law imposes a due diligence requirement, that DeWeerth failed to exercise reasonable diligence in locating the painting after its disappearance, and that her action for recovery was untimely,[177] the court reasoned as follows: it noted that in actions for recovery of stolen property New York is governed by the demand-and-refusal rule as to good-faith purchasers,[178] and that the demand may not be unreasonably delayed;[179] that the fact that the plaintiff's action was brought soon after refusal does not end the inquiry;[180] and that the plaintiff's argument that her actions before she discovered the defendant's identity could not be subject to the unreasonable-delay rule was without merit, since an obligation to attempt to locate stolen property is consistent with New York's protective treatment of the good-faith purchaser—that is, the

> plaintiff's proposed exception to the rule would rob it of all of its salutary effect: The thief would be immune from suit after [New York's statutory limitations period expires], while the good-faith purchaser would remain exposed as long as his identity did not fortuitously come to the property owner's attention.[181]

The court went on to note:

> Other jurisdictions have adopted limitations rules that encourage property owners to search for their missing goods. In virtually every state except New York, an action for conversion accrues when a good-faith purchaser acquires stolen property; demand and refusal are unnecessary. . . . It is true that New York has chosen to depart from the majority view. Nevertheless, the fact that plaintiff's interpretation of New York law would exaggerate its inconsistency with the law of other jurisdictions weighs against adopting such a view.[182]

The court held that DeWeerth failed to meet the diligent-search requirement by neglecting to conduct any search for twenty-four years from 1957 until 1981. Her "failure to consult the *Catalogue Raisonné*," which enabled her nephew to identify the Wildenstein gallery within three days, was "particularly inexcusable."

The three-pronged rule of *DeWeerth* was upheld in the yet-more-recent suit of *Guggenheim v. Lubell.*[183] In that case the Guggenheim Museum sought the return in 1986 of a Marc Chagall painting titled "Menagerie" from defendant Julia Lubell, a good-faith purchaser. Lubell and her late husband had bought the painting in 1967 from "a reputable art dealer, Robert Elkon," and it hung in the defendant's apartment in New York City except on two occasions when it was exhibited publicly at the Robert Elkon Gallery in 1969 and 1973.

The Guggenheim had acquired the Chagall in 1937, and it had remained in the collection (except for some short-time loans) until some time after April 1965 when it was reported missing. The report was not confirmed until 1969 when the museum inventoried its paintings.

In August 1985 a transparency of "Menagerie" was brought to Sotheby's for an appraisal and seen by a former employee of the museum, who identified the Chagall as the one missing from the Guggenheim collection. Upon ascertaining the identity of the art dealer's client (Mrs. Lubell), the museum in January 1986 requested the return of the painting. Mrs. Lubell refused and the museum subsequently brought an action for its possession.

In dismissing the museum's suit as time-barred, the New York Supreme Court, relying heavily on the *DeWeerth* case, noted that the museum did nothing for twenty years except search its premises and that, at a minimum, it should have routinely contacted such agencies as the police department, the FBI, INTERPOL, and the ADAA to aid in its search for the missing Chagall. Because the museum had failed to seek the painting's recovery diligently, the statute of limitations period, which began to run in 1973 when the painting was publicly displayed at the Elkon Gallery in Manhattan the second time in four years, was not tolled. Accordingly, due to the passage of time, the museum lost any right to recover title to the painting.

At least one other state—New Jersey in *O'Keeffe v. Snyder*[184]—has recently dealt with the issue of accrual in a limitations statute in the context of stolen art, and has likewise imposed a duty of reasonable investigation. In still another New Jersey case focusing on whether or not the owner acted with due diligence in pursuing personal property, the court held that, when a good-faith bailee prevails on the defense of the statute of limitations, that bailee, like a good-faith purchaser, gets good title to the chattel in question, enabling the bailee to convey good title to a third party.[185]

Recovery of Stolen Property

Legislation: California is the only state that has legislation governing the accrual of a cause of action in the case of a stolen artwork or artifact. Highly protective of prior owners, it provides that an action must be brought within three years of "the discovery of the whereabouts" of the work "by the aggrieved party."[186] Apparently, the claimant need make no effort to locate the work, and ignorance or neglect does not appear to count against the claimant. If so, the California statute is more benevolent toward the claimant than the *DeWeerth* and *Guggenheim* cases, which require the claimant to make diligent efforts to locate the work. In contrast (and *pre-DeWeerth*), bills were proposed in both 1985 and 1986 in the New York legislature based on the California statute, which would have overruled *Menzel v. List* with respect to museums. The bills failed because they were deemed not to have balanced fairly the legitimate interests of museums, foreign countries seeking to recover lost or stolen art, and other innocent prior owners.

Misattribution

In cases in which, for example, a buyer discovers that a work of art is inauthentic and is not, as was alleged, by a given artist or from a given culture, the statute of limitations for a suit against the seller is governed by the UCC. In the majority of states the UCC provides that "an action for breach of any contract for sale must be commenced within four years after the cause of action has accrued."[187] The parties "by the original agreement" may "reduce the period of limitation to not less than one year," but they "may not extend it."[188] Moreover, "a cause of action accrues when the breach occurs, regardless of the aggrieved party's lack of knowledge of the breach."[189] Except in cases where a warranty explicitly extends to future performance of the goods, a breach occurs when tender of delivery is made.[190]

In the recent case of *Wilson v. Hammer Holdings, Inc.*,[191] for example, the plaintiffs in 1961 purchased for more than $11,000 a painting entitled "Femme Debout" from the Hammer Galleries and received a written guarantee that the painting was an original work of art by the French artist Vuillard. In 1984 the plaintiffs had the painting examined by an expert in preparation for selling it. When the expert determined that the painting was not by Vuillard and refused to authenticate it, the plaintiffs returned the painting to the Hammer Galleries and filed an action seeking damages for breach of warranty and negligence. The federal district court dismissed the case on the ground that it was time-barred by the applicable statute of limitations. On appeal, the First Circuit affirmed. Citing the applicable provision of the UCC as codified in Massachusetts, it noted the four-year limitation period from accrual that applies to actions for breach of sales contracts.[192] The court further noted that the breach occurred when "tender of delivery" of the painting was made. Moreover, the court held that this was not a warranty extending to future performance of the goods—where the cause of action accrues when the breach is or should have been discovered,[193] nor was it a cause of action in negligence under a different section of the UCC designed to address breach-of-warranty actions that are in essence product-liability actions.[194]

In most cases, the UCC's four-year statute should be viewed as controlling, but a lawyer in any jurisdiction should be alert for statutes inconsistent or in conflict with the UCC's provision. In New York, for example, if the action was based on mistake rather than breach of warranty of authenticity, the permissible period within which to bring suit for an alleged wrongdoing is six years from the occurrence of the wrongdoing, rather than four years under the UCC provision.[195]

If, subsequent to the purchase, a buyer learns that a work of art is misattributed, the buyer may revoke acceptance of it if he or she does so in a timely way when the misattribution substantially impairs the work's value, provided the original acceptance "was reasonably induced either by the difficulty of discovery before acceptance or by the seller's assurances."[196]

Principles of Contract and Tort Law

As is made clear below, the burdens borne by and the remedies available to an aggrieved purchaser through the application of existing contract and tort law principles are generally less than satisfactory.

Innocent Mistake

In the case of mutual mistake, in which both the buyer and the seller of a work of art are mistaken as to a material aspect of that work—for example, the identity of the artist—the sole form of relief ordinarily available to the aggrieved party is rescission and restitution.[197] If a sold object is discovered to be significantly more valuable than both parties had assumed, the seller may rescind the sale.[198] Similarly, if the object is significantly less valuable than both buyer and seller thought, the buyer may seek recourse.[199] When a seller, ignorant of its value, sells an item, and the item turns out to be worth much more than its purchase price, generally the seller may get no relief. Presumably conscious of his or her ignorance, the seller made no operative mistake of fact that would justify any relief.[200] If in a transaction, however, a mistake is the fault of the seller or the seller knows or has reason to know of a mistake, a buyer may obtain rescission and restitution, even if the mistake was unilateral on the buyer's part.[201]

Fraud

The tort of fraud occurs when the seller of a work of art makes an intentional or knowing[202] misrepresentation of a material existing fact about the artwork, either by positive conduct or by willful nondisclosure or concealment, intending the misrepresentation to be relied on, and where the representation is, in fact, relied on by the purchaser to the purchaser's detriment.[203] The misrepresentation must ordinarily be one of fact, not mere opinion or the seller's puffing.[204] If, however, a seller represents himself or herself as possessing an expertise with respect to the artwork to be sold, the seller's misrepresenting opinion may be sufficient for fraud.[205] In addition, if a seller presents a matter as fact, rather than opinion, that statement may be actionable.[206]

By virtue of the tortious character of fraud, an injured party has a choice of remedies: he or she can, as in the case of innocent misrepresentation or mutual mistake, rescind the transaction and obtain restitution of the money paid on redelivery of the artwork to the seller, or the injured party can elect to affirm the contract and collect damages proximately resulting from the fraud.[207]

Negligent Misrepresentation

Like fraud, negligent misrepresentation is a tort. However, unlike fraud, which generally requires intent or knowledge of the misrepresentation, negligent misrepresentation may lead to recovery even if the wrongdoer believed the false statements to be true, provided the statements were made without reasonable grounds.[208] As in a case of fraud, a party bringing suit in negligent misrepresentation can elect either to rescind the transaction and obtain restitution or to affirm the contract and collect proximate damages.[209]

Comparisons with Breach of Warranty

There are several important distinctions between fraud or negligent misrepresentation and breach of warranty. First, in fraud and negligent misrepresentation the buyer must be able to prove the requisite state of mind of the seller at the time the false statement was made; such proof is not necessary in an action for breach of warranty.[210] Second, since the concepts of both warranty and mistake are contractual, the rules governing venue and the statute of limitations are those applicable to contract actions; fraud and negligent misrepresentation are governed by rules applicable to actions in tort.[211] Finally, since a warranty is a term of the sales contract, the buyer cannot offer extrinsic evidence of its exclusion or modification unless the requirements of the parol evidence rule are first satisfied.[212]

Arts and Consumer Legislation

In addition to the redress offered the injured buyer by the UCC and by tort and contract law, a number of states have enacted legislation to provide further protections to the consumer. Below is a brief survey of some of that legislation.

Penal Statutes

Most applicable penal statutes throughout the United States are concerned with forgery and fraud. The relevant forgery statutes focus on written instruments, which include certificates of authenticity and other documents related to the purchase, consignment, and sale of artwork. The forgery statutes are of a general nature and require proof of criminal intent to injure or defraud,[213] as well as proof of the forged or counterfeit nature of the work.[214] In most states the relevant forgery statutes range from mid- to lower-level felonies to misdemeanors. Depending on the nature of the forgery and the laws of the jurisdiction, penalties range from prison terms of up to twenty years[215] to payment of a small fine.[216]

In addition, a number of states have enacted what are generally known as criminal-simulation statutes.[217] Typical is New York's statute, which provides for criminal penalties for the making or altering of any object so that "it appears to have an antiquity, rarity, source or authorship which it does not in fact possess."[218] As with forgery, the criminal simulation statutes require proof of criminal intent to defraud or injure,[219] as well as proof of the altered or counterfeit nature of the work.[220] Violation of the statute in most states constitutes a high-level misdemeanor, although a few states have statutes predicating the level of the crime on the value of the object altered or forged.[221]

Warranties of Authenticity

To date, New York and Michigan have enacted art legislation[222] providing assurances as to the authenticity of art purchases beyond those found in the UCC. Both statutes hold art merchant sellers responsible to nonmerchant buyers for any statement pertinent to the authorship of a work of fine art, notwithstanding that the statement may be merely the seller's opinion. In addition, the Michigan statute provides that "an art merchant whose warranty of authenticity of authorship was made in good faith shall not be liable for damages beyond the return of the purchase price which he receives."[223] However, such a warranty made in bad faith may entitle the buyer to consequential damages, rather than the mere return of the purchase price.[224]

Those statutes clarify the express warranty provision of the UCC[225] by (1) ensuring that the identification of a work of fine art with any authorship in a written instrument is itself part of the basis of the bargain and (2) abolishing, insofar as authorship is concerned, the distinction between fact and the seller's mere opinion.

Under the New York statute reproduced in part below, a standard for determining liability for breach of warranty has evolved—that is, whether the representations by the art merchant had a reasonable basis in fact at the time the representations were made, as shown by the testimony taken as a whole.[226]

Notwithstanding any provision of any other law to the contrary:

1. Whenever an art merchant, in selling or exchanging a work of fine art, furnishes to a buyer of such work who is not an art merchant a certificate of authenticity or any similar written instrument it:
   (a) Shall be presumed to be part of the basis of the bargain; and
   (b) Shall create an express warranty for the material facts stated as of the date of such sale or exchange.

Native American Arts

A number of states have enacted legislation addressing the representations of authenticity made in connection with Native American arts.[227] Those statutes render it a crime for a seller to place a state-registered label on fake Indian arts and crafts or otherwise to represent those items as being authentic for the purpose of reselling them. Violations of the statutes are generally classified as misdemeanors.

The Print Market: Disclosure Statutes

Prints may be either (1) reproductions of original works in other media produced in limited editions and signed by the artist or (2) art-making in primary form, with the artist working directly on the stone, plate, or block. Except for the artists who do their own printing, prints are the result of collaboration between the artist and a fine printer. For the print to be deemed "original,"[228]

1. The artist alone must create the master image in or on the plate, stone, woodblock, or other material;
2. The print must be made from such material by the artist or pursuant to his directions; or
3. The finished print must be approved by the artist.

Prints traditionally appear in limited editions; their usual form of numbering is a fraction, with the denominator giving the edition size and the numerator giving the sequential number of the print in hand. The edition size is adjusted to the potential market, with the asking price for a print often bearing an inverse relation to the size of the edition.

Over the years, the print market has suffered an array of abusive practices, including

- "Stretching" editions,[229]
- Issuing different numbered editions (for example, an Arabic-numbered edition of 200 and a Roman-numbered edition of 100 or an American edition of 100 and a European edition of 100),
- Publishing subsequent editions,
- Forging an artist's signature to commercial reproductions, and
- Wholesaling signed blank sheets of paper on which reproductions of a painting or drawing are subsequently printed and that are then numbered and issued as original prints.

To protect the consumer, a number of states[230] have recently enacted print-disclosure statutes requiring the prospective purchaser to be furnished with detailed information covering the sale of fine prints. As the most inclusive, New York's statute[231]—which applies to all prints sold after the statute's effective date, regardless of when the prints were made—requires the disclosure of extensive information, including whether the print is based on an image produced in another medium; whether the print was signed by the artist or, if not, the source of the artist's name on the multiple; the year when the multiple was produced; whether the print is a posthumous multiple; and the number of multiples in a limited edition.[232] The New York statute should be reviewed carefully by all persons involved with any aspect of prints.

Although predating the New York Print Disclosure Statute, regulation 30,[233] enacted in New York City as part of its Consumer Protection Law, supplements the print statute by offering additional prohibitions regarding deceptive advertising and labeling of alleged "limited edition" products.

The Sculpture Market

As in the print market, reproduction of sculpture has seen widespread abuse. Among the all too common practices here and abroad are the following:[234]

- Surmoulage, which is casting bronzes not from the artist's approved master waxes or plasters but from other bronzes made either by the artist in life or by the artist's estate;
- Enlargement of a sculptor's work by someone other than the artist; and
- Casting a sculptor's work in a medium other than that clearly intended by the sculptor for the final version of his work without authorization.

Those practices are inimical to the interests of both the artist and the public. They denigrate the artist's right of control over his or her own castings; they violate the quality of the original sculptures, since the making of a second edition from a bronze rather than a master wax or plaster is of diminished definition; they cause the owners of the original work to see their piece devalued; and they cause confusion in the public mind as to the origins of a particular work.

To provide protection for the consumer beyond existing statutes, arts groups have advocated additional statutory protection by requiring disclosure to the prospective buyer of vital information concerning the sculpture to be purchased. Although at this writing no specific state statutes exist, New York came close to passing a sculpture disclosure law in 1987.[235]

New York Home Solicitation Act

Enacted to afford consumers of goods primarily for personal or household purposes a cooling-off period from high-pressure sales tactics when payment of the purchase price is deferred over time, the New York Home Solicitation Act has been applied in at least one judicial case to the purchase of art by a collector.

In the previously discussed *Vom Lehn* case[236] (see pages 77-78), in which the New York Supreme Court found that the purchase price for twenty jade carvings was unconscionable and, therefore, would not enforce the contract requiring the plaintiffs to pay the balance of the purchase price, the court applied the Home Solicitation Sales Act to enable plaintiffs to recover their down payment on the carvings along with reasonable legal fees. In the course of its discussion, the court noted that the purchase price was to be paid in five installments, the defendants solicited the sale at the buyers' home, and there were no prior negotiations at the defendants' shop.[237]

Magnuson-Moss Warranty Act

Supplementary to and not in restriction of existing consumer rights and remedies under federal and state law, the Magnuson-Moss Warranty Act[238] mandates that sellers who give written warranties with respect to the sale of consumer products adhere to certain requirements:

1. If a consumer product costs more than $5, the seller must adhere to the FTC's rules relating to the disclosure of warranty terms.[239]
2. The seller must clearly and conspicuously designate the written warranty as either a "full warranty" or a "limited warranty."[240] A "full warranty" must conform to certain federal minimum standards.[241] A "limited warranty" need not meet those standards but must be clearly and conspicuously labeled as a limited warranty.[242] Not subject to those designation provisions are general statements of policy concerning consumer satisfaction,[243] such as statements indicating "satisfaction guaranteed or your money back."
3. A seller may not make what is deemed to be a deceptive warranty under the Act. A deceptive warranty includes any written warranty that: (a) contains an affirmation of

> fact, false or fraudulent representations, or promises or descriptions that would mislead a reasonable person exercising due care; (b) fails to contain sufficient information to prevent its terms from being misleading; or (c) uses the terms "guarantee" or "warranty" when other terms limit the breadth and the scope of the protection apparently granted, so as to deceive a reasonable person.[244]

The rules and regulations under the Warranty Act are promulgated by the FTC.[245] In order for the Act to apply to a transaction, the following conditions must be fulfilled:

1. The subject of the transaction must be a "consumer product."[246]
2. The seller must have issued a written warranty in connection with the subject of the sale.[247] (Nothing in the Act, however, requires that such a warranty be given.)
3. The product must either be distributed in interstate commerce or affect trade, traffic, transportation, or commerce.[248] Consequently, if an artwork is produced locally and sold locally, without the use of the mails, the Act may not apply.

Truth-in-Lending Act

If a collector buys a work of art on credit with the price payable in more than four installments or if a finance charge is imposed, the disclosure of the credit terms in accordance with the federal Truth-in-Lending Act[249] may be required. Willful and knowing failure to comply with the Act triggers criminal penalties—a fine of up to $5,000 or imprisonment for up to one year or both.[250] Civil liability may also be incurred for failure to comply with certain provisions of the Act.[251]

Federal Trade Commission

The FTC prohibits unfair or deceptive acts or practices in commerce.[252] Accordingly, a collector who believes that a dealer is engaged in deceptive acts or practices in the sale of artwork may lodge a complaint with the FTC. As noted earlier in this chapter (see page 54), the FTC has brought at least two actions[253] in which it has sought temporary, preliminary, and permanent injunctive relief as well as rescission and restitution for injured consumers.

New York City Truth in Pricing Law

The New York City Truth in Pricing Law,[254] which dates back to 1971, has only recently been enforced against art galleries located in New York City. The New York City Department of Consumer Affairs (DCA) has interpreted the law to require all retail establishments—that is, art galleries—to post prices next to exhibited works, list those prices in a public space at the art gallery or have sheets listing those prices readily available to members of the public. The new attention to art galleries resulted from the DCA's investigation of the auction industry, which led to the recently revised New York City auction rules discussed in chapter 3. In March 1988 DCA inspectors visited numerous art galleries and issued seventeen citations for failure conspicuously to display prices. Most art galleries have complied with the requirement of posting prices, although we understand that at least one art gallery may challenge the requirement in court.[255]

SALES BY COLLECTORS

When a collector undertakes to sell a work of art, he or she is bound by most of the same principles and statutes that circumscribe the conduct of dealers. However, some allowances are made for the collector's relative lack of expertise concerning both art objects and the trade, resulting in a somewhat less stringent code of required behavior by the collector as seller. The more important of the variances—which are found in the UCC, in principles of common law, and in arts and consumer legislation—are set forth below.

Express Warranties

For purposes of determining the existence of an express warranty in the absence of words of guarantee or warranty, statements by a collector concerning the attributes of a work of art, including authenticity, that are not stated as fact are more likely to be considered opinion than if those statements were made by a dealer.[256]

Implied Warranty of Merchantability

Although the implied warranty of merchantability is not applicable to a sale by someone who is not a merchant with respect to the type of goods being sold,[257] the nonmerchant-seller is nevertheless obligated on principles of good faith to disclose to the buyer any knowledge he or she has with respect to any hidden defects in the goods.[258]

Warranty of Title

As earlier indicated, a warranty of title is statutorily imposed in every sales contract unless the warranty is specifically disclaimed or modified. However, when a nonmerchant is the seller, the warranty does not include an implied representation that the goods are free of any rightful claim of patent or trademark infringement by a third person.[259]

Statute of Frauds

A contract for the sale of goods of $500 or more must be evidenced by a signed writing. An exception to that rule exists for a sale between merchants;[260] the exception is not available to a sale by a collector who is not a merchant of the goods sold.

Voidable Title

A seller with voidable title can transfer good title to a good-faith purchaser for value. However, a private collector, unlike an art dealer, cannot pass good title when the collector is entrusted with a work of art by another not intending to pass title.[261]

Buyer in the Ordinary Course of Business

All purchasers of art, whether dealers or not, must meet the test of being a buyer in the ordinary course of business within the meaning of the UCC in order to acquire unchallenged clear title. Although a more stringent standard is required of merchants who would be buyers in the ordinary course of business, a nonmerchant, to meet the test, must buy from a merchant in good faith and without knowledge that the sale would be in violation of third party ownership rights. "Good faith" for nonmerchant buyers means "honesty in fact."[262]

Sale on Approval/Sale or Return

A sale on approval occurs when a work, which may be returned even though it conforms to the contract, is delivered to a buyer who intends it primarily for use rather than resale.[263] Although such a sale does not render the work subject to the claims of the buyer's creditors until acceptance,[264] once the work is accepted, it can be reached by the buyer's creditors unless a security interest is reserved or a financing statement is filed. A sale or return, on the other hand, occurs when a work, which may be returned even though it conforms to the contract, is delivered primarily for resale.[265] In that case the work is subject to the claims of the dealer's creditors while it is in the dealer's possession[266] unless it can be established that the dealer's creditors know that the dealer is engaged in selling the goods of others or there is compliance with the UCC filing provisions of the article on secured transactions. (See pages 27-28.)

Risk of Loss

Generally, when a work of art is purchased from a merchant, the risk of loss passes to the buyer on the receipt of the work by the buyer.[267] When a work of art is purchased from a nonmerchant seller, the risk of loss passes to the buyer on notification necessary to enable the buyer to take delivery of the work.[268]

Arts and Consumer Legislation

The express warranty of authenticity of authorship, as set forth by statute in New York and Michigan,[269] is not applicable to a collector in the sale of a work of fine art.

IMMUNITY FROM SEIZURE OF ARTWORK

When a collector lends a work for exhibition out of state, the collector—absent special protection—risks having the work seized and attached by his or her creditors or claimants in that jurisdiction, thus rendering the collector subject to the courts of that state. The parallel situation exists in the United States on a national level; in organizing loan exhibitions, musuems must often conquer the reluctance of museums in foreign countries to lend their works of art to the United States, where they may be subject to judicial seizure. To cope with that predicament and to encourage the benefits to be derived from cultural exchange, state and federal legislatures have enacted immunity statutes.

A Brief Comparison of Two Statutes

The federal immunity statute[270] permits a grant of immunity from judicial seizure to cultural objects imported into the United States by nonprofit organizations for temporary display, provided that, before the object enters the country, (1) the United States Information Agency (USIA) determines that the object is of cultural significance, and (2) the USIA, in conjunction with the Department of State, finds that the temporary exhibition of the object is in the national interest. The federal statute further requires that a notice to such effect be published in the *Federal Register*, and indicates that, if a dispute arises over the shipping cost of an otherwise protected artwork, it may, in that limited connection, become subject to judicial seizure.

Like the federal statute, the New York statute[271] is restricted to objects entering the jurisdiction for display by a museum or other nonprofit organization. Although it covers only works of fine art, whereas the federal statute also embraces works of cultural significance, the New York statute does operate automatically, without the need to file an application or secure a finding that the exhibition or display is in the public interest.

SECURED TRANSACTIONS

A number of art transactions concern people who have a financial interest in a particular work of art and yet are not parties to the transaction. Examples are the artist who consigned a work to a dealer who, in turn, sold it to a purchaser; the bank that underwrites the dealer's business; and the creditor who has supplied the dealer with, for instance, framing services and has a long-standing account receivable. In addition, dealers and, to an ever-greater extent, collectors are borrowing money to purchase works of art and are pledging artworks as security for loans. Citibank in New York City has pioneered in the lending of money secured by artwork. All those situations give rise to an array of issues, such as: (1) how to secure collateral; (2) the rights of a creditor in and to collateral, as against the rights of other creditors; and (3) the risk assumed by a consignor that a dealer can convey to a third party good title in artwork, leaving the consignor unpaid. Those issues are dealt with in article 9 of the UCC on secured transactions. A brief survey of the subject as it applies to dealing in art is set forth below.

Creation of the Security Interest

In a security interest there must be a creditor and a debtor. The creditor is a lender of money, goods, or services, and the debtor is a borrower of the money, goods, or services. The debtor is also the grantor of the security interest.[272] For a security interest to exist between a creditor and a debtor, it must attach to the collateral given as security for the loan,[273] and it is limited by the extent of the rights of the debtor in the collateral.[274] For a secured party—that is, the creditor—to enjoy the maximum protection afforded by article 9, he or she must ensure that the security interest in the collateral (1) attaches and (2) is perfected.[275]

Attachment

Attachment of the security interest is a prerequisite to perfection (a condition that generally must occur in order for the secured party to prevail over third-party claims to the collateral, and must occur before a creditor can sue to enforce his or her rights under the UCC).[276] There are three requirements for attachment:

1. The debtor must execute a security agreement, or the collateral must be in the possession of the secured party;
2. The secured party must give value; and
3. The debtor must have rights in the collateral.[277]

Those three prerequisites to attachment may take place in any order; the time of attachment is the time when the last of the three, whichever that may be, occurs.[278]

Collateral is grouped into three major categories:[279]

1. Tangible personal property or goods;
2. Semi-intangibles, encompassing instruments, documents, and chattel paper; and
3. Pure intangibles, encompassing accounts, contract rights, and general intangibles.

Tangible collateral, pertinent to most secured transactions involving art, are divided into four classifications:[280]

1. Consumer goods, used primarily for personal, household, or family purposes;
2. Equipment, a catchall term meaning goods "used or bought for use primarily in business";
3. Farm products, meaning goods of a described type not subjected to a manufacturing process and in the possession of a debtor who is a farmer; and
4. Inventory, meaning goods held for sale or lease or to be furnished under service contracts, raw materials, work in process, and materials used or consumed in a business.

The four classes of tangibles are mutually exclusive,[281] and the proper classification of collateral hinges on its principal use or intended principal use by the debtor.[282] Thus, if a debtor owns a large sculpture for purposes of display in his or her home, the sculpture is classified a consumer good, whereas, if the same debtor holds the same piece of sculpture in his or her gallery for sale, the sculpture is classified as an item of inventory.[283]

Perfection

As noted earlier,[284] the security interest in the collateral must be perfected in order for the creditor to receive priority against adverse claims by third parties to the collateral. There are three basic methods of perfection: (1) perfection by filing, (2) perfection by taking possession, and (3) perfection on attachment (that is, automatic perfection).[285]

The most common method of perfection is that of filing,[286] and a brief financing statement may be filed in the appropriate state or county office[287] in lieu of the actual security agreement.[288] Filing is deemed to occur at the time of presentation to the filing officer,[289] and may be made before the security interest attaches and even before the security agreement is executed.[290] The financing statement is effective for five years after the date of filing and may be renewed for additional five-year periods by filing successive continuation statements.[291]

In perfection by possession, an alternative to filing, the collateral or pledge may be taken either by the secured party or by an agent on the secured party's behalf.[292] Perfection here occurs when the secured party takes possession of the collateral or when the collateral is in the hands of the party's agent when the agent receives notice of the secured party's interest.[293] The secured party must use "reasonable care in the custody and preservation of collateral" in his or her possession.[294]

The third method, perfection on attachment, occurs in art transactions most commonly in situations involving the purchase-money security interest.[295] Thus, an art gallery that sells a painting on credit has a perfected security interest at the time of the sale without the necessity of filing a financing statement. That is, when the buyer executes a security agreement, the gallery gives value in the form of an extension of credit, and the buyer receives a contractual right to the goods.[296] A party other than the seller may have a purchase-money security interest, as would be the case when a lender of money takes a security interest to secure the loan to a buyer to enable the debtor to buy the painting, and the debtor in fact uses the money to acquire the collateral.[297]

Priorities

Most secured transaction litigation deals with the issue of who has first claim on the collateral—the secured party or a competing third-party claimant.[298] In most cases involving art, the competing claimant is (1) a lien creditor, (2) another secured party, or (3) a buyer from the debtor.[299]

Secured Party Versus Lien Creditor: Generally, an unperfected security interest is subordinate to the rights of one who becomes a lien creditor before the security interest is perfected.[300] Thus, secured party *X*, who on March 1 obtains a security interest in a painting owned by a debtor-gallery and lends the gallery funds, but fails to file a financing statement until March 8, is subordinate to the claims of an unsecured creditor who on March 4 obtains a judicial lien against the gallery by way of judgment and levy.

An exception occurs with purchase-money security interests[301] in which a secured party who files within ten[302] days after the debtor takes possession of the collateral prevails over one who becomes a lien creditor between the time the security interest attaches and the time of filing. Thus, an art dealer who sells a painting on March 1 to a debtor-art gallery on credit and delivers it the same day prevails over one who becomes a judicial lienholder on March 4, even though the secured party neglects to file until March 8.

Secured Party Versus Secured Party: When a debtor grants a security interest in the same collateral to two different lenders and subsequently defaults on the loans, both secured parties may assert claims to the collateral. Here are some of the general rules of priority:[303]

1. When neither security interest is perfected, the first to attach prevails.[304]
2. When one security interest is perfected and the other is not, the perfected interest prevails.[305]
3. When both security interests are perfected, one by a means other than filing, the first party to file or perfect, whichever occurs earlier, prevails.[306]
4. When both security interests are perfected by filing, the first party to file or perfect, whichever occurs earlier, prevails.[307]
5. When the collateral is other than inventory, a purchase-money security interest prevails over conflicting claims[308] if it is perfected within ten days[309] after the debtor takes possession of the collateral. Moreover, the interest holder automatically has a security interest in the proceeds of that collateral.[310] When the collateral is inventory, a purchase-money security interest prevails over conflicting claims in the same inventory and in identifiable cash pro-

ceeds received by the time of delivery of the inventory to a buyer if, before the debtor takes possession of the collateral, the purchase-money security interest is perfected and all secured parties with perfected interests in the same collateral receive written notice of that interest.[311]

6. One who delivers goods under a *consignment* that is not a security interest, and who is required to file a financing statement under the UCC,[312] prevails over a secured creditor of the consignee. The consignor also prevails as to identifiable cash proceeds received by the time of delivery of the goods to the buyer, provided (a) the consignor complies with the filing provisions of the UCC[313] before the consignee takes possession of the goods, and (b) the secured creditors receive written notice of the filing, in accordance with the UCC.[314]

Secured Party Versus Buyer: In art transactions a secured creditor may reach collateral in the hands of a buyer except for the four instances below:

1. When the creditor has authorized the sale or other disposition of the collateral "in the security agreement or otherwise,"[315] his or her security interest does not survive the authorized transaction.
2. When the creditor has an unperfected security interest, the buyer prevails if he or she gives value and receives delivery without knowledge of the security interest before it is perfected.[316]
3. When there is a buyer in the ordinary course of business, the buyer takes possession free of a perfected security interest, even if the buyer is aware of it, unless the buyer knows that the sale violates the security agreement's terms.[317]
4. In the case of a consumer-to-consumer sale, the holder of a purchase-money security interest in consumer goods may perfect without filing, but the holder must file in

order to prevail over one who buys for personal, household, or family use without knowledge of the security interest.[318]

Creditor's Rights on Default

Once a default has occurred, the secured creditor may proceed under the UCC against the collateral.[319] In addition, since the options are not mutually exclusive,[320] the creditor may proceed outside the UCC by bringing suit on the debt.[321] Some of the alternatives available to the secured creditor are noted in the following discussion.

When Default Occurs

Although not defined in the UCC,[322] default most commonly occurs on the debtor's failure to make payments when due.[323] In addition, default generally occurs whenever the parties have contractually so agreed. The well-drafted security agreement specifies which acts or occurrences are to be events of default.[324] Virtually all security agreements contain an acceleration clause, requiring immediate payment under prescribed conditions of the entire remainder of the loan.[325] Such clauses in consumer agreements, however, are nullified in states that have adopted non-UCC consumer-protection legislation whereby the debtor may cure default by paying delinquent installments.[326]

Bringing Suit on the Debt

On default, the secured creditor may bring suit outside the UCC on the debt, procure a judgment, obtain a levy on the debtor's property, and receive from the sheriff, after a public auction, whatever proceeds are required to satisfy the debt. When the collateral's value is substantially less than the outstanding debt, the lien of a postjudgment levy reaches all the debtor's property, not just the collateral subject to the security interest.[327]

Realizing on Tangible Collateral—Right to Repossession

The secured party may proceed under the UCC to repossess the collateral either through self-help, if it can be accomplished without committing a breach of the peace, or through judicial action.[328] Once the collateral is repossessed, either through self-help or after the procurement of a judgment, the creditor may realize on the collateral by reselling or retaining it.[329]

Retention of the Collateral in Satisfaction of the Debt

The secured party may, under the UCC[330] and in compliance with the UCC's notice provisions, resort to strict foreclosure. The collateral is retained, and the debt is discharged, with the debtor neither liable for a deficiency nor entitled to any surplus if the creditor later sells.[331] Strict foreclosure is feasible only when the collateral's value approximates the unpaid balance of the debt, plus the anticipated costs of disposition.[332] However, when the collateral is consumer goods and the debtor has paid at least 60 percent of the loan or cash price, the secured party must dispose of the collateral under the UCC[333] within ninety days after taking possession or risk exposure in conversion or other liabilities under the UCC.[334]

Sale or Other Disposition of Collateral

By far the most common method of realization on tangible collateral is by its sale or other disposition.[335] Disposition, which must be in compliance with the UCC's notice provisions,[336] can occur by auction, by private sale, or by contract,[337] so long as the disposition is commercially reasonable[338] as to method, time, manner, place, and terms.[339] Proceeds from the disposition are applied, first, to the reasonable expenses of repossession and sale; second, to the satisfaction of the debt; and third, to the satisfaction of third-party security interests.[340] Any surplus is turned over to the debtor.[341] When the proceeds cannot cover the unpaid balance of the debt, plus expenses, the debtor is personally liable for the deficiency unless it has been otherwise agreed.[342]

Debtor's Right of Redemption

Under any circumstances, until the secured party has sold the collateral or otherwise discharged the debt, the debtor may redeem the collateral by paying all the obligations secured by the collateral, plus reasonable expenses, including attorneys' fees.[343]

Liability of the Secured Party

When there is misconduct by the secured party in repossessing and realizing on the collateral, the debtor and other creditors may avail themselves of a number of remedies. One remedy is judicial intervention; a court may enjoin, for instance, a wrongful repossession or commercially unreasonable disposition.[344] A second remedy, if an improper disposition has already occurred, is a right of recovery by the debtor or other creditors against the secured party.[345] Other remedies not mentioned in the applicable provision of the UCC but recognized in a number of jurisdictions include liability in conversion,[346] other tort liability on grounds (such as trespass and invasion of privacy),[347] and denial of the secured party's right to recover a deficiency.[348]

NOTES
to Chapter 2

1. *See* IFARREPORTS, Dec. 1986, at 4.

2. N.Y. TIMES, Feb. 10, 1988, at B1.

3. See discussion on the statute of limitations, at pp. 82-90.

4. For an excellent general discussion of artwork title disputes, including a review of some of the resources available for recovering and investigating title to artwork, see Hoover, *Title Disputes in the Art Market: An Emerging Duty of Care for Art Merchants*, 51 GEO. WASH. L. REV. 443 (1983).

5. The United States maintains its membership in INTERPOL pursuant to 22 U.S.C. § 263(a)(1978). In 1977, the Justice and Treasury Departments assumed responsibility for representing the interests of the United States in INTERPOL.

6. State v. Wright Hepburn Webster Gallery, Ltd., 64 Misc. 2d 423, 314 N.Y.S.2d 661 (Sup. Ct. 1970), *aff'd*, 37 A.D.2d 698, 323 N.Y.S.2d 389 (1st Dep't 1971).

7. *Id.*, 64 Misc. 2d at 427, 314 N.Y.S.2d at 667.

8. WALL ST. J., July 17, 1987.

9. IFARREPORTS, Jan. 1989, at 4.

10. FTC v. Federal Sterling Galleries, Inc., No. 87-2072 (D. Ariz. filed Jan. 12, 1989).

11. FTC v. Austin Galleries, No. 88 C 3845 (N.D. Ill. Nov. 7, 1988).

12. N.Y. TIMES, Feb. 15, 1987, at Arts and Leisure § 2, at 1, col. 2. See further discussion in chapter 3.

13. See discussion on the sculpture market at p. 96.

14. *See* L. DUBOFF, DESKBOOK OF ART LAW 390-91 (1977 & Supp. 1984).

15. See discussion of expert opinions and liability in chapter 5 at pp. 243-50.

16. Radiocarbon dating, used to test materials derived from once-living organisms, gives estimates of the time elapsed since an organism's death by measuring the quantity of a particular radiation emitted by those materials.

17. Mainly applicable to ceramic ware or fired clay, thermoluminescent analysis measures the thermoluminescence or light of the material, thereby indicating the time elapsed since the last firing of the clay. The technique is especially suitable to sculpture and antiquities.

18. X-ray photography includes a variety of X-ray techniques: X-radiographs, which provide insights into the structure of paintings in general; X-ray diffraction, which determines the degree and character of the internal structure of such materials as jewelry, glass, pigments, and glazes; autoradiography, which permits the identification and examination of the pigments in a painting.

19. In comparative analysis, the expert examines characteristic composition patterns that can be compared with a known sample, thus permitting the scientist to deduce the information sought.

20. Chemical analysis is used primarily to date fossil bones and teeth from a single area when they are preserved under comparable conditions by measuring, in particular, the accumulation in the bones of two elements, fluorine and uranium.

21. N.Y. Arts & Cult. Aff. Law § 13.01 (McKinney 1984 & Supp. 1988).

22. *See, e.g.*, Mich. Comp. Laws Ann. §§ 442.321-.325 (West Supp. 1987).

23. *See* Steiner v. Jarrett, 130 Cal. App. 2d 869, 280 P.2d 235 (1954); Cole v. Weber, 69 Cal. App. 394, 231 P. 353 (1924).

24. U.C.C. § 2-313.

25. U.C.C. § 2-313 comments l, 4.

26. U.C.C. § 2-313 comment 8.

27. U.C.C. § 2-313(2); Overstreet v. Norden Laboratories, Inc., 669 F.2d 1286 (6th Cir. 1982); Gladden v. Cadillac Motor Car Div., 83 N.J. 320; 416 A.2d 394 (1980).

28. McKnelly v. Sperry Corp., 642 F.2d 1101 (8th Cir. 1981).

29. Crest Container Corp. v. R.H. Bishop Co., 445 N.E.2d 19 (Ill. Ct. App. 1982).

30. Eddington v. Dick, 87 Misc. 2d 793, 386 N.Y.S.2d 180 (Sup. Ct. 1976).

31. Sylvestri v. Warner & Swasey Co., 398 F.2d 598 (2d Cir. 1968).

32. U.C.C. § 2-313 comment 7.

33. U.C.C. § 2-202; Young & Cooper, Inc. v. Vestring, 214 Kan. 311, 521 P.2d 281 (1974).

34. U.C.C. § 2-313 (1)(a).

35. *Id.*

36. *Id.*

37. U.C.C. § 2-313(1)(b).

38. U.C.C. § 2-313(1)(b) comment 5.

39. *Id.*

40. U.C.C. § 2-313(2).

41. *Id.*

42. Grinnel v. Charles Pfizer & Co., 274 Cal. App. 2d 424, 79 Cal. Rptr. 369 (1969).

43. U.C.C. § 2-316 comment 8.

44. *Id.*

45. *See* Overstreet v. Norden Laboratories, Inc., *supra* note 27, at 1291.

46. Cox v. DeSoto Crude Oil Purchasing Corp., 55 F. Supp. 467 (W.D. La. 1944); Morse v. Howard Park Corp., 50 Misc. 2d 834, 272 N.Y.S.2d 16 (Sup. Ct. 1966).

47. U.C.C. § 2-316 comment 8.

48. U.C.C. § 2-316(1).

49. *Id.*

50. N.Y. Arts & Cult. Aff. Law § 13.01(4) (McKinney 1984 & Supp. 1988).

51. Mich. Comp. Laws Ann. § 442.323 (West Supp. 1987).

52. *See* U.C.C. § 2-316; Giusti v. Sotheby Parke Bernet, Inc., N.Y.L.J., July 16, 1982, at 24 (Sup. Ct. 1982).

53. Weiscz v. Parke-Bernet Galleries, Inc., 67 Misc. 2d 1077, 325 N.Y.S.2d 576 (Civ. Ct. 1971), *rev'd*, 77 Misc. 2d 80, 351 N.Y.S.2d 911 (App. Term 1st Dep't 1974).

54. *Id.*, 67 Misc. 2d at 1082, 325 N.Y.S.2d at 582.

55. *Supra* note 53, 77 Misc. 2d at 80, 351 N.Y.S.2d at 912.

56. U.C.C. § 2-202.

57. U.C.C. § 2-202(a).

58. U.C.C. § 2-202(b).

59. Implied Warranty of Merchantability: U.C.C. § 2-314; Implied Warranty of Fitness for a Particular Purpose; U.C.C. § 2-315.

60. U.C.C. § 2-314.

61. U.C.C. § 2-314(1).

62. U.C.C. § 2-104(1).

63. U.C.C. § 2-104 comment 2.

64. *Id.*

65. *See, e.g.*, Daniell v. Ford Motor Co., 581 F. Supp. 728 (D.N.M. 1984); Hinderer v. Ryan, 7 Wash. App. 434, 499 P.2d 252 (1972).

66. U.C.C. § 2-314(2).

67. U.C.C. § 2-314 comment 2.

68. U.C.C. § 2-314 comment 8.

69. U.C.C. § 2-315 & comment 1.

70. Price Bros. Co. v. Philadelphia Gear Corp., 649 F.2d 416 (6th Cir.), *cert. denied*, 454 U.S. 1099 (1981).

71. U.C.C. § 2-315 comment 4.

72. U.C.C. § 2-316(3)(b).

73. *Id.*

74. U.C.C. § 2-316 comment 8.

75. *Id.*

76. *Id.*

77. U.C.C. § 2-316.

78. U.C.C. § 2-316(2) & comments 3, 5.

79. U.C.C. § 2-316(2) & comment 3; U.C.C. § 1-201(10).

80. U.C.C. § 2-316(2) & comment 3.

81. U.C.C. § 2-316(3)(a) & comment 7.

82. U.C.C. § 2-316(2).

83. *Id.*

84. *Id.*

85. U.C.C. § 2-316(3)(a) & comment 7.

86. U.C.C. § 2-316(3)(c).

87. Alger v. Abele Tractor & Equip. Co., 92 A.D.2d 677, 460 N.Y.S.2d 202 (3d Dept. 1983); FMC Fin. Corp. v. Murphree, 632 F.2d 413 (5th Cir. 1980).

88. U.C.C. §§ 2-316(2), 1-201(10). *See, e.g.*, Lupa v. Jock's, 131 Misc. 2d 536, 500 N.Y.S.2d 962 (Sup. Ct. 1986); Natale v. Martin Volkswagen, Inc., 92 Misc. 2d 1046, 402 N.Y.S.2d 156 (Sup. Ct. 1978).

89. U.C.C. § 2-302. *See, e.g.*, Industralease Automated Scientific & Equip. Corp. v. R.M.E. Enters., Inc. 58 A.D.2d 482, 396 N.Y.S.2d 427 (2d Dep't 1977).

90. *See, e.g.*, CAL. CIV. CODE §§ 1790 *et seq.* (West Supp. 1988); ME. REV. STAT. tit. 11, § 2-316(5) (West Supp. 1987); MD. COM. LAW CODE ANN. § 2-316.1

(Supp. 1987); MASS. GEN. LAWS ANN. ch. 106, § 2-316A (West Supp. 1988); OR. REV. STAT. tit. 8, ch. 72.8050 (1987); WASH. REV. CODE § 2-316(4) (West Supp. 1988).

91. Consumer goods are generally defined in the statutes as goods purchased primarily for personal, family, or household use.

92. U.C.C. § 2-318 comment 3.

93. *See, e.g.*, Mayes v. Harnischfeger Corp., 60 Misc. 2d 308, 302 N.Y.S.2d 658 (Sup. Ct. 1969).

94. Lonzrick v. Republic Steel Corp., 6 Ohio St. 2d 227, 218 N.E.2d 185 (1966).

95. 1 R. ANDERSON, UNIFORM COMMERCIAL CODE § 2-103:18 (3d ed. 1981 & Supp. 1987); 3 R. ANDERSON, UNIFORM COMMERCIAL CODE § 2-314:97 (3d ed. 1983 & Supp. 1987).

96. U.C.C. § 2-312.

97. U.C.C. § 2-312(1)(a).

98. *Id.*

99. U.C.C. § 2-312(1)(b).

100. U.C.C. § 2-312(3).

101. U.C.C. § 2-312(2).

102. *Id. See also* Duesenberg & King, *Sales and Bulk Transfers*, 3 BENDER'S U.C.C. SERV. 1987 § 5.03.

103. Sunseri v. RKO-Stanley Warner Theatres, Inc., 374 A.2d 1342 (Pa. Super. 1977).

104. Duesenberg & King, *supra* note 102, at § 5.03. *See also, e.g.*, Simmons Mach. Co. v. M&M Brokerage, Inc., 409 So. 2d 743 (Ala. 1981).

105. U.C.C. § 2-312 comment 5. But note that the warranty against infringement may be excluded by agreement between the parties. *See* Duesenberg & King, *supra* note 102, at § 5.04[5].

106. U.C.C. § 2-312 comment 5.

107. *See, e.g.*, Cady v. Pitts, 625 P.2d 1089 (Idaho 1981); Smith v. Taylor, 261 S.E.2d 19 (N.C. Ct. App. 1979).

108. Menzel v. List, 49 Misc. 2d 300, 267 N.Y.S.2d 804 (Sup. Ct. 1966), *modified as to damages*, 28 A.D.2d 516, 279 N.Y.S.2d 608 (1st Dep't 1967), *rev'd as to modifications*, 24 N.Y.2d 91, 246 N.E.2d 742, 298 N.Y.S.2d 979 (1969). See discussion related to the statute of limitations at pp. 82-90.

109. *Supra* note 108, 24 N.Y.2d at 97, 246 N.E.2d at 745, 298 N.Y.S.2d at 983.

110. The Perls did not pursue their cause of action against the Parisian art dealer, as he was then deceased.

111. *Supra* note 108, at 98, 246 N.E.2d at 745, 298 N.Y.S.2d at 983.

112. U.C.C. § 2-714(2).

113. Koerner v. Davis, No. 85 Civ. 0752 (S.D.N.Y. May 21, 1987).

114. U.C.C. § 2-607.

115. U.C.C. § 1-201(25), (26).

116. U.C.C. § 2-607(3)(a).

117. U.C.C. § 2-609 comment 4.

118. U.C.C. § 2-607(5)(a).

119. U.C.C. § 2-201(2).

120. U.C.C. § 2-201(3).

121. National Historic Shrines Found. v. Dali, 4 U.C.C. Rep. Serv. (Callaghan) 71 (N.Y. Sup. Ct. 1967).

122. U.C.C. § 2-302. But note that this provision is omitted entirely in the state of California.

123. Vom Lehn v. Astor Art Galleries, Ltd., 86 Misc. 2d 1, 11, 380 N.Y.S.2d 532, 541 (Sup. Ct. 1976).

124. Vom Lehn, *supra* note 123, at 10, 380 N.Y.S.2d at 541.

125. *Id.*

126. *Id.*

127. *Supra* note 123.

128. *Id.* at 13, 380 N.Y.S.2d at 543.

129. *See, e.g.*, Bassett v. Spofford, 45 N.Y. 387 (1871). *See also* Menzel v. List, *supra* note 108, 49 Misc. 2d at 315, 267 N.Y.S.2d at 819.

130. U.C.C. § 2-403(1).

131. *See, e.g.*, Ross v. Leuci, 194 Misc. 345, 85 N.Y.S.2d 497 (City Ct. 1949); Crocker v. Crocker, 31 N.Y. 507 (1865).

132. U.C.C. § 2-403(2).

133. U.C.C. § 1-201(9).

134. U.C.C. § 2-103(1)(b).

135. Porter v. Wertz, 68 A.D.2d 141, 416 N.Y.S.2d 254 (1st Dep't 1979), *aff'd*, 53 N.Y.2d 696, 421 N.E.2d 500, 439 N.Y.S.2d 105 (1981) (mem.) *See also* Phillips, *The Commercial Culpability Scale*, 92 Yale L.J. 228 (1982).

136. Porter v. Wertz, *supra* note 135, at 145, 416 N.Y.S.2d at 257.

137. Porter v. Wertz, *supra* note 135; *see also* Taborsky v. Maroney, No 83-2533, 745 F.2d 60 (7th Cir. 1984) (unpublished); Taborsky v. Bolen Gallery, Inc., No 83-2560, 745 F.2d 60 (7th Cir. 1984) (unpublished), *reproduced in* 2 F. Feldman, S. Weil & S. Biederman, Art Law § 9.2.4, (1986). *See* Autocephalous Greek Orthodox Church v. Goldberg, IP 89-304C (S.D. Ind. Aug. 3, 1989).

138. *See* Taborsky, *supra* note 137. See also discussion on sales by collectors at pp. 99-102.

139. *Supra* note 137.

140. *Id.*

141. *Id.*

142. *Id.*

143. *Id.*

144. Van Rijn v. Wildenstein, No. 85 Civ. 3597 (S.D.N.Y. 1987).

145. U.C.C. § 2-327(2)(b).

146. U.C.C. § 2-503; *see also* U.C.C. § 2-509.

147. U.C.C. § 2-509(3); Conway v. Larsen Jewelers, Inc., 104 Misc. 2d 872, 429 N.Y.S.2d 378 (Small Claims Ct. 1980).

148. Bassett, *supra* note 129, at 391.

149. *See* D. Dobbs, Handbook on the Law of Remedies 399 (1973).

150. *Id.* at 403.

151. Petrovich, *The Recovery of Stolen Art: of Paintings, Statues & Statutes of Limitations*, 27 UCLA L. Rev. 1122, 1125 (1980). Petrovich provides a comprehensive treatment of the theories of accrual in statutes of limitations.

152. *Id.* at 1127.

153. *Id.*

154. *Id.* at 1128.

155. *Id.*

156. *Id.* at 1129.

157. *See generally*, Petrovich, *supra* note 151.

158. *See, e.g.*, Redmond v. New Jersey Historical Soc'y, 132 N.J. Eg. 464, 28 A.2d 189 (1942). Note: a thief who takes and conceals property cannot get title, however long he holds the property—that is, the statute of limitations does not begin to run. He can, however, take title through adverse possession, since in that case he openly and notoriously holds the property, so the owner could have a reasonable chance of knowing its whereabouts and asserting title. *See* 51 Am. Jur. 2d *Limitation of Actions* § 124, at 694 (1970, Supp. 1989).

159. Petrovich, *supra* note 151, at 1141.

160. *Id.* at 1142.

161. *Id.*

162. *Id.* at 1142-43.

163. *Id.* at 1146.

164. *Id.*

165. 51AM. JUR. 2D *Limitation of Actions* § 125, at 694 (1970, Supp. 1989). *See also* W. KEETON, R. KEETON, D. DOBBS & D. OWEN, PROSSER AND KEETON ON THE LAW OF TORTS 93-94 (5th ed. 1984 & Supp. 1988).

166. *Id.*

167. *Id.*

168. *See* Koerner v. Davis, 85 Civ. 0752 (S.D.N.Y. May 21, 1987); PROSSER AND KEETON, *supra* note 165, at 94 n.50.

169. *See* Menzel v. List, *supra* note 108.

170. *Id.*

171. Petrovich, *supra* note 151, at 1133.

172. *Id.* at 1139.

173. Kunstsammlungen Zu Weimar v. Elicofon, 536 F. Supp. 829 (E.D.N.Y. 1981), *aff'd*, 678 F.2d 1150 (2d Cir. 1982).

174. DeWeerth v. Baldinger, 836 F.2d 103 (2d Cir.), *rev'g* 658 F. Supp. 688 (S.D.N.Y. 1987).

175. *Id.*

176. *Id.* at 104.

177. *Id.* at 112.

178. *Id.* at 106.

179. *Id.* at 106-07.

180. *Id.* at 108-109.

181. *Id.* at 109.

182. *Id.* at 112.

183. Guggenheim v. Lubell, N.Y.L.J., Feb. 15, 1989, at 1, col. 1.

184. O'Keeffe v. Snyder, 170 N.J. Super. 75, 405 A.2d 840 (1979), *rev'd*, 83 N.J. 478, 416 A.2d 862 (1980). For a discussion of the *O'Keeffe* decision, see Ward, *The Georgia Grind: Can the Common Law Accommodate the Problems of Title in the Art World, Observations on a Recent Case*, 8 J. COLLEGE & U.L. 533 (1981-1982).

185. Desiderio v. D'Ambrosio, 190 N.J. Super 424, 463 A.2d 986 (1983).

186. CAL. CIV. PROC. CODE § 338.3 (West Supp. 1985).

187. U.C.C. § 2-725(1).

188. *Id.*

189. U.C.C. § 2-725(2).

190. *Id.*

191. Wilson v. Hammer Holdings, Inc., 850 F.2d 3 (1st Cir. 1988). *See also* Roser v. Spanierman Gallery, 87 Civ. 9045 (S.D.N.Y. filed Apr. 25, 1989).

192. *Id.* at 4-5.

193. *Id.* at 6.

194. *Id.* at 7.

195. N.Y. CIV. PRAC. L. & R. 213(6) (McKinney 1972 & Supp. 1989).

196. U.C.C. § 2-608.

197. *See* 3 A. CORBIN, CORBIN ON CONTRACTS § 605 (1960 & 1971 Supp.); *see also* 13 S. WILLISTON, WILLISTON ON CONTRACTS §§ 1543, 1557 (3d. ed. 1970 & Supp. 1986).

198. *See, e.g.*, Ohio Co. v. Rosemeir, 32 Ohio App. 2d 116, 288 N.E.2d 326 (1972).

199. *See, e.g.*, Chapman v. Cole, 12 Gray (Mass.) 141 (1858).

200. 3 CORBIN, *supra* note 197, at § 605.

201. 13 WILLISTON, *supra* note 197 at § 1543.

202. Aside from knowledge and belief, reckless disregard for a representation's truth or falsity and awareness of a lack of sufficient basis of information to make a representation are two states of mind that also support a suit in fraud. *See* PROSSER AND KEETON, *supra* note 165, at §§ 105, 107.

203. 12 WILLISTON, *supra* note 197, at §§ 1487, 1487-A (Supp. 1987); PROSSER AND KEETON, *supra* note 165, at § 105.

204. PROSSER AND KEETON, *supra* note 165, at § 109.

205. *Id.*

206. *Id.* Here, as in the text immediately above, the seller, depending on the circumstances, may also be liable for breach of warranty.

207. *Id.* at § 105.

208. *Id.* at § 107.

209. *Id.* at § 105.

210. See discussion of breach of warranties at pp. 91-92.

211. R. Duffy, Art Law: Representing Artists, Dealers, and Collectors 16 (1977).

212. U.C.C. § 2-202. See also discussion of parol evidence at p. 64.

213. A few statutes, such as Ohio's and Pennsylvania's, permit a suit in forgery on proof of mere knowledge, rather than intent, to defraud or injure. Ohio Rev. Code Ann. § 2913.31 (Baldwin Supp. 1987); Pa. Cons. Stat. Ann. § 4101 (Purdon Supp. 1987).

214. *See, e.g.*, N.Y. Penal Law § 170.05 (McKinney 1975 & Supp. 1988). *See also* Note, *Legal Control of the Fabrication and Marketing of Fake Paintings*, 24 Stan. L. Rev. 930, 940-41 (1972).

215. Mont. Code Ann. § 45-6-325 (Supp. 1987).

216. Conn. Gen. Stat. Ann. § 53a-140 (West Supp. 1988).

217. *See, e.g.*, Ala. Code § 13A-9-10 (Supp. 1987); Alaska Stat. § 11.46.530 (Supp. 1987); Ariz. Rev. Stat. Ann. § 13-2004 (Supp. 1987); Ark. Code § 5-37-213 (Supp. 1987); Colo. Rev. Stat. § 18-5-110 (Supp. 1986); Conn. Gen. Stat. Ann. § 53a-141 (West Supp. 1987); Ky. Rev. Stat. § 516.110 (Supp. 1986); N.J. Stat. Ann. § 2C:21-2 (Supp. 1987); Ohio Rev. Code Ann. § 2913.32 (Supp. 1987); Pa. Cons. Stat. Ann. § 4102 (Purdon Supp. 1987); Tex. Ann. Code § 32.22 (Supp. 1988); Utah Code Ann. § 76-6-501 (Supp. 1987); Vt. Stat. Ann. § 2023 (Supp. 1987); Wis. Stat. Ann. § 943.38(3)(a) (Supp. 1987).

218. N.Y. Penal Law § 170.45 (McKinney 1975 & Supp. 1988). *See also* People v. Haifif, 128 Misc. 2d 713, 491 N.Y.S.2d 226 (Sup. Ct. 1985).

219. Again, some state statutes, such as Ohio's and Pennsylvania's, *supra* note 213, permit the bringing of suit upon mere proof of knowledge of injury or deception rather than intent.

220. *See, e.g.*, Ohio's statute, *supra* note 217.

221. *See, e.g.*, Utah's statute, *supra* note 217.

222. Mich. Comp. Laws Ann., *supra* note 22; N.Y. Arts & Cult. Aff. Law, *supra* note 21.

223. Mich. Comp. Laws Ann., *supra* note 22, at § 442.324.

224. Lawson v. London Arts Group, 708 F.2d 226 (6th Cir. 1983).

225. U.C.C. § 2-313.

226. Englehard v. Duffy, N.Y.L.J., Oct. 27, 1983, at 13; Dawson v. Malina, Inc., 463 F. Supp. 461 (S.D.N.Y. 1978).

227. *See, e.g.*, Ariz. Rev. Stat. Ann. § 44-1231.01 (West 1987); Colo. Rev. Stat. §§ 12-44.5-101 to -108 (1986); Okla. Stat. Ann. tit. 78, §§ 71-75 (West Supp. 1988).

228. See also discussion of forgeries at pp. 52-57.

229. Here, additional examples may be signed and numbered or inscribed by the artist, or one or more "printer's proofs" or "artist's proofs" may be signed.

230. *See* Ark. Stat. Ann. §§ 4-73-301 to -305 (1987); Cal. Civ. Code §§ 1740-1745.5 (West Supp. 1988); Ga. Code Ann. §§ 106-2001 to -2008 (Supp. 1986); Hawaii Rev. Stat. §§ 481F-1 to -9 (Supp. 1987); Ill. Rev. Ann. ch. 121½, §§ 361-369 (West Supp. 1987); Md. Com. Law Code Ann. §§ 14-501 to -505 (1987); Mich. Stat. Ann. §§ 19.4091-.40917 (Callaghan 1987); Minn. Stat. Ann. §§ 324.06-.10 (West Supp. 1987); N.Y. Arts & Cult. Aff. Law art. 15, §§ 15.01-.19 (McKinney Supp. 1988); Or. Rev. Stat. §§ 359.300-.315 (1987); S.C. Code Ann. §§ 39-16-10 *et seq.* (Law. Co-op. 1986).

231. N.Y. Arts & Cult. Aff. Law art. 15, §§ 15.01–.19 (McKinney Supp. 1988).

232. *Supra* note 230.

233. *See* N.Y. City Admin. Code tit. A, ch. 64, reg. 206.

234. For an excellent discussion of sculpture abuse and available means of protection, see DuBoff, *Bronze Sculptures: Casting Around for Protection*, 3 Cardozo Arts & Ent. L.J. 235 (1984).

235. See N.Y. Assembly Bill No. 5953, which proposed the addition of article 16 of the New York Arts and Cultural Affairs Law. The bill was introduced into the 1987-1988 regular session of the New York legislature, but subsequently withdrawn for further study.

236. *Supra* note 123.

237. *Id.* at 11, 380 N.Y.S.2d at 542.

238. 15 U.S.C. §§ 2301 *et seq.* (1989).

239. 15 U.S.C. § 2302(e) (1989); 16 C.F.R. § 701 (1989).

240. 15 U.S.C. § 2303(a)(1989).

241. *Id.* §§ 2303(a)(1), 2304 (1989).

242. *Id.* § 2303(a)(2) (1989).

243. *Id.* § 2303(b) (1989).

244. *Id.* § 2310(c)(2) (1989).

245. *Id.* §§ 2302, 2312(c) (1989).

246. *Id.* § 2302 (1989).

247. *Id.*

248. 15 U.S.C. § 2311 (1989).

249. *Id.* §§ 1601 *et seq.* (1989).

250. *Id.* § 1611 (1989).

251. *Id.* § 1640 (1989).

252. *Id.* § 45(a) (1989).

253. *Supra* notes 10 and 11.

254. N.Y. City Admin. Code tit. 15, ch. 5, subch. 2, §§ 20-707 to -711 (1988).

255. *See* N.Y. Times, Mar. 3, 1988, § 1, at 25; N.Y. Times, Mar. 20, 1988, § 2, at 33; ARTnewsletter, Sept. 6, 1988.

256. *See*, *e.g.*, Royal Business Machs., Inc. v. Lorraine Corp., 633 F.2d 34 (7th Cir. 1980).

257. U.C.C. § 2-314(1) & comment 3.

258. U.C.C. § 2-314 comment 3.

259. U.C.C. § 2-312(3).

260. U.C.C. § 2-201(2).

261. U.C.C. § 2-403(2).

262. Taborsky, *supra* note 137.

263. U.C.C. § 2-326(1)(a).

264. U.C.C. § 2-326(2).

265. U.C.C. § 2-326(1)(b).

266. U.C.C. § 2-326(2).

267. U.C.C. § 2-509(3). *See also* Conway v. Larsen Jewelers, Inc., *supra* note 147.

268. U.C.C. §§ 2-503, 2-509(3).

269. *See supra* note 230.

270. 79 Stat. 985, codified at 22 U.S.C. § 2459 (1988).

271. N.Y. Arts & Cult. Aff. Law, *supra* note 21, at § 12.03.

272. U.C.C. § 9-105(1).

273. U.C.C. § 9-203.

274. 8 R. Anderson, Uniform Commercial Code § 9-203:44 (1985 & Supp. 1987).

275. *See* D. Baker, A Lawyer's Guide to Basic Secured Transactions 67 (1983). It is beyond the scope of this book to present a detailed treatment of secured transactions. The Baker work, frequently cited here, provides an excellent basic text on the subject.

276. Baker, *supra* note 275, at 67.

277. U.C.C. § 9-203(1).

278. U.C.C. § 9-203(2).

279. Baker, *supra* note 275, at 39. *See also* U.C.C. §§ 9-105, 9-106. Although the terms "tangible," "semi-intangible," and "pure intangible" are not mentioned in article 9, they are widely recognized. *See* Baker, *supra* note 275, at 39.

280. U.C.C. § 9-109.

281. U.C.C. § 9-109 comment 2.

282. *Id.*; *see also* Baker, *supra* note 275, at 41.

283. U.C.C. § 9-109(1), (4), comment 2.

284. See discussion of attachment at pp. 104-05.

285. Baker, *supra* note 275, at 89.

286. *Id.* at 99.

287. *Id.*

288. U.C.C. § 9-402 & comment 1.

289. U.C.C. § 9-403(1).

290. U.C.C. § 9-402(1).

291. U.C.C. § 9-403(2), (3).

292. U.C.C. § 9-305 comment 2.

293. U.C.C. § 9-305.

294. U.C.C. § 9-207(1).

295. U.C.C. § 9-302(1)(d).

296. *Id. See also* Baker, *supra* note 275, at 91.

297. U.C.C. § 9-107 & comment 1.

298. Baker, *supra* note 275, at 147.

299. *Id.*

300. U.C.C. § 9-301(1)(b).

301. U.C.C. § 9-301(2).

302. In a number of states, including New York, the secured party has a grace period of twenty days, rather than ten days, in which to file.

303. As it is beyond the scope of this book to enumerate every rule of priority, the reader is referred to Baker, *supra* note 275, at 152 *et seq.*, for a more exhaustive listing of priorities.

304. U.C.C. § 9-312(5)(b).

305. U.C.C. §§ 9-301(1)(a), 9-312(5)(a).

306. U.C.C. § 9-312(5)(a).

307. *Id.*

308. U.C.C. § 9-312(4).

309. In a number of states, including New York, the secured party has a grace period of twenty days, rather than ten days, in which to file.

310. U.C.C. § 9-312(4).

311. U.C.C. § 9-312(3)(a), (b).

312. In accordance with U.C.C. § 2-326(3)(c).

313. *Id.*

314. U.C.C. §§ 2-326(3)(c), 9-114(1).

315. U.C.C. § 9-306(2).

316. U.C.C. § 9-301(1)(c).

317. U.C.C. § 9-307(1) & comment 2.

318. U.C.C. § 9-307(2).

319. U.C.C. § 9-501. *See also* BAKER, *supra* note 275, at 297.

320. U.C.C. § 9-501(1). *See also* BAKER, *supra* note 275, at 297-98.

321. U.C.C. § 9-501(1). *See also* BAKER, *supra* note 275, at 301.

322. BAKER, *supra* note 275, at 298-99.

323. *Id.* at 299.

324. *Id.* Insolvency or bankruptcy of the debtor, loss of or damage to the collateral, death or dissolution of the debtor, and, in general, nonperformance of any of the debtor's obligations under the security agreement are among the events commonly listed. In the absence of contractual stipulation, a court may well find that an occurrence other than nonpayment is not an event of default. *See* BAKER, *supra* note 275, at 299.

325. *Id.*

326. *Id.* at 300.

327. *Id.* at 301-02.

328. U.C.C. § 9-503.

329. BAKER, *supra* note 275, at 305.

330. U.C.C. § 9-505(2).

331. U.C.C. § 9-505 comment 1.

332. BAKER, *supra* note 275, at 306.

333. U.C.C. § 9-504. Unless, that is, the debtor has signed after default a statement renouncing his rights. *See* U.C.C. § 9-505(1).

334. U.C.C. §§ 9-505(1), 9-507(1).

335. U.C.C. § 9-504(1). *See also* BAKER, *supra* note 275, at 309.

336. U.C.C. § 9-504(3).

337. *Id.*

338. U.C.C. §§ 9-504(3), 9-507(2).

339. U.C.C. § 9-504(3).

340. U.C.C. § 9-504(1).

341. U.C.C. § 9-504(2).

342. *Id. See also* BAKER, *supra* note 275, at 310-11.

343. U.C.C. § 9-506.

344. U.C.C. § 9-507(1) & comment 1.

345. U.C.C. § 9-507(1). Since the amount recoverable for actual loss in small-ticket consumer transactions is often insufficient to discourage creditor misconduct, the consumer-debtor may choose between actual damages and a minimum recovery, for which no proof of loss is required, consisting of the "credit service charge plus 10 percent of the principal amount of the debt or the time price differential plus 10 percent of the cash price." *See* U.C.C. § 9-507(1).

346. BAKER, *supra* note 275, at 323.

347. *Id.*

348. *Id.*

FORMS

FORM

MODEL COLLECTOR-DEALER CONSIGNMENT AGREEMENT

THIS AGREEMENT made and entered into this day of ______________, 198__, by and between ______________________________ ______________________________________, New York, New York 10022, (hereinafter referred to as "Owner") and ______________________, ____________________, ____________________, ____________________; (hereinafter referred to as "Dealer").

W I T N E S S E T H

WHEREAS, Dealer is engaged in the business of the sale of works of art; and

WHEREAS, Owner is the owner of ______________________________ (hereinafter referred to as the "Painting"); and

WHEREAS, Owner wishes to consign the Painting to Dealer for sale.

NOW THEREFORE, in consideration of the mutual promises contained herein, each party agrees as follows:

1. A. Owner hereby grants to Dealer the sole and exclusive right throughout the world, for a period of time commencing on ____________ and terminating on ______________ ("the Consignment Period") renewable monthly thereafter in writing by both parties hereto, to offer the Painting for sale at a gross sales price ("G.S.P.") which shall realize net proceeds to Owner after payment of any and all commissions to Dealer pursuant to Paragraph 6 of this Agreement, of no less than ______________ Dollars ($ ______________), hereinafter referred to as the Net Proceeds.

B. During the Consignment Period Dealer or its agents shall not present the image of the Painting, or the Painting itself to more than ______________ prospective purchasers.

C. Owner shall during the Consignment Period refer to Dealer all inquiries regarding the Painting's purchase.

D. Dealer may retain such other dealers and entities as it deems appropriate to the effectuation of the sale of the Painting, subject to Paragraph 1B above, and provided that any payments due such dealers or entities shall be the sole responsibility of Dealer.

2. Owner represents and warrants that he is the sole and absolute owner of the Painting, has the full right to sell and transfer same, and

that the Painting is free and clear of any and all liens, mortgages, security interests or other encumbrances; and further agrees to indemnify and hold Dealer, its officers, and directors harmless from any and all demands, claims, suits, judgments, or other liability (including all expenses incurred by Dealer in connection therewith) asserted by or awarded any person or entity arising by reason of Owner's ownership, possession and sale of the Painting. Title to the Painting shall pass to a buyer upon payment in full of the Net Proceeds in good funds to Owner, at which time Owner agrees to transfer ownership and title and to provide such documentation as is reasonably required upon sale.

3. Owner shall not be responsible for any costs which Dealer may incur in connection with its efforts to sell the Painting, unless otherwise approved in advance in writing by Owner, PROVIDED, HOWEVER, if Dealer sells the Painting within the initial Consignment Period, it shall be entitled to receive reimbursement from Owner for costs incurred by Dealer directly attributable to the sale of the Painting up to a maximum amount of ________________ thousand Dollars ($________________). Owner will at his expense provide to Dealer two color transparencies, and at his expense will ship the Painting to Dealer at any one location Dealer may specify.

4. Dealer shall arrange and pay for insurance for the Painting against any loss or damage in the amount of the Net Proceeds. Such insurance shall be provided from the moment the Painting is shipped to Dealer and until it is returned to Owner or to the buyer upon payment in full. Before any shipment of the Painting from the address of Owner, Dealer will specifically inform its insurance company directly of the address and means of transportation of the Painting, and this information shall be taken with full confidentiality directly between the insurance company and Dealer. Dealer agrees to use its best efforts and all due care in handling the Painting.

5. A. Dealer shall use its best efforts to sell the Painting during the Consignment Period. In the event that Dealer receives a bona fide offer to purchase the Painting for an all cash gross sales price equal to or greater than that which shall realize the full Net Proceeds, Dealer may accept such offer without further authorization from Owner.

B. Should Dealer receive a bona fide offer to purchase for a gross sales price which would realize less than the full Net Proceeds, or an offer to purchase on terms other than all cash, Dealer shall inform

Owner of such offer, and Owner shall expeditiously inform Dealer in writing whether it accepts or rejects such an offer.

6. A. In the event that the Painting is sold during the Consignment Period, all proceeds from the sale of the Painting shall initially be paid to Dealer. Dealer shall be entitled to receive ____________ (______%) per cent of the gross sales price as a commission in consideration of its services. Dealer shall deduct this commission and the amount as determined under Paragraph 3 above and forward the balance to Owner within seven (7) days of receipt by it of the sales proceeds.

B. In the event that the Painting is not sold during the Consignment Period, Dealer shall, unless otherwise agreed in writing to extend this contract, return the Painting at its expense to Owner within seven (7) days of the expiration of the Consignment Period, or deliver it to a location in New York City as specified by Owner within such seven (7) day period.

C. In the event that Owner or his agent(s) sell(s) the Painting within six (6) months after the termination date of the Consignment Period or its extension, to one of the ____________ individuals or entities to whom Dealer or its agent(s) have shown the Painting during the Consignment Period, Dealer shall receive its full commission as provided in Paragraph 6A above. This provision shall not apply after the expiration of such six (6) month period.

7. A. Title to, and a security interest in, the Painting (and any proceeds thereof) is reserved in Owner until sale of the Painting by Dealer whereupon the proceeds of such sale shall be held by Dealer for Owner and delivered (except for such commission set forth above) to Owner as herein provided.

B. Dealer agrees to immediately sign Form UCC-1 evincing Owner's security interest in the Painting. Dealer agrees to inform any purchaser of the Painting of the existence of Owner's security interest in the Painting.

C. In the event of any default under this Agreement by Dealer, Owner shall have all of the rights of a secured party under the Uniform Commercial Code. Owner agrees to file Form UCC-3 terminating Owner's security interest on receipt from Dealer of the Net Proceeds.

8. This Agreement represents the entire understanding of all the Parties hereto, supersedes any and all other and prior agreements between the Parties and declares all such prior agreements between the Parties null and void. The terms of this Agreement may not be modified

or amended, except in writing. This Agreement and all matters relating to it shall be governed by the Uniform Commercial Code and the laws of the State of New York.

IN WITNESS WHEREOF, the Parties hereto have hereunto signed their hands and seals the day and year first above written.

____

Owner –

____

Dealer –

FORM

COLLECTOR CONSIGNMENT WITH SECURITY AGREEMENT

[DATE]

ABC Galleries, Inc.
1234 Madison Avenue
New York, NY 10000

You hereby acknowledge receipt of the following oil painting owned by me (the "Painting"):

Title:
Medium:
Size:
Signature:
Date:

The purchase price of the Painting less your commission of ______ per cent shall be delivered by you to me within ten (10) days from and after the date on which delivery shall be made by you under any sale or contract of sale. Title to, and a security interest in, the Painting (and any proceeds thereof) is reserved in me until sale of the Painting by you whereupon the proceeds of such sale shall be held for me and delivered (except for such commission set forth above) to me as herein provided. You shall have no right to sell the Painting until the Form UCC-1 is signed by you and returned to me for recording.

In the event of any default by you, I shall have all of the rights of a secured party under the Uniform Commercial Code.

You agree to hold the Painting for sale at a price of $ __________. You agree that you will not sell the Painting for a price less than $ __________ without permission from me.

You agree to specifically inform any purchaser of the Painting from you of the existence of my security interest as stated herein. I agree to sign and file a Form UCC-3 termination statement once I have approved the terms of the sale of the Painting.

Notwithstanding the foregoing, at any time prior to any sale of the Painting by you, at my request you will deliver the Painting to me immediately upon receipt of any instruction from me.

____
Collector

The foregoing is confirmed and
agreed to: ABC Galleries, Inc.

By:______________________________

FORM - GALLERY BILL OF SALE

ABC GALLERY CORP.

Bill of Sale

Date: ____

Parties: ABC Gallery Corp., with principal office at __________ Street, New York, N.Y. _______ ("Seller"); and

____

____(Buyer")

1. **SALE**. For the sum of $_________ (the "Purchase Price"), Seller hereby sells to Buyer, subject to the terms and

conditions hereinafter set forth, the following described work of art (the "Work"):

Title:

Artist:

Medium:

Size:

How and where signed:

How and where dated:

Number of other identifying marks:

Additional information (e.g., provenance):

2. **PURCHASE PRICE**. (a or b)

a. Full Payment: The Purchase Price shall be paid in full at or prior to delivery of the Work to the Buyer. All drafts, checks or other instruments given in payment of the Purchase Price shall be accepted subject to collection.

b. Terms: ____

____

____

3. **SALES TAX**. Buyer agrees to pay all applicable sales tax due on the sale of the Work. The sales tax due on this sale is $________, which amount is in addition to the Purchase Price.

4. **REPRESENTATIONS AND WARRANTIES OF SELLER**. Seller does hereby represent and warrant that:

(a) The authenticity of authorship of the Work is in accordance with the description contained herein.

(b) Seller has all legal authority to sell the Work, and the sale thereof is free and clear of all liens, encumbrances or restrictions except as specifically set forth below in paragraph 7.

(c) The Work is in satisfactory condition unless otherwise specified below in paragraph 7.

(d) The warranties and representations made herein are limited. No other warranties, express or implied, including, without limitations, warranties of merchantability and fitness for a particular purpose, have been made except as set forth herein. Buyer's sole remedy for a breach of warranty shall be an action for rescission. Under no circumstances shall Seller be liable for any special, incidental or consequential damages.

(e) The warranties and representations made herein are made by Seller solely for the benefit of Buyer and are not assignable to any subsequent owner or any person who may have or acquire any interest in the work sold hereunder and not expressly named herein.

5. **REPRODUCTION**. This sale is made subject to all provisions of the federal copyright laws and, where applicable, the provisions of Article 14, §14.01 of the New York Arts and Cultural Affairs Law, which limits the transfer of reproduction rights.

6. **PAYMENT**. If the Purchase Price is payable in installments as provided in Section 2(b) hereof, then Buyer agrees to execute the Security Agreement annexed hereto and such other documents, including one or more Financing Statements, as may be reasonably requested by Seller, and furthermore, expressly authorizes Seller to sign and file one or more Financing Statements on Buyer's behalf, to evince Seller's security interest in the Work.

7. **COMMENTS**. ______________________________

____

____

ABC Gallery Corp.

By: ______________________________
President (Seller)

____
(Buyer)

ABC GALLERY CORP.

SECURITY AGREEMENT

The Buyer agrees to pay the total Purchase Price indicated in Section 1 of the Bill of Sale in such installments as are indicated in Section 2b thereof. In order to secure the prompt payment when due of said Purchase Price and each such installment, the Buyer hereby grants and conveys to Seller a security interest in the Work described on the attached Bill of Sale and any and all proceeds of any sale or disposition thereof. Any default in the payment of the Purchase Price or of any installment or interest payment when due shall be a default under this Security Agreement. Upon any such default, the entire unpaid balance of the Purchase Price shall become due and payable without further demand, and Seller shall be entitled to exercise all of the rights and remedies of a secured party under the Uniform Commercial Code. In the event of any default the unpaid portion of the Purchase Price shall bear interest at the rate of the lesser of 15% per annum or the maximum rate permitted by law from the date of default until the date that the actual payment of the Purchase Price plus all costs of collection and interest herein shall be made.

The Buyer agrees to reimburse Seller for all costs and expenses (including reasonable attorneys' fees) incurred by it in protecting and enforcing this Security Agreement. The Buyer shall execute and deliver to Seller and expressly authorizes the execution and filing on its behalf by Seller of one or more Financing Statements or other evidences of this security interest as may be reasonably requested by Seller.

The Buyer agrees to obtain an all risks insurance policy insuring the Work in the amount of $_________ and to name the Seller as an insured to the extent of Seller's interest therein.

The Buyer agrees to specifically inform any purchaser of the Work from Buyer of the existence of Seller's security interest as stated herein. If necessary, Seller agrees to sign and file a Uniform Commercial Code termination statement once payment of the Purchase Price, plus and any other amounts that may be due under this Agreement, has been made in full.

Dated: ________________ 19___

New York, New York

____

Buyer

Witness: ______________________

Auctions

3

GENERALLY

Art can be sold in a variety of ways. In chapter 2 the process of traditional one-to-one retail sale was treated at length; this chapter delves into the intricacies of sales by auction. In recent years in the United States, art auctions have emerged as a vital, sizable business. The nation's two largest auction houses alone, Sotheby's, Inc. (Sotheby's) and Christie, Manson & Woods International, Inc. (Christie's), handled a combined national sales volume in the 1987-88 season of approximately $2.4 billion dollars. Sotheby's and Christie's expect the 1988-89 volume to exceed $3 billion. Moreover, numerous smaller auction houses flourish throughout the nation. Although Sotheby's and Christie's tend to receive the majority of publicity, they are by no means the only way to sell property at auction. There are hundreds of smaller auction houses, and there are some that are highly specialized.

Two types of auctions can be found in the American art market: the Dutch auction and, far more commonly, the English auction. Although the objective of each auction is to secure the highest possible price for an item from a group of bidders in one location, the procedures governing the two types of auctions are markedly different. In the Dutch auction, seen only rarely in the United States, the auctioneer starts with the highest price believed to be remotely obtainable and solicits offers at that level. If none is forthcoming, the auctioneer gradually lowers the price until an offer is made. The Dutch auction, as a rule, generates very little drama and suspense.

Operating under different ground rules and often surrounded in mystery, suspense, and excitement is the more prevalent English auction, typified by auctions at Sotheby's and Christie's. In the English auction the auctioneer starts the bidding at a low price, and bidders competitively make higher offers until the last responsive offer is made and the hammer falls. A variation of the English auction, found infrequently in the art market, is the silent auction. In the silent auction, each bidder may place only one bid, and the seller retains the option of either accepting the highest bid or rejecting it.

An auction sale is one in which property is presented for sale to be bid on by assembled bidders and sold for the highest offer. A bid constitutes an offer by a prospective buyer to pay a specified price for the property being auctioned. Put in traditional contract terms: property for sale is presented by the auctioneer as an invitation to make an offer; bidders make offers for the property, with higher bids canceling lower ones as the bidding progresses; a contract is formed when an offer in the form of the highest bid is accepted by the auctioneer. Bids are usually made orally by those attending the sale, but a raised paddle, for example, as a means of visual communication arranged with the auctioneer, is a common way to convey a bid. On occasion, more elaborate or secretive bidding signals, such as a wink of an eye, a flick of a finger, or a pat on the chin, are worked out with the auctioneer in advance.

At the auctioneer's discretion, a bidder need not personally attend the sale; rather, he or she may make order bids—that is, bids made in writing. Several major auction houses, including Christie's and Sotheby's, permit that practice and place bids on behalf of the order bidder on a particular item or lot (items sold together) up to the maximum figure stated by the customer. Such bids are placed in competition with the bids of those attending the sale; if the order bidder is successful, he or she acquires the property for a price determined by the next bidding increment over and above the last bid in the auction room as long as the order bidder's maximum written bid is not exceeded. For example, X places an order bid by mail to Sotheby's of a maximum of $100,000 for a particular work of art up for auction. During the course of the auction, bidding for the work is conducted in increments of $1,000, and the auctioneer has duly submitted bids on X's behalf up to $100,000. If the bidding for the work reaches $75,000 with no further bids offered, X will acquire the work for $76,000.

APPLICATION OF UCC

The Uniform Commercial Code (UCC) supplements and clarifies some of the contractual laws attendant to auction sales. All the provisions of express warranties,[1] warranty of title,[2] the implied warranties of merchantability[3] and fitness for a particular purpose,[4] and the exclusion or modification of warranties[5] discussed with respect to private sales in chapter 2 apply as well to auctions. In addition, other provisions of the UCC apply uniquely to auctions. If goods are offered for sale in lots, for example, the UCC provides that each lot is the subject of a separate sale.[6] The sale of a lot is completed and the bidder's offer is accepted when the auctioneer so indicates by the fall of a hammer (knocking down) or some other customary manner.[7] A bidder may retract his or her bid, however, at any time before the auctioneer's announcement of the completion of the sale.[8] Moreover, the fall of a hammer need not always complete the sale if the auctioneer fully disclosed the identity of the principals and if the sale is conditioned on the approval of the principals.[9]

When a bid is made during the fall of the auctioneer's hammer in acceptance of a prior bid, the auctioneer, under the Code, may, at his or her discretion, either reopen the bidding or declare the goods sold for the bid on which the hammer was falling.[10]

Marx v. Sotheby Parke Bernet, Inc.[11]

In May 1980, the plaintiffs, Leonard and Virginia Marx, both knowledgeable and sophisticated collectors of American antiques, participated in an estate auction conducted by Sotheby's at Pokety Farms in Cambridge, Maryland. The auction was held in a large tent, open at the sides, with between 1,200 and 1,500 people sitting inside the tent and others standing or sitting outside the tent. John Marion, an experienced auctioneer and chairman of Sotheby's, was conducting the auction. Stationed throughout the tent were other Sotheby's employees known as spotters. The Marxes bid on a Federal turned and inlaid mahogany wall sofa, and the hammer came down on their $22,000 bid.

Approximately eight to ten seconds later, a spotter drew John Marion's attention to a bidder near the rear of the tent who had bid $22,000 at approximately the same time as the Marx bid. Since there was now confusion as to which of the $22,000 bids the auctioneer had accepted, he reopened the bidding; again the sofa went to the Marx couple—this time for $34,000. The plaintiffs made no protest at the reopening of the bidding, but, rather, purchased the sofa and made arrangements for its shipment. The plaintiffs' first protest to Sotheby's was registered three days after the incident in the form of a letter offering Sotheby's a check in the sum of $22,000 plus the standard 10 percent buyer's premium. Sotheby's rejected the check, insisting on full payment of the $34,000 plus the 10 percent buyer's premium. The New York Supreme Court, whose holding was confirmed by the Appellate Division, found in favor of Sotheby's—that is, the plaintiffs owed the defendant the sum of $34,000 plus the buyer's premium, costs, and disbursements. In its reasoning and taking all the circumstances particular to the case into consideration, the court relied on the provision of the Code (the gist of which was also found in Sotheby's sales contract) that mandates that, when a bid is made while the hammer is falling in acceptance of a prior bid, the auctioneer at his or her election may either reopen the bidding or declare the goods sold for the prior bid.

The Statute of Frauds

The statute of frauds provision of the Code[12] applies to auctions as well as to private sales. Generally a contract for the sale of goods costing $500 or more is unenforceable unless there is a written document sufficient to indicate that the contract of sale was made between the parties. The memorandum must be signed by the party against whom enforcement is sought or by his or her authorized agent or broker. Therefore, in the absence of other statutory provisions, if a work of art costs more than $500, the buyer has to sign a memorandum with respect to an offer to buy the work in order to be bound. A number of states, notably New York and California,[13] have enacted specific legislation permitting the auctioneer to bind the successful bidder by entering a memorandum in a sales book or by other similar procedure. New York's statute provides that notwithstanding the UCC, if goods are sold at public auction and at such time the auctioneer "enters in a sale book, a memorandum specifying the nature and price of the property sold, the terms of the sale, the name of the purchaser, and the name of the person on whose account the sale was made," the memorandum has the same effect as a note of the contract or sale signed by the party against whom enforcement is sought.[14]

In states lacking such specific legislation, a written order bid signed by the purchaser should satisfy the statute of frauds. The typical oral or visual bid, however, requires the auctioneer to memorialize carefully the result of the bidding on each lot offered at auction or incur liability for damages if the consignor suffers loss and can establish negligence on the part of the auctioneer.

INTERRELATIONSHIPS AMONG THE PARTIES

By its nature, an auction sale often involves the participants in relationships of labyrinthine complexity. A description of the major relationships and some of the attendant issues and responsibilities follows.

1. *The consignor-auctioneer relationship.* The consignor relies on the auctioneer for the following:

    - A determination whether the artwork is auctionable;
    - The decision whether the artwork, if auctionable, should be placed in a major or minor auction and in the company of which other artwork;
    - The suggestion of an estimated price;
    - The suggested reserve price;
    - The collection of sales proceeds; and
    - Standing, as an expert, behind the authenticity of the artwork in the event the authenticity is questioned. The auctioneer, on the other hand, relies on the consignor to support the consignor's ownership of title to the work if its provenance is ever questioned.

2. *The purchaser-auctioneer relationship.* The purchaser or successful bidder at auction depends on the auctioneer for a determination that the artwork purchased is authentic and that the estimated purchase price was reasonable. All bidders at an auction are entitled to assume that the auction process has integrity and to base their bids on that assumption. If the auctioneer engages in the practice, unbeknownst to the bidders, of knowingly receiving a bid on the seller's behalf or if the seller makes or procures such a bid, the buyer may choose either to void the sale or to take the goods at the price of the last good-faith bid before the completion of the sale.[15] In addition, the purchaser relies on the auctioneer for some assurance that the auctioneer will be granting the purchaser clear title to the artwork.

3. *The purchaser-consignor relationship.* Although the buyer is aware that works sold at auction are generally owned by third parties, with the auctioneer serving as agent of a generally undisclosed principal, the following question repeatedly arises: To whom does the buyer look for recourse when either the title to or the authenticity of the work is questioned? If the issue is one of authenticity, the buyer may claim against the auctioneer, regardless of whether the identity of the principal (the consignor) is known to the buyer. The purchaser of the work has presumably relied on the credibility and the expertise of the auctioneer and on the representations contained in the auctioneer's catalog. If the issue is one of title, the purchaser looks to the auctioneer when the identity of the principal is undisclosed. If, however, the principal is known, the buyer should be able to seek recourse from both the principal and the auctioneer. The following is a summary of a recent case illustrating the potential for complexities among the parties.

Abrams v. Sotheby Parke Bernet, Inc.[16]

In June 1984 Sotheby's sold at auction a number of important Hebrew books and manuscripts that were known to have been in the possession of a German seminary and to have been smuggled out of the country before World War II. At first, Sotheby's refused to disclose the identity of the consignor. The Attorney General of the State of New York, on behalf of members of the public who might wish to consult the items for religious or scholarly purposes and on the grounds that it was questionable whether the undisclosed consignor could transfer good title, sought to void the sale and have the books and manuscripts returned to the Jewish people. The case raised a number of provocative issues including the following:

- Could the seminary under the circumstances have transferred good title to anyone?
- How did the consignor receive possession of the documents—that is, was the consignor a smuggler or a good-faith purchaser for value?
- Could Sotheby's justify its refusal to disclose the identity of the consignor?
- What rights did the buyer have against either the auctioneer or the consignor if title was found to be defective?
- What standing did the New York attorney general have to question the proposed sale?
- What laws governed each aspect of the transaction?

In the complaint the attorney general asserted claims under two state laws[17] relating to consumer fraud that enable the attorney general to void consumer transactions when innocent buyers have been misled. Further, the attorney general asserted a claim based on particular restitution laws promulgated by the Occupation forces after World War II.[18] These restitution laws carry a presumption that a transfer of property without consideration, during specific years in parts of Germany, is void as having been performed under duress.

The consignor questioned whether the attorney general was acting properly in pursuing the action in the first place, because the attorney general had failed to take any action in comparable situations. However, the case was settled in July 1985 without any determination of the legal issues involved.

By the reported terms of settlement, Sotheby's was to reclaim approximately thirty of the fifty-nine manuscripts and books sold at auction and to donate them to several institutions for the study of Jewish cultural and religious history. Under the settlement agreement, any buyer who could demonstrate that a copy of the work that buyer purchased was available in an institution for public use would not have to return it to Sotheby's. Such sales, the parties believed, would generate proceeds in excess of $1 million, which were to be distributed to various institutions to be used to purchase rare, scholarly Jewish materials. Finally, the consignor, Professor Alexander Guttmann, a teacher at Hebrew Union College, was to receive approximately $900,000, about half the amount that had been raised by the auction and a separate contemporaneous sale to the Jewish Theological Seminary of two of the most valuable documents.

The court invited public comment on the proposed settlement, and met with considerable protest. Hebrew Union College submitted a memorandum urging that Guttmann, the consignor, never owned the collection of books and manuscripts and should not receive the $900,000 due him according to the settlement. The college went on to write that "concealment of the materials for 44 years, never divulging that they survived the Nazi era or that he possessed them, is the fact that dominates any assessment of his credibility."[19] (Guttmann was subsequently dismissed from Hebrew Union College.[20])

THE AUCTION HOUSE AND THE CONSIGNOR

The relationship between the consignor and the auctioneer is a fiduciary one. The auctioneer stands as an agent on behalf of the consignor with an obligation to "act in the utmost good faith and in the interest of [the consignor] throughout their relationship."[21] A breach of that fiduciary duty gives rise to liability on the part of the agent for damages caused to the consignor-principal, whether the cause of action is based on contract or on negligence.[22] This section of the chapter examines some of the specific rights and obligations flowing between auctioneer and consignor.

Standard of Care

The auction house, as the consignor's agent, is considered the bailee of the consigned goods. As such, the auction house is responsible for the safe custody of the works delivered to the auction house for the purpose of sale and is liable to the consignor if the works are lost or damaged as a result of the auction house's negligence or that of its agents or employees (including the auctioneer). It has long been the law[23] that an auction house is bound to take care of a consignor's goods as if they were its own, but is not liable for a loss arising from misfortune or unavoidable accidents. That is, auction houses are governed by the common rules of bailment law, discussed in some detail in chapter 5. To limit further the potential for exposure, the auction houses look to the terms of the consignment agreement and seek insurance coverage.

Duty of Disclosure

An auction house must disclose to the consignor any internal disagreement as to the auctionability of the consigned property. If some within the auction house believe the property, though valuable, is not likely to excite the bidding public and would be better placed with a private dealer, that fact must be brought to the consignor's attention.[24] Further, an auction house may have an obligation not to attempt to auction property if the undertaking reasonably appears to be impossible or impracticable.[25] If an auction house is inclined to accept property on consignment, it must disclose to the consignor the risk of loss of value that may occur if the property is offered for sale at auction and fails to sell.[26]

Auctioneer's Commission

Because the auctioneer acts as an agent of the consignor, the consignor pays the auctioneer's commission. Although the major auction houses currently charge consignors a commission of 10 percent of the sale price of a work of art when the sale price is $5,000 or more, that percentage is often negotiable. Otherwise, a consignor might be faced, for example, with a commission fee of $5 million for a Van Gogh that sold for $50 million.

Duty to Obtain Best Price

As fiduciary of the consignor, the auctioneer is under an obligation to obtain the best possible validly offered price for the consignor's offering. That obligation, however, may have been compromised by the development over the past fifteen to twenty years of two auction policies: the buyer's premium and the guaranteed price.

Buyer's Premium

With the opening of its New York salesroom in May 1977, Christie's introduced the concept of the buyer's premium into the United States, already in effect in London at both Christie's and Sotheby's. (Christie's announced the new policy in London in July 1975, and Sotheby's followed suit three days later.) Under the buyer's premium policy, the commission charged to consignors may be reduced, but a 10 percent premium is imposed on the hammer price payable by the buyer. Unlike the consignor's commission, the buyer's premium appears to be uniformly imposed and largely nonnegotiable.[27] The buyer's premium as introduced in this country by Christie's was adopted here by Sotheby's in January 1979 amid a wave of protest. Art dealers complained that the buyer's premium yielded extraordinary advantages to auction houses, their competitors, in that the auctioneers could now reduce or even eliminate the commissions charged to consignors. The buyer's premium may still redound to the ultimate disadvantage of the consignor by depressing the prices that buyers are willing to pay at auction, as the buyer must pay an additional 10 percent over the bid price. The art dealers questioned the legality of an auctioneer's acceptance of payment from the buyer for whom the auctioneer is rendering no service considering that by law he is the consignor-seller's agent.[28] Dealers' efforts to overturn the buyer's premium in New York and London have been unsuccessful.

Guaranteed Price

Under the guaranteed price arrangement, introduced in New York by Sotheby's in November 1972, the auction house may appraise a work of art and offer to guarantee a portion of its market value. If the auction does not yield the guaranteed price, the auction house purchases the work from the consignor at the guaranteed price. Although a standard agreement for guaranteed prices has yet to be developed by Sotheby's or Christie's, the concept is clear: for the security of knowing that the artwork will be purchased for some minimum amount, the consignor pays a premium commission, computed on the guaranteed price, over and above the standard auction commission. When the auction house becomes the owner of the artwork under those circumstances, several conflict-of-interest questions may arise. For example, what if net purchase price to the auction house turns out to be significantly below fair market value? The consignor may claim that the auction house did not use its best efforts to get the market price, since the factors determining an auction's success are within the control of the auctioneer—that is, the auctioneer can affect the purchase price of a consigned work by, for example, failing to advertise adequately or failing to catalog or display the work prominently. Failure to use best efforts to get the highest price would violate the fiduciary relationship between the consignor and the auctioneer.

When an auction house is selected because of its special skill, a consignor may rely on its judgment and integrity, and the auction house "has an implied good faith obligation to use [its] best efforts to promote the [consignor's] product."[29] When an auction house, having acquired artwork through guaranteed pricing, subsequently resells that art as the principal, it sets its own reserve price.[30] Questions may be raised about the legal consequences of that practice in the event of an unconsummated sale, at least in New York and California, where mock auctions are illegal.[31] It could be alleged, for example, that an auction house was engaged in conducting a mock auction if the auctioneer, not in good faith, sets an artificially high reserve price.

Duty to Recommend Appropriate Reserve Price

Because the consignor generally relies on the auction house as a market expert, the auction house has an obligation to recommend an appropriate reserve price.[32] Secretly agreed to by the consignor and the auction house, the reserve price is the lowest price at which the consigned property may be purchased by someone other than the consignor. Under the UCC, unless expressly stated to the contrary, auctions are deemed to be using reserve prices.[33] In New York City, under special auction regulations that became effective in April 1987,[34] when property is being sold subject to a reserve price, that fact must be indicated by the auction house in the catalog.[35] The reserve price defends the consignor from involuntarily selling his or her consigned property at a figure far below the anticipated bids. If the hammer price does not reach the reserve price, then, in the absence of a guaranteed price agreement with the auctioneer, the consignor becomes the successful bidder and is said to have "bought-in" the work. In return for that security, the consignor pays the auctioneer a commission (generally 5 percent and occasionally negotiable) based on the buy-in price or the last independent bid. In all cases in New York City, when the reserve price is not bid, the revised auction regulations require the auctioneer to announce that the lot has been "withdrawn" or "bought-in."[36]

When a principal has consigned several works to a single lot or a series of lots in a given auction, there may be combined reserve prices and floating reserve prices. With combined reserve prices, the consignor and the auctioneer agree that the reserve price on each work will be determined by the price brought or expected to be brought by the other works covered by the combined reserve price. With floating reserve prices, the reserve price may be changed as a particular sale progresses, with the consignor waiting to evaluate the market strength before committing himself or herself to a minimum price.

Historically, one controversial aspect of reserve prices has been their secrecy. Those against secrecy cite the unfairness of inducing prospective buyers to waste time and, frequently, traveling expenses to bid on merchandise they have no hope of acquiring. They also criticize auctioneers for accepting bids for items at far below the reserve price when the auction, in effect, begins only when the reserve price is reached.

Although those objections are valid, they recently failed to hold sway in New York City. Under New York City's revised auction regulations of April 13, 1987, reserve prices may remain secret—although, as noted earlier, if a sale carries a reserve price, that fact—but not the price itself—must be indicated in the auction catalog. Moreover, the response of the auction houses and the professional auctioneers favoring the secrecy of reserve prices is equally valid. They argue that the use of floating and combined reserve prices, or even fixed reserve prices that may be changed at the last minute, makes the advance publication of reserve prices impractical. And, citing their primary obligation to obtain the best price for the consignor, the auctioneers allege that they can best do so by opening the bidding below the reserve price and allowing the drama and suspense to build with the rising bids. Moreover, the major auction houses, including Sotheby's and Christie's, incorporate presale high and low estimates of the expected sale price of consigned works in their catalogs, providing at least a preliminary idea whether a prospective purchaser has a chance to bid successfully on a given item. The low estimated sales price is usually in excess of the reserve price. In New York City in any event, under no circumstance may the reserve price exceed the estimated high price.[37]

Liability as Market Expert

An auction may be canceled or objects withdrawn from the auction wholly at the discretion of the auctioneer.[38] An auction house, having an obligation to render to its consignor truthful opinions as to the value of the consigned work,[39] may incur liability to the consignor under various theories of tort law for an incorrect appraisal (assessment of the monetary value of a work) or authentication (assessment of the genuineness of a work). Those theories of liability include disparagement, defamation (only rarely), and negligent misrepresentation—all of which are treated at some length in chapter 5. What follows here is a brief description of a recent case arising from an incorrect appraisal that illuminates the auction house's all-too-real potential for exposure in the course of its daily business.

Cristallina, S.A. v. Christie, Manson & Woods International, Inc.[40]

In February 1981, Dimitry Jodidio, the principal officer of Cristallina, a foreign corporation solely in the business of buying and selling artwork, told David Bathurst, then-president of Christie's, that his company wanted to raise $10 million through the sale of several of its paintings. Bathurst examined some of Cristallina's Impressionist paintings and gave Jodidio estimates of their value in three possible contexts: a private sale, a low bid at public auction, and a high bid at public auction. Eight paintings were chosen on Bathurst's advice. Bathurst estimated that the eight could be sold privately for approximately $8 million and that at public auction they could be sold for between $8.5 million (the cumulative low bid) and $12.6 million (the cumulative high bid). Christie's agreed to arrange and pay for the shipment of the paintings to New York and to promote the sale. Christie's further agreed to reduce its seller's commission to 4 percent, with the understanding that, if the total proceeds did not exceed $9.4 million, the auction house would forgo its commission entirely and accept only the buyer's premium.

Christie's was subsequently engaged to sell the eight paintings, and it duly advertised and solicited media coverage for the auction. In February 1981, Bathurst and Jodidio tentatively agreed on a reserve price for each of the paintings; however, the final reserve prices were not established until a day before the auction, which was set for May 19, 1981. In addition to the final reserve prices, Christie's established a floating reserve price of $150,000, which it could add to the established reserve price on any painting if circumstances so dictated. Although all the tickets for the auction were sold, the results of the auction were disappointing; only one painting was sold, bringing a price of $2.2 million. The remaining seven paintings were bought in, since no bid reached the reserve price.

In an apparent effort to avoid embarrassment for all parties, Christie's issued a press release announcing that three of the Cristallina paintings had been sold for a total of $5.6 million. Christie's did inform Jodidio that, in fact, only one painting had been sold, and the unsold paintings were subsequently returned to Cristallina.

Cristallina brought suit against Christie's, alleging that Bathurst and Christie's misrepresented their abilities to accurately address current market conditions and to accurately estimate the value of the Cristallina paintings. That is, Cristallina alleged that the initial estimates given by Bathurst at the February 1981 meetings were false and were given solely to induce Cristallina to engage Christie's services. Cristallina further alleged that the reserve price for each picture was too high in relation to its actual value, thereby diminishing its chances of being sold at auction. Cristallina also alleged that Christie's failed to warn it of the dangers inherent in an auction—that is, that the failure to sell a painting has an adverse effect on its value in any future sale.

The lower court dismissed the action,[41] and, on Cristallina's appeal, the Appellate Division modified the decision so as to deny, on six of the eight causes of action, the defendant's motion to dismiss the case.[42] In January 1987, after the case had been on trial for a week, the parties reached a settlement, whereby Cristallina dropped all of its charges against Christie's and Cristallina was awarded a cash payment of an undisclosed amount, estimated, in one account, to be possibly more than $1 million. Cristallina had originally sought $5.5 million, including $2.2 million in interest, which it contended was the amount that it lost because of the decrease in value of the paintings after they had failed to sell at auction.[43]

Consignment Contracts

When artwork is consigned to an auctioneer for the purpose of sale, the relationship that arises between the consignor and the auctioneer is governed by general fiduciary principles. The specifics of the consignor-auctioneer relationship, however, are controlled by the auctioneer's consignment contracts and other agreements relating to auction sales. The two major auction houses, Sotheby's and Christie's, have, over the years, developed elaborate consignment documents, the latest versions of which are reproduced at the close of this chapter. The following is a brief description of some of the major points covered by the documents, along with a notation of any significant differences in the treatment of the points by the two auction houses.

General Points

Before exploring some of the areas covered by the consignment documents, we should first state that the doctrine of *contra preferentem* is still viable in New York. Under that rule, ambiguous language in a form contract, such as a consignment agreement between a consignor and an auctioneer, may be construed against the drafter of the contract. New York courts, however, have recognized that the doctrine is to be used as a matter of last resort, after other aids of construction have failed to resolve ambiguities.[44] When a consignment agreement is not ambiguous, the courts may enforce its express terms.[45]

Auctioneer's Discretion

The auction house reserves absolute discretion as to the following:

- The place and the date of the sale
- The manner of conducting the sale
- The grouping of property into lots
- Consultations, if any, with experts
- Providing catalogs and other descriptions of the property

Commission

For the auctioneer's services as the seller's agent in organizing, promoting, and holding the auction sale, the auctioneer charges the seller a commission. At each house, the commission is 20 percent of the sale price per lot selling under $1,000, 15 percent of the sale price per lot selling between $1,000 and $4,999, and 10 percent of the sale price per lot selling at $5,000 or more. Sotheby's charges a minimum commission of $100 per lot sold, and Christie's charges a minimum of $75. Each auction house further charges a premium of 10 percent of the sale price, to be collected by the auction house from the buyer (see discussion of buyer's premium at page 153).

Settlement of Account

Thirty-five days after the date of the sale, the auction house pays the seller the net sales proceeds minus its commissions and reimbursable expenses.

Seller's Representations and Warranties

The seller must warrant and represent to the auctioneer and the purchaser that the seller has the right and the title to consign the property for sale and that the property is free and clear of all liens, claims, and encumbrances.

Indemnification

Both Sotheby's and Christie's require broad indemnifications from the seller. Sotheby's exacts indemnifications from the seller to both the auction house and the purchaser.

Copyright Matters

The auction house reserves an unrestricted right to photograph and to reproduce and distribute photographs of the property consigned for sale. The auction house retains copyright in all blocks, prints, plates, and other illustrations and depictions of the property that it creates.

Buyer's Nonpayment

If the buyer does not pay, the auction houses reserve the right to cancel the sale and to return the property to the seller. In such a case, the seller is not required to pay any commission to the auction house. Christie's contract provides that it may, at its sole election, enforce payment by the buyer. Sotheby's contract specifically provides that it has no obligation to enforce payment by any purchaser.

Reserve Prices

Christie's contract provides that, unless the reserve price is mutually agreed to by the seller and by Christie's and is confirmed by the seller in writing, the reserve price is determined by Christie's in its sole discretion and that, if the bidding does not reach the reserve price on any lot, the auctioneer will withdraw the lot from sale. Sotheby's contract provides that, unless a different reserve price is mutually agreed to by the seller and by Sotheby's and is confirmed by the seller in writing, the reserve price is the following percentage of its latest low presale estimate: 25 percent per lot with a low estimate of less than $300; 40 percent per lot with a low estimate of between $300 and $999; 60 percent per lot with a low estimate of $1,000 or more. The reserve price may not exceed Sotheby's high presale estimate. The seller agrees not to bid on the property; all bids to protect the seller's reserve prices are made by Sotheby's. Lots bought-in are so announced, and the commission thereon is 5 percent of the reserve price, subject to a minimum handling charge. Both Sotheby's and Christie's retain the right to sell any lot below its reserve price, provided the seller receives the net amount to which he or she would be entitled had the lot been sold at its reserve price.

Rescission

The auction house may rescind the sale of any property if the auction house determines that the sale offering subjects either the auction house or the seller to any liability.

Packing, Shipping, and Delivery

The seller bears all the expenses of packing, shipping, and delivering the consigned property to the auction house premises.

THE AUCTION HOUSE AND THE PURCHASER

Although no fiduciary relationship exists between the auctioneer and the purchaser, the parties are nevertheless bound by certain rights and obligations. The major ones are noted below.

Jurisdiction over Bidders: The *Franklyn* Case

With out-of-state bidders this question often arises: If a prospective purchaser's bids are taken seriously, do the courts of the state where the auction house is located have jurisdiction over that party if he or she decides not to go through with the sale? The answer is generally yes, an out-of-state bidder subjects himself or herself to the jurisdiction of the local forum of the auction house. The process of bidding, either personally or through an agent, serves to bind the successful bidder to a contract enforceable under the substantive and procedural rules of the jurisdiction where the auction house is located.

That issue was decided in New York some years ago[46] when, in March 1967, Dr. Robert Franklyn, living in California, received a catalog from Parke-Bernet Galleries describing some paintings to be sold at auction at its New York City galleries on April 6. Franklyn notified Parke-Bernet by letter that he wished to bid up to $71,000 for a particular painting. On the day before the auction, Franklyn called Parke-Bernet and requested that the auction house set up telephone communication during the auction so that Franklyn could participate during the bidding. He confirmed his desire to participate in that manner by telegram, in which he further stated that he might also bid on additional lots.

The auction house accordingly opened a telephone line the evening of the auction and assigned a Parke-Bernet employee to apprise Franklyn continuously of the bids being made in the auction room and to relay, in turn, Franklyn's bids. At the close of the auction, Franklyn had acquired two paintings, a Roger a de La Fresnaye and a Paul Klee, for $70,000 and $26,000, respectively. After billing Franklyn and receiving no payment, Parke-Bernet sued him for the amount owed. Franklyn moved to dismiss the suit on the ground that the court lacked jurisdiction over his person.

The New York long-arm statute,[47] similar to long-arm statutes in other states,[48] vests the New York courts with personal jurisdiction over any nondomiciliary who in person or through an agent transacts any business within the state if a cause of action arises from that transaction. The New York courts in the past had concluded that it was the purpose of the long-arm statute to extend the jurisdiction of the state courts to nonresidents who have "engaged in some purposeful activity [here] in connection with the matter in suit . . . [and that] a single transaction in New York would satisfy this statutory requirement."[49] The court in the Franklyn case emphasized that physical presence was not required under the long-arm statute and that, indeed, "one can engage in extensive purposeful activity here without ever actually setting foot in the State."[50] The court further noted that the case "falls between the situation where a defendant was physically present at the time the contract was made—the clearest sort of case in which our courts would have [long-arm] jurisdiction—and the situation where a defendant merely telephones a single order from outside the State—a case in which our courts would not have such jurisdiction."[51] The court then noted Franklyn's active participation in the bidding, assisted by the Parke-Bernet employee, and concluded that "[w]hether we view this case as one in which the defendant had personally engaged in purposeful activity here or as one in which . . . he had engaged in such activity 'through an agent' present here, there is ample basis for concluding that the defendant is subject to the jurisdiction of our courts with respect to a cause of action arising out of the auction."[52]

Sales Tax

Purchasers of artwork at auction must be aware that they may be liable for sales taxes on their purchases. The sales tax is now 8.25 percent for property sold in New York City. Many cities and states impose sales taxes on property sold within their borders. The applicable sales taxes are collected by the auction house from the purchasers and are then remitted to the appropriate taxing authorities. If the purchaser is an out-of-state resident and the artwork purchased is delivered to the purchaser out-of-state, the sales tax would not apply, but often a use tax in the purchaser's home state is due. Purchasers sometimes believe that they can avoid the sales tax by having an art dealer (who has a resale certificate, exempting him from paying the sales tax) buy the artwork on the purchaser's behalf. That belief is not correct, since the art dealer then becomes legally obligated to collect the sales tax from the ultimate purchaser.

Authenticity

The artwork that a purchaser acquires at auction must be, in terms of authorship, what it is described to be. New York lawmakers on both the state level and the local level have been remarkably responsive to that concern of buyers, resulting in the enactment of legislation over the past twenty or twenty-five years that goes to considerable lengths to alleviate purchasers' fears. Before 1966, a New York auction house acted solely as the seller's agent, contending that the buyer must seek any recourse against the seller, a frequently remote figure unidentified to the buyer. In keeping with that assertion, auctioneers, as a rule, disclaimed all warranties and representations and virtually all responsibility with respect to the works offered for sale. Then in 1966, in response to claims of auctioneer unconscionability, New York enacted legislation addressing the creation and the negation of express warranties in the sale of works of fine art.[53] Legislation in 1968 limited the application of the warranties to sales by art merchants to nonmerchants and further curtailed the power to negate such warranties.[54] The amended legislation, calling for greater particularity in disclaimers, does not permit any disclaimer to be coupled with a written instrument (defined to include an auction catalog) that unqualifiedly states that a particular work of fine art is by a particular artist. Sotheby's accordingly revised its auction catalog; its later version had fewer unqualified statements of authorship and greater specificity in its disclaimers.

In the wake of the legislative diminution of disclaimers arose the 1971 case of *Weiscz v. Parke-Bernet Galleries, Inc.*,[55] discussed in more detail in chapter 2, in which the lower court ruled that the plaintiff-purchasers could recover the purchase prices paid for paintings that Parke-Bernet had incorrectly described as being by Raoul Dufy. As one of its defenses, Parke-Bernet had submitted the traditional plea that it was acting only as an agent and that the purchasers should pursue the responsible party—that is, the consignor. The lower court dismissed that argument, possibly in view of the developing legislation. Although the lower court was reversed by the appellate court, which noted that, at the time of that public auction, the law did not recognize the expressed opinion of the seller as giving rise to any implied warranty of authenticity of authorship,[56] the case augured a judicial deathblow to the auctioneer's historical stance as a nonculpable agent.

Limited Warranties

In response to the evolving legislative and judicial perception of the auctioneer as a responsible and potentially culpable party, Sotheby's reversed its former position. Beginning in September 1973, on lots sold in its New York salesroom, it guaranteed for five years (1) the authorship of any work executed after 1869 and (2) that the work was not a counterfeit in the case of works executed before 1870. Christie's, on entering the New York market in 1977, offered a similarly limited warranty. The most recent versions of those warranties are included at the close of this chapter. Note that those warranties extend solely to a work's authorship and do not address either its physical condition or its provenance. Nevertheless, the combined effect of the legislative, judicial, and trade developments in New York have done much to bolster the protection and the confidence of the purchaser.

Indeed, in a recent case involving the authenticity of a Fabergé egg, Christie's was impelled by the purchaser to agree to a settlement. A summary of the dispute follows.

The Case of the Fabergé Egg[57]

On April 27, 1977, an Iranian-born businessman, Eskandar Aryeh, purchased at auction from Christie's in Geneva a Fabergé imperial enameled Easter egg. The hammer price of $250,000 was, at the time, the highest price paid for a Fabergé imperial egg. Shortly after the auction, Aryeh began to doubt the authenticity of the egg because of its slight discoloration and the quality of the workmanship; consequently, he refused to accept delivery or to pay for it unless he was provided with proof that the egg was genuine. In response, Christie's Geneva issued a letter certifying the egg as an authentic piece from the workshop of Fabergé. After Aryeh refused to accept Christie's certification as adequate proof of authenticity, Christie's brought civil and criminal proceedings against him in Switzerland.

During the course of the proceedings, Christie's delivered to Aryeh, living in New York, a second letter of authentication. That letter, signed by A. Kenneth Snowman, one of the world's foremost experts on Fabergé, persuaded Aryeh to proceed with the purchase. Accordingly, Aryeh paid the $250,000 for the egg, along with $150,000 in legal fees, interest, and other expenses sought by Christie's,[58] and the pending lawsuits against Aryeh were dropped.

Aryeh subsequently placed the egg in a New York City bank vault, where it remained until the fall of 1985, when he decided to sell it at Christie's New York. At a recent sale at Sotheby's, another Fabergé imperial Easter egg had sold for $1.6 million.[59] The sale of Aryeh's egg, scheduled for October 16, 1985, was withdrawn by Christie's on October 3 after Snowman revised his opinion to state that although the egg was by Fabergé, it had been doctored, whereupon Aryeh commenced suit against Christie's.

In the course of the proceedings, Aryeh alleged that the 1977 sale to him was fraudulent; that, on the eve of the 1977 auction, Snowman had examined the egg and had advised Christie's Geneva of his reservations about the egg's authenticity; and that the delivery to him of the alleged Snowman letter in December 1977 was, therefore, part of the fraudulent scheme to induce him to proceed with the purchase of the egg.

Christie's moved to dismiss the complaint, asserting, among other allegations, that the applicable statute of limitations had expired. However, before the proceedings had advanced much further, Christie's reached a settlement of the case with Esther Aryeh; her husband, Eskandar, had died during the course of the action.

Had the case not been settled, however, it is likely that Aryeh would have prevailed on the statute-of-limitations issue, assuming that he could establish a prima facie case of fraudulent conspiracy. That may not have been so difficult to establish, since Snowman himself admitted to the *London Times* that, on the eve of the 1977 auction, he relayed to Christie's Geneva his doubts about the egg's authenticity.[60]

Where fraud has been secretly practiced and a cause of action has not been discovered because of the fraudulent concealment, in most jurisdictions the running of the statute of limitations is suspended until the cause of action either becomes known or should have been discovered.[61] Even if the facts of a case do not indicate a concealed fraud, the running of the limitations statute can still be postponed on evidence of acts or conduct designed to mislead, deceive, or lull inquiry.[62] Surely, in the Fabergé egg case, the December 1977 letter from Snowman, a leading Fabergé expert, authenticating the egg, would have served to lull inquiry on the part of Aryeh. In fact, Aryeh apparently relied on the contents of that letter when he ultimately decided to consummate the purchase of the egg. Since the egg was in a bank vault until he sought to sell it in 1985, Aryeh did not discover his cause of action, nor was there any reason for him to do so, until the egg was withdrawn by Christie's from the impending auction. Once Aryeh determined that he had an action, he wasted no time in initiating the suit.

Title

Another major concern of the buyer at auction is that the work he or she purchases carries free and clear title. Under the UCC,[63] any sale, whether by auction or otherwise, conveys a warranty of title. The scope of the warranty includes freedom from a security interest "of which the buyer at the time of contracting has no knowledge."[64] In the United States it has long been held that an auctioneer selling the works of an undisclosed principal stands behind the representations and warranties of title that exist in every contract of sale.[65] It has also been held that one who enters into a contract as an agent without disclosing the name of the principal becomes liable on the contract, even though the agent is known to be acting for another.[66] As to the liability of the auctioneer for warranty of title when the principal is disclosed under the revised auction regulations in New York City (discussed later in this chapter), the auction house retains its liability and, in any event, cannot disclaim the warranty of title, whether or not the principal is disclosed.[67] Moreover, an auctioneer who sells goods that are stolen or that are subject to a lien is liable to the true owner or the lien holder without regard to the auctioneer's actual or constructive knowledge of the consignor's lack of title or authority to sell.[68] The measure of damages is the value of the item at the time the buyer is required to return it.[69] Moreover, an auctioneer may be liable for conversion of property fraudulently obtained by a consignor when the auctioneer has knowledge of the fraud.[70]

Disclaimers of Warranties

Although, as noted both here and in chapter 2, the law looks dimly on disclaimers of warranties, particularly disclaimers of warranties of title by auctioneers, that does not mean that disclaimers by auctioneers of other warranties will not, at times, be upheld. In fact, in 1982 the New York Supreme Court in New York County, applying the UCC, upheld the disclaimer of an auction house printed in its auction catalog. A brief summary of the case follows.

Giusti v. Sotheby Parke Bernet, Inc.[71]

In April 1974, the plaintiff, Antonio Giusti, purchased at auction at Sotheby's a diamond ring for which he paid $115,000. The auction catalog described the ring as being an emerald-cut diamond of approximately 9.10 carats on a platinum mount, flanked by two baguette diamonds. The description further noted that the central diamond was "certified to be very fine color and flawless."[72] A few days before purchasing the ring, Giusti had examined it at Sotheby's and was advised that the ring was "E" color and flawless; he was further advised that before the sale Sotheby's would procure the original certificate from the Gemological Institute of America (GIA). Giusti was the highest bidder for the ring at auction, and he signed, without reading, a "Memorandum of Successful Bid" presented to him by a Sotheby employee immediately after the close of the bidding. On the memorandum was imprinted the following legend: "The Buyer Acknowledges Familiarity With the 'Conditions of Sale' Governing Purchase at Auction As Published In the Catalog." Those conditions of sale contained the following disclaimer:[73]

> Except as so specifically provided in the "Terms of Guarantee" with respect to authenticity of authorship, all property is sold "as is" and neither the Galleries nor the Consignor makes any warranties or representations of any kind or nature with respect to, nor shall they be held responsible or liable for, the correctness of the catalog or other description of the physical condition, size, quality, rarity, importance, provenance, exhibition, literature and historical relevance of the property. . . .

After the auction, Giusti was given a photocopy of the GIA certificate and was advised that the original would be forthcoming. In the ensuing few weeks, Giusti still had not received the original certificate; by then he had learned that the stone bore some slight imperfections.

The ring had been consigned to Sotheby's in February 1974 by Lee Vandervelde of California, who had represented to Sotheby's that the ring weighed 9.09 carats and had been graded "E" color and either "flawless" or "internally flawless" by GIA. Vandervelde further represented that a certificate stating the foregoing had been issued and would be furnished to Sotheby's; that representation, however, was false. In fact, in 1969 and 1973, Vandervelde procured two GIA certificates as to the diamond. The 1969 certificate assessed the diamond's weight at 9.00 carats, its clarity as "internally flawless," and its color as "F" (one grade inferior to "E"). The 1973 certificate assessed the diamond's weight as 9.09 carats, the color grade as "E," but the clarity as "VVS1"—that is, having very slight surface imperfections. What Vandervelde ultimately forwarded to Sotheby's in 1974 for the sale was not a true GIA certificate but, rather, a composite of the 1969 and 1973 certificates. Thus, Vandervelde had willfully misrepresented the characteristics of the ring to Sotheby's.

When Sotheby's received the ring in 1974, pursuant to its consignment agreement, its appraiser made a limited examination of the mounted stone and satisfied himself that it conformed reasonably well to the characteristics Vandervelde had described. After the sale to Giusti and after some extended correspondence among Giusti, Sotheby's, and Vandervelde, the ring was returned to Sotheby's in December 1974 for re-examination by GIA as an unmounted stone. The resultant assessment included a clarity grade of "VVS," potentially flawless, and a color grade of "F." The examination revealed a small bruise on one facet of the diamond. Giusti accordingly brought suit against Sotheby's and Vandervelde, seeking rescission; damages for breach of warranty, breach of contract, and negligent and reckless misrepresentation against Sotheby's; and seeking damages for breach of warranty and fraudulent misrepresentations against Vandervelde.

The court dismissed the complaint, holding that no recovery was warranted under any theory. The court found that Sotheby's had made neither negligent nor reckless misrepresentations nor any representations that were relied on by Giusti. Moreover, the court found that, although Vandervelde misrepresented the certificate he forwarded to Sotheby's, Giusti placed no reliance on either that misrepresentation or the certificate; rather, by his own testimony, the principal reason he decided to bid on the ring was because he liked it after having looked at it. Further, the court noted, even if Giusti was found to have relied on Sotheby's or Vandervelde's representations, the question would remain as to whether that reliance was justified in the face of his admitted disregard of the conditions of sale prominently set forth in the catalog and on signs posted throughout the gallery. As the court stated:

> The fact that Giusti neither read this notice in the catalog nor the "as is" disclaimer posted throughout the gallery on the conditions of sale signs, does not in the least diminish the force of the disclaimers nor enhance Giusti's right to recovery. He is bound by the terms of the sale and the limitations clearly imposed thereon and his claimed lack of actual knowledge of them through negligence or inexcusable trustfulness will not relieve him of his contract.[74]

The court noted that Giusti's reliance on the UCC was likewise unavailing and that any express or implied warranties imposed on the transaction by virtue of the UCC provisions are effectively modified or excluded, as provided in the Code,[75] by the conspicuously placed "as is" disclaimers.

NEW YORK CITY REGULATION OF AUCTIONEERS

Beginning in December 1984, the New York Department of Consumer Affairs conducted a two-year study of the procedures and practices of the auction industry. As a result of the study, regulations that were promulgated in 1974 have been updated to address current market conditions and to monitor courses of conduct that have developed since 1974. The following is a summary of some of the major provisions of the revised regulations. A complete copy of the new regulations, which became effective April 13, 1987, is included at the end of this chapter.

Written Contract

There must be a written contract between the consignor and the auctioneer for the auctioning of property (Regulation 8).

Disclosure to Consignors

Fees, commissions, and other charges payable by the consignor to the auctioneer must be disclosed (Regulation 9(a)).

Consignor Warrants Good Title

Each consignor-auctioneer contract must contain a provision whereby the consignor (1) warrants that, as of the date of the auction, he or she had complete and lawful title in the property auctioned, (2) indemnifying the auctioneer against any defect of title, and (3) acknowledging that the intended beneficiary of the warranty is the ultimate purchaser at auction (Regulation 9(b)).

Disclosure to Prospective Buyers

Any interest by the auctioneer in the auction property, other than the right to a commission on the sale, must be disclosed. The disclosure must appear in connection with any description of the object in the auction catalog or in any other printed materials published or distributed in connection with the sale (Regulation 11).

- The auctioneer must disclose in the auction catalog whether the consignor is entitled to a rebate commission or may bid on his or her own property at the sale (Regulation 12).
- If there is a reserve price on an article, that fact must be disclosed in the auction catalog. If there is no reserve price, the auctioneer cannot imply that there is one (Regulations 13(a) and 13(b)).
- If an auctioneer makes loans to consignors or prospective buyers, that fact must be disclosed in the auction catalog (Regulation 15).
- Whenever an estimated value of an item or lot is published in a catalog, a general description of the estimate and its

meaning and function must also be included in the publication (Regulation 17).

- If any lot has been bought-in, the auctioneer must disclose that fact at the auction before the bidding on the next lot starts (Regulation 20).
- If the auctioneer intends to bid up to the reserve price on behalf of the seller, he or she must disclose that fact both in the catalog and on signs posted at the entrance to and inside the auction room (Regulation 21).

Conduct of the Auction

- Once the bidding on a lot or an item has reached the reserve price, the auctioneer may not bid or accept bids on behalf of the consignor or of the auction house (Regulation 22(a)).
- In no event shall the reserve price for any lot exceed its published presale maximum estimated value (Regulation 23).
- The auctioneer may not disclaim warranty of title of any item sold at auction (Regulation 24).

Puffing

Although the legitimacy of various auction practices is frequently dictated by state statutes and by local regulations, such as those recently enacted in New York City, two prevalent practices have historically been declared unlawful: (1) puffing up the sale price by sellers or their agents and (2) chill bidding to depress the auction price. The UCC expressly proscribes puffing[76] and implicitly prohibits chill bidding.[77]

An auctioneer may not knowingly receive a bid on the seller's behalf, nor may the seller make or procure such a bid without prior notice to the buyer that the seller has retained the right to do so. Case law has consistently held fictitious bids to be fraudulent and illegal.[78] In the event of such bidding, the UCC provides options for the buyer: The buyer may either rescind the sale or take the goods "at the price of the last good faith bid prior to the completion of the sale."[79] When a single buyer is making a bid in competition with a fraudulent bid, it has been suggested that the purchase price should be the last good-faith bid before the first fraudulent overbid.[80]

Chill Bidding

Generally illegal under common law[81] was the practice of chill bidding—that is, an agreement between two or more persons to refrain from competitive bidding in order to depress the sales price. As with puffing, the practice is fraudulent, since it prevents a fair price from being determined by fair competition and it distorts, to the detriment of the consignor and the auctioneer, the actual extent of competition among willing buyers. Proof of its existence under common law provided the seller with two options: (1) the right to withdraw his or her goods from any party involved in the chill, even when the auction was conducted without reserve prices, and (2) the right, predicated on rescission for fraud, to recover the goods sold to a chill bidder.[82] The practice of chill bidding spawned the growth of bidding rings that purchased auctioned goods at artificially low prices, defrauding auctioneers and consignors.

The following is a brief description of a ring in operation. An auction is attended, for example, by a group of six prospective purchasers who know each other, each interested in acquiring the same work of art. The six agree among themselves that rather than bid against each other, thus raising the purchase price for the consignor's benefit, only one of their number will bid to acquire the artwork. They further agree to later hold a private knockout auction among themselves for the work, if their designated bidder is successful. The profit made by the seller in the second auction—the amount over what he or she bid in the previous auction—is divided among the five unsuccessful bidders at the knockout auction, benefiting all but the consignor and the auctioneer.

Bidding rings were such a problem in England that Parliament enacted prohibitive legislation. The 1927 Auctions (Bidding Agreements) Act,[83] also known as the Knockout Act, made such arrangements expressly illegal, although it permitted joint-account bidding, provided the agreement was in writing and was deposited with the auctioneer before the purchase. Although there does not appear to be comparable legislation in the United States, an organized ring may be prosecuted under federal or state law as a combination in restraint of trade, provided that proof of the ring's existence is established. In the face of informal arrangements, however, proving it could be no mean feat. It has also been suggested that common-law rules governing fraud may obtain, since such an agreement may defraud both the consignor and the auctioneer.[84] Indeed, in jurisdictions throughout the United States, it has been held that any agreement or combination intending to stifle fair competition and to chill bidding is unenforceable as being against public policy and will cause a sale to be set aside.[85] However, the courts look to the intention of the parties; if the intention is fair and honest—with the parties' primary purpose being not to suppress competition but, rather, to advance their own interests or protect their rights—the arrangements will be upheld.[86]

NOTES to Chapter 3

1. U.C.C. § 2-313.

2. U.C.C. § 2-312.

3. U.C.C. § 2-314.

4. U.C.C. § 2-315.

5. U.C.C. § 2-316. Note: Mississippi now omits this section of the Code.

6. U.C.C. § 2-328(1).

7. U.C.C. § 2-328(2).

8. U.C.C. § 2-328(3). Note, however, that a bidder's retraction does not revive any previous bid.

9. Dulman v. Martin Fein & Co., 66 A.D.2d 809, 411 N.Y.S.2d. 358 (2d Dept. 1978).

10. U.C.C. § 2-328(2).

11. Marx v. Sotheby Parke Bernet, Inc., No. 7561/81 (Sup. Ct.), *aff'd*, 102 A.D.2d 729, 476 N.Y.S.2d 482 (1st Dep't 1983).

12. U.C.C. § 2-201.

13. *See* N.Y. Gen. Oblig. Law § 5-701(a)(6) (McKinney 1989); Cal. Civ. Code § 2363 (West 1988).

14. *Id.*

15. U.C.C. § 2-328(4). *See also* Nevada Nat'l Leasing Co. v. Hereford, 38 U.C.C. Rep. Serv. 716 (Callaghan), 36 Cal. 3d 146, 680 P.2d 1077 (1984).

16. Abrams v. Sotheby Parke Bernet, Inc., Index No. 42255/84 (N.Y. Sup. Ct. 1984).

17. N.Y. Exec. Law § 63(12) (McKinney 1982); N.Y. Gen. Bus. Law § 349 (McKinney 1988).

18. Article 5 of Military Restitution Law No. 59 and Article 4 of the Berlin Restitution Law.

19. N.Y. TIMES, Aug. 2, 1985, at C11, col. 1.

20. N.Y. TIMES, Aug. 7, 1985, at C15, col. 5.

21. Cristallina S.A. v. Christie, Manson & Woods, Int'l Inc., 117 A.D.2d 284, 292, 502 N.Y.S.2d 165, 171 (lst Dept. 1986).

22. *Id.*

23. Maltby v. Christie, 1 Esp. 340, 179 Eng. Rep. 378 (K.B. 1795).

24. Cristallina, *supra* note 21, 117 A.D.2d at 292-93, 502 N.Y.S.2d at 171. *See also* RESTATEMENT (SECOND) OF AGENCY § 381 (1958 & App. Supp. 1988).

25. Cristallina, *supra* note 21, 117 A.D.2d at 292-93 n.7, 502 N.Y.S.2d at 171 n.7, *citing* RESTATEMENT, *supra* note 24, at § 384.

26. Cristallina, *supra* note 21, 117 A.D.2d at 293, 502 N.Y.S.2d at 171; *see also* RESTATEMENT, *supra* note 24, at § 381.

27. See Sconyers v. Bowers & Ruddy Galleries, Inc., N.Y.L.J., Aug. 7, 1987, at 12, col. 1 (Sup. Ct. 1987), where the court in granting summary judgment to the defendant auctioneer held that the plaintiff purchaser of coins, in alleging that the auctioneer orally agreed to a 50 percent discount on the buyer's premium, failed to refute the auctioneer's defense that no such agreement existed.

28. *Id.*

29. Cristallina, *supra* note 21, 117 A.D.2d at 293, 502 N.Y.S.2d at 172.

30. *See, e.g.*, Sotheby's Conditions of Sale ¶ 8, *infra*.

31. N.Y. GEN. BUS. LAW § 24 (McKinney 1988); CAL. ANN. PENAL CODE vol. 49, § 535 (West Supp. 1989).

32. Cristallina, *supra* note 21, 117 A.D.2d at 294, 502 N.Y.S.2d at 172.

33. U.C.C. § 2-328(3).

34. *See* Auction Regulation, *infra* pp. 172-76.

35. Auction Regulation 13(a).

36. Auction Regulation 20.

37. Auction Regulation 23.

38. Benjamin v. First Citizens Bank & Trust Co., 248 A.D. 610, 287 N.Y.S. 947 (2d Dept. 1936).

39. Cristallina, *supra* note 21, 117 A.D.2d at 294, 502 N.Y.S.2d at 172.

40. Cristallina, *supra* note 21.

41. *Id.*

42. *Id.*

43. ARTNEWSLETTER, Feb. 3, 1987, at 1.

44. Schering Corp. v. Home Ins. Co. 712 F.2d 4, 10 n.2 (2d Cir. 1983).

45. DeBruno v. Sotheby Parke Bernet, Inc., Civ. Action No. 84-3021, Bench Opinion (D.N.J. Nov. 8, 1984). The case is reproduced in 2 F. FELDMAN, S. WEIL & S. BIEDERMAN, ART LAW 249 (1986).

46. Parke-Bernet Galleries, Inc. v. Franklyn, 26 N.Y.2d 13, 256 N.E.2d 506, 308 N.Y.S.2d 337 (1970).

47. N.Y. CIV. PRAC. L. & R. 302(a), ¶1 (McKinney 1972 & Supp. 1989).

48. *See* Annotation, *Construction and Application of State Statutes or Rules of Court Predicating in Personam Jurisdiction Over Nonresidents or Foreign Corporations on Making or Performing a Contract Within the State*, 23 A.L.R.3D 551.

49. *Supra* note 46, 26 N.Y.2d at 16, 256 N.E.2d at 507-08, 308 N.Y.S.2d at 339.

50. *Id.* at 17, 256 N.E.2d at 508, 308 N.Y.S. at 340.

51. *Id.*

52. *Id.* at 17-18, 256 N.E.2d at 508, 308 N.Y.S.2d at 340.

53. N.Y. GEN. BUS. LAW art. 12-D, §§ 219-b to -e, subsequently repealed as of December 31, 1983, the within provisions now being covered by N.Y. ARTS & CULT. AFF. LAW art. 13 (McKinney 1984 & Supp. 1989).

54. N.Y. ARTS & CULT. AFF. LAW art. 13 (McKinney 1984 & Supp. 1989).

55. Weisz v. Parke-Bernet Galleries, Inc., 67 Misc. 2d 1077, 325 N.Y.S.2d 576 (Civ. Ct. 1971), *rev'd*, 77 Misc. 2d 80, 351 N.Y.S.2d 911 (App. Term 1974).

56. 77 Misc. 2d 80, 351 N.Y.S.2d 911, 912 (App. Term 1974).

57. Aryeh v. Christie's Int'l, Index No. 1030/86 (N.Y. Sup. Ct. 1986).

58. ARTNEWSLETTER, Feb. 2, 1988, at 3.

59. Aryeh v. Christie's, *supra* note 57.

60. LONDON TIMES, Oct. 1985.

61. *See, e.g.*, Myers v. Canton Nat'l Bank, 109 F.2d 31 (7th Cir. 1940); Rozell v. Kaye, 197 F. Supp. 733 (S.D. Tex. 1961); Sylvester v. Bernstein, 283 A.D. 333, 127 N.Y.S.2d 746 (1st Dep't), *aff'd*, 307 N.Y. 778, 121 N.E.2d 616 (1954).

62. *See, e.g.*, Norris v. Haggin, 136 U.S. 386 (1890); Pratt v. Thompson, 133 Wash. 218, 233 P. 637 (1925); Van Ingin v. Duffin, 158 Ala. 318, 48 So. 507 (1909).

63. U.C.C. § 2-312.

64. U.C.C. § 2-312(1)(b).

65. *See, e.g.*, Universal C.I.T. Credit Corp. v. State Farm Mut. Auto. Ins. Co., 493 S.W.2d 385 (Mo. App. 1973). *See also* Itoh v. Kimi Sales, Ltd., 74 Misc. 2d 402, 345 N.Y.S.2d 416 (Civ. Ct. 1973); Meyer v. Redmond, 205 N.Y. 478, 98 N.E. 906 (1912).

66. *See, e.g.*, DeRemer v. Brown, 165 N.Y. 410, 419 (1901); M.N. Bank v. Gallaudet, 120 N.Y. 298, 307 (1890). *See also* H. Reuschlein & W. Gregory, Agency & Partnership § 6 (1979).

67. Auction Regulation 24. *See also* Auction Regulations 9(b) and 8.

68. Levy Bros. v. Karp, 124 Misc. 901, 209 N.Y.S. 720 (Sup. Ct. 1924). But note that in a small number of jurisdictions an auctioneer who has neither actual nor constructive knowledge of a claim by a third party is not liable to that third party. *See* Annotation, *Auctioneer Liability for Conversion*, 96 A.L.R.2d 308, 314.

69. *See* Menzel v. List, 24 N.Y.2d 91, 298 N.Y.S.2d 979 (1969). *See also* Itoh v. Kimi Sales, *supra* note 65.

70. Grossman v. Walter, 58 Hun. 603, 11 N.Y.S. 471, *aff'd*, 132 N.Y. 594, 30 N.E. 1151 (1890).

71. Giusti v. Sotheby Parke Bernet, Inc., Index No. 6843/76 (N.Y. Sup. Ct. 1982); N.Y.L.J., July 16, 1982, at 24.

72. *Id.*

73. *Id.*

74. *Id.*

75. U.C.C. § 2-316(1), (3).

76. U.C.C. § 2-328(4).

77. *But see* W. Hawkland, Uniform Commercial Code Series § 2-328:05, at 568 (1985) (suggesting that "chill bidding" may actually be proscribed by the Code). Hawkland argues that the practice, illegal under common law, continues to be illegal under U.C.C. § 1-103. That section provides that, unless displaced by specific provisions of the UCC, the principles of law and equity—including the law merchant, contract law, and the law of agency—will supplement the Code.

78. *See, e.g.*, Nevada Nat'l Leasing Co. v. Hereford, 36 Cal. 3d 146, 680 P.2d 1077, 203 Cal. Rptr. 118 (1984); Berg v. Hogan, 322 N.W.2d 448 (N.D. 1982); Feaster Trucking Serv., Inc. v. Parke-Davis Auctioneers, Inc., 211 Kan. 78, 505 P.2d 612 (1973).

79. U.C.C. § 2-328(4).

80. 1 W. Hawkland, A Transactional Guide to the Uniform Commercial Code 40 (1964).

81. *See* Hawkland, *supra* note 80, at 41. *But see also* Rawlings v. General Trading Co., 90 K.B. 404 (1921), which, despite a strong dissent indicating that the bidding combination at issue was contrary to public policy as being in restraint of trade, held that an agreement between two prospective purchasers to chill bidding was not illegal.

82. Hawkland, *supra* note 80, at 41.

83. Auctions (Bidding Agreements) Act, 1927, 17 & 18 Geo. 5, ch. 12, 4 Halsbury's Statutes 5 (4th ed. 1987).

84. Hawkland, *supra* note 80, at 41.

85. *See, e.g.*, Preske v. Carroll, 178 Md. 543 (1940); Konen v. Konen, 165 La. 288, 115 So. 490 (1928); Stewart v. Severance, 43 Mo. 322 (1869).

86. *See, e.g.*, Jones v. Clary, 194 Va. 804, 75 S.E.2d 504 (1953); Henderson v. Henrie, 61 W. Va. 183, 56 S.E. 369 (1907); Smith v. Ullman, 58 Md. 183 (1881); James v. Fulcrod, 5 Tex. 512 (1851).

FORMS

CITY OF NEW YORK
ADMINISTRATIVE CODE

Title 20
Department of Consumer Affairs

Chapter 2
Licenses

Subchapter 13
AUCTIONEERS

§ 20-278. License required. It shall be unlawful for any person to engage in the business of auctioneer without a license therefor.

§ 20-279. Fee; bond. a. The annual fee for such license shall be two hundred dollars.

b. Each applicant for such license shall file with the commissioner, a bond with two good sureties, in the penal sum of two thousand dollars, which bond shall meet with the approval of the commissioner.

HISTORICAL NOTE: Amended by Local Law No. 44 for 1970, August 10.

§ 20-280. Requirements for auctioneers. Each auctioneer shall cause his or her name and license number to be conspicuously displayed at any place where he or she shall conduct an auction sale during such sale.

§ 20-281. Persons acting as auctioneers. It shall be unlawful for any person not licensed as an auctioneer to represent or circulate or place before the public any announcement, or to insert or cause to be inserted in any city, business or telephone directory, any notice that he or she is conducting the business of auctioneering.

HISTORICAL NOTE: Amended by Local Law No. 172 for 1939, November 20; Local Law No. 20 for 1973, June 5.

§ 20-282. Advertising. Every auctioneer in his or her own name, shall give notice in one or more of the public newspapers printed in the city, of every auction sale to be conducted by him or her. In the event that such auctioneer shall be connected with any firm or other person his or her name shall in all cases precede the name of such firm or other person.

HISTORICAL NOTE: Amended by Local Law No. 20 for 1973, June 5.

§ 20-283. *Night auctions.* a. The sale by public auction of all goods except as set forth in subdivision b hereof shall be made in the daytime, between eight o'clock in the morning and eight o'clock in the evening.

b. Any sale by auction of the following goods after eight o'clock in the evening shall be conducted pursuant to a special permit issued by the commissioner, in his or her discretion and upon such reasonable conditions as he or she shall prescribe:

1. Books and prints;
2. Goods sold in the original package, as imported, according to a printed catalogue, of which samples shall have been opened and exposed to public inspection at least one day previous to the sale;
3. Horses and live stock;
4. Fruit and other farm products;
5. Paintings, statuary, bronzes and other works of art and specimens of natural history, which shall have been on public exhibition in the city for at least one day immediately preceding the time of sale, provided that public notice of the time and place of such exhibition shall have been given by advertisement for at least one day immediately preceding the day of such exhibition, in one or more of the designated daily newspapers printed in the city.

c. The commissioner from time to time, by a notice to be filed in his or her office and printed for five consecutive days in the City Record, shall designate the newspapers in which such advertisements may be printed, and the commissioner, at any time, by a like notice may revoke the designation of any such newspapers.

HISTORICAL NOTE: Amended by Local Law No. 20 for 1973, June 5.

§ 20-284. Sale of jewelry. a. Each auctioneer shall cause to be delivered to the purchaser of diamonds, precious stones or other jewelry, a signed document containing a description of the article sold and the representations made in regard thereto at the time of the sale.

b. Each article of jewelry sold at public auction shall have affixed thereto a tag, on which shall be printed or written a correct description of such article.

§ 20-285. Restrictions. a. It shall be unlawful for any auctioneer, his or her agent, employee or servant to sell at public auction or expose for such sale:

1. Any dry-goods, clothing, hardware, household furniture, woodenware or tinware by retail or in small parcels or pieces, in any street or public place;

2. Any goods, wares, merchandise or other things to any person who, at the time of bidding for or while examining such articles, shall be on any street;

3. Any goods, wares, merchandise or other things in any street or public place, or place them thereon, unless he or she first shall obtain the consent or permission, in writing, of the occupant of the lot or building before which such articles or any part thereof shall be placed or exposed for sale.

b. It shall be unlawful to employ any means of attracting the attention of purchasers, other than a sign or flag, at or near any place of sale, auction room, residence of any auctioneer, or at or near any auction whatsoever. c. Every article sold or exposed for sale at public auction, in any street or public place, shall be removed therefrom by sunset on the day of such sale or display.

HISTORICAL NOTE: Amended by Local Law No. 172 for 1939, November 20; Local Law No. 20 for 1973, June 5.

§ 20-286. Sale of real property; fees. a. It shall be unlawful for any auctioneer to demand or receive for his or her services, in selling, at public auction, any real estate directed to be sold by any judgment or decree of any court of this state, a greater fee than fifty dollars for each parcel separately sold, except that in all sales of real estate conducted by any auctioneer pursuant to a judgment or decree of any court of this state in any action brought to foreclose a mortgage or other lien on real estate, the fees of such auctioneers shall be as follows:

1. in all cases where the judgment of foreclosure is for an amount not exceeding five thousand dollars, the fee shall be fifteen dollars;

2. in all cases where the judgment of foreclosure is for an amount in excess of five thousand dollars, but not exceeding twenty-five thousand dollars, the fee shall be twenty-five dollars;

3. in all cases where the judgment of foreclosure is for an amount in excess of twenty-five thousand dollars, the fee shall be fifty dollars.

b. Where such sale is made at any public salesroom, such auctioneer may demand and receive such further amount not exceeding ten dollars for each parcel separately sold as he or she may have actually paid for the privilege or right of making the sale in such salesroom. c. Where one or more lots are so sold at public auction with the option to the purchaser of taking one or more additional lots at the same rates or price, nothing herein contained shall be construed to prevent the auctioneer making such sale from demanding and receiving for his or her services the compensation or fee above allowed, for each additional lot taken by such purchaser under such option.

HISTORICAL NOTE: Subdivision b as amended by Law, Chapter 83 for 1947, March 8.

§ 20-287. Split fees. It shall be unlawful for any auctioneer, either directly or indirectly, to allow or pay to the receiver, referee, sheriff, or other officer under whose direction a sale is made, pursuant to section 20-276 of this subchapter or to any of the attorneys in the action or proceeding from which such sale arises, any portion of his or her fee or compensation.

§ 20-288. False or fraudulent representations. Any auctioneer who shall have knowledge of any false or fraudulent representations or statements or who makes or causes any such statements to be made in respect to the character of any sale, or the party authorizing the same, or the quality, condition, ownership, situation or value of any property, real or personal, exposed, put up, or offered by him or her for sale at public auction, shall be deemed guilty of a misdemeanor, and, upon conviction thereof, shall be punished by imprisonment not exceeding one year or by a fine not exceeding one thousand dollars.

HISTORICAL NOTE: Amended by Local Law No. 20 for 1973, June 5.

§ 20-289. Complaints. a. The commissioner may take testimony, under oath, relating to and upon the complaint of any person who claims he or she has been defrauded by any auctioneer, his or her clerk, agent or assignee, or relating to and upon the complaint of any person who has consigned real or personal property for sale and to whom such auctioneer shall not have accounted fully. The license of each such auctioneer may be revoked and his or her bond declared forfeited if, in the opinion of the commissioner, such charge is sustained. Any such person whose license has been revoked for cause shall not be granted another such license.

b. The commissioner may take testimony, under oath, relating to and upon the complaint of any person who claims that any auctioneer, his or her clerk, agent or assignee, has been guilty of misconduct relating to the business transacted under such auctioneer's license, and if such charge, in his or her opinion, shall be sustained, the commissioner may suspend such license for a period not to exceed six months.

§ 20-290. Marshals exempt. Nothing in this subchapter shall apply to a duly appointed marshal, who, by virtue of his or her office sells real or personal property, levied upon by him or her under legal process.

HISTORICAL NOTE: Auctioneers were licensed by the Department of Licenses (since 1968, the Department of Consumer Affairs) beginning in 1938.

REGULATIONS

I. *STANDARDS, LICENSES AND APPLICATION OF REGULATIONS*

1. The auctioneer will be held responsible for the truth of any statement contained in any catalogue, advertisement, announcement, press release or other public statement made by the auctioneer relating to any auction.

2. The auctioneer shall be held responsible for full compliance by his employer or principal with all rules and regulations of the Department and pertinent provisions of law.

3. Each application for a license shall be accompanied by the affidavits of three citizens who are residents of New York City and who have known the applicant not less than two years.

4. The fee for a permit to auction publicly after 8 p.m. the goods or any of them specified in Section 20-283 of the Administrative Code shall be ten dollars for the first permit in any license year. Subsequent permits issued during the same license year may be issued without fee.

5. Each applicant for a permit to auction publicly after 8 p.m. shall furnish with the application for the permit a catalogue of the articles to be auctioned, and a copy of the advertisement to be published in connection with said auction. In the case of an auction of fruit, vegetables or other farm products, the catalogue shall be filed as soon as it has been printed.

6. All licensed auctioneers and auction houses must include their Department of Consumer Affairs license number, or the license

number assigned to their auction house or principal auctioneer and identify it as such in all advertisements in any medium, and on all written contracts, catalogues and announcements, relating to auction activity in New York City.

7. These rules and regulations do not apply to auction sales of real property.

II. *REQUIREMENTS AND OBLIGATIONS OF LICENSEES*

8. *Contracts Required*—No personal property may be auctioned except pursuant to a written contract between the consignor or his or her agent or authorized representative and the auctioneer, unless auctioned pursuant to an order of a court of competent jurisdiction.

9. Every contract required pursuant to Regulation 8 must contain the following provisions:

a. All fees, commissions and charges to be paid by the consignor to the auctioneer or his or her agents, principals, employees, employers or assigns shall (i) to the extent practicable, be itemized and specified as to amount (which may be stated as a percentage of the reserve price or any final bid), and (ii) if such itemization and specification as to amount is not practicable, be described with sufficient particularity to inform the consignor of the nature of the services for which such fees, commissions and charges will be imposed.

b. That as of the date of the auction the consignor warrants that he or she has complete and lawful right, title and interest in the property auctioned, and that the consignor shall indemnify the auctioneer, his or her agents, principals, employees, employers or assigns in the event of any defect in title, and that an intended beneficiary of this warranty is the ultimate purchaser at auction.

10. Where articles are referred to by catalogue or advertisement as having been obtained from any specific person, place or source, such articles must be separately enumerated and identified.

11. If an auctioneer or public salesroom has any interest, direct or indirect, in an article, including a guaranteed minimum, other than the selling commission, the fact such interest exists must be disclosed in connection with any description of the article or articles in the catalogue or any other printed material published or distributed in relation to the sale. Such notice may be denoted by a symbol or letter which will refer the reader to an explanation of the nature

of the interest the symbol or letter denotes. For the purpose of this regulation advertisements in newspapers or other periodicals shall not constitute printed material. Where no printed material is provided in connection with an auction, the auctioneer shall have available during any advertised inspection period, information [of] as to whether such an interest exists with relation to a particular item and shall announce before he or she commences the auction that such information is available upon request.

12. Where a consignor is to receive a rebate commission in whole or in part, or where he or she will be permitted to bid upon and to buy back his or her own article at the sale, disclosure of such a condition must be made in connection with any description of the item or items so affected in the catalogue or any other printed material published or distributed in relation to the sale. The existence of such a condition may be denoted by a symbol or letter which will refer the reader to an explanation of the nature of the interest the symbol or letter denotes. For the purpose of this regulation, advertisements in newspapers or other periodicals shall not constitute printed material. Where no printed material is provided in connection with the auction, the auctioneer shall have available during any advertised inspection period information of whether such a condition exists with relation to a particular item and shall announce before he or she commences the auction that such information is available upon request.

13.a. If the consignor has fixed a price below which an article will not be sold, the "reserve price," the fact that the lot is being sold subject to reserve must be disclosed in connection with the description of any lot so affected in the catalogue or any other printed material published or distributed in relation to the sale. The existence of a reserve price may be denoted by a symbol or letter which will refer the reader to an explanation of reserve price. For the purpose of this regulation, advertisements in newspapers or other periodicals shall not constitute printed material. Where no printed material is provided in connection with the auction an auctioneer shall have available during any advertised inspection period information as to whether a particular lot is to be sold subject to reserve and shall anounce before he or she commences the auction that such information is available upon request.

b. When a lot is not subject to a reserve price, the auctioneer shall not indicate in any manner that the lot is subject to a reserve price.

14. The auctioneer shall:

(a) Provide information as to the number of jewels, approximate number of carats, number of points (diamond), principal metal content, and manufacturer's name, if known, for all articles of jewelry, including watches. The information required by this regulation shall be provided either in the catalogue descriptions of such items or by attaching to each such item a tag or marking containing the information.

(b) Issue or cause to be issued to each purchaser an invoice which shall contain all the following information:

1. The auctioneer's name, business address and license number;
2. The name and address of the auctioneer's employer or principal;
3. the date of sale;
4. The lot number, description, quantity and selling price of each lot;
5. The total amount of purchase with a separate statement of sales tax;
6. All deposits made against the purchase price.

This does not apply to the auction sale of fruit, vegetables or other farm products.

(c) Notify the Department of the change of address of any business location or salesroom within seventy-two hours of such change.

(d) Notify the Department ten days in advance regarding the name and address of a new employer or the new location of activity.

(e) Advertise each auction sale at least once in the seven day period immediately preceding the auction.

(f) Notify the person whose property is being auctioned (and any other person entitled to be notified according to law) as to the date, place and time of sale.

(g) Permit (prior to the start of the auction) prospective purchasers to inspect each and every article to be offered for sale.

(h) Furnish to any buyer, consignor or owner of an article, upon request, information as to the whereabouts of that article that comes into his or her possession or that is sold or offered for sale by him or her.

(i) Send check for net amount received on all sales to persons entitled to the proceeds thereof within fourteen days of date of sale (except as otherwise agreed in writing or otherwise provided by law) together with a complete detailed statement including lot number, quantity, description and selling price of each lot; total amount received on sale; and disbursements listing commission, cost of advertisement, labor, charges and allowances, and sundry expenses.

(j) Report to the Department of Consumer Affairs the date and place of any sale of merchandise which includes a scale, in time to permit the Department to have an inspector present at the sale.

(k) Notify the Department in advance if he or she is unable because of sickness or other valid reason to conduct a duly advertised auction; and then a licensed auctioneer may act as his or her substitute.

(l) When an auctioneer has a number of the same kind of articles to be sold and intends to dispose of each of them at the amount at which the first is sold, he or she shall make an announcement to that effect prior to opening the sale of the first article.

15. If an auctioneer makes loans or advances money to consignors and/or prospective purchasers, this fact must be conspicuously disclosed in the auctioneer's catalogue or printed material. If the auctioneer does not provide any such printed material, he or she shall make the disclosure, either by conspicuously posting a sign, or in another similarly conspicuous manner, at the time of any advertised inspection periods prior to the auctions. For the purpose of this regulation advertisements in newspapers or other periodicals shall not constitute printed material.

16. Except to implement a reserve price, and subject to Regulation 21, no auctioneer, his or her consignor, employee, employer, assignee or agent for any of them may bid for his or her own account at any auction if any of them shall have access to information not otherwise available to the public regarding reserves, value or other material facts relating to the articles which are the subject of the auction, unless their "insider" status and intended participation is disclosed in the auctioneer's catalogue and any printed material and on signs posted at the auction.

17. Wherever an estimate or estimated value of an item or lot

is published in a catalogue or any other printed material published or distributed in relation to an auction sale, a general description of the estimate and its meaning and function must be included in such printed material. For the purpose of this regulation, advertisements in newspapers or other periodicals shall not constitute printed material. Where no printed material is provided, and an estimate or estimated value is announced or disseminated in any manner, a general description of the estimate and its meaning and function must be available for distribution and its availability must be announced at the commencement of the auction.

18. In any advertisement indicating an auction sale due to a business' loss of lease or liquidation, the auctioneer must include the name of the consignor or business authorizing the auction. In any sale advertised as pursuant to a security agreement, the name of the debtor shall be indicated conspicuously.

19. The following newspapers published in the City of New York are hereby designated as newspapers in which auctioneers shall advertise as required by Sections 20-282 and 20-283 of the Administrative Code:

New York Times
New York Journal of Commerce
New York Post
New York Daily Fruit Reporter
Newsday
Staten Island Advance
New York Daily News
New York Law Journal
American Banker
Action
Il Progresso
China Post
China Times
Chinese Journal
France-Amerique
Aufbau
National Herald
Novoye Russkoye Slovo
El Diario
El Mirador
Svoboda
Jewish Daily Forward
Barbininkas

III. *RESERVES*

20. If the reserve price is not bid, the auctioneer may withdraw a lot from sale. At the time of such withdrawal, and before bidding on another lot begins, the auctioneer shall announce that the withdrawn lot has been "passed", "withdrawn", "returned to owner" or "bought-in".

21. *Affirmative Disclosure.* Before bidding on any lot has reached its reserve price no auctioneer may make or place consecutive or successive bids, or place bids in response to bids from others,

on behalf of the consignor, unless the fact that the auctioneer will or may bid in such a manner is clearly and conspicuously disclosed in any catalogue and any other printed material published or distributed in connection with the sale. For the purposes of this regulation advertisements in newspapers or other periodicals shall not constitute printed material. This disclosure must also be made on signs prominently displayed in the auction room and at the entrance thereto, and must be announced by the auctioneer immediately prior to the commencement of any auction.

The sign required by this regulation must be at least 12 inches by 18 inches in dimension with letters at least one inch high, and must read as follows, or convey a substantially similar disclosure:

> The Auctioneer may open bidding on any lot by placing a bid on behalf of the seller. The auctioneer may further bid on behalf of the seller, up to the amount of the reserve, by placing successive or consecutive bids for a lot, or by placing bids in response to other bidders.

22. After bidding has reached the reserve price of a lot:

a. the auctioneer may not bid on behalf of the consignor or the auction house; and

b. the auctioneer may only accept bids from persons other than the consignor or the auction house except absentee telephone, order or other agent's bids;

c. This Regulation shall not apply to auction sales conducted pursuant to an order of a court of competent jurisdiction, including an order of a bankruptcy judge or trustee, or a sale of secured property pursuant to the Uniform Commercial Code, or the sale of property which is subject to a lien or assignment pursuant to the laws of the State of New York.

23. In no event shall the reserve price for any lot exceed the maximum estimated value of the lot as published in any catalogue or other printed material distributed by the auctioneer.

IV. *PROHIBITED PRACTICES*

24. An auctioneer may not disclaim warranty of title of any item sold at auction. The auctioneer shall reimburse any purchaser in an amount equal to the successful bid at auction plus any buyer's commission paid in the event it is determined that the purchaser has not acquired transferable title to the item.

25. At the auction sale premises only exterior signs may be dis-

played advertising the auction sale but the same shall not be excessive in size.

26. An auctioneer may not:

(a) Offer more than one article for sale at any one time unless the combining of articles or lots is so indicated prior to the initial bid.

(b) Represent an article to be guaranteed by the manufacturer or the owner unless a manufacturer's or owner's guarantee accompanies the article.

(c) Offer an article contained in a carton, package or other container commonly known as a blind article unless prior to the offer it is announced that the highest bidder may reject the article if not satisfactory to him or her. This provision does not refer to an auction of articles in bulk where a sample is displayed and balance of articles are represented to conform with the sample.

(d) Use a loudspeaker outlet located within ten feet of any entrance or exit or which is beamed in any direction except away from said entrance or exit. In any event loudspeaker apparatus must not attract attention from outside auction premises.

(e) Accept as payment or exchange any article previously knocked down or sold to a successful bidder. The article knocked down or sold must be delivered to the bidder or, if the auctioneer is willing and at the bidder's election, the purchase price refunded in full. No other article may be offered to said bidder as a substitute or replacement. Such refund shall take place within a reasonable time or may be applied as part payment or payment for any other article purchased at auction by the same bidder.

V. *RECORDS; MISCELLANEOUS*

27. An auctioneer must keep a written record of all details of each sale including copies of advertisements; lot number, quantity, description and selling price of each lot; record of disbursements; and net amount sent to persons entitled to proceeds of sale for a period of six years from the date of the auction.

28. *Exceptions*—Rules and regulations 10 through 12 inclusive above shall not apply to:

(a) Any auction sale involving a printed catalogue when all of the following conditions are met:

(1) the printed catalogue is distributed and available for a reasonable period of time prior to the auction being held;

(2) said catalogue contains a precise, detailed description of

the items to be auctioned and the terms used to describe the items have a widely accepted, standardized usage in the field;

(3) the value of the items described in said catalogue can be verified by reference to standard recognized reference sources commonly known of and utilized in the field; and

(4) the sale of the item at the auction is not final until the purchaser has had a reasonable opportunity to verify independently that the item purchased was accurately described in said catalogue.

(b) Any auction sales conducted for primarily commercial purposes where all of the bidders at such auction can reasonably be anticipated to be purchasing for use in a commercial endeavor and not for use by the purchaser, or the purchaser's family, as consumer goods as that term is defined in the Consumer Protection Law of 1969 of The City of New York (Administrative Code of The City of New York, Chapter 64, Title A, Section 2203(d)-1.0 et seq).

HISTORICAL NOTE: Regulations were amended as the result of a two-year study of the auction industry conducted by the Department. These regulations were amended to update those existing in order to conform to current conditions and to regulate new practices that had developed in the period since the previous regulations had been enacted. Regulations were published twice for comments in the City Record, they were published for adoption on March 13, 1987, and became effective April 13, 1987.

SOTHEBY'S

FOUNDED 1744

1334 York Avenue, New York, New York 10021 (212) 606-7000

MASTER CONSIGNMENT AGREEMENT

Thank you for consigning your property to Sotheby's. This confirms our agreement under which all property which you consign to us from time to time and which we accept (the "Property") will be offered by us as your agent at public auction subject to the following terms and our standard Conditions of Sale and Terms of Guarantee printed in our catalogue. As used herein, "we," "us" and "our" mean Sotheby's, Inc. You acknowledge that you have received and read our Conditions of Sale and Terms of Guarantee currently in effect.

1. The Auction. We will inform you of our acceptance of Property for auction by a confirmation notice. In connection with the auction, we will have absolute discretion as to (a) consulting any expert, (b) grouping the Property into lots and providing catalogue and other descriptions as we believe appropriate, (c) the date or dates of the auction, and (d) the manner of conducting the sale.

2. Commission. You agree to pay us a commission equal to 20% of the successful bid price for each lot sold for less than $1,000, 15% of the successful bid price for each lot sold for $1,000 or more but less than $5,000, and 10% of the successful bid price for each lot sold for $5,000 or more, subject to a minimum commission of $100 on each lot sold. In any case, you also authorize us, as your agent, to collect from the purchaser and retain as our additional commission a premium of 10% of the successful bid price for each lot sold (the "buyer's premium").

3. Settlement. Thirty-five days after the last session of the auction (the "Settlement Date"), we will mail to you the sale proceeds we collect and receive, after deducting our commissions and reimbursable expenses (the "net sale proceeds"), unless the purchaser has notified us of intention to rescind the sale (as provided in paragraph 10). We may also deduct and retain from the net sale proceeds any other amount you owe us, whether arising out of the sale of the Property or otherwise.

We have no obligation to enforce payment by any purchaser. If a purchaser does not pay, and you and we do not agree on another course of action, we reserve the right to cancel the sale and return the Property to you. You authorize us, in our discretion, to impose on the purchaser and retain for our account a late charge if payment is not made in accordance with the Conditions of Sale.

4. Reserves. Each lot of the Property will be offered subject to a reserve determined as follows:

Unless a different reserve has been agreed upon by us and confirmed by you in writing and received by us before the auction, the reserve will be the following percentage of our latest announced or published low presale estimate: (i) 25% for any lot having a low estimate of less than $300, (ii) 40% for any lot having a low estimate of $300 or more up to $1,000, or (iii) 60% for any lot having a low estimate of $1,000 or more. However, we may sell any lot of the Property at a price below the reserve, provided that we pay you on the Settlement Date the net amount which you would have been entitled to receive had such lot of the Property been sold at the reserve (that is, the reserve less our selling commission, reimbursable expenses and any amount you owe us). The reserve will not exceed our high presale estimate.

You agree not to bid on the Property; all bids to protect your reserves will be made by us. If, however, you violate your foregoing commitment and you or your agent become the successful bidder on your Property, you will pay us the commission set forth in paragraph 2 (including buyer's premium) on the hammer price, the Property may be sold without any reserve, and you will not be entitled to the benefit of any of the Terms of Guarantee.

The commission for any lot which is bought-in for failing to reach its reserve will be 5% of the reserve, subject to a minimum handling charge of $75 on each bought-in lot.

In the event any lot is bought-in, we will make an announcement that such lot has been "passed, returned to owner, withdrawn or bought-in."

5. Sotheby's Arcade Auctions. If we deem it appropriate, we may, in our sole discretion, include in a Sotheby's Arcade Auction any Property with a low presale estimate, in our opinion, of $5,000 or less. In such event, or if you and we agree to include any Property in a Sotheby's Arcade Auction, we will offer the Property subject to the provisions of this Agreement and our Conditions of Sale for Sotheby's Arcade Auctions printed in the catalogue, except that the Settlement Date will be twenty-one days after the last session of the auction, and the minimum commission on each sold and bought-in lot will be $75.

6. Representations and Warranties; Indemnity. You represent and warrant to us and to the purchaser that you have the right to consign the Property for sale; that it is now and until its sale will be kept free of all liens, claims and encumbrances of others including, but not limited to, claims of governments or governmental agencies; that good title and right to possession will pass to the purchaser free of all liens, claims and encumbrances; and that there are no restrictions on our right to make, reproduce, or distribute photographs of it. We retain the exclusive copyright to all catalogue and other illustrations and descriptions of the Property created by us.

You agree to indemnify and hold us and the purchaser harmless from and against any and all claims, actions, damages, losses, liabilities, and expenses (including reasonable attorneys' fees) relating to the breach or alleged breach of any of your agreements, representations or warranties in this Agreement.

Your representations, warranties and indemnity will survive completion of the transactions contemplated by this Agreement.

7. Expenses. You agree to bear the expenses of (a) our assumption of risk of loss or damage to the Property (as provided in paragraph 8), (b) our standard fees then in effect for catalogue illustration, (c) packing, shipping and customs duties to our premises, (d) agreed-upon special advertising, and (e) other services, such as framing, restoration and gemological tests, approved by you. There will be a 20% service charge on the cost of any services performed by others and paid by us for your account. In addition to other remedies available to us by law, we reserve the right to impose a late charge of 1½% per month on any amount due us and remaining unpaid more than fifteen days after we notify you.

8. Responsibility for Loss or Damage. We will assume responsibility for loss of or damage to the Property from the time of our receipt until it ceases to be in our custody and control, or until 60 days after the sale, whichever occurs first, at a rate equal to the following percentage of the amount of our maximum liability described in the following paragraph: (a) 1% for all Property receipted by us at our auction premises or any of our warehouses in New York City, or (b) 1½% for all Property receipted by us at one of our branch offices or any other location.

LIMITED LIABILITY. Our liability under the preceding paragraph for loss of or damage to any Property will not exceed: (a) the successful bid price (excluding buyer's premium) if the Property has been sold, (b) the reserve (but not more than the mean of our latest presale estimates) if the Property has been bought-in, or (c) the mean of our latest presale estimates if the Property has not otherwise been sold at the time of loss or damage. In no event will our liability include our expenses or commissions, nor will we be liable for damage to frames or glass covering prints, paintings or other works, or for damage caused by restorers, framers or other independent contractors employed with your consent, changes in humidity or temperature, or inherent conditions or defects.

9. Withdrawal. You may not withdraw any Property from sale after the date on which we issue a receipt. Regardless of whether we have previously issued a receipt, published a catalogue including the Property or advertised its sale, we may withdraw any Property at any time before sale if we believe (a) there is doubt as to its authenticity or attribution, (b) any of your representations or warranties concerning it are inaccurate, or (c) you have breached any provision of this Agreement. If you withdraw any Property in breach of your foregoing commitment, or if we withdraw any Property under (b) or (c) of the preceding sentence, you will pay us 20% of the mean of our latest presale estimates for the withdrawn Property, and we will then return such Property to you at your expense. There will be no charge for any Property withdrawn under (a) above, which will be returned to you at your expense.

10. Rescission. You authorize us to rescind the sale of any Property in accordance with the Terms of Guarantee, or if we learn that the Property is inaccurately described in the catalogue, or if we learn that the Property is a counterfeit (a modern forgery intended to deceive). If we receive from a purchaser notice of intention to rescind and we determine that a lot of the Property is subject to rescission under the Terms of Guarantee, we will credit the purchaser with the purchase price, you will return to us any sale proceeds paid by us to you for such Property, and we will return the Property to you upon your reimbursing us for our expenses incurred in connection with the rescinded sale, and paying us any other amounts you owe us.

11. Private Sales. If any lot fails to reach its reserve and is bought-in for your account, you authorize us, as your exclusive agent, for a period of 60 days following the auction to sell the lot privately for a price that will result in a payment to you of not less than the net amount (after our selling commission and expenses) to which you would have been entitled had the lot been sold at a price equal to the agreed reserve. In such event, your obligations to us hereunder with respect to such lot are the same as if it had been sold at auction.

12. Treatment of Unsold Property. If any Property remains unsold for any reason after the auction, we will notify you. If such Property has not been sold privately pursuant to paragraph 11, and if it is not reconsigned to us for sale on mutually agreed-upon terms or picked up within 60 days after such notification, we may return it to you at your expense or sell it at public auction without reserve at a place and date determined by us. The proceeds of any such sale will be applied to any amount you owe us, including but not limited to our standard commissions and expenses, and any excess will be remitted to you. Unless and until we reoffer and sell such Property or return it to you, we will hold it without charge for a period of 30 days after the auction in which it is offered but not sold; thereafter, a handling charge of 1% per month of the reserve or the mean of our presale estimates, whichever is greater, will be payable by you to cover our costs of storage and handling.

13. Estimates; Catalogue Descriptions. Presale estimates, if any, are intended as guides for prospective bidders; we make no representation or warranty of the anticipated selling price of any Property and no estimate anywhere by us of the selling price of Property may be relied upon as a prediction of the actual selling price. Estimates included in receipts, catalogues or elsewhere are preliminary only and subject to revision by us from time to time in our sole discretion.

We will not be liable for any errors or omissions in catalogue or other descriptions of Property and make no guarantees, representations or warranties whatsoever to you with respect to the Property, its authenticity, condition, value or otherwise.

14. Use of Name. We may use your name as owner of the Property when we offer it for sale or advertise or otherwise promote the sale, both before or after the auction, unless you initial the box below. If we may use your name, but in a form other than that appearing on the first page of this Agreement, please type or print it on the line below and place your initials in the box next to it.

You may not use my name: ☐
You may use my name as follows:

______________________________ ☐.

15. Legal Status. If you are acting as a fiduciary in executing this Agreement and in the transactions contemplated hereunder, please initial "Fiduciary" below and sign and return to us our standard "Fiduciary Agreement."

Fiduciary [   ]

If you are acting as an agent for someone who is not signing this Agreement, you and your principal jointly and severally assume your obligations and liabilities hereunder to the same extent as if you were acting as principal.

16. Term of Agreement; Amendment. Either you or we may terminate this Agreement at any time upon 30 days' prior written notice to the other. No such termination shall permit you to withdraw from sale any Property previously delivered to us or relieve either you or us of any obligations or liabilities incurred prior to the effective date of such notice.

Neither you nor we may amend, supplement or waive any provision of the Agreement other than by means of a writing signed by both parties, except that if at any time we propose by written notice to amend or supplement any provision of this Agreement, or provide additional terms or conditions as to your future consignments, you will be deemed to have agreed thereto with respect to any Property received by us at any time after such notice, unless you notify us in writing to the contrary before such Property is received by us.

17. Miscellaneous. This Agreement shall be governed by and construed and enforced in accordance with the laws of the State of New York. In the event of a dispute hereunder, you hereby consent to the exclusive jurisdiction of the state courts of, and the federal courts sitting in, the State of New York. This Agreement shall be binding upon your heirs, executors, beneficiaries, successors and assigns, but you may not assign this Agreement without our prior written consent. Any notices given hereunder to you or us shall be in writing to the respective address indicated on the first page of this Agreement (or to such other address as you or we may notify the other in writing) and shall be deemed to have been given five calendar days after mailing to such address. The paragraph headings contained in this Agreement are for convenience of reference only and shall not affect in any way the meaning or interpretation of this Agreement.

Please confirm your agreement with the foregoing by dating, signing and returning to us the duplicate copy of this Agreement.

SOTHEBY'S, INC.

By ______________________________

ACCEPTED AND AGREED TO:

____
Consignor

Dated: ______________________________

JOHN L. MARION
PRINCIPAL AUCTIONEER
LICENSE #524728

SOTHEBY'S

FOUNDED 1744

1334 York Avenue, New York, New York 10021 (212) 606-7000

CONDITIONS OF SALE

This catalogue, as amended by any posted notices or oral announcements during the sale, is Sotheby's, Inc. and the Consignor's entire agreement with the purchaser relative to the property listed herein. The following Conditions of Sale, the Terms of Guarantee and any glossary contained herein are the complete and only terms and conditions on which all property is offered for sale. The property will be offered by us as agent of the Consignor, unless the catalogue indicates otherwise.

1. The authenticity of the authorship of property listed in the catalogue is guaranteed as stated in the Terms of Guarantee; except as provided therin all provided therein all property is sold "AS IS," and neither we nor the Consignor make any warranties or representations of the correctness of the catalogue or other description of the physical condition, size, quality, rarity, importance, provenance, exhibitions, literature or historical relevance of the property and no statement anywhere, whether oral or written, shall be deemed such a warranty or representation. Prospective bidders should inspect the property before biddng to determine its condition, size and whether or not it has been repaired or restored. We and the Consignor make no representation or warranty as to whether the purchaser acquires any copyrights, including but not limited to any reproduction rights, in the property.

2. A premium of 10% of the successful bid price will be added thereto and is payable by the purchaser as part of the total purchase price.

3. We reserve the right to withdraw any property before sale.

4. Unless otherwise announced by the auctioneer, all bids are per lot as numbered in the catalogue.

5. We reserve the right to reject any bid. The highest bidder acknowledged by the auctioneeer will be the purchaser. In the event of any dispute between bidders, or in the event of doubt on our part as to the validity of any bid, the auctioneer will have the final discretion either to determine the successful bidder or to reoffer and resell the article in dispute. If any dispute arises after the sale, our sale record is conclusive. Although in our discretion we will execute order bids or accept telephone bids as a convenience to clients who are not present at auctions, we are not responsible for any errors or omissions in connection therewith.

6. If the auctioneer decides that any opening bid is below the value of the article offered, he may reject the same and withdraw the article from sale, and if, having acknowledged an opening bid, he decides that any advance thereafter is insufficient, he may reject the advance.

7. On the fall of the auctioneer's hammer, title to the offered lot will pass to the highest bidder acknowledged by the auctioneer, subject to fulfillment by such bidder of all of the conditions set forth herein, and such bidder thereupon (a) assumes full risk and responsiblity therefor, (b) will sign a confirmation of purchase thereof, and (c) will pay the full purchase price therefor or such part as we may require. In addition to other remedies available to us by law, we reserve the right to impose a late charge of 1½% per month of the total purchase price if payment is not made in accordance with the condition set for herein. All property must be removed from our premises by the purchaser at his expense not later than 3 business days following its sale and, if it is not so removed, (i) a handling charge of 1% of the purchase price per month until its removal will be payable to us by the purchaser, with a minimum of 5% for any property not so removed within 60 days after the sale, and (ii) we may send the purchased property to a public warehouse for the account, risk and expense of the purchaser. If any applicable conditions herein are not complied with by the purchaser, in addition to other remedies available to us and the Consignor by law, including without limitation the right to hold the purchaser liable for the totai purchase price, we at our option may either (a) cancel the sale, retaining as liquidated damages all payments made by the purchaser or (b) resell the property at public auction without reserve, and the purchaser will be liable for any deficiency, costs, including handling charges, the expenses of both sales, our commission on both sales at our regular rates, all other charges due hereunder and incidental damages. In addition, a defaulting purchaser will be deemed to have granted us a security

interest in, and we may retain as collateral security for such purchaser's obligations to us, any property in our possession owned by such purchaser. We shall have all of the rights afforded a secured party under the New York Uniform Commercial Code with respect to such property and we may apply against such obligations all monies held or received by us for the account of, or due from us to, such purchaser. At our option, payment will not be deemed to have been made in full until we have collected funds represented by checks, or, in the case of bank or cashier's checks, we have confirmed their authenticity.

8. Lots marked with ■ immediately preceding the lot number are offered subject to a reserve, which is the confidential minimum price below which such lot will not be sold. We may implement such reserves by bidding on behalf of the Consignor. In certain instances, the Consignor may pay us less than the standard commission rate where a lot is "bought-in" to protect its reserve. Where the Consignor is indebted to or has a monetary guarantee from us, and in certain other instances, where we or our affiliated companies may have an interest in the offered lots and the proceeds therefrom other than our commissions, we may bid therefor to protect such interests.

9. Unless exempted by law, the purchaser will be required to pay the combined New York State and local sales tax or any applicable compensating use tax of another state on the total purchase price. The rate of such combined tax is 8¼% in New York City and ranges form 4¼% to 8¼% elsewhere in New York State.

10. These Conditions of Sale as well as the purchaser's and our respective rights and obligations herunder shall be governed by and construed and enforced in accordance with the laws of the State of New York. By bidding at an auction, whether present in person or by agent, order bid, telephone or other means, the purchaser shall be deemed to have consented to the jurisdiction of the state courts of, and the federal courts sitting in, the State of New York.

11. We are not responsible for the acts or omissions of carriers or packers of purchased lots, whether or not recommended by us. Packing and handling of purchased lots by us is at the entire risk of the purchaser.

12. In no event will our liability to a purchaser exceed the purchase price actually paid.

CONDITIONS OF SALE FOR SOTHEBY'S ARCADE AUCTIONS

This catalogue, as amended by any posted notices or oral announcements during the sale, is Sotheby's, Inc. (herein referred to as "we," "us," or "our") and the Consignor's entire agreement with the purchaser relative to the property listed herein. The following Conditions of Sale are the complete and only terms and condtions on which all property is offered for sale. The property will be offered by us as agent for the Consignor, unless the catalogue indicates otherwise.

1. All property is sold "AS IS," and neither we nor the Consignor make any guarantees, warranties or representations, expressed or implied, with respect to the property or the correctness of the catalogue or other description of the authenticity of authorship, physical condition, size, quality, rarity, importance, provenance, exhibitions, literature or historical relevance of the property or otherwise. No statement anywhere, whether oral or written, shall be deemed such a guarantee, warranty or representation. Prospective bidders should inspect the property before bidding to determine its condition, size and whether or not is has been repaired or restored. We and the Consignor make no representation or warranty as to whether the purchaser acquires any copyrights, including but not limited to any reproduction rights, in the property.

2. However, if within 14 calendar days of the sale of any lot, the purchaser gives notice in writing to us that the lot is counterfeit and within 14 calendar days after such notice, the purchaser returns the lot to us in the same condition as when sold, and demonstrates to our satisfaction that the lot is a counterfeit, we will refund the purchase price.

3. A premium of 10% of the successful bid price will be added thereto and is payable by the purchaser as part of the total purchase price.

4. We reserve the right to withdraw any property before sale.

5. Unless otherwise announced by the auctioneer, all bid are per lot as numbered in the catalogue.

6. We reserve the right to reject any bid. The highest bidder acknowledged by the auctioneer will be the purchaser. In the event of any dispute between bidders, or in the event of doubt on our part as to the validity of any bid, the auctioneer will have the final discretion either to determine the successful bidder or to reoffer and resell the article in dispute. If any dispute arises after the sale, our sale record is conclusive. Although in our discretion we will execute order bids or accept telephone bids as a convenience to clients who are not present at auctions, we are not responsible for any errors or omissions in connection therewith.

7. If the auctioneer decides that any opening bid is below the value of the article offered, he may reject the same and withdraw the article from sale, and if, having acknowledged an opening bid, he decides that any advance thereafter is insufficient, he may reject the advance.

8. On the fall of the auctioneer's hammer, title to the offered lot will pass to the highest bidder acknowledged by the auctioneer, subject to fulfillment by such bidder of all of the conditions set forth herein, and such bidder thereupon (a) assumes full risk and responsibility therefor, and (b) will pay the full purchase price therefor or such part as we may require. In addition to other remedies available to us by law, we reserve the right to impose a late charge of 1½% per month of the total purchase price if payment is not made in accordance with the conditions set forth herein. All property must be removed from our premises by the purchaser at his expense not later than 3 business days following its sale and, if it is not so removed, (i) a handling charge of $10 per day for (A) each rug or furniture lot, (B) up to five lots of decorative arts other than furniture and (C) all other lots until removal will be payable to us by the purchaser, and (ii) in addition, we may send the purchased property to a public warehouse for account, risk and expense of the purchaser.

9. If any applicable conditions herein are not complied with by the purchaser, in addition to other remedies available to us and the Consignor by law, including without limitation the right to hold the purchaser liable for the total purchase price, we at our option may either (a) cancel the sale, retaining as liquidated damages all payments made by the purchaser or (b) resell the property at public auction without reserve, and the purchaser will be liable for any deficiency, costs, including handling charges, the expenses of both sales, our commission on both sales at our regular rates, all other charges due hereunder and incidental damages. In addition, a defaulting purchaser will be deemed to have granted us a security interest in, and we may retain as collateral security for such purchaser's obligation to us, any property in our possession owned by such purchaser. We shall have all of the rights afforded a secured party under the New York Uniform Commercial Code with respect to such purchaser. At our option, payment will not be deemed to have been made in full until we have collected funds represented by checks, or, in the case of bank or cashier's checks, we have confirmed their authenticity.

10. Lots marked with • immediately preceding the lot number are offered subject to a reserve, which is the confidential minimum price below which such lot will not be sold. We may implement such reserves by bidding on behalf of the Consignor. In certain instances, the Consignor may pay us less than the standard commission rate where a lot is "bought-in" to protect its reserve. Where the Consignor is indebted to or has a monetary guarantee from us, and in certain other instances, where we or our affiliated companies may have an interest in the offered lots and the proceeds therefrom other than our commissions, we may bid therefor to protect such interests.

11. Unless exempt by law, the purchaser will be required to pay the combined New York State and local sales tax or any applicable compensating use tax of another state on the total purchase price. The rate of such combined tax is 8¼% in New York City and ranges from 4¼% to 8¼% elsewhere in New York State.

12. These Conditions of Sale as well as the purchaser's and our respective rights and obligations hereunder shall be governed by and construed and enforced in accordance with the laws of the State of New York. By bidding at an auction whether present in person or by agent, order bid, telephone or other means, the purchaser shall be deemed to have consented to the jurisdiction of the state courts of, and the federal courts sitting in, the State of New York.

13. We are not responsible for the acts or omissions of carriers or packers of purchased lots, whether or not recommended by us. Packing and handling of purchased lots by us is at the entire risk of the purchaser. In no event will we be liable for damage to glass or frames, regardless of the cause.

14. In no event will our liability to a purchaser exceed the purchase price actually paid.

30 day trade terms not applicable at Sotheby's Arcade Auctions.

TERMS OF GUARANTEE

We guarantee the authenticity of Authorship of each lot contained in this catalogue on the terms and conditions set forth below.

1. Definition of Authorship

"Authorship" means the identity of the creator, the period, culture, source of origin of the property, as the case may be, as set forth in the BOLD TYPE HEADING of such catalogue entry.

2. Guarantee Coverage

Subject to the exclusions of (i) attributions of paintings, drawings or sculpture executed prior to 1870, and (ii) periods or dates of execution of the property, as explained in Paragraph 5 below, if within five (5) years from the date of the sale of any lot, the original purchaser of record tenders to us a purchased lot in the same condition as when sold through us and it is established that the identification of Authorship (as defined above) of such lot set forth in the BOLD TYPE HEADING of the catalogue description of such lot (as amended by any posted notices or oral announcements during the sale) is not substantially correct based on a fair reading of the catalogue including the terms of any Glossary contained herein, the sale of such lot will be rescinded and the original purchase price refunded.

3. Non-Assignability

It is specifically understood that the benefits of this Guarantee are not assignable and shall be applicable only to the original purchaser of the lot from us and not to the subsequent owners or others who have or may acquire an interest therein.

4. Sole Remedy

It is further specifically understood that the remedy set forth herein, namely the rescission of the sale and refund of the original purchase price paid for the lot, is exclusive and in lieu of any other remedy which might otherwise be available as a matter of law.

5. Exclusions

The Guarantee covers only the correctness of description of Authorship (as defined in 1 above) as indentified in the BOLD TYPE HEADING of the catalogue item but does *not* extend to (i) the identify of the creator of paintings, drawings and sculpture executed before 1870 unless these works are determined to be counterfeits, as this is a matter of current scholarly opinion which can change, (ii) the identification of the periods or dates of execution of the property which may be proven inaccurate by means of scientific process not generally accepted for use until after publication of the catalogue, or (iii) titles or other identification of offered lots or descriptions of physical condition and size, quality, rarity, importance, provenance, exhibitions and literature of historical relevance, which information normally appears in lower case type below the BOLD TYPE HEADING identifying the Authorship. Although our best judgment is used in attributing paintings, drawings and sculpture created prior to 1870 through the appropriate use of glossary terms, and due care is taken to insure the correctness of the supplemental material which appears below the BOLD TYPE HEADING of each entry in the catalogue, the Guarantee does not extend to any possible errors or omission therein.

SOTHEBY'S, INC. SETS FORTH THE FOLLOWING WARRANTY AND DISCLOSURE IN ITS AUCTION CATALOGUES

Conditions of Sale

This catalogue, as amended by any posted notices or oral announcements during the sale, is Sotheby's, Inc.'s and the Consignor's entire agreement with the purchaser relative to the property listed herein. The following Conditions of Sale, the Terms of Guarantee and any glossary contained herein are the complete and only terms and conditions on which all property is offered for sale. The property will be offered by us as agent for the Consignor, unless the catalogue indicates otherwise.

1. The authenticity of the Authorship of property listed in the catalogue is guaranteed as stated in the Terms of Guarantee; except as provided therein, all property is sold **"AS IS,"** and neither we nor the Consignor make any warranties or representations of the correctness of the catalogue or other description of the physical condition, size, quality, rarity, importance, medium, provenance, exhibitions, literature or historical relevance of the property and no statement anywhere, whether oral or written, shall be deemed such a warranty or representation. Prospective bidders should inspect the property before bidding to determine its condition, size and whether or not it has been repaired or restored. We and the Consignor make no representations and warranties as to whether the purchaser acquires any copyrights, including but not limited to, any reproduction rights in the property.

* * * *

Terms of Guarantee

We guarantee the authenticity of Authorship of each lot contained in this catalogue on the terms and conditions set forth below.

1. **Definition of Authorship.** "Authorship" means the identity of the creator, the period, culture, source of origin of the property, as the case may be, as set forth in the **Bold Type Heading** of such catalogue entry.

2. **Guarantee Coverage.** Subject to the exclusions of (i) attributions of paintings, drawings or sculpture executed prior to 1870, and (ii) periods or dates of execution of the property, as explained in Paragraph 5 below, if within five (5) years from the date of the sale of any lot, the original purchaser of record tenders to us a purchased lot in the same condition as when sold through us, and it established that the identification of Authorship (as defined above) of such lot set forth in the **Bold Type Heading** of this catalogue description of such lot (as amended by any posted notices or oral announcements during the sale) is not sub-

stantially correct based on a fair reading of the catalogue including the terms of any Glossary contained herein, the sale of such lot will be rescinded and the original purchase price refunded.

3. **Non-Assignability.** It is specifically understood that the benefits of this Guarantee are not assignable and shall be applicable only to the original purchaser of the lot from us and not to the subsequent owners or others who have or may acquire an interest therein.

4. **Sole Remedy.** It is further specifically understood that the remedy set forth herein, namely the rescission of the sale and refund of the original purchase price paid for the lot, is exclusive and in lieu of any other remedy which might otherwise be available as a matter of law.

5. **Exclusions.** The Guarantee covers only the correctness of description of Authorship (as defined in 1 above) as identified in the **Bold Type Heading** of the catalogue item but does not extend to (i) the identity of the creator of paintings, drawings and sculpture executed before 1870 unless these works are determined to be counterfeits, as this is a matter of current scholarly opinion which can change, (ii) the identification of the periods or dates of execution of the property which may be proven inaccurate by means of scientific processes not generally accepted for use until after publication of the catalogue, or (iii) titles or other identification of offered lots or descriptions of physical condition and size, quality, rarity, importance, provenance, medium, exhibitions and literature of historical relevance, which information normally appears in lower case type below the **Bold Type Heading** identifying the Authorship. Although our best judgment is used in attributing paintings, drawings and sculpture created prior to 1870 through the appropriate use of glossary terms, and due care is taken to insure the correctness of the supplemental material which appears below the **Bold Type Heading** of each entry in the catalogue, the Guarantee does not extend to any possible errors or omissions therein.

REF: **DATE:**

CHRISTIE'S

CONSIGNMENT AGREEMENT BETWEEN

NAME:
("Seller")

AND

CHRISTIE, MANSON & WOODS INTERNATIONAL INC. (CHRISTIE'S)

ADDRESS:

502 PARK AVENUE
NEW YORK, NY 10022
(212) 546-1000

219 EAST 67th STREET
NEW YORK, NY 10021
(212) 606-0400

TELEPHONE: (   )

CONDITIONS OF ACCEPTANCE

We confirm our agreement with you as follows:

1. **CONSIGNMENT:** Seller hereby consigns to Christie's the property identified in the attached schedule (the "Property") which Christie's, as Seller's agent, will offer for sale at public auction, unless otherwise agreed and subject to the provisions set forth below and Christie's standard CONDITIONS OF SALE and LIMITED WARRANTY (if any) in effect at the time of the auction.

2. **COMMISSION:** For its services, Christie's will receive and retain from the proceeds of the sale as a commission from Seller (i) an amount equal to 10% of the final bid on each lot sold for $5,000 or more, 15% of the final bid on each lot sold for $1,000 or more but less than $5,000 and 20% of the final bid on each lot sold for less than $1,000 and (ii) a premium of 10% of the final bid to be collected by Christie's from the buyer. There will be a minimum commission charge of $75 per lot for each lot sold.

3. **INSURANCE:** The Property will be insured, at Seller's expense, from the time of receipt by Christie's until it ceases to be in Christie's custody for an amount equal to the mean of the pre-sale estimates if unsold or for the amount of the final bid if sold (either amount, as the case may be, is referred to herein as the "valuation base"). Insurance for Property received at Christie's auction premises will be charged to Seller at a rate of 1.0% of the valuation base. Insurance for Property received at one of Christie's regional offices or at any location other than its auction premises will be charged to Seller at a rate of 1.5% of the valuation base unless the Property is breakable, such as porcelain or glass, or consists of photographs, in which event the rate shall be 2.0% of the valuation base. Christie's liability to Seller resulting from loss of or damage to any Property shall not exceed the above-mentioned insurance coverage of such Property. While Christie's undertakes to exercise reasonable care in handling the Property, it shall not be responsible for any damage to any Property caused by climatic or atmospheric conditions, nor shall it be responsible for any damage to picture frames.

4. **PACKING, TRANSPORT AND DELIVERY:** Seller agrees to pay all costs and expenses of packing, transport and delivery of the Property to Christie's premises. While Christie's will on request suggest a carrier, it accepts no responsibility therefor, and packing, transport and delivery of the Property will be at Seller's sole expense and risk. Christie's reserves the right to arrange for storage of the Property in a warehouse at Seller's expense.

5. **ILLUSTRATION:** Seller agrees to pay all costs and expenses relating to catalogue illustrations of the Property according to the following schedule of charges: $800 per color plate with text opposite; $600 per color plate with text beneath; $150 per full page black and white plate; $100 per half page black and white plate; and $75 per quarter page (or smaller) black and white plate.

6. **TESTS AND PROCEDURES:** Seller agrees to pay all costs and expenses of tests or procedures which, in Christie's sole opinion, may be necessary to verify the authorship, attribution, quality or authenticity of any Property, including gemological tests of jewelry and related items.

7. **SPECIAL CHARGES:** Seller agrees to pay all costs and expenses of agreed-upon restoration procedures, as well as special advertising and promotional efforts relating to the sale of the Property, together with such additional costs and expenses not set forth in paragraphs 3 through 7 hereof as may be agreed to by Seller. Expenses incurred by Christie's for the Seller's account pursuant to paragraphs 4, 6 and 7 of this Agreement shall include a 10% service charge.

8. **DISCRETIONARY MATTERS:** Christie's shall have complete discretion as to (i) the place and date of sale and the manner in which such sale is conducted, including the CONDITIONS OF SALE then in effect, (ii) the illustration, if any, and/or the description of the Property in its catalogues or other literature, (iii) seeking the views of any expert, and (iv) the combination or division of the Property into such lots and/or separate auctions as may, in Christie's sole opinion, be deemed appropriate.

9. **SELLER'S RESERVE; ESTIMATES:** Unless otherwise agreed, all Property will be sold subject to a reserve which is the confidential minimum price below which the Property will not be sold. However, Christie's may sell any Property below the reserve if Seller receives from the proceeds of the sale the net amount which he would have received had the Property been sold at the reserve. Unless the reserve is mutually agreed upon between Seller and Christie's and confirmed by Seller in writing, which confirmation is received by Christie's at least five days before the sale, the reserve will be determined by Christie's in its absolute discretion. The reserve and any printed pre-sale estimates shall not include the buyer's premium referred to in paragraph 2 above or taxes. Christie's shall act to protect the reserve as agent of Seller by bidding through the auctioneer. If bidding does not reach the reserve on any lot, such lot will be withdrawn from sale by the auctioneer. Any appraisal, estimate or other statement of Christie's or its representatives with respect to the estimated or expected selling price of any article (whether or not in writing) is a statement of opinion only and shall not be relied upon by Seller or any third party as a prediction or guarantee of the actual selling price. In no event shall Christie's be liable for the failure of any Property to be sold at such estimated or expected price or to reach the reserve.

10. NO BIDDING BY SELLER: Under no circumstances shall Seller, its principal, if any, its representatives, employees or agents (other than Christie's acting as Seller's agent in accordance with paragraph 9 hereof), enter or cause to be entered a bid on any Property being offered for sale.

11. WITHDRAWAL: No Property may be withdrawn after the date of this Agreement without Christie's consent. In the event that Christie's consents to such a withdrawal, the Property may be withdrawn upon payment of 20% of the reserve price or 20% of the valuation base (as defined in paragraph 3 hereof) where the reserve has not yet been set, plus all out-of-pocket expenses incurred by Christie's. Christie's reserves the right to withdraw any Property at any time before actual sale if in Christie's sole judgment (i) there is doubt as to its attribution or to its authenticity, (ii) there is doubt as to the accuracy of Seller's representations or warranties set forth herein in any respect, (iii) Seller has breached or is about to breach any provision of this Agreement, (iv) or for other just cause.

12. SETTLEMENT OF ACCOUNT: Provided Christie's has received payment in full from the buyer, Christie's will pay Seller the net proceeds received and collected from the sale of the Property thirty-five calendar days after the sale after deducting its commissions, any reimbursable expenses incurred by Christie's and any other amounts due Christie's or any of its affiliates (whether arising out of the sale of the Property or otherwise), unless Christie's shall have received notice of the buyer's intention to rescind the sale or of any other claim relating to the Property or its sale or shall for any reason have refunded such proceeds to the buyer prior to the expiration of such thirty-five day period.

13. NON-PAYMENT BY BUYER: In the event of non-payment by the buyer, Christie's in its sole discretion may cancel the sale and return the Property to Seller, enforce payment by the buyer or take any other actions permitted by law. Christie's shall not, under any circumstances, be liable for any incidental or consequential damages resulting to Seller as a result of a breach or failure by the buyer.

14. RESCISSION OF SALE: Christie's, as Seller's agent, is authorized to accept the return and rescind the sale of any Property at any time if Christie's, in its sole judgment, determines that the offering for sale of any Property has subjected or may subject Christie's and/or Seller to any liability, including any liability under warranty of authenticity or title. In such event, Christie's is further authorized to refund or credit to the buyer the purchase price of such returned Property, and if Christie's has already remitted to Seller any proceeds of the rescinded sale, Seller forthwith shall pay Christie's on request an amount equal to the remitted proceeds.

15. UNSOLD PROPERTY: For each lot offered but not sold, there will be a service charge of 2% of the seller's reserve price. Property remaining unsold and not being kept for sale must be collected at Seller's expense within ten days after notice requiring Seller to do so. Thereafter, Seller will incur a storage charge of $5.00 per day on each lot. Seller shall not be entitled to reclaim any unsold Property until all commissions, expenses and other amounts owed to Christie's have been paid in full. Any Property not picked up or reconsigned for sale within ten days of such notice to collect may be sold at public auction by Christie's, at Christie's standard commission rates and charges, with reserve price set at Christie's absolute discretion. The proceeds of such sale shall first be applied to the expenses of such sale, then to the indebtedness owing to Christie's, and any excess will be remitted to Seller, or held by Christie's for Seller's account, at Christie's sole discretion.

16. SELLER'S REPRESENTATIONS AND WARRANTIES: Seller represents and warrants that Seller has the right and title to consign the Property for sale; that the Property is, and until the completion of sale by Christie's will be, free and clear of all liens, claims and encumbrances of others or restrictions on Christie's right to offer and sell the Property at auction, and that good title and right to possession will pass to the buyer free of any such liens, claims, encumbrances or restrictions. Seller agrees that such representations and warranties are for the benefit of Christie's and buyers of the Property from Christie's and that such representations and warranties shall survive the completion of the transactions contemplated hereby. Seller agrees to notify Christie's promptly in writing of any events or circumstances that may cause the foregoing representations and warranties to be inaccurate or breached in any way. If Seller is acting as an agent for a principal, Seller and principal, jointly and severally, assume all of the obligations under this Agreement.

17. COPYRIGHT MATTERS: Seller represents and warrants that there are not and until the completion of sale by Christie's there will not be any restrictions on Seller's or Christie's right to photograph or reproduce photographs of the Property or to exhibit the Property for sale and that Christie's shall retain all rights in and to all blocks, prints and plates and the right of reproduction therefrom.

18. INDEMNIFICATION: Seller shall indemnify and defend Christie's from and against any and all claims, liabilities and expenses (including interest, penalties and attorney's fees and amounts paid in investigation, defending or settling any of the foregoing) arising out of or in connection with: (a) any acts by or omissions of Seller, its agents or employees, or allegations based upon such acts or omissions, relating to or affecting the Property consigned to Christie's hereunder, (b) any inaccuracy of any representation or warranty made by Seller in connection with the transactions contemplated herein, (c) the claims of third parties claiming or challenging title to any Property consigned hereunder, or claiming infringement of any copyrights or similar proprietary interests, and/or (d) the claims of buyers, persons claiming for buyers or any other person resulting from Christie's offering for sale or selling any Property consigned hereunder, whether or not the Property has been offered, sold or returned to Christie's.

19. MISCELLANEOUS: All prior negotiations, representations, contracts or agreements, if any, between the parties hereto relating to the Property are hereby merged into this Agreement and this Agreement is complete, entire and the only Agreement between us. In the event of any disputes arising hereunder, Christie's shall not be liable to Seller for any incidental or consequential damages. This Agreement shall be governed by and construed in accordance with the laws of the State of New York.

Seller agrees to the foregoing by signing in the space provided below.

Date:

Agreed to by:

CHRISTIE, MANSON & WOODS
INTERNATIONAL INC.

________________________ by ________________________

SELLER

Licensed by the New York City
Department of Consumer Affairs

Principal Auctioneer, Christopher J. Burge
License #761543

N-5-42/EN-5-19A (Rev. 2-88)

CHRISTIE'S NEW YORK PLACES THE FOLLOWING LANGUAGE IN ITS AUCTION CATALOGUES

"Limited Warranty"

> Christie's warrants the authenticity of authorship on the terms and conditions and to the extent set forth herein. SUBJECT TO THE PROVISIONS OF THE LAST PARAGRAPH HEREOF, Christie's warrants for a period of six years from the date of sale that any article described in headings printed in UPPER CASE TYPE in this catalogue (as such description may be amended by any sale room notice or announcement) which is unqualifiedly stated to be the work of a named author or authorship, is authentic and not counterfeit. The term "author" or "authorship" refers to the creator of the article or to the period, culture, source or origin, as the case may be, with which the creation of such article is identified in the description of the article in this catalogue. Only UPPER CASE TYPE headings of lots in this catalogue (i.e. headings having capital-letter type) indicate the degree of authenticity of authorship warranted by Christie's. If this catalogue has a "glossary", the terms used in such headings are further explained therein. ANY HEADING WHICH IS STATED IN THE "GLOSSARY" TO REPRESENT A QUALIFIED OPINION IS NOT SUBJECT TO THE WARRANTY CONTAINED HEREIN. Christie's warranty does not apply to supplemental material which appears below the UPPER CASE TYPE heading of each lot in this catalogue and Christie's is not responsible for any errors or omissions in such supplemental material.

The benefits of this warranty are not assignable and shall be applicable only to the original buyer of the lot and not subsequent assigns, purchasers, heirs, owners, or others who have or may acquire an interest therein and is conditioned upon the buyer returning the lot to Christie's, 502 Park Avenue, New York, N.Y., 10022, in the same condition as at the time of sale.

The buyer's sole remedy under this warranty shall be the rescission of the sale and refund of the original purchase price paid for the article. This remedy shall be exclusive and is in lieu of any other remedy which might otherwise be available as a matter of law, and the seller and Christie's shall not be liable for any incidental or consequential damages.

CHRISTIE'S LIMITED WARRANTY DOES NOT APPLY TO THE ATTRIBUTION OF PAINTINGS, DRAWINGS, GRAPHIC ART OR SCULPTURE CREATED BEFORE 1870, AS THE ATTRIBUTION OF SUCH IDENTITY IS BASED ON CURRENT SCHOLARLY OPINION, WHICH MAY CHANGE.

* * * *

Absence of Other Warranties

EXCEPT AS SPECIFICALLY PROVIDED ABOVE UNDER "LIMITED WARRANTY", ALL PROPERTY IS SOLD "AS IS" AND NEITHER CHRISTIE'S, THE SELLER'S AGENT, NOR THE SELLER MAKES ANY EXPRESS OR IMPLIED WARRANTY OR REPRESENTATION OF ANY KIND OR NATURE WITH RESPECT TO THE PROPERTY. IN NO EVENT SHALL CHRISTIE'S OR THE SELLER BE RESPONSIBLE FOR THE CORRECTNESS OF, OR BE DEEMED TO HAVE MADE, ANY REPRESENTATION OR WARRANTY OF MERCHANTABILITY, FITNESS FOR PURPOSE, DESCRIPTION, GENUINENESS, ATTRIBUTION, PROVENANCE OR CONDITION CONCERNING THE PROPERTY, AND NO STATEMENT IN THIS CATALOGUE OR MADE AT THE SALE OR IN THE BILL OF SALE OR INVOICE OR ELSEWHERE, WHETHER ORAL OR WRITTEN, SHALL BE DEEMED SUCH A WARRANTY OR REPRESENTATION OR AN ASSUMPTION OF LIABILITY. However, the foregoing disclaimer of implied warranties does not apply to articles produced after July 3, 1975.

CHRISTIE'S AND THE SELLER MAKE NO WARRANTY OR REPRESENTATION, EXPRESS OR IMPLIED, THAT THE BUYER OF ANY WORK OF ART OR OTHER PROPERTY WILL ACQUIRE ANY COPYRIGHT OR REPRODUCTION RIGHTS THERETO.

* * * *

Important Notice

All property is sold "AS IS" in accordance with the section entitled ABSENCE OF OTHER WARRANTIES, and neither Christie's nor the seller makes any express or implied warranty or representation as to the condition of any lot offered for sale, and no statement made at any time, whether oral or written, shall constitute such a warranty or representation. Descriptions of condition are not warranties. The descriptions of the conditions of articles in this catalogue, including all references to damage or repairs, are provided as a service to interested persons and do not negate or modify the section entitled ABSENCE OF OTHER WARRANTIES. Accordingly, all lots should be viewed personally by prospective buyers to evaluate the condition of the articles offered for sale.

4

Commissioned Works

Commissioning an artist to create a work of art is fraught with problems. What must the artist do, and who is to determine if the agreement has been fulfilled? Having a clear and understandable agreement is important to both the artist and the purchaser.

PRIVATE COMMISSIONS

There should always be a written agreement between the artist and the person who commissions the artist to create a work of art. Any agreement should include the following terms and conditions:

- A brief description of what is to be created;
- The medium to be used;
- The size of the work;
- The time when the work of art is to be completed;
- Agreement as to sketches and models;
- Location of delivery and installation, and who pays for any shipping charges and the cost of installation;
- The price and a payment schedule for the work;
- Agreement as to who owns the copyright;
- What happens if the artist becomes ill or dies before completion, and what happens if the artist simply does not complete the work;
- Inspection of the work in progress;
- Insurance coverage during creation; and
- Satisfaction of the purchaser.

This last item causes the most misunderstanding and problems. The artist may think he or she has created a masterpiece, while the collector may be completely dissatisfied. The general rule is that, if the agreement provides that the individual who commissioned the work must be satisfied, the fact that the individual's dissatisfaction is completely unreasonable is not relevant. That rule is illustrated by two old cases on point.

In *Zaleski v. Clark*,[1] an action was brought in 1876 by the artist, Zaleski, against Mrs. Clark, for whom the artist had made a bust of her deceased husband. The artist never dealt directly with Mrs. Clark; he was represented by another individual acting as his agent. The agent for the artist, without the artist's knowledge, represented to Mrs. Clark that there was no risk, since "she need not take it [the bust] unless she was satisfied with it." The court looked at what the parties had agreed to and found that the artist's agent had general authority to make the contract, and that under the contract Mrs. Clark had to be satisfied; therefore, the artist had not completed the contract. The court stated:

> It is not enough to say that she [Mrs. Clark] ought to be satisfied with it, and that her dissatisfaction is unreasonable. She, and not the court, is entitled to be the judge of that. The contract was not to make one that she ought to be satisfied with, but to make one that she would be satisfied with.[2]

In *Pennington v. Howland*[3] an action was brought in 1898 by the artist Pennington against Howland, for whom the artist had painted a portrait of his wife. Howland testified that over his objections, the artist began to paint the portrait of Mrs. Howland in street dress and hat. Howland said that the artist stated, "it was an artistic idea which he wished to carry out and that if it was not satisfactory he would paint the defendant one 'until satisfied.'" The artist testified that the defendant accepted the portrait. The court held:

> When the subject of the contract is one which involves personal taste or feeling, an agreement that it shall be satisfactory to the

> buyer necessarily makes him the sole judge whether it answers that condition. He cannot be required to take it because other people might be satisfied with it; for that is not what he agreed to do. Personal tastes differ widely, and if one has agreed to submit his work to such a test he must abide by the result.[4]

The court distinguished the line of cases that require work to be performed in "a satisfactory manner" from the instant situation, in which the work had to be performed to the satisfaction of Howland.

There is no substitute for a clear written contract that spells out the agreement between the parties. The artist needs an agreement that defines the acceptance of the work of art when a model or sketches are approved by the purchaser. On the other hand, the purchaser needs an agreement that reserves the decision on acceptance until the work is complete and the purchaser is completely satisfied. See the private commission agreement at the end of this chapter.

More recently, Richard Weisman, a well-known collector, brought suit in 1988 against various persons, alleging that they acquired portraits of athletic stars that he commissioned Andy Warhol to paint. Andy Warhol may have completed portraits other than those he delivered to Weisman. If an agreement existed that gave Weisman all rights to the portraits he commissioned and prohibited Warhol from making extra paintings, Weisman should prevail. The case is still in litigation.

PUBLIC COMMISSIONS

An unprecedented boom in the public commission of works of art has resulted from the laws passed by various states that require commercial buildings to allocate a percentage of total construction costs for the purchase of artwork for display in public areas of the building, the efforts of the General Services Administration and the National Endowment for the Arts, and the efforts of countless municipalities that want their own artwork.

Although there are many public commissions of paintings, most public commissions seem to be sculptures, which demand more time, materials, and expense for the artist. There is always a formal contract for a public commission, and an artist should always have legal representation before signing any commission agreement for a public work of art.[5]

Checklist for Public Commissions

At the end of this chapter is the model form of the General Services Administration contract for fine-arts services. The contract is the result of the United States government's art-in-architecture program, under which major works of art are commissioned for incorporation into federal buildings. Public-commission contracts for municipalities and other public agencies vary, but cover the same general issues discussed below. Each issue must be discussed with the artist before he or she becomes involved in a public commission that, if not complied with or not understood, can turn into an unpleasant experience for the artist.

- *Manner of selection.* Generally, a public commission is awarded after a competition or a review by a selection committee. The artist should fully understand how the process works, who is on the selection committee, and what happens to any models or sketches submitted.
- *Terms defined.* As in any good contract, a section should define as many terms peculiar to the contract as possible, including design, fabrication, transportation, completion, acceptance, permanent installation, access, site, artist's illness, materials, and labor.
- *Artist's services.* What is the artist to do, and how is it to be done? The contract should be specific when it comes to the artist's responsibility for fabrication, transportation, and installation. The contract should accurately describe the materials, size, color, and purpose of the artwork. Most public commissions require a model and detail speci-

fications on full-scale construction costs. If the artist is to have artistic freedom to vary the design, even slightly, that flexibility must be written into the contract. The artist must be able to price his or her costs, since public commissions are generally fixed-price contracts, not cost-plus contracts. The artist must understand that the costs of materials and labor may increase over the period during which the work of art is made, and some flexibility for that increase should be built into the contract.

- *Completion time.* The artist must be given a reasonable amount of time to complete the work of art. The artist may not be able to meet the deadline for the opening of the building if enough time is not allowed. The artist, particularly one who has not previously worked on a public commission, must be made to understand that he or she has responsibility to complete the work in a timely fashion. If possible, some leeway should be in the contract to cover illness or other unusual personal circumstances of the artist or unusual fabrication or installation problems that were unforeseen at the inception. Obviously, strikes, material shortages, fires, and the like are beyond the control of the artist.

  The commission may call for periodic progress reports and inspections. The artist who believes that it may interfere with his or her creative abilities should not accept a public commission. The artist is dealing with a bureaucracy, and its rules demand compliance.
- *Structural requirements.* The public commission may require the artist to obtain a structural engineer's report and the artist must include that report in his or her costs. Even if such a report is not required, the artist is well advised to obtain as complete an engineering report as possible for his or her own protection should the work of art fall or break and injure someone.

- *Installation and maintenance.* The contract should be specific as to exactly where the work of art is to be installed. Although the contract may call for the installation to be permanent, circumstances may require its removal. The artist should attempt to obtain a provision that requires the artist to be consulted if the work of art is to be removed to another site. (See the discussion below on the "Tilted Arc" case.)

  The contract should specify who is to prepare the site for installation, the cost of the preparation, and the timing of the preparation.

  The contract must cover the responsibility for the work of art during its on-site installation. Often, an artist resides hundreds of miles from the installation site, and the work must be protected during the time the artist is not present.
- *Payment.* The artist must obtain a schedule of payments, so that he or she does not face large bills for fabrication costs with no funds to pay the bills. Ideally, the artist should have the entity that commissioned the work of art pay the engineering, materials, fabrication, and other costs directly, based on specific estimates. The contract should also provide a fee schedule for payment to the artist and the method and timing of final acceptance of the work and final payment.
- *Nonperformance clause.* A nonperformance clause should cover both the artist and the entity that commissioned the work of art. The artist must be protected for costs and expenses, should full funding for the commission not be forthcoming. The entity that commissioned the work of art must also be protected, should the artist not complete the artwork in a timely manner or not complete it in accordance with agreed-upon specifications.
- *Insurance coverage.* The artist may be required to take out a comprehensive liability insurance policy, and, if the contract is not examined carefully, it may require the artist to

pay the full premium. The artist may not realize until too late that the cost of the insurance wipes out his entire profit on the commission. The artist or the artist's representative must examine the indemnification provisions and understand just what the artist is responsible for. Generally, the artist bears the risk of loss until the work of art is finally accepted, and any risk should be covered by insurance.

- *Warranties.* The public commission may require the artist to warrant the work of art against defective materials and workmanship. The artist's attorney should argue that any such warranty be only for a limited period of time. If the work of art is a painted sculpture that is to be located outdoors, provision should be made for repainting it, and the contract should specify who pays for the repainting. The language pertaining to the sculpture's not presently being a danger to any person should be modified so that, once the work of art is accepted, the responsibility for the safety of the public shifts to the entity that commissioned the work. Any warranty clause must be examined and reviewed with the artist in detail.
- *Models and sketches.* Ownership of models and sketches must be addressed in the commission contract.
- *Copyright.* If the public commission is from the federal government, the copyright cannot be retained by the artist. In other public commissions, the artist may retain the copyright, and that fact can be provided in the contract. The artist may want to protect the work of art from being used on posters, stationery, T-shirts, and the like. Further, the contract may require the artist to warrant that the work of art being created is unique and that no future work will be the same or similar. The contract must define just what future works may be prohibited, so as not to unduly restrict the artist's creative abilities. The word "similar" is too broad and should be defined with specific-

ity. The commissioning entity needs protection against the artist's creating identical works of art for someone else that would detract from the value and the uniqueness of the commissioned work of art.

- *Repair and restoration.* The contract should provide how and when any repairs or restoration should be done and, if the artist is alive, that the artist be consulted and paid for his or her time on any repair or restoration that may change the work of art.
- *Acceptance of the artwork.* Acceptance should not be subjective and dependent on final satisfaction of the entity that ordered the public commission. The work should be deemed approved on the basis of the model or sketches and —if built, made, constructed, or painted to specifications —it should be deemed accepted. That is an objective test, as opposed to the subjective test of satisfaction the artist may encounter when dealing with a private commission.
- *Sales taxes.* If any sales taxes are due and have to be collected by the artist, the contract should provide that the entity that ordered the public commission pay those taxes.
- *Local laws.* Sometimes local zoning laws or other local laws or ordinances can cause delays or other problems with the installation. The contract should make the entity that ordered the public commission responsible for obtaining all permits and dealing with any local law problems.

Problem Areas

Removal of the Artwork

The recent case of *Serra v. United States General Services Administration*[6] illustrates the problems that can be encountered with a public commission. The case, which has received enormous publicity, involved a commission awarded to the artist Richard Serra under the United States government's art-in-architecture program, which is administered by the General Services Administration (GSA). The GSA had a contract with Serra for an outdoor sculpture to be located in Federal Plaza in lower Manhattan. The sculpture was a 120-foot-long piece of steel, twelve feet tall, weighing seventy-three tons, entitled "Tilted Arc." The sculpture cost $175,000. The GSA contract that Serra signed provides: "All designs, sketches, models and the work produced under this agreement . . . shall be the property of the United States of America."[7]

The work was completed in December 1981, and Serra signed a general release in favor of the United States.

As soon as "Tilted Arc" was installed, the GSA began receiving complaints. Eventually, the complaints grew into an avalanche, with the submission of petitions with thousands of signatures calling for the sculpture's removal. The GSA held public hearings, which generated great passion on both sides. Serra contended that his sculpture was site-specific and that its removal would effect a destruction of the work and would violate both the GSA contract and his constitutional rights. On the other side, some said that a once beautiful plaza was rendered useless by an ugly rusted steel wall.

Serra's complaint was cast in multiple claims: breach of contract, copyright violation, trademark violation, violation of New York statutory law, and violation of Serra's first and fifth amendment rights.

District Court. The United States District Court for the Southern District of New York held that it lacked jurisdiction to adjudicate Serra's contract, copyright, trademark, and state-law claims, because the United States had not waived its sovereign immunity. Under the doctrine of sovereign immunity, the United States government may not be sued without its consent, and the existence of consent is a prerequisite for jurisdiction.[8] The court so held even though Serra had not sued the United States directly, but, instead, had sued the GSA and its three senior officials.

Serra argued that sovereign immunity was inapplicable, since the United States government had consented to district court jurisdiction to resolve the GSA contract claim under either the Tucker Act or the Administrative Procedure Act.[9] The court held that the United States government had not so consented under either Act.

The court held that the Administrative Procedure Act expressly denies jurisdiction in the district court for Serra's copyright claim,[10] and that no statute of the United States contains a consent from the United States that it may be sued for trademark infringement.[11] The court further noted that the trademark of the sculpture "Tilted Arc" was not even at issue in the case, which was dealing with the location of the sculpture. The court further dismissed any state-law claim, since no state had jurisdiction.[12]

Serra's constitutional claims were interesting, although they were also dismissed. Serra contended that his sculpture, "Tilted Arc," is a constitutionally protected expression of free speech and that the United States government's actions to remove it were a violation of his first amendment rights. He further argued that the action to remove the sculpture was in violation of the procedural due process requirement of the fifth amendment.

The court outlined the extensive administrative procedures followed by the GSA and found no procedural due process violation.

The court finally addressed the first amendment question as to whether "Tilted Arc" is a constitutionally protected expression and whether the GSA's decision to relocate the sculpture violated Serra's freedom of speech.[13] Without deciding whether "Tilted Arc" is speech entitled to first amendment protection, the court assumed for the purpose of its decision that the sculpture is expression protected to some extent by the first amendment. The court noted that, even if "Tilted Arc" is speech, Serra's first amendment rights must be balanced against the authority and mission of the GSA stemming from the Constitution itself and against the fact that Serra conveyed title in the work to the GSA.[14]

The court weighed Serra's first amendment rights against the legitimate government interest, as determined by the GSA. The court found no evidence in the record that the GSA's decision to relocate the sculpture was based on the content of its message. The court concluded:

> GSA's decision to relocate Tilted Arc is a valid content-neutral determination. It furthers an important governmental interest unrelated to the suppression of speech and the incidental restriction on alleged First Amendment freedoms and is no greater than is essential to the furtherance of that interest.[15]

The government had not attempted to ban Serra's sculpture generally, and the argument that the sculpture is site-specific is not sufficient to paralyze the GSA's ability reasonably to manage government buildings. Therefore, the decision of the GSA to relocate the sculpture "Tilted Arc" did not violate Serra's first amendment rights.[16]

Court of Appeals. Serra appealed the decision to the United States Court of Appeals for the Second Circuit, which affirmed the judgment of the district court.[17] The appeal was heard based on alleged violation of Serra's first amendment right of freedom of speech and Serra's fifth amendment right of due process.

The court once again reviewed the facts in the case specifically recognizing that the contract that Serra signed provided that "all designs, sketches, models, and the work produced under this Agreement . . . shall be the property of [the United States]."[18]

The court first discussed the first amendment and noted that the purpose of the first amendment is to protect private expression, and nothing in the guarantee precludes the government from controlling its own expression or that of its agents.[19] The court found that the artistic expression belongs to the government rather than to Serra, a private individual, since under the contract he signed he transferred all ownership rights to the government. Serra had the opportunity to bargain for the right to control the duration of the exhibition of his work when he made the contract for its sale. The court concluded that: "The Government's action in this case is limited to an exercise of discretion with respect to the display of its own property. . . . [N]othing GSA has done here encroaches in any way on Serra's or any other individual's right to communicate."[20]

The court went on to observe that even assuming that Serra retains some first amendment interest in the continued display of "Tilted Arc," the removal of the sculpture is a permissible time, place, and manner restriction. (First amendment rights may be restricted provided that the restrictions are justified without reference to the content of the regulated speech, that they are narrowly tailored to serve a significant governmental interest, and that they leave open ample alternative channels for communication of the information.[21])

The court found that the GSA has a significant interest in keeping the plaza where the sculpture was installed unobstructed, an interest that may be furthered only by removing the sculpture. Further, the relocation of "Tilted Arc" does not preclude Serra from communicating his ideas in other ways. The court observed that the first amendment protects the freedom to express one's views, not the freedom to continue speaking forever. The court went on to affirm the view of the district court that:

> [t]here is no evidence in the record that GSA's decision to relocate the sculpture was based on the content of its message. . . . GSA's decision to relocate the structure was undertaken for functional purposes—in order to regain the openness of the plaza.[22]

Serra also argued that under the holding of *Board of Education v. Pico*[23] he was entitled to a jury trial to determine whether in fact the removal of the sculpture was impermissibly content-based. The court recognized that the *Serra* case posed at least the potential for a *Pico*-type first amendment violation. However, the court concluded that:

> Even if we assume, without deciding, that Serra has standing to assert a *Pico*-type claim, it is clear that under any reading of the record in this case, the removal of "Tilted Arc" did not violate the principles of *Pico*. . . . Serra has failed to present any facts to

support a claim that Government officials acted in a narrowly partisan or political manner.[24]

In fact, the court went further when it stated that to the extent the GSA's decision may have been motivated by the sculpture's lack of aesthetic appeal, the decision to remove it was still entirely permissible. Finally, the court concluded that Serra's due process claim failed as a matter of law even accepting his factual allegations as true. The lengthy and comprehensive hearing that was provided was more process than what was due.[25]

In March 1989, "Tilted Arc" was removed from its location in New York's Federal Plaza. The decision of the General Services Administration was that, if possible, it should remain in its present location until another suitable site was located. However, the relocation process proved to be more difficult than originally anticipated, and the sculpture is currently being stored in a warehouse in Brooklyn.[26]

Any artist contemplating a commissioned work would do well to review the *Serra* case carefully so he or she is aware of the scope of the government's rights in connection with a commissioned work of art.

Temporary Artwork

Not all art is created to be permanent. An artist sometimes creates an installation piece—that is, a work of art designed for a particular space, often in conjunction with a show of the artist's work. The artwork may have no practical sale value and is meant to be destroyed at the end of the show. At other times, an artist creates a work under a public or private commission and, in either case, the work has an impact on public space, even though it is intended to be of only a temporary nature.

For example, the artist Christo has hung a curtain across a deep valley in Colorado, has made a fence of white nylon fabric running across twenty-four miles of Marin County, and has wrapped in cloth the Pont Neuf in Paris. Those public-space works of art were intended to be only temporary in nature.

The creation of an installation work or other temporary work should, as described above, be covered by a written agreement. In addition to the terms described above, the agreement should specify: the duration of the work's existence, who has the authority to remove the work, how it should be removed, who will pay for its removal, whether it can be sold, what is to be done with any left-over materials, who owns any sketches or photographs, who owns the copyright, and sometimes whether the work can be removed before the end of its agreed-upon existence if the work is for some reason offensive to the general public—for example, if the work is pornographic or defamatory. If the work is on public property (à la Christo), permission from the appropriate authority has to be obtained, and the agreement should specify whose responsibility it is to obtain that permission.

NOTES
to Chapter 4

1. Zaleski v. Clark, 44 Conn. 218 (1876). *See also* Zaleski v. Clark, 45 Conn. 397 (1877).

2. Zaleski v. Clark, 44 Conn. at 219.

3. Pennington v. Howland, 21 R.I. 65, 41 A. 891 (1898).

4. *Id.*, 21 R.I. at 66.

5. *See generally* J. MERRYMAN & A. ELSEN, LAW, ETHICS, AND THE VISUAL ARTS ch. 5 (2d ed. 1987); 1 F. FELDMAN, S. WEIL & S. BIEDERMAN, ART LAW ch. 4 (1986); Committee on Art Law of the Association of the Bar the City of New York, *Commissioning a Work of Public Art: An Annotated Model Agreement*, 10 COLUM. J.L. & ARTS 1 (1985); Balfe & Wyszominski, *Public Art and Public Policy*, 15 J. ARTS MGMT. & L. 5 (Winter 1986); Martin & Smith, *Commissioning Public Works of Sculpture: An Examination of the Contract*, 12 COLUM. J.L. & ARTS 505 (1988).

6. Serra v. United States Gen. Servs. Admin., 667 F. Supp. 1042 (S.D.N.Y. 1987), *aff'd*, 847 F.2d 1045 (2d Cir. 1988). *See also* Serra v. United States Gen. Servs. Admin., 664 F. Supp. 798 (S.D.N.Y. 1987).

7. Serra, *supra* note 6, 667 F. Supp. at 1044.

8. Serra, *supra* note 6, 667 F. Supp. at 1046; United States v. Mitchell, 463 U.S. 206 (1983).

9. Tucker Act, 28 U.S.C. § 1346(a)(2) (1982), grants jurisdiction in the district court in certain limited situations covering claims against the United States in amounts not exceeding $10,000. The limited jurisdiction over contract claims was withdrawn by the Contract Disputes Act 41 U.S.C. §§ 601-613 (1982). *See also* Administrative Procedure Act, 5 U.S.C. § 702 (1982).

10. Serra, *supra* note 6, 667 F. Supp. at 1051; 5 U.S.C. § 707 (1982); 28 U.S.C. § 1498(b) (1982).

11. Serra, *supra* note 6, 667 F. Supp. at 1051.

12. Serra, *supra* note 6, 667 F. Supp. at 1052. Serra's state law claim was based on N.Y. ARTS & CULT. AFF. LAW § 14.03 (McKinney 1984), which prohib-

its the public display of an artwork in an altered, defaced, mutilated, or modified form without the artist's consent.

13. See chapter 7 for a detailed discussion of the first amendment rights of artists.

14. Serra, *supra* note 6, 667 F. Supp. at 1055.

15. Serra, *supra* note 6, 667 F. Supp. at 1056.

16. Serra, *supra* note 6, 667 F. Supp. at 1057.

17. Serra, *supra* note 6, 847 F.2d 1045.

18. Serra, *supra* note 6, 847 F.2d at 1047.

19. Serra, *supra* note 6, 847 F.2d at 1048.

20. Serra, *supra* note 6, 847 F.2d at 1049.

21. Clark v. Community for Creative Non-Violence, 468 U.S. 288, 293 (1984).

22. Serra, *supra* note 6, 847 F.2d at 1050.

23. 457 U.S. 853 (1982), where the Supreme Court held, in a case involving the removal of books from a school library by the local school board, that such discretion may not be exercised in a narrowly partisan or political manner.

24. Serra, *supra* note 6, 847 F.2d at 1050-51.

25. Serra, *supra* note 6, 847 F.2d at 1052.

26. As an example of the difficulty in situations like this, Richard Serra was a defendant in a lawsuit in the early 1970s involving a worker helping to install a two-piece sculpture by Serra; the worker was killed when one of the steel plates fell over. The jury found that the fault was with the steel fabricator, for using a poor technique in making the piece, and the rigger, for failing to follow instructions. Serra was absolved of any blame in the accident. In October 1988, two workers were injured when a sixteen-ton steel sculpture by Serra toppled over when the workers were removing the sculpture from the Leo Castelli gallery. *See* N.Y. Times, Oct. 27, 1988, at B6.

FORMS

PRIVATE COMMISSION AGREEMENT
SCULPTURE

THIS AGREEMENT, made and entered into this ____ day of ____, 19__, by and between ________, ________, ____, ________ (hereinafter referred to as the "Artist"), and ________, ____, ________, ____ (hereinafter referred to as the "Patron").

WITNESSETH

WHEREAS, the Artist is engaged in the creation of works of art; and

WHEREAS, the Patron is desirous of commissioning the Artist to create a work of art for him (hereinafter referred to as the "Sculpture").

NOW THEREFORE, in consideration of the mutual promises contained herein, each party agrees as follows:

1. The Artist agrees to create a Sculpture to be entitled "____." The Sculpture is described as [*brief description*].

2. The Sculpture will be constructed as follows:
   a. Size—all dimensions:______________
   b. Materials to be used:______________
   c. Manner of construction:______________
   d. Location of construction:______________
   e. Final location of Sculpture:______________

3. The Artist agrees to prepare two drawings and a scale model for the Patron's approval. Under all circumstances, other than that specified in Paragraph 12 of this Agreement, the drawings and model shall be the property of the Patron.

4. The Sculpture will be completed by [*Completion Date*], PROVIDED, HOWEVER, under extenuating circumstances that prevent the Artist from working, the Artist may extend the time ___ months.

5. The Patron shall pay all costs of removing the Sculpture from the Artist's studio, transporting it to the final location, and installing it at the final location. The Artist agrees to submit a site plan and to supervise the installation at the final location. The cost of preparing the site shall be paid by the Patron. The Patron agrees to pay the Artist's transportation and living costs during the installation at the final location.

6. The Artist shall arrange for and pay for all fabricating and construction costs.

7. The Artist agrees to transfer the copyright to the Sculpture to the Patron.

8. The Patron agrees to pay the Artist as follows:

a. $______________ upon the signing of this Agreement.

b. $______________ upon the approval by the Patron of the sketches and model.

c. $______________ upon the completion of one-half of the Sculpture.

d. $______________ upon the completion of the Sculpture, its final approval and acceptance by the Patron, and prior to its removal from the Artist's studio.

e. The amount paid under (a) and (b) above shall not be refundable.

9. The Artist at his expense agrees to keep the Sculpture fully insured until final approval and delivery at the Artist's studio. The Patron agrees at his expense to insure the Sculpture from the time it leaves the Artist's studio until it is installed at the final location.

10. If the Artist becomes ill, dies, or is otherwise unable to complete the Sculpture by the Completion Date, the Artist agrees to refund to the Patron all amounts paid to the Artist other than the amounts paid in Paragraphs (a) and (b) of Clause 8 of this Agreement. Under such circumstances the sketches, model, and Sculpture (to the extent completed) shall be the property of the Patron.

11. The Artist represents that the Sculpture is unique and that no identical or greatly similar sculpture will be created by him.

12. Final approval and acceptance of the Sculpture shall be solely within the discretion of the Patron. The Patron agrees to accept or reject the Sculpture by ______________. If the Sculpture is rejected, the amounts paid under Paragraphs (a), (b), and (c) of Clause 8 of this Agreement shall be retained by the Artist, and the Patron shall not be required to pay the amount specified in Paragraph (d) of Clause 8 of this Agreement. If the Sculpture is rejected by the Patron, it, the sketches, the model, and the copyright shall be the property of the Artist.

13. This Agreement represents the entire understanding of the Parties hereto, supersedes any and all other and prior agreements between the Parties, and declares all such prior agreements between the Parties null and void. The terms of this Agreement may not be modified or amended, except in writing. This Agreement and all matters relating to it shall be governed by the Uniform Commercial Code and the laws of the State of ____________________.

IN WITNESS WHEREOF, the Parties hereto have hereunto signed their hands and seals the day and year first above written.

____

Artist-

____

Patron-

GENERAL SERVICES ADMINISTRATION
PUBLIC BUILDINGS SERVICE
CONTRACT FOR FINE ARTS SERVICES

On this ______ day of ______, 19__, the United States of America (hereinafter referred to as the Government), acting by and through the General Services Administration, and ______________ (hereinafter referred to as the Artist), an individual whose address is ____________________________, do hereby mutually agree as follows:

ARTICLE 1. Definitions

(a) The term "head of the agency" as used herein means the Administrator of General Services, and the term "his duly authorized representative" means any person or persons or board (other than the Contracting Officer) authorized to act for the head of the agency.

(b) The term "Contracting Officer" as used herein means the person executing this contract on behalf of the Government and includes a duly appointed successor or authorized representative.

ARTICLE 2. Scope of Services

(a) The Artist shall perform all services and furnish all supplies, material and equipment as necessary for the design, execution and installation of _____ (hereinafter referred to as "the work") to be placed in _______ at the location shown on Contract Drawing No. __ attached hereto. The Artist shall execute the work in an artistic, professional manner and in strict compliance with all terms and conditions of this contract.

(b) The Artist shall determine the artistic expression, subject to its being acceptable to the Government. The Artist shall submit to the Government a sketch or other document which conveys a meaningful presentation of the work which he/she proposes to furnish in fulfillment of this contract; he/she shall allow __ calendar days for the Government to determine acceptability of the proposed artistic expression.

(c) The work shall be of a material and size mutually acceptable to the Government and to the Artist.

(d) The Artist shall install the work, in the location shown on the attached drawings.

(e) The Artist shall be responsible for prepayment of all mailing or shipping charges on sketches, models or other submissions to the Government.

(f) Upon installation the artist is to provide written instructions to the contracting officer for appropriate maintenance and preservation of the artwork. The Government is responsible for the proper care and maintenance of the work.

(g) The Artist shall furnish the Government with the following photographs of the finished work as installed:

1. One black and white negative 4″ x 5″
2. One color negative 4″ x 5″
3. Two black and white prints 8″ x 10″
4. Two color prints 8″ x 10″
5. One color transparency 4″ x 5″
6. Five representative 35mm color slides

ARTICLE 3. Changes

(a) The Artist shall make any revision necessary to comply with such recommendations as the Contracting Officer may make for practical (non-aesthetic) reasons.

(b) If the Contracting Officer makes any recommendations within the scope of paragraph (a) above, after approval of any submission by the Artist, the Artist's fee shall be equitably adjusted for any increase or decrease in the Artist's cost of, or time required for, performance of any services under this contract; the contract shall be modified in writing to reflect any such adjustment. Any claim of the Artist for adjustment under this clause must be asserted in writing within 30 days from the date of receipt by the Artist of the recommendation, unless the Contracting Officer grants a further period of time before the date of final payment under the contract.

(c) If the Contracting Officer makes any recommendations within the scope of paragraph (a) above, prior to the approval of any submission by the Artist, the Artist shall make the revisions necessary to comply with these recommendations, at no additional cost to the Government.

(d) No services for which an additional cost or fee will be charged by the Artist shall be furnished without the prior written authorization of the Contracting Officer.

ARTICLE 4. Inspection and Care

(a) The Artist shall furnish facilities for inspection of the work in progress by authorized representatives of the Contracting Officer. The Government will contact the Artist in advance of any inspection to arrange a mutually convenient time.

(b) The Artist shall be responsible for the care and protection of all work performed by him/her until completion of the installed work and acceptance by the Contracting Officer and shall repair or restore any damaged work; provided, however, that the Artist shall not be responsible for any damage which occurs after installation is complete and before acceptance by the Contracting Officer which is not caused by any acts or omissions of the Artist or any of his/her agents or employees.

(c) The Artist shall give the Contracting Officer at least 10 days advance written notice of the date the work will be fully completed and ready for final inspection. Final inspection will be started within 10 days from the date specified in the aforesaid notice unless the Contracting Officer determines that the work is not ready for final inspection and so informs the Artist.

ARTICLE 5. Time for Completion

The Artist shall complete all work as follows:

(a) The preliminary submittal as required by Article 2. (b): ___ calendar days after the receipt of notice to proceed.

(b) The completed work in place: ___ calendar days after receipt of notice to proceed.

ARTICLE 6. Ownership

All designs, sketches, models, and the work produced under this Agreement for which payment is made under the provisions of this contract shall be the property of the UNITED STATES OF AMERICA. All such items may be conveyed by the Contracting Officer to the National Collection of Fine Arts-Smithsonian Institution for exhibiting purposes and permanent safekeeping.

The Artist shall neither publicly exhibit the final work, nor shall he/she make exact reproductions or reductions of the finished work except by written permission of the Contracting Officer.

ARTICLE 7. Fee and Payment

In consideration of the Artist's performance of the services required by this contract, the Government shall pay the artist a fixed fee not to exceed $____________. The fee shall be paid in installments as follows:

(a) $____________ upon approval of the proposed artistic expression as required by Article 2.(b).

(b) $____________ when the work is completed, approved and ready for installation.

(c) $____________ upon completion, and acceptance by the Government, of all services required under this contract.

The Contracting Officer shall advise the Artist in writing of the approval or reasons for disapproval within 30 days after (i) receipt of the document(s) showing the artistic expression, (ii) receipt of the notice that the work is completed and ready for installation, or (iii) after inspection of the installed work.

Upon approval and/or acceptance (whichever is applicable) of the work performed under this contract, the amount due the Artist shall be paid as soon as practicable after receipt of a correct billing from the Artist. Prior to the final payment the Artist shall furnish the Government with a release of all claims against the Government under this Agreement, other than such claims as the Artist may except. The Artist shall describe and state the amount of each excepted claim.

ARTICLE 8. Travel

All travel by the Artist and his/her agents or employees as may be necessary for proper performance of the services required under this contract is included in the fee amount set out in Article 7, above, and shall be at no additional cost to the Government.

ARTICLE 9. Responsibility of the Artist

(a) Neither the Government's review, approval or acceptance of, nor payment for, any of the services required under this contract shall be construed to operate as a waiver of any rights under this contract or of any cause of action arising out of the performance of this contract, and the Artist shall be and remain liable to the Government in accordance with applicable law for all damages to the Government caused by the Artist's negligent performance of any of the services furnished under this contract.

(b) The rights and remedies of the Government provided for under this contract are in addition to any other rights and remedies provided by law.

(c) The Artist guarantees all work to be free from defective or inferior materials and workmanship for one year after the date of final acceptance by the Government. If within one year the Contracting Officer finds the work in need of repair because of defective materials or workmanship, the Artist shall, without additional expense to the Government, promptly and satisfactorily make the necessary repairs.

ARTICLE 10. Suspension of Work

(a) The Contracting Officer may order the Artist in writing to suspend all or any part of the work for such period of time as he may determine to be appropriate for the convenience of the Government.

(b) If the performance of all or any part of the work is for an unreasonable period of time, suspended or delayed by an act of the Contracting Officer in the administration of this contract, or by his failure to act within the time specified in this contract (or if no time is specified, within a reasonable time), an adjustment shall be made for any increase in cost of performance of this contract (excluding profit) necessarily caused by such unreasonable suspension or delay, and the contract modified in writing accordingly. However, no adjustment shall be made under this clause for any suspension or delay to the extent (1) that performance would have been suspended or delayed by any other cause, including the fault or negligence of the Artist or (2) for which an equitable adjustment is provided for or excluded under any other provision of this contract.

(c) No claim under this clause shall be allowed (1) or any costs incurred more than 20 days before the Artist shall have notified the Contracting Officer in writing of the act or failure to act involved (but this requirement shall not apply as to a claim resulting from a suspension order), and (2) unless the claim, in an amount stated, is asserted in writing as soon as practicable after the termination of such suspension or delay, but not later than the date of final payment. No part of any claim based on the provisions of this clause shall be allowed if not supported by adequate evidence showing that the cost would not have been incurred but for a delay within the provisions of this clause.

ARTICLE 11. Termination

(a) The Contracting Officer may, by written notice to the Artist, terminate this contract in whole or in part at any time, either for the Government's convenience or because of the failure of the Artist to fulfill his/her contractual obligations. Upon receipt of such notice, the Artist shall immediately discontinue all services affected (unless the notice directs otherwise).

(b) If the termination is for the convenience of the Government, the Artist shall at his/her option have the right to either:

(1) An equitable adjustment in the price (without allowance for anticipated profit on unperformed services) in which event the Government shall have the right to possession and transfer of title to all sketches, designs, models, the work (whether completed or uncompleted) and all other items produced by the Artist in the course of performing the contract prior to the date of termination, which right may be exercised or not at the sole discretion of the Contracting Officer; or

(2) The possession of all sketches, designs, models or other documents or materials produced and submitted to the Government in the course of the Artist's performance of the work prior to termination, in which case the Artist shall remit to the Government a sum equal to all payments (if any) made pursuant to this contract prior to the termination.

(c) If the termination is due to the failure of the Artist to fulfill his contract obligations, the Government shall return to the Artist all sketches, designs, models or other documents or materials produced and submitted to the Government in the course of the Artist's performance of the work prior to termination, in which case the Artist shall remit to the Government a sum equal to all payments (if any) made pursuant to this contract prior to the termination.

(d) If, after notice of termination for failure to fulfill contract obligations, it is determined that the Artist had not so failed, the termination shall be deemed to have been effected for the convenience of the Government. In such event, the provisions of paragraph (b) of this Article shall be deemed applicable.

Loans, Libel, and Other Liabilities 5

This chapter focuses on certain situations in which the art collector may be thrust into the role of plaintiff in a lawsuit. Such situations, addressed in this chapter, include (1) events calling into question a work's uniqueness, (2) circumstances taking issue with a work's reputation, and (3) incidents casting doubt on a work's physical condition. The chapter also discusses the risks an appraiser runs when rendering an expert opinion.

UNIQUENESS

The art collector has an interest in preserving the uniqueness of his or her acquisitions. Uniqueness can be threatened either by outright duplication of a work by a third party or by the artist's creation of new works bearing a similarity to the earlier one the collector owns. Recent case law treats the two situations quite differently.

Copyright Infringement

Duplicating a work without the consent of the copyright holder (normally, the artist or the collector) constitutes a form of copyright infringement. Infringement of copyright is defined as the violation of any one of the exclusive rights of the copyright holder:[1] the rights of reproduction, distribution, adaptation, performance, and display.[2] Other than the distribution right, the exclusive rights involve, in different ways, the copyright holder's authority to keep others from copying the work without consent.[3] Generally, to establish copyright infringement, the copyright holder need not show that another has actually copied from the earlier work; rather, recent case law has held that copyright infringement lies where the infringer's work captures the "total concept and feel" of the protected work.[4] Moreover, for an infringement to occur, it is not necessary that the work be copied in the same medium in which it was originally produced.[5] Further, innocent or unintentional copying is no defense against a charge of copyright infringement.[6]

Common Source

The copying of a common source should be distinguished from actionable infringement. Actionable infringement does not occur when a third party has independently duplicated a work,[7] as when a photographer has taken a picture of the same scene from the same perspective as that in a prior copyrighted photograph. When the source is not protected by copyright, as stated by Mr. Justice Holmes, "[o]thers are free to copy the original. They are not free to copy the copy."[8] However, indirect copying, through the creation or the assemblage of a common source, is prohibited. For example, an artist infringes on another's copyrighted painting of a still life if he assembles the items used in the earlier still-life painting and arranges them in substantially the same manner as the objects in the copyrighted painting.[9]

Fair Use

Described as the primary defense against an action of copyright infringement,[10] the fair-use doctrine creates a privilege to use the work of another in a reasonable manner, even though that use may technically constitute an infringement. As to what constitutes fair use, the current federal Copyright Act has provided the following factors to be considered:

- The nature of the copyrighted work;
- The amount and the substantiality of the portion used in relation to the work as a whole;
- The purpose and the character of the use, including whether that use is of a commercial nature or is for non-profit educational purposes; and
- The effect of the use on the potential market for the work.[11]

Although the Copyright Act does not indicate the weight to be assigned to each of those factors, it has been suggested[12] that the fourth factor is the most crucial in determining whether or not fair use has occurred. If the new work competes with and supplants the need for the original work, the use is most likely not fair use.

Generally, fair use occurs when one is using another's creation in the context of a new work, usually for purposes of criticism, comment, teaching, news reporting, scholarship, or research.[13] Examples include the taking of a photograph of a painting loaned by a collector to a university or some other institution for a review of the exhibition, or a reproduction for the institution's documentary files.

Prerequisites to an Infringement Suit

To maintain an action charging infringement, the copyright holder of a work must have satisfied the statutory requirements of both registration and, where applicable, recordation. As to registration, the federal Copyright Office has issued brief and self-explanatory forms specific for the type of work being registered. The registration form must be accompanied by one or two deposit copies of the work[14] and a registration fee of $10.[15] Copyright registration is deemed effective as of the date the Copyright Office receives the application, the deposit copy or copies, and the fee.[16]

In addition to the registration requirement, there was, regarding transfers of copyright occurring prior to March 1, 1989, a second prerequisite: recordation.[17] The plaintiff had to first record in the Copyright Office the instrument of transfer under which the plaintiff asserted ownership of the rights allegedly infringed. The Copyright Act, for a nominal fee, permits the recordation not only of the transfer instrument but of all the documents relating to copyright ownership, including exclusive licenses and nonexclusive licenses. Recordation gives constructive notice to the world of all the facts set forth in the documents recorded.[18] However, effective as of March 1, 1989 with the enactment of the Berne Convention Implementation Act of 1988 amending the Copyright Act (discussed in chapter 8), recordation of instruments of transfer is no longer a prerequisite to an infringement suit.

Remedies for Infringement

The prevailing copyright holder in an infringement suit can obtain substantial damages. For example, he or she may recover not only the actual damages sustained as a result of the infringement but also any profits the infringer received that are attributable to the infringement.[19] As an alternative, the prevailing copyright holder may elect to recover statutory damages based on set amounts per infringement, those amounts being determined by the court in its discretion.[20] Injunctive relief[21] is also available and, in appropriate circumstances, infringing articles may be impounded or destroyed.[22] The court may award costs and attorney's fees to the prevailing party.[23]

Claims Against the Artist

Duplication of a Prior Theme

What happens when a collector who holds the copyright to a work learns that the artist, the original copyright owner, is creating subsequent works of art involving the same subject matter, vision, or technique as the earlier work? Would the collector prevail in an infringement action against the artist under those circumstances? Although some early cases[24] seem to hold in favor of the collector, more recent holdings seem inclined to favor the artist when there is a question of whether the artist actually copied the earlier work.

In a 1978 case, the Franklin Mint[25] and the artist Albert Earl Gilbert were sued for copyright infringement by the National Wildlife Art Exchange. A few years earlier, Gilbert had been commissioned by Ralph H. Stewart to paint a watercolor of cardinals. Stewart paid the artist both for the watercolor and for the transfer of copyright. Shortly thereafter, Stewart incorporated the National Wildlife Art Exchange and transferred the Gilbert painting to it. A few years later, Gilbert agreed to paint a series of four watercolor bird pictures, including one of cardinals, for Franklin Mint. The Mint made engravings of the four paintings. In painting "The Cardinal," Gilbert used some of the same source material he had used for the earlier work, including sketches, photographs, and slides. The federal court of appeals, however, affirmed the district court's finding, reached after hearing extensive testimony, that the artist had not copied the Exchange's painting when he painted "The Cardinal," citing evidence, for example, that the artist used slides created subsequent to the earlier watercolor as well as some of the same source material.[26]

Duplication and the Artist's Duty to Inform

Although courts today are loath to limit artistic expression by an easy finding of infringement on the part of the artist, that does not mean that an artist cannot be found to infringe, nor does it mean that an artist cannot be held to other related responsibilities. Fairly recently, for example, in a 1978 suit against Frank Stella,[27] who painted three paintings entitled "Marquis de Portago," a California superior court found against Stella, ruling that an artist is bound to inform the purchaser of the existence of any duplicate work that would materially affect the value or the marketability of the work purchased.

EXPERT OPINIONS

For the art collector, the question of authenticity poses a constant specter of concern in a market flooded with fakes[28] or forgeries.[29] Before purchasing valuable works of art, the wise collector may engage an art expert to render an opinion as to the work's authenticity.

The art expert must exercise care that is reasonable in the light of the expert's skill and knowledge or else risk liability to the collector under various theories of tort law.[30] Three major theories of art expert liability are negligent misrepresentation, disparagement, and defamation.

Negligent Misrepresentation

Struna v. Wolf[31]

In February 1982, Lewis Sharp, the curator of the American Wing of the Metropolitan Museum of Art, examined a work by the sculptor Elie Nadelman entitled "La Femme Assise" at the request of an art dealer who thought that the museum might want to acquire the sculpture, and who was showing it on behalf of the plaintiff, William Struna. Sharp subsequently advised the dealer that the museum would not buy the work, but he afterward contacted Erving and Daniel Wolf, private collectors, who were interested and who agreed to purchase the sculpture for $120,000. On February 11, 1982, the Wolfs paid Struna $15,000 and executed a promissory note for the balance of $105,000, payable February 16, 1982. In addition, the Wolfs issued Struna a check for $105,000, postdated February 16, 1982.

The balance was never paid, the postdated check "bounced" when it was deposited, and Struna sued both the Wolfs and the museum for breach of contract and for payment of the note and the check. Struna contended that, although neither the note nor the check was signed by anyone at the Metropolitan Museum of Art, the museum was liable as a party to the contract, because

Struna understood that the museum was the real party acquiring the sculpture, with payment to be made by the Wolfs as the museum's benefactors—that is, the purchase was being conducted as a joint venture between the Wolfs and the museum. As an alternative cause of action against the museum, Struna asserted negligent misrepresentation. He claimed that the museum appraised the sculpture and advised him that it was genuine, whereupon, relying on that appraisal, Struna purchased the sculpture; if the sculpture was not, in fact, authentic, the museum acted negligently in its appraisal, causing Struna to sustain damages of at least $100,000.

The court granted the museum's motion to dismiss the case with the following reasoning: Since neither Struna nor the dealer ever advised the museum that, at the time the appraisal was allegedly requested and rendered, Struna was not the actual owner of the sculpture but, rather, a mere consignee, there was no indication that either the museum or its curator knew or should have known that Struna planned to rely on the appraisal. (The court did not reach any question of whether the work was or was not authentic.) Further, the museum could in no way have realized that its rendering of an erroneous appraisal could have served to the detriment of Struna. As the court noted:

> [C]ases [alleging negligent misrepresentation] routinely require the existence of a "special relationship" between the parties creating a duty of care owed to the plaintiff thus entitling the plaintiff to rely upon the defendant's representations. Whether or not a "special relationship" exists depends on many considerations . . . more often than not . . . it arises out of a contract where the defendant was specifically employed for the purpose of rendering an appraisal to the plaintiff knowing that the plaintiff intended to rely on it. Here, on the other hand, by the plaintiff's own admission . . . [he] was acting at arm's length in attempting to achieve a sale of the sculpture to the museum. This relationship . . . appears to be the very antithesis of the "special relationship" ordinarily required. . . .[32]

Duty of Care

Negligent misrepresentation is the making of a false, material misrepresentation to another person without a reasonable belief that the representation is true, whereupon another person reasonably relies on the representation and is induced to act to his or her detriment.[33] The representation may be one of fact or, under certain circumstances, one of opinion.[34] Misrepresentations of opinion may be a basis of relief, for example, when the parties stand in a relation of trust and confidence, such as partners, attorneys and their clients, and close friends. If it is a representation of opinion given by an expert, it may be relied on as if it were a statement of fact.[35]

To avoid liability for negligent misrepresentation, the art expert must have knowledge of the subject and apply it properly. Liability for an opinion that turns out to be erroneous may be found if it is shown that:[36]

1. The expert lacks the minimal necessary knowledge, whether or not he or she is aware of it.
2. The expert's information is distorted or outdated to such an extent that his or her knowledge really amounts to mere belief. Again, the expert may or may not be aware of the shortcoming.
3. The expert either intentionally or inadvertently neglects to apply his or her knowledge; for example, a stylistic expert may fail to consider one or more major stylistic conventions of a historical period when authenticating a work.
4. The expert has the proper knowledge but applies it badly; for example, an expert may fail to draw the proper conclusions from comparative analyses.

The proper standard of care, however, is not an absolute; rather, it depends in part on the extent of the expert's responsibilities in a given situation—responsibilities that are largely determined by the express and implied understandings about the scope of the expert's opinion.[37] Moreover, an expert's qualifications also play a major role in determining his or her responsibilities.[38] An expert specializing in scientific methods, for example, might not be held responsible for stylistic considerations.

Once the extent of the responsibilities assumed are determined, the appropriate standard of care can be addressed. For example, an expert who represents that he or she has special skills and knowledge is held to apply and exercise those special skills and knowledge.[39] An expert who claims to have only less than the minimum amount of skill common to art experts is bound to exercise only that lower level of skill.[40] An expert who makes no representations about skills or knowledge is held to a minimum standard of knowledge in the field.[41] An expert, for example, on the works of Rembrandt who offers an opinion on the authenticity of one of his self-portraits must use care that is reasonable in light of his or her special knowledge and may be found negligent, in view of such special knowledge, if he or she furnishes an erroneous opinion. On the other hand, an expert who does not specialize in Rembrandt per se but who does possess general knowledge of the art produced within Rembrandt's historical period, may not, under the same circumstances, be found negligent if he or she furnishes an erroneous opinion about the self-portrait, assuming the expert's skill and knowledge were not misrepresented. Of course, an expert with little knowledge of the works of Rembrandt or of his historical period who nonetheless furnishes an opinion on the portrait's authenticity may be found negligent if he or she gives an erroneous opinion based on inadequate knowledge.

The case of *Travis v. Sotheby Parke Bernet, Inc.*,[42] illustrates the proper standard of care that must be rendered by an art expert expressing an opinion. Plaintiff Travis wanted to contribute a painting he owned to the Metropolitan Museum of Art in order to obtain an income tax charitable deduction. There was a question whether this particular painting, purchased by him at a Plaza Art

Gallery auction in New York for $17,000, was by Joshua Reynolds or by Tilly Kettle. If the painting was by Reynolds it would be worth considerably more than $17,000.

In 1978, within a year after purchasing the painting, Travis asked Sotheby's for an opinion as to its value. Sotheby's expert, Brenda Auslander, determined that the painting was by Tilly Kettle and not by Joshua Reynolds. However, apparently on two previous occasions having nothing to do with Travis, Sotheby's or its predecessor firm had described the painting as a Reynolds. Therefore, Travis claimed in his lawsuit that Sotheby's must have been negligent on at least one of those occasions. If the painting was really by Reynolds he was losing a valuable tax deduction, and if it was by Tilly Kettle, then Sotheby's prior opinions led him astray in purchasing the painting when he did so at auction.

The court found the expert, Brenda Auslander, not to be negligent, reasoning that she had examined the painting; she had looked the painting up in an authoritive book on Reynolds by Sir Ellis Waterhouse; and when she did not find the painting in the book, she actually got in touch with Waterhouse, who was the prime authority on Joshua Reynolds. He advised her that he considered the painting to be a Tilly Kettle. Auslander was actually found to have gone beyond the call of duty by seeking out the prime authority on Reynolds.

As to Sotheby's, the court held that even if its earlier pronouncements that the painting was by Reynolds had been negligent, Sotheby's had no duty of care to Travis at the time they were made. On top of this, Travis suffered no damages for he had acquired a painting that according to his own experts was worth anywhere from $5,000 to $450,000.

Also addressing the issue of the standard of care—this time with a finding of negligence on the part of the appraiser—is the recent case of *Estate of Querbach v. A&B Appraisal Service*,[43] in which the defendant appraiser at the request of the plaintiff estate conducted an item-by-item appraisal of the tangible personal property at the decedent's residence, including three small unframed oil paintings appraised at $50 each. When an acquaintance of the plaintiff subsequently purchased one of the three oils and then had it appraised for insurance purposes, the painting, found to be a work by Jasper Francis Cropsey, a highly regarded artist of the Hudson River Valley School, was valued at $14,800. Apparently, the artist's signature had appeared on both the front and back of the painting and the defendant appraiser had missed it entirely. When the plaintiff learned of the true value of the painting and brought an action for damages against the defendant appraiser on a theory of negligence, the estate was able to recover the sum of $14,700 along with prejudgment interest.

Certification programs for appraisers have been instituted by the Appraiser's Association of America and the American Society of Appraisers. Both organizations have guidelines of proper appraisal methodology to be followed by appraisers. Following proper appraisal methodology will go a long way in avoiding liability for negligent misrepresentation.

Plaintiffs and Damages

Not only a collector but anyone with an interest to protect who engages an art expert to render an opinion is a potential plaintiff in a negligent misrepresentation suit.[44] The expert's duty is readily ascertained from the contractual relationship;[45] equally ascertainable, under ordinary circumstances, is the expert's extent of liability—that is, the measure of damages.[46] Thus, an expert who negligently advises a client that a Picasso is not genuine when, in fact, it is, causing the client to sell the Picasso at a reduced price, incurs liability. The extent of the liability is ordinarily the true fair market value of the Picasso minus the actual sale price.[47] Likewise, the expert who negligently concludes that a Picasso is authentic when, in fact, it is a forgery is liable to a buyer who commissioned his or her opinion, whether the buyer is a collector, a dealer, or a museum. The measure of damages in that case is the purchase price paid minus the fair market value or salvage value of the forged work.[48]

Moreover, the expert may be liable to the dealer or the auctioneer who is merely holding a work on consignment if that person engaged the expert and relied on his or her negligent, erroneous opinion. If the consignee or another party takes a security interest in an inauthentic work of art in reliance on a solicited expert opinion, the measure of damages is the amount of the obligation in default covered by the security interest minus the fair market value of the security interest in the inauthentic art object.[49]

Defenses

One defense to a charge of negligent misrepresentation is contributory negligence.[50] That defense can be asserted if the person suing the expert supplied the expert with false information that materially contributed to the mistaken opinion. It can also be asserted that the person relying on the expert's opinion should have known that it was wrong.

If, therefore, an expert advises a dealer that a Utrillo the dealer is planning to buy is genuine, the expert is not held liable if the dealer should have known that the Utrillo is inauthentic. Another defense, possible but extremely remote, is assumption of risk.[51] If, say, a collector and prospective buyer is advised by an expert that a work of art is a fake, the expert probably cannot assert the defense that the collector assumed the risk of the expert's opinion. If, however, eleven experts, for example, advise that collector that a work of art is a fake and then the twelfth expert advises the collector that it is genuine, perhaps, as to the twelfth expert, the collector has assumed the risk.

More fruitful than exploring defenses after the fact is the policy of prevention. When commissioned to render an opinion, the expert can effectively limit exposure to claims of negligent misrepresentation by the careful drafting of an agreement.[52] First, the expert can circumscribe the scope of his or her responsibility. If a contract discloses, for example, that an expert lacks scientific expertise and acknowledges that scientific testing may be material, the party relying on the expert's opinion cannot complain that the expert did not conduct scientific tests. Second, the expert can limit the number of potential claimants by indicating in writing that the opinion is solely for the commissioning party and not for dissemination to others. In that way, the expert is not chargeable with knowledge that other people are depending on the opinion.

In any event, the expert can take comfort from an awareness that the crux of an action for negligent misrepresentation is an erroneous opinion and that, in order to prove that an opinion is incorrect, the complaining party must be able to persuade the court that most judgments about authenticity can be made objectively and conclusively. The reality, of course, is that the universe of art throughout the ages has been and continues to be governed by laws of relativity and fluctuating frames of reference. Sometimes, of course, the law, too, is in a state of rapid flux, as in the torts of disparagement and defamation.

Disparagement

Hahn v. Duveen[53]

On June 17, 1920,[54] the *New York World* made history by publishing a comment by Sir Joseph Duveen (later Baron Duveen of Millbank), one of the most spectacular art dealers of all time.

Andrée Hahn, a stunning French warbride, had received as a gift from her godmother upon her marriage to Harry Hahn, an American serviceman, a painting supposedly by Leonardo da Vinci, "La Belle Ferroniere." The Hahns moved to the United States and in 1920 brought the painting here, billing it as "the first Leonardo to arrive in America" and announcing its prospective sale to the Kansas City Art Gallery for $250,000. The *New York World* sent a reporter to solicit Duveen's opinion, advising him that the painting had been authenticated by a well-known French art expert, Georges Sortais. Duveen, having seen no more than a photograph of the work, replied that the Hahn painting was a

> copy, hundreds of which have been made of this and other Leonardo subjects, and offered in the market as genuine. . . . [Leonardo's] original *La Belle Ferroniere* is in the Louvre. Georges Sortais' certificate is worthless, if it really relates to the Kansas City picture. He is not an expert in the works of Leonardo.[55]

The Kansas City sale fell through, and Andrée Hahn sued Duveen for $500,000, alleging that his disparagement of her painting made it virtually worthless anywhere in the world. Duveen responded that the sacred right of free speech would be destroyed if he could not render a statement of opinion in good faith.

The case was ultimately tried in New York in 1929, resulting in a court decision that was not satisfactory to either party. After a long jury trial in which a parade of experts gave conflicting testimony as to the authenticity of both the Hahn painting and the Louvre painting, the jury was unable to reach the required unanimous verdict, and the judge ordered a retrial.[56] One month before the retrial, a settlement was reached, no doubt casting a chilling effect on the volubility of the art expert. Duveen paid the Hahns $60,000 in damages plus costs.

In 1985, after many years in storage and a few odd years in various museums, mainly as a subject of study or special exhibition, the Hahn painting once again surfaced on the market. Its current owner billed it as an original Leonardo, but its history trailed it like a poisoned vapor as the owner attempted to make a sale.[57]

Elements of Disparagement

An action for disparagement may be against a person whose false statement about an artwork has reduced the market value of the work.[58] A plaintiff in a disparagement case must prove that:[59]

1. A legally protected interest was affected by the comment.
2. The comment had an injurious character.
3. The comment was false.
4. The comment was published.

5. The circumstances of publication were such that reliance on the comment by a third party was reasonably foreseeable.
6. The third-party recipient understood the comment in its injurious sense.
7. The third-party recipient understood the comment as applicable to the plaintiff's interests.
8. The pecuniary loss resulted from the publication.
9. The defendant knew his or her statement was false or acted with reckless disregard of its truth or falsity.

Example 1: Suppose that at a cocktail party an art appraiser sees a painting by Jan Doe, a famous living artist, hanging on the wall. A fellow guest informs the art appraiser that a mutual friend is trying to decide whether or not to buy the painting from a dealer. The art appraiser then approaches his friend, who is surrounded by people, and, knowing that his statement is false, announces that there is a diminishing secondary market for Jan Does, and that the painting is not a good investment. The friend heeds the appraiser's remark and does not buy the painting. The result? The art appraiser would be subject to liability to the dealer for disparagement.

Example 2: The facts are the same except that this time the appraiser merely has a high degree of awareness of the probable falseness of his statement. The result is the same: the appraiser would be subject to liability to the dealer for disparagement. Reckless disregard of the truth or falsity of one's statement renders the speaker liable, as surely as does knowledge of a statement's falsity.

Example 3: Again, the facts are the same except that this time, the friend approaches the art appraiser, draws him into a private room, tells him that he is trying to decide whether or not to buy the Jan Doe, and asks for his input. The appraiser, believing in good faith that his statement is true and that he has a sufficient knowledge of the market to justify it although, in fact, his statement is false and would be shown to be false by a reasonably diligent investigation, gives the friend advice about the Jan Doe. The friend heeds the appraiser's remark and does not buy the painting. The result: the appraiser would not be liable to the dealer, because when communicating a statement to a prospective buyer at the buyer's request, the art appraiser may avail himself of the conditional privilege of "protection of interests of third persons."[60] That the prospective buyer—that is, someone with an interest to protect—has made the request for information indicates that he regards the matter as sufficiently important to justify the publication of any defamatory material that may be involved in response to his request for information. Therefore, the art appraiser who publishes that information or causes it to be published—in the example, a verbal or written statement about the Jan Doe work to anyone other than the dealer or Jan Doe—is not required to evaluate microscopically the interest the prospective buyer seeks to protect, nor is he required to compare (as he otherwise would be required, had he volunteered his opinion) the harm likely to be done to the dealer if his statement is false with the harm likely to be done to his friend if his statement is true. In this example, of course, the statement is false. Nevertheless, the appraiser is protected by the conditional privilege as long as he does not make the statement with either knowledge of its falsity or reckless disregard as to its truth or falsity.[61]

In addition to the conditional privilege described above, the appraiser may be able to avail himself of the absolute privilege of consent.[62] Indeed, had his friend already purchased the Jan Doe when he came to the appraiser for an opinion, he would be held to have consented to whatever the appraiser told him about it—disparaging or not—so long as the statement did not exceed the scope of his consent. Of course, if the appraiser were relaying his opinion solely to his friend as owner of the Jan Doe, there would be no action for disparagement in any event, as publication would not have occurred. However, in relaying the information to his friend, the prospective buyer, the appraiser could argue that the dealer, in letting his painting out on approval, assumed the risk of negative opinions.[63]

Facts Versus Opinions and Malice

At least two issues of law on disparagement are unsettled: (1) the distinction, if any, to be made between statements of fact and statements of opinion and (2) the basis and the degree of bad intent (malice) required to sustain a claim.

At common law, a disparaging statement could be one of fact or one of opinion.[64] There are at least three types of expressions of derogatory opinion:

1. A deductive opinion, in which the publisher implies or deduces a disparaging fact about the plaintiff on the basis of true information available to the public;
2. An evaluative opinion, in which the publisher makes a derogatory value judgment about the plaintiff on the basis of true information available to the public; and
3. An informational opinion, in which the publisher's expression of a derogatory opinion gives rise to an inference that it is based on undisclosed facts justifying the opinion.[65]

The deductive and evaluative opinions are pure opinions based on disclosed facts. The informational opinion is a mixed opinion based on undisclosed facts. Under common law, an action in disparagement can be based on statements of pure opinions and of mixed opinions and on statements of facts.

The same held true for defamation—but not anymore. In defamation, an action based on a pure opinion appears to have been rendered unconstitutional.[66] In the earlier Jan Doe examples, if the appraiser accurately pointed out particular concrete aspects of the Jan Doe painting to his friend and his guests and announced that, on the basis of those aspects, he thought that the Jan Doe painting was little more than a piece of junk (even though he was lying when he expressed his opinion) and that his friend should not buy the Jan Doe, chances are that his statement could no longer sustain an action in defamation because the only injurious and false portion of that statement was his opinion, which was based on concrete, accurately disclosed facts. The above statement was an example of an evaluative opinion. It remains to be seen if any distinction between pure opinions are made, permitting an action in defamation on a deductive opinion in which there is an unreasonable or dishonest deduction of a false fact.[67] It also remains to be seen if the Constitution will be read to place the same strictures on disparagement, thereby freeing from liability for disparagement the publisher of a disparaging statement of pure opinion or a certain type of pure opinion.

Related to that is the future viability of fair comment. Under common law, everyone had a qualified privilege of fair comment[68] on matters of public interest, which clearly include exhibitions of art.[69] That privilege is applicable to both defamation and disparagement[70] and has been largely viewed to apply solely to statements of pure opinion.[71] However, if pure opinion of all types is held to be nonactionable in both disparagement and defamation, the qualified privilege of fair comment no longer serves any purpose.[72] If, however, pure opinions based on unreasonable or dishonest deductions of false facts are deemed actionable, the common law privilege of fair comment may still have some vitality.[73]

The second unsettled issue of law in disparagement, the requisite degree of malice, also takes its cue from defamation. A number of older authorities, drawing an analogy between disparagement and defamation, held that disparagement was governed by strict liability[74]—that is, that liability attached to any false disparaging statement no matter how innocently expressed. More recent authorities assert that disparagement was never governed by strict liability but that any of four states of mind under common law gave rise to liability:

1. Knowledge of a statement's falsity,
2. Reckless disregard as to its falsity,
3. Motivation by ill will (factual malice or spite), or
4. Intent to harm.[75]

It is currently clear that either of the first two states of mind gives rise to liability for disparagement. It is unclear whether either of the other two states of mind is, by itself, sufficient to do so today. The Supreme Court, in evolving a standard of liability for defamation, has indicated that some showing of fault as to the issue of liability,[76] not merely spite or intent to harm,[77] is required to sustain such an action. It remains to be seen whether that principle of the Court's decisions will be applied to disparagement.

Defamation

Under the common law, one who intentionally published defamatory material was, as to its truth or falsity, liable without consideration of fault.[78] Then, in the 1964 landmark case of *New York Times v. Sullivan*,[79] the Supreme Court held that a public official cannot recover for defamation unless it is proven that the defamatory statement was made with knowledge of its falsity or reckless disregard of its truth or falsity. The Court labeled that standard "actual malice" and, in the ensuing ten years, expanded its application to include public figures[80] and then public and private individuals involved in matters of public concern.[81] In 1974, however, the Supreme Court backtracked. Now valuing the individual's interest in reputation over freedom of expression, the Court held that plaintiffs who are private individuals in a defamation suit against media defendants need not prove actual malice in order to recover[82] but left it to the individual states to determine their appropriate standards of liability, so long as those standards included at least some degree of fault.[83]

Differences Between Defamation and Disparagement

Although both defamation and disparagement involve incurring liability for injuries sustained through false statements about the plaintiff published to third parties, differences abound. A disparagement suit centers on the economic interests of the injured party,[84] whereas a defamation suit is to protect the personal reputation and the good name of the injured party.[85] Publication is defamatory if it tends to harm the reputation of another, lowering the party in the estimation of the community or deterring third persons from associating or dealing with the party.[86] Damages in defamation can be more comprehensive than damages in disparagement.[87]

The two theories of liability can overlap, and the injured party may simultaneously sue on both theories, as long as the damages are not duplicated.[88] But in doing an appraisal or an attribution, one runs the risk of a defamation suit only if an oral or written statement is published that goes beyond reflecting on the quality of the work of art to constitute a direct attack on the reputation of the seller[89] by implying that he or she is dishonest or lacking in integrity or that he or she is perpetrating a fraud on the public by selling something he or she knows to be defective.[90]

To return to the earlier examples concerning the art appraiser's volunteered opinion that there is a diminishing secondary market for Jan Does, and, therefore, the painting would not be a good investment—the appraiser's statement, although possibly defamatory to Jan Doe,[91] is in no way personally defamatory to the dealer. It implies no dishonesty, fraud, or lack of integrity in him and focuses solely on the painting. If, on the other hand, the appraiser had gone on to add, with at least a negligent disregard for the falsity of the statement, that the dealer was aware that Jan Does were not a good investment and that, consequently, he was dumping all his Jan Does, as well as a few fakes he was passing off as Jan Does, the appraiser would, in most jurisdictions,[92] be asking for a potful of trouble in the form of a suit in defamation by the dealer.

In summary as to disparagement and defamation, the expert may safely venture reasoned and reasonable opinions when asked to do so by someone with an interest to protect, such as a collector who is a serious prospective buyer. In that case, the privileges of consent and protection of third persons ordinarily free the expert to make any reasonable statement in good faith, regardless of whether it is a statement of fact, a statement of opinion, or a mixture of both. Generally, it is only when the expert volunteers an opinion that he or she risks suits for disparagement and defamation. And even when the expert volunteers, he or she should be on safe ground with comments made in good faith without knowledge of falsity, or reckless disregard for truth or falsity, as long as the comments focus solely on the artwork and not on any personality.

ARTWORK ON LOAN

On occasion, the collector may lend a work of art from his or her collection to a third party, such as a museum, a historical society, or some other institution; and the loan may create a bailment, imposing certain obligations upon the borrowing institution. After the discussion of bailments from the collector's perspective, this chapter closes with a review of bailments from the institution's point of view—for example, how to handle old loans that the institution is unable to return.

Bailments: The Collector's Perspective

When a collector loans works of art to a museum or some other institution, a legal relationship is created between the collector and that institution, a bailment usually for the benefit of the bailee.

Duty of Care

Under common law, the standard of care to which a bailee was held depended on the nature of the bailment[93]—that is, the highest duty of care was imposed on bailments for the sole benefit of the bailee, with an intermediate standard imposed on bailments of mutual benefit, and a less strict obligation attached to bailments solely benefiting the bailor. However, the distinction among degrees of negligence is often difficult to determine, so some case law appears to dispense with those distinctions in favor of an ordinary or reasonable standard of care[94] appropriate to the particular circumstances. That means, for example, that when a collector delivers a work of art to a museum for a particular purpose, such as an exhibition, with the understanding that the property will be returned when the purpose is concluded, the museum (the bailee) need not under every circumstance return the property in order to avoid liability. If something happens to the artwork while it is in the museum's custody—it is damaged or stolen, for example—it may be sufficient for the museum to account for it by noting that the artwork was stolen or damaged. If the lender is subsequently able to prove that the artwork's theft or damage was due to the museum's negligence while the artwork was in its custody, he or she may be able to recover damages. However, if negligence cannot be established on the part of the museum, the lender, under the law of bailment, as illustrated below, has no basis of recovery for damage to his or her property.

In *Colburn v. Washington State Art Association*,[95] the plaintiff, a lapidary and manufacturer of jewelry, was approached by a curator of the museum maintained in Seattle by the defendant and was invited to put some of his goods on exhibition in the museum's rooms. After some urging by the museum, the plaintiff agreed to do so, with the understanding that he could place his business cards by the exhibit as a form of advertising, thus creating a bailment for the benefit of both parties. When the plaintiff went to examine the exhibit case in which his goods were to be put, he requested the use of a padlock on the case for further security. The museum refused to comply, not wanting to tamper with the cases, and advised the jeweler that all the cases, none of which had padlocks, were securely wired together and that, moreover, a watchman was on duty to enhance security. The plaintiff thereupon left his goods with the museum and visited his exhibit several times over the next few months. The plaintiff's goods had been placed there without any agreement as to their remaining any particular length of time, and it was clear that he was free to remove them at any time.

About six months after the goods were placed on exhibition, some of them were stolen from the exhibit case. At the time a museum officer was aware of suspicious behavior on the part of two youths in the museum, sought to apprehend them, failed, and went to the police. The plaintiff sued the museum, arguing that the goods were placed on exhibition under a contract amounting to a warranty for their return. The trial court agreed and found for the plaintiff for an amount equal to the value of the goods stolen and not recovered. The appeals court reversed, however, holding that the situation was nothing more than a "bailment for the mutual benefit of both appellant and respondent. This being the nature of the relation between them . . . it seems plain . . . that appellant was bound to exercise ordinary diligence only. . . ."[96] Moreover, the court found that the museum had exercised reasonable care under the circumstances. The court then noted the general rule in bailment law: When a bailor sues a bailee to recover damages for goods placed in the bailee's possession that are not accounted for in any manner and are not returned to the bailor on demand, there is a presumption of negligence against the bailee. However, in cases of loss by burglary, larceny, fire, and other causes that, by themselves, do not indicate negligence on the part of the bailee, the bailee has met the prima facie case of negligence against him, and the burden then shifts to the plaintiff, as in any other case of alleged negligence.[97]

Under bailment law, reckless indifference may be equivalent to negligence, thus giving rise to liability. So that, in a case wherein the plaintiff loaned the defendant museum a diamond brooch for exhibition, with no pecuniary advantage accruing to the plaintiff, and the defendant's custody of the brooch was so casual that the defendant did not know "when or how the brooch was lost, or if stolen by whom, when and in what circumstances. . . ."[98] and, when the loss was finally noticed, refrained from informing the plaintiff for two months more, the prima facie case of negligence established by the plaintiff was not overcome by the defendant museum.[99]

The Loan Agreement

If bailment law remained the sole underpinning for the loans of artwork to museums and similar institutions, chances are that most loans would founder, since the lender is generally afforded little protection against loss or damage to his or her work. That loans continue to flourish must be attributed to the practice of using loan agreements, which provide that certain risks on the part of the lender, although not covered by the law of bailment, are to be covered by insurance. Since the loan agreement and the related insurance policy should fit seamlessly and since those insurance policies themselves are not uniform, not all loan agreements are alike. Nevertheless, certain provisions are common to virtually all loan arrangements between lenders and museums. Those provisions are discussed below.

Dates of exhibition. The agreement notes the dates or period of time during which the artwork will be exhibited.

Lender's identification. The lender indicates his or her name, address, phone number, and the exact form of his or her name for the exhibition label and the catalog.

The work being loaned. The loan agreement generally includes a questionnaire seeking to ascertain basic facts about the work being loaned—for example, the name of the artist, the title of the work, the medium or materials used, the date of the work (if it appears at all), whether the work is signed, and its size.

Insurance. The museum undertakes to insure the borrowed work for an amount specified by the lender. The insurance normally covers all forms of risk except those arising from inherent vice, governmental action, war, invasion, hostilities, rebellion, insurrection, nuclear damage, and so on.[100] However, a loss caused by one of those extended perils, although not insured against, may still leave the museum liable as a bailee if the lender can prove either actual negligence or reckless indifference. If the lender chooses to rely on his or her own insurance, rather than the museum's insurance, the lender is generally required by the borrower to add the museum as an additional assured or to provide a waiver of subrogation against the museum. If the lender fails to do so, he or she is deemed, under most loan agreements, to release the museum from any liability in connection with the loan.

Catalog and publicity. The museum may want to obtain photographs of the work for catalog reproduction and publicity. It may also want to reproduce the work in its publications and for publicity purposes in connection with the exhibition. The museum may also seek permission to use the work for telecasts for publicity or educational purposes. In addition, it may wish to make and distribute slides for educational use.

Framing. The agreement addresses the condition of the work's framing, if any. The museum may also seek permission to reframe or remat the work for the exhibition.

Shipping. The agreement sets forth the pickup and delivery dates agreed to by the parties. It also details the shipping arrangements for the work of art and notes how the cost of crating, shipping, and transporting is to be borne.

Additional conditions regarding the loan. The agreement generally includes a schedule of additional conditions governing the loan. Some of the more common conditions include a statement as to the standard of care to which the museum will adhere (usually, care comparable to that given to its own property); a notice of any change of address on the part of the lender; the notices to be given if the ownership of the work changes during the pendency of the loan; in the absence of a specified term of duration, a ceiling on the length of term of the loan.

Unreturnable loans. To cover those situations in which the museum, through no fault of its own, is unable to return a work of art at the end of the loan, a number of museums have added to their agreements a provision similar to the following:

> The Museum's right to return the work shall accrue absolutely at the termination date of the loan. If reasonable efforts to return the work fail, then the Museum shall have the right to place the work in storage at Lender's expense for storage fees and the cost of insurance, and to have and enforce a lien for such fees and costs. If the work is not claimed after three years from the date of commencement of this loan, Lender hereby gives all right, title, and interest in the work as an unrestricted and unredeemable absolute charitable gift to the Museum.[101]

Old Loans

Until quite recently, American museums followed the practice of accepting works of art on indefinite loan. Unfortunately, that procedure gave rise to an array of complications, including cluttering the storerooms of old museums with objects of doubtful circumstance. Some of those long-stored objects may well be infested, thus threatening the preservation of other stored works of perhaps greater value. Unsure whether the ownership of those objects has somehow attached to the museum, the museum's staff may hesitate even to treat those infested objects and, if they do, the museum has borne expenses for objects that (1) it probably does not own and (2) it certainly is not exhibiting. Moreover, even when the owner of an artwork does surface, the owner may have difficulty reclaiming the work on demand if the museum does not keep accurate records. An example of that is dealt with in the following case, in which the New Jersey Historical Society, in asserting ownership through adverse possession, refused to turn over a Gilbert Stuart to the lender's heirs.

Redmond v. New Jersey Historical Society:[102] The Defense of Adverse Possession

At issue in this case was the question of who was entitled to the exclusive right of possession of a Gilbert Stuart portrait of Captain James Lawrence—his only descendants (great, great grandchildren) or the New Jersey Historical Society? The portrait was in the possession of Mary Lawrence Redmond, the sole surviving grandchild of Captain Lawrence, at the time of her death in 1887. She was survived by her fourteen-year-old son, Preston Redmond. By her will she devised and bequeathed all her property to her son and his heirs, providing that, if her son left no descendants, the Gilbert Stuart portrait was to go to the New Jersey Historical Society. A few months later an executor of her estate delivered the portrait to the Historical Society, where it remained. In 1938 Preston Redmond died, survived by a widow and three children. By his will Preston Redmond devised and bequeathed all his property to his wife and, on her death, the remainder to his three children. His widow, individually and as the executrix of his estate, assigned and transferred all her interest in and to the portrait to her three children.

Shortly after Preston Redmond's death his three children, the complainants in the action, demanded the portrait's return from the New Jersey Historical Society. The demand was refused, whereupon the complainants, in March 1939, commenced a suit in replevin to recover the portrait. Among the defenses asserted by the Historical Society were those of adverse possession and the statute of limitations—that is, that the Historical Society by the time of the suit had the exclusive right of possession of the portrait and that in any event the complainants were time-barred from bringing suit. The court noted, however, that, to establish adverse possession, the party asserting the defense had to prove each element of the defense by a preponderance of the evidence—that is, the Historical Society had to prove that its possession of the portrait was "hostile as well as actual, visible, exclusive and continuous. . . . It must be 'adversary', it 'must begin, and continue for the whole term, in hostility.'"[103]

The Historical Society took the position that the delivery of the portrait by Mary Lawrence Redmond's executor, its receipt by the Historical Society, and the Society's claim to it each constituted a conversion of the portrait and commenced the running of the limitations statute. The court, on the other hand, disagreed with the Historical Society's contentions and found that the Society's records "besp[o]ke no assertion of ownership. The first assertion of ownership by the Society was in 1938, when it refused to deliver the portrait to complainants, and the statute of limitations did not begin to run until that time."[104]

Moreover, the court noted, since the Historical Society made several announcements that the portrait was bequeathed to it under Mary Redmond's will and testament, the Society failed to prove that its possession of the portrait was adversary or hostile.[105]

When Does the Statute of Limitations Begin to Run?

Although this question was discussed in some detail in chapter 2,[106] it is addressed here solely with respect to bailment situations. Relatively recent case law holds that, for bailments of an indefinite term, the statute of limitations does not commence until an actual demand for the return of the goods is made, usually by way of a presentment of a receipt.[107] That does not mean that the bailor is permitted to postpone the demand indefinitely so as to defeat the policy of the statute of limitations. Rather, it has been held that a duty rests with the bailor to make a demand within a reasonable time for the return of the property, the issue of reasonableness to be determined by the facts and the circumstances of each case.[108] In the 1980 case of *Houser v. Ohio Historical*

Society,[109] the court observed: "In Ohio, and in a majority of other jurisdictions, a reasonable time within which the demand must be made is ordinarily presumed to be the period of the statute of limitations applicable to the bailor's cause of action for return of the property."[110] The court, however, did recognize the well-known exception "that a demand will not be presumed if to do so would be contrary to the express terms of the agreement between the parties, or if the circumstances indicate that the parties contemplated a quick demand or an unusual delay in making the demand."[111]

In a situation involving an indefinite loan, in which nothing occurs to begin the running of any statute of limitations—that is, no demand for the return of the property has been made—the time for the return of the goods can seemingly be extended indefinitely, enabling distant heirs of the bailor to recover the bailed property.[112]

Legislative Solutions: A General Survey

In view of some of the problems engendered by old loans, museums in a number of states in recent years have urged enactment of legislation to ameliorate the situation. Generally, the purpose of the old loan legislation is to establish a method to determine the ownership of loaned cultural property that has been abandoned by the lender, to establish uniform procedures for the termination of loans of property to museums, to allow museums to conserve loaned property under certain conditions, and to limit actions to recover loaned property. Washington adopted such a statute in 1975,[113] and in subsequent years a number of other states followed suit, including Arizona, California, Iowa, Louisiana, Maine, Montana, North Carolina, North Dakota, Oregon, South Carolina, Tennessee, and Texas.[114] To date there is no old-loan statute in the state of New York, although we understand that such legislation may soon be proposed.

NOTES
to Chapter 5

1. 17 U.S.C. § 501(a) (1989), as amended by Berne Convention Implementation Act of 1988 (hereinafter 1988 Act).

2. 17 U.S.C. § 106 (1989), as amended by 1988 Act.

3. Berkowitz & Leafer, *Copyright and the Art Museum*, 8 ART & L. 249, 309 (1984).

4. *See, e.g.*, Walker v. Time-Life Films, Inc., 784 F.2d 44 (2d Cir. 1986); Atari, Inc. v. North Am. Phillips, 672 F.2d 607 (7th Cir. 1982). Note that still more recent case law has indicated that the unprotectable elements of the copyrighted work must be disregarded when comparing the works as a whole to determine whether the defendant's work captures the total concept and feel of the protected work. Trust Co. Bank v. Putnam Publishing Group, ___ F. Supp. ___ (C.D. Cal. 1988). The case is not reported but is available on WESTLAW, 1988 WL 62755 C.D. Cal., and is reproduced in 4 COPYRIGHT L.J. 52 (1988). The concepts of "access" and "substantial similarity" also play an important role in determining whether an infringement has occurred. *See, e.g.*, Steinberg v. Columbia Pictures Indus., Inc., 663 F. Supp. 706 (S.D.N.Y. 1987), in which the artist, Saul Steinberg, sued Columbia Pictures and other parties for infringement of an illustration drawn for the *New Yorker* magazine, which appeared on the cover of the March 29, 1976, issue. Steinberg claimed that the defendants' promotional poster for their motion picture, "Moscow on the Hudson," infringed his illustration known as a parochial New Yorker's view of the world. In holding for Steinberg, on a motion for summary judgment as against certain defendants, the court noted that where proof of access exists, as was conceded here, the required degree of similarity between the original work and the infringing copy, in meeting the infringement standard of "substantial similarity," may be somewhat less than would be necessary in the absence of such proof.

5. 3 M. NIMMER, NIMMER ON COPYRIGHT § 13.03[E][2] (1987).

6. *See* Berkowitz & Leafer, *supra* note 3, at 310.

7. *Id.*

8. Bleistein v. Donaldson Lithographing Co., 188 U.S. 239, 249 (1903).

9. Gross v. Seligman, 212 F. 930 (2d Cir. 1914).

10. *See* Berkowitz & Leafer, *supra* note 3, at 313.

11. *Id.*

12. *See* 3 NIMMER, *supra* note 5, §§ 13.05[A](4), 13.05[B], for an analysis of that factor.

13. 17 U.S.C. § 107 (1989), as amended by 1988 Act.

14. 17 U.S.C. § 408(b) (1989), as amended by 1988 Act. One deposit copy in the case of an unpublished work; two deposit copies in the case of a published work. *Id.*

15. 17 U.S.C. § 708 (1989), as amended by 1988 Act.

16. 17 U.S.C. § 410(d) (1989), as amended by 1988 Act.

17. *See* 3 NIMMER, *supra* note 5, § 12.08.

18. 17 U.S.C. § 205(c) (1989), as amended by 1988 Act.

19. 17 U.S.C. § 504(b) (1989), as amended by 1988 Act.

20. 17 U.S.C. § 504(c) (1989), as amended by 1988 Act.

21. 17 U.S.C. § 502(a) (1989), as amended by 1988 Act.

22. 17 U.S.C. § 503 (1989), as amended by 1988 Act.

23. 17 U.S.C. § 505 (1989), as amended by 1988 Act.

24. *See, e.g., Gross v. Seligman, supra* note 9.

25. Franklin Mint Corp. v. National Wildlife Art Exch., 575 F.2d 62 (3d Cir. 1978).

26. *Id.* at 66.

27. Factor v. Stella, No.C58832 (Cal. Sup. Ct. Nov. 2, 1978). The case is reproduced in 1 F. FELDMAN, S. WEIL & S. BIEDERMAN, ART LAW 275 (1986).

28. Fakes are defined as works in the style of an artist in which forged signatures and documents are frequently used to establish authenticity. *See* Karlen, *Fakes, Forgeries and Expert Opinions*, 16 J. ARTS MGMT. & L. 21 (1986); *see also* F. ARNAU, THE ART OF THE FAKER: THREE THOUSAND YEARS OF DECEPTION (1961).

29. Forgeries are duplicates of authentic pieces that are either intentionally created to deceive or else innocently created but later passed off as original works of the well-known artist. Such pieces include works created by forgers, innocent copyists, and artists of the Master's school whose works are later sold as those of the Master. *See* Karlen, *supra* note 28, at 21; *see also* L. DUBOFF, THE DESK BOOK OF ART LAW 388-94 (1977 & Supp. 1984).

30. See, for example, the Appraisers Association of America and American Society of Appraisers Joint Uniform Standards of Professional Appraisal Practice for the "Personal Property Discipline," issued in 1986, reproduced at the end of this chapter.

31. Struna v. Wolf, 126 Misc. 2d 1031, 484 N.Y.S.2d 392 (Sup. Ct. 1985).

32. *Id.* at 1036, 484 N.Y.S.2d at 397. The *Struna* case was subsequently settled out of court; Struna recovered the sculpture and accepted payment of an undisclosed sum of money from the Wolfs. *See also* Rosen v. Spanierman Gallery, 87 Civ. 9045 (S.D.N.Y. filed Apr. 25, 1989), which, in granting defendants' motion for summary judgment on a variety of claims, including negligent misrepresentation, held, inter alia, that the relationship between the plaintiffs and the gallery, which both sold the painting to the plaintiffs and subsequently appraised the painting for the plaintiffs, was a mere "contractual relationship, insufficient to sustain a cause of action for negligent misrepresentation . . . ," and that the appraisals in this case could not create the special relationship necessary to give rise to a cause of action for negligent misrepresentation as the appraisals were conducted after the sale of the painting and "were not part of the sale at issue."

33. *See* Restatement (Second) of Torts §§ 528, 552 (1977); W. Keeton, R. Keeton, D. Dobbs & D. Owen, Prosser and Keeton on Torts §§ 105, 107 (5th ed. 1984 & Supp. 1988).

34. *See* Prosser, *supra* note 33, at § 109.

35. *Id.*

36. *See* Karlen, *supra* note 28, at 9.

37. *Id.* at 10

38. *Id.*

39. *See* Restatement, *supra* note 33, at § 299A.

40. *Id.*

41. *Id.*

42. Travis v. Sotheby Parke Bernet, Inc., Index No. 4290/79, (N.Y. Sup. Ct. Nov. 11, 1982).

43. Estate of Querbach v. A&B Appraisal Serv., No. L-089362-85 (N.J. Super. Ct. July 15, 1987). The case is reproduced in 1 F. Feldman, S. Weil & S. Biederman, Art Law 282 (1988 Supp.).

44. *See* Restatement, *supra* note 33, at § 552(2)(a).

45. *Id.* at § 299A comment c.

46. *See* Karlen, *supra* note 28, at 13.

47. *Id.*

48. *See* Restatement, *supra* note 33, at § 552B. There is a split of authority here, in that a number of courts may also allow benefit-of-the-bargain damages in cases of negligent misrepresentation; that is, the claimant may be able to

receive the fair market value of what he or she should have acquired minus the fair market value of what was actually acquired.

49. *See* Karlen, *supra* note 28, at 13.

50. *See* RESTATEMENT, *supra* note 33, at §§ 463, 464, 552A.

51. *See* PROSSER, *supra* note 33, at § 68. Prosser records powerful arguments for eliminating this defense. Prosser also cites the state of New Jersey as taking the lead in abolishing this doctrine completely.

52. *See* Karlen, *supra* note 28, at 15.

53. Hahn v. Duveen, 133 Misc. 871, 234 N.Y.S. 185 (Sup. Ct. 1929).

54. For an excellent summary of the history of the problem-ridden painting to be discussed here, "La Belle Ferroniere," *see* Decker, *The Multimillion Dollar Belle*, ARTNEWS, Summer 1985, at 86.

55. *Id.* at 89.

56. Hahn v. Duveen, 133 Misc. 871, 234 N.Y.S. 185 (Sup. Ct. 1929).

57. For additional background information concerning "La Belle Ferroniere," *see* SIMPSON, ARTFUL PARTNERS: BERNARD BERENSON AND JOSEPH DUVEEN 241-43 (1986).

58. The action in disparagement protects economic interests of an injured party; whereas the similar, but distinct, action in defamation protects the personal reputation of an injured party.

59. *See* RESTATEMENT, *supra* note 33, at § 651.

60. *See* RESTATEMENT, *supra* note 33, at §§ 646A, 595 comment j.

61. *See* RESTATEMENT, *supra* note 33, at § 595 comment a, for other ways, not pertinent to the example discussed in the text, in which this privilege can be abused, thus causing a loss of its protection.

62. *See* RESTATEMENT, *supra* note 33, at § 635 comments a, b.

63. *See* Stebbins, *Possible Tort Liability for Opinions Given by Art Experts*, in F. FELDMAN & S. WEIL, ART WORKS: LAW, POLICY, PRACTICE 988 (1974).

64. *See* RESTATEMENT, *supra* note 33, at §§ 623A comment e, 566 comment b.

65. *See* PROSSER, *supra* note 33, at 813.

66. Gertz v. Robert Welch, Inc., 418 U.S. 323, 339 (1974); *see also* RESTATEMENT, *supra* note 33, at § 566 comment c.

67. *See* PROSSER, *supra* note 33, at 831.

68. *See* PROSSER, *supra* note 33, at 813.

69. *See* PROSSER, *supra* note 33, at 832.

70. *See* Restatement, *supra* note 33, at § 646A; *see also* Prosser, *supra* note 33, at 974.

71. *See* Restatement, *supra* note 33, at § 566 comment b.

72. *See* Prosser, *supra* note 33, at 815.

73. *See* Prosser, *supra* note 33, at 831.

74. Smith, *Disparagement of Property*, 13 Colum. L. Rev. 13 (1913), the argument of which was incorporated in 3 Restatement of Torts § 625 (1938). *See* Prosser, *supra* note 33, at 969.

75. *See* Restatement, *supra* note 33, at § 623A comment d.

76. *See* Gertz, *supra* note 66, at 347.

77. *See* Restatement, *supra* note 33, at §§ 623A comment d, 580A comment d, 580B comment c.

78. *See* Prosser, *supra* note 33, at 804.

79. New York Times v. Sullivan, 376 U.S. 254 (1964).

80. Curtis Publishing Co. v. Butts, 388 U.S. 130 (1967); Associated Press v. Walker, 389 U.S. 997 (1967).

81. Rosenbloom v. Metromedia, 403 U.S. 29 (1971).

82. *See* Gertz, *supra* note 66, at 347. *Gertz* also held, however, that a private defamation plaintiff who establishes the liability of a media defendant without proof of "actual malice" may recover only compensatory damages, not punitive damages. A subsequent case, Dun & Bradstreet v. Greenmoss Builders, 472 U.S. 749 (1985), limited *Gertz* by holding that private individuals not involved in matters of public concern could recover both compensatory and punitive damages without a showing of "actual malice."

83. In Chapadeau v. Utica Observer Dispatch, Inc., 38 N.Y.2d 196, 341 N.E.2d 569, 379 N.Y.S.2d 61 (1975), the New York Court of Appeals adopted a standard of gross irresponsibility for private plaintiffs involved in matters of public interest that is not far removed from the *New York Times* actual-malice test.

84. *See* Restatement, *supra* note 33, at § 623A comment g.

85. *See* Prosser, *supra* note 33, at 771.

86. *See* Restatement, *supra* note 33, at § 559; *see also* Prosser, *supra* note 33, at 774.

87. Damages in disparagement are generally limited to the pecuniary loss flowing directly and immediately from the conduct of third parties resulting from the disparaging remark, plus the cost of measures reasonably necessary to counteract the disparaging publication. Damages in defamation can range from nominal damages in the absence of substantial harm to general damages for

impairment of reputation and mental suffering to punitive damages in particular cases of actual malice. *See* RESTATEMENT, *supra* note 33, at §§ 620, 621, 622, 633.

88. *See* RESTATEMENT, *supra* note 33, at § 623A.

89. *See* RESTATEMENT, *supra* note 33, at § 573 comment c.

90. *See* RESTATEMENT, *supra* note 33, at § 623A comment g.

91. *See* PROSSER, *supra* note 33, at 771-83.

92. As noted earlier (*supra* notes 66 *et seq.*), *Gertz*, with respect to private plaintiffs, left it to the individual states to determine their appropriate standards of liability, excluding strict liability. A number of states may well require a greater degree of fault than negligence.

93. *See*, *e.g.*, Breckinridge County v. Gannaway, 243 Ky. 49, 47 S.W.2d 934 (1932); Harlan State Bank v. Banner Fork Coal Corp., 202 Ky 639, 261 S.W. 16 (1924); Nuell v. Forty-North Corp., 358 S.W.2d 70 (Mo. App. 1962).

94. *See*, *e.g.*, Mickey v. Sears, Roebuck & Co., 196 Md. 326, 72 A.2d 350 (1950); First Nat'l Bank v. Ocean Nat'l Bank 60 N.Y. 278 (1875).

95. Colburn v. Washington State Art Ass'n, 80 Wash. 662, 141 P. 1153 (1914).

96. *Id.* at 668, 141 P. at 1155.

97. *Id.* at 669, 141 P. at 1156.

98. Gardini v. Museum of City of N.Y., 173 Misc. 791, 792; 19 N.Y.S.2d 96, 97 (City Ct. 1940).

99. *Id.* at 793, 19 N.Y.S.2d at 98.

100. Some art insurance policies that will compensate a collector for the theft of an artwork will not, as a matter of public policy, compensate him or her for any ransom payments the collector may have to pay to recover the work, even if the sum is only a fraction of what the insurer will have to pay if the work is not recovered. That policy is not always the case, however, as in Kraut v. Morgan & Bros. Manhattan Storage Co. 38 N.Y.2d 445, 343 N.E.2d 744, 381 N.Y.S.2d 25 (1976). In that case, when the defendant storage company was concededly negligent in permitting rare Russian enamels to be stolen from its premises, the plaintiff, who was forced to make ransom payments to secure their return, sought to recover that sum, along with the value of the items not returned, and the New York Court of Appeals held for the plaintiff, rejecting the defendant's public policy argument.

101. The Art Institute of Chicago Loan Agreement, Michigan Avenue at Adams Street, Chicago, Illinois 60603.

102. Redmond v. New Jersey Historical Soc'y, 132 N.J. Eq. 464, 28 A.2d 189 (1942).

103. *Id.* at 474, 28 A.2d at 194.

104. *Id.* at 475, 28 A.2d at 195.

105. *Id.*

106. See discussion in Chapter 2 on statute of limitations, addressing accrual, pp. 82-84, 87-88.

107. Houser v. Ohio Historical Soc'y, 62 Ohio St. 2d 77, 403 N.E.2d 965 (1980).

108. *Id.* at 81, 403 N.E.2d at 967; Lowney v. Knott, 83 R.I. 505, 120 A.2d 552, 125 A.2d 98 (1956).

109. Houser v. Ohio Historical Soc'y, *supra* note 107.

110. *Id.* at 81, 403 N.E.2d at 968.

111. *Id.*

112. *In re* Estate of Therese Davis McCagg, 450 A.2d 414 (D.C. 1982).

113. WASH. REV. CODE ANN. § 27.40.034 (1988). (The statute governs only the state museum at the University of Washington.)

114. ARIZ. REV. STAT. ANN. §§ 44-351 to -356 (1987); CAL. CIV. CODE §§ 1899 to 1899.11 (West Supp. 1988); Iowa-Senate File 370 (enacted 1988); LA. REV. STAT. ANN. § 25.345 (West Supp. 1988) (the statute applies only to the State Museum); ME. REV. STAT. ANN. ch. 27, § 601 (Supp. 1988); MONT. CODE ANN. §§ 22-3-501 to -510, 22-3-521 to -523 (1987); N.C. Gen. Stat. §§ 121-2 and 121-7 (Supp. 1988); N. DAK. CENT. CODE § 47-07-14 (1987); OR. REV. STAT. §§ 358.415-.440 (Supp. 1987); S.C. CODE §§ 27-45-10 to -100 (1987); TENN. CODE ANN. §§ 66-29-201 to -204 (Supp. 1988); TEX. PROP. CODE ANN. §§ 80.001-80.008 (Vernon Supp. 1988).

FORMS

FORM—MODEL APPRAISAL AGREEMENT

Appraiser's Letterhead

Dear :

This letter will confirm our agreement as to the preparation of the appraisal to be done on .

The property to be appraised is broadly described as follows:

The property is located where you will arrange for us to physically inspect the property. You agree to supply us with any factual information within your knowledge that we may request from you. In preparing the appraisal, will inspect the property, prepare a detailed description of the property, evaluate it and submit a written and signed report to you. We will use acceptable appraisal methodology in preparing the appraisal. The appraisal will be prepared for you for the purpose of and will be used by you only for such purpose.

The fee for said appraisal shall be per hour/day. In addition, expenses or travelling and other out-of-pocket expenses shall be charged to you. The fee and expenses shall be due and payable upon delivery of the written report. An advance of percent of the estimated fee and/or expenses is due (upon signing this letter of agreement) (upon commencement of the appraisal inspection). An additional fee will be charged for any required future services pertaining to this appraisal.

Our appraisal will represent our best judgment and opinion as to the current fair market value and other factors stated in the appraisal of the appraised property. The appraisal will not be a statement or representation of fact nor will it be a representation or warranty with respect to authenticity, genuineness, provenance or condition of the appraised property.

You represent and warrant that you own the property free and clear of any claims, liens, encumbrances or interests of others and agree to indemnify and hold us harmless from any claims, actions, damages or expenses incurred by us as a result of claims by third persons based on the appraisal.

Any controversy or claim arising out of or relating to this contract, or the breach thereof, shall be settled by arbitration in accordance with the Commercial Arbitration Rules of the American Arbitration Association, and judgment upon the award rendered by the Arbitrator(s) may be entered in any Court having jurisdiction thereof.

If you are in agreement with these terms, please sign and return one copy of this letter to us at your earliest convenience.

Looking forward to working with you, we are,

Very truly yours,

Appraiser Client

Date Date

FORM
INFORMATION REQUIRED TO BE CONTAINED IN AN APPRAISAL OF TANGIBLE PERSONAL PROPERTY BEING CONTRIBUTED TO CHARITY FOR WHICH A DEDUCTION WILL BE CLAIMED FOR FEDERAL INCOME TAX PURPOSES

QUALIFIED APPRAISAL

The following information is required pursuant to Treas. Reg. Section 1.170A-13(b)(2)(ii). Donors of tangible personal property to charity should require the appraiser to include the following information in the appraisal.

1. DESCRIPTION OF THE PROPERTY—in sufficient detail for a person who is not generally familiar with the type of property to ascertain that the property that was appraised is the property that was—or will be—contributed.

   Description should include dimensions, color, materials used, and, if known, date of creation, maker, location of origin and whatever other factual details would be helpful.
2. PHYSICAL CONDITION of the property—the appraisal should note any repairs, defects, worn elements, fading, etc.
3. DATE—OR EXPECTED DATE—OF CONTRIBUTION TO Charity.
4. DATE OR DATES ON WHICH THE PROPERTY WAS VALUED by the appraiser—note that the appraisal can not be prepared more than 60 days prior to the actual date of contribution of the appraised property.
5. METHOD OF VALUATION used to determine the fair market value—such as comparable sales approach or replacement cost-less-depreciation approach.
6. SPECIFIC BASIS FOR VALUATION, if any, such as specific comparable sales transactions.
7. TERMS OF ANY AGREEMENT—or understanding between the donor and the donee charity relating to the use, sale or other disposition of the property. If none, the appraisal should so state, or if there are, the appraisal should explain.
8. FEE ARRANGEMENT between donor and appraiser—fees based on a percentage of the value will render the appraisal invalid for income tax contribution purposes.
9. QUALIFICATIONS of the APPRAISER including background, experience, education and membership, if any, in professional

appraiser associations. There should be included, in addition, specific examples of qualifications by way of experience or background to appraise the particular items which are the subject of the appraisal.

10. FAIR MARKET VALUE—the appraised value of the property which is the subject of the appraisal as of the date (or expected date) of contribution.
11. PURPOSE OF APPRAISAL—a statement that the appraisal was prepared for federal income tax purposes.
12. SIGNATURE of appraiser on the appraisal. The name, address and taxpayer identification number of the appraiser must be on the appraisal.

FORM

MODEL LOAN AGREEMENT

[Based on loan agreement used by the Art Institute of Chicago and model loan agreement appearing in M. MALARO, A LEGAL PRIMER ON MANAGING MUSEUM COLLECTIONS 170 (1985).]

Name of Museum
Address of Museum
Telephone number of Museum

The undersigned Lender hereby lends to _______ Museum the objects described herein for the purposes and subject to the terms and conditions set forth below.

LENDER: Name
Address
Telephone number
Credit line for exhibition, catalog, publicity

OBJECT: Artist
Title
Date
Medium
Dimensions
Signed
How
Where
Accession number

PERIOD: The period of the loan shall be from ______ to ______.

CATALOG: Name of copyright holder
If photographs exist, furnish
_______ black and white
_______ color transparencies
_______ color slides
Do you agree that ____________ Museum may photograph, film, tape, or reproduce in any medium the above object for catalog, educational and publicity purposes? ____ (initial to signify yes)

INSURANCE: Subject to conditions set forth below

Do you wish ______ Museum to insure object? ____

Do you wish to maintain your own insurance? ____

What is the value in United States currency of the object? ______

SHIPPING: List special shipping instructions:

________ Museum will contact you to arrange pick-up and packing on or about __________. ____________ Museum will inform you of proposed installation method at Museum.

COSTS: ________ Museum will pay costs of packing, shipping, insurance, and ________.

SPECIAL CONDITIONS:______________________

CONDITIONS GOVERNING LOANS

Care, Preservation, and Exhibition

1. The Museum will give to objects borrowed the same care it gives comparable property of its own. Precautions will be taken to protect objects from fire, theft, mishandling, dirt, and insects, and from extremes of light, temperature, and humidity while in the Museum's custody. It is understood by the Lender and the Museum that all tangible objects are subject to gradual inherent deterioration for which neither party is responsible.

2. Evidence of damage at the time of receipt or while in the Museum's custody will be reported immediately to the Lender. It is understood that objects that, in the opinion of the Museum, may be damaged by infestation may be fumigated at the discretion of the Museum.

3. The Lender will be requested to provide written authorization for any alteration, restoration, or repair. The Museum, for its own purposes, may examine objects by all modern scientific methods.

4. The Museum retains the right to determine when, if, and for how long objects borrowed will be exhibited. The Museum retains the right to cancel the loan upon reasonable notice to the Lender.

Transportation and Packing

1. The Lender certifies that the objects lent are in such condition as to withstand ordinary strains of packing and transportation and handling. A written report of the condition of objects prior to shipment must be sent by the Lender to the Museum. Otherwise, it will be assumed that objects are received in the same condition as when leaving the Lender's possession. Condition records will be made at the Museum on arrival and departure.

2. Costs of transportation and packing will be borne by the Museum unless the loan is at the Lender's request. The method of shipment must be agreed upon by both parties.

3. Governmental regulations will be adhered to in international shipments. As a rule, the Lender is responsible for adhering to his country's import/export requirements and the borrower is responsible for adhering to its country's import/export requirements.

4. The Lender will assure that said objects are adequately and securely packed for the type of shipment agreed upon, including any special instructions for unpacking and repacking. Objects will be returned packed in the same or similar materials as received unless otherwise authorized by the Lender.

Insurance

1. Objects will be insured for the amount specified herein by the Museum under its "all-risk" wall-to-wall policy subject to the following standard exclusions: wear and tear, gradual deterioration, insects, vermin, or inherent vice; repairing, restoring, or retouching process; hostile or warlike action, insurrection, rebellion, etc.; nuclear reaction, nuclear radiation, or radioactive contamination. Insurance will be placed in the amount specified by the Lender herein, which must reflect fair market value. If the Lender fails to indicate an amount, the Museum, with the implied concurrence of the Lender, will set a value for purposes of insurance for the period of the loan. Said value is not to be considered an appraisal.

2. If the Lender elects to maintain his own insurance coverage, then, prior to shipping, the Museum must be supplied with a certificate of insurance naming the Museum as an additional insured or waiving rights of subrogation. If the Lender fails to provide that certificate, this failure shall constitute a waiver of insurance by the Lender (see No. 4

below). The Museum shall not be responsible for any error or deficiency in information furnished by the Lender to the insurer or for any lapses in such coverage.

3. In the case of long-term loans, it is the responsibility of the Lender to notify the Museum of current insurance valuations.

4. If insurance is waived by the Lender, that waiver shall constitute the agreement of the Lender to release and hold harmless the Museum from any liability for damages to or loss of the loan property.

5. The amount payable by insurance secured in accordance with this loan agreement is the sole recovery available to the Lender from the Museum in the event of loss or damage.

Reproduction and Credit

Unless otherwise notified in writing by the Lender, the Museum may photograph or reproduce the objects lent for educational, catalog, and publicity purposes. It is understood that objects on exhibit may be photographed by the general public. Unless otherwise instructed in writing, the Museum will give credit to the Lender as specified on the face of this agreement in any publications. Whether individual labels are provided for objects on display is at the discretion of the Museum.

Change in Ownership or Address

It is the responsibility of the Lender or his agent to notify the Museum promptly in writing if there is any change in ownership of the objects (whether through *inter vivos* transfer or death) or if there is a change in the identity or address of the Lender. The Museum assumes no responsibility to search for a Lender (or owner) who cannot be reached at the address of record.

Return of Loans

1. Unless otherwise agreed in writing, a loan terminates on the date specified on the face of this agreement. If no date is specified, the loan shall be for a reasonable period of time, but in no event to exceed three years. Upon termination of a loan, the Lender is on notice that a return or renewal must be effected, or else a gift of the objects will be inferred.

2. Objects will be returned only to the Lender of record or to a location mutually agreed upon in writing by the Museum and the Lender of record. In case of uncertainty, the Museum reserves the right to require a Lender/claimant to establish title by proof satisfactory to the Museum.

3. When the loan is returned, the Museum will send the Lender a receipt form. If that form is not signed and returned within thirty days after mailing, the Museum will not be responsible for any damage or loss.

4. If the Museum's efforts to return objects within a reasonable period following the termination of the loan are unsuccessful, then the objects will be maintained at the Lender's risk and expense for a maximum of ______ years. If after ______ years the objects have not been claimed, then and in consideration of maintenance and safeguarding, the Lender/owner shall be deemed to have made the objects an unrestricted gift to the Museum.

Applicable Law

This agreement shall be construed in accordance with the law of ____[jurisdiction]____.

I have read and agree to the above conditions and certify that I have full authority to enter into this agreement.

Signed: ________[Lender*]________ Date: ______________

Title: ______________________________

*If the Lender is not the owner, complete the following two lines:

Name of Owner: ______________________________

Address of Owner: ______________________________

APPROVED FOR THE MUSEUM:

Signed: ______________________________ Date: ______________

Title: ______________________________

(Please sign and return both copies.)

UNIFORM STANDARDS OF PROFESSIONAL APPRAISAL PRACTICE PERSONAL PROPERTY DISCIPLINE

A. Preamble:

It is essential that a professional personal property appraiser arrive at and communicate his or her analyses, conclusions, opinions and valuations in a manner appropriate to the function of the appraisal and of transcending clarity to the client, to any third parties involved, to the public or to any other legitimately interested entities. The intent of these standards is to guide the practicing professional personal property appraiser; to serve as establishing present appropriate standards, as well as a foundation for any further future development, in personal property appraising; and to make users of appraisal services and the public aware of these standards. Appraisers who maintain today's highest level of professional practice will observe these standards when developing and communicating an appraisal, analysis, opinion or valuation conclusion.

These standards are intended to apply to appraisers of personal property as that term is generally understood by the public, e.g., paintings, antiques, jewelry, household furnishings, collectibles, etc.

Aware that some professions may recognize personal property as including machinery, equipment, intangibles and certain business assets, we endorse action to establish uniform standards of professional appraisal practice in those disciplines by committees most closely associated with the discipline of Machinery and Equipment Appraising and the discipline of Business Valuation.

B. Competency:

Prior to agreeing to perform a personal property appraisal, the appraiser must carefully consider the knowledge, training and experience that will be required to complete the appraisal competently, and either:

1. has been tested and certified in the required field of expertise by a major recognized testing and certifying appraisal society, or
2. assumes personal responsibility in presenting alternate substantial evidence that he or she has the specialized knowledge, training, experience and resources to complete the appraisal competently, or
3. immediately discloses the lack of required knowledge, training, experience or resources to the client, allowing the client to engage appraisal services elsewhere, or, with the client's

approval, take all steps necessary and appropriate to complete the appraisal competently, such as use of necessary experts etc.

C. Definitions:

For the purpose of these standards, the following definitions apply:

Appraisal: the act or process of estimating value

Appraisal Report: any communication, written or oral, of an appraisal; the document that is transmitted to the client upon completion of an appraisal assignment.

Client: any party for whom an appraiser performs a service.

Personal Property: identifiable portable and tangible objects which are considered by the general public as being "personal", e.g., furnishings, artwork, antiques, gems and jewelry, collectibles, etc.

D. Standards:

Standard I.

In developing a personal property appraisal, an appraiser must be aware of, understand, and correctly employ those recognized methods and techniques that are necessary to produce a credible appraisal.

Rules for Standard I

Rule 1. In developing a personal property appraisal, an appraiser must:

a) be aware of, understand, and correctly employ those recognized methods and techniques that are necessary to produce a credible appraisal;

b) not commit a substantial error of omission or commission that significantly affects an appraisal;

c) not render appraisal services in a careless or negligent manner, such as improper or incomplete research or a series of minor errors that, considered individually, may not significantly affect the results of an appraisal, but which, when considered in the aggregate, would be misleading.

Rule 2. In developing a personal property appraisal, an appraiser must observe the following specific appraisal guidelines:

a) adequately identify the object(s) to be evaluated including the method of identification if other than or in addition to a personal physical inspection;

b) state and clearly define the purpose and function of the appraisal including any special limiting conditions;

c) identify the effective date of the appraisal clearly distinguishing the appraisal date from the report date when appropriate;

d) define the value to be considered consistent with the function of the appraisal, e.g., retail replacement value for most insurance appraisals; fair market value for charitable donations or estate tax valuation of property, etc.;
e) value the object by an appropriate appraisal method or technique;
f) collect, verify, analyze and reconcile such comparable sales data as are available, adequately identifed and described, to indicate a value conclusion;
g) ALL PERTINENT INFORMATION MUST BE INCLUDED;
h) when applicable, consider and analyze the effect on value of:
   1. any damage or imperfections relevant to the object(s);
   2. the object(s)' importance as compared to other items of the same type and classification, or as it relates to an artist's total work, or as enhancing other parts of a specific collection;
   3. any historical factors (provenance) which would affect the value of the object(s);
   4. the market acceptability of the style and scale of the object(s);
   5. the object(s)' utility, if any, in today's society as it relates to the object(s)' originally intended use;
   6. any prior sales of the object(s) being appraised.

Standard II.
In a personal property appraisal report, an appraiser must communicate his or her analyses, opinons, conclusions and valuations in a manner that is clear and not misleading.

Rules for Standard II

Rule 1. Each written or oral appraisal report must:
a) clearly and accurately set forth the appraisal in a manner that will not be misleading;
b) contain sufficient information to enable the person(s) who receive or rely on the report to understand it properly;
c) clearly and accurately disclose any extraordinary assumption or limiting condition that directly affects the appraisal and indicate the impact on value of such assumptions or conditions.

Rule 2. Each written appraisal report must comply with the following specific reporting guidelines:
a) identify and describe the personal property being appraised;
b) define the purpose, function and scope of the appraisal;
c) define the value to be estimated;

d) set forth the effective date of the appraisal and the date of the report;
e) set forth all assumptions and limiting conditions that affect the analyses, opinions, conclusions and valuations;
f) where appropriate, set forth the information considered, the appraisal procedures followed, and the reasoning that supports the analyses, opinions, conclusions and valuations;
g) as the use of comparable sales is the normal valuation approach for the appraisal of personal property, explain and support the use of a different valuation approach;
h) set forth any additional information that may be appropriate to show compliance with the requirements of Standard I;
i) include a signed certification in accordance with the following Rule 3.

Rule 3. Each written appraisal report must contain a certification consisting of the following elements which the appraiser certifies to the best of his or her knowledge and belief:
a) the statements of fact contained in the appraisal report are true and correct;
b) the reported analyses, opinions and conclusions are limited only by the reported assumptions and limiting conditions, and are the appraiser's personal, unbiased, professional analyses, opinions, conclusions and valuations;
c) the appraiser has no present nor contemplated future interest in the object(s) which is the subject of the report (unless specified to the contrary);
d) the appraiser has no personal interest or bias with respect to the parties involved (unless specified to the contrary);
e) the appraiser does not have a personal or business relationship with the parties involved which would lead a reasonable person to question the objectivity and validity of the report;
f) the appraiser's compensation is not contingent on an action or event resulting from the analyses, opinions, or conclusions in, or the use of, the report;
g) the appraiser's compensation is not to be dependent upon the amount of value which he or she determines at the conclusion of his or her work, neither as a fixed percentage of that value determination, nor as compensation connected to a predetermined scale relating fee to value range;
h) the appraiser has made a personal, physical inspection of the

object(s) specified in the report (unless specified to the contrary);

i) the appraiser received no separate significant professional assistance (unless specified to the contrary in which case the name of the individual(s) providing such assistance must be stated and, where appropriate, should sign the report);

j) the analyses, opinions, conclusions and valuations in the report were developed, and the report prepared, in conformity with the Uniform Standards of Professional Appraisal Practice For the Personal Property Discipline.

Rule 4. To the extent that it is both possible and appropriate, each oral appraisal report, including expert testimony, must address the substantive matters set forth in these Standards I and II.

E. Jurisdictional Exceptions:

If any part of these standards is contrary to the law of any jurisdiction or public policy clearly affirmed by competent authority in a jurisdiction, only that part shall be void and of no force or effect in that jurisdiction.

6 International Transportation of Art and Cultural Property

The illicit international trade in cultural property is a major problem. In the course of acquiring works of art, museums, dealers, and collectors must all take into consideration United States laws, international treaties, and the laws of foreign nations governing the international trade in art objects. Generally, those domestic and international restrictions focus on the preservation of cultural property. The term "cultural property" includes all objects produced or adopted by a given culture—that is, works of art with special historical, archaeological, or ethnological values.

The United States, as a wealthy country, has had a policy of favoring the free flow of works of art into the United States. That policy contrasts with the policy of protecting the cultural heritage of individual nations through international cooperation. This chapter summarizes the law in this area and alerts the purchaser of works of art to the problem areas.[1]

CIVIL ACTIONS

Legal remedies available in the United States to foreign nations and citizens of foreign nations from which cultural property has been stolen or smuggled have proved to be cumbersome and inadequate. To recover smuggled property, the country of origin or the owners of title have to sue under the laws of the United States, prove title to the property and the right to possession, or prove that the defendant took the property without the plaintiff's consent.[2] In addition, the country of origin must bring its action within the time set by the applicable statute of limitations. If the claim of a foreign nation is based on a violation of its export restrictions, the foreign nation cannot recover the object or its value in the United States in the absence of treaties or other international agreements. A work of art is not illegally imported into the United States merely because it was exported in violation of another country's laws.[3] Further, the exporting nation that is claiming the rights of an owner of stolen art may not have standing to sue in the United States for the return of the work of art.[4]

Political and public pressure may be one of the best ways a nation has for retrieving stolen cultural property. For example, in October 1973 an important religious object of worship from the Kingdom of Kom in the United Republic of Cameroon was discovered in New York in the possession of a New York dealer. The object, the Afo-A-Kom, had been stolen by a member of the royal court and then sold to smugglers. After much publicity, the object was acquired by the Museum of African Art in Washington, D.C., from the dealer who had possession of it, and it was returned to the people of Kom. No lawsuit was filed.[5]

In *India v. Simon*[6] suit was brought by the government of India in London, New York, and Los Angeles against Norton Simon for the recovery of the tenth century religious sculpture Sivapuram Nataraja. That idol, smuggled from India twenty years earlier, surfaced in 1969, when it was purchased by the art dealer Ben Heller. An Indian export permit had been obtained, but the Indian government claimed that the permit was invalid, since it improperly described the object. Heller sold the idol to Norton Simon for $900,000. India sued Simon claiming title to the statue and alleging that Simon knew the statue was stolen when he bought it. The case was settled privately. Simon agreed to return the idol to India but retained the right to exhibit it for ten years.

Guatemala v. Hollinshead[7] was a civil court action brought by the government of Guatemala against Hollinshead, a dealer in pre-Columbian artifacts, to recover a Mayan stela. (The criminal action involved in the case is discussed below.) Guatemala had enacted a statute vesting ownership of all cultural property in the government to prevent the destruction of its historic and archaeological treasures. The statute enabled Guatemala to have standing to sue in a United States court. The case was settled out of court, and Guatemala recovered the work.

In both *India v. Simon* and *Guatemala v. Hollinshead*, the governments claimed title to the works of art and alleged that the works of art were illegally exported, as well as stolen. Although the governments in those cases were successful, civil actions for replevin are costly and time-consuming and provide only a limited remedy for the recovery of cultural property.[8]

CRIMINAL ACTIONS AND THE NATIONAL STOLEN PROPERTY ACT

The National Stolen Property Act (NSPA) makes it a federal crime to "transport in foreign commerce goods known to be stolen or to receive, conceal or sell such goods."[9] For many years that statute was routinely applied to stolen automobiles and appliances but not to cultural property (artifacts), since, in order to obtain a criminal conviction, the prosecutor must prove that the defendant had knowledge that the property was stolen. *United States v. Hollinshead*[10] was the first criminal conviction in the United States under the NSPA for the illegal transport of cultural property. Hollinshead, an art dealer, was charged with illegally transporting a Mayan stela in interstate commerce. Under Guatemalan law the stela was considered stolen property under a statute that vests ownership of all cultural property in the government. Hollinshead was convicted, and his conviction was affirmed. The Ninth Circuit Court of Appeals held that, since Hollinshead knew that the Mayan stela was stolen, it was not necessary for the prosecutor to prove that Hollinshead knew that the law of Guatemala vested title to the stela in the state.[11]

In 1979 the Fifth Circuit decided *United States v. McClain*,[12] finding that pre-Columbian artifacts from Mexico had been smuggled by individuals who had knowledge of the Mexican law concerning ownership of excavated and unexcavated materials from Mexico. The court upheld the criminal convictions, based on conspiracy to violate the NSPA, even though there was no evidence offered to show how the artifacts had been acquired from Mexico. The *McClain* case has been criticized, since it allows for the imposition of criminal sanctions without specific evidence that the defendant stole the work from the country of origin.[13] Since the NSPA is a criminal statute, it does not in and of itself guarantee seizure, forfeiture, or return of artifacts. Generally, the NSPA action is applied in conjunction with a technical customs law violation, such as an incorrect customs declaration, which allows the Customs Service to seize the artifacts and arrange for their return to the country of origin.

TREATY WITH MEXICO

The United States signed a treaty with Mexico in July 1970, that prohibits exportation of any pre-Columbian items from Mexico.[14] The treaty contains an agreement by the parties to use all the legal means at their disposal to recover and return stolen archaeological, historical, and cultural properties. No provision is made for compensation to innocent purchasers of those objects. Thus, any purchaser of important pre-Columbian art is subject to the risk that it will be seized and returned to Mexico without any compensation to the purchaser. The treaty states that regular customs procedures shall not be followed in regard to seized cultural property.

The United States entered into a similar agreement with Peru in 1981.[15]

PRE-COLUMBIAN STATUTE OF 1972

The Pre-Columbian Statute of 1972[16] authorizes seizure and forfeiture by the United States Customs Service under United States customs laws if any architectural sculpture or mural or fragment thereof from a pre-Columbian Indian culture enters the United States without a proper export license issued by the country of origin. The art covered by the statute does not have to be stolen to be considered illegally exported; thus, the statute gives effect to the export laws of thirteen Latin American countries. However, the statute only protects architectural sculptures or murals from a pre-Columbian Indian culture. The United States Customs Service may seize the art without prior request of the exporting country.

UNITED STATES CUSTOMS RULES

Anyone who imports works of art or cultural property into the United States must be familiar with the rules and regulations of the United States Customs Service.[17] The Customs Service not only enforces the import restrictions on cultural property described above but also favors the enforcement of the *McClain* case under the NSPA. A 1982 Customs directive instructs Customs officials to detain any pre-Columbian artifact from any Latin American country.[18]

Original works of art whose importation is not otherwise prohibited are exempt from any customs duty. Before 1959 there were interpretive problems as to whether specific objects could be classified as "art" and thus be exempt. In 1959 the Tariff Act was amended to broaden the definition of "art" so that works representing some school, kind, or medium of fine arts would be admitted duty-free. However, the collector of customs may require the importer to furnish proof by a museum or art expert that the item is art.

Replicas, reproductions, and copies are subject to customs duty. Customs regulations require that a declaration accompany the imported work of art.

UNESCO CONVENTION AND CULTURAL PROPERTY ACT

The 1970 United Nations Educational, Scientific, and Cultural Organization (UNESCO) Convention[19] is the most comprehensive international treaty dealing with the international trade of cultural property. Its purpose was "to provide a common framework among nations for alleviating abuses in the international trade of cultural property."[20] The UNESCO Convention resulted from a growing international concern that the high demand for cultural objects in the art market had generated rampant pillaging of archaeological and ethnological materials, particularly in countries with few resources to protect their cultural heritage. The United States ratified the UNESCO Convention in 1972.[21] As of December 1988 a total of sixty-four countries were parties to the UNESCO Convention.[22]

Under the UNESCO Convention, the member countries agreed:

- No article of cultural property that is documented as stolen from a member country and as belonging to a museum, or a religious or secular public monument, or similar institution may be imported into another member's country; and
- A member country whose archaeological or ethnological property that is a part of a country's national patrimony is in jeopardy from pillage may request the other member countries to impose import restrictions.[23]

Although the United States ratified the UNESCO Convention in 1972, it was not until 1983 that the necessary implementing legislation was passed that enabled the UNESCO Convention to apply to the United States.[24] A provision included in the Senate's ratification of the UNESCO Convention in 1972 stated that the United States understood that the convention was not self-executing and that formal ratification was not effective until Congress passed the implementing legislation. That it took the United States eleven years to pass the necessary implementation legislation is probably because the United States is a wealthy, art-importing country that favors the unrestricted import of art.[25]

The Cultural Property Act[26] was signed into law by President Ronald Reagan in January 1983. The United States instrument of acceptance was deposited with UNESCO and entered into force in December 1983. The Cultural Property Act implements articles 7 and 9 of the UNESCO Convention.

Article 7, as implemented by the Cultural Property Act, prohibits the importation of stolen cultural property into the United States if that property is part of the documented inventory of a museum or a religious or secular public monument or a similar institution. However, article 7 applies only to cultural property stolen after April 12, 1983, the effective date of the act.[27] Cultural property stolen before April 12, 1983, must be recovered through other means, as discussed in earlier sections of this chapter.

Article 9, as implemented by the Cultural Property Act, allows United States import restrictions to be applied to archaeological and ethnological materials that are part of a country's national patrimony that is in jeopardy from pillage. However, the import restrictions are available only to member countries of the UNESCO Convention and only after a specific request for that protection to cover listed artifacts has been submitted to the President of the United States. Once import restrictions are in place, the artifacts are denied entry into the United States unless the artifacts are accompanied by an export certificate issued by the country of origin. Restrictions may be imposed expeditiously in emergency situations.

The United States Information Agency is responsible for carrying out the presidential decision-making functions under the Cultural Property Act.[28] The United States Commissioner of Customs issued regulations under the Cultural Property Act that went into effect on March 31, 1986.[29] The first United States import restrictions were imposed on September 11, 1987, as a response to an emergency request submitted by the Government of El Salvador.[30]

The participation of the United States in the UNESCO Convention and the enactment of the Cultural Property Act are the result of many compromises between the competing interests of those favoring the unrestricted flow of cultural property into the United States and those wanting to protect a country's cultural heritage. The result is a statutory scheme that is cumbersome and difficult to implement.[31]

IMPORTATION OF NONCULTURAL PROPERTY

As previously noted, a work of art that is not cultural property is not illegally imported into the United States merely because it was exported in violation of another country's laws.[32] The case of *Jeanneret v. Vichey*[33] illustrates that principle. Anna Vichey, a United States citizen, inherited a painting by Henri Matisse from her father, who died in Italy. The painting was brought to the United States, and no export license or permit was obtained from the Italian government. There was extensive expert testimony as to whether or not an export license or permit was actually required under Italian law, and the court never decided the issue.[34] Anna Vichey subsequently sold the painting to Marie Jeanneret, an art dealer based in Geneva. Marie Jeanneret was unable to sell the painting and claimed that there was a cloud on its title, since no export license had been obtained, and Italy could then reclaim the painting if it ever entered Italy. Jeanneret sued Vichey on breach of express and implied warranties of title, false and fraudulent misrepresentation, and breach of contract. The lower court found for the plaintiff, Jeanneret, on the basis of a breach of an implied warranty of title and a breach of contract.

On appeal to the Second Circuit, the lower court was reversed. The Second Circuit held in 1982 that nothing showed that the defendant breached the warranty described in section 2-312(1)(a) of the Uniform Commercial Code.[35] The court found that the Italian government had neither a security interest in nor other lien or encumbrance on the painting. As long as the painting was not brought back to Italy, it could not be confiscated, and neither the owner nor a purchaser from her was subject to monetary liability to Italy. Notwithstanding the foregoing, the court noted that, if the painting could not be sold in the normal course of business because of the fear of a claim by the Italian government, indeed there was a cloud, if not on then, over the title. In reversing the lower court, the Second Circuit remanded the case for further proceedings that would produce more definitive evidence.

Prior to the commencement of a new trial, Jeanneret voluntarily withdrew the federal action after allegedly receiving a judgment in Italy which allowed her to sell the painting. Although under *Jeanneret v. Vichey* it is clear that failure to have an export license for a noncultural property work of art is not, in itself, a breach of warranty of title, it is recommended that a collector require the seller to produce the required export license to prevent any questions.

An interesting postscript to *Jeanneret v. Vichey* is the still pending New York State Court action in which Vichey sued Jeanneret for damages allegedly caused by malicious prosecution based upon criminal and civil complaints filed by Jeanneret in Switzerland and in Italy; and damages allegedly caused by Jeanneret's abuse of process in a former state court action and in the above discussed federal action. On October 4, 1988 the court denied Jeanneret's motion for summary judgment dismissing the complaint and held that Vichey has stated a cause of action for malicious prosecution and for abuse of process.[36] The case is still pending.

NOTES
to Chapter 6

1. *See* R. Duffy, Art Law: Representing Artists, Dealers and Collectors 343 (1977); Bator, *An Essay on the International Trade in Art*, 34 Stan. L. Rev. 275 (1982); McAlee, *From the Boston Raphael to Peruvian Pots: Limitations on the Importation of Art into the United States*, 85 Dick. L. Rev. 565 (1981); Hofkin, *The Cultural Property Act: The Art of Compromise*, 12 Colum. J.L. & Arts 423 (1988); Partington & Sage, *The American Reponse to the Recovery of Stolen and Illegally Exported Art: Should the American Courts Look to the Civil Law?*, 12 Colum. J.L. & Arts 395 (1988); Curbing Illicit Trade in Cultural Property: U.S. Assistance under the Convention on Cultural Property Implementation Act, U.S.I.A. (1988); J. Merryman & A. Elsen, Law, Ethics, and the Visual Arts 46-139 (2d ed. 1985) (containing a comprehensive discussion with citations on the illicit international trade in art).

2. Rogers, *The Legal Response to the Illicit Movement of Cultural Property*, 5 L. & Pol'y Int'l Bus. 932 (1973).

3. Bator, *supra* note 1, at 287.

4. McAlee, *supra* note 1, at 593; Hofkin, *supra* note 1, at 429.

5. *See* N.Y. Times, Oct. 25, 1973; Merryman & Elsen, *supra* note 1, at 56.

6. L. DuBoff, The Deskbook of Art Law 109-14 (1977 & Supp. 1984).

7. Guatemala v. Hollinshead, No. 6771 (Cal. Super. Ct. filed Dec. 29, 1972).

8. Hofkin, *supra* note 1, at 431.

9. 18 U.S.C. § 2314 (1982).

10. United States v. Hollinshead, 495 F.2d 1154 (9th Cir. 1974).

11. *Id.* at 1156.

12. United States v. McClain, 593 F.2d 658 (5th Cir. 1979). In United States v. McClain, 545 F.2d 988 (5th Cir. 1977), the court had initially reversed the conviction of the defendants on the ground that Mexico did not declare ownership of all pre-Columbian art until 1972.

13. *See* Hofkin, *supra* note 1, at 433.

14. Treaty of Cooperation for the Recovery and Return of Stolen Archaeological, Historical and Cultural Property, July 17, 1970, United States-Mexico, 22 U.S.T. 494, T.I.A.S. No. 7088.

15. Agreement with Peru for the Recovery and Return of Stolen Archaeological, Historical and Cultural Properties, Sept. 15, 1981, United States-Peru, T.I.A.S. No. 10136.

16. Importation of Pre-Columbian Monumental or Architectural Sculpture or Murals Act, 19 U.S.C. §§ 2091-2095 (1982).

17. 19 U.S.C. § 1202 (1982). *See* P. FELLER, U.S. CUSTOMS AND INTERNATIONAL TRADE GUIDE (1987).

18. *See* McAlee, *supra* note 1, at 834.

19. 1970 UNESCO Convention on the Means of Prohibiting and Preventing the Illicit Import, Export, and Transfer of Ownership of Cultural Property, 823 U.N.T.S. 231 (1972).

20. M. MALARO, A LEGAL PRIMER ON MANAGING MUSEUM COLLECTIONS 73 (1985).

21. S. Res. 374, 92d Cong., 2d Sess., 118 CONG. REC. 27,924-25 (1972).

22. *See* United States Information Agency booklet entitled, *Information on U.S. Assistance under the Convention on Cultural Property Implementation Act* (July 1988). The booklet is available by writing to the United States Information Agency, Cultural Property Staff, Ann J. Guthrie, Executive Director, 301 Fourth Street, S.W., Rm. 247, Washington, D.C. 20547.

23. *See* UNESCO Convention arts. 7(b)(1), 9, *supra* note 19.

24. See discussion below of the Cultural Property Implementation Act of 1983.

25. *See* Bator, *supra* note 1; *see also* McAlee, *supra* note 1.

26. Convention on Cultural Property Implementation Act, 19 U.S.C. § 2601 (1982). Hofkin, *supra* note 1, at 438, contains an excellent discussion of the mechanics of the Cultural Property Implementation Act.

27. *See supra* note 22.

28. Exec. Order No. 12555 (Mar. 1986).

29. 19 C.F.R. § 12.104 (1988).

30. *See supra* note 22, at 9.

31. *See* Hofkin, *supra* note 1, at 450, where she comments that the Cultural Property Act fails in its essential purpose.

32. *See supra* note 3.

33. Jeanneret v. Vichey, 693 F.2d 259 (2d Cir. 1982), *rev'g* 541 F. Supp. 80 (S.D.N.Y. 1982).

34. The expert testimony involved the application of the Regulations for the Execution of Law No. 364 of June 20, 1909, art. 129 of which required anyone desiring to export objects of historical, archaeological, paleontological, artistic, or numismatic interest to present them to a royal office for the exportation of antiquities and objects. The court also had to consider a statute of the Mussolini regime entitled, "Protection of items of artistic or historical interest," Law No. 1089 of June 1, 1939.

35. Section 2-312 of the UCC provides:

(1) Subject to subsection (2) there is in a contract for sale a warranty by the seller that

- (a) the title conveyed shall be good, and its transfer, rightful; and
- (b) the goods shall be delivered free from any security interest or other lien or encumbrance of which the buyer at the time of contracting has no knowledge. . . .

36. Vichey v. Jeanneret, N.Y.L.J., Oct. 4, 1988, at 21 (N.Y. Sup. Ct.).

Artists' Rights III

First Amendment Rights 7

FREEDOM OF EXPRESSION

A fundamental concern of the fine artist is whether the creation, exhibition, and placement of artwork is a protected form of speech. Although this area of art law is profoundly unsettled, the answer appears to be yes, with many qualifications, particularly in the placement of the artwork. Exacerbating this unsettled state of jurisprudence is the emergence of certain new art forms, such as site-specific art and graffiti art. Site-specific art, such as the recently notorious "Tilted Arc" by Richard Serra,[1] is generally viewed by the art community as being one of a piece with the environment for which it is specifically created; removal of the work from the environment is usually perceived by the artist as being a violation of the work. The creation and exhibition of graffiti art, now generally recognized as an authentic art form, is often stymied by the enactment of local antigraffiti ordinances.[2] This chapter explores the current state of the law and its limits as it relates to freedom of artistic expression.

Pure Speech, Visual Speech, and Conduct

Over the years, artistic expression has frequently been characterized as symbolic or visual speech, thus differentiating it from verbal or written communication, known as pure speech. Historically, distinctions have been drawn between the two types of speech, as well as between speech in general and physical conduct, another form of expression frequently protected by the first amendment.[3] Although the law has not been perfectly consistent, it can, in general, be said that of the three categories, pure speech traditionally has received the most protection under the Constitution. Visual speech, because of its greater immediate effect on the viewer and its less fundamental manner of expression, has generally been subjected to somewhat greater restriction than has pure speech. Physical conduct, the third category, has traditionally received the least protection.

Recently, there has been a tendency to treat cases involving either visual speech or physical conduct to the kind of first amendment analysis customarily applied to instances of pure speech,[4] with resolution under some of the same legal theories, but the protection of visual speech remains a largely unsettled body of law.

Art as Visual Speech

Far more than being merely decorative, works of fine art throughout history have served as powerful purveyors of political and religious ideas, as well as portrayers of social commentary and satire. From as early as the Paleolithic or Old Stone Age, about 20,000 years ago, when images of animals were painted, incised, or sculpted on the rock surfaces of caves, presumably as part of a magic ritual to ensure a successful hunt, to the later narrative scenes of biblical themes depicted in the vast and intricate wall mosaics of Early Christian art and to the still later frescoes by Michelangelo in the Sistine Chapel, art has been permeated with the religious ideas of those in power. Political ideology, too, has been protrayed in works of art. Witness, for example, the painting "The Death of Marat," depicting with stunning realism the death of one of the political leaders of the French Revolution and considered by many[5] to be the greatest picture by the artist Jacques-Louis David, an activist in the French Revolution. Social commentary has found voice in the paintings of such artists as Hieronymus Bosch, William Hogarth, Honore Daumier, and, in contemporary times, Andy Warhol. In Warhol's "Race Riot" series—his work that incorporates a photograph of a middle-aged, white policeman, perhaps symbolizing state power and authority, juxtaposed with a news photo portraying black protesters injured by police during a race riot—the artist rendered critical commentary on the values depicted by the component images.[6] Satire, too, is evident in works of art: one of the most famous examples is Picasso's masterpiece, "Guernica," a notorious and powerful expression of the horrors of war and a denunciation of those responsible for it.

The courts, perhaps adhering to the echoes of history, have been inclined in recent years to grant constitutional protection to works of art possessing such communicative objectives.

Ideas

In one instance,[7] the court found that a proposed mural portraying the difficulties of Mexican-American laborers was a form of expression entitled to protection under the Constitution. There, the plaintiffs—members of a community organization in Illinois promoting Hispanic culture and the artist engaged by the organization to paint a mural depicting the struggles of Mexican-American laborers—leased an outside wall of a restaurant for the mural, and secured a grant from a state agency to finance the project. The defendants—who included the mayor, the building commissioner, and other local officials—sought to prohibit the creation of the mural by means of local city ordinances regulating the size and the location of signs, including advertising and business signs.

Holding for the plaintiffs, the court observed that the mural did not direct attention to a product, person, or institution, but, rather, sought to portray an idea, precisely the sort of expression that, the court noted, is protected by the first amendment from government interference. The court also indicated that the defendants were misapplying an ordinance that regulates commercial communication only and were thereby threatening the plaintiffs' free exercise of their right to communicate.

Social Commentary

Lawsuits attempting to restrain visual expression have proliferated in recent years; they have used a variety of theories, ranging from defamation to copyright and trademark infringement. In one notable case,[8] the defendant published a picture of figures resembling the plaintiff's trade characters "Poppin' Fresh" and "Poppie Fresh" engaged in sexual intercourse and fellatio. Also featured in the picture were the plaintiff's barrelhead trademark and its jingle, the refrain of a two-stanza song entitled "The Pillsbury Baking Song."

In bringing suit against the defendant, the plaintiff alleged, among other claims, several counts of copyright infringement, trademark infringement, and tarnishment of its trade characters.

The court found that there was no tortious tarnishment of trade characters and no trademark infringement, but it did find that several of the plaintiff's copyrights were, in fact, infringed. However, the court determined that the defendant's use of the plaintiff's copyrighted works was protected under the fair use doctrine. In so concluding, the court noted that the defendant's use was "more in the nature of an editorial or social commentary than . . . an attempt to capitalize financially on the plaintiff's original work"[9] and that, although the "court does not condone the manner in which [the defendant] chose to assault the corporate citadel . . . value judgments have no place in this analysis."[10]

Visual speech as a vehicle for social commentary was again affirmed in the slightly later case of *Silberman v. Georges.*[11] "The Mugging of the Muse," a painting by the artist Paul Georges, was intended to criticize the aesthetic views of several of the artist's New York colleagues, who subsequently brought suit in defamation. Apparently, the plaintiffs and the defendant, all artists known in the art world and friends for some time, parted ways after a dispute over refinements of respective views concerning aspects of their art. Amidst those troubled relationships, the defendant painted the offending picture, depicting an apparent attempted assassination of a scantily clad woman on a city street by three men armed with knives. The painting was exhibited before the Alliance of Figurative Artists. The two plaintiffs claimed that they were depicted in the painting by the masks on the faces of the two downstage assassins; that, being equated with muggers and robbers, they were held up to ridicule and scorn; that they had been accused of criminal conduct; and that their reputations had been impaired. The defendant averred that the portrayal was allegorical only and constituted no more than an expression of opinion. The appellate court, reversing the decision of the lower court, agreed with the defendant, finding the painting to be nothing more than "rhetorical hyperbole," and dismissed the case. The court wrote: "Far worse commentary is written almost daily by newspaper and magazine critics of every aspect of the arts and is deemed to be no more than an expression of opinion."[12] Further, the court found no proof that the plaintiffs were injured by exhibition of the painting, nor of malice, as defined by New York law, on the part of the defendant.

Satire

From the earliest drawings on cave walls, caricature has been used throughout the ages to express opinions on matters of public interest. Thus, Hogarth in eighteenth-century England and Daumier in nineteenth-century France produced critical and satirical commentary on the social and political issues of the day. However, unlike Daumier, who was imprisoned for six months for directing a satirical cartoon at King Louis Philippe,[13] practitioners of visual satire in the United States have significant constitutional protection. That protection enabled the caricaturist Thomas Nast, for example, in the 1870s to help destroy the corrupt political regime of "Boss" Tweed and the Tammany Ring by means of a series of deadly political cartoons.

Nevertheless, the limits of constitutional protection of visual satire are tested from time to time. One example of such testing is the well-known case of *Yorty v. Chandler*,[14] in which Samuel Yorty, who was then mayor of Los Angeles and apparently interested in being appointed to President Nixon's cabinet as Secretary of Defense, sued the *Los Angeles Times*, its parent company, and the artist Paul Conrad on charges of defamation. It seems that in November 1968 the paper published on its editorial page a cartoon depicting Mayor Yorty seated at his office desk talking on the telephone and surrounded by four white-coated medical orderlies. One orderly is holding a straitjacket behind his back while another beckons the mayor with his finger. The caption reads, "I've got to go now. . . . I've been appointed Secretary of Defense and the Secret Service men are here!"

Yorty alleged, among other contentions, that the defendants intended to intimate to their readers that he was unfit to serve as Secretary of Defense and that, because he believed he was so qualified, he was mentally ill. The trial court dismissed the complaint, and the appellate court affirmed the dismissal, concluding that the cartoon was not reasonably susceptible to the interpretation placed on it by the plaintiff. In the course of its reasoning, the court noted that a cartoon, like any other form of depiction or representation, may be found defamatory if it maliciously presents as fact derogatory material that is false.[15] But because, as the court further noted, a political cartoon presents critical opinion in imaginative and symbolic form, a court must ferret out the underlying themes of the cartoon in cases of alleged defamation and determine whether those themes can reasonably be considered libelous.[16] Given, as the court reasoned, that mere expressions of opinion, no matter how critical, are not defamatory and further, as the court found, that the defendants published not a factual report of news intended to be read at face value but, rather, a cartoon intended to present an editorial comment on the mayor's qualifications for high national office, it is clear why the court dismissed the case.

In another case involving an effort to curb visual expression,[17] the artist John Sefick brought suit against the city of Chicago and its officials, requesting that the defendants be compelled to display one of his exhibits, consisting of three life-size plaster figures in a Chicago version of Grant Wood's famous painting, "American Gothic." The tableau, entitled "The Bilandics," satirized the handling by then-mayor Michael Bilandic of the snow-removal operation in Chicago necessitated by the city's record snowfall in the winter of 1979. The tableau depicted Bilandic seated in an easy chair, with his wife, Heather, on the arm of the chair and a child nearby. A tape recording accompanying the tableau portrayed the mayor commenting on the heavy snowfall, telling Heather to put another log on the fire, and asking her what they should do about the snow.

Sefick, an artist specializing in environmental sculpture, had exhibited his works in a number of establishments in and around Chicago and had received permission to exhibit some of his work for a three-week period at the city's Richard J. Daley Civic Center. After his proposal had been approved, Sefick supplied the appropriate city official with more detailed information concerning the intended exhibits. Three separate tableaux were to be exhibited, one at a time for a week each. On the second exhibition day of the offending tableau, Sefick was notified that it was unsuitable for display in the Daley Center and that it would have to be removed. Meanwhile, the city placed a blanket over the exhibit to prevent others from viewing it. Sefick brought suit, and the court, in determining that the tableau "constitutes speech within the meaning of the first amendment,"[18] ordered the city of Chicago to honor its commitment to exhibit the work.

In so holding, the court noted that although the city was under no constitutional compulsion to provide a public forum for art exhibits, once the public display area in the Daley Center was voluntarily opened to such exhibits, constitutional guarantees come into play.[19] The court further noted that—in those circumstances not involving obscenity, defamation, speech creating a clear and present danger to other individuals, or regulations involving the manner, time, and place of speech—a government body cannot ordinarily select which issues are worth discussing or which views should be heard when public facilities are involved.[20] As the court acknowledged, that does not mean that the government is completely powerless to regulate speech; rather, the government must show that the regulation is in furtherance of a substantial governmental interest and not merely the product of disagreement with the message of the speaker.[21]

The court's holding in the Bilandic case should influence the result in an ongoing suit also in Chicago involving many of the same issues. In the case now pending,[22] the plaintiff, David Nelson, a graduating student of the School of the Art Institute of Chicago (SAIC) participated in May 1988 in a three-day private exhibition of student artwork held by and at the school. In accordance with SAIC practice, Nelson selected those of his works he wished to exhibit, including a painting depicting the late Chicago Mayor Harold Washington wearing women's undergarments.

On May 11, 1988, during the first day of the exhibit, a few Chicago police officers and Chicago aldermen, allegedly acting under color of state law, entered the SAIC, viewed the painting, disapproved of it, seized it, and removed it from the premises. On the following day, after the defendants' refusal to return the painting, the plaintiff retained counsel and demanded the painting's return from the city's Corporation Counsel. Later that evening, the painting was returned to the plaintiff bearing a conspicuous gash.

The plaintiff brought suit for declaratory judgment and damages, alleging, among other claims, violation of his first amendment rights of free expression, as well as damage to his professional reputation, mental and emotional distress, humiliation, and embarrassment. The case is currently pending in an Illinois federal district court.

On the basis of the facts alleged in the complaint, it seems that the plaintiff-artist stands on solid ground. The painting, although offensive to some, cannot be considered obscene, nor did it cause a threat of civil unrest or disturbance beyond the ability of the police to control, nor could defamation be an issue here, since the deceased cannot be defamed. The defendants were allegedly acting under color of state law and, as noted in the Bilandic case, the government, if it is to regulate speech, must show that such regulation furthers a substantial governmental interest and is not merely the product of disagreement with the message of the speaker. Finally, the painting was displayed in a private exhibition; no one needed to be a captive audience[23] to it, and those who were offended could have easily avoided it.

However, it remains to be seen what direction the court will take in the determination of this case.

THE FLAG AS A VEHICLE OF PROTEST

An array of cases heard by the courts involving art and other exhibitions of the American flag in various guises, as well as conduct involving the American flag, have thrown into sharp relief the following issues: (1) whether art is entitled to constitutional consideration as visual speech and (2) whether conduct may be entitled to such consideration. In recent years, until June 1989 the courts, led by the United States Supreme Court, have generally held that—absent a showing of obscenity, violation of flag desecration statutes, or an indication that the public health, safety, or well-being of a community is threatened—visual speech or conduct having a clearly communicative aspect is entitled to constitutional protection, no matter how obnoxious it may be to the prevailing views of the majority.

Then in the case of *Texas v. Gregory Lee Johnson*,[24] discussed below, the United States Supreme Court, evoking a storm of controversy, ruled in June 1989 that no laws could prohibit political protesters from burning the American flag. The 5–4 decision threw into question the constitutionality of the flag-desecration laws of forty-eight states as well as a similar federal statute as to instances of peaceful political expression.[25] Only Alaska and Wyoming do not make flag-burning a crime.

The Flag, Conduct, and Constitutional Protection

One of the purposes of a flag-desecration statute is to ensure the preservation of the public peace.[26] The federal law, which has made it a crime publicly to mutilate the American flag, reads in part as follows:

> Whoever knowingly casts contempt upon any flag of the United States by publicly mutilating, defacing, defiling, burning, or trampling upon it shall be fined not more than $1,000 or imprisoned for not more than one year, or both.[27]

New York's statute,[28] fairly representative of state enactments, provides, in substance, that any person who, for exhibition or display, places a mark or design on the American flag or the state flag, or who exhibits or sells an article of merchandise bearing a representation of the flag, or who publicly mutilates, defiles, tramples on, or casts contempt on the flag shall be guilty of a misdemeanor.

Over the years the courts have heard a variety of cases addressing flag-related conduct, many of those cases involving the particular state's flag-desecration statute. Thus, in *People v. Street*[29] the United States Supreme Court reversed the conviction of a defendant who, on hearing of the shooting of the civil rights leader James Meredith, burned an American flag on a street corner, saying, "We don't need no damn flag." The reversal rested on the fact that it could not be determined which part of Street's conviction was based on uttering constitutionally protected words and which part was based on his act of setting fire to the flag, and thus the conviction could not be upheld. However, the Court expressly left open the question of the validity of Street's conviction insofar as it was sustained on the basis of flag burning "even though the burning was an act of protest."[30] The case was remanded to the New

York Court of Appeals, and a new trial was ordered, solely for the defendant's act of burning the flag. In subsequent years, convictions in state courts for violating flag-desecration statutes were obtained for, among other acts, the displaying on the same staff and above the American flag of a Communist-type flag with a hammer and sickle, [31] the wearing of a vest from a cut-up American flag,[32] the hanging and displaying of an American flag covered with red-brownish paint,[33] and the burning of an American flag.[34] Of course, these and other convictions for similar violations of the flag-desecration statutes will have to be reassessed in light of the June 1989 ruling in *Texas v. Gregory Lee Johnson.*

However, even prior to this ruling, flag-desecration statutes were not sacrosanct. For example, the Massachusetts statute was held to be unconstitutional when applied to a person wearing a "small cloth version of the American flag on the seat of his pants."[35] A provision in New Jersey's statute requiring school students to show respect for the flag by standing at attention during the pledge of allegiance was found unconstitutional,[36] as was the application of Georgia's statute to a protestor who burned an American flag in protest of United States policy toward Iran, where there was no clear and present danger of imminent public unrest.[37]

In 1974, the United States Supreme Court reversed a state court conviction of a defendant who had been found guilty of violating a Washington statute proscribing improper uses of the flag.[38] The defendant Spence, a college student, in protest against the then recent invasion of Cambodia by the United States and the killings at Kent State University, had hung a United States flag from his apartment window in an upside-down position and attached on both of its sides a peace symbol fashioned of removable black tape. The Court, in holding for the defendant, adopted a two-step analysis: first, a determination of whether flag-related conduct is within the protections of the first amendment and, second, whether, in a given case, the state's interests are so substantial as to justify an infringement of constitutional rights. The Court found that Spence's use of the flag constituted the expression of an idea through activity and that his conduct was sufficiently communicative to bring it within the ambit of constitutionally protected speech. Moreover, the Court found that no state interest had been sufficiently impaired by Spence's activity to warrant the imposition of criminal sanctions.[39]

Other conduct not directly related to the American flag has also been held sufficiently communicative to find protection under the first amendment. Thus, a daily ceremony conducted by a defendant at a children's summer camp during which the children raised the Soviet flag and pledged allegiance to it was permitted to continue.[40] Reversing a conviction for that action under a California statute making it a criminal offense to display a red flag as a symbol of opposition to organized government, an invitation to anarchistic action, or an aid to propaganda of a seditious character, the Supreme Court found that, if the defendant had been convicted for flying the flag as a symbol of opposition, her first amendment right to freedom of expression had been breached.[41] Other constitutionally protected conduct includes nude dancing in a business establishment,[42] verbal criticism and challenge directed at police officers in the performance of their duty,[43] all musical expression,[44] the wearing of black armbands to school by students to protest the Vietnam War,[45] vulgar gestures made by a student toward a teacher off school grounds and after school hours,[46] and peaceful leafleting and picketing.[47]

Nevertheless, not all forms of conduct, however communicative, have found constitutional protection. In *O'Brien v. United States*,[48] for example, the defendant O'Brien had publicly burned his draft card on the South Boston courthouse steps, thereby attracting a crowd, and the Supreme Court held that a federal statute proscribing the destruction of draft cards was not an unconstitutional abridgement of freedom of speech.

O'Brien contended, among other points, that the action he took with his draft card was a communication of his ideas about the conduct of the war and the draft, but the Court responded as follows:

> [E]ven on the assumption that the alleged communicative element in O'Brien's conduct is sufficient to bring into play the First Amendment, it does not necessarily follow that the destruction of a registration certificate is constitutionally protected activity. . . . [A] government regulation is sufficiently justified if it is within the constitutional power of the Government; if it furthers an important or substantial governmental interest; if the governmental interest is unrelated to the suppression of free expression; and if the incidental restriction on alleged First Amendment freedoms is no greater than is essential to the furtherance of that interest.[49]

The standard set forth in *O'Brien* was referred to but not applied in the recent, previously noted case of *Texas v. Gregory Lee Johnson*.[50] There the United States Supreme Court affirmed a state appeals court's overturn of a conviction on constitutional grounds. The defendant Gregory Johnson, during the 1984 Republican National Convention, in participating in a political demonstration to protest the policies of the Reagan administration and some Dallas-based corporations, burned an American flag while protesters chanted "America, the red, white and blue, we spit on you."[51] In holding that Johnson's conviction of flag desecration was inconsistent with the first amendment, the United States Supreme Court determined that Texas did not assert an interest in support of Johnson's conviction that was

> unrelated to the suppression of expression and would therefore permit application of the test set forth in *United States v. O'Brien* whereby an important governmental interest in regulating nonspeech can justify incidental limitations on First Amendment freedoms when speech and nonspeech elements are combined in the same course of conduct.[52]

Exhibition of the Flag as Art

In a number of instances, state and federal courts have granted constitutional protection to the use of the American flag as art.

Thus, the exhibition of photographs of a nude woman draped with an American flag has passed constitutional muster,[53] as did, ultimately, the exhibition at an art gallery of three-dimensional works of the American flag in the forms of a phallic symbol, a human form hanging from a noose, and a gun caisson wrapped in a flag. However, in that case, involving Stephen Radich, the proprietor of a New York City art gallery,[54] vindication was nearly seven years in coming.

In December 1966, Radich displayed in his second-floor Madison Avenue art gallery three-dimensional constructions by the artist Marc Morrel, partly composed of portions of the United States flag and partly of other objects, including a Vietcong flag, a Russian flag, a Nazi swastika, and a gas mask. Three of the thirteen art works in the exhibit were singled out for particular attention by the state courts: an object resembling a gun caisson wrapped in a flag, a flag stuffed into the shape of a six-foot human form hanging by the neck from a yellow noose, and a seven-foot "cross with a bishop's mitre on the head-piece, the arms wrapped in ecclesiastical flags and an erect penis wrapped in an American flag protruding from the vertical standard."[55] Both Radich and Hilton Kramer, art news editor of the *New York Times*, asserted that in their expert opinions the constructions were, by contemporary standards, art. Radich also asserted that he intended no disrespect for the American flag; rather, the constructions were intended solely to express protest against the American involvement in Vietnam and against war in general. Radich further testified that during the exhibition antiwar protest music, audible throughout the entire gallery, was played from a tape recorder.

Radich was convicted in the New York City Criminal Court of violating the state's flag-desecration statute. The conviction was affirmed by New York's appellate courts and again by the United States Supreme Court. When he applyed for habeas corpus relief in the United States District Court for the Southern District of New York, Radich was vindicated. The federal court found that New York's flag-desecration statute was unconstitutional as it applied to him. In its reasoning, the court, as had the Supreme Court in the *Spence* case,[56] addressed three principal issues that could have conceivably justified state action against flag desecration:

1. Prevention of breach of the peace,
2. Protection of the sensibilities of passersby, and
3. Preservation of the American flag as an unalloyed symbol of our country.

In vindicating Radich, the federal court: (1) was unable to find any objective evidence that a breach of the peace was either likely to occur or an imminent result of Radich's exhibition; (2) noted that Radich did not thrust his ideas on a captive audience, but, rather, displayed the constructions in the privacy of his second-floor art gallery; and (3) found that—unlike the flag that is burned, destroyed, or otherwise permanently disfigured—the flag as used by the artist was simply transferred as a symbol from its traditional surroundings to the realm of protest and dissent, which did not rob the flag of its universal symbolism.[57]

EMBLEMS AND INSIGNIA

Federal law limits the right of persons to reproduce or use the following emblems, insignia, characters, and names:

- The manufacture, sale, or possession of any badge, identification card, or other insignia, of the design prescribed by the head of any department or agency of the United States for use by any officer or employee thereof, or any colorable imitation thereof is prohibited.[58] The making of any print, photograph, engraving, or impression thereof is also prohibited.[59]
- The wearing, manufacture, or sale of any armed forces decoration or medal or any "colorable imitation thereof" is prohibited.[60]
- The manufacture, reproduction, sale, or purchase for

resale of any badge, medal, emblem, or other insignia or any colorable imitation thereof, of any veterans' organization incorporated by enactment of Congress is prohibited.[61] One who knowingly prints, lithographs, engraves or otherwise reproduces on any poster, circular, periodical, magazine, newspaper, or other publication, or circulates or distributes any such printed matter bearing a reproduction of such badge, medal, emblem or other insignia or any colorable imitation thereof, except when authorized under rules and regulations prescribed by any such organization is subject to fine or imprisonment or both.[62]

- The use of the emblem of a Greek red cross on a white ground or any sign or insignia made or colored in imitation thereof or the words "Red Cross" or "Geneva Cross" or any combination of these words is prohibited.[63]
- The use of the 4-H Club emblem or any sign, insignia, or symbol in colorable imitation thereof, or the words "4-H Club" or "4-H Clubs" or any combination of these or other words or characters in colorable imitation thereof is prohibited.[64]
- The manufacture, reproduction, or use of the characters or the names "Smokey the Bear" or "Woodsy Owl" is prohibited without appropriate authorization.[65]
- The display of the seal of the President or the Vice President of the United States or any facsimile thereof for the purpose of conveying the false impression of sponsorship or approval by the United States government is prohibited.[66] The manufacture, reproduction, sale, or purchase for resale of reproductions of those seals or any article to which is appended any likeness of those seals is prohibited unless authorized under regulations promulgated by the President.[67]
- The manufacture, reproduction, or use of the Golden Eagle insignia "in such a manner as is likely to cause confusion, or to cause mistake, or to deceive" is prohibited.[68]

In light of the *Spence* and *Radich* decisions discussed earlier, it could be argued that the constitutionality of the restrictions imposed on the reproduction and the use of any particular emblem, insignia, characters, or name must be determined by considering the validity of the governmental interest involved and the nature of the use to which the reproduction is placed.

State laws also generally prohibit the use or the reproduction of certain signs and emblems. For example, under New York law it is a violation for anyone to willfully wear or attach to any motor vehicle, unless entitled to do so, any badge, insignia, or emblem of the Police Conference of New York, the New York State Fire Fighters Association, any order recognized as Masonic by the Grand Lodge of Free and Accepted Masons of the State of New York, the Order of the Eastern Star of the State of New York, and the like.[69]

GRAFFITI ART

Although graffiti are generally considered an authentic form of art, that does not mean that their application goes totally unfettered. As the existence of flag-desecration statutes prohibits certain artistic creations, so, too, do local antigraffiti ordinances restrict the creation and display of graffiti art.[70]

PUBLIC ART

There is frequently an innate conflict between the rights of the majority users of public space and the rights of an artist to that space. The conflict brings into play issues of the artist's first amendment rights of expression versus claims of public nuisance and aesthetic and environmental objections. It is clear that an artist has no absolute right to exhibit in a particular place.[71] Indeed, in the long-awaited decision in the "Tilted Arc" case,[72] the United States Court of Appeals for the Second Circuit affirmed a decision by the district court, finding that the first amendment has only limited application in the case in which artistic expression belongs to the government, rather than a private individual.[73]

In *Serra*, the plaintiff-artist was commissioned by the General Services Administration to create a sculpture for the plaza of the Jacob K. Javits Federal Building at 26 Federal Plaza in lower Manhattan. The sculpture, a 120-foot-long piece of steel twelve feet tall that bisected the plaza, was installed in 1981. Almost immediately after its installation, the General Services Administration received a considerable number of complaints concerning the presence of the work, characterizing it as an obstruction. In 1985, the regional administrator of the General Services Administration announced that he might have the work removed because it obstructed the plaza, and the next year, after a public hearing, the agency recommended its removal. In his suit against the Government, the artist, Richard Serra, claimed that the three-day hearing before a five-member panel named by the General Services Administration regional administrator was biased and that his rights to due process were violated. In the decision of the court of appeals, the judges ruled that "pursuant to Serra's contract, the sculpture is the property of GSA, not the artist."[74] In addition, the court noted that

> Government can be a significant patron of the arts. Its incentive to fulfill that role must not be dampened by unwarranted restrictions on its freedom to decide what to do with the art it has purchased.[75]

Attempts to use public space for temporary artistic expression have, in the United States, met with mixed results. The artist Christo, for example, was able to realize the fulfillment of such projects as "Valley Curtain," in which a curtain was hung across a deep valley in Colorado, and "Running Fence," in which a fence of white nylon fabric was run across twenty-four miles of Marin County. In all his pieces, it should be noted, the controversy involved in securing legal permission from public and private parties is viewed as part of the performance of the artwork. Indeed, the obtaining of public support and involvement in realizing each project is a crucial element of the creative process.[76] Although the actual physical presence of the works is of brief duration, permanence is achieved through the filmed record of each installation process.[77] Because Christo uses only private funds to support his work, it seldom becomes a major political issue. However, that is not always the case when other considerations come to the fore, as happened in a recently attempted project of his, "The Gates." Christo proposed to install in New York City's Central Park between 11,000 and 15,000 steel-supported, golden-orange banners on twenty-five miles of park pathways for a two-week period in the autumn sometime between 1982 and 1985. In denying Christo's permit application, the city parks and recreation commissioner felt, as guardian of the physical space of Central Park, an obligation to protect the park's structure from "the substantial unknown risks inevitable in such a venture."[78]

LIMITATIONS ON FREEDOM OF EXPRESSION

As has been noted earlier, the first amendment does not constitute an unbridled license for freedom of expression.[79] Clearly, an artist may not damage private or public property in the name of artistic expression; injury to private property would constitute a trespass, enabling the owner to enjoin the activity and recover damages from the artist; damage to public property is usually a crime under the laws of the applicable jurisdiction. Moreover, the laws against obscenity, defamation,[80] invasion of privacy, and speech and conduct likely to cause a breach of the peace provide limits, albeit evolving ones, within which constitutionally protected expression must fall. The remainder of this chapter explores both the limitations of constitutional expression and the emerging trends in the laws limiting the scope of the first amendment.

Obscenity

Many states, recognizing the artist's need of freedom of expression to create, have enacted either broad policy statements addressing the freedom of artistic expression or exceptions to state obscenity laws for artistic works.[81] Other states assign to their arts councils the task of preserving the freedom of artistic expression.[82] That said, it must nevertheless be acknowledged that the Supreme Court has several times altered its view of what may be deemed obscene and that there has always been some line of demarcation beyond which visual representations may not go. A capsulization of the law of obscenity as it has evolved over the past twenty years follows.

Evolution of the Current Guidelines

Although the Supreme Court has endeavored to deal with the problem, it has never managed to provide a concise definition of obscenity. Obscenity was in 1957 held by the Supreme Court to be outside of the protection of the first amendment in *Roth v. United States*.[83] There, in affirming a conviction of a New York publisher and distributor of books, photographs, and magazines for violating a federal obscenity statute by mailing obscene circulars and advertising an obscene book, the Court attempted to set a standard for defining obscenity—that is,

> whether to the average person, applying contemporary community standards, the dominant theme of the material taken as a whole appeals to prurient interest.[84]

A final aspect of the allegedly obscene material to be considered was whether it had "even the slightest redeeming social importance."[85] If it did, the material was constitutionally protected. In a subsequent case,[86] the Court in 1964 held that the standards referred to in *Roth* were national, rather than local, community standards.

In 1966 in *Memoirs v. Massachusetts*,[87] in which the Attorney General of Massachusetts sought to have the book *Fanny Hill* declared obscene, the Supreme Court refused to do so, holding that the mere risk that a work may be exploited by panderers because of its pervasive treatment of sexual matters is not sufficient to make it obscene. Rather, the Court held that, to establish obscenity, the prosecution must prove three separate elements:

1. the dominant theme of the material taken as a whole appeals to a prurient interest in sex;
2. the material is patently offensive because it affronts contemporary community standards relating to the description or representation of sexual matters; and
3. the material is utterly without redeeming social value.[88]

However, in 1973 the test of *Memoirs* was modified substantially, and the national interpretation of standards was overruled.

The Current Test

In *Miller v. California*,[89] the appellant had been convicted under California law for the unsolicited mailing of obscene material. The Supreme Court noted that the context of review was a limited one, involving the interest of a state to prohibit the dissemination of obscene material when the mode of distribution carries with it the "significant danger of offending the sensibilities of unwilling recipients or of exposure to juveniles."[90]

However, following an interval of nearly eight years after it announced the *Memoirs* test, the Court, unhappy with the abstract nature of the guidelines established for determining obscenity, decided to try again. Thus, *Miller* held that, henceforth, whether a work is adjudged obscene depends on:

- Whether "the average person, applying contemporary community standards" would find that the work, taken as a whole, appeals to the prurient interest;

- Whether the work depicts or describes, in a patently offensive way, sexual conduct specifically defined by the applicable state law; and
- Whether the work, taken as a whole, lacks serious literary, artistic, political, or scientific value.[91]

From those new guidelines emerged two significant revisions in the constitutional standards. First, the Court totally rejected the *Memoirs* requirement that a work must be "utterly without redeeming social value" in order to be obscene; in doing so, it noted that the *Memoirs* test, in calling on the prosecution to prove a negative—that is, that the material was "utterly without redeeming social value"[92]—placed on it a burden virtually impossible under our criminal standards of proof.[93] The Court also concluded that the *Memoirs* test too readily permitted an opportunity for the exploitation of obscene works:

> Sex and nudity may not be exploited without limit by films or pictures exhibited or sold in places of public accommodation any more than live sex and nudity can be exhibited or sold without limit in such public places. At a minimum, prurient, patently offensive depiction or description of sexual conduct must have serious literary, artistic, political or scientific value to merit First Amendment protection.[94]

Second, the Court promulgated the local community standard guideline, so that a work not considered obscene in one state or county or town may constitutionally be considered obscene in another.

> It is neither realistic nor constitutionally sound to read the First Amendment as requiring that the people of Maine or Mississippi accept public depiction of conduct found tolerable in Las Vegas or New York City. . . . People in different states vary in their tastes and attitudes, and this diversity is not to be strangled by the absolutism of imposed uniformity.[95]

The community-standards guideline, however, did not provide the states with free rein to set their own standards of obscenity, nor was that the Court's intention. As the Court made clear in "prong (b)" of the three-pronged standard, only materials depicting sexual conduct can be limited by obscenity regulation. Although the Court did not attempt to propose specific regulatory guidance for states faced with conforming their obscenity statutes to the Miller guidelines, it did provide several examples of the type of sexual conduct of which the depiction or description could be properly regulated by state law:

- Patently offensive representations or descriptions of ultimate sexual acts, normal or perverted, actual or simulated; and
- Patently offensive representation or descriptions of masturbation, excretory functions, and lewd exhibition of the genitals.[96]

The Court, on several occasions, also made it clear that it considered only hard-core pornography to be obscene and, therefore, subject to regulation by the states. The Court characterized its holding in *Miller* and its companion cases,[97] known as the *Miller* "quintuplets,"[98] as insuring that henceforth

> no one will be subject to prosecution for the sale or exposure of obscene materials unless these materials depict or describe patently offensive "hard core" sexual conduct specifically defined by the regulating state law, as written or construed.[99]

Aftermath of Miller

The years after *Miller* have found the state courts wrestling with the new standards for determining obscenity established in that landmark case. Some of the great difficulties posed for the states have been in attempting to define what constitutes a community for the purposes of ascertaining its moral standards[100] and in drafting a state statute that would comply with the Supreme Court's specificity requirement.[101] In addition, courts grappled with the extent of the discretion permitted communities in determining what is obscene. A notorious example of that issue is encapsulated in *Jenkins v. Georgia*,[102] noted below.

In *Jenkins v. Georgia*, the Supreme Court reversed a conviction of the manager of a theater in Albany, Georgia, for the showing of the film "Carnal Knowledge," which the trial jury deemed to be obscene. The Supreme Court, in finding that there was nothing patently offensive about the film, rejected the argument of the state of Georgia that the trial jury's determination of the issue is conclusive. The Court stated:

> Even though questions of appeal to the "prurient interest" or of "patent offensiveness" are "essentially questions of fact," it would be a serious misreading of *Miller* to conclude that juries have unbridled discretion in determining what is "patently offensive." Not only did we there say that "the First Amendment values applicable to the States through the Fourteenth Amendment are adequately protected by the ultimate power of appellate courts to conduct an independent review of constitutional claims when necessary" [citation omitted] but we made it plain that under the holding "no one will be subject to prosecution for sale or exposure of obscene materials unless these materials depict or describe patently offensive 'hard core' sexual conduct. . . ."[103]

In the course of its opinion in *Jenkins*, the Court noted that so long as hard-core pornography is involved, the states can define obscenity in terms of local community standards either specifically or by referring the issue to the understanding of the local jury. Since, however, the motion picture "Carnal Knowledge" did not involve, in the Court's view, the public depiction of hard-core sexual behavior for its own sake and for ensuring commercial gain, made punishable by *Miller*, the conviction could not stand.[104]

Many of the appellate decisions following *Miller* appear to focus on the method of determining community standards. Although no definitive rule has emerged, a number of jurisdictions appear to prefer statistical evidence to indicate a community's acceptance of certain materials. For example, it was found that a

Texas trial court had erroneously excluded a Harris County theater operator's statistical evidence of community patronage of "Deep Throat" (a film comparable to that shown by the defendant), offered as circumstantial evidence of contemporary community standards.[105] Ultimately, however, trial judges retain a considerable degree of discretion as to the relevance of tendered evidence.[106] But however such community standards are determined, the question of a work's obscenity rests on the local standards of that community in which the work is located or displayed. Thus, a fine-art multiple produced in an edition of 200 and marketed nationwide may be subjected to as many as 200 local community standards, as well as the federal standard under the Comstock Act.[107] A copy of the work not considered obscene in New York City may be considered obscene, for instance, in Cheyenne, Wyoming.

The method of marketing a work of art may also be of special significance in determining the issue of its obscenity. If pandering is present, the work will most likely be considered obscene. Pandering is defined as "the business of purveying textual or graphic matter openly advertised to appeal to the erotic interest of their customers."[108] Thus, it is conceivable that a jury may determine that a work of art has some slight artistic value, but, nevertheless, find the dealer in whose gallery it is exhibited guilty because the artwork was solely advertised and promoted as sexually provocative.[109]

Sale or Distribution Versus Private Possession

The Court has restricted the application of obscenity statutes when the materials in question are privately possessed. In *Stanley v. Georgia*,[110] the Court held that, although public dissemination of obscene materials may be regulated, states cannot make private possession of those materials a crime.[111] However, the Court did draw narrow boundaries around the zone of privacy afforded by *Stanley*. In *United States v. 12 200-Ft. Reels of Super 8MM Film*,[112] the Court held that the importation of obscene materials can be regulated even if those materials are intended for private use, and today the zone of privacy is not likely to extend far beyond the confines of one's home. By virtue of Court decisions,[113] a gallery open to the public cannot with impunity possess or display obscene works. Moreover, it is conceivable that the possession of such works in an artist's studio, from which works may be sold from time to time to the public, may also be constitutionally unprotected.

The Captive Audience

Since, in obscenity cases, the Supreme Court in its reflections considers the rights and the interests of the state and offended viewers, as well as the rights of the speaker, performer, or exhibitor, works displayed to a captive or unwilling audience are more likely to be deemed constitutionally unprotected than are those not so displayed. In *Close v. Lederle*,[114] a federal court of appeals held that, where there is, in effect, a captive audience, people have a right to protection against "assault upon individual privacy" short of legal obscenity.[115] In *Close v. Lederle*, the plaintiff, an art instructor at the University of Massachusetts, exhibited, at the invitation of a superior, his paintings on the walls of a corridor in the student union. The exhibition, involving clinically explicit nudes, proved to be controversial and was removed after being up for five of the twenty-four days scheduled for its display. The plaintiff, claiming that his constitutional rights were invaded sought to have the space made available for his exhibit for the equivalent of the unexpired period. In dismissing the complaint the federal appellate court drew an analogy between visual speech and pure speech by noting as follows:

> There are words that are not regarded as obscene, in the constitutional sense, that nevertheless need not be permitted in every context. Words that might properly be employed in a term paper about *Lady Chatterley's Lover*, or in a novel submitted in a creative writing course, take on a very different coloration if they are

bellowed over a loudspeaker at a campus rally or appear prominently on a sign posted on a campus tree.[116]

"Freedom of speech," the court continued, "must recognize, at least within limits, freedom not to listen."[117] As the paintings were displayed in a passageway regularly used by the public, including children, the court reasoned that the university officials could consider the primary use of the corridor as a public thoroughfare, with the public, in effect, a captive audience; therefore, the officials had a right to afford protection against assault on individual privacy.[118]

In a similar vein and citing the holding of *Close*, a Massachusetts federal district court, in 1988, upheld a regulation banning nude bathing at a Cape Cod national park seashore.[119] In holding that the regulation did not ban the first amendment rights of women who wished to bathe in the nude to protest the exploitation of women in American society, the court noted that "not only is a public beach an unlikely and unnecessary showcase for nude expression, but also nudity there significantly intrudes upon others who did not seek it out and may be offended by it."[120]

Artwork and Minors

In an exhibition of artwork depicting nudity or sexual conduct, consideration should also be given to the interests of minors. Works that are not obscene may, nevertheless, be regulated by states to the extent appropriate to protect minors.[121] Some states have specific statutes restricting the display or the sale to minors of works depicting nudity. A New York statute, for example, prohibits the sale to a minor of any artwork depicting nudity, sexual conduct, or sadomasochistic abuse.[122]

The Rights of Privacy and of Publicity

Although the right of publicity is occasionally described as an extension of the right of privacy, the two are emerging as quite different prerogatives. The right of privacy is more of a personal nature, whereas the right of publicity is evolving principally as a property right. Each is discussed in turn below.

Privacy

An artist, in the course of his or her work, does not generally have the right under the first amendment to invade the privacy of a person. A person's privacy is invaded by an artist, for example, if the artist, however accurately, paints a picture portraying that person as ill and secluded in a hospital bed and publicly displays it without permission. That prerogative, at its core, is the right to be free from unwanted or unwarranted publicity; it is the right to be left alone. In one form or another, the right of privacy is recognized in virtually all jurisdictions.[123] In some states—for example, New York, Virginia, and Nebraska[124]—it is recognized by statute, and in other states it is recognized by case law alone. Some authorities argue that the law of privacy comprises several distinct kinds of invasion of different interests of the plaintiff:[125]

1. Unreasonable intrusion, by physical means or otherwise, on the plaintiff's solitude or seclusion;
2. Public disclosure of sensitive or highly objectionable private information about the plaintiff, even if the information is true; and
3. Publicity that places the plaintiff in a false light in the public eye.

Because it is a personal right, the prerogative of privacy generally ceases with a person's death. The action for defamation and the action for invasion of privacy should be carefully distinguished; the action for defamation is to protect a person's interest in a good name and reputation, whereas the action for invasion of privacy is to protect a person's interest in being let alone. Invasion of privacy as an action is available when the plaintiff can show that some matter has been made public or some right of privacy or solitude has been invaded in an unreasonable or unjustifiable manner. Unlike what is needed in an action for defamation, the falsity of the publication need not be established in an action for invasion of privacy.[126]

As an example of legislation of that prerogative, is New York's right of privacy statute, which provides:

> A person, firm or corporation that uses for advertising purposes, or for the purposes of trade, the name, portrait or picture of any living person without having first obtained the written consent of such person, or if a minor of his or her parent or guardian, is guilty of a misdemeanor.[127]

Publicity

Unlike the right of privacy, the right of publicity centers on the freedom to exploit and to exclude others from exploiting the commercial value inherent in, for instance, one's own name, voice, signature, photograph, image, or likeness. That prerogative has been described as a person's "right to profit from [his or her] general notoriety."[128]

The right of publicity was first directly recognized in *Haelan Laboratories, Inc. v. Topps Chewing Gum, Inc.*,[129] a 1953 case in which a federal court of appeals held that an exclusive contract right to photograph a person was legally cognizable. In the ensuing years, the right of publicity gradually gained acceptance. Judicial recognition has been granted in a substantial number of jurisdictions,[130] and statutory recognition in at least several states.[131]

To the extent that it resembles a property right, the right of publicity raises a question as to its survivability—that is, is it descendible? The courts have been divided on that question. In New York, the right of publicity is viewed as descendible.[132] In California, however, the opposite result has obtained. In *Lugosi v. Universal Pictures*,[133] a state appellate court held that the family of the late Bela Lugosi could not prevent Universal Pictures from using the actor's name or likeness on T-shirts, toys, and other memorabilia, as such rights as Lugosi may have originally had could only have been exercised by him during his lifetime. However, since a statutory enactment of 1984,[134] the right of publicity in California can be preserved and protected for up to fifty years after an individual's death, provided that the name, voice, likeness, signature, or photograph of that particular person had "commercial value at the time of his or her death."[135] Protection under the statute is offered for individuals who died as long ago as January 1, 1935.

Although visual artists who, under New York law, paint unauthorized likenesses of legendary deceased figures, such as John Lennon and Pablo Picasso, for purposes of trade, do not risk violating New York's right of privacy statute (as it is a right terminable at death), those artists do risk violating those figures' common-law property right of publicity. As noted in a 1977 New York appellate court case:

> In New York there is a distinction between the statutory right which protects living persons from commercial exploitation of their name and pictures without their written consents, as embodied in sections 50 and 51 of the New York Civil Rights Law, and the common-law property right in one's public personality. The statutory right is deemed a "right of privacy" . . . . [That right] is not assignable during one's lifetime and terminates at death . . . [but the common-law] right to publicity, i.e., the property right in one's name, photograph and image is under no such inhibition.[136]

On the other hand, were visual artists to be painting such individual portraits under California law, they would be on safe ground, since that state's right of publicity statute specifically exempts from liability "single and original works of fine art."[137] However, fine artwork made in multiples, such as an edition of alabaster busts or a lithograph series, places the artist on less sure footing. Unless the artworks are shown to be published for political purposes, thereby exempting them under another portion of the statute, the creation of such works can give rise to an action for damages. Such an action occurred at least once when in 1987 Andy Warhol, shortly before his death, was sued by Wayne Enterprises, which claimed, among other allegations, that Warhol's unauthorized use of the late John Wayne's likeness in print had violated the publicity rights that Wayne Enterprises had purchased.[138] In February 1988, however, the suit was dismissed and California's publicity statute as applied here was found to be unconstitutional as violative of the first amendment. The defense had argued that since the statute exempted books, newspapers, and the like printed in multiple copies, visual speech produced in multiple form should not be accorded harsher treatment: Warhol, as the argument went, could have chosen to bind the portfolio of prints, hence making it exempt as a book, and constitutional issues should not be resolved on such a trifling basis.

A few other states have enacted right-of-publicity legislation, such as, for example, Kentucky, Tennessee, and Texas.[139] Moreover, there are certain privacy statutes, such as that of Florida,[140] that specifically create a limited right of publicity after death. It remains to be seen how those statutory enactments, as well as decisional law, will apply the right of publicity to artwork. It is to be hoped that the expanding right of publicity does not significantly impoverish the visual references that artists have felt free to incorporate into their work.

Postscript

As this book went to press the artist's first amendment right to freedom of expression was once again threatened. The controversy arose from an amendment proposed by Sen. Jesse Helms to a Department of the Interior appropriations bill. The amendment, which was approved on July 26, 1989, by a voice vote in the Senate, would bar the National Endowment for the Arts from supporting "obscene or indecent" work by prohibiting the use of federal arts funds to "promote, disseminate or produce obscene or indecent materials, including but not limited to depictions of sadomasochism, homoeroticism, the exploitation of children, or individuals engaged in sex acts; or material which denigrates the objects or beliefs of the adherents of a particular religion or non-religion." The amendment was a reaction to controversial photographic exhibitions of the works of Andres Serrano and the late Robert Mapplethorpe that were supported by National Endowment art funds.

We question the constitutionality of the proposed Helms amendment. If enacted into law, it would cast a shadow on the artist's freedom of expression that far exceeds the boundaries circumscribed by the Supreme Court's test of obscenity. It should also be declared void for vagueness. Neither the language nor the spirit of this amendment has any place in a society such as ours that prizes the creation and dissemination of diversified expression.

NOTES
to Chapter 7

1. See discussion of commissioned works in chapter 4.

2. *See, e.g.*, N.Y. City Admin. Code tit. 10, ch. 1, § 10-117 (1988).

3. *See, e.g.*, Healy v. James, 408 U.S. 169 (1972); Brown v. Louisiana, 383 U.S. 131, 142 (1966); Wood v. Moore, 350 F. Supp. 29, 31 (W.D.N.C. 1972).

4. *See, e.g.*, Melton v. Young, 328 F. Supp. 88 (D. Tenn. 1971), *aff'd*, 465 F.2d 1332 (6th Cir.), *cert. denied*, 411 U.S. 951 (1973).

5. *See* H. Janson, History of Art 462 (1974).

6. Krieg, *Copyright, Free Speech and the Visual Arts*, 15 J. Arts Mgmt. & L. 59, 60 (Winter 1986).

7. Latin Am. Advisory Council v. Withers, No. 74 Civ. 2717 (N.D. Ill. Nov. 22, 1974) (mem. and order). The case is reproduced in 1 F. Feldman, S. Weil & S. Biederman, Art Law 39 (1986). *See also* Schwartz v. Planning & Zoning Comm'n, 208 Conn. 146 (1988), in which the Connecticut Supreme Court, in not reaching first amendment issues, held that a kinetic sculpture, to be placed at a shopping plaza's entrance, did not constitute a "sign" within the meaning of zoning regulations. *But see* N.Y. Times, July 14, 1987, at B1, col. 1, where a zoning ordinance was used to force the removal of a twelve-by-eleven-foot cartoon-style painting of a porpoise shown in the yard of a New Jersey art gallery: the work was viewed as an "oversized sign" in violation of a local building code provision. This case might be distinguishable from the *Latin American Advisory* case in that the latter involved exhibition of a work of greater political import, thus rendering more equitable there the denial of full force to a local ordinance.

8. Pillsbury Co. v. Milky Way Prods., Inc., 215 U.S.P.Q. 124 (N.D. Ga. 1981).

9. *Id.* at 131.

10. *Id.* at 132.

11. Silberman v. Georges, 91 A.D.2d 520, 456 N.Y.S.2d 395 (lst Dep't 1982).

12. *Id.* at 521, 456 N.Y.S.2d at 397.

13. D. Robb & J. Garrison, Art in the Western World 590 (1963).

14. Yorty v. Chandler, 13 Cal. App. 3d 467, 91 Cal. Rptr. 709 (1971).

15. *Id.* at 472, 91 Cal. Rptr. at 711.

16. *Id.* at 472, 91 Cal. Rptr. at 712.

17. Sefick v. City of Chicago, 485 F. Supp. 644 (N.D. Ill. 1979).

18. *Id.* at 648.

19. *Id.* at 649.

20. *Id.*

21. *Id.* at 651.

22. Nelson v. Certain Police Officers & Aldermen, No. 88-C-5434 (N.D. Ill. 1988). Note also a controversy in Philadelphia concerning an "Art in City Hall" show featuring a photographic exhibition of mummers' costumes relating to Philadelphia's long-time traditional New Year's Day Mummers' Parade. The crux of the controversy involved photographs of mummers who appeared to be in blackface. In response to civil rights groups, blackface had been banned by court order from the parade since 1964. Among the objectors to the photographic exhibition was Philadelphia Mayor Wilson Goode, who, on December 29, 1987, ordered the removal from the exhibition of a number of photographs. In response to that action, several photographers from the exhibition said they would pull their works from the show. PHILADELPHIA INQUIRER, Jan. 5, 1988, at A8, F1; *Id.*, Jan. 6, 1988, at A14, col. 3; N.Y. TIMES, Dec. 31, 1987, at C15, col. 3; Id., Jan. 10, 1988, at 35, col. 4.

23. See discussion of the captive-audience concept at pp. 340-41.

24. Texas v. Gregory Lee Johnson, United States Supreme Court, No. 88-155, June 21, 1989, *aff'g* 755 S.W.2d 92 (Tex. Crim. App. 1988).

25. N.Y. TIMES, June 22, 1989, at A-1.

26. *See, e.g.*, Halter v. Nebraska, 205 U.S. 34 (1907). The United States government has enacted a flag-desecration statute, as has each of the nation's states. *See* 18 U.S.C. § 700 (1988); N.Y. GEN. BUS. LAW § 136 (McKinney 1988); Jones v. Wade, 479 F.2d 1176 (5th Cir. 1973).

27. 18 U.S.C. § 700(a) (1988).

28. N.Y. GEN. BUS. LAW § 136 (McKinney 1988).

29. People v. Street, 20 N.Y.2d 231, 229 N.E.2d 187, 282 N.Y.S.2d 491 (1967), *rev'd*, 394 U.S. 576 (1969), *on remand*, 24 N.Y.2d 1026, 250 N.E.2d 250, 302 N.Y.S.2d 848 (1969).

30. *Id.*, 394 U.S. at 594.

31. Commonwealth v. Lorene, 281 A.2d 743 (D.C. 1971).

32. People v. Cowgill, 274 Cal. App. 2d Supp. 923, 78 Cal. Rptr. 853 (1969).

33. People v. Verch, 63 Misc. 2d 477, 311 N.Y.S.2d 637 (Sup. Ct. 1970).

34. People v. Burton, 27 N.Y.2d 198, 265 N.E.2d 66, 316 N.Y.S.2d 217 (1970).

35. Smith v. Goquen, 415 U.S. 566 (1974).

36. Lipp v. Morris, 579 F.2d 834 (3d Cir. 1978).

37. Monroe v. State Court, 739 F.2d 568 (11th Cir. 1984).

38. Spence v. Washington, 418 U.S. 405 (1974).

39. *Id.* at 415.

40. Stromberg v. California, 283 U.S. 359 (1931).

41. *Id.* at 369.

42. International Food & Beverage Sys. v. City of Fort Lauderdale, 794 F.2d 1520 (11th Cir. 1986).

43. City of Houston v. Hill, 107 S. Ct. 2502 (1987).

44. Cinevision Corp. v. City of Burbank, 745 F.2d 560 (9th Cir. 1984), *cert. denied*, 471 U.S. 1054 (1985).

45. Tinker v. Des Moines School Dist., 393 U.S. 503 (1969).

46. Klein v. Smith, 635 F. Supp. 1440 (D. Me. 1986).

47. Knolls Action Project v. Knolls Atomic Power Laboratory (KAPL), 600 F. Supp. 1353 (N.D.N.Y. 1985), *aff'd*, 771 F.2d 46 (2d Cir. 1985).

48. O'Brien v. United States, 376 F.2d 538 (1st Cir. 1967), *vacated*, 391 U.S. 367 (1968). *See also* United States v. Miller, 367 F.2d 72 (2d Cir. 1966), *cert. denied*, 386 U.S. 911 (1967).

49. O'Brien v. United States, *supra* note 48, 391 U.S. at 376.

50. *Supra* note 24.

51. *Id.*

52. *Id.*

53. People v. Keough, 31 N.Y.2d 281, 290 N.E.2d 819, 338 N.Y.S.2d 618 (1972).

54. People v. Radich, 53 Misc. 2d 717, 279 N.Y.S.2d 680 (Sup. Ct. 1967), *aff'd*, 57 Misc. 2d 1082, 294 N.Y.S.2d 285 (App. Term 1968), *aff'd*, 26 N.Y.2d 114, 257 N.E.2d 30, 308 N.Y.S.2d 846 (1970), *aff'd*, 401 U.S. 531 (1971); United States *ex rel.* Radich v. Criminal Court, 459 F.2d 745 (2d Cir. 1972), *on remand*, 385 F. Supp. 165 (S.D.N.Y. 1974).

55. People v. Radich, 53 Misc. 2d at 718, 279 N.Y.S.2d at 682.

56. Spence v. Washington, 418 U.S. at 412 (1974).

57. United States *ex rel.* Radich v. Criminal Court, *supra* note 54, 385 F. Supp. 165.

58. 18 U.S.C. § 701 (1988).

59. *Id.*

60. 18 U.S.C. § 704 (1988).

61. 18 U.S.C. § 705 (1988).

62. *Id.*

63. 18 U.S.C. § 706 (1988).

64. 18 U.S.C. § 707 (1988).

65. 18 U.S.C. §§ 711, 712(a) (1988).

66. 18 U.S.C. § 713(a) (1988).

67. 18 U.S.C. § 713(b) (1988).

68. 18 U.S.C. § 715 (1988).

69. N.Y. Gen. Bus. Law § 137 (McKinney 1988).

70. N.Y. City Admin. Code tit. 10, ch. 1, § 10-117 (McKinney 1988).

71. Silvette v. Art Comm'n, 413 F. Supp. 1342 (E.D. Va. 1976).

72. Serra v. United States Gen. Servs. Admin., 664 F. Supp. 798, 667 F. Supp. 1042 (S.D.N.Y. 1987), *aff'd*, 847 F.2d 1045 (2d Cir. 1988).

73. This case is discussed at length in chapter 4 at pp. 222-27.

74. Serra, *supra* note 72, 847 F.2d at 1052.

75. *Id.* at 1051.

76. Balfe & Wyszomirski, *Public Art and Public Policy*, 15 J. Arts Mgmt. & L. 5, 10 (Winter 1986).

77. *Id.*

78. Davis, *Report and Determination in the Matter of Christo: The Gates*, *cited in* 1 F. Feldman, S. Weil & S. Biederman, Art Law 84 *et seq.* (1986).

79. *See, e.g.*, Cohen v. California, 403 U.S. 15 (1971).

80. Defamation and the state of the current law are discussed in chapter 5 at pp. 261-63.

81. *See, e.g.*, Colo. Rev. Stat. § 18-7-104(a), (b) (Supp. 1985); Ga. Code Ann. § 16-12-80(b)(2) (1984); Iowa Code Ann. § 728.7 (1979); Minn. Stat. Ann. § 617.241(a) (West Supp. 1989); Mo. Ann. Stat. §§ 573.010, 573.050 (Vernon 1979 & Supp. 1989); Mont. Code Ann. § 45-8-201(3)(b) (1987); Neb. Rev. Stat. §§ 28-813(1)(c), 28-815(1) (1985); Nev. Rev. Stat. § 201-237 (1986);

N.H. REV. STAT. ANN. §§ 650:1(IV(c)), 650:5(III & IV) (1986); OKLA. STAT. ANN. tit. 21, § 1021.1 (West 1983); OR. REV. STAT. §§ 167.085(2), 167.089 (Supp. 1987); R.I. GEN. LAWS § 11-31-1 (1981); S.C. CODE ANN. § 16-15-280(5) (Law. Co-op. 1985); S.D. CODIFIED LAWS ANN. §§ 22-24-27(4)(c), 22-24-37(2) (1988); TENN. CODE ANN. §§ 39-6-1101(5)(c), 39-61-1117(3) (1988); UTAH CODE ANN. §§ 76-10-1201(11)(iii), 76-10-1203(1)(c) (1988); VT. STAT. ANN. tit. 13, §§ 2801(6)(c), 2805(b)(3), 2805(c) (Supp. 1988); VA. CODE §§ 18.2-372, 18.2-383(2) (1988); W. VA. CODE § 61-8A-1(7)(c) (1989).

82. *See, e.g.*, ALA. CODE § 41-9-45(4) (1982); ALASKA STAT. § 44.27.050(4) (Supp. 1988); ARIZ. REV. STAT. ANN. § 41-982(B)(4) (1985); CONN. GEN. STAT. ANN. § 10-370 (West Supp. 1989); GA. CODE ANN. § 50-12-23(4) (1986); IND. CODE ANN. § 4-23-2-2(d) (Burns 1986); MICH. COMP. LAWS ANN. § 2.124(4) (1981); MINN. STAT. ANN. § 139.10(2)(a) (West 1979 & Supp. 1989); MISS. CODE ANN. § 39-11-7(4) (1972); MO. ANN. STAT. § 185.040(4) (Vernon Supp. 1989); MONT. CODE ANN. § 22-2-106(4) (1987); NEB. REV. STAT. § 82-312(4) (1987); N.H. REV. STAT. ANN. § 19-A:1 (1970); N.J. REV. STAT. ANN. § 52:16A-26(c) (1986); N.D. CENT. CODE § 54-54-05.4 (1982); S.D. CODIFIED LAWS ANN. § l-22-6 (1985); WYO. STAT. § 9-2-903(a)(v) (1987).

83. Roth v. United States, 354 U.S. 476 (1957). In its holding, the Court rejected the test of Regina v. Hicklin, 3 L.R.-Q.B. 360 (1868), which had been to judge the material according to the effect of an isolated excerpt on particularly susceptible persons.

84. Roth v. United States, 354 U.S. at 489.

85. *Id.* at 484.

86. Jacobellis v. Ohio, 378 U.S. 184 (1964).

87. Memoirs v. Massachusetts, 383 U.S. 413 (1966).

88. *Id.* at 418.

89. Miller v. California, 413 U.S. 15 (1973).

90. *Id.* at 19.

91. *Id.* at 24.

92. *Id.* at 22.

93. *Id.* The burden of proof difficulties posed by the *Memoirs* test, as noted by *Miller*, were also stressed in a case subsequent to *Miller*: Hamling v. United States, 418 U.S. 87 (1974).

94. Miller v. California, 413 U.S. at 25-26.

95. *Id.* at 32-33.

96. *Id.* at 25.

97. *Miller* had four companion cases: Paris Adult Theatre I v. Slaton, 413 U.S. 49, *injunction aff'd*, 231 Ga. 312, 201 S.E.2d 456 (1973), *cert. denied*, 418 U.S. 939 (1974); Kaplan v. California, 413 U.S. 115 (1973); United States v. Orito, 413 U.S. 139 (1973); United States v. 12 200-ft. Reels of Super 8MM Film, 413 U.S. 123 (1973).

98. L. DuBoff, The Deskbook of Art Law 258 n.1 (1977 & Supp. 1984).

99. Miller v. California, 413 U.S. at 27.

100. *See, e.g.*, Davison v. State, 288 So. 2d 483 (Fla. 1973), *stay denied*, 415 U.S. 943 (1974).

101. *See, e.g.*, Papp v. State, 281 So. 2d 600 (App. 1973), *vacated*, 298 So. 2d 374 (Fla. 1974).

102. Jenkins v. Georgia, 418 U.S. 153 (1974).

103. *Id.* at 160.

104. *Id.* at 161.

105. Keller v. State, 606 S.W.2d 931 (Tex. Crim. App. 1980). *See also* People v. Nelson, 88 Ill. App. 3d 196, 410 N.E.2d 476 (1980).

106. *See, e.g.*, United States v. Battista, 646 F.2d 237 (6th Cir.), *cert. denied*, 454 U.S. 1046 (1981).

107. 18 U.S.C. § 1461 (1988).

108. Pinkus v. United States, 436 U.S. 293, 303 (1978).

109. *See, e.g.*, Splawn v. California, 431 U.S. 595, 598 (1977); Hamling v. United States, 418 U.S. 87, 130 (1974); Ginzburg v. United States, 383 U.S. 463, 470 (1966).

110. Stanley v. Georgia, 394 U.S. 557 (1969).

111. *See also* United States v. Reidel, 402 U.S. 351 (1971).

112. *Supra* note 97.

113. *See, e.g.*, Paris Adult Theatre I v. Slaton, 418 U.S. 939 (1974); United States v. Orito, 413 U.S. 139 (1973).

114. Close v. Lederle, 424 F.2d 988 (1st Cir.), *cert. denied*, 400 U.S. 903 (1970).

115. *Id.* at 990.

116. *Id., citing* Wright, *The Constitution on the Campus*, 22 Vand. L. Rev. 1027, 1058 (1969).

117. Close v. Lederle, 424 U.S. at 991.

118. *But see* Cohen v. California, 403 U.S. 15, 21 (1971), which has since limited the application of the captive-audience theory to those instances in which

"substantial privacy interests are being invaded in an essentially intolerable manner." However, as subsequently noted in Sefick v. City of Chicago, 485 F. Supp. at 651, the "facts of *Close* are such that the action of the university might well be justifiable even in light of *Cohen*."

119. Craft v. Hodel, 683 F. Supp. 289 (D. Mass. 1988).

120. *Id.* at 294.

121. Ginsberg v. New York, 390 U.S. 629 (1968).

122. N.Y. PENAL LAW § 235.21 (McKinney 1980 & Supp. 1989).

123. P. KEETON, E. KEETON, B. DOBBS & G. OWEN, PROSSER AND KEETON ON THE LAW OF TORTS 851 (5th ed. 1984 & Supp. 1988). Prosser notes that as of 1980, the only state not recognizing a right of privacy in some form was Rhode Island. *Id.*

124. *See, e.g.*, N.Y. CIV. RIGHTS LAW §§ 50, 50-a, 50-b, 51 (McKinney 1976 & Supp. 1988); VA. CODE 1950, §§ 2.1-377 to -386 (1986); NEB. REV. STAT. §§ 20-201 to -211, 25-804.01 (1981). *See also* CAL. CIV. CODE § 3344 (1988).

125. *See, e.g.*, PROSSER AND KEETON, *supra* note 123, at 851. Prosser argues that the tort involves invasions of four distinct interests: (1) appropriation of name and likeness; (2) intrusion upon another's seclusion; (3) public disclosure of private facts; and (4) false liqht in the public eye. *Id.* at 851 *et seq. But see also* Felcher & Rubin, *Privacy, Publicity, and the Portrayal of Real People by the Media*, 88 YALE L.J. 1577, 1588 (1979), whereby Prosser's "appropriation of name and likeness" is characterized as the right of publicity.

126. PROSSER AND KEETON, *supra* note 123, at 856.

127. N.Y. CIV. RIGHTS LAW §§ 50 (McKinney 1976 & Supp. 1988); *see also* N.Y. CIV. RIGHTS LAW §§ 50-a, 50-b, 51 (McKinney 1976 & Supp. 1988).

128. Felcher & Rubin, *supra* note 125, at 1589.

129. Haelan Laboratories, Inc. v. Topps Chewing Gum, Inc., 202 F.2d 866 (2d Cir.), *cert. denied*, 346 U.S. 816 (1953).

130. Felcher & Rubin, *supra* note 125, at 1589.

131. *See, e.g.*, Personal Rights Protection Act of 1984, TENN. CODE ANN. §§ 47-25-1101 to -1108 (1985); KY. REV. STAT. § 391.170 (1984).

132. *See, e.g.*, Lombardo v. Doyle, Dane & Bernbach, Inc., 58 A.D.2d 620, 396 N.Y.S.2d 661 (2d Dep't 1977).

133. Lugosi v. Universal Pictures, 25 Cal. App. 3d 813, 603 P.2d 425, 160 Cal. Rptr. 323 (1979).

134. CAL. CIV. CODE § 990 (1988); Note, *Right of Publicity Runs Riot: The Case for a Federal Statute*, 60 SO. CAL. L. REV. 1179 (1987).

135. CAL. CIV. CODE § 970(h) (1988).

136. Lombardo v. Doyle, Dane, & Bernbach, Inc., 58 A.D.2d at 621, 396 N.Y.S.2d at 664.

137. CAL. CIV. CODE § 970(n)(3) (1988).

138. F. FELDMAN, S. WEIL, S. BIEDERMAN, ART LAW SUPPLEMENT 15 (1988).

139. KY. REV. STAT. § 391.170 (1984); Personal Rights Protection Act of 1984, TENN. CODE ANN. §§ 47-25-1101 to -1108 (1985); TEX. PROP. CODE ANN. §§ 26.001-.015 (Vernon Supp. 1988). *See also* FLA. STAT. ANN. § 540.08 (1972); NEB. REV. STAT. § 20-208 (1983); VA. CODE § 8.01-.40, 18.2-216.1 (Supp. 1988); OKLA. STAT. ANN. tit. 21, § 839.1-.3 (West 1983).

140. FLA. STAT. ANN. § 540.08 (West 1972). *See also* OKLA. STAT. ANN. tit. 21, §§ 839.1-.3 (West 1983).

8

Copyrights

Copyright as a field of inquiry occupies a pivotal role in art law. It is the body of law that addresses the right to reproduce an artist's work, and it is conceptually linked to issues of moral rights, resale rights, and constitutional protections. Copyright law occupies volumes of thought and treatises beyond the scope of this book. This chapter, however, provides an overview: a brief history; the basic elements of copyright law, including the Acts of both 1976 and 1909 as they apply to artists and works of fine art; ownership of copyright, including the exclusive bundle of rights that inhere in the copyright holder, joint ownership, and works made for hire; procedures of copyright; utilitarian objects and copyright; the impact of subject matter on copyright, such as works in the public domain, works by noncitizens, and obscene works; and an update on recent legislative developments. Throughout this chapter the terms author and artist and their derivatives are used interchangeably.

HISTORY

Historically, copyright has existed in two distinct forms: common-law copyright and statutory copyright. Common-law copyright evolved from court precedent, and statutory copyright has its origins in federal legislation. Common-law copyright afforded protection to works upon creation without any copyright notice, and the protection lasted forever unless the work was published or registered. Statutory copyright affords protection solely to works registered with the Copyright Office or published with copyright notice, and the protection extends for a fixed period of time.

The United States Constitution, article I, section 8, furnishes the basis for copyright protection in the United States: it provides that Congress shall have the power

> To promote the Progress of Science and useful Arts, by securing for limited Times to Authors and Inventors the exclusive Right to their respective Writings and Discoveries.

In 1791 Congress enacted the nation's first federal copyright statute, providing copyright for an initial term of fourteen years, plus a renewal term of fourteen years, covering the making of copies of books, maps, and charts. The law was amended several times over the years to address successively broader categories of works of authorship and to provide increasingly longer periods of copyright protection. The federal Copyright Act of 1909 and Copyright Act of 1976 constitute the present statutory basis for American copyright law, with the earlier Act continuing to apply to works created before January 1, 1978.

The Copyright Act of 1976 eliminates common-law copyright almost entirely, thereby simplifying the copyright system. All works created on or after January 1, 1978, are protected by statutory copyright from the time of creation in fixed tangible form, regardless of registration or publication with copyright notice.[1]

ELEMENTS OF COPYRIGHT

Fixation

Copyright protection begins when an artist has fixed his or her work in a tangible medium of expression—that is, the artistic expression of the work must be placed in a material object, be it a block of alabaster, a sheet of paper, or a canvas. In addition, a copyrighted work must be tangible, as well as fixed. That means the work must be rendered in a sufficiently permanent and stable form. That requirement generally eliminates from eligibility for copyright protection such artworks as Christo's temporary installation pieces.[2]

Distinction Between the Work and the Copyright in the Work

A distinction must be made between ownership of the material object in which the copyrighted work is embodied and ownership of the copyright itself. A copyrighted work may be "a literary work printed on the pages of a book," for example, or "pigment painted on a canvas, or a musical work pressed into the grooves of a phonorecord."[3] Under today's law, sale of the material object, such as a book, painting, or phonorecord of the copyrighted work, does not convey ownership of copyright in and to that work or transfer any rights under copyright.[4] Rather, any transfer of copyright other than one by operation of law requires a writing signed by the owner of the rights conveyed or the owner's duly authorized agent.[5] Therefore, the person who purchases a work of art does not obtain the copyright to that work of art unless there is a transfer in writing by the copyright owner to the purchaser.

Before the 1976 Act became effective on January 1, 1978, unconditional sale of a copyrighted work automatically transferred the common-law copyright and the right to reproduce the work.[6] To retain his or her common-law copyright in a work sold, an artist or owner was required to make an express reservation of that right when the work was sold. Otherwise, the law presumed that all rights, including reproduction rights, were intended to be transferred in connection with the sale.[7]

However, before the 1976 Act became law, New York[8] and California[9] enacted legislation that reversed the presumption that sale of a work of art transferred the copyright to the buyer. The legislation generally provided that, when an artist or the artist's heirs sold or otherwise transferred a work of art, the right of reproduction continued to be reserved to the transferor until such time as it passed into the public domain, unless the reproduction right was expressly transferred by a document in writing.

Idea and Expression

Copyright protects only the expression of ideas, not the ideas themselves.[10] For example, the creation of an elaborate theory of art or the construction of an ingenious method for installing an exhibition belongs to the realm of ideas and is, therefore, unprotectible under copyright law.[11] If, however, that theory or method were reduced to written form, it would then constitute a protectible work of authorship and would preclude the unlicensed copying of the expression of that theory or method, even if that theory or method per se constituted an unprotectible idea.[12] Although the idea/expression dichotomy was first recognized by statute under the 1976 Act, it has long been recognized by the courts,[13] and was neither enlarged nor diminished by the 1976 Act.[14]

Originality

To receive copyright protection, a work of authorship must be original. That requirement was inferred by the courts from the 1909 Act[15] and expressly stated in the 1976 Act.[16] Generally, an original work of authorship is one that originates with the author and exhibits at least a minimal amount of creativity.[17] It need not be novel; as long as the work is independently created and not copied from a prior existing work, it is granted copyright protection even if it is substantially similar to—or, in fact, identical with—a prior work.[18] Moreover, artistic merit plays no role in determining what constitutes minimal creativity.[19]

A minimum standard of originality applies to the creation of art, as to any other work: the artist need only add a "distinguishable variation," beyond the mere trivial, arising from independent effort, to secure copyright protection.[20] A work copied without distinguishable variation from a prior work—even though the duplication may require special skill, training, knowledge, and independent judgment on the part of the copyist—is not, in itself, sufficiently original to qualify for a copyright. Thus, in *L. Batlin & Son v. Snyder*,[21] a federal appeals court held that the "physical skill" and "special training" required to convert a cast-iron Uncle Sam bank into plastic form did not display originality sufficient to support a claim of copyright.

Publication

The 1909 Act

Under the 1909 Act, which is applicable to works created before January 1, 1978, publication was an event of critical importance: it marked the end of state common-law copyright protection of a work and the commencement of federal copyright protection. If a work was not published, it could theoretically endure forever under state common-law copyright. An author had to affix proper notice to all copies of a work when published, or else the work would be injected into the public domain.

An Illinois state court in 1948 held that there was a publication of the murals that the plaintiff was commissioned to paint on the walls of a room in a Chicago hotel.[22] On completion of her work, the plaintiff failed to secure a copyright, whereupon the defendants, interior decorators engaged to redecorate that room, placed an advertisement in a national magazine involving several photographs of the newly decorated room, including the plaintiff's murals. The artist's suit for copyright infringement was unsuccessful, for, as the court noted, "[I]t is universally held that where the work is made available to the public . . . without restriction, there has been a publication."[23] Since the murals were available to the public when they were painted on the hotel room walls, and were open to the inspection of anyone who visited the hotel, that constituted a publication, causing the plaintiff to lose her common-law right in the murals.[24]

Although a number of other cases decided before the 1976 Act became law held that mere public exhibition of a work of art constitutes its publication,[25] the principle was qualified by the United States Supreme Court. In *American Tobacco Co. v. Werckmeister*,[26] the court held under prior law that, even though publicly exhibited, a general publication of a work of art does not occur if the public is admitted to view the art with the understanding that no copying take place and with measures taken to enforce that restriction.

As to what constitutes publication, the 1909 Act contained no statutory definition of the concept. A definition did evolve, however, through case law, indicating:

> [P]ublication occurs when by consent of the copyright owner, the original or tangible copies of a work are sold, leased, loaned, given away, or otherwise made available to the general public, or when an authorized offer is made to dispose of the work in any such manner even if a sale or other such disposition does not in fact occur.[27]

It is, therefore, paramount for any party acquiring copyright to a work of art created in the United States before 1978 to determine the circumstances relating to its publication. Although doing so may be difficult without the proper records, it is worth the effort. Otherwise, the acquiring party—be it a museum or some other institution, a private collector, or a gallery—may be unhappily surprised to find that the work has been injected into the public domain.

The Copyright Act of 1976

Although publication is of diminished significance under current law, the event still holds some import. For one thing, notice is required on all copies of a work published prior to March 1, 1989, and notice confers certain procedural and substantive rights. The registration certificate, for example, of a work registered within five years of its first publication can constitute prima facie evidence of the validity of that work's copyright. Moreover, if registration is effected within three months of a work's first publication, the copyright holder can avail himself or herself of statutory damages and attorney's fees when appropriate.[28]

Unlike under the 1909 Act, copyright protection of a work created under the 1976 Act and published prior to March 1, 1989, is not forfeited if proper notice is not affixed to each and every copy of such a work. However, the work can be injected into the public domain if notice is omitted from a substantial number of its copies.[29] Moreover, any work under the 1976 Act can be injected into the public domain if registration of the work is not made within five years of its publication. In addition to registration, a reasonable effort to add notice to copies of works published prior to March 1, 1989, where omitted, is required to save the copyright on such works.[30] In most cases, there will not be multiple copies of a work of art—only the original. See the discussion at pages 389-90 concerning change in the notice requirement for works of art published on or after March 1, 1989.

The 1976 Act defines publication:

> "Publication" is the distribution of copies . . . of a work to the public by sale or other transfer of ownership, or by rental, lease or lending. The offering to distribute copies . . . to a group of persons for purposes of further distribution, public performance, or public display, constitutes publication. A public performance or display of a work does not of itself constitute publication.[31]

Duration

The Constitution mandates that the federal term of copyright protection be for a limited time only. For works created on or after January 1, 1978, the basic term of copyright begins on creation and lasts for the life of the artist plus fifty years after the artist's death.[32] That period of duration accounts for all works that are not anonymous, pseudonymous, or made for hire.[33]

The term of copyright protection for works created and published before January 1, 1978, is governed by the 1909 Act. Under that law the term of copyright begins on the date of the work's first publication. The 1909 Act created a system of two copyright terms: a first term of twenty-eight years and a renewal term of twenty-eight years, for a total of fifty-six years. To obtain the renewal term, a copyright owner was required to make timely filing of a renewal claim in the Copyright Office. Failure to do so injected the work into the public domain.[34] Those renewal provisions (discussed in detail later in this chapter) still apply to all works copyrighted under the 1909 Act and in their first term of copyright as of January 1, 1978.[35] Thus, the copyright of a piece of sculpture published in 1975 must be renewed in 2002 or 2003. If the work was in its first term of copyright when the 1976 Act became effective, the renewal term, which still must be timely and properly claimed, is now extended from twenty-eight years to forty-seven years,[36] for a total period of copyright protection of seventy-five years. If, however, the work was in its renewal term when the 1976 Act became effective, that renewal term is automatically extended for another nineteen years, giving a renewal term of forty-seven years[37] and a total protection period of seventy-five years, with nothing further to be done to acquire that additional protection time.

For works created but not published before January 1, 1978, copyright protection subsists from January 1, 1978, and endures for the life of the artist plus fifty years, but in no event will protection terminate before December 31, 2002. If an unpublished work is published on or before December 31, 2002, the term of copyright will not expire before December 31, 2027.[38]

EXCLUSIVE RIGHTS

Under the 1976 Act, when a work of authorship is created, its copyright is born. The copyright vests in the creator of the work and consists of a bundle of five exclusive rights:

1. The right to reproduce
2. The right to adapt
3. The right to distribute
4. The right to perform and
5. The right to display[39]

Each of those rights is subject to restrictions. Moreover, copyright infringement does not occur unless an unauthorized use of the copyrighted work falls within the scope of one of the five enumerated rights. The performance right applies not to pictorial, graphic, or sculptural works, but rather to literary, musical, dramatic, and choreographic works, along with pantomimes, motion pictures, and other audiovisual works.[40] A discussion of the four exclusive rights that do apply to works of art follows, along with the relevant restrictions attached to those rights.

The Right to Reproduce

Perhaps the most basic of the exclusive rights consists of the right to reproduce the copyrighted work—that is, material objects in which the work of authorship is fixed[41]—in copies.[42] For a work to be fixed, its embodiment in a copy must be sufficiently permanent to permit it to be perceived, reproduced, or otherwise communicated for a period of more than transitory duration.[43] Thus, the duplication of a pictorial image on the sand or its projection on a television screen—although perhaps violative of, for example, the display right—does not violate the reproduction right. By requiring some permanence of a work's embodiment before copying could be found, the 1976 Act makes explicit what was usually,[44] but not always,[45] the law under the 1909 Act.

Infringement may occur even if the work is reproduced in a different medium or dimension, such as a sketch copied from a photograph[46] or a doll copied from a cartoon.[47] Moreover, in order for an infringement to arise, the copy need not be exact, as long as it is substantially similar to the copyrighted work.[48]

Restrictions

With respect to artwork, there are a few restrictions on the exclusive right of reproduction. For example, if artwork is lawfully reproduced in or on useful articles that have been offered for sale or other distribution to the public, it is not a copyright infringement under the 1976 Act to make, distribute, or display photographs of those articles in connection with advertisements or commentaries related to the distribution or display of the articles or in connection with news reports.[49]

For another example, a library, under certain circumstances, has a limited right to reproduce an illustration when the illustration is an accompaniment to explanatory text.[50]

The Right to Adapt

The copyright holder has the exclusive right to make derivative works based on the underlying work of authorship.[51] Derivative works are based on existing works and include translations, motion picture versions, and art reproductions.[52] If the derivative work is not itself an infringing work, and if it meets the requirements of originality—that is, a "distinguishable variation that is more than 'merely trivial' "[53]—it is separately copyrightable.[54] As in any copyright case, the standard for infringement is one of substantial similarity.[55] Copyright in a derivative work covers only those elements in the derivative work that are original to that work.[56] If the underlying work is protected by copyright, then copyright in the derivative work does not affect the protection accorded the underlying work.[57] If the underlying work is in the public domain, a copyright in the derivative work does not render the underlying work protectible.[58] Despite a line of earlier cases in conflict with the above principles,[59] the 1909 Act contained similar statutory language.[60]

The Right to Distribute

The third exclusive right enumerated by the 1976 Act—the right of distribution—accords to the copyright owner the exclusive right to distribute copies of the copyrighted work to the public by sale or other transfer of ownership or by rental, lease, or lending.[61] Thus, the distribution right, in essence, is the right to control the publication of a work. Although the copyright holder's rights of public distribution cease with respect to a particular copy once he or she has parted with copyright ownership, such rights do not cease if the copyright holder has parted with mere possession of that copy.[62] Infringement of the distribution right can occur, for example, when a museum or bookstore sells posters or postcards duplicated without authorization from the copyright holder. Infringement occurs even if the objects were bought from a third party and innocently sold by the museum or bookstore without knowledge of the circumstances of duplication.

Restrictions

Under the 1976 Act, the restriction on the distribution right applicable to works of art is known as the first-sale doctrine. That doctrine provides that the owner of a particular lawfully made copy or any person authorized by the owner may, without the authority of the copyright owner, sell or otherwise dispose of the possession of that copy.[63] The 1909 Act contained a similar provision: "[N]othing in this title shall be deemed to forbid, prevent, or restrict the transfer of any copy of a copyrighted work, the possession of which has been lawfully obtained."[64] Thus, for example, a museum, private collector, or gallery that owns a work of art may sell it to another, as long as it was acquired from a party who had lawful ownership. The first-sale doctrine applies only to the right to resell a copy of the work; it does not permit other exploitation of it except, under certain circumstances, to display that copy publicly to viewers present at the place where the copy is located.[65]

Under that doctrine, then, the copyright owner may make a profit on the first sale of his or her work, but not on a further resale or rental of the work. However, influenced by such European nations as France and Germany, which recognize continuing resale rights for artists, California enacted a Resale Royalties Act in 1976, enabling artists under certain limited circumstances to recover a portion of the profit of the work as it passes through successive owners.[66] Responsive to California's initiative, as well as to the European experience, and influenced by pressure from artists' rights groups, at least one bill was introduced in the 100th Congress (but not acted on) calling for a study of the resale royalties issue to be conducted jointly by the National Endowment for the Arts and the Register of Copyrights. That bill, along with other legislative developments, is discussed at the conclusion of this chapter, as well as at the conclusion of chapters 9 and 10.

The Right of Public Display

The fourth exclusive right applicable to works of art and codified for the first time in the 1976 Act is the right to display the work publicly.[67] To display a work is to show a copy of it either directly or by a device or process. A motion picture, for example, is *displayed* when its frames are shown nonsequentially; when shown in sequence, however, the motion picture is considered *performed*.[68] To display "publicly" means to display a work:

> [A]t a place open to the public or at any place where a substantial number of persons outside of a normal circle of a family and its social acquaintances is gathered; or to transmit or otherwise communicate a . . . display of the work [to such place] by means of any device or process, whether the members of the public capable of receiving the . . . display receive it in the same place or in separate places and at the same time or at different times.[69]

Restrictions

One restriction on the display right applicable to works of art permits the owner of a lawfully made copy of a work to display it directly or by projection of no more than one image at a time to viewers present at the place where the copy is located.[70] If, for example, a museum or a gallery owns a piece of sculpture, even if it is not the copyright holder in and to that work, it may show the sculpture to the public directly or by projection, as long as the display takes place on museum grounds or on gallery premises and is not further projected to distant sites.

Divisibility of Copyright

The 1909 Act

The 1909 Act was based on the premise of a single copyright with a single legal title held by "the copyright proprietor."[71] Accordingly, the courts inferred that the bundle of rights accruing to a copyright owner were "indivisible,"[72] and a transfer of anything less than such a totality was deemed a "license," rather than an assignment.[73] Since only the copyright proprietor could bring an infringement action,[74] the doctrine of indivisibility protected alleged infringers from the harassment of successive lawsuits. It took the evolution of the communications media—that is, the development of motion pictures, television, phonograph records, and legitimate stage productions—along with the emergence of performing rights societies to redefine commercial reality. Today, "copyright" is a label for a collection of diverse, separately marketable property rights.[75]

The Copyright Act of 1976

By recognizing the principle of divisibility, the 1976 Act acknowledges the ever-expanding commercial possibilities inherent in copyright ownership. For example, the original copyright holder (or his or her transferee) of a painting can now sell the right of reproduction to Company *X*, sell the right of distribution to Company *Y*, retain the right of adaptation for himself or herself, and grant a university a two-year exclusive license for the display of the work. Each one of those transferees now becomes an owner of a copyright interest in and to the painting. "Copyright owner" is defined as referring to the owner of any one or more of the exclusive rights in a copyright,[76] and the copyright owner has standing to sue for infringement of that right.[77] Also, "transfer of copyright ownership" is defined as an assignment, exclusive license, and any other grant except a nonexclusive license.[78]

Licenses and Assignments

Under the 1976 Act, a copyright holder may exercise ownership prerogatives in a number of ways. He or she may assign the entire copyright interest to another, who then becomes the copyright holder, or may assign only one or more of the exclusive rights. In addition, the copyright holder may convey a license in and to a work. A license is a right amounting to a less-than-complete ownership interest in a work. If the grantor agrees not to convey that right to anyone else, it is an exclusive license; if the grantor also conveys the same right to a third party, it is a nonexclusive license. As noted in the preceding section, assignments and exclusive licenses are considered transfers of copyright. To be effective under the 1976 Act, they must be accompanied by a signed writing.[79] The writing should clearly denote the principal terms of the conveyance, such as the royalty provisions, its duration, the name to be carried on the copyright notice, any termination provisions, and the responsibilities for maintaining an infringement suit against third parties.[80] Although nonexclusive licenses may be conveyed orally, it is prudent to put them into writing.

Joint Ownership

The 1976 Act defines a "joint work" as one "prepared by two or more authors with the intention that their contributions be merged into inseparable or interdependent parts of a unitary whole."[81] The intention at the time of creation controls.[82] Case law under the 1909 Act, on the other hand, stressed "fusion of effort," rather than intent at the time of creation.[83] One recent notable instance of joint works of art were those canvases created by the artists Andy Warhol and Jean Michel Basquiat. Decisional law dating from the 1909 Act provides that, in the absence of specific agreement to the contrary, all joint authors share equally in the ownership of the joint work, even if their respective contributions to the work are not equal,[84] and that, on the death of each joint owner, his or her heirs or legatees acquire his or her respective share of the joint work.[85] Under the 1976 Act, the duration of copyright of a joint work consists of the life of the last surviving author plus fifty years.[86] For joint works created under the 1909 Act, succession to the right to obtain a renewal copyright is controlled by the relevant statutory provisions of that Act.[87] Under both the 1976 Act and the 1909 Act, a joint owner may grant a nonexclusive license in the work without obtaining the consent of the other joint owners.[88] Moreover, in the absence of an agreement to the contrary, one joint owner may always transfer his or her interest in a joint work to a third party, but cannot transfer the interest of another joint owner without that joint owner's consent.[89]

Anonymous and Pseudonymous Works

Any anonymous work is a work on whose copies no natural person is identified as the author.[90] A pseudonymous work is a work on whose copies the author is identified under a fictitious name.[91] For all such works created on or after January 1, 1978, the copyright endures for a term of seventy-five years from the year of first publication of the work or a term of 100 years from the year of its creation, whichever expires first.[92] For works created before January 1, 1978, the provisions noted earlier in this chapter under "Duration" apply (see pages 361-62).

Collective Works

Under the 1976 Act, a collective work is one, such as an anthology or encyclopedia, in which a number of contributions, themselves separate and independent works, are assembled into a collective whole.[93] The contributions to the collective work may emanate from the same or from different authors. Such a work qualifies for copyright by reason of the original effort expended in the process of compilation, even if no new matter is added.[94] A calendar, for example, illustrated by copies of twelve separate works of art by disparate artists, but having a common theme, may well be copyrightable. As with derivative works, discussed earlier in this chapter, the amount of originality generally required to render a collective work protectible is a "distinguishable variation that is more than 'merely trivial.'"[95] As with a derivative work, a collective work copyright does not of itself make the pre-existing works on which the later work is based copyrightable, nor does the collective work copyright affect any copyright protection or lack of protection accorded the pre-existing works.[96] Generally, the above principles relating to collective works under the 1976 Act also applied under the 1909 Act because of the earlier Act's similar statutory language.[97]

Works Made for Hire

Under the 1976 Act, a work made for hire is either (1) a work prepared by an employee within the scope of employment or (2) certain work specially commissioned for a statutorily prescribed use if both parties expressly agree in a written instrument signed by them that the work shall be considered a work made for hire.[98] In the first category, several factors may be considered in determining the existence of the employer-employee relationship, the most crucial being whether the employer has the right to direct and supervise the employee's work.[99] If such a relationship is found to exist and the work is prepared by an employee within the scope of employment, it is a work made for hire, with ownership vesting in the employer. Note that one may be an employee whether paid on a conventional periodic salary basis, on a piece-work basis, on a fee or royalty basis, or even with no compensation at all.[100]

Specially commissioned works are works made for hire only if the parties expressly agree to that effect in a signed writing and the works fall into one of the following nine categories:[101]

- Contributions to collective works
- Parts of motion pictures or other audiovisual works
- Translations
- Supplementary works
- Compilations
- Instructional texts
- Tests
- Answer materials for tests
- Atlases

A commissioned portrait, therefore, is not a work made for hire because it does not fit any of the above categories. Nevertheless, to avoid any confusion, the artist should not sign anything indicating that such a commissioned work is a work made for hire.

The issue of the scope of a work made for hire was recently addressed by the United States Supreme Court. In *Community for Creative Non-Violence (CCNV) v. Reid*,[102] Mitch Snyder, a member and trustee of CCNV, a nonprofit association devoted to the welfare of homeless people, retained the artist, James Earl Reid, in the fall of 1985 to create a sculptured Nativity scene dramatizing the plight of the homeless to be exhibited in the annual Christmastime Pageant of Peace in Washington, D.C. The agreement was made verbally with little more than a handshake. After the sculpture was completed and displayed near the site of the Pageant, both Reid and Snyder, the latter acting in his capacity as CCNV's trustee, filed competing certificates of copyright registration. Mr. Snyder claimed he supervised and directed every step of the creation of the sculpture and, therefore, that the sculpture was a work made for hire with the copyright vesting in CCNV. Mr. Reid, on the other hand, claimed that he as the artist created the sculpture, that under the 1976 Act it was not a work made for hire, and accordingly, that he owned the copyright. The legal question presented was whether the sculpture created was a work made for hire under the 1976 Act.

The federal district court, reasoning that Reid had been an "employee" of CCNV within the meaning of the 1976 Act's "work made for hire" provision because CCNV was the motivating force in the statue's production, held that Snyder, as trustee for CCNV, was the exclusive owner of the copyright in the sculpture. The United States Court of Appeals for the District of Columbia reversed the district court's decision: it reasoned that under agency law, Reid was an independent contractor and that, therefore, the work was not prepared by an employee under the 1976 Act's work made for hire provision. The court of appeals further noted that the sculpture was not a work made for hire under the provision's second section: the sculpture did not fall within one of the nine categories of works enumerated under that section nor did the parties agree in writing that the sculpture be a work made for hire. Accordingly, the court of appeals held that Reid owned the copyright (but remanded for a determination whether the sculpture was a joint work under the Copyright Act).[103]

The United States Supreme Court affirmed the holding that the sculpture was not a work made for hire. In its reasoning it noted as follows:

> To determine whether a work is for hire under the [Copyright] Act, a court should first ascertain, using principles of general common law of agency, whether the work was prepared by an employee or an independent contractor. After making this determination, the court can apply the appropriate subsection of [the work made for hire provision].[104]

Here the Supreme Court found that Reid was an independent contractor.

> True, CCNV members directed enough of Reid's work to ensure that he produced a sculpture that met their specifications. . . . *But the extent of control the hiring party exercises over the details of the product is not dispositive.*[105] (emphasis added)

As to the second section of the work made for hire provision, CCNV conceded that the sculpture could not fall within that category. The Supreme Court did note, however, as did the court of appeals, that the sculpture might be a joint work if, on remand, the district court determines that "CCNV and Reid prepared the work 'with the intention that their contributions be merged into inseparable or interdependent parts of a unitary whole.'"[106]

Under the 1976 Act, works made for hire differ from other works in several ways. First, the copyright term of a work made for hire is not the life of the author plus fifty years; rather, it is a term of seventy-five years from the year of its first publication or 100 years from creation, whichever expires first.[107] Second, the author of a work made for hire, unlike the author of other works, does not have the right to terminate the copyright holder's ownership of copyright after thirty-five years.[108] Termination of copyright in general is discussed later in this chapter (see pages 382-83).

Under the 1909 Act, there was a legal presumption that employers owned the copyright to works created by their employees by virtue of the employment relationship.[109] Moreover, through case law, the for-hire rule was often presumed to exist for specifically commissioned works. Whether the copyright was initially vested in the commissioning party or in the independent contractor depended on the parties' intention, when cognizable.[110] When that intention was not expressly stated, most case law generally held that the copyright in the work was vested in the party commissioning the work.[111] Thus, in two respects the 1909 Act granted broader rights to the commissioning party than does the 1976 Act: first, the copyright could be vested in the commissioning party despite the absence of a written agreement to that effect, and, second, a commissioning party could claim the copyright as against the independent contractor whether or not the work belonged to one of the nine prescribed categories previously cited.[112]

PROCEDURES OF COPYRIGHT

Unlike most nations throughout the world, the United States requires adherence to certain formalities in order to preserve both the copyright and certain remedies under the copyright. Recently, with the passage of the Berne Convention Implementation Act of 1988 (the 1988 Act)[113] amending the 1976 Act and causing the United States to become an adherent to the Berne Convention, such formalities have been relaxed. They have not, however, been altogether abolished. The 1988 Act became effective March 1, 1989. As it has no retroactive effect, the requirements of the law as it existed prior to March 1, 1989, will continue to apply to preexisting issues. The 1988 Act is discussed in greater detail at pages 388-90, and a copy of the 1988 Act is included at the end of this chapter.

Notice

As to copies of works publicly distributed by authority of the copyright owner on or after March 1, 1989, the 1976 Act, as amended, makes the required notice provisions permissive rather than mandatory.[114] Nevertheless, we strongly recommend that all artists wishing to retain the copyright in works of art created by them correctly affix the copyright notice specified in the 1976 Act. As to copies of works publicly distributed by authority of the copyright owner under the 1976 Act prior to March 1, 1989, a copyright notice is required.[115] Notice was also required under the 1909 Act.[116] Unlike the earlier Act, however, the 1976 Act provides that omission of the notice or an erroneous notice no longer causes immediate forfeiture of the copyright and can be corrected by registration within five years.[117]

Form and Placement of Notice

The Copyright Act of 1976

The prescribed copyright notice must be affixed to all "visually" perceptible copies of a work "publicly distributed" anywhere "by authority of the copyright owner."[118] The required form of notice consists of three elements:[119]

1. "©," "Copyright," or "Copr."
2. The year of the work's first publication
3. The name of the owner of the copyright in the work

However, on a pictorial, graphic, or sculptural work that accompanies textual matter or that is reproduced on greeting cards, post cards, stationery, jewelry, dolls, toys, or any useful articles, the date may be omitted.[120]

As to its placement, the notice "shall be affixed to the copies in such manner and location as to give reasonable notice of the claim of copyright."[121] The notice for a two-dimensional work must be affixed directly or by label to the front or the back of the work or another material to which the copy is permanently attached. The same requirement is applicable to a three-dimensional work except that the notice must be affixed on a visible portion of the work.[122] As to copies of works publicly distributed under the 1976 Act by authority of the copyright owner on or after March 1, 1989, the codified requirements as to the correct form and placement of the copyright notice are permissive rather than mandatory.[123]

The 1909 Act

The prescribed copyright notice was required to be affixed on each copy of a work "published or offered for sale in the United States by authority of the copyright proprietor."[124] The required form of notice for works of art was identical to the 1976 Act except that the year of the work's first publication was not required.[125] Moreover, for works of art an alternative short-form notice was available, consisting of "©" plus the mark or symbol of the copyright proprietor, provided that the proprietor's name appeared on some accessible portion of the copy of the work.[126]

As to placement of the notice, the 1909 Act, unlike the 1976 Act, had no statutory requirement. Case law, however, dictated that the notice be placed on an integral part of the artwork that provided the public, on inspection, with notice of the proprietor's claim of copyright.[127] That was certainly not the case in *Sherr v. Universal Match Corporation.*[128] There, the copyright claimant affixed a notice on the back of a very tall statue depicting a charging infantryman. The notice was placed approximately twenty-two feet from the ground and was not visible to anyone inspecting the statue. The court held that the notice was inadequate and that exhibition of the statue injected it into the public domain.[129]

International Protection

Under both the 1976 Act and the 1909 Act, the foregoing forms of notice, when required, are sufficient to provide domestic copyright protection. If, however, the artist or other copyright owner seeks to control international reproduction, the copyright notice must conform to the requirements established in the applicable conventions. The United States, long a member nation of both the Universal Copyright Convention and the Buenos Aires Convention, has, as of March 1, 1989, also become an adherent to the Berne Convention. Although the Berne Convention does not require placement of a notice of copyright on a work, the other two conventions do. The Universal Copyright Convention requires that the year of publication, as defined by the Convention, be on the copyright notice for all works, including works of art. In addition, "©" should be used instead of "Copyright" or "Copr."[130] To adhere to the Buenos Aires Convention, the copyright holder should include the phrase "All Rights Reserved" in the copyright notice,[131] indicating a reservation of the property right.

Omission of Notice

Under the 1976 Act, with respect to authorized public distribution of copies of works prior to March 1, 1989, an omission of the required copyright notice "from no more than a relatively small number of copies . . . distributed to the public"[132] is excused, regardless of whether the omission was by accident[133] and regardless of whether the copyright owner had sought to comply with the 1976 Act.[134] Under the 1909 Act, an omission of copyright notice from a "particular copy or copies" invalidated the copyright unless the copyright proprietor could demonstrate attempted compliance with the copyright notice provisions of the Act.[135] Thus, an omission by accident or oversight (which is contrary to demonstrating attempted compliance) was not excused under the 1909 Act. Moreover, under those circumstances where notice is required, the 1976 Act offers the copyright owner increased protection in the event of failure to apply the notice to copies of a published work in two additional respects. The work is protected (1) if the copyright owner registers the work within five years after the publication without the notice and makes a reasonable effort to add the notice to all copies publicly distributed in the United States[136] or (2) if the notice was omitted by a third person in violation of the express written requirement of the copyright owner.[137]

Defective Notice

Under the 1976 Act, with respect to authorized public distributions of copies of works prior to March 1, 1989, when such copies omit the copyright owner's name or the date in the copyright notice, when it is required, the work is deemed to have been published without any notice and is governed by the provisions discussed in the immediately preceding section, "Omission of Notice."[138] In the case of an error in name, the ownership and the validity of the copyright are not affected, but an innocent infringer may have a complete defense if that party can prove that he or she was misled by the notice.[139] The 1909 Act contained no provisions expressly addressing defective notice.

Registration

The Copyright Act of 1976

Under the 1976 Act, registration is not a condition of copyright protection,[140] but failure to register can have deleterious effects on the copyright. Registration can be obtained at any time during the existence of the copyright in any published or unpublished work.[141] The owner of the copyright or of any exclusive right in a work of art, including "pictorial, graphic, or sculptural works," may register by delivering to the Copyright Office (1) the application form VA for copyright registration; (2) the $10 fee for registration and issuance of a certificate of registration; and (3), for an unpublished work, one deposit copy or, for a published work, two deposit copies of the work's "best edition."[142]

The certificate of registration is issued once it is determined that the material deposited is copyrightable and that the "other legal and formal requirements" of the law have been met.[143] The certificate includes the information given in the application, along with the number and the effective date of the registration.[144] If registration is refused, the applicant receives written notification of the reasons.[145]

Various provisions of the law encourage prompt registration. If, for example, registration is made before or within five years after publication without copyright notice, where such notice is required, it can prevent invalidation of the copyright.[146] Registration is also required for the filing of a renewal claim.[147] Moreover, whether or not a work is published, the holder of the copyright, except for Berne Convention works whose country of origin is not the United States, cannot bring an infringement suit unless the work has first been registered.[148]

Requirement of Deposit

Aside from being required as part of registration, copies of published works, whether or not those works bear a notice of copyright, must be deposited in the Copyright Office for the use of the Library of Congress.[149] The owner of the copyright or of the exclusive right of publication in the work must deposit two complete copies of the work's best edition within three months after the date of its publication in the United States.[150] Failure to make a timely deposit results in the imposition of fines.[151] The deposit may simultaneously fulfill the deposit requirements of registration. For copyright holders of pictorial, graphic, or sculptural works, the Register of Copyrights is empowered either to exempt a work from the deposit requirement or to devise an alternate form of deposit for the purpose of easing any practical or financial hardship on the depositor.[152] Most artists fulfill the requirement of deposit by filing color transparencies of their work.[153]

The 1909 Act

Works created and published before January 1, 1978, had to be registered with the Copyright Office "promptly" after publication;[154] however, failure to register the work did not result in loss of copyright.[155] Registration was necessary to bring a copyright infringement action,[156] as well as to renew the copyright.[157] Works of art and photographs could be registered before publication; however, reproductions, prints, and pictorial illustrations must have been published before registration. If a work registered as unpublished was later published with a notice of copyright, it was necessary to reregister the work.[158] Registration was effected in generally the same manner as provided under the 1976 Act and, regarding works of art, the Register of Copyrights in its discretion was empowered to permit alternative forms of registration when the statutory provisions would be unduly burdensome to the depositor.[159] The 1909 Act had no deposit requirements apart from those needed for registration.

Recordation

The Copyright Act of 1976

Under the 1976 Act, any signed transfer of copyright ownership or other signed documents "pertaining to a copyright" may, if they meet certain conditions, be recorded in the Copyright Office.[160] Although permissive, rather than mandatory, prompt recordation is desirable for several reasons. First, recordation provides constructive notice of the facts stated in the recorded document.[161] Even if a third party did not have actual notice of the document, he or she is presumed to have had that information. However, for the constructive notice to be effective, the underlying work must have been registered.[162] Second, recordation, along with registration, is a prerequisite to an infringement suit regarding transfers prior to March 1, 1989.[163] Third, recordation establishes the priority between conflicting transfers.[164] If an artist, for example, conveys a copyright in a piece of sculpture to a university in December 1988 and conveys the copyright in the same work to Collector *X* in January 1989, the university, as the first transferee, has a grace period of one month to record the copyright conveyance in and to the sculpture in the Copyright Office, after which recording becomes a race between the two transferees. If the university is then last to record, it forfeits its right of copyright.[165] Finally, recordation determines the priority between a conflicting transfer of ownership and a nonexclusive license.[166]

The 1909 Act

As with the 1976 Act, the 1909 Act required a written instrument of assignment for the transfer of statutory copyright.[167] Although the Copyright Office did not have explicit authority to record the assignment of any rights less than the full copyright interest,[168] the Office did accept such partial assignments for recordation. Recordation under the 1909 Act did not necessarily serve as constructive notice to all persons of the contents of the recorded document,[169] and the grace period for recording documents was somewhat longer than in the 1976 Act.[170]

Renewals

The concept of copyright renewal was codified in the 1909 Act.[171] The rationale for the renewal provision was to provide authors, who frequently sold their copyrights outright to publishers for a relatively small sum, with a second chance to exploit their work. The provision was particularly pertinent to authors who initially sold the copyrights in and to their works to publishers for a pittance and later witnessed large profits made from their works by those same publishers.[172] As the Supreme Court noted, the "basic consideration of public policy underlying the renewal provision" was the author's right to "sell his 'copyright' without losing his renewal interest."[173]

Although the concept of copyright renewal has been abolished under the 1976 Act and replaced by the idea of termination, a multitude of copyrighted works published before 1978 are now in their first or second term of copyright. For works in their first term of copyright as of January 1, 1978, the renewal provisions of the 1909 Act have been retained, with the renewal term extended from twenty-eight to forty-seven years.[174] If renewal is not timely made, copyrights in their first term on January 1, 1978, will expire twenty-eight years after copyright was originally secured.[175] Any such work that is a posthumous work or a work made for hire copyrighted by the employer should be renewed by the copyright proprietor.[176] Any other work in its first copyright term as of January 1, 1978, should be renewed by the author, if still living. If the author is deceased, the renewal should be by the author's surviving spouse or children or, absent those, by his or her executor or the author's next of kin in the absence of a will.[177]

Application for renewal may be made during the last calendar year of the first term of copyright. If renewal is not effective by December 31 of the twenty-eighth calendar year, the work is injected into the public domain.[178]

Termination of Transfers

For works in their renewal term of copyright as of January 1, 1978, and for works created on or after that date, the concept of copyright renewal does not apply. Instead, the 1976 Act introduces the concept of termination of transfers, that is, a reversion of the transferred copyrights in and to a work back to the author of that work.[179] The rationale for including a reversion of rights in the 1976 Act was to protect authors against unprofitable transfers of copyright arising from the authors' unequal bargaining positions due, in part, to the impossibility of determining a work's value until it has been exploited. The substitution of the concept of reversion for renewal was an attempt to prevent the unwitting injection of works into the public domain caused by failure to renew.[180]

Works Created on or After January 1, 1978

The artist or, if deceased, his or her heirs may reclaim future copyright ownership of the work by terminating a transfer or license of copyright between the thirty-fifth and the fortieth years after the date of its grant.[181] The right applies to all works except works made for hire, and it cannot be bargained away. Moreover, the right applies solely to grants executed by a living artist on or after January 1, 1978; grants by will are not subject to termination.[182] Notice of termination specifying the actual termination date, which must be within the appropriate five-year period, must be given in writing by the artist or by his or her heirs. The notice must be given between two and ten years before the termination date. If the termination rights are not exercised in a timely manner, the grantee of the copyright interest will benefit for the entire duration of copyright.[183] The estate planning problems that result from the right of termination are discussed in chapter 13.

Works in Their Renewal Term as of January 1, 1978

Termination of transfer also applies to the renewal term of a work's copyright,[184] which has been extended from twenty-eight to forty-seven years. The termination right addresses those additional nineteen years of protection and applies only to transfers made before January 1, 1978.[185] Thus, with respect to those works, an artist or his or her heirs may terminate any transfer of a copyright interest and recover all or part of the additional nineteen years of the renewal term. The termination right, which does not apply to works made for hire or to grants made by will, may take effect at any time during the five-year period beginning either fifty-six years after the date that copyright in the work was originally secured or on January 1, 1978, whichever date is later.[186] The terminating party must give written notice of the termination between two and ten years before its effective date and, in doing so, must comply with regulations prescribed by the Register of Copyrights.[187]

UTILITARIAN OBJECTS AND COPYRIGHT

Although works of applied art are largely outside the scope of this book, a brief discussion of copyright issues as they apply to such works seems appropriate. In *Mazer v. Stein*[188] the United States Supreme Court addressed the issue of whether a lamp manufacturer whose lamps used statuettes of male and female dancing figures made of semivitreous china as bases could copyright those bases. The Court, in determining that the item could be copyrighted, indicated that, as far back as the Copyright Act of 1870, Congress had eliminated any "[v]erbal distinctions between purely aesthetic articles and useful works of art. . . ."[189] The Court also noted: "[T]he legislative history of the [1909 Act] and the practice of the Copyright Office unite to show that 'works of art' are terms that were intended by Congress to include the authority to copyright these statuettes."[190] Therefore, although *Mazer v. Stein* extended copyright protection to applied art, the Copyright Office was impelled to develop distinctions between useful articles that would be granted such protection as works of art and articles that would not. The distinction was often delicate. A 1978 case, in applying the 1909 Act,[191] upheld the determination of the Register of Copyrights that the overall shape or configuration of outdoor lighting fixtures was not copyrightable. In so holding, the court noted that attempts to distinguish between "copyrightable 'works of art' and noncopyrightable industrial designs" has long been an issue of concern to the Copyright Office.[192] The court further noted[193] that the House Report on the 1976 Act,[194] indicating that the Act was intended to draw as clear a distinction as possible between the two categories, illustrates the distinction with the concept of "conceptual separability"—that is,

> [u]nless the shape of an . . . industrial product contains some element that, physically or conceptually, can be identified as separable from the utilitarian aspects of that article, the design would not be copyrighted under the [1976 Act]. [As to] [t]he test of separability and independence from the utilitarian aspects of the article . . . only [those] elements, if any, which can be identified separately from the useful article as such are copyrightable [and even then] copyright protection would extend only to that element and would not cover the over-all configuration of the utilitarian article as such.[195]

In a slightly later case applying the 1976 Act,[196] a federal court of appeals—in upholding the copyrights granted to a designer of sculptured, ornamental belt buckles cast in precious metals—found in the designer's belt buckles conceptually separable elements as, the court noted, did the buckles' wearers, who used them as ornamentation for parts of the body other than the waist. Relying on the foregoing decision, the same federal court five years later, in 1985, in applying the test of "conceptual separability," denied copyright protection to the creator of mannequins of partial human torsos.[197] In so doing, the court noted:

> Congress has explicitly refused copyright protection for works of applied art or industrial design which have aesthetic or artistic features that cannot be identified separately from the useful article. Such works are not copyrightable regardless of the fact that they may be "aesthetically satisfying and valuable."[198]

The court distinguished its present holding from that in the earlier case by noting that the

> ornamented surfaces of the buckles were not in any respect required by their utilitarian functions; the artistic and aesthetic features could . . . be conceived of as having been added to, or superimposed upon, an otherwise utilitarian article. The unique artistic design was wholly unnecessary to performance of the utilitarian function.[199]

In 1987, citing the two preceding cases, a New York federal district court noted that animal-shaped children's backpacks were entitled to copyright protection when "the artistic aspect of the backpack, that is, the animal image, is separate from the useful function of the packs."[200]

Patents as Additional Protection

It may be appropriate for an artist on rare occasions to consider procuring patent protection in addition to copyright protection. Such circumstances may include, for example, creation on the cutting edge of video art. There are three types of patents (utility, plant, and design patents) that may overlap with copyright. A patent protects the discoveries of the inventor against the unauthorized making, using, or selling of the invention in the United States. The invention must be useful, new, and nonobvious, representing a significant advance over prior art.

The novelty and nonobviousness of an invention constitute a far stricter test for patent protection than does the originality required for copyrightability. A design patent is valid for fourteen years. Utility and plant patents are each valid for seventeen years. There is no renewal period for any patent.

The Patent Act of 1952, as amended, is found in title 35 of the United States Code. Patent matters are administered by the Patent and Trademark Office in the United States Department of Commerce.[201]

SUBJECT MATTER AND COPYRIGHT

Addressed here briefly are matters in which the obtaining of copyright protection may be problematical or prohibited.

Works in the Public Domain

Under both the 1976 Act and the 1909 Act, copyright protection is available only if the work has not been placed in the public domain.

Works by Noncitizens

Under the 1976 Act, unpublished works receive copyright protection "without regard to the nationality or domicile of the author."[202] Published works governed by the 1976 Act[203] and all works under the 1909 Act[204] that are created by an artist who is a national, domiciliary, or sovereign authority of a foreign nation or state are *not* copyrightable unless

1. The artist is domiciled within the United States when the work is first published;
2. On the date of its first publication, the artist was a national or domiciliary or sovereign authority of a foreign nation that is a member of either the Universal Copyright Convention or the Buenos Aires Convention;

3. The work was first published in a foreign nation that, on the date of first publication, was a party to the Universal Copyright Convention;
4. The work is a Berne Convention work; or
5. The work comes within the scope of a presidential proclamation.

In addition to the foregoing and under the 1976 Act only, works first published in the United States are entitled to copyright protection, regardless of the author's nationality or domicile.[205]

Manufacturing Clause

The 1909 Act required in its manufacturing clause that books, periodicals, lithographs, and photoengravings of domestic origin must be manufactured in the United States in order to be eligible for copyright protection.[206] Exceptions were made for, among other things, works of foreign origin and works protected under the Universal Copyright Convention.

The manufacturing requirements under the 1976 Act were considerably more relaxed and, as of July 1, 1986, are no longer applicable.[207] Under the 1976 Act, manufacture in the United States or Canada was required of copies imported into or publicly distributed in the United States of a copyrighted work "consisting preponderantly of nondramatic literary material"[208] in the English language. As with the 1909 Act, there were certain exemptions from the manufacturing requirements involving circumstances, for example, in which the author was a nondomestic national or domiciliary.[209] Works of art under the 1976 Act were not subject at all to the manufacturing requirement unless the works were part of a nondramatic literary work in the English language.[210]

Under the 1976 Act, the importation or public distribution of copies in violation of the manufacturing clause did not invalidate copyright protection, but it did, in any civil or criminal infringement action for the unlawful reproduction or distribution of copies, provide the infringer with a complete defense against charges of infringement.[211]

Works of Illegal Content or Use

In a thoughtful and thorough analysis of the matter, a federal appeals court in *Mitchell Bros. Film Group v. Cinema Adult Theater*[212] held that a work is not excluded from copyright protection by reason of its obscene content. Although that is the currently prevailing view, a number of courts in the past took the view that obscene works are not eligible for copyright.[213] *Mitchell* further observed that an obscenity restriction on copyrightability "would be antithetical to [the underlying purpose of copyright] promotion of creativity. The pursuit of creativity requires freedom to explore into the gray areas, to the cutting edge, and even beyond."[214] The *Mitchell* finding goes beyond the issue of obscenity. It suggests that, notwithstanding the scant authority to the contrary,[215] copyright may not be denied to a work because of its seditious or libelous content.

For works of a fraudulent or deceptive nature, at least one early decision did withhold copyright on those grounds,[216] but the *Mitchell* principle again suggests that such grounds do not justify a denial of copyright protection.

CURRENT DEVELOPMENTS

Berne Convention Implementation Act of 1988

As noted earlier in this chapter, the United States has long been a member of the Universal Copyright Convention, an international treaty promoting the international copyright protection of the works of authors of member nations. In addition, and effective as of March 1, 1989, the United States became an adherent of the Berne Convention. That treaty, more than 100 years old and having approximately seventy-six member nations, has grown to be the highest internationally recognized standard for the protection of works of authorship of all kinds. It is expected that one major benefit to the United States in its adherence to the Berne Convention will be enhanced political credibility in its efforts to strengthen copyright standards, to suppress piracy, and to secure in all the nations of the world a realistic minimum standard of protection for creative works.

On October 31, 1988, President Reagan signed the 1988 Act, which became effective March 1, 1989. The 1988 Act enables the United States to become a member of the Berne Convention, and amends the current Copyright Act in a number of ways in order to conform to the Berne Convention. The highlights of the 1988 Act as they apply to artists and works of fine art are summarized below.

Moral Rights

The 1988 Act specifically states that it does not expand or reduce that bundle of rights known as "moral rights" that may be currently available to artists.[217] (Moral rights are the subject of chapter 9 of this book.)

Architectural Plans

The 1988 Act amends the 1976 Act to include architectural plans as a class of works to receive copyright protection.[218]

Copyright Notice

The 1988 Act amends the 1976 Act by eliminating the requirement of a copyright notice and substituting a permissible notice.[219] If the notice is placed on the work, then no weight is to be given to a defendant's interposition of a defense based on innocent infringement in mitigation of actual or statutory damages.[220] We still strongly recommend that artists affix the copyright notice to works of art created by them.

Copyright Registration

The 1988 Act amends the 1976 Act by eliminating the notice requirement as a condition of registration and deposit.[221]

Other Changes

There are other technical amendments to the 1976 Act dealing with, among other issues, infringement and remedies.

Cochran Bill and Kennedy Bill

Other pertinent legislation debated but not acted on in the 100th Congress included the Cochran bill, S. 1223, and the Kennedy bill, S. 1619. The intention of the Cochran bill was to amend the 1976 Act by narrowing the application of the work made for hire doctrine. The bill would have limited the application of the doctrine to traditional employer-employee relationships specifically defined in the bill and would have rendered eight of the nine categories of work now eligible for work made for hire treatment[222] as special orders or commissions completely ineligible.[223] Undoubtedly, the net effect of the bill, if acted on, would have permitted many freelance artists and other artists working on special orders or commissions to retain the copyrights in and to the artwork or other work products they produced. The United States Supreme Court's opinion in *CCNV v. Reid* discussed earlier in this chapter, which clarifies significantly the employer-employee relationship needed to qualify a work as one made for hire, has solved part of the problem addressed by the Cochran bill.

The objective of the Kennedy bill, also known as the Visual Artists Rights Act, was to address three areas of major concern to visual artists: the copyright notice requirement, moral rights, and resale royalties. As to notice, the bill would have eliminated the requirement that copyright notice be affixed to visual art. However, as previously discussed, the enabling legislation making the United States an adherent to the Berne Convention will, in any event, largely eliminate the notice requirement. As to moral rights, the Kennedy bill sought to amend the 1976 Act by granting the right of paternity and the right of integrity to the visual artist. Under at least one version of the bill, the right of paternity would have ensured the artist's right to claim authorship of any publicly displayed work and, conversely, to disclaim authorship of such publicly displayed work if it had been distorted, mutilated, or otherwise altered. The right of integrity would have granted the artist the exclusive right, under an array of circumstances, to prevent unauthorized distortion, mutilation, alteration, or destruction of a work of art in the hands of future owners.[224] As to resale royalties, the last 1988 version of the bill called for the issue to be studied by the National Endowment for the Arts in conjunction with the Register of Copyrights.[225]

The Kennedy bill was introduced in the 101st Congress.[226]

Copyright, Moral Rights, and Film Colorization

A currently controversial issue in the worlds of both art and commerce is the colorization of old black-and-white films.[227] In favor of the process are colorization firms and such television moguls as Ted Turner, who not long ago acquired MGM's collection of over 3,000 old motion pictures. In opposition to the process are film directors and such organizations as the Screen Actors Guild and the Directors Guild of America. Film critics and film viewers are found on both sides of the issue.

The crux of the controversy addresses the issue of copyright ownership of a film as opposed to creative rights in and to that film. Directors, generally opposed to colorization, argue that black-and-white films, rather than being merely films from which color is absent, are composed of an array of creative choices. Accordingly, their integrity should be preserved. Such an argument by directors, in the United States at least, has little, if any, legal impact.

Under the 1976 Copyright Act, motion pictures are generally deemed "works made for hire" with copyright vesting in the employer for whom the work is prepared. Usually the employer is a production company or a studio, which distributes the film. This means that the production company or studio, as copyright owner of a given film, controls the exclusive bundle of prerogatives comprising the copyright—including the right to prepare and distribute derivative works based upon the original, copyrighted work. In the case of motion pictures, a colorized film is a derivative work based on the original black-and-white film. It should be noted in any event, however, that the limited term of protection afforded a copyrighted work by the Copyright Act ensures that virtually all black-and-white films will fall into the public domain, at which time they can be colorized by anyone without securing permission.

In contrast, in those nations that recognize the moral rights of the creator of a work, particularly the right of integrity, the "author" of a black-and-white film may well be able to prevent its colorization. This is particularly true because, in *droit moral* nations, owners of the copyright in a motion picture include such creative contributors to the work as directors and film editors. The Berne Convention, of which most *droit moral* nations are members, regulates the assertion of moral rights by specifically defining and circumscribing the types of alterations to which creative contributors may object.

It has been asserted that no federal law in the United States today prevents the colorization of black-and-white films despite artistic objections to the colorization process, and that perhaps the viewing public should be the ultimate judge of the future viability of colorized films.[228]

NOTES
to Chapter 8

1. Berkowitz & Leaffer, *Copyright and the Art Museum*, 8 ART & L. 249, 255 (1984). The article provides an excellant treatment of both the 1976 Act and the 1909 Act as they apply to works of fine art.

2. See discussion of site-specific art in chapter 7.

3. *See* Berkowitz & Leaffer, *supra* note 1, at 258.

4. 17 U.S.C. § 202 (1988), as amended by Berne Convention Implementation Act of 1988, Pub. L. No. 100-568, 102 Stat. 2853 (1988) (effective March 1, 1989) (hereinafter 1988 Act).

5. 17 U.S.C. § 204(a) (1988), as amended by 1988 Act.

6. *See, e.g.*, Pushman v. New York Graphic Soc'y, 287 N.Y. 302, 39 N.E.2d 249 (1942).

7. *Id.* at 308, 39 N.E.2d at 251. *See also* Grandma Moses Properties, Inc. v. This Week Magazine, 117 F. Supp. 348 (S.D.N.Y. 1953).

8. N.Y. GEN. BUS. LAW art. 12-E (McKinney 1966).

9. CAL. CIV. CODE § 982 (West Supp. 1976).

10. 17 U.S.C. § 102(b) (1988), as amended by 1988 Act.

11. *See* Berkowitz & Leaffer, *supra* note 1, at 260.

12. 1 M. NIMMER, NIMMER ON COPYRIGHT § 2.03[D] (1988).

13. *See, e.g.*, Mazer v. Stein, 347 U.S. 201 (1954).

14. *See* 1 NIMMER, *supra* note 12, at § 2.03[D].

15. *Id.* at § 2.01.

16. 17 U.S.C. § 102(a) (1988), as amended by 1988 Act.

17. *See* Berkowitz & Leaffer, *supra* note 1, at 261.

18. *See* 1 NIMMER, *supra* note 12, at § 2.01[A].

19. Bleistein v. Donaldson Lithographing Co., 188 U.S. 239 (1903).

20. *See* 1 NIMMER, *supra*, note 12, at § 2.01[B].

21. L. Batlin & Son v. Snyder, 536 F.2d 486 (2d Cir. 1976).

22. Morton v. Raphael, 334 Ill. App. 399, 79 N.E.2d 522 (1948).

23. *Id.* at 402, 79 N.E.2d at 523.

24. *Id.* at 403, 79 N.E.2d at 524.

25. *See, e.g.*, William A. Meier Glass Co. v. Anchor Hocking Glass Corp., 95 F. Supp. 264 (W.D. Pa. 1951); Pierce & Bushnel Mfg. Co. v. Werckmeister, 72 F. 54 (1st Cir. 1896).

26. American Tobacco Co. v. Werckmeister, 207 U.S. 284 (1907). Letter Edged in Black Press, Inc. v. Public Bldg. Comm'n, 320 F. Supp. 1303 (N.D. Ill. 1970), in following the *American Tobacco* rule, held that a public exhibition of a Picasso statue constituted a divestment of common-law copyright, noting that in that case there had been no restrictions on copying and no guards to prevent copying. The court also found that there had been an unrestricted distribution of photographs of the statue bearing no copyright notice.

27. *See* 1 Nimmer, *supra* note 12, at § 4.04.

28. *See* Berkowitz & Leaffer, *supra* note 1, at 271.

29. 17 U.S.C. § 405(a)(1) (1988), as amended by 1988 Act.

30. 17 U.S.C. § 405(a)(2) (1988), as amended by 1988 Act.

31. 17 U.S.C. § 101 (1988), as amended by 1988 Act.

32. 17 U.S.C. § 302(a) (1988), as amended by 1988 Act.

33. See discussion of anonymous and pseudonymous works, *infra* at p. 369; see also discussion of works made for hire, *infra* at pp. 370-74.

34. 17 U.S.C. § 24 (1909) (superseded 1976).

35. 17 U.S.C. § 304(a) (1988), as amended by 1988 Act.

36. *Id.*

37. 17 U.S.C. § 304(b) (1988), as amended by 1988 Act.

38. 17 U.S.C. § 303 (1988), as amended by 1988 Act.

39. 17 U.S.C. § 106 (1988), as amended by 1988 Act.

40. 17 U.S.C. § 106(4) (1988), as amended by 1988 Act.

41. 17 U.S.C. § 101 (1988), as amended by 1988 Act.

42. 17 U.S.C. § 106(1) (1988), as amended by 1988 Act.

43. 17 U.S.C. § 101 (1988), as amended by 1988 Act.

44. *See, e.g.*, MGM Distrib. Corp. v. Wyatt, 21 Copyright Office Bull. 203 (D. Md. 1932); Tiffany Prods., Inc. v. Dewing, 50 F.2d 911 (D. Md. 1931); Mura v. Columbia Broadcasting Sys., 245 F. Supp. 587 (S.D.N.Y. 1965).

45. Patterson v. Century Prods., Inc., 93 F.2d 489 (2d Cir. 1937); *see also* Pathe Exch. v. I.A.T.S.E., 3 F. Supp. 63 (S.D.N.Y. 1932).

46. Habersham Plantation Corp. v. Country Concepts, 209 U.S.P.Q. 711 (N.D. Ga. 1980).

47. *See, e.g.*, Ideal Toy Corp. v. Kenner Prods., 443 F. Supp. 291 (S.D.N.Y. 1977); King Features Syndicate v. Fleischer, 299 F. 533 (2d Cir. 1924).

48. *See* 2 Nimmer, *supra* note 12, at § 8.01[G].

49. 17 U.S.C. § 113(c) (1988), as amended by 1988 Act.

50. 17 U.S.C. § 108(h) (1988). *See also* Berkowitz & Leaffer, *supra* note 1, at 289 n.176.

51. 17 U.S.C. § 106(2) (1988), as amended by 1988 Act.

52. 17 U.S.C. § 101 (1988), as amended by 1988 Act.

53. *See* 1 Nimmer, *supra* note 12, at § 3.03. *But see also* Gracen v. Bradford Exch., 698 F.2d 300 (7th Cir. 1983), which required that the derivative work be "substantially different from the underlying work [in order] to be copyrightable." *Id.* at 305.

54. *See* Nimmer, *supra* note 12, at § 3.01.

55. *See* Berkowitz & Leaffer, *supra* note 1, at 290.

56. 17 U.S.C. § 103(b) (1988), as amended by 1988 Act. *See also* 1 Nimmer, *supra* note 12, at § 3.04.

57. *Id.*

58. *Id.*

59. *See, e.g.*, Hartfield v. Peterson, 91 F.2d 998 (2d Cir. 1937); Leon v. Pacific Tel. & Tel., 91 F.2d 484 (9th Cir. 1937); Amplex Mfg. Co. v. ABC Plastic Fabricators, Inc., 184 F. Supp. 285 (E.D. Pa. 1960); Yale Univ. Press v. Row, Peterson & Co., 40 F.2d 290 (S.D.N.Y. 1930).

60. Section 7 of the 1909 Act read, in pertinent part: "but the publication of any such new works shall not affect the force or validity of any subsisting copyright upon the matter employed or any part thereof, or be construed to imply an exclusive right to such use of the original works, or to secure or extend copyright in such original works."

61. 17 U.S.C. § 106(3) (1988), as amended by 1988 Act.

62. H. Henn, Copyright Law: A Practitioner's Guide 165 (2d ed. 1988 & Supp. 1989).

63. 17 U.S.C. § 109(a) (1988), as amended by 1988 Act.

64. 17 U.S.C. § 27 (1909) (superseded 1976).

65. 17 U.S.C. § 109(c) (1988), as amended by 1988 Act.

66. Cal. Civ. Code § 986 (1988). See discussion of resale rights *infra* chapter 10.

67. 17 U.S.C. § 106(5) (1988), as amended by 1988 Act.

68. 17 U.S.C. § 101 (1988), as amended by 1988 Act.

69. *Id.*

70. 17 U.S.C. § 109(c) (1988), as amended by 1988 Act.

71. *See* 3 Nimmer, *supra* note 12, at § 10.01[A].

72. *See, e.g.*, Goldwyn Pictures Corp. v. Howells Sales Co., 282 F. 9 (2d Cir. 1922); M. Witmark & Sons v. Pastime Amusement Co., 298 F. 470 (E.D.S.C. 1924); New Fiction Publishing Co. v. Star Co., 220 F. 994 (S.D.N.Y. 1915); Ed. Brawley, Inc. v. Gaffney, 399 F. Supp. 115 (N.D. Cal. 1975).

73. *See* 3 Nimmer, *supra* note 12, at § 10.01[A], citing such cases as Hirshon v. United Artists Corp. 243 F.2d 640 (D.C. Cir. 1957); Goldwyn Pictures Corp. v. Howells Sales Co., 282 F. 9 (2d Cir. 1922); Hiawatha Card Co. v. Colourpicture Publishers, Inc., 255 F. Supp. 1015 (E.D. Mich. 1966).

74. *See* 3 Nimmer, *supra* note 12, at § 10.01[A].

75. *Id.*

76. 17 U.S.C. § 101 (1988), as amended by 1988 Act.

77. 17 U.S.C. § 501(b) (1988), as amended by 1988 Act.

78. 17 U.S.C. § 101 (1988), as amended by 1988 Act.

79. 17 U.S.C. § 204(a) (1988), as amended by 1988 Act.

80. *See* Berkowitz & Leaffer, *supra* note 1, at 301.

81. 17 U.S.C. § 101 (1988), as amended by 1988 Act.

82. *See* Henn, *supra* note 62, at 71.

83. *Id.* at n.11.

84. Sweet Music, Inc. v. Melrose Music Corp., 189 F. Supp. 655 (S.D. Cal. 1960); Eliscu v. T.B. Harms Co., 151 U.S.P.Q. 603 (N.Y. Sup. Ct. 1966).

85. Edward B. Marks Corp. v. Wonnell, 61 F. Supp. 722 (S.D.N.Y. 1945).

86. 17 U.S.C. § 302(b) (1988), as amended by 1988 Act.

87. 17 U.S.C. § 24 (1909) (superseded 1976). *See also* 1 Nimmer, *supra* note 12, at § 6.09.

88. *See, e.g.*, Meridith v. Smith, 145 F.2d 620 (9th Cir. 1944); Noble v. D. Van Nostrand Co., 63 N.J. Super. 534, 164 A.2d 834 (1960).

89. *See* 1 Nimmer, *supra* note 12, at § 6.11.

90. 17 U.S.C. § 101 (1988), as amended by 1988 Act.

91. *Id.*

92. 17 U.S.C. § 302(c) (1988), as amended by 1988 Act.

93. 17 U.S.C. § 101 (1988), as amended by 1988 Act.

94. *See* 1 Nimmer, *supra* note 12, at § 3.03.

95. *See* 1 Nimmer, *supra* note 12, at § 3.03 n.19.

96. *See* 1 Nimmer, *supra* note 12, at § 3.04.

97. *See* 1 Nimmer, *supra* note 12, at § 3.04, and referring to note 10 therein. But note, also, a line of cases decided under the earlier Act in conflict with the Act's statutory language. Those cases, however, were criticized by Nimmer, who asserted that "these cases are incorrect in that they fail to apply the standard of originality as it is understood in the law of copyright." *Id.*

98. 17 U.S.C. § 101 (1988), as amended by 1988 Act.

99. Other factors to consider are whether the employee was creating something related to his employment duties and whether the employer was the motivating factor in the creation of the work. *See* Berkowitz & Leaffer, *supra* note 1, at 305.

100. *See* 1 Nimmer, *supra* note 12, at § 5.03[B][1][a].

101. 17 U.S.C. § 101 (1988), as amended by 1988 Act.

102. Community for Creative Non-Violence (CCNV) v. Reid, 109 S. Ct. 2166 (1989), *aff'g and remanding* 846 F.2d 1485 (D.C. Cir. 1988).

103. 846 F.2d 1485 (D.C. Cir. 1988). *See* Easter Seal Soc'y for Crippled Children & Adults v. Playboy Enters., 815 F.2d 323 (5th Cir. 1987), *cert. denied,* 108 S. Ct. 1280 (1988); Alson Accessories Ltd. v. Spiegel, Inc., 738 F.2d 548 (2d Cir.), *cert. denied,* 469 U.S. 982 (1984); Evans Newton, Inc. v. Chicago Sys. Software, 793 F.2d 889 (7th Cir.), *cert. denied,* 107 S. Ct. 434 (1986).

104. 109 S. Ct. 2166 (1989).

105. *Id.*

106. *Id.*

107. 17 U.S.C. § 302(c) (1988), as amended by 1988 Act.

108. 17 U.S.C. § 203(a) (1988), as amended by 1988 Act.

109. 17 U.S.C. § 26 (1909) (superseded 1976). *See also* 1 Nimmer, *supra* note 12, at § 5.03[B].

110. *See* 1 Nimmer, *supra* note 12, at § 5.03[B].

111. *Id.*

112. *Id.*

113. *Supra* note 4.

114. 17 U.S.C. § 401(a) (1988), as amended by 1988 Act.

115. *Id.*; 1988 Act *supra* note 4, § 13(b).

116. 17 U.S.C. § 10 (1909) (superseded 1976).

117. *See* HENN, *supra* note 62, at 93; 1988 Act, *supra* note 4, § 13(b).

118. 17 U.S.C. § 401(a) (1988), as amended by 1988 Act; 1988 Act, *supra* note 4, § 13(b).

119. 17 U.S.C. § 401(b) (1988), as amended by 1988 Act; 1988 Act, *supra* note 4, § 13(b).

120. *Id.*

121. 17 U.S.C. § 401(c) (1988), as amended by 1988 Act; 1988 Act, *supra* note 4, § 13(b).

122. *See* Berkowitz & Leaffer, *supra* note 1, at 277.

123. 17 U.S.C. § 401(b), (c) (1988), as amended by 1988 Act.

124. 17 U.S.C. § 10 (1909) (superseded 1976).

125. 17 U.S.C. § 19 (1909) (superseded 1976).

126. *Id.*

127. Coventry Ware, Inc. v. Reliance Picture Frame Co., 288 F.2d 193 (2d Cir. 1961), *rev'g* 186 F. Supp. 798 (S.D.N.Y. 1960), *cert. denied*, 368 U.S. 818 (1961); Sherr v. Universal Match Corp., 297 F. Supp. 107 (S.D.N.Y. 1967).

128. Sherr v. Universal Match Corp., 297 F. Supp. 107 (S.D.N.Y. 1967), *aff'd*, 417 F.2d 497 (2d Cir. 1969), *cert. denied*, 397 U.S. 936 (1970).

129. *Id.* at 112.

130. *See* HENN, *supra* note 62, at 95.

131. *Id.*

132. 17 U.S.C. § 405(a)(1) (1988), as amended by 1988 Act; 1988 Act, *supra* note 4, § 13(b).

133. Beacon Looms, Inc. v. S. Lichtenberg & Co., 552 F. Supp. 1305 (S.D.N.Y. 1982).

134. *See* 1 NIMMER, *supra*, note 12, at § 7.13[A][1].

135. 17 U.S.C. § 21 (1909) (superseded 1976).

136. 17 U.S.C. § 405(a)(2) (1988), as amended by 1988 Act; 1988 Act, *supra* note 4, § 13(b).

137. 17 U.S.C. § 405(a)(3) (1988), as amended by 1988 Act; 1988 Act, *supra* note 4, § 13(b).

138. 17 U.S.C. § 406(c) (1988), as amended by 1988 Act; 1988 Act, *supra* note 4, § 13(b).

139. 17 U.S.C. § 406(a) (1988), as amended by 1988 Act; 1988 Act, *supra* note 4, § 13(b).

140. 17 U.S.C. § 408(a) (1988), as amended by 1988 Act.

141. *Id.*

142. *Id.*; 17 U.S.C. §§ 408(b), 708(a) (1988), as amended by 1988 Act; 37 C.F.R. §§ 202.3(a), 202.3(b)(1)(iii), 202.3(b)(2), 202.3(c)(1), 202.3(c)(2) (1988); *see also* 37 C.F.R. § 202.10(a) (1988). "Best edition" means the edition of the work, "published" in the United States at any time before the date of deposit, that the Library of Congress determines to be most suitable for its purposes. 17 U.S.C. § 101 (1988), as amended by 1988 Act.

143. 17 U.S.C. § 410(a) (1988), as amended by 1988 Act.

144. *Id.*

145. 17 U.S.C. § 410(b) (1988), as amended by 1988 Act.

146. 17 U.S.C. § 405(a)(2) (1988), as amended by 1988 Act; 1988 Act, *supra* note 4, § 13(b).

147. *See* Henn, *supra* note 62, at 122.

148. 17 U.S.C. § 411(a) (1988), as amended by 1988 Act.

149. *See generally* 17 U.S.C. § 407 (1988), as amended by 1988 Act.

150. 17 U.S.C. § 407(a) (1988), as amended by 1988 Act.

151. 17 U.S.C. § 407(d) (1988), as amended by 1988 Act.

152. 17 U.S.C. § 407(c) (1988), as amended by 1988 Act.

153. From a conversation with a specialist in the United States Copyright Office.

154. 17 U.S.C. § 13 (1909) (superseded 1976).

155. Key West Hand Print Fabrics, Inc. v. Serbin, Inc., 269 F. Supp. 605 (S.D. Fla.), *aff'd*, 381 F.2d 735 (11th Cir. 1966).

156. 17 U.S.C. § 13 (1909) (superseded 1976).

157. 17 U.S.C. § 24 (1909) (superseded 1976).

158. R. Duffy, Art Law: Representing Artists, Dealers and Collectors 154-55 (1977).

159. 17 U.S.C. § 13 (1909) (superseded 1976).

160. 17 U.S.C. § 205(a) (1988), as amended by 1988 Act.

161. 17 U.S.C. § 205(c) (1988), as amended by 1988 Act.

162. *Id.*

163. 17 U.S.C. § 205(d) (1988), as amended by 1988 Act; 1988 Act, *supra* note 4, § 13(b).

164. 17 U.S.C. § 205(d) (1988), as amended by 1988 Act.

165. *See* Berkowitz & Leaffer, *supra* note 1, at 302.

166. 17 U.S.C. § 205(e) (1988), as amended by 1988 Act.

167. 17 U.S.C. § 30 (1909) (superseded 1976).

168. *Id.*

169. 3 Nimmer, *supra* note 12, at § 10.07[B].

170. 17 U.S.C. § 30 (1909) (superseded 1976).

171. 17 U.S.C. § 24 (1909) (superseded 1976).

172. 2 Nimmer, *supra* note 12, at § 9.02.

173. Fred Fisher Music Co. v. M. Witmark & Sons, 318 U.S. 643, 653-54 (1943).

174. 17 U.S.C. § 304(a) (1988), as amended by 1988 Act.

175. 17 U.S.C. §§ 304(a), 305 (1988), as amended by 1988 Act. The terminal date of copyright terms discussed in the "Renewals" section of this chapter is actually the close of the calendar year in which they would otherwise expire. *Id.* at § 305.

176. 17 U.S.C. § 304(a) (1988), as amended by 1988 Act.

177. *Id.*

178. *See* Henn, *supra* note 62, at 146.

179. 3 Nimmer, *supra* note 12, at § 11.01.

180. *Id.*

181. 17 U.S.C. § 203(a) (1988), as amended by 1988 Act.

182. *Id.*

183. *See* Berkowitz & Leaffer, *supra* note 1, at 285.

184. 17 U.S.C. § 304(c) (1988), as amended by 1988 Act.

185. *Id.*

186. *Id.*

187. *Id.*

188. Mazer v. Stein, 347 U.S. 201 (1954).

189. *Id.* at 211.

190. *Id.* at 213.

191. Esquire, Inc. v. Ringer, 591 F.2d 796, 799 n.8 (D.C. Cir. 1978): "The Copyright Act of 1976 . . . does not apply to this case . . . [as the] Act does not provide copyright protection for any work that goes into the public domain before January 1, 1978."

192. *Id.* at 801.

193. *Id.* at 803.

194. H.R. Rep. No. 1476, 94th Cong., 2d Sess. 50, 55 (1976).

195. *See* Esquire, Inc. v. Ringer, *supra* note 191, at 803 (citing from the House Report).

196. Kieselstein-Cord v. Accessories by Pearl, Inc., 632 F.2d 989 (2d Cir. 1980).

197. Carol Barnhart Inc. v. Economy Cover Corp., 773 F.2d 411 (2d Cir. 1985).

198. *Id.* at 418.

199. *Id.* at 419.

200. Act Young Imports, Inc. v. B & E Sales Co., 673 F. Supp. 672 (S.D.N.Y. 1987).

201. *See generally* Henn, *supra* note 62, at 2-3.

202. 17 U.S.C. § 104(a) (1988), as amended by 1988 Act.

203. 17 U.S.C. § 104 (1988), as amended by 1988 Act.

204. 17 U.S.C. § 9 (1909) (superseded 1976).

205. For this section on works by noncitizens, see generally Henn, *supra* note 62, at 63 *et seq.*; 1 Nimmer, *supra* note 12, at § 5.05.

206. 17 U.S.C. § 16 (1909) (superseded 1976).

207. 17 U.S.C. § 601(a)(1988), as amended by 1988 Act.

208. *Id.*

209. 17 U.S.C. § 601(b) (1988), as amended by 1988 Act.

210. 17 U.S.C. § 601 (1988) (historical note).

211. 17 U.S.C. § 601(d) (1988), as amended by 1988 Act.

212. Mitchell Bros. Film Group v. Cinema Adult Theater, 604 F.2d 852 (5th Cir. 1979).

213. *See, e.g.*, Barnes v. Miner, 122 F. 480 (S.D.N.Y. 1903); Martinetti v. Maguire, 16 F. Cas 920 (C.C. Cal. 1867) (No. 9173).

214. *See* Mitchell, *supra* note 212, at 856.

215. *See* Hoffman v. LeTraunik, 209 F. 375 (N.D.N.Y. 1913).

216. Stone & McCarrick, Inc. v. Dugan Piano Co., 220 F. 837 (5th Cir. 1915).

217. 1988 Act, *supra* note 4, § 3(b).

218. 1988 Act, *supra* note 4, § 4(a)(1)(A).

219. 1988 Act, *supra* note 4, § 7(a)(2).

220. 1988 Act, *supra* note 4, § 7(a)(4).

221. 1988 Act, *supra* note 4, § 9(a).

222. See discussion of works made for hire at pp. 370-74 *supra*.

223. Under the bill, only works commissioned for use as a part of a motion picture would have remained eligible for work made for hire treatment.

224. See discussion of moral rights in general, chapter 9.

225. See discussion of resale rights in general, chapter 10.

226. See chapter 9 at pp. 436-37.

227. For a thorough examination of the issue, see Kohs, *When Art and Commerce Collide: Colorization and the Moral Right*, 18 J. ARTS MGMT. & L. 13 (1988).

228. *Id.* at 34.

APPENDIX

BERNE CONVENTION IMPLEMENTATION ACT OF 1988 PUB. L. NO. 100-568, 102 STAT. 2853 (1988)

Section 1. Short Title and References to Title 17, United States Code.

(a) SHORT TITLE.—This Act may be cited as the "Berne Convention Implementation Act of 1988".

(b) REFERENCES TO TITLE 17, UNITED STATES CODE.—Whenever in this Act an amendment or repeal is expressed in terms of an amendment to or a repeal of a section or other provision, the reference shall be considered to be made to a section or other provision of title 17, United States Code.

SEC. 2. DECLARATIONS.

The Congress makes the following declarations:

(1) The Convention for the Protection of Literary and Artistic Works, signed at Berne, Switzerland, on September 9, 1886, and all acts, protocols, and revisions thereto (hereafter in this Act referred to as the "Berne Convention") are not self-executing under the Constitution and laws of the United States.

(2) The obligations of the United States under the Berne Convention may be performed only pursuant to appropriate domestic law.

(3) The amendments made by this Act, together with the law as it exists on the date of the enactment of this Act, satisfy the obligations of the United States in adhering to the Berne Convention and no further rights or interests shall be recognized or created for that purpose.

SEC. 3. CONSTRUCTION OF THE BERNE CONVENTION.

(a) RELATIONSHIP WITH DOMESTIC LAW.—The provisions of the Berne Convention—

(1) shall be given effect under title 17, as amended by this Act,

and any other relevant provision of Federal or State law, including the common law; and

(2) shall not be enforceable in any action brought pursuant to the provisions of the Berne Convention itself.

(b) CERTAIN RIGHTS NOT AFFECTED.—The provisions of the Berne Convention, the adherence of the United States thereto, and satisfaction of United States obligations thereunder, do not expand or reduce any right of an author of a work, whether claimed under Federal, State, or the common law—

(1) to claim authorship of the work; or

(2) to object to any distortion, mutilation, or other modification of, or other derogatory action in relation to, the work, that would prejudice the author's honor or reputation.

SEC. 4. SUBJECT MATTER AND SCOPE OF COPYRIGHTS.

(a) SUBJECT AND SCOPE.—Chapter 1 is amended—

(1) in section 101—

(A) in the definition of "Pictorial, graphic, and sculptural works" by striking out in the first sentence "technical drawings, diagrams, and models" and inserting in lieu thereof "diagrams, models, and technical drawings, including architectural plans";

(B) by inserting after the definition of "Audiovisual works", the following:

"The 'Berne Convention' is the Convention for the Protection of Literary and Artistic Works, signed at Berne, Switzerland, on September 9, 1886, and all acts, protocols, and revisions thereto.

"A work is a 'Berne Convention work' if—

"(1) in the case of an unpublished work, one or more of the authors is a national of a nation adhering to the Berne Convention, or in the case of a published work, one or more of the authors is a national of a nation adhering to the Berne Convention on the date of first publication;

"(2) the work was first published in a nation adhering to the Berne Convention, or was simultaneously first published in a nation adhering to the Berne Convention and in a foreign nation that does not adhere to the Berne Convention;

"(3) in the case of an audiovisual work—

"(A) if one or more of the authors is a legal entity, that author has its headquarters in a nation adhering to the Berne Convention; or

"(B) if one or more of the authors is an individual, that author is domiciled, or has his or her habitual residence in, a nation adhering to the Berne Convention; or

"(4) in the case of a pictorial, graphic, or sculptural work that is incorporated in a building or other structure, the building or structure is located in a nation adhering to the Berne Convention.

For purposes of paragraph (1), an author who is domiciled in or has his or her habitual residence in, a nation adhering to the Berne Convention is considered to be a national of that nation. For purposes of paragraph (2), a work is considered to have been simultaneously published in two or more nations if its dates of publication are within 30 days of one another."; and

(C) by inserting after the definition of "Copyright owner", the following:

"The 'country of origin' of a Berne Convention work, for purposes of section 411, is the United States if—

"(1) in the case of a published work, the work is first published—

"(A) in the United States;

"(B) simultaneously in the United States and another nation or nations adhering to the Berne Convention, whose law grants a term of copyright protection that is the same as or longer than the term provided in the United States;

"(C) simultaneously in the United States and a foreign nation that does not adhere to the Berne Convention; or

"(D) in a foreign nation that does not adhere to the Berne Convention, and all of the authors of the work are nationals, domiciliaries, or habitual residents of, or in the case of an audiovisual work legal entities with headquarters in, the United States;

"(2) in the case of an unpublished work, all the authors of the work are nationals, domiciliaries, or habitual residents of the United States, or, in the case of an unpublished audiovisual work, all the authors are legal entities with headquarters in the United States; or

"(3) in the case of a pictorial, graphic, or sculptural work incorporated in a building or structure, the building or structure is located in the United States.

For the purposes of section 411, the 'country of origin' of any other Berne Convention work is not in the United States.";

(2) in section 104(b)—

(A) by redesignating paragraph (4) as paragraph (5); and

(B) by inserting after paragraph (3) the following new paragraph:

"(4) the work is a Berne Convention work; or";

(3) in section 104 by adding at the end thereof the following:

"(c) EFFECT OF BERNE CONVEN-

TION.—No right or interest in a work eligible for protection under this title may be claimed by virtue of, or in reliance upon, the provisions of the Berne Convention, or the adherence of the United States thereto. Any rights in a work eligible for protection under this title that derive from this title, other Federal or State statutes, or the common law, shall not be expanded or reduced by virtue of, or in reliance upon, the provisions of the Berne Convention, or the adherence of the United States thereto."; and

(4) by inserting after section 116 the following new section:

"§ 116A. Negotiated licenses for public performances by means of coin-operated phonorecord players

"(a) APPLICABILITY OF SECTION.—This section applies to any nondramatic musical work embodied in a phonorecord.

"(b) LIMITATION ON EXCLUSIVE RIGHT IF LICENSES NOT NEGOTIATED.—

"(1) APPLICABILITY.—In the case of a work to which this section applies, the exclusive right under clause (4) of section 106 to perform the work publicly by means of a coin-operated phonorecord player is limited by section 116 to the extent provided in this section.

"(2) DETERMINATION BY COPYRIGHT ROYALTY TRIBUNAL.—The Copyright Royalty Tribunal, at the end of the 1-year period beginning on the effective date of the Berne Convention Implementation Act of 1988, and periodically thereafter to the extent necessary to carry out subsection (f), shall determine whether or not negotiated licenses authorized by subsection (c) are in effect so as to provide permission to use a quantity of musical works not substantially smaller than the quantity of such works performed on coin-operated phonorecord players during the 1-year period ending on the effective date of that Act. If the Copyright Royalty Tribunal determines that such negotiated licenses are not so in effect, the Tribunal shall, upon making the determination, publish the determination in the Federal Register. Upon such publication, section 116 shall apply with respect to musical works that are not the subject of such negotiated licenses.

"(c) NEGOTIATED LICENSES.—

"(1) AUTHORITY FOR NEGOTIATIONS.—Any owners of copyright in works to which this section applies and any operators of coin-operated phonorecord players may negotiate and agree upon the terms and rates of royalty payments for the performance of such works and the proportionate division of fees paid among copyright owners, and may designate common agents to negotiate, agree to, pay, or receive such royalty payments.

"(2) ARBITRATION.—Parties to such a negotiation, within such time as may be specified by the Copyright Royalty Tribunal by regulation, may determine the result of the negotiation by arbitration. Such arbitration shall be governed by the provisions of title 9, to the extent such title is not inconsistent with this section. The parties shall give notice to the Copyright Royalty Tribunal of any determination reached by arbitration and any such determination shall, as between the parties to the arbitration, be dispositive of the issues to which it relates.

"(d) LICENSE AGREEMENTS SUPERIOR TO COPYRIGHT ROYALTY TRIBUNAL DETERMINATIONS.—License agreements between one or more copyright owners and one or more operators of coin-operated phonorecord players, which are negotiated in accordance with subsection (c), shall be given effect in lieu of any otherwise applicable determination by the Copyright Royalty Tribunal.

"(e) NEGOTIATION SCHEDULE.—Not later than 60 days after the effective date of the Berne Convention Implementation Act of 1988, if the Chairman of the Copyright Royalty Tribunal has not received notice, from copyright owners and operators of coin-operated phonorecord players referred to in subsection (c)(1), of the date and location of the first meeting between such copyright owners and such operators to commence negotiations authorized by subsection (c), the Chairman shall announce the date and location of such meeting. Such meeting may not be held more than 90 days after the effective date of such Act.

"(f) COPYRIGHT ROYALTY TRIBUNAL TO SUSPEND VARIOUS ACTIVITIES.—The Copyright Royalty Tribunal shall not conduct any ratemaking activity with respect to coin-operated phonorecord players unless, at any time more than one year after the effective date of the Berne Convention Implementation Act of 1988, the negotiated licenses adopted by the parties under this section do not provide permission to use a quantity of musical works not substantially smaller than the quantity of such works performed on coin-operated phonorecord players during the one-year period ending on the effective date of such Act.

"(g) TRANSITION PROVISIONS; RETENTION OF COPYRIGHT ROYALTY TRIBUNAL JURISDICTION.—Until such time as licensing provisions are determined by the parties under this section, the terms of the compulsory license under section 116, with respect to the public performance of nondramatic musical works by means of coin-operated phonorecord players, which is in effect on the day before the effective date of the Berne Convention Implementation Act of 1988, shall remain in force. If a negotiated license authorized by this section comes into force so as to supersede previous determinations of the Copyright Royalty Tribunal, as provided in subsection (d), but thereafter is terminated or expires and is not replaced by another licensing agreement, then section 116 shall be effective with respect to musical works that were the subject of such terminated or expired licenses.".

(b) TECHNICAL AMENDMENTS.—(1) Section 116 is amended—

(A) by amending the section heading to read as follows:

"§116. Scope of exclusive rights in nondramatic musical works: compulsory licenses for public performances by means of coin-operated phonorecord players";

(B) in subsection (a) in the matter preceding paragraph (1), by inserting after "in a phonorecord," the following: "the performance of which is subject to this section as provided in section 116A,"; and

(C) in subsection (e), by inserting "and section 116A" after "As used in this section".

(2) The table of sections at the beginning of chapter 1 is amended by striking out the item relating to section 116, and inserting in lieu thereof the following:

"116. Scope of exclusive rights in nondramatic musical works: Compulsory licenses for public performances by means of coin-operated phonorecord players.

"116A. Negotiated licenses for public performances by means of coin-operated phonorecord players.".

SEC. 5. RECORDATION.

Section 205 is amended—

(1) by striking out subsection (d); and

(2) by redesignating subsections (e) and (f) as subsections (d) and (e), respectively.

SEC. 6. PREEMPTION WITH RESPECT TO OTHER LAWS NOT AFFECTED.

Section 301 is amended by adding at the end thereof the following:

"(e) The scope of Federal preemption under this section is not affected by the adherence of the United States to the Berne

Convention or the satisfaction of obligations of the United States thereunder.".

SEC. 7. NOTICE OF COPYRIGHT.

(a) VISUALLY PERCEPTIBLE COPIES.—Section 401 is amended—

(1) in subsection (a), by amending the subsection heading to read as follows:

"(a) GENERAL PROVISIONS.—";

(2) IN SUBSECTION (A), BY STRIKING OUT "SHALL BE PLACED ON ALL" AND INSERTING IN LIEU THEREOF "MAY BE PLACED ON";

(3) IN SUBSECTION (B), BY STRIKING OUT "THE NOTICE APPEARING ON THE COPIES" AND INSERTING IN LIEU THEREOF "IF A NOTICE APPEARS ON THE COPIES, IT"; AND

(4) BY ADDING AT THE END THE FOLLOWING:

"(D) EVIDENTIARY WEIGHT OF NOTICE.—If a notice of copyright in the form and position specified by this section appears on the published copy or copies to which a defendant in a copyright infringement suit had access, then no weight shall be given to such a defendant's interposition of a defense based on innocent infringement in mitigation of actual or statutory damages, except as provided in the last sentence of section 504(c)(2).".

(b) PHONORECORDS OF SOUND RECORDINGS.—Section 402 is amended—

(1) in subsection (a), by amending the subsection heading to read as follows:

"(a) GENERAL PROVISIONS.—";

(2) in subsection (a), by striking out "shall be placed on all" and inserting in lieu thereof "may be placed on";

(3) in subsection (b), by striking out "The notice appearing on the phonorecords" and inserting in lieu thereof "If a notice appears on the phonorecords, it"; and

(4) by adding at the end thereof the following new subsection:

"(d) EVIDENTIARY WEIGHT OF NOTICE.—If a notice of copyright in the form and position specified by this section appears on the published phonorecord or phonorecords to which a defendant in a copyright infringement suit had access, then no weight shall be given to such a defendant's interposition of a defense based on innocent infringement in mitigation of actual or statutory damages, except as provided in the last sentence of section 504(c)(2).".

(c) PUBLICATIONS INCORPORATING UNITED STATES GOVERNMENT WORKS.—Section 403 is amended to read as follows:

"Sections 401(d) and 402(d) shall not apply to a work published in copies or phonorecords consisting predominantly of one or more works of the United States Government unless the notice of copyright appearing on the published copies or phonorecords to which a defendant in the copyright infringement suit had access includes a statement identifying, either affirmatively or negatively, those portions of the copies or phonorecords embodying any work or works protected under this title.".

(d) NOTICE OF COPYRIGHT; CONTRIBUTIONS TO COLLECTIVE WORKS.—Section 404 is amended—

(1) in subsection (a), by striking out "to satisfy the requirements of sections 401 through 403", and inserting in lieu thereof "to invoke the provisions of section 401(d) or 402(d), as applicable"; and

(2) in subsection (b), by striking out "Where" and inserting in lieu thereof "With respect to copies and phonorecords publicly distributed by authority of the copyright owner before the effective date of the Berne Convention Implementation Act of 1988, where".

(e) OMISSION OF NOTICE.—Section 405 is amended—

(1) in subsection (a), by striking out "The omission of the copyright notice prescribed by" and inserting in lieu thereof "With respect to copies and phonorecords publicly distributed by authority of the copyright owner before the effective date of the Berne Convention Implementation Act of 1988, the omission of the copyright notice described in";

(2) in subsection (b), by striking out "omitted," in the first sentence and inserting in lieu thereof "omitted and which was publicly distributed by authority of the copyright owner before the effective date of the Berne Convention Implementation Act of 1988,"; and

(3) by amending the section heading to read as follows:

"§ 405. Notice of copyright: Omission of notice on certain copies and phonorecords"

(f) ERROR IN NAME OR DATE.—Section 406 is amended—

(1) in subsection (a) by striking out "Where" and inserting in lieu thereof "With respect to copies and phonorecords publicly distributed by authority of the copyright owner before the effective date of the Berne Convention Implementation Act of 1988, where";

(2) in subsection (b) by inserting "before the effective date of the Berne Convention Implementation Act of 1988" after "distributed";

(3) in subsection (c)—

(A) by inserting "before the effective date of the Berne Convention Implementation Act of 1988" after "publicly distributed"; and

(B) by inserting after "405" the following: "as in effect on the day before the effective date of the Berne Convention Implementation Act of 1988"; and

(4) by amending the section heading to read as follows:

"§406. Notice of copyright: Error in name or date on certain copies and phonorecords".

(g) CLERICAL AMENDMENT.—The table of sections at the beginning of chapter 4 is amended by striking out the items relating to sections 405 and 406 and inserting in lieu thereof the following:

"405. Notice of copyright: Omission of notice on certain copies and phonorecords.

"406. Notice of copyright: Error in name or date on certain copies and phonorecords".

SEC. 8. DEPOSIT OF COPIES OR PHONORECORDS FOR LIBRARY OF CONGRESS.

Section 407(a) is amended by striking out "with notice of copyright".

SEC. 9. COPYRIGHT REGISTRATION.

(a) REGISTRATION IN GENERAL.—Section 408 is amended—

(1) in subsection (a), by striking out "Subject to the provisions of section 405(a), such" in the second sentence and inserting in lieu thereof "Such";

(2) in subsection (c)(2)—

(A) by striking out "all of the following conditions—" and inserting in lieu thereof "the following conditions:";

(B) by striking out subparagraph (A); and

(C) by redesignating subparagraphs (B) and (C) as subparagraphs (A) and (B), respectively.

(b) INFRINGEMENT ACTIONS.—

(1) REGISTRATION AS A PREREQUISITE.—Section 411 is amended—

(A) by amending the section heading to read as follows:

"§ 411. Registration and infringement actions";

(B) in subsection (a) by striking out "Subject" and inserting in lieu thereof "Except for actions for infringement of copyright in Berne Convention works whose country of origin is not the United States, and subject"; and

(C) in subsection (b)(2) by inserting ", if required by subsection (a)," after "work".

(2) TABLE OF SECTIONS.—The table of sections at the beginning of chapter 4 is amended by striking out the item relating to section 411 and inserting in lieu thereof the following:

"411. Registration and infringement actions.".

SEC. 10. COPYRIGHT INFRINGEMENT AND REMEDIES.

(a) INFRINGEMENT.—Section 501(b) is amended by striking out "sections 205(d) and 411," and inserting in lieu thereof "section 411,".

(b) DAMAGES AND PROFITS.—Section 504(c) is amended—

(1) in paragraph (1)—

(A) by striking out "$250", and inserting in lieu thereof "$500"; and

(B) by striking out "$10,000", and inserting in lieu thereof "$20,000"; and

(2) in paragraph (2)—

(A) by striking out "$50,000.", and inserting in lieu thereof "$100,000."; and

(B) by striking out "$100.", and inserting in lieu thereof "$200.".

SEC. 11. COPYRIGHT ROYALTY TRIBUNAL.

Chapter 8 is amended—

(1) in section 801, by adding at the end of subsection (b) the following: "In determining whether a return to a copyright owner under section 116 is fair, appropriate weight shall be given to—

"(i) the rates previously determined by the Tribunal to provide a fair return to the copyright owner, and

"(ii) the rates contained in any license negotiated pursuant to section 116A of this title."; and

(2) by amending section 804(a)(2)(C) to read as follows:

"(C)(i) In proceedings under section 801(b)(1) concerning the adjustment of royalty rates as provided in section 115 [*sic, 116*], such petition may be filed in 1990 and in each subsequent tenth calendar year, and at any time within 1 year after negotiated licenses authorized by section 116A are terminated or expire and are not replaced by subsequent agreements.

"(ii) If negotiated licenses authorized by section 116A come into force so as to supersede previous determinations of the Tribunal, as provided in section 116A(d), but thereafter are terminated or expire and are not replaced by subsequent agreements, the Tribunal shall, upon petition of any party to such terminated or expired negotiated license agreement, promptly establish an interim royalty rate or rates for the public performance by means of a coin-operated phonorecord player of non-dramatic musical works embodied in phonorecords which had been subject to the terminated or expired negotiated license agreement. Such interim royalty rate or rates shall be the same as the last such rate or rates and shall remain in force until the conclusion of proceedings to adjust the royalty rates applicable to such works, or until superseded by a new negotiated license agreement, as provided in section 116A(d).".

SEC. 12 WORKS IN THE PUBLIC DOMAIN.

Title 17, United States Code, as amended by this Act, does not provide copyright protection for any work that is in the public domain in the United States.

SEC. 13. EFFECTIVE DATE; EFFECT ON PENDING CASES.

(a) EFFECTIVE DATE.—This Act and the amendments made by this Act take effect on the date on which the Berne Convention (as defined in section 101 of title 17, United States Code) enters into force with respect to the United States.

(b) EFFECT ON PENDING CASES.—Any cause of action arising under title 17, United States Code, before the effective date of this Act shall be governed by the provisions of such title as in effect when the cause of action arose.

9

Moral Rights

In France, Germany, and Italy, as well as in most other European and some Latin American nations, there is a recognition of a cluster of prerogatives personal to the creator of a work of art and unrelated to the artist's pecuniary interests. Those prerogatives arise from the belief that an artist, in the process of creation, injects some of his or her spirit into the art and that, consequently, the artist's personality, as well as the integrity of the work, should be protected and preserved. Known as moral rights or the *droit moral* and subscribed to by the approximately seventy-six member nations of the Berne Copyright Convention,[1] that cluster of prerogatives is the focus of this chapter. The following pages address the origins of moral rights, their various categories, their characteristics abroad, the extent of their recognition in the United States through case law and current state legislation, and some of the various attempts made to amend the federal copyright law of the United States to incorporate at least several of the moral rights.

EUROPEAN ORIGINS

Some commentators trace certain of the beginnings of the *droit moral* to the philosophy of individualism that accompanied the French Revolution, as well as to doctrines in civil law nations that developed slowly in the nineteenth century and more rapidly in the twentieth.[2] By 1880, French jurisprudence had begun to recognize at least several of the moral rights. However, the central debate over the nature of artists' rights occurred in Germany near the close of the nineteenth century: an intellectual work had either a dualist *Doppelrecht*—that is, an incorporeal property giving rise to personal rights of either a patrimonial or a moral nature—or a monist nature, whereby both the personal and the patrimonial rights were inseparable parts of a single *Persönlichkeitsrecht*. The debate over those two views was resolved in the first half of the twentieth century. The dualist view prevailed in France, where to this day the author's rights are viewed as an incorporeal cluster of prerogatives separable into moral and patrimonial rights. In Germany the monist view predominated, with moral rights and exploitative interests uniting in a single right that expires seventy years after the artist's death.[3] As the *droit moral* is considered to have originated in France and as that country remains its foremost champion,[4] the following discussion enumerating the categories of the droit moral focuses primarily, though not exclusively, on the French conception of those rights.

CATEGORIES OF MORAL RIGHTS

The following cluster of rights is, under French law, retained by the author of a work even after the work has entered the stream of public commerce.

Right of Disclosure (*Droit de Divulgation*)

The recognition that public disclosure of a work affects an artist's reputation provided a basis for the *droit de divulgation* (the right of disclosure)—that is, the artist has the sole prerogative to determine when and how to make his or her work public.[5] That right, codified under the French law of March 11, 1957, and under the German law of September 9, 1965, actually received its most famous judicial endorsement at the turn of the century. In the case of *Whistler v. Eden*, the Paris Court of Appeals excused the artist James McNeill Whistler, who had been commissioned to paint a portrait of the wife of Lord Eden, from specific performance. Apparently a dispute had arisen as to payment, whereupon Whistler, claiming to be dissatisfied with the work, painted out Lady Eden's head, painted in another head, and refused to deliver the portrait. When Lord Eden sued for breach of contract, Whistler, although required to pay damages for nonperformance, was not compelled to deliver the portrait. The decision reflects the French view that, even when the right of disclosure may impair contractual obligations, an artist retains the absolute right to determine when to disclose his or her work to the public.

Right to Withdraw from Publication or to Make Modifications (*Droit de Retrait ou de Repentir*)

Recognized in Italian and German law, as well as in French law,[6] the *droit de retrait ou de repentir* permits an artist to withdraw a work from publication or to modify the work even if exploitation rights in the work have been transferred, so long as the artist indemnifies the transferee before exercising the right. Clearly, both situations can give rise to tremendous practical difficulties, and, in fact, since 1957, few French cases have even addressed the right.

Right of Authorship (*Droit á la Paternité*)

Over the course of time, the *droit á la paternité* has expanded into three rights.[7] The first of those rights permits an artist to be recognized by name as the author of his or her work or, if the artist wishes, to publish anonymously or pseudonymously. In France the right has been broadly interpreted, so that an artist's name must appear on all copies of a work, as well as on the original piece, and on all publicity materials preceding or accompanying its sale, even if the author has contracted otherwise. A reproduction of a painting, sculpture, or architectural model must bear the name of the original artist. In addition, all publicity materials preceding or accompanying the sale of a work of art—be it an original, a copy, or a reproduction—must bear the name of the original artist, regardless of any contractual arrangements to the contrary. The second of the rights of authorship confers on the artist the right to prevent his or her work from being attributed to someone else. With the third right of authorship, the artist may prevent the use of his or her name on works that he or she did not, in fact, create. That right has been applied in at least two types of instances: first, an artist (or an heir) may remove the artist's name from distorted editions of the work, and, second, the artist may protest the use without permission of his or her name in advertisements.

According to at least one commentator,[8] *droit á la paternité* may be the least problematic of the moral rights to enforce. Perhaps for that reason, the right of paternity is one of the two moral rights reflected in the Berne Copyright Convention and one of the two such rights primarily protected by most of the legal systems acknowledging the droit moral today, the other such right being the right of integrity. Moreover, the rights of paternity and integrity are the two rights adopted by those few states in the United States that have enacted moral rights statutes. A state-by-state summary of such legislation is found later in this chapter.

Right of Integrity (*Droit au Respect de l'Oeuvre*)

Considered by all scholars to be the most essential prerogative of moral rights,[9] the right of integrity empowers the artist, even after title to a work is transferred, affirmatively to prevent any tampering with it. Recognized in France as early as 1874, the right evolved rapidly during the twentieth century and has received exceedingly broad application in recent German case law.[10] The right of paternity and the right of integrity constitutes the two moral rights most frequently protected in the jurisprudence of those governments—be they state or national—that recognize the doctrine of *droit moral*. Further, the right of integrity, like the right of paternity, is reflected in the Berne Copyright Convention.

Note, however, that the right to protect a work against tampering does not necessarily include protection against its complete destruction. In France the law on that issue remains unsettled.[11] In the United States the existence of the right of protection against destruction depends on how the right of integrity is perceived by a particular jurisdiction. In California, Massachusetts, New Mexico, and Pennsylvania, the right of integrity stresses preservation of the artwork; therefore, the statutes in those jurisdictions protect against destruction of a work of art. In New York, Louisiana, Maine, and Rhode Island, on the other hand, the right of integrity is perceived as harboring the more modest intention of preventing harm to the artist's reputation; therefore, the statutes of those states merely prohibit public display of any "altered, defaced, mutilated or modified" work of art, and total destruction is permitted. If, in a jurisdiction, the right of integrity is deemed to emphasize the artist's personality, the pertinent moral-rights statute generally does not include the right to protect against destruction. In such a case, total destruction is apparently deemed less abhorrent than the ongoing display of an altered or mutilated work that misrepresents the artist. If, however, the right of integrity is perceived in a jurisdiction to stress the public interest in preserving the culture, the right to protect against destruction is ordinarily included in the applicable moral rights statute.

CHARACTERISTICS OF MORAL RIGHTS IN EUROPE

To varying degrees, depending on the laws of a particular jurisdiction, moral rights in Europe may be characterized as (1) personal, (2) perpetual, and (3) inviolable and unassignable.[12]

The Personal Right

French law acknowledges that the *droit moral* attaches to the author of a work, rather than to the work itself, and, therefore, remains vested in the artist even after the work is transferred. To claim moral rights in France, the author of a work must be a natural person. That proviso is not uniform throughout Europe; Portuguese law, for example, provides that the moral right to a work that is injected into the public domain attaches to the state, which, in turn, exercises the right through cultural institutions.

The Perpetual Right

French law clearly provides that the *droit moral* is perpetual. Although that may contradict the tenet that the *droit moral* vests solely in the person of the creator of the work, French law distinguishes between the moral right itself and the right to exercise it. Thus, the artist's heirs inherit only the right to exercise the prerogative, not the prerogative itself. Moreover, certain moral rights do, indeed, expire at the author's death. Such rights include the right to withdraw a work from publication and the right to make modifications in it. Generally, the rights of authorship and of integrity survive the author. More problematical is the right of disclosure. Although French law provides that the right is inheritable, a troublesome reality is that the heirs may issue the right. Thus, French law further provides that, in a case of serious misuse, the courts can mandate appropriate measures, including administering the right themselves.

Inviolability and Unassignability

French law pronounces the *droit moral* to be inviolable. Not only may an artist not renounce the prerogative, but the artist may not transfer the rights to a third party, even when that party has become the owner of the material object and the transferee of exploitative rights in it. In reality, however, contractual clauses requiring a transfer of the *droit moral* as a condition of employment are often enforced by the French courts, and the statutory pronouncement of inviolability is checkered with exceptions.

German statutory law is more flexible than the French law regarding the assignment of an artist's moral rights, and the Berne Convention disregards the principle of assignability altogether.

DROIT MORAL AND THE UNITED STATES

In 1790, Congress passed the first American copyright act. The principles of that law were derived from England's Statute of Anne, which was viewed as a three-way compromise[13] among the interests of publishers, authors, and censors. Historically, in both the United States and Britain, statutory copyright protection covered only those property interests conferred by the statute on the copyright owner, who is not necessarily the author. In the United States today, the artist's property rights in his or her work are secured by the Copyright Act of 1976, which also serves to protect the work from unauthorized exploitation. Moreover, neither the current Act nor any of its federal predecessors in the United States accords any recognition of moral rights. Recognizing the injustice wrought by that omission under particular circumstances, the courts have sought to acknowledge the existence of at least part of the *droit moral*, either under copyright or under such labels as unfair competition, breach of contract, defamation, or invasion of privacy.[14] A discussion of early attitudes in the United States toward moral rights as reflected by judicial law and alternative approaches to preserve the rights of injured parties follows.

Early Attitudes

In the 1940s in New York, the judicial climate was not particularly hospitable to moral rights. At least one well-known case—*Crimi v. Rutgers Presbyterian Church*, discussed below—repudiated the contention that such rights have any application to United States law. With the passage of time, however, particularly in recent years, case law has begun to accord at least a limited recognition of moral rights to the artist. That such recognition frequently comes under the guise of other theories of action, rather than under the federal Copyright Act, has served to spur a number of states to enact their own legislation, recognizing to varying extents the artist's *droit moral*.

In *Crimi v. Rutgers Presbyterian Church*,[15] the plaintiff, artist

Alfred Crimi, had in 1937 won a competition sponsored by the defendant to design and execute a mural to be placed on a rear wall of the church. A contract was drawn by the parties' attorneys, and, as per the contract, the work was completed on time, the agreed-on price was paid in full, the work was copyrighted, and the copyright was assigned to the church. As the years passed, a number of parishioners objected to some of the content of the mural, and in 1946, when the church was redecorated, the mural was painted over without first giving notice to the artist. When he learned of the overpainting, the artist brought an action for equitable relief, seeking to compel the church to remove the paint covering the mural or to permit him to remove the mural at the church's expense or to pay money damages. The plaintiff artist alleged that the "artist has a continued limited proprietary interest in his work after its sale, to the extent reasonably necessary to the protection of his honor and reputation as an artist,"[16] and that within that protection is the right of the work's continued existence without destruction, alteration, mutilation, or obliteration.[17] The court noted that the Berne Convention upheld the doctrine of *droit moral* for its member nations, but held that the United States was not a signatory to the Berne Convention. Further to bolster its holding that no rights in the mural were reserved by the artist and that all right, title, and interest in and to the mural was sold and transferred to the church, the court cited both treatise and case law affirming that the concept of moral rights, although recognized and developed in the civil law countries, has not yet received acceptance in the laws of the United States.[18]

The "Monty Python" Case

In the case of *Gilliam v. American Broadcasting Cos., Inc.*,[19] the United States Court of Appeals for the Second Circuit directed the district court to issue a preliminary injunction to restrain the American Broadcasting Companies (ABC) from broadcasting edited versions of three separate programs originally written and performed by the plaintiffs for broadcast by the British Broadcasting Corporation (BBC). The plaintiffs were a group of mainly British writers and performers known as "Monty Python." Since 1969, when the group was formed, it attained popularity through its thirty-minute television programs created for the BBC as part of a comedy series entitled "Monty Python's Flying Circus." Under an agreement between the plaintiffs and the BBC, the plaintiffs wrote and delivered scripts for use in the television series to the BBC. Although the agreement conferred on the BBC final authority to make changes, the writers exercised optimum control over the scripts consistent with the BBC's authority, and only minor changes were permitted without prior consultation with the writers. The agreement further provided that the BBC could license the transmission of recordings of the television programs in any overseas territory.

In October 1973, the BBC empowered Time-Life Films to distribute the Monty Python series in the United States, with permission to edit the programs only to insert commercials and meet requirements of time and applicable censorship or governmental rules and regulations. In July 1975, ABC agreed with Time-Life to broadcast two ninety-minute specials, each consisting of three thirty-minute Monty Python programs not previously shown in the United States.

ABC aired the first of the specials in October 1975, omitting twenty-four of the original ninety minutes recorded. The writers, appalled at the resultant mutilated broadcast, learned that ABC planned to air the second special in December 1975 and, after futile negotiations with ABC concerning that program's editing, brought suit to enjoin the broadcast and for damages.

In ordering the district court to grant the preliminary injunction sought by the plaintiffs, the appellate court held that the defendant, ABC, may have committed a copyright infringement as well as a possible violation of section 43(a) of the Lanham Trade-Mark Act.[20]

As to the possible copyright infringement, the court, in applying the then-current Copyright Act of 1909, noted that the recorded program, as a dramatization of the copyrighted script, is regarded as a new work subject to copyright and entitled to copyright protection as a derivative work and that one who obtains permission to use a copyrighted script in the production of such a derivative work may not exceed the specific purpose for which the permission was granted. The court observed that a situation such as the one before it, in which a licensee makes an unauthorized use of the underlying work (the script) by publishing it in "a truncated version," constitutes the rationale for a finding of copyright infringement.[21]

As to the possible violation of the Lanham Trade-Mark Act, the plaintiffs claimed that the editing done for ABC mutilated the original work and that, consequently, the broadcast of those programs as the creation of Monty Python gave rise to a federal violation. The court observed that the Lanham Trade-Mark Act (the federal counterpart of state unfair competition laws) has been invoked to prevent misrepresentations injurious to a plaintiff's business or personal reputation. The court further noted that a representation of a product that, although technically true, creates a false impression of the product's origin is sufficient to violate the act.

Although the court viewed the facts in the case as likely being in violation of the Lanham Act, it noted that the cause of action, which sought redress for deformation of an artist's work, is rooted in the concept of the *droit moral*, which includes "the right of the artist to have his work attributed to him in the form in which he created it."[22] The court commented:

> American copyright law, as presently written, does not recognize moral rights or provide a cause of action for their violation, since the law seeks to vindicate the economic, rather than the personal, rights of [artists and] authors. Nevertheless, the economic incentive for . . . creation . . . cannot be reconciled with the inability of artists to obtain relief for mutilation or misrepresentation of their work to the public on which the artists are financially dependent.

> Thus courts have long granted relief . . . by relying on theories outside the statutory law of copyright. . . . Although such decisions are clothed in terms of proprietary right in one's creation, they also properly vindicate the author's personal right to prevent the presentation of his work to the public in a distorted form.[23]

The finding of copyright infringement in *Gilliam* was reinforced and carried a step further in another case six years later. In a suit involving "superstation" WGN,[24] which brought an infringement action against United Video, the cable television distributor of its evening news show, for deleting WGN's teletext of news stories and replacing it with a Dow Jones teletext of business news, the Seventh Circuit upheld WGN's claim of infringement: it reasoned that because the teletext was transmitted along with the news show it was covered by the same copyright. In *Gilliam*, the court's holding of copyright infringement was based on a finding that the substantial deletion caused the work's integrity to be severely damaged. No such finding of damage was made in *WGN* to support the court's holding of infringement.[25]

Other Case Law

Aggrieved artists do not lack ingenuity. Since United States law includes no federal statutory recognition of the *droit moral*, artists, in an effort to establish authorship rights, have resorted to other theories of action, in addition to that of copyright infringement and violation of the Lanham Act, with some success. Thus, on a theory of unfair competition, the creator of the famous "Mutt and Jeff" cartoon characters was able to restrain a publisher from publishing, without his consent, other cartoons designated as "Mutt and Jeff" drawn by another cartoonist, lest unauthorized and perhaps inferior depictions of the cartoon characters deceive the public and reduce the characters' financial value to the creator.[26]

On a theory of defamation, an author, who was both a lawyer and a writer, prevailed when he alleged that a publisher had impaired his reputation by publishing a revised, error-ridden edition of his book bearing his name on the title page without indicating that he had not done the revision.[27]

By bringing suit under a privacy statute, a marine painter was able to keep a magazine publisher from selling a crude reproduction of one of his paintings as a pattern for embroidered sofa and pillow cushions. The suit was for the unauthorized use of the artist's name for purposes of trade.[28]

Problems

In many instances, the aggrieved artist was left without relief. One such notable incident occurred in 1980. In 1975, the Bank of Tokyo Trust Company in New York City commissioned the renowned Japanese artist Isamu Noguchi to create a sculpture for its United States headquarters near Wall Street. Designed particularly for the space, the sculpture was a seventeen-foot-long rhomboid suspended point downward from the ceiling of the lobby. Five years later, the bank decided to remove the massive sculpture from the lobby and, without notifying the artist, ordered the work cut up, removed, and banished to storage, thus effectively destroying the work. Noguchi viewed that as an act of "vandalism and very reactionary."[29] Others in the New York arts community were similarly outraged. However, since Noguchi had transferred all his rights in and to the sculpture to the bank, then-current law provided him with no relief. The bank, after all, was simply exercising a traditional property right—the right to destroy.[30]

Noguchi's plight was not an isolated case. In 1979, a change of ownership at the Samoset Resort in Rockport, Maine, brought about the dismantling of a twenty-five-foot-high sculpture by the artist Bernard Langlais that had been installed at the resort's entrance five years earlier. The dismantling, done by means of a chain saw, was accomplished without informing Langlais's widow in advance. Adding insult to injury, the resort left the fragments of the dismantled sculpture uncovered in a heap throughout a summer and an autumn at the rear of the resort's main entrance.[31]

In still another instance, two stone Art Deco sculptures, embedded in the facade of the Bonwit Teller building in New York City since the building's construction in 1928, were smashed by jackhammers in 1980 in the course of razing the building to make way for Trump Tower. The Metropolitan Museum of Art had been interested in acquiring the pieces, and the developer was willing to donate them to the museum if the removal costs were not unreasonable. In the end, although the removal costs were not preemptive, the developer calculated that the costs in terms of delay would be too great. Accordingly, the pieces were destroyed, much to the surprise and dismay of the museum and others who had sought the sculptures' safekeeping.[32]

The publicity generated by those instances and others stoked the fires of public awareness of and sympathy to the plight of the artist. Thus, in 1979 the state of California pioneered moral rights legislation in the United States with the enactment of the California Art Preservation Act (discussed later in this chapter). However, even as recently as 1982, an artist in New York could not seek redress for violation of a moral right by looking to New York legislation, but, rather, was compelled to consider other theories. The artist Frank Stella, for example, had to resort to a stolen property theory to recover two rain-damaged canvases he had intended to discard, but that had disappeared from the landing outside his studio, only to turn up for sale in the defendant's art gallery. Stella's purpose in bringing suit was to prevent the damaged paintings from being represented as his work, thereby harming his reputation as an artist.[33] The parties ultimately settled the case out of court, and Stella recovered and destroyed the paintings. The next year, 1983, New York enacted a moral rights statute that would have been responsive to Stella's plight.

Moral Rights and State Legislation

In recent years several states have enacted limited moral rights legislation. In most of the states, the moral rights granted to artists are versions of paternity and integrity rights. Understandably, no state has adopted the moral right of the artist to withdraw or modify his or her work once it has entered the stream of commerce. To permit such a right to exist in the United States would wreak havoc with established courses of trade and with such bodies of law as the Uniform Commercial Code. The following is a state-by-state survey of the moral rights legislation that has been enacted as of this writing.

California Art Preservation Act[34]

California was the first state in the nation to enact moral rights legislation. Adopted in 1979, the California Art Preservation Act secures rights of paternity and integrity for the artist. It prohibits intentional "defacement, mutilation, alteration, or destruction" of "fine art" and empowers the artist to claim authorship or "for just and valid reason" (which is not defined) to disclaim authorship. "Fine art" includes original paintings, sculpture, drawings, and works of art in glass "of recognized quality." The quality is determined by the trier of fact. Remedies include injunctive relief, actual damages, punitive damages, reasonable attorney and expert witness fees, and other proper relief. Rights exist for the life of the artist plus fifty years, and may be exercised by the artist's heir, legatee, or personal representative. The rights may only be waived by an express, signed, written instrument. The artist must enforce his or her rights within one year of discovery of, or three years after, the act complained of, whichever is later.

In addition, the California Cultural and Artistic Creations Preservation Act,[35] enacted in 1982, permits certain public and charitable institutions to enforce some of the rights granted to artists under the Art Preservation Act if the works of fine art are "of recognized quality and of substantial public interest."

California's approach to *droit moral* legislation is to protect both the artist's reputation and the public interest in preserving the integrity of cultural and artistic creations. Moreover, California's legislation declares that fine art is an expression of the artist's personality; accordingly, its destruction or alteration is prohibited. That is true whether it is in the public eye or not; the art need only be "of recognized quality."

New York Artists' Authorship Rights Act[36]

New York was the second state in the nation to adopt moral rights legislation. Like the California statute, New York's law, enacted in 1983, grants artists the right of paternity—that is, the artist may claim authorship or "for just and valid reason" disclaim authorship. "Just and valid reason" includes unauthorized alteration, defacement, mutilation, or other modification when damage to the artist's reputation has resulted or is reasonably likely to result. However, unlike the California statute, New York's legislation grants a right of integrity that merely prevents public display of a work of fine art that is "altered, defaced, mutilated or modified" if the artwork is displayed as being the work of the artist and damage to the artist's reputation is reasonably likely to result therefrom. The thrust of the New York statute is the preservation of the artist's reputation. Accordingly, the statute applies solely to works on public display on the assumption that an artist's reputation cannot be damaged by acts occurring in private. Moreover, New York's law does not forbid the total destruction of a work; apparently, an artist's reputation cannot be demeaned by a work that has ceased to exist. Works of "fine art" include, without limitation, paintings, sculpture, drawings, works of graphic art, prints, and, for purposes of the *droit moral* statute only, limited-edition multiples of not more than 300 copies. Remedies include legal and injunctive relief. The artist must enforce his or her rights within one year of discovery of, or three years after, the act complained of, whichever is longer.

Louisiana Artists' Authorship Rights Act[37]

Signed into law in 1986, the Louisiana statute, though modeled on New York's legislation, has at least one pertinent, noteworthy difference. As under New York law, the artist retains the right to claim authorship of his or her work of fine art—and to disclaim authorship for just and valid reason. "Just and valid reason" is defined similarly to New York's statute. Unlike that of New York, however, Louisiana's right of integrity prohibits the unauthorized, knowing, public display of a work of fine art or its reproduction in an "altered, defaced, mutilated, or modified form" or the unauthorized public display of such work attributed to the artist under circumstances reasonably likely to result in damages to the artist's reputation. That is, it is unclear whether the artist, under the Louisiana statute, would have to prove damage to reputation in the event his or her work is subjected to unauthorized public display in a changed form: if the artist does not have to prove damage to reputation, the burden of sustaining a claim under this statute is considerably lighter. Works of "fine art" include, without limitation, paintings, drawings, prints, photographic prints, and limited-edition sculpture of no more than 300 copies. Both remedies and the time frame within which an action must be brought are modeled on the New York statute.

Maine Moral Rights Statute[38]

In 1985, Maine enacted a moral rights statute based on the New York model. The paternity rights and the right of integrity are substantially similar to those of New York's statute. Works of "fine art" include, without limitation, paintings, drawings, prints, photographic prints, or limited-edition sculpture of no more than 300 copies. Both remedies and the time frame within which an action must be brought are modeled on the New York statute.

Massachusetts Moral Rights Statute[39]

Enacted in 1984, the Massachusetts Moral Rights Statute is based on the California legislation, granting the rights of paternity and integrity. The Massachusetts statute does, however, differ from California's law in a number of details, including the following: in the Massachusetts statute the forbidden intentional defacement also includes defacement by gross negligence; "fine art" is more broadly defined to include, without limitation, paintings, prints, drawings, sculpture, craft objects, photographs, audio and video tapes, films, and holograms "of recognized quality" as determined by the court (not by the trier of fact); remedies available to artists and certain artists' organizations include injunctive and declaratory relief, actual damages, attorney and expert witness fees, and other proper relief; rights are for the artist's life plus fifty years and are exercisable by the artist's heir, legatee, or personal representative or by the state attorney general if the artist is deceased and the work of art is in public view; rights may be waived by an express, signed, written instrument referring to the specific work concerned; rights must be enforced within one year of discovery of, or two years after, the act complained of, whichever is longer.

New Mexico Act Relating to Fine Art in Public Buildings[40]

Effective June 19, 1987, the New Mexico act follows the California approach and uses language similar to that in the Massachusetts law, but limits certain coverage to art in "public buildings." Paternity and integrity rights are granted. The forbidden intentional defacement also includes defacement by gross negligence. To be protected under the statute, the art must be "fine art" in "public view." "Fine art" includes paintings, prints, drawings, sculpture, crafts, objects, photographs, audio and video tapes, films, and holograms "of recognized quality." "Public view" means on the exterior or interior of a "public building"—that is, a building owned by the state or a political subdivision. The artist may claim "credit," or "for just and valid reason" may disclaim authorship. Rights may be waived by an express, signed, written instrument referring to the particular work involved. No specific period of limitation is included in the Act.

Pennsylvania Fine Arts Preservation Act[41]

Enacted late in 1986, Pennsylvania's statute is based on the California legislation, with its grant of paternity and integrity rights, but the Pennsylvania law applies only to works "displayed in a place . . . accessible to the public." Artists' remedies include injunctive relief, actual damages, punitive damages (payable to a charitable or educational organization), attorney and expert witness fees, and other proper relief. Rights exist for fifty years after the artist's death and are exercisable by the artist's heir, legatee, or personal representative. Rights may be waived by an express, signed, written instrument. The artist must enforce his or her rights within one year after discovery of, or three years after, the violation complained of, whichever is longer.

Rhode Island Artists' Rights Act[42]

Enacted in 1987, Rhode Island's legislation follows New York's statutory approach. It prohibits the unauthorized knowing display in a public place of a work of "fine art" in an altered, defaced, mutilated, or modified form under circumstances in which it would reasonably be regarded as being the work of the artist. The New York requirement, however, that damage to the artist's reputation be reasonably likely to result from the display is *not* included here. "Fine art" includes, without limitation, paintings, drawings, prints, photographic prints, and limited-edition sculpture of no more than 300 copies. The artist may claim authorship or "for just and valid reason" disclaim authorship. "Just and valid reason" is defined as it is in the New York law. Provisions regarding remedies and time periods during which rights must be enforced are substantially similar to those in the

New York law. As in the New York law, there is no provision forbidding the destruction of a work.

Utah Percent-for-Art Statute, Moral Rights Provision[43]

Adopted in 1985, the Utah limited moral rights provision grants a full right of paternity over work created by artists working on commission in the state's public art program. The statute also grants such artists a right of first refusal should the state decide to sell the commissioned work.

MORAL RIGHTS LEGISLATION AND JUDICIAL SCRUTINY

Case law is beginning to test recently enacted moral rights legislation. For example, New York's statute was subjected to scrutiny in *Newmann v. Delmar Realty Co.*,[44] in which the plaintiff, the established fine artist Robert Newmann, secured a court order enabling him to complete his mural, pending the result of further litigation. In February 1982, Newmann signed an agreement with the defendant, Delmar Realty, owner of the building known as the Palladium, and with its tenant, Ron Delsener, a rock-music promoter, whereby Newmann would create a mural by May 1983 to be displayed on the rear wall of the Palladium until March 1988. The agreement also provided that, should Delmar sell or lease the Palladium, it would notify Newmann and use its best efforts to persuade the new tenant to agree to the project. In March 1983, Delmar entered into a fifteen-year lease with Muidallap, also a named defendant, and was apparently unsuccessful in its efforts to persuade Muidallap to continue with the mural project. In April 1983, Muidallap stopped Newmann's work, despite the artist's claim that he could complete the project in a matter of days. Apparently, Muidallap planned to install a new entrance in the rear wall and intended to paint the wall black.[45] Newmann, seeking to enjoin the defendants Delmar Realty and Muidallap from interfering with the completion and the integrity of the mural in progress, maintained, among other points, that he was protected by the recently enacted New York moral rights statute. The court, although noting that denial of access to the uncompleted mural resulted in the mural's display in an unfinished form to the probable detriment of the artist, held in favor of the artist on a contractual basis. Thus, the court was relieved from determining whether the display of an uncompleted work was within the protective scope of a statute that addressed itself to the display of a work in "altered, defaced, mutilated or modified form." Newmann, accordingly, was permitted to finish his mural if he chose to do so, understanding that, when the case was finally decided, Muidallap might be entitled to destroy it.

In a later development in the case, Newmann sought an order of contempt of court against Muidallap for punching two holes in the wall near the artwork. The artist was unsuccessful in that effort.[46]

FEDERAL LEGISLATION: PAST ATTEMPTS AND RECENT CHANGES

The increased awareness in the United States of the desirability of protecting the artist's reputation—if not personality, of which reputation is one factor—has led to attempts on the federal level to amend the current Copyright Act to include some provision for moral rights. Noted below are a few of the recent attempts and changes.

The Visual Artists' Rights Act

As noted in the preceding chapter on copyright, the most recent of the efforts to provide for artists' moral rights, all unsuccessful to date, was the Visual Artists' Rights Act (S. 1619), introduced by Senator Edward M. Kennedy in the 100th Congress, 1st Session, in 1987. Among other provisions, the bill recognized the right of paternity and the right of integrity. In addition, the bill sought to protect works of "fine art"—that is, pictorial, graphic, and sculptural work "of recognized stature"—against intentional destruction or destruction by gross negligence, whether or not the work was publicly displayed. The bill provided that the term of rights was for the life of the artist plus fifty years. S. 1619 substituted for a substantially similar bill from a previous congress—S. 2796, 99th Cong., 2d Sess. (1986). A bill having the substance of S. 1619, which was not passed in the 100th Congress, was introduced in the 101st Congress by Senator Kennedy. A copy of the new bill (S. 1198) follows this chapter.

The Berne Convention Implementation Act

As mentioned in the preceding chapter on copyright, the Berne Convention Implementation Act was signed into law on October 31, 1988, and became effective March 1, 1989. The Berne Act is the requisite legislation that enables the United States to become a member of the Berne Convention. Article *6bis* of the Berne Convention provides in pertinent part:

> 1. Independently of the author's economic rights, and even after the transfer of the said rights, the author shall have the right to claim authorship of the work and to object to any distortion, mutilation, or other modification of, or other derogatory action in relation to, the said work, which would be prejudicial to his honor or reputation.
> 2. The rights granted to the author in accordance with the preceding paragraph shall, after his death, be maintained, at least until the expiry of the economic rights, and shall be exercisable by the persons or institutions authorized by the legislation of the country where protection is claimed.
> 3. The means of redress for safeguarding the rights granted by this Article shall be governed by the legislation of the country where protection is claimed.[47]

Although the United States has become a signatory to the Berne Convention, the Berne Act (as was noted in chapter 8 on copyright) specifically states that it does not expand or reduce the moral rights, if any, that are currently available to artists. In the 100th Congress, at least one bill was proposed to amend the current Copyright Act to implement the Berne Convention and to adopt the moral rights of paternity and integrity for the artist,[48] but that bill was not passed into law.

Future of Moral Rights

Although it appears that the adoption of moral rights throughout the United States by amending the current Copyright Act is an idea whose time has not yet arrived, we believe that that time will be forthcoming. We acknowledge that some of the moral rights—for example, the right to withdraw a work from publication and the right to modify it even after the transferral of exploitation rights, would wreak havoc with our nation's commercial practices and laws.[49] We feel, however, that the artist is entitled to the rights of integrity and paternity as to his or her work, and that the current Copyright Act should be amended to include those two moral rights. Further, although we believe that such an amendment should be premised on the broader concept of art as an extension of the artist's personality that must be preserved, we bow to what is probably the inevitable—that is, legislation for moral rights based on the preservation of the artist's reputation and of the artwork. Most likely, moral rights based on such a rationale would address only those situations involving public display of artwork. We could live with that; however, those rights should be nonwaivable. Otherwise, the artist, who all too often suffers from an inferior negotiating posture in transactions, would be too easily compelled to bargain those rights away.

NOTES
to Chapter 9

1. International Union for the Protection of Literary and Artistic Works, signed at Berne, Sept. 9, 1886; Additional Act and Declaration, signed at Paris, May 4, 1896; revised at Berlin, Nov. 13, 1908; Additional Protocol, signed at Berne, Mar. 20, 1914; revised at Rome, June 2, 1928; revised at Brussels, June 26, 1948; revised at Stockholm, July 14, 1967 (but not ratified by a sufficient number of member states to bring the Stockholm Act into force); revised at Paris, July 24, 1971.

2. For a thoughtful and comprehensive article on moral rights, see DaSilva, *Droit Moral and the Amoral Copyright: A Comparison of Artists' Rights in France and the United States*, 28 Bull. Copyright Soc'y 1, 9 (1980). *See also* Horowitz, *Artists' Rights in the United States: Toward Federal Legislation*, 25 Harv. J. Legis. 153, 155 (1988) (an in-depth discussion of the need for federal legislation protecting artists' rights).

3. DaSilva, *supra* note 2, at 11.

4. Damich, *The New York Artists' Authorship Rights Act: A Comparative Critique*, 84 Colum. L. Rev. 1733, 1734 (1984).

5. *See* DaSilva, *supra* note 2, at 17.

6. *Id.* at 23-24.

7. See *id.* at 26 for a more in-depth discussion of *droit á la paternité.*

8. *Id.* at 28.

9. *Id.* at 31.

10. *Id.*

11. *Id.* at 33.

12. See *id.* at 11 for an in-depth discussion.

13. *Id.* at 38.

14. 2 M. Nimmer, Nimmer on Copyright § 8.21[B] (1988); *see also* Horowitz, *supra* note 2, at 172.

15. Crimi v. Rutgers Presbyterian Church, 194 Misc. 570, 89 N.Y.S.2d 813 (Sup. Ct. 1949).

16. *Id.* at 573, 89 N.Y.S.2d at 816.

17. *Id.*

18. *Id.* at 574-75; 89 N.Y.S.2d at 817-18.

19. Gilliam v. American Broadcasting Cos., Inc., 538 F.2d 14 (2d Cir. 1976).

20. 15 U.S.C.A. § 1125(a) (West 1982 & Supp. 1989). That statute provides in part: Any person who shall affix, apply, or annex, or use in connection with any goods or services, . . . a false designation of origin, or any false description or representation . . . and shall cause such goods or services to enter into commerce. shall be liable to a civil action by any person . . . who believes that he is or is likely to be damaged by the use of any such false description or representation.

See also Verbit, *Moral Rights and Section 43(a) of the Lanham Act: Oasis or Illusion*, 9 COMM/ENT L.J. 383 (1987) (a thoughtful discussion of moral rights protection through the use of section 43[a]).

21. *Id.* at 20-21.

22. *Id.* at 24.

23. *Id.*

24. WGN Continental Broadcasting Co. v. United Video, Inc., 693 F.2d 622 (7th Cir. 1982).

25. *Id.* at 439-41.

26. Fisher v. Star Co., 231 N.Y. 414, 132 N.E. 133 (1921).

27. Clevenger v. Baker Voorhis & Co., 8 N.Y.2d 187, 168 N.E.2d 643, 203 N.Y.S.2d 812 (1933).

28. Neyland v. Home Pattern Co., 65 F.2d 363 (2d Cir.), *cert. denied*, 290 U.S. 667 (1933).

29. Glueck, *Bank Cuts Up a Noguchi Sculpture and Stores It*, N.Y. TIMES, Apr. 19, 1980, at 1.

30. *See* Note, *Sculptures Vandalized*, 68 ART IN AM. 202 (1980).

31. *See* ARTNEWS, Dec. 1979, at 12.

32. *See* McFadden, *Bonwit Art Deco Sculptures Ruined*, N.Y. TIMES, June 6, 1980.

33. Stella v. Mazoh, No. 07585-82 (N.Y. Sup. Ct. Apr. 1, 1982).

34. CAL. CIV. CODE § 987 (West Supp. 1988).

35. CAL. CIV. CODE § 989 (West Supp. 1988).

36. N.Y. ARTS & CULT. AFF. LAW § 14.03 (McKinney 1988).

37. 1986 La. Acts 599, ch. 32.

38. Me. Rev. Stat. Ann. tit. 27, § 303 (1987 Supp.).

39. Mass. Ann. Laws ch. 231, § 85S; ch. 260 § 2c (1984).

40. 1987 N.M. Laws ch. 70, N.M. Stat. Ann. § 13-4B-1 (Supp. 1989).

41. 1986 Pa. Laws No. 161, Pa. Stat. Ann. tit. 73, §§ 2101, 2121 (Purdon 1987).

42. 1987 R.I. Pub. Laws 566.

43. Utah Code Ann. § 64-2a-9 (1985).

44. Newmann v. Delmar Realty Co., N.Y.L.J., June 11, 1984, at 1.

45. *See Manhattan Wall Spurs Test Case over Art*, N.Y. Times, Mar. 3, 1984, at 13.

46. *See* ARTnewsletter, Nov. 27, 1984, at 5.

47. *See* 4 Nimmer, *supra* note 14, at app. 27.

48. *E.g.*, H.R. 1623, 100th Cong., 1st Sess.

49. The moral right *droit de divulgation*, or "right of disclosure," was, under the 1909 Copyright Act, largely protected in the United States by common law copyright. Under the current Copyright Act, the right of first publication still belongs to the author so long as the author has not transferred his or her copyright, but the right is now a matter of federal law and is no longer perpetual.

APPENDIX

CHAPTER 3
PRODUCTS OF THE MIND

§980. Invention, Literature and Art Protected.

(a) (1) The author of any original work of authorship that is not fixed in any tangible medium of expression has an exclusive ownership in the representation or expression thereof as against all persons except one who originally and independently creates the same or similar work. A work shall be considered not fixed when it is not embodied in a tangible medium of expression or when its embodiment in a tangible medium of expression is not sufficiently permanent or stable to permit it to be perceived, reproduced, or otherwise communicated for a period of more than transitory duration, either directly or with the aid of a machine or device.

(2) The author of an original work of authorship consisting of a sound recording initially fixed prior to February 15, 1972, has an exclusive ownership therein until February 15, 2047, as against all persons except one who independently makes or duplicates another sound recording that does not directly or indirectly recapture the actual sounds fixed in such prior sound recording, but consists entirely of an independent fixation of other sounds, even though such sounds imitate or simulate the sounds contained in the prior sound recording.

(b) The inventor or proprietor of any invention or design, with or without delineation, or other graphical representation, has an exclusive ownership therein, and in the representation or expression thereof, which continues so long as the invention or design and the representations or expressions thereof made by him remain in his possession. **Leg.H.** 1872, 1947 ch. 1107, 1949 ch. 921, 1982 ch. 574.

Ref.: Cal. Fms Pl. & Pr., "Literary Property and Copyright," "Patents."

§981. Joint Invention or Authorship.

(a) Unless otherwise agreed, an original work of authorship not fixed in any tangible medium of expression and in the creation of which several persons are jointly concerned, is owned by them in equal proportion.

(b) Unless otherwise agreed, an invention or design in the production of which several persons are jointly concerned is owned by them as follows:

(1) If the invention or design is single, in equal proportions.

(2) If it is not single, in proportion to the contribution of each. **Leg.H.** 1872, 1947 ch. 1107, 1949 ch. 921, 1982 ch. 574.

Ref.: Cal. Fms Pl. & Pr., "Literary Property and Copyright," "Patents."

§982. Assignment or Transfer—Right of Reproduction.

(a) The owner of any rights in any original works of authorship not fixed in any tangible medium of expression may transfer the ownership therein.

(b) The owner of any invention or design, or of any representation or expression thereof, may transfer his or her proprietary interest in it.

(c) Notwithstanding any other provision in this section, whenever a work of fine art is transferred, whether by sale or on commission or otherwise, by or on behalf of the artist who created it, or that artist's heir, legatee, or personal representative, the right of reproduction thereof is reserved to such artist or such heir, legatee, or personal representative until it passes into the public domain by act or operation of law, unless that right is expressly transferred by a document in writing in which reference is made to the specific right of reproduction, signed by the owner of the rights conveyed or that person's duly authorized agent. If the transfer is pursuant to an employment relationship, the right of reproduction is transferred to the employer, unless it is expressly reserved in writing. If the transfer is pursuant to a legacy or inheritance, the right of reproduction is transferred to the legatee or heir, unless it is expressly reserved by will or codicil. Nothing contained herein, however, shall be construed to prohibit the fair use of such work of fine art.

(d) As used in subdivision (c):

(1) "Fine art" means any work of visual art, including but not limited to, a drawing, painting, sculpture, mosaic, or photograph, a work of calligraphy, a work of graphic art (including an etching, lithograph, offset print, silk screen, or a work of graphic art of like nature), crafts (including crafts in clay, textile, fiber, wood, metal, plastic, and like materials), or mixed media (including a collage, assemblage, or any combination of the foregoing art media).

(2) "Artist" means the creator of a work of fine art.

(3) "Right of reproduction", at the present state of commerce and technology shall be interpreted as including, but shall not be limited to, the following: reproduction of works of fine art as prints suitable for framing; facsimile casts of sculpture; reproductions used for greeting cards; reproductions in general books and magazines not devoted primarily to art, and in newspapers in other than art or news sections, when such reproductions in books, magazines, and newspapers are used for purposes similar to those of material for which the publishers customarily pay; art films; television, except from stations operated for educational purposes, or on programs for educational purposes from all stations; and reproductions used in any form of advertising, including magazines, calendars, newspapers, posters, billboards, films or television.

(e) The amendments to this section made at the 1975-76 Regular Session shall only apply to transfers made on or after January 1, 1976. **Leg.H.** 1872, 1947 ch. 1107, 1949 ch. 921, 1975 ch. 952, 1982 ch. 574.

Ref.: Cal. Fms Pl. & Pr., "Art," "Literary Property and Copyright," "Patents."

§983. Dedication by Publication.

If the owner of any invention or design intentionally makes it public, a copy or reproduction may be made public by any person, without responsibility to the owner, so far as the law of this state is concerned. **Leg.H.** 1872, 1947 ch. 1107, 1949 ch. 921, 1982 ch. 574.

Ref.: Cal. Fms Pl. & Pr., "Literary Property and Copyright," "Patents."

§984. Enacted 1872. Repealed 1947 ch. 1107.

A new §984 follows.

§984. When Not Made Public.

If the owner of an invention or design does not make it public, any other person subsequently and originally producing the same thing has the same right therein as the prior inventor, which is exclusive to the same extent against all persons except the prior inventor, or those claiming under him. **Leg.H.** 1949 ch. 921.

Ref.: Cal. Fms Pl. & Pr., "Literary Property and Copyright," "Patents."

§985. Letters and Private Writings—Title—Publication.

Letters and other private communications in writing belong to the person to whom they are addressed and delivered; but they cannot be published against the will of the writer, except by authority of law. **Leg.H.** 1872.

Ref.: Cal. Fms Pl. & Pr., "Literary Property and Copyright."

§987. The California Art Preservation Act.

(a) The Legislature hereby finds and declares that the physical alteration or destruction of fine art, which is an expression of the artist's personality, is detrimental to the artist's reputation, and artists therefore have an interest in protecting their works of fine art against such alteration or destruction; and that there is also a public interest in preserving the integrity of cultural and artistic creations.

(b) As used in this section:

(1) "Artist" means the individual or individuals who create a work of fine art.

(2) "Fine art" means an original painting, sculpture, or drawing, or an original work of art in glass, of recognized quality, but shall not include work prepared under contract for commercial use by its purchaser.

(3) "Person" means an individual, partnership, corporation, association or other group, however organized.

(4) "Frame" means to prepare, or cause to be prepared, a work of fine art for display in a manner customarily considered to be appropriate for a work of fine art in the particular medium.

(5) "Restore" means to return, or cause to be returned, a deteriorated or damaged work of fine art as nearly as is feasible to its original state or condition, in accordance with prevailing standards.

(6) "Conserve" means to preserve, or cause to be preserved, a work of fine art by retarding or preventing deterioration or damage through appropriate treatment in accordance with prevailing standards in order to maintain the structural integrity to the fullest extent possible in an unchanging state.

(7) "Commercial use" means fine art created under a work-for-hire arrangement for use in advertising, magazines, newspapers, or other print and electronic media.

(c) (1) No person, except an artist who owns and possesses a work of fine art which the artist has created, shall intentionally commit, or authorize the intentional commission of, any physical defacement, mutilation, alteration, or destruction of a work of fine art.

(2) In addition to the prohibitions contained in paragraph (1), no person who frames, conserves, or restores a work of fine art shall commit, or authorize the commission of, any physical defacement, mutilation, alteration, or destruction of a work of fine art by any act constituting gross negligence. For purposes of this section, the term "gross negligence" shall mean the exercise of so slight a degree of care as to justify the belief that there was an indifference to the particular work of fine art.

(d) The artist shall retain at all times the right to claim authorship, or, for just and valid reason, to disclaim authorship of his or her work of fine art.

(e) To effectuate the rights created by this section, the artist may commence an action to recover or obtain any of the following:

(1) Injunctive relief.

(2) Actual damages.

(3) Punitive damages. In the event that punitive damages are awarded, the court shall, in its discretion, select an organization or organizations engaged in charitable or educational activities involving the fine arts in California to receive such damages.

(4) Reasonable attorneys' and expert witness fees.

(5) Any other relief which the court deems proper.

(f) In determining whether a work of fine art is of recognized quality, the trier of fact shall rely on the opinions of artists, art dealers, collectors of fine art, curators of art museums, and other persons involved with the creation or marketing of fine art.

(g) The rights and duties created under this section:

(1) Shall, with respect to the artist, or if any artist is deceased, his heir, legatee, or personal representative, exist until the 50th anniversary of the death of such artist.

(2) Shall exist in addition to any other rights and duties which may now or in the future be applicable.

(3) Except as provided in paragraph (1) of subdivision (h), may not be waived except by an instrument in writing expressly so providing which is signed by the artist.

(h) (1) If a work of fine art cannot be removed from a building without substantial physical defacement, mutilation, alteration, or destruction of such work, the rights and duties created under this section, unless expressly reserved by an instrument in writing signed by the owner of such building and properly recorded, shall be deemed waived. Such instrument, if properly recorded, shall be binding on subsequent owners of such building.

(2) If the owner of a building wishes to remove a work of fine art which is a part of such building but which can be removed from the building without substantial harm to such fine art, and in the course of or after removal, the owner intends to cause or allow the fine art to suffer physical defacement, mutilation, alteration, or destruction, the rights and duties created under this section shall apply unless the owner has diligently attempted without success to notify the artist, or, if the artist is deceased, his heir, legatee, or personal representative, in writing of his intended action affecting the work of fine art, or unless he did provide notice and that person failed within 90 days either to remove the work or to pay for its removal. If such work is removed at the expense of the artist, his heir, legatee, or personal representative, title to such fine art shall pass to that person.

(3) Nothing in this subdivision shall affect the rights of authorship created in subdivision (d) of this section.

(i) No action may be maintained to enforce any liability under this section unless brought within three years of the act complained of or one year after discovery of such act, whichever is longer.

(j) This section shall become operative on January 1, 1980, and shall apply to claims based on proscribed acts occurring on or after that date to works of fine art whenever created.

(k) If any provision of this section or the application thereof to any person or circumstance is held invalid for any reason, such invalidity shall not affect any other provisions or applications of this section which can be effected without the invalid provision or application, and to this end the provisions of this section are severable. Leg.H. 1979 ch. 409, 1982 ch. 1517 §1, 1609 §2.5.

1979 Note: This act shall be known and may be cited as "The California Art Preservation Act." Stats. 1979 ch. 409 §2.

§988. Reservation of Ownership Rights in Reproduced, Displayed or Performed Work of Art.

(a) For the purpose of this section:

(1) The term "artist" means the creator of a work of art.

(2) The term "work of art" means any work of visual or graphic art of any media including, but

not limited to, a painting, print, drawing, sculpture, craft, photograph, or film.

(b) Whenever an exclusive or nonexclusive conveyance of any right to reproduce, prepare derivative works based on, distribute copies of, publicly perform, or publicly display a work of art is made by or on behalf of the artist who created it or the owner at the time of the conveyance, ownership of the physical work of art shall remain with and be reserved to the artist or owner, as the case may be, unless such right of ownership is expressly transferred by an instrument, note, memorandum, or other writing, signed by the artist, the owner, or their duly authorized agent.

(c) Whenever an exclusive or nonexclusive conveyance of any right to reproduce, prepare derivative works based on, distribute copies of, publicly perform, or publicly display a work of art is made by or on behalf of the artist who created it or the owner at the time of the conveyance, any ambiguity with respect to the nature or extent of the rights conveyed shall be resolved in favor of the reservation of rights by the artist or owner, unless in any given case the federal copyright law provides to the contrary. **Leg.H.** 1982 ch. 1319.

Ref.: Cal. Fms Pl. & Pr., "Art."

§989. Injunctive Relief to Preserve or Restore Integrity of Fine Art Work.

(a) The Legislature hereby finds and declares that there is a public interest in preserving the integrity of cultural and artistic creations.

(b) As used in this section:

(1) "Fine art" means an original painting, sculpture, or drawing, or an original work of art in glass, of recognized quality, and of substantial public interest.

(2) "Organization" means a public or private not-for-profit entity or association, in existence at least three years at the time an action is filed pursuant to this section, a major purpose of which is to stage, display, or otherwise present works of art to the public or to promote the interests of the arts or artists.

(3) "Cost of removal" includes reasonable costs, if any, for the repair of damage to the real property caused by the removal of the work of fine art.

(c) An organization acting in the public interest may commence an action for injunctive relief to preserve or restore the integrity of a work of fine art from acts prohibited by subdivision (c) of Section 987.

(d) In determining whether a work of fine art is of recognized quality and of substantial public interest the trier of fact shall rely on the opinions of those described in subdivision (f) of Section 987.

(e) (1) If a work of fine art cannot be removed from real property without substantial physical defacement, mutilation, alteration, or destruction of such work, no action to preserve the integrity of the work of fine art may be brought under this section. However, if an organization offers some evidence giving rise to a reasonable likelihood that a work of art can be removed from the real property without substantial physical defacement, mutilation, alteration, or destruction of the work, and is prepared to pay the cost of removal of the work, it may bring a legal action for a determination of this issue. In that action the organization shall be entitled to injunctive relief to preserve the integrity of the work of fine art, but shall also have the burden of proof. The action shall commence within 30 days after filing. No action may be brought under this paragraph if the organization's interest in preserving the work of art is in conflict with an instrument described in paragraph (1) of subdivision (h) of Section 987.

(2) If the owner of the real property wishes to remove a work of fine art which is part of the real property, but which can be removed from the real property without substantial harm to such fine art, and in the course of or after removal, the owner intends to cause or allow the fine art to suffer physical defacement, mutilation, alteration, or destruction the owner shall do the following:

(A) If the artist or artist's heir, legatee, or personal representative fails to take action to remove the work of fine art after the notice provided by paragraph (2) of subdivision (h) of Section 987, the owner shall provide 30 days' notice of his or her intended action affecting the work of art. The written notice shall be a display advertisement in a newspaper of general circulation in the area where the fine art is located. The notice required by this paragraph may run concurrently with the notice required by subdivision (h) of Section 987.

(i) If within the 30-day period an organization agrees to remove the work of fine art and pay the cost of removal of the work, the payment and removal shall occur within 90 days of the first day of the 30-day notice.

(ii) If the work is removed at the expense of an organization, title to the fine art shall pass to that organization.

(B) If an organization does not agree to remove the work of fine art within the 30-day period or fails to remove and pay the cost of removal of the work of fine art within the 90-day period the owner may take the intended action affecting the work of fine art.

(f) To effectuate the rights created by this section, the court may do the following:

(1) Award reasonable attorney's and expert witness fees to the prevailing party, in an amount as determined by the court.

(2) Require the organization to post a bond in a reasonable amount as determined by the court.

(g) No action may be maintained under this section unless brought within three years of the act complained of or one year after discovery of such act, whichever is longer.

(h) This section shall become operative on January 1, 1983, and shall apply to claims based on acts occurring on or after that date to works of fine art, whenever created.

(i) If any provision of this section or the application thereof to any person or circumstances is held invalid, such invalidity shall not affect other provisions or applications of this section which can be given effect without the invalid provision or application, and to this end the provisions of this section are severable. **Leg.H.** 1982 ch. 1517 §4.

Ref.: Cal. Fms Pl. & Pr., "Art."

CHAPTER 4 OTHER KINDS OF PERSONAL PROPERTY

§990. Deceased Personality's Name, Voice, Signature, Photograph, or Likeness in Advertising or Soliciting.

(a) Any person who uses a deceased personality's name, voice, signature, photograph, or likeness, in any manner, on or in products, merchandise, or goods, or for purposes of advertising or selling, or soliciting purchases of, products, merchandise, goods, or services, without prior consent from the person or persons specified in subdivision (c), shall be liable for any damages sustained by the person or persons injured as a result thereof. In addition, in any action brought under this section, the person who violated the section shall be liable to the injured party or parties in an amount equal to the greater of seven hundred fifty dollars ($750) or the actual damages suffered by the injured party or parties, as a result of the unauthorized use, and any profits from the unauthorized use that are attributable to the use and are not taken into account in computing the actual damages. In establishing these profits, the injured party or parties shall be required to present proof only of the gross revenue attributable to the use and the person who violated the section is required to prove his or her deductible expenses. Punitive damages may also be awarded to the injured party or parties. The prevailing party or parties in any action under this section shall also be entitled to attorneys' fees and costs.

(b) The rights recognized under this section are property rights, freely transferable, in whole or in part, by contract or by means of trust or testamentary documents, whether the transfer occurs before the death of the deceased personality, by the deceased personality or his or her transferees, or, after the death of the deceased personality, by the person or persons in whom such rights vest under this section or the transferees of that person or persons.

(c) The consent required by this section shall be exercisable by the person or persons to whom such right of consent (or portion thereof) has been transferred in accordance with subdivision (b), or if no such transfer has occurred, then by the person or persons to whom such right of consent (or portion thereof) has passed in accordance with subdivision (d).

(d) Subject to subdivisions (b) and (c), after the death of any person, the rights under this section shall belong to the following person or persons and may be exercised, on behalf of and for the benefit of all of those persons, by those persons who, in the aggregate, are entitled to more than a one-half interest in such rights:

(1) The entire interest in those rights belong to the surviving spouse of the deceased personality unless there are any surviving children or grandchildren of the deceased personality, in which case one-half of the entire interest in those rights belong to the surviving spouse.

(2) The entire interest in those rights belong to the surviving children of the deceased personality and to the surviving children of any dead child of the deceased personality unless the deceased personality has a surviving spouse, in which case the ownership of a one-half interest in rights is divided among the surviving children and grandchildren.

(3) If there is no surviving spouse, and no surviving children or grandchildren, then the entire interest in those rights belong to the surviving parent or parents of the deceased personality.

(4) The rights of the deceased personality's children and grandchildren are in all cases divided among them and exercisable on a per stirpes basis according to the number of the deceased personality's children represented; the share of the children of a dead child of a deceased personality can be exercised only by the action of a majority of them. For the purposes of this section, "per stirpes" is defined as it is defined in Section 240 of the Probate Code.

(e) If any deceased personality does not transfer his or her rights under this section by contract, or by means of a trust or testamentary document, and there are no surviving persons as described in subdivision (d), then the rights set forth in subdivision (a) shall terminate.

(f) (1) A successor-in-interest to the rights of a deceased personality under this section or a licensee thereof may not recover damages for a use prohibited by this section that occurs before the successor-in-interest or licensee registers a claim of the rights under paragraph (2).

(2) Any person claiming to be a successor-in-interest to the rights of a deceased personality under this section or a licensee thereof may register that claim with the Secretary of State on a form prescribed by the Secretary of State and upon payment of a fee of ten dollars ($10). The form shall be verified and shall include the name and date of death of the deceased personality, the name and address of the claimant, the basis of the claim, and the rights claimed.

(3) Upon receipt and after filing of any document under this section, the Secretary of State may microfilm or reproduce by other techniques any of the filings or documents and destroy the original filing or document. The microfilm or other reproduction of any document under the provision of this section shall be admissible in any court of law. The microfilm or other reproduction of any document may be destroyed by the Secretary of State 50 years after the death of the personality named therein.

(4) Claims registered under this subdivision shall be public records.

(g) No action shall be brought under this section by reason of any use of a deceased personality's name, voice, signature, photograph, or likeness occurring after the expiration of 50 years from the death of the deceased personality.

(h) As used in this section, "deceased personality" means any natural person whose name, voice, signature, photograph, or likeness has commercial value at the time of his or her death, whether or not during the lifetime of that natural person the person used his or her name, voice, signature, photograph, or likeness on or in products, merchandise or goods, or for purposes of advertising or selling, or solicitation of purchase of, products, merchandise, goods or service. A "deceased personality" shall include, without limitation, any such natural person who has died within 50 years prior to January 1, 1985.

(i) As used in this section, "photograph" means any photograph or photographic reproduction, still or moving, or any videotape of live television transmission, of any person, such that the deceased personality is readily identifiable. A deceased personality shall be deemed to be readily identifiable from a photograph when one who views the photograph with the naked eye can reasonably determine who the person depicted in the photograph is.

(j) For purposes of this section, a use of a name, voice, signature, photograph, or likeness in connection with any news, public affairs, or sports broadcast or account, or any political campaign, shall not constitute a use for which consent is required under subdivision (a).

(k) The use of a name, voice, signature, photograph, or likeness in a commercial medium shall not constitute a use for which consent is required under subdivision (a) solely because the material containing such use is commercially sponsored or contains paid advertising. Rather it shall be a question of fact whether or not the use of the deceased personality's name, voice, signature, photograph, or likeness was so directly connected with the commercial sponsorship or with the paid advertising as to constitute a use for which consent is required under subdivision (a).

(*l*) Nothing in this section shall apply to the owners or employees of any medium used for advertising, including, but not limited to, newspapers, magazines, radio and television networks and stations, cable television systems, billboards, and transit ads, by whom any advertisement or solicitation is violation of this section is published or disseminated, unless it is established that such owners or employees had knowledge of the unauthorized use of the deceased personality's name, voice, signature, photograph, or likeness as prohibited by this section.

(m) The remedies provided for in this section are cumulative and shall be in addition to any others provided for by law.

(n) This section shall not apply to the use of a deceased personality's name, voice, signature, photograph, or likeness, in any of the following instances:

(1) A play, book, magazine, newspaper, musical composition, film, radio or television program, other than an advertisement or commercial announcement not exempt under paragraph (4).

(2) Material that is of political or newsworthy value.

(3) Single and original works of fine art.

(4) An advertisement or commercial announcement for a use permitted by paragraph (1), (2), or (3). **Leg.H.** 1984 ch. 1704.

Ref.: Cal. Fms Pl. & Pr., "Privacy."

NEW YORK ARTS AND CULTURAL AFFAIRS LAW

TITLE C—TRANSACTIONS INVOLVING ARTISTS AND THEIR WORKS

Former Title C. Title, comprising former articles 11, 13, 14, 14–A and 15, was added L.1983, c. 876, § 1; and repealed by L.1984, c. 849, § 1.

ARTICLE 11—DEFINITIONS

§ 11.01. Definitions

As used in this title:

1. "Artist" means the creator of a work of fine art or, in the case of multiples, the person who conceived or created the image which is contained in or which constitutes the master from which the individual print was made.

2. "Art merchant" means a person who is in the business of dealing, exclusively or non-exclusively, in works of fine art or multiples, or a person who by his occupation holds himself out as having knowledge or skill peculiar to such works, or to whom such knowledge or skill may be attributed by his employment of an agent or other intermediary who by his occupation holds himself out as having such knowledge or skill. The term "art merchant" includes an auctioneer who sells such works at public auction, and except in the case of multiples, includes persons, not otherwise

defined or treated as art merchants herein, who are consignors or principals of auctioneers.

3. "Author" or "authorship" refers to the creator of a work of fine art or multiple or to the period, culture, source or origin, as the case may be, with which the creation of such work is identified in the description of the work.

4. "Creditors" means "creditor" as defined in subdivision twelve of section 1-201 of the uniform commercial code.

5. "Counterfeit" means a work of fine art or multiple made, altered or copied, with or without intent to deceive, in such manner that it appears or is claimed to have an authorship which it does not in fact possess.

6. "Certificate of authenticity" means a written statement by an art merchant confirming, approving or attesting to the authorship of a work of fine art or multiple, which is capable of being used to the advantage or disadvantage of some person.

7. "Conservation" means acts taken to correct deterioration and alteration and acts taken to prevent, stop or retard deterioration.

8. "Craft" means a functional or non-functional work individually designed, and crafted by hand, in any medium including but not limited to textile, tile, paper, clay, glass, fiber, wood, metal or plastic; provided; however, that if produced in multiples, craft shall not include works mass produced or produced in other than a limited edition.

9. "Fine art" means a painting, sculpture, drawing, or work of graphic art, and print, but not multiples.

10. "Limited edition" means works of art produced from a master, all of which are the same image and bear numbers or other markings to denote the limited production thereof to a stated maximum number of multiples, or are otherwise held out as limited to a maximum number of multiples.

11. "Master" when used alone is used in lieu of and means the same as such things as printing plate, stone, block, screen, photographic negative or other like material which contains an image used to produce visual art objects in multiples.

12. "On consignment" means that no title to, estate in, or right to possession of, the work of fine art or multiple that is superior to that of the consignor vests in the consignee, notwithstanding the consignee's power or authority to transfer or convey all the right, title and interest of the consignor, in and to such work, to a third person.

13. "Person" means an individual, partnership, corporation, association or other group, however organized.

14. "Print" in addition to meaning a multiple produced by, but not limited to, such processes as engraving, etching, woodcutting, lithography and serigraphy, also means multiples produced or developed from photographic negatives, or any combination thereof.

15. "Proofs" means multiples which are the same as, and which are produced from the same masters as, the multiples in a limited edition, but which, whether so designated or not, are set aside from and are in addition to the limited edition to which they relate.

16. "Reproduction" means a copy, in any medium, of a work of fine art, that is displayed or published under circumstances that, reasonably construed, evinces an intent that it be taken as a representation of a work of fine art as created by the artist.

17. "Reproduction right" means a right to reproduce, prepare derivative works of, distribute copies of, publicly perform or publicly display a work of fine art.

18. "Signed" means autographed by the artist's own hand, and not by mechanical means of reproduction, after the multiple was produced, whether or not the master was signed or unsigned.

19. "Visual art multiples" or "multiples" means prints, photographs, positive or negative, and similar art objects produced in more than one copy and sold, offered for sale or consigned in, into or from this state for an amount in excess of one hundred dollars exclusive of any frame. Pages or sheets taken from books and magazines and offered for sale or sold as visual art objects shall be included, but books and magazines are excluded.

20. "Written instrument" means a written or printed agreement, bill of sale, invoice, certificate of authenticity, catalogue or any other written or printed note or memorandum or label describing the work of fine art or multiple which is to be sold, exchanged or consigned by an art merchant.
(Added L.1984, c. 849, § 1.)

Effective Date. Section effective Dec. 31, 1984, pursuant to L.1984, c. 849, § 3.

Derivation. Former sections 11.01, 13.01, 14.01, 14.51 and 15.01.

Said section 11.01, L.1983, c. 876, § 1; amended L.1983, c. 73, § 1; and repealed by L.1984, c. 849, § 1, was from General Business Law § 219, added L.1966, c. 984, § 1; amended L.1969, c. 321, § 1; L.1975, c. 85, § 1; L.1983, c. 73, § 1; and repealed by L.1983, c. 876, § 5.

Said section 13.01, L.1983, c. 876, § 1; repealed by L.1984, c. 849, § 1, was from General Business Law §§ 219–b(pt.), 219–f(pt.), 219–h(pt.), 228–a(pt.). Said section 219–b, added L.1968, c. 454, § 1, formerly § 221; renumbered 219–b and amended L.1975, c. 107, §§ 1, 11, was repealed by L.1983, c. 876, § 5. Said section 219–f, added L.1966, c. 668, § 2, formerly § 223; renumbered 219–f, L.1975, c. 107, § 5, was repealed by L.1983, c. 876, § 5, and L.1983, c. 993, § 1, without reference to L.1983, c. 876, § 5. Said section 219–h, added L.1969, c. 320, § 1, formerly § 225; renumbered 219–h, L.1975, c. 107, § 7, was repealed by L.1983, c. 876, § 5. Said section 228–a, added L.1975, c. 301, § 1, was repealed by L.1983, c. 876, § 5.

Said section 14.01, added L.1983, c. 993, § 1; repealed by L.1984, c. 849, § 1, was from General Business Law § 219–f, added L.1983, c. 993, § 1; and repealed by L.1983, c. 876, § 5.

Said section 14.51, added L.1983, c. 994, § 3; repealed by L.1984, c. 849, § 1, was from General Business Law § 228–m, added L.1983, c. 994, § 3; and repealed by L.1983, c. 876, § 5.

Said section 15.01, L.1983, c. 876, § 1; repealed by L.1984, c. 849, § 1, was from General Business Law § 220–a, added L.1981, c. 992, § 2; amended L.1982, c. 77, § 1; and repealed by L.1983, c. 876, § 5.

Former section 11.03. Section, L.1983, c. 876, § 1, which related to artist and art dealer relationships, was repealed by L.1984, c. 849, § 1. See now section 12.01.

Savings Provision. Section 2 of L.1984, c. 849, eff. Dec. 31, 1984, provided: "2. The repeal of any provision of law by this act [enacting this title and repealing former title C] shall not be construed to take away, impair or affect any right or remedy acquired or given by the provisions hereby repealed; and all existing suits or proceedings may be continued and completed; and all offenses committed or penalties or forfeitures incurred shall continue and remain in force with the same effect as though this act had not become law."

ARTICLE 12—ARTIST-ART MERCHANT RELATIONSHIPS

Section

12.01. Artist-art merchant relationships.

12.03. Exemption from seizure.

12.01. Artist-art merchant relationships

1. Notwithstanding any custom, practice or usage of the trade, any provision of the uniform commercial code or any other law, statute, requirement or rule, or any agreement, note, memorandum or writing to the contrary:

(a) Whenever an artist or craftsperson, his heirs or personal representatives, delivers or causes to be delivered a work of fine art, craft or a print of his own creation to an art merchant for the purpose of exhibition and/or sale on a commission, fee or other basis of compensation, the delivery to and acceptance thereof by the art merchant establishes a consignor/consignee relationship as between such artist or craftsperson and such art merchant with respect to the said work, and:

(i) such consignee shall thereafter be deemed to be the agent of such consignor with respect to the said work;

(ii) such work is trust property in the hands of the consignee for the benefit of the consignor;

(iii) any proceeds from the sale of such work are trust funds in the hands of the consignee for the benefit of the consignor;

(iv) such work shall remain trust property notwithstanding its purchase by the consignee for his own account until the price is paid in full to the consignor; provided that, if such work is resold to a bona fide third party before the consignor has been paid in full, the resale proceeds are trust funds in the hands of the consignee for the benefit of the consignor to the extent necessary to pay any balance still due to the consignor and such trusteeship shall continue until the fiduciary obligation of the consignee with respect to such transaction is discharged in full; and

(v) no such trust property or trust funds shall be subject or subordinate to any claims, liens or security interest of any kind or nature whatsoever.

(b) Waiver of any provision of this section is absolutely void except that a consignor may lawfully waive the provisions of clause (iii) of paragraph (a) of this subdivision, if such waiver is clear, conspicuous, in writing and subscribed by the consignor, provided:

(i) no such waiver shall be valid with respect to the first two thousand five hundred dollars of gross proceeds of sales received in any twelve-month period commencing with the date of the execution of such waiver;

(ii) no such waiver shall be valid with respect to the proceeds of a work initially received on consignment but subsequently purchased by the consignee directly or indirectly for his own account; and

(iii) no such waiver shall inure to the benefit of the consignee's creditors in any manner which might be inconsistent with the consignor's rights under this subdivision.

2. Nothing in this section shall be construed to have any effect upon any written or oral contract or arrangement in existence prior to September first, nineteen hundred sixty-nine or to any extensions or renewals thereof except by the mutual written consent of the parties thereto.

(Added L.1984, c. 849, § 1.)

Effective Date. Section effective Dec. 31, 1984, pursuant to L.1984, c. 849, § 3.

Derivation. Former section 11.03, L.1983, c. 876, § 1; repealed by L.1984, c. 849, § 1. Said section 11.03 was from General Business Law § 219–a, added L.1966, c. 984, § 1, formerly § 220; renumbered 219–a and amended L.1969, c. 321, §§ 2, 3; amended L.1975, c. 85, §§ 2 to 4; and repealed by L.1983, c. 876, § 5.

§ 12.03. Exemption from seizure

No process of attachment, execution, sequestration, replevin, distress or any kind of seizure shall be served or levied upon any work of fine art while the same is enroute to or from, or while on exhibition or deposited by a nonresident exhibitor at any exhibition held under the auspices or supervision of any museum, college, university or other nonprofit art gallery, institution or organization within any city or county of this state for any cultural, educational, charitable or other purpose not conducted for profit to the exhibitor, nor shall such work of fine art be subject to attachment, seizure, levy or sale, for any cause whatever in the hands of the authorities of such exhibition or otherwise.

(Added L.1984, c. 849, § 1.)

Effective Date. Section effective Dec. 31, 1984, pursuant to L.1984, c. 849, § 3.

Derivation. Former section 13.11, L.1983, c. 876, § 1; repealed by L.1984, c. 849, § 1. Said section 13.11 was from General Business Law § 219-k, added L.1968, c. 1065, § 1, formerly § 228; renumbered § 219-k, L.1975, c. 107, § 10; and repealed by L.1983, c. 876, § 5.

ARTICLE 13—EXPRESS WARRANTIES

Section

§ 13.01. Express warranties

Notwithstanding any provision of any other law to the contrary:

1. Whenever an art merchant, in selling or exchanging a work of fine art, furnishes to a buyer of such work who is not an art merchant a certificate of authenticity or any similar written instrument it:

(a) Shall be presumed to be part of the basis of the bargain; and

(b) Shall create an express warranty for the material facts stated as of the date of such sale or exchange.

2. Except as provided in subdivision four of this section, such warranty shall not be negated or limited provided that in construing the degree of warranty, due regard shall be given the terminology used and the meaning accorded such terminology by the customs and usage of the trade at the time and in the locality where the sale or exchange took place.

3. Language used in a certificate of authenticity or similar written instrument, stating that:

(a) The work is by a named author or has a named authorship, without any limiting words, means unequivocally, that the work is by such named author or has such named authorship;

(b) The work is "attributed to a named author" means a work of the period of the author, attributed to him, but not with certainty by him; or

(c) The work is of the "school of a named author" means a work of the period of the author, by a pupil or close follower of the author, but not by the author.

4. (a) An express warranty and disclaimers intended to negate or limit such warranty shall be construed wherever reasonable as consistent with each other but subject to the provisions of section 2-202 of the uniform

commercial code on parol or extrinsic evidence, negation or limitation is inoperative to the extent that such construction is unreasonable.

(b) Such negation or limitation shall be deemed unreasonable if:

(i) the disclaimer is not conspicuous, written and apart from the warranty, in words which clearly and specifically apprise the buyer that the seller assumes no risk, liability or responsibility for the material facts stated concerning such work of fine art. Words of general disclaimer are not sufficient to negate or limit an express warranty; or

(ii) the work of fine art is proved to be a counterfeit and this was not clearly indicated in the description of the work; or

(iii) the information provided is proved to be, as of the date of sale or exchange, false, mistaken or erroneous.

(Added L.1984, c. 849, § 1.)

Effective Date. Section effective Dec. 31, 1984, pursuant to L.1984, c. 849, § 3.

Derivation. Former section 13.03, L.1983, c. 876, § 1; repealed by L.1984, c. 849, § 1. Said section 13.03 was from General Business Law § 219–c, added L.1968, c. 454, § 1, formerly § 222; renumbered 219–c, L.1975, c. 107, § 2; and repealed by L.1983, c. 876, § 5.

Former Section 13.01. Section L.1983, c. 876, § 1, which related to definitions concerning works of fine arts, prints and posters, was repealed by L.1984, c. 849, § 1. See now section 11.01.

§ 13.03. Falsifying certificates of authenticity or any similar written instrument

A person who, with intent to defraud, deceive or injure another, makes, utters or issues a certificate of authenticity or any similar written instrument for a work of fine art attesting to material facts which the work does not in fact possess is guilty of a class A misdemeanor.

(Added L.1984, c. 849, § 1.)

Effective Date. Section effective Dec. 31, 1984, pursuant to L.1984, c. 849, § 3.

Derivation. Former section 13.09, L.1983, c. 876, § 1; repealed by L.1984, c. 849, § 1. Said section 13.09 was from General Business Law § 219–i, added L.1969, c. 320, § 1, formerly § 226; renumbered 219–i, L.1975, c. 107, § 8; and repealed by L.1983, c. 876, § 5.

Former Section 13.03. section, L.1983, c. 876, § 1, which related to express warranties of art merchants, was repealed by L.1984, c. 849, § 1. See now section 13.01.

§ 13.05. Express warranties for multiples

1. When an art merchant furnishes the name of the artist of a multiple, or otherwise furnishes information required by this title for any time period as to transactions including offers, sales or consignments, the provisions of section 13.01 of this article shall apply except that said section shall be deemed to include sales to art merchants. The existence of a reasonable basis in fact for information warranted shall not be a defense in an action to enforce such warranty, except in the case of photographs produced prior to nineteen hundred fifty, and multiples produced prior to nineteen hundred.

2. The provisions of subdivision four of section 13.01 of this article shall apply when an art merchant disclaims knowledge as to a multiple about which information is required by this title, provided that in addition, such disclaimer shall be ineffective unless clearly, specifically and categorically stated as to each item of information and contained in the physical context

of other language setting forth the required information as to a specific multiple.

(Added L.1984, c. 849, § 1.)

Effective Date. Section effective Dec. 31, 1984, pursuant to L.1984, c. 849, § 3.

Derivation. Former sections 13.05 and 15.13.

Said section 13.05, L.1983, c. 876, § 1; repealed by L.1984, c. 849, § 1, was from General Business Law § 219–d, added L.1968, c. 454, § 1, formerly § 222–a; renumbered 219–d, L.1975, c. 107, § 3; and repealed by L.1983, c. 876, § 5.

Said section 15.13, L.1983, c. 876, § 1; repealed by L.1984, c. 849, § 1, was from General Business Law § 220–g, added L.1981, c. 992, § 2; amended L.1982, c. 77, § 5; and repealed by L.1983, c. 876, § 5.

§ 13.07. Construction

1. The rights and liabilities created by this article shall be construed to be in addition to and not in substitution, exclusion or displacement of other rights and liabilities provided by law, including the law of principal and agent, except where such construction would, as a matter of law, be unreasonable.

2. No art merchant who, as buyer, is excluded from obtaining the benefits of an express warranty under this article shall thereby be deprived of the benefits of any other provision of law.

(Added L.1984, c. 849, § 1.)

Effective Date. Section effective Dec. 31, 1984, pursuant to L.1984, c. 849, § 3.

Derivation. Former section 13.21, L.1983, c. 876, § 1; repealed by L.1984, c. 849, § 1. Said section 13.21 was from General Business Law § 219–e, added L.1968, c. 454, § 1, formerly § 222–b; renumbered 219–e, L.1975, c. 107, § 4; and repealed by L.1983, c. 876, § 5.

Former Sections 13.07 to 13.19. Section 13.07, L.1983, c. 876, § 1, which related to the right to reproduce works of fine art, was repealed by L.1984, c. 849, § 1. See now section 14.01.

Section 13.09, L.1983, c. 876, § 1, which related to falsifying certificates of authenticity of works of fine art, was repealed by L.1984, c. 849, § 1. See now section 13.03.

Section 13.11, L.1983, c. 876, § 1, which related to exemption of works of fine art from seizure, was repealed by L.1984, c. 849, § 1. See now section 12.03.

Section 13.13, L.1983, c. 876, § 1, which related to the application of former sections 13.17 through 13.21, was repealed by L.1984, c. 849, § 1.

Section 13.15, L.1983, c. 876, § 1, which related to the description of fine prints as being signed, was repealed by L.1984, c. 849, § 1.

Section 13.17, L.1983, c. 876, § 1, which related to alteration of fine prints, was repealed by L.1984, c. 849, § 1.

Section 13.19, L.1983, c. 876, § 1, which related to the penalty for violations of former sections 13.15 or 13.17, was repealed by L.1984, c. 849, § 1.

ARTICLE 14—WORKS OF FINE ART AND MULTIPLES GENERALLY

Section

§ 14.01. Right to reproduce works of fine art

1. Whenever a work of fine art is sold or otherwise transferred by or on behalf of the artist who created it, or his heirs or personal representatives, the reproduction right thereto is reserved to the grantor until it passes into

the public domain by act or operation of law unless such right is sooner expressly transferred by an instrument, note or memorandum in writing signed by the owner of the rights conveyed or his duly authorized agent.

2. Whenever an exclusive or non-exclusive conveyance of any reproduction right is made by the holder of such right, or his duly authorized agent, ownership of the physical work of fine art shall be presumed to remain with and be reserved to the grantor unless expressly transferred in writing by an instrument, note or memorandum or by other written means, signed by the grantor or his duly authorized agent.

3. This article shall not apply to the sale, conveyance, donation or other transfer of the physical work of fine art which does not include a conveyance of a reproduction right in such work.

4. Nothing herein contained, however, shall be construed to prohibit the fair use of such work of fine art.

5. Nothing in this section shall operate or be construed to conflict with any rights or liabilities under federal copyright law.

(Added L.1984, c. 849, § 1.)

Effective Date. Section effective Dec. 31, 1984, pursuant to L.1984, c. 849, § 3.

Derivation. Subd. 1. Former section 13.07, L.1983, c. 876, § 1; repealed by L.1984, c. 876, § 1. Said section 13.07 was from General Business Law § 219–g, added L.1966, c. 668, § 2, formerly § 224; renumbered 219–g, L.1975, c. 107, § 6; and repealed by L.1983, c. 876, § 5.

Subd. 2. Former section 14.03, subd. 2, added L.1983, c. 993, § 1; and repealed by L.1984, c. 849, § 1.

Subd. 4. Former section 14.03, subd. 3, added L.1983, c. 993, § 1; and repealed by L.1984, c. 849, § 1.

Subd. 5. Former section 14.03, subd. 4, added L.1983, c. 993, § 1; and repealed by L.1984, c. 849, § 1.

Former Section 14.01. Section, added L.1983, c. 993, § 1, which related to definitions concerning conveyances of rights in works of art, was repealed by L.1984, c. 849, § 1. See now section 11.01.

§ 14.03. Artists authorship rights

1. Except as limited by subdivision three of this section, on and after January first, nineteen hundred eighty-five, no person other than the artist or a person acting with the artist's consent shall knowingly display in a place accessible to the public or publish a work of fine art or limited edition multiple of not more than three hundred copies by that artist or a reproduction thereof in an altered, defaced, mutilated or modified form if the work is displayed, published or reproduced as being the work of the artist, or under circumstances under which it would reasonably be regarded as being the work of the artist, and damage to the artist's reputation is reasonably likely to result therefrom, except that this section shall not apply to sequential imagery such as that in motion pictures.

2. (a) Except as limited by subdivision three of this section, the artist shall retain at all times the right to claim authorship, or, for just and valid reason, to disclaim authorship of such work. The right to claim authorship shall include the right of the artist to have his or her name appear on or in connection with such work as the artist. The right to disclaim authorship shall include the right of the artist to prevent his or her name from appearing on or in connection with such work as the artist. Just and valid reason for disclaiming authorship shall include that the work has been altered, defaced, mutilated or modified other than by the artist, without the artist's consent, and damage to the artist's reputation is reasonably likely to result or has resulted therefrom.

(b) The rights created by this subdivision shall exist in addition to any other rights and duties which may now or in the future be applicable.

3. (a) Alteration, defacement, mutilation or modification of such work resulting from the passage of time or the inherent nature of the materials will not by itself create a violation of subdivision one of this section or a right to disclaim authorship under subdivision two of this section; provided such alteration, defacement, mutilation or modification was not the result of gross negligence in maintaining or protecting the work of fine art.

(b) In the case of a reproduction, a change that is an ordinary result of the medium of reproduction does not by itself create a violation of subdivision one of this section or a right to disclaim authorship under subdivision two of this section.

(c) Conservation shall not constitute an alteration, defacement, mutilation or modification within the meaning of this section, unless the conservation work can be shown to be negligent.

(d) This section shall not apply to work prepared under contract for advertising or trade use unless the contract so provides.

(e) The provisions of this section shall apply only to works of fine art or limited edition multiples of not more than three hundred copies knowingly displayed in a place accessible to the public, published or reproduced in this state.

4. (a) An artist aggrieved under subdivision one or subdivision two of this section shall have a cause of action for legal and injunctive relief.

(b) No action may be maintained to enforce any liability under this section unless brought within three years of the act complained of or one year after the constructive discovery of such act, whichever is longer.
(Added L.1984, c. 849, § 1.)

Effective Date. Section effective Dec. 31, 1984, pursuant to L.1984, c. 849, § 3.

Derivation. Subd. 1. Former section 14.53, added L.1983, c. 994, § 3; and repealed by L.1984, c. 849, § 1.

Subd. 2. Former section 14.55, added L.1983, c. 994, § 3; and repealed by L.1984, c. 849, § 1.

Subd. 3. Former section 14.57, added L.1983, c. 994, § 3; and repealed by L.1984, c. 849, § 1.

Subd. 4. Former section 14.59, added L.1983, c. 994, § 3; and repealed by L.1984, c. 849, § 1.

Former Section 14.03. Section, added L.1983, c. 993, § 1, which related to the right to reproduce works of art, was repealed by L.1984, c. 849, § 1. See now section 14.01.

Law Review Commentaries

The New York artists' authorship rights act: a comparative critique. Damich. 84 Columbia L.Rev. 1733 (1984).

The New York artists' authorship rights act: increased protection and enhanced status for visual artists. 70 Cornell L.Rev. 158 (1984).

Notes of Decisions

1. **Construction with other laws**

Claim alleging violation of New York statute [N.Y.McKinney's Arts and Cultural Affairs Law § 14.03], which provides that right of reproduction of work of art which is sold or transferred remains with grantor unless it passes into public domain, or is expressly transferred in writing, was preempted by copyright law. Ronald Litoff, Ltd. v. American Exp. Co., D.C.N.Y.1985, 621 F.Supp. 981.

ARTICLE 14-A—ARTISTS' AUTHORSHIP RIGHTS

[§§ 14.51 to 14.59. Repealed. L.1984, c. 849, § 1, eff. Dec. 31, 1984]

Section 14.51, added L.1983, c. 994, § 3, related to definitions concerning artists' authorship rights. See now section 11.01.

Section 14.53, added L.1983, c. 994, § 3, related to public display, publication and reproduction of works of fine art. See now section 14.03.

Section 14.55, added L.1983, c. 994, § 3, related to artists' authorship rights. See now section 14.03.

Section 14.57, added L.1983, c. 994, § 3, related to limitations of applicability of former sections 14.53 and 14.55. See now section 14.03.

Section 14.59, added L.1983, c. 994, § 3, related to relief for persons aggrieved under former sections 14.53 and 14.55. See now section 14.03.

ARTICLE 15—SALE OF VISUAL ART OBJECTS PRODUCED IN MULTIPLES

§ 15.01. Full disclosure in the sale of certain visual art objects produced in multiples

1. An art merchant shall not sell or consign a multiple in, into or from this state unless a written instrument is furnished to the purchaser or consignee, at his request, or in any event prior to a sale or consignment, which sets forth as to each multiple the descriptive information required by this article for the appropriate time period. If a prospective purchaser so requests, the information shall be transmitted to him prior to the payment or placing of an order for a multiple. If payment is made by a purchaser prior to delivery of such an art multiple, this information shall be supplied at the time of or prior to delivery. With respect to auctions, this information may be furnished in catalogues or other written materials which are readily available for consultation and purchase prior to sale, provided that a bill of sale, receipt or invoice describing the transaction is then provided which makes reference to the catalogue and lot number in which such information is supplied. Information supplied pursuant to this subdivision shall be clearly, specifically and distinctly addressed to each item as required by this article for any time period unless the required data is not applicable. This section is applicable to transactions by and between merchants, non-merchants, and others considered art merchants for the purposes of this article.

2. An art merchant shall not cause a catalogue, prospectus, flyer or other written material or advertisement to be distributed in, into or from this state which solicits a direct sale, by inviting transmittal of payment for a specific multiple, unless it clearly sets forth, in close physical proximity to the place in such material where the multiple is described, the descriptive

information required by this article for the appropriate time period. In lieu of this required information, such written material or advertising may set forth the material contained in the following quoted passage, or the passage itself, containing terms the nonobservance of which shall constitute a violation of this article, if the art merchant then supplies the required information prior to or with delivery of the multiple:

"Article fifteen of the New York arts and cultural affairs law provides for disclosure in writing of certain information concerning multiples of prints and photographs when sold for more than one hundred dollars ($100) each, exclusive of any frame, prior to effecting a sale of them. This law requires disclosure of such matters as the identity of the artist, the artist's signature, the medium, whether the multiple is a reproduction, the time when the multiple was produced, use of the master which produced the multiple, and the number of multiples in a 'limited edition'. If a prospective purchaser so requests, the information shall be transmitted to him prior to payment or the placing of an order for a multiple. If payment is made by a purchaser prior to delivery of such an art multiple, this information will be supplied at the time of or prior to delivery, in which case the purchaser is entitled to a refund if, for reasons related to matter contained in such information, he returns the multiple substantially in the condition in which received, within thirty days of receiving it. In addition, if after payment and delivery, it is ascertained that the information provided is incorrect the purchaser may be entitled to certain remedies."

This requirement is not applicable to general written material or advertising which does not constitute an offer to effect a specific sale.

3. In each place of business in the state where an art merchant is regularly engaged in sales of multiples, the art merchant shall post in a conspicuous place, a sign which, in a legible format, contains the information included in the following passage:

"Article fifteen of the New York arts and cultural affairs law provides for the disclosure in writing of certain information concerning prints and photographs. This information is available to you in accordance with that law."

(Added L.1984, c. 849, § 1.)

Effective Date. Section effective Dec. 31, 1984, pursuant to L.1984, c. 849, § 3.

Derivation. Former section 15.03, L.1983, c. 876, § 1; repealed by L.1984, c. 849, § 1. Said section 15.03 was from General Business Law § 220–b, added L.1981, c. 992, § 2; amended L.1982, c. 77, § 2; and repealed by L.1983, c. 876, § 5.

Former Section 15.01. Section, L.1983, c. 876, § 1, which related to definitions concerning the sale of visual art objects produced in multiples, was repealed by L.1984, c. 849, § 1. See now section 11.01.

§ 15.03. Information required

The following information shall be supplied, as indicated, as to each multiple produced on or after January first, nineteen hundred eighty-two:

1. Artist. State the name of the artist.

2. Signature. If the artist's name appears on the multiple, state whether the multiple was signed by the artist. If not signed by the artist then state the source of the artist's name on the multiple, such as whether the artist placed his signature on the master, whether his name was stamped or estate stamped on the multiple, or was from some other source or in some other manner placed on the multiple.

3. Medium or process. (a) Describe the medium or process, and where pertinent to photographic processes the material, used in producing the multiple, such as whether the multiple was produced through etching, engraving, lithographic, serigraphic or a particular method and/or material used in the photographic developing processes. If an established term, in accordance with the usage of the trade, cannot be employed accurately to describe the medium or process, a brief, clear description shall be made.

(b) If the purported artist was deceased at the time the master was made which produced the multiple, this shall be stated.

(c) If the multiple or the image on or in the master constitutes a mechanical, photomechanical, hand-made or photographic type of reproduction, or is a reproduction, of an image produced in a different medium, for a purpose other than the creation of the multiple being described, this information and the respective mediums shall be stated.

(d) If paragraph (c) of this subdivision is applicable, and the multiple is not signed, state whether the artist authorized or approved in writing the multiple or the edition of which the multiple being described is one.

4. Use of master. (a) If the multiple is a "posthumous" multiple, that is, if the master was created during the life of the artist but the multiple was produced after the artist's death, this shall be stated.

(b) If the multiple was made from a master which produced a prior limited edition, or from a master which constitutes or was made from a reproduction of a prior multiple or of a master which produced prior multiples, this shall be stated.

5. Time produced. As to multiples produced after nineteen hundred forty-nine, state the year or approximate year the multiple was produced. As to multiples produced prior to nineteen hundred fifty, state the year, approximate year or period when the master was made which produced the multiple and/or when the particular multiple being described was produced. The requirements of this subdivision shall be satisfied when the year stated is approximately accurate.

6. Size of the edition. (a) If the multiple being described is offered as one of a limited edition, this shall be so stated, as well as the number of multiples in the edition, and whether and how the multiple is numbered.

(b) Unless otherwise disclosed, the number of multiples stated pursuant to paragraph (a) of this subdivision shall constitute an express warranty, as defined in section 13.01 of this title, that no additional numbered multiples of the same image, exclusive of proofs, have been produced.

(c) The number of multiples stated pursuant to paragraph (a) of this subdivision shall also constitute an express warranty, as defined in section 13.01 of this title, that no additional multiples of the same image, whether designated "proofs" other than trial proofs, numbered or otherwise, have been produced in an amount which exceeds the number in the limited edition by twenty or twenty percent, whichever is greater.

(d) If the number of multiples exceeds the number in the stated limited edition as provided in paragraph (c) of this subdivision, then state the number of proofs other than trial proofs, or other numbered or unnumbered multiples, in the same or other prior editions, produced from the same master as described in paragraph (b) of subdivision four of this section, and whether and how they are signed and numbered.

(Added L.1984, c. 849, § 1.)

Effective Date. Section effective Dec. 31, 1984, pursuant to L.1984, c. 849, § 3.

Derivation. Former section 15.05, L.1983, c. 876, § 1; repealed by L.1984, c. 849, § 1. Said section 15.05 was from General Business Law § 220–c, added L.1981, c. 992, § 2; amended L.1982, c. 77, § 3; and repealed by L.1983, c. 876, § 5.

Former Section 15.03. Section, L.1983, c. 876, § 1, which related to full disclosure in the sale of certain visual art objects produced in multiples, was repealed by L.1984, c. 849, § 1. See now section 15.01.

§ 15.05. Information required; nineteen hundred fifty to January first, nineteen hundred eighty-two

The information which shall be supplied as to each multiple produced during the period from nineteen hundred fifty to January first, nineteen hundred eighty-two, shall consist of the information required by section 15.03 of this article except for paragraph (d) of subdivision three, paragraph (b) of subdivision four and paragraphs (c) and (d) of subdivision six of such section.

(Added L.1984, c. 849, § 1.)

Effective Date. Section effective Dec. 31, 1984, pursuant to L.1984, c. 849, § 3.

Derivation. Former section 15.07, L.1983, c. 876, § 1; repealed by L.1984, c. 849, § 1. said section 15.07 was from General Business Law § 220–d, added L.1981, c. 292, § 2; and repealed by L.1983, c. 876, § 5.

Former Section 15.05. Section, L.1983, c. 876, § 1, which related to information required in the sale of visual art objects produced in multiples, was repealed by L.1984, c. 849, § 1. See now section 15.03.

§ 15.07. Information required; nineteen hundred to nineteen hundred forty-nine

The information which shall be supplied as to each multiple produced during the period from nineteen hundred through nineteen hundred forty-nine shall consist of the information required by section 15.03 of this article except for paragraphs (b), (c) and (d) of subdivision three and subdivisions four and six of such section.

(Added L.1984, c. 849, § 1.)

Effective Date. Section effective Dec. 31, 1984, pursuant to L.1984, c. 849, § 3.

Derivation. Former section 15.09, L.1983, c. 876, § 1; repealed by L.1984, c. 849, § 1. Said section 15.09 was from General Business Law § 220–e, added L.1981, c. 992, § 2; amended L.1982, c. 77, § 4; and repealed by L.1983, c. 876, § 5.

Former Section 15.07. Section, L.1983, c. 876, § 1, which related to information required as to art multiples produced between 1950 to Jan. 1, 1982, was repealed by L.1984, c. 849, § 1. See now section 15.05.

§ 15.09. Information required; pre-nineteen hundred

The information which shall be supplied as to each multiple produced prior to nineteen hundred shall consist of the information required by section 15.03 of this article except for subdivision two, paragraphs (b), (c) and (d) of subdivision three and subdivisions four and six of such section 15.03.

(Added L.1984, c. 849, § 1.)

Effective Date. Section effective Dec. 31, 1984, pursuant to L.1984, c. 849, § 3.

Derivation. Former section 15.11, L.1983, c. 876, § 1; repealed by L.1984, c. 849, § 1. Said section 15.09 was from General Business Law § 220–f, added L.1981, c. 992, § 2; amended L.1982, c. 77, § 4; and is now covered by L.1983, c. 876, § 5.

Former Section 15.09. Section, L.1983, c. 876, § 1, which related to information required as to art multiples produced from 1900 to 1949, was repealed by L.1984, c. 849, § 1. See now section 15.07.

§ 15.11. Express warranties

Information provided pursuant to the provisions of this article shall create an express warranty pursuant to section 13.05 of this title. When such information is not supplied because not applicable, this shall constitute an express warranty that such required information is not applicable.

(Added L.1984, c. 849, § 1.)

Effective Date. Section effective Dec. 31, 1984, pursuant to L.1984, c. 849, § 3.

Derivation. Former section 15.13, L.1983, c. 876, § 1; repealed by L.1984, c. 849, § 1. Said section 15.13 was from General Business Law § 220–g, added L.1981, c. 992. § 2; amended L.1982, c. 77, § 5; and repealed by L.1983, c. 876, § 5.

Former Section 15.11. Section, L.1983, c. 876, § 1, which related to information required as to art multiples produced before 1900, was repealed by L.1984, c. 849, § 1. See now section 15.09.

§ 15.13. Construction

1. The rights, liabilities and remedies created by this article shall be construed to be in addition to and not in substitution, exclusion or displacement of other rights, liabilities and remedies provided by law, except where such construction would, as a matter of law, be unreasonable.

2. Whenever an artist sells or consigns a multiple of his own creation, the artist shall incur the obligations prescribed by this article for an art merchant, but an artist shall not otherwise be regarded as an art merchant.

3. An artist or merchant who consigns a multiple to a merchant for the purpose of effecting a sale of the multiple shall have no liability to a purchaser under this article if such consignor, as to the consignee, has complied with the provisions of this article.

4. When a merchant has agreed to sell a multiple on behalf of a consignor, who is not an art merchant, or when an artist has not consigned a multiple to a merchant, but the merchant has agreed to act as the agent for an artist for the purpose of supplying the information required by this article, such merchant shall incur liabilities of other merchants prescribed by this article as to a purchaser.

5. When an art merchant or merchant is liable to a purchaser pursuant to the provisions of this article, as a result of providing information in the situations referred to above in this section, as well as when such a merchant purchased such a multiple from another merchant, if the merchant or art merchant can establish that his liability results from incorrect information which was provided by the consignor, artist or merchant to him in writing, the merchant who is liable in good faith relied on such information, the consignor, artist or merchant shall similarly incur such liabilities as to the purchaser and such merchant.

(Added L.1984, c. 849, § 1.)

101st CONGRESS
1st Session

S. 1198

To amend title 17, United States Code, to provide certain rights of attribution and integrity to authors of works of visual art.

IN THE SENATE OF THE UNITED STATES

June 16 (legislative day, January 3), 1989

Mr. Kennedy (for himself and Mr. Kasten) introduced the following bill; which was read twice and referred to the Committee on the Judiciary

---

A BILL

To amend title 17, United States Code, to provide certain rights of attribution and integrity to authors of works of visual art.

Be it enacted by the Senate and House of Representatives of the United States of America in Congress assembled,

SECTION 1. SHORT TITLE.

This Act may be cited as the "Visual Artists Rights Act of 1989".

SEC. 2. WORK OF VISUAL ART DEFINED.

Section 101 of title 17, United States Code, is amended by inserting after the paragraph defining "widow" the following:

"A 'work of visual art' is a painting, drawing, print, sculpture, or still photographic image produced for exhibition purposes only, existing in a single copy, in a limited edition of 200 copies or fewer, or, in the case of a sculpture, in multiple cast sculptures of 200 or fewer. A work of visual art does not include—

"(1) any version that has been reproduced in other than such limited edition prints or cast sculptures;

"(2)(A) any poster, map, globe, chart, technical drawing, diagram, model, applied art, motion picture or other audio visual work, book, magazine, periodical, or similar publication;

"(B) any merchandising item or advertising, promotional, descriptive, covering, or packaging material or container;

"(C) any portion or part of any item described in subparagraph (A) or (B);

"(3) any work made for hire;

"(4) any reproduction, depiction, portrayal, or other use of a work in, upon, or in any connection with any item described in paragraph (1), (2), or (3); or

"(5) any work not subject to copyright protection under section 102 of this title.".

SEC. 3. RIGHTS OF ATTRIBUTION AND INTEGRITY.

(a) RIGHTS OF ATTRIBUTION AND INTEGRITY.—Chapter 1 of title 17, United States Code, is amended by inserting after section 106 the following new section:

"§ 106A. Rights of certain authors to attribution and integrity

"(a) RIGHTS OF ATTRIBUTION AND INTEGRITY.—Subject to section 107 and independent of the exclusive rights provided in section 106, the author of a work of visual art—

"(1) shall have the right—

"(A) to claim authorship of that work, and

"(B) to prevent the use of his or her name as the author of any work of visual art which he or she did not create;

"(2) shall have the right to prevent the use of his or her name as the author of the work of visual art in the event of a distortion, mutilation, or other modification of the work as described in paragraph (3); and

"(3) subject to the limitations set forth in section 113(d), shall have the right—

"(A) to prevent any distortion, mutilation, or other modification of that work which would be prejudicial to his or her honor or reputation, and any intentional or grossly negligent distortion, mutilation, or modification of that work is a violation of that right, and

●S 1198 IS

"(B) to prevent any destruction of a work of recognized stature, and any intentional or grossly negligent destruction of that work is a violation of that right.

In determining whether a work is of recognized stature, a court or other trier of fact may take into account the opinions of artists, art dealers, collectors of fine art, curators of art museums, conservators of recognized stature, and other persons involved with the creation, appreciation, history, or marketing of works of recognized stature. Evidence of commercial exploitation of a work as a whole, or of particular copies, does not preclude a finding that the work is a work of recognized stature.

"(b) SCOPE AND EXERCISE OF RIGHTS.—The author of a work of visual art has the rights conferred by subsection (a), whether or not the author is the copyright owner, and whether or not the work qualifies for protection under section 104. Where the author is not the copyright owner, only the author shall have the right during his or her lifetime to exercise the rights set forth in subsection (a).

"(c) EXCEPTIONS.—(1) The modification of a work of visual art which is a result of the passage of time or the inherent nature of the materials is not a destruction, distortion, mutilation, or other modification described in subsection (a)(3) unless the modification was the result of gross negligence in maintaining or protecting the work.

"(2) The modification of a work of visual art which is the result of conservation is not a destruction, distortion, mutilation, or other modification described in subsection (a)(3) unless the modification is caused by gross negligence.

"(d) DURATION OF RIGHTS.—(1) With respect to works of visual art created on or after the effective date set forth in section 10(a) of the Visual Artists Rights Act of 1989, the rights conferred by subsection (a) shall endure for a term consisting of the life of the author and fifty years after the author's death.

"(2) With respect to works of visual art created before the effective date set forth in section 10(a) of the Visual Artists Rights Act of 1989, but not published before such effective date, the rights conferred by subsection (a) shall be coextensive with, and shall expire at the same time as, the rights conferred by section 106.

"(3) All terms of the rights conferred by subsection (a) run to the end of the calendar year in which they would otherwise expire.

"(e) TRANSFER AND WAIVER.—(1) Except as provided in paragraph (2), the rights conferred by subsection (a) may not be waived or otherwise transferred.

"(2) After the death of an author, the rights conferred by subsection (a) on the author may be exercised by the person to whom such rights pass by bequest of the author or by the applicable laws of intestate succession.

"(3) Ownership of the rights conferred by subsection (a) with respect to a work of visual art is distinct from ownership of any fixation of that work, or of a copyright or any exclusive right under a copyright in that work.".

(b) CONFORMING AMENDMENT.—The table of sections at the beginning of chapter 1 of title 17, United States Code, is amended by inserting after the item relating to section 106 the following new item:

"106A. Rights of certain authors to attribution and integrity.".

SEC. 4. REMOVAL OF WORKS OF VISUAL ART FROM BUILDINGS.

Section 113 of title 17, United States Code, is amended by adding at the end thereof the following:

"(d)(1)(A) Where—

"(i) a work of visual art has been incorporated in or made part of a building in such a way that removing the work from the building will cause the destruction, distortion, mutilation, or other modification of the work as described in section 106A(a)(3), and

"(ii) the author or, if the author is deceased, the person described in section 106A(e)(2), consented to the installation of the work in the building in a written instrument signed by the owner of the building and the author or such person,

then the rights conferred by paragraphs (2) and (3) of section 106A(a) shall not apply, except as may otherwise be agreed in a written instrument signed by such owner and the author or such person.

"(B) An agreement described in subparagraph (A) that the rights conferred by paragraphs (2) and (3) of section 106A(a) shall apply shall not be binding on any subsequent owner of the building except where such subsequent owner had actual notice of the agreement or where the instrument evidencing the agreement was properly recorded, before the transfer of the building to the subsequent owner, in the applicable State real property registry for such building.

"(2) If the owner of a building wishes to remove a work of visual art which is a part of such building and which can be removed from the building without the destruction, distortion, mutilation, or other modification of the work as described in section 106A(a)(3), the author's rights under paragraphs (2) and (3) of section 106A(a) shall apply unless—

"(A) the owner has made a diligent, good faith attempt without success to notify the author or, if the author is deceased, the person described in section 106A(e)(2), of the owner's intended action affecting the work of visual art, or

"(B) the owner did provide such notice by registered mail and the person so notified failed, within 90 days after receiving such notice, either to remove the work or to pay for its removal.

If the work is removed at the expense of the author or the person described in section 106A(e)(2), title to that fixation of the work shall be deemed to be in the author or such person, as the case may be. For purposes of subparagraph (A), an owner shall be presumed to have made a diligent, good faith attempt to send notice if the owner sent such notice by registered mail to the last known address of the author or, if the author is deceased, to the person described in section 106A(e)(2).

"(3) The Register of Copyrights shall establish a system of records whereby any author of a work of visual art that has been incorporated in or made part of a building, or persons described in section 106A(e)(2) with respect to that work, may record their identities and addresses with the Copyright Office. The Register shall also establish procedures under which such authors or persons may update the information so recorded, and procedures under which owners of buildings may record with the Copyright Office evidence of their efforts to comply with this subsection.".

SEC. 5. PREEMPTION.

Section 301 of title 17, United States Code, is amended by adding at the end the following:

"(f)(1) On or after the effective date set forth in section 10(a) of the Visual Artists Rights Act of 1989, all legal or equitable rights that are equivalent to any of the rights conferred by section 106A with respect to works of visual art to which the rights conferred by section 106A apply are governed exclusively by section 106A and section 113(d) and the provisions of this title relating to such sections. Thereafter, no person is entitled to any such right or equivalent right in any work of visual art under the common law or statutes of any State.

"(2) Nothing in paragraph (1) annuls or limits any rights or remedies under the common law or statutes of any State with respect to—

"(A) any cause of action from undertakings commenced before the effective date set forth in section 10(a) of the Visual Artists Rights Act of 1989; or

"(B) activities violating legal or equitable rights that are not equivalent to any of the rights conferred by section 106A with respect to works of visual art.".

SEC. 6. INFRINGEMENT ACTIONS.

(a) In General.—Section 501(a) of title 17, United States Code, is amended—

(1) by inserting after "118"; the following: "or of the author as provided in section 106A(a)"; and

(2) by striking out "copyright." and inserting in lieu thereof "copyright or right of the author, as the case may be. For purposes of this chapter (other than section 506), any reference to copyright shall be deemed to include the rights conferred by section 106A(a).".

(b) EXCLUSION OF CRIMINAL PENALTIES.—Section 506 of title 17, United States Code, is amended by adding at the end thereof the following:

"(f) RIGHTS OF ATTRIBUTION AND INTEGRITY.— Nothing in this section applies to infringement of the rights conferred by section 106A(a).".

(c) REGISTRATION NOT A PREREQUISITE TO CERTAIN REMEDIES.—(1) Section 411(a) of title 17, United States Code, is amended in the first sentence by inserting after "United States" the following: "and an action brought for a violation of the rights of the author under section 106A(a)".

(2) Section 412 of title 17, United States Code, is amended by inserting "an action brought for a violation of the rights of the author under section 106A(a) or" after "other than".

SEC. 7. STATUTE OF LIMITATIONS.

Section 507(b) of title 17, United States Code, is amended by adding at the end the following: "For purposes of an action brought for infringement of the rights under section 106A(a) of an author of a work of visual art, the claim accrues when the author (or person described in section 106A(e)(2), as the case may be) knew or should have known of the violation of the author's rights under section 106A(a).".

SEC. 8. FAIR USE.

Section 107 of title 17, United States Code, is amended by striking out "section 106" and inserting in lieu thereof "sections 106 and 106A".

SEC. 9. STUDY ON RESALE ROYALTIES.

(a) IN GENERAL.—The Register of Copyrights, in consultation with the Chair of the National Endowment for the Arts, shall conduct a study on the feasibility of implementing—

(1) a requirement that, after the first sale of a work of art, a royalty on any resale of the work, consisting of a percentage of the price, be paid to the author of the work; and

(2) other possible requirements that would achieve the objective of allowing an author of a work of art to share monetarily in the enhanced value of that work.

•S 1198 IS

(b) GROUPS TO BE CONSULTED.—The study under subsection (a) shall be conducted in consultation with other appropriate departments and agencies of the United States, foreign governments, and groups involved in the creation, exhibition, dissemination, and preservation of works of art, including artists, art dealers, collectors of fine art, and curators of art museums.

(c) REPORT TO CONGRESS.—Not later than 18 months after the date of the enactment of this Act, the Register of Copyrights shall submit to the Congress a report containing the results of the study conducted under this section, and any recommendations that the Register may have as a result of the study.

SEC. 10. EFFECTIVE DATE.

(a) IN GENERAL.—Subject to subsection (b) and except as provided in subsection (c), this Act and the amendments made by this Act take effect 6 months after the date of the enactment of this Act.

(b) APPLICABILITY.—The rights created by section 106A of title 17, United States Code, shall apply to works created but not published before the effective date set forth in subsection (a), and to works created on or after such effective date, but shall not apply to any destruction, distortion, mutilation, or other modification (as described in section 106A(a)(3) of such title) of any work which occurred before such effective date.

(c) SECTION 9.—Section 9 takes effect on the date of the enactment of this Act.

O

Resale Rights 10

The artist's resale royalty right was first established in France in 1920 and is often referred to as a *droit de suite.*[1] The right has since been adopted in varying forms in a number of other nations, although a greater number have rejected it. At the present time, the United States has not included a *droit de suite* in its statutes, although California does.[2]

A *droit de suite* is the right of an artist to participate in the proceeds realized from the resale of the tangible embodiment of his or her work. It was conceived of as an attempt to equate the copyright status of artists to that of authors;[3] it is a technique designed to allow artists to participate in the appreciation in value of their works when they are sold after the initial sale.

The question whether an artist should be entitled to resale rights has generated enormous controversy. Generally, an artist receives the major part of his or her income from the original sale of the artwork. Although the artist may still own the copyright in the work, the artist is not selling multiple copies of the original work of art. A writer, on the other hand, receives the major part of his or her income from the sale of multiple copies of the written work. The copyright law allows the writer to receive a royalty on the sale of each copy of the written work. That disparity in copyright protection between the artist and the writer is addressed in the resale rights debate.

THE EUROPEAN CONCEPT

France

The *droit de suite* was conceived in France. Under French law as originally enacted, the artist received a pecuniary right, parallel to that afforded an author through copyright, that allowed the artist to collect 3 percent of the total sales price of the artwork each time it was sold at public auction.[4] The right was inalienable and inured to the artist for his or her life plus fifty years. The French law was expanded in 1957 so that it would apply to sales by dealers, as well as sales at public auction.[5] However, the revision of the French law requires implementing rules, and those rules have not been issued. As a result, the French *droit de suite* is still applicable only to sales at public auction.

To be protected under the French law, an artist is required to register the work with the French government. The data required for registration include name, address, and signature of the artist. The registration requirement was thought to be helpful for purposes of establishing a proved record of authentication. As a practical matter, French artists joined an organization known as *Societe de la Propriete Artistique et des Dessins et Modeles* (SPADEM), an organization whose purpose is to collect the royalties of artists, much as the American Society of Composers, Authors, and Publishers (ASCAP) does for performing artists in the United States.[6] SPADEM works closely with the French auction houses to obtain the necessary data to provide the royalties required by the French *droit de suite*.

West Germany, Italy, and Other Countries

The West German statute follows the French approach in that it gives the artist a percentage of the total resale price, whether the resale is at a profit or at a loss. The Italian statute gives the artist a percentage of the difference between the seller's purchase price and the resale price when the work of art is sold at a gain.[7] The

Italian system is more difficult to administer and enforce, and is used infrequently.

Other countries with some form of *droit de suite* statutes are Belgium, Luxembourg, Tunisia, and Sweden. Uruguay has enacted a similar law, but has not adopted the enabling legislation. Czechoslovakia and Poland have included a *droit de suite* in their copyright laws. Still others—including Austria, Spain, Great Britain, Norway, Holland, Portugal, and Switzerland—have considered enacting *droit de suite* statutes, but have not done so.[8]

Our review of the current written materials and current state of effectiveness of droit de suite legislation in the various countries throughout the world indicates that the statutes are difficult to enforce and often ignored. Even in those places where the law is followed, few artists receive any meaningful benefits.

THE UNITED STATES CONCEPT

Federal Legislation

Many efforts have been made to introduce the *droit de suite* concept into federal legislation. Senator Jacob K. Javits of New York was a strong advocate for artists' resale rights, and the cause has most recently been taken up by Senator Edward M. Kennedy of Massachusetts. A brief examination of the most recent legislative attempts helps to illustrate the current state of favor of any potential federal *droit de suite* legislation.[9]

The Visual Artists Rights Act of 1987,[10] as introduced but not passed, contained a resale royalty provision patterned on the Italian concept. The 1987 bill would have established a system for the payment of royalties on the resales of works of art. The royalty payment was to be made by the seller at the rate of 7 percent of the difference between the seller's purchase price and the amount the seller receives in exchange for the work. The royalty would not have applied to resale prices of less than $1,000 or if the seller made less than a 50 percent gain on the sale. Administration was to be by the Copyright Office, and the artist would be required to register to be eligible to receive royalties.

The Visual Artists Rights Act of 1988[11] took a dramatic turn. The 1988 bill had no resale royalty provision. Instead, the bill obligated the National Endowment for the Arts to conduct a one-year study to analyze the economic effects and the means of implementing new initiatives to enable artists to participate in the commercial exploitation of their work after the first sale of the work, including but not limited to a resale royalty right for artists. Although the bill did not pass, it is expected to be reintroduced in the 101st Congress.[12] We believe that the elimination of a federal *droit de suite* should enhance the possibility of the bill's future passage into law, since the main opposition to the bill was generated by the resale royalty provision.

State Legislation

California is the only state that has adopted *droit de suite* legislation.[13] The law was enacted in 1976 and became effective on January 1, 1977. The California Resale Royalties Act is reproduced, as amended in 1982, at the end of this chapter. The California legislation attracted little attention before passage, and it was enacted without consulting the art community beyond a limited number of artists who strongly supported the legislation.[14] Some of the important features of the California statute are described below.[15]

Subject Matter

The statute applies to the sale of a work of fine art,[16] which is defined as an original painting, sculpture, or drawing or an original work of art in glass.[17]

First-Sale Exclusion

The statute does not apply to the initial sale of a work of art when legal title to the work is vested in the artist.[18] The statute is designed to apply only to the resale of works of art and contains various other special exclusions from the payment of royalties.[19]

Required Situs

In order for the statute to apply, either the seller must be a resident of California at the time of the sale, or the sale must take place in California.[20] In addition, the artist must be either a citizen of the United States or a resident of California for a minimum of two years.[21]

Royalty Amount

When a work of fine art that is subject to the statute is sold, the artist is entitled to be paid by the seller or the seller's agent a royalty equal to 5 percent of the gross amount of the sales price.[22] The statute requires a gallery representative, dealer, broker, museum official, or other person acting as the agent for the seller to withhold 5 percent of the amount of the sale, locate the artist, and pay the artist.[23] No royalty is payable if the gross sales price is less than $1,000[24] or if the gross sales price is less than the purchase price previously paid by the seller.[25]

Limitation and Termination

If the artist does not receive the royalty, he or she may bring an action for damages, but that action must be taken within three years following the date of sale or one year after discovery of the sale, whichever is later.[26] No royalty is due for any resale occurring after the artist's death,[27] except that, if the artist dies after January 1, 1983, his rights under the statute continue and inure to his heirs or estate for twenty years after the artist's death.[28]

Waiver of Rights

Under the statute, an artist's royalty rights are not transferable and may not be waived unless the artist is compensated in an amount in excess of 5 percent of the amount of the sale as consideration for the waiver.[29] The statute was amended in 1983 to provide that an artist may assign the right to collect the royalty payment to another individual or entity. Presumably, this was done to allow an entity similar to ASCAP to operate for artists.

Case Law Under the California Statute

The California *droit de suite* statute has withstood one judicial challenge. *Morseburg v. Balyon*[30] was brought after an intentional violation of the California statute in order to challenge its validity. Howard Morseburg, an art dealer, sold two paintings that required the payment of royalties and then challenged the constitutionality of the California Resale Royalties Act. Morseburg claimed that the Act was unconstitutional because it was preempted by the 1909 Copyright Act[31] and that it violated the due process and contracts clauses of the United States Constitution.

The court first discussed the preemption issue and twice emphasized that its holding applied only to the 1909 Copyright Act. A preemption issue is raised when federal law and state law conflict, so that federal law occupies the field.[32] In other words, are the rights created under state law (the California statute) equivalent to one or more rights contained in federal law (the Copyright Act)? If there are equivalent federal and state rights, the federal rights preempt the state rights.

The court in *Morseburg* held that there was no federal preemption by the 1909 Copyright Act. The court based its conclusion on *Goldstein v. California*,[33] in which the Supreme Court held valid a California statute making it a criminal offense to pirate recordings produced by others, an activity against which the copyright holder at that time had no protection. In *Goldstein* the Court refused to interpret the copyright clause of the Constitution as foreclosing the existence of all state power to grant to authors the exclusive right to their writings. In *Morseburg* the court reasoned that the California statute in no way impaired any right created under the 1909 Copyright Act, and that, therefore, the federal law did not preempt the California Resale Royalties Act.

The court was concerned with the word "vend" in section 1 of the 1909 Copyright Act and whether that provision preempted any state law that might limit the right of the artist to vend. The court held:

> Prior to the initial sale he [the artist] holds title to the work and, assuming proper steps have been taken, all rights given to him by reason of his copyright. None of these provide the right afforded to him by the California Resale Royalties Act. This is an additional right similar to the additional protection afforded by California's anti-pirating statute upheld in Goldstein. It is true that under the California Act the right it bestows cannot be waived or transferred. This limits the right created by state law but not any right created by the copyright law.

It would be proper to brand this conclusion as sophistry were it true that the right "to vend" provided by section 1 of the 1909 Act meant a right to transfer the works at all times and at all places free and clear of all claims of others. It is manifest that such is not its meaning. It merely means that the artist has "the exclusive right to transfer the title for a consideration to others."[34] The California Act does not impair this right; it merely creates a right in personam against a seller of a "work of fine art."[35]

The court also concluded that the California statute does not violate the contracts clause or the due process provisions of the Constitution.

There still exists, however, some question as to the constitutionality of the California Resale Royalties Act. The court in *Morseburg* emphasized in its holding that it was applicable only under the 1909 Copyright Act, which left the California statute open to challenge as preempted under the 1976 Copyright Act. In his treatise on copyright law, Professor Nimmer notes that if state law creates a right that inhibits the reproduction, performance, distribution, or display of a work of authorship, it is "equivalent" to copyright and is, therefore, preempted, even if the state-created right is either broader or narrower than the comparable right under the Copyright Act.[36] Nimmer observes that the California statute and the Copyright Act both deal with the right to sell, but they contain different rights and concludes, "broader or narrower, it is the same conduct in relation to the same subject matter that triggers either rights or immunities under both federal [Copyright Act] and state [California Resale Royalties Act] law. From this it would necessarily follow that the state law is preempted."[37]

THE CONTRACTUAL ALTERNATIVE

In the early 1970s several efforts were made to draft a model contract agreement that would provide to artists the equivalent of a *droit de suite*. The most widely distributed form was drafted by New York attorney Robert Projansky and was titled "The Artist's Reserved Rights Transfer and Sale Agreement."[38] In its original form the model contract required a royalty payment to the artist of 15 percent of the gross profit on each resale of the work of art. Further, the contract required a purchaser to agree that the work could not be resold or otherwise transferred without the purchaser's personally guaranteeing that any subsequent purchasers or other transferees would agree to pay the royalty on a resale and similarly bind other purchasers or transferees. In other words, a chain of privity would connect the artist to every subsequent owner for the artist's life plus twenty-one years.

The major problem with the Projansky contract is that there is no way to make the contract binding on subsequent owners of the work of art. The artist can bind only the person with whom he or she directly deals. The artist has no privity of contract with the purchaser who buys the work of art from the person who originally bought it from the artist. Few purchasers were willing to bind themselves as guarantors for future royalties to the artist, and the form contract was rarely used.[39]

A later form contract was prepared by another New York attorney, Charles Jurrist.[40] That form also called for a 15 percent royalty on any gross resale profit, but made it applicable only to the first resale. Even with that modification, the form contract has not been used. The form contract does, however, present a useful checklist of rights that may be contracted for, separate and apart from resale rights.

An artist can legally bind a purchaser who buys a work either from the artist or from the artist's agent to pay a resale royalty on the first resale in the manner set forth in the Jurrist contract. Subsequent resales, however, cannot be legally tied to the artist, since there is no privity of contract and no manner of giving notice to a bona fide purchaser in good faith.[41] Accordingly, we feel that the contract approach to resale rights is not a viable alternative.

FUTURE OF RESALE RIGHTS

The concept of *droit de suite* has been widely debated in the art community.[42] Despite its initial appeal in California, the *droit de suite* does not appear to have been a benefit to many artists and certainly not to the young, less financially successful artists. Nor does there seem to be a great economic benefit to artists in the various European countries that have adopted a *droit de suite*, and the statutes are difficult to enforce and often ignored. We believe that the *droit de suite*, although popular for artists in theory, affords the artist little real benefit, since the profitable resale of artwork is not so common as the auction houses would like us to believe. Moreover, the time, effort, and cost of enforcing such legislation would be disproportionately high in comparison with the benefits achieved. Accordingly, we do not believe a federal *droit de suite* should be passed in the United States.

NOTES
to Chapter 10

1. *See* R. DUFFY, ART LAW: REPRESENTING ARTISTS, DEALERS AND COLLECTORS 263 (1977); J. MERRYMAN & A. ELSEN, LAW, ETHICS, AND THE VISUAL ARTS 213 (1987); F. FELDMAN, S. WEIL & S. BIEDERMAN, ART LAW 555 (1986); L. DUBOFF, THE DESKBOOK OF ART LAW 855 (1977 & Supp. 1984); Merryman, *Visual Arts Law*, 17 CAL. W. INT'L L. REV. 266 (1987).

2. CAL. CIV. CODE § 986 (1988). The statute is discussed in detail later in the chapter.

3. M. NIMMER, NIMMER ON COPYRIGHT 8-272 (1988); Price & Price, *Right of Artists: The Case of the* Droit de Suite, 31 ART J. 144 (Winter 1971).

4. *See* Hauser, *The French* Droit de Suite: *The Problem of Protection for the Underprivileged Artist under the Copyright Law*, 11 COPYRIGHT L. SYMP. (ASCAP) 1 (1962); Price, *Government Policy and Economic Security for Artists: The Case of the* Droit de Suite, 77 YALE L.J. 1333 (1968).

5. France, Law of March 11, 1957, No. 296, art. 42, *reproduced in* MERRYMAN & ELSEN, *supra* note 1.

6. Societe de la Propriete Artistique et des Dessins et Modeles. The exclusive representative of SPADEM in the United States is the Visual Artists and Galleries Association, Inc. located in New York City.

7. *See* MERRYMAN & ELSEN, *supra* note 1, at 215.

8. *See* Schulder, *Art Proceeds Act: A Study of the* Droit de Suite *and a Proposed Enactment For the United States*, 61 NW. U.L. REV. 19 (1966).

9. Visual Artists Rights Act of 1987, S. 1619, H.R. 3221 (1987).

10. Visual Artists Rights Act of 1987 (as introduced by Representative Waxman); Visual Artists Rights Act of 1986, H.R. 4366 (as introduced by Representative Downey).

11. Visual Artists Rights Act of 1988, S. 1619, H.R. 3221 (1988).

12. See discussion of other aspects of the bill in chapter 8 at pp. 390-91, chapter 9 at pp. 436-37.

13. CAL. CIV. CODE § 986 (1988). New York State has, from time to time, considered *droit de suite* legislation. There is strong resistance to such legislation in New York from the auction houses and art dealers.

14. *See* MERRYMAN & ELSEN, *supra* note 1, at 231; Emley, *The Resale Royalties Act: Paintings, Preemption and Profit*, 8 GOLDEN GATE U.L. REV. 239 (1978); Bolch, Damon & Hinshaw, *An Economic Analysis of the California Art Royalty Statute*, 10 CONN. L. REV. 689 (1978).

15. *See* NIMMER, *supra* note 3, at 8-272.3.

16. CAL. CIV. CODE § 986(a) (1988).

17. *Id.* § 986(c)(2) (1988).

18. *Id.* § 986(b)(1) (1988).

19. *Id.* § 986(b) (1988).

20. *Id.* § 986(a) (1988).

21. *Id.* § 986(c)(1) (1988).

22. *Id.* § 986(a) (1988).

23. *Id.* § 986(a)(1) (1988). If the artist cannot be located within ninety days of the sale, the royalty must be deposited with the California Arts Council.

24. *Id.* § 986(b)(2) (1988).

25. *Id.* § 986(b)(4) (1988).

26. *Id.* § 986(a)(3) (1988).

27. *Id.* § 986(b)(3) (1988).

28. *Id.* § 986(a)(7) (1988).

29. *Id.* § 986(a) (1988).

30. Morseburg v. Balyon, 621 F.2d 972 (9th Cir.), *cert. denied*, 449 U.S. 983 (1980).

31. The 1976 Copyright Act became effective after the sales in question.

32. *See* Note, *The Preemption Doctrine: Shifting Perspectives on Federalism and The Burger Court*, 75 COLUM. L. REV. 623 (1975).

33. Goldstein v. California, 412 U.S. 546 (1973).

34. *See* Bauer v. O'Donnell, 229 U.S. 1, 11 (1912).

35. Morseburg, supra note 30, 621 F.2d at 977.

36. *See* NIMMER, *supra* note 3, at 8-272.5.

37. *See* NIMMER, *supra* note 3, at 8-272.6. For a contrary view, see Jones, Morseburg v. Balyon—*The High Court Grants Royalty A Reprieve: Constitutional Challenges to the California Resale Royalties Act*, 3 COMM. & ENT. L.J. 1 (1980).

38. The contract form is reproduced in MERRYMAN & ELSEN, *supra* note 1, at 4-144ff.

39. *See* MERRYMAN & ELSEN, *supra* note 1, at 230.

40. The contract form is reproduced at the end of this chapter.

41. *See* U.C.C. § 2-312(1)(b).

42. *See* authorities cited, *supra* note 1.

FORMS

CALIFORNIA RESALE ROYALTIES ACT
Cal. Civ. Code Sec. 986 (1988)

Sec. 986. **Residual Rights in Artist for Sale of Work.**

(a) Whenever a work of fine art is sold and the seller resides in California or the sale takes place in California, the seller or the seller's agent shall pay to the artist of such work of fine art or to such artist's agent 5 percent of the amount of such sale. The right of the artist to receive an amount equal to 5 percent of the amount of such sale may be waived only by a contract in writing providing for an amount in excess of 5 percent of the amount of such sale. An artist may assign the right to collect the royalty payment provided by this section to another individual or entity. However, the assignment shall not have the effect of creating a waiver prohibited by this subdivision.

(1) When a work of fine art is sold at an auction or by a gallery, dealer, broker, museum, or other person acting as the agent for the seller, the agent shall withhold 5 percent of the amount of the sale, locate the artist and pay the artist.

(2) If the seller or agent is unable to locate and pay the artist within 90 days, an amount equal to 5 percent of the amount of the sale shall be transferred to the Arts Council.

(3) If a seller or the seller's agent fails to pay an artist the amount equal to 5 percent of the sale of a work of fine art by the artist or fails to transfer such amount to the Arts Council, the artist may bring an action for damages within three years after the date of sale or one year after the discovery of the sale, whichever is longer. The prevailing party in any action brought under this paragraph shall be entitled to reasonable attorney fees, in an amount as determined by the court.

(4) Moneys received by the council pursuant to this section shall be deposited in an account in the Special Deposit Fund in the State Treasury.

(5) The Arts Council shall attempt to locate any artist for whom money is received pursuant to this section. If the council is unable to locate the artist and the artist does not file a written claim for the money received by the council within seven years of the date of sale of the work of fine art, the right of the artist terminates and such money shall be transferred to the council for use in acquiring fine art pursuant to the Art in Public Buildings program set forth in Chapter 2.1 (commencing with Sec-

tion 15813) of Part 10b of Division 3 of Title 2, of the Government Code.

(6) Any amounts of money held by any seller or agent for the payment of artists pursuant to this section shall be exempt from enforcement of a money judgment by the creditors of the seller or agent.

(7) Upon the death of an artist, the rights and duties created under this section shall inure to his or her heirs, legatees, or personal representative, until the 20th anniversary of the death of the artist. The provisions of this paragraph shall be applicable only with respect to an artist who dies after January 1, 1983.

(b) Subdivision (a) shall not apply to any of the following:

(1) To the initial sale of a work of fine art where legal title to such work at the time of such initial sale is vested in the artist thereof.

(2) To the resale of a work of fine art for a gross sales price of less than one thousand dollars ($1,000).

(3) Except as provided in paragraph (7) of subdivision (a), to a resale after the death of such artist.

(4) To the resale of the work of fine art for a gross sales price less than the purchase price paid by the seller.

(5) To a transfer of a work of fine art which is exchanged for one or more works of fine art or for a combination of cash, other property, and one or more works of fine art where the fair market value of the property exchanged is less than one thousand dollars ($1,000).

(6) To the resale of a work of fine art by an art dealer to a purchaser within 10 years of the initial sale of the work of fine art by the artist to an art dealer, provided all intervening resales are between art dealers.

(7) To a sale of a work of stained glass artistry where the work has been permanently attached to real property and is sold as part of the sale of the real property to which it is attached.

(c) For purposes of this section, the following terms have the following meanings:

(1) "Artist" means the person who creates a work of fine art and who, at the time of resale, is a citizen of the United States, or a resident of the state who has resided in the state for a minimum of two years.

(2) "Fine art" means an original painting, sculpture, or drawing, or an original work of art in glass.

(3) "Art dealer" means a person who is actively and principally engaged in or conducting the business of selling works of fine art for which business such person validly holds a sales tax permit.

(d) This section shall become operative on January 1, 1977, and shall apply to works of fine art created before and after its operative date.

(e) If any provision of this section or the application thereof to any person or circumstance is held invalid for any reason, such invalidity shall not affect any other provisions or applications of this section which can be effected, without the invalid provision or application, and to this end the provisions of this section are severable.

(f) The amendments to this section enacted during the 1981-82 Regular Session of the Legislature shall apply to transfers of works of fine art, when created before or after January 1, 1983, that occur on or after that date. Leg. H. 1976 ch. 1228, 1982 ch. 497, operative July 1, 1983, chs. 1601, 1609 § 1.5.

JURRIST CONTRACT FORM

AGREEMENT, made this___ day of _____________ , 19___ , between _______________ (hereinafter referred to as the "Artist"), residing at _______________, and _______________ (hereinafter referred to as the "Collector"), residing at _______________.

WITNESSETH:

WHEREAS the Artist has created a certain work of art (hereinafter referred to as the "Work"), which is fully described in Paragraph 1 below; and

WHEREAS the Collector desires to purchase the Work from the Artist and the Artist is willing to sell the Work to the Collector upon the terms set forth in this Agreement and not otherwise,

NOW, THEREFORE, in consideration of the mutual promises set forth in this Agreement, as well as other good and valuable consideration, the receipt of which is hereby mutually acknowledged, the parties do hereby covenant and agree as follows:

1. *The Transaction.* The Artist hereby sells to the Collector, and the Collector hereby purchases from the Artist, for a total price of $___ , the Work, which is described and identified as follows:

Medium:_______________
Dimensions:_______________
Title:_______________
Date (or approximate period of creation):_______________
Size of edition:_______________

2. *Edition and Provenance.* (a) Unless otherwise indicated in the space "Size of edition" in Paragraph 1 of this Agreement, the Work is unique. If the Work is unique, the Artist hereby covenants that he shall not produce any exact duplicate of the Work; if the Work is one of an edition, the Artist hereby covenants that the size of the edition shall not be increased after the date of execution of this Agreement.

(b) Upon receipt of a written request from the Collector, the Artist shall provide the Collector with a written statement attesting to the authenticity of the Work and setting forth the size of the edition, if any, of which the Work is a part.

3. *Care of Work.* (a) So long as the Work remains in the Collector's possession, the Collector covenants to exercise reasonable care in maintaining the Work and further covenants not intentionally to alter or destroy the Work.

(b) If the Work is damaged in any manner, the Collector shall notify the Artist of the occurrence and the nature of the damage and shall afford the Artist a reasonable opportunity to conduct, or to supervise, the restoration of the Work.

(c) If the Artist does not take steps to commence the restoration of the Work within thirty (30) days after receipt of notice of damage from the Collector, the Collector shall be free to make whatever arrangements he deems appropriate for the restoration of the Work.

(d) Nothing contained in this Paragraph 3 shall be construed to require that the Collector cause or permit the Work to be moved from the place where it is usually kept in order to allow the Artist to conduct, or to supervise, its restoration.

4. *Artist's Right to Borrow.* (a) The Artist reserves the right, upon giving the Collector reasonable notice of his intention to do so, to borrow the Work from the Collector in order to include it in a public exhibition of the Artist's works. The Collector shall have the right, before permitting the Artist to borrow the Work, to demand the submission, by the Artist or by the exhibiting institution, of documents evidencing adequate insurance coverage on the Work and prepayment of shipping charges to and from the exhibiting institution.

(b) The Artist shall not be entitled to borrow the Work more than once in any twelve-month period or for any single period longer than six (6) weeks.

(c) If the Artist borrows the Work for inclusion in a public exhibition, it shall be the Artist's responsibility to ensure that the exhibiting institution identifies the Work as belonging to the Collector.

5. *Notices to Be Supplied by Collector.* (a) If the Collector moves from the address set forth at the opening of this Agreement, he shall promptly notify the Artist of his new address. The Collector shall also promptly notify the Artist of any subsequent changes of address.

(b) If the Collector lends the Work to any museum, gallery, or other institution for purposes of exhibition or otherwise, the Collector shall promptly notify the Artist that the Work has been so lent. If the Work is to be publicly exhibited, such notice shall include the name of the exhibiting institution, the title of the exhibition, the dates of the exhibition, and the name of the curator or other person, if any, in charge of the exhibition.

6. *Reproduction.* (a) The Collector shall be entitled to permit the reproduction of the Work in books, art magazines, and exhibition catalogues, as he shall see fit.

(b) Except as provided in subparagraph (a), the Artist hereby reserves all rights whatsoever to copy or reproduce the Work and the Collector agrees not to permit such reproduction without first securing the written consent of the Artist.

(c) Nothing contained in this Paragraph 6 shall be construed as requiring that the Collector afford access to the Work for purposes of its being photographed, copied, or reproduced.

(d) (There may be inserted here a subparagraph governing the division between Artist and Collector of any fees received for a reproduction of the Work which the Artist authorizes pursuant to 6(b).)

7. *Transfer of Work.* (a) If the Collector, at any time after the execution of this Agreement, sells the Work, he shall pay to the Artist a sum equal to fifteen percent (15%) of the excess of the gross amount realized from the sale of the Work over the price set forth in Paragraph 1 of this Agreement.

(b) If the Collector, at any time after the execution of this Agreement, exchanges, barters, or trades the Work for another work of art, he shall pay to the Artist a sum equal to fifteen percent (15%) of the excess of the fair market value of the work of art which he receives over the price set forth in Paragraph 1 of this Agreement.

(c) The Collector may, at any time, donate the Work to a museum and, in the event of such donation, no payment shall be required to be made to the Artist. If, however, at any time after the execution of this Agreement, the Collector donates the Work to any institution other than a museum and takes a tax deduction in respect of such donation, he shall pay to the Artist a sum equal to fifteen percent (15%) of the excess of the tax deduction so taken over the price set forth in Paragraph 1 of this Agreement.

(d) If the Collector, at any time after the execution of this Agreement, gives or transfers the Work to any person in any manner other than those enumerated in subparagraphs (a) through (c) of this Paragraph 7, he shall pay to the Artist a sum equal to fifteen percent (15%) of the excess of the fair market value of the Work at the time of such transfer over the price set forth in Paragraph 1 of this Agreement.

8. *Duration and Effect.* This Agreement shall remain in full force and effect until five (5) years after the death of the Artist and shall operate to bind the parties as well as their heirs, legatees, executors, and administrators. However, the obligations imposed upon the Collector by Paragraphs 3(b) and 4 of this Agreement shall terminate immediately upon the death of the Artist.

9. *Construction.* This Agreement shall be construed in accordance with the laws of the State of ____________.

10. *Headings.* Paragraph headings have been included in this Agreement solely for purposes of convenience and such headings shall not have legal effect or in any way affect the extent or interpretation of any of the terms of this Agreement.

IN WITNESS WHEREOF the parties have signed this Agreement as of the date first above written.

____
Artist

____
Collector

IV

Collectors

11 *The Collection as an Investment Property*

Maintaining a collection in good condition is expensive: expenses may include framing, reframing, lighting, air conditioning and humidity controls, cleaning and other maintenance, security devices, publications, and insurance. Travel and other buying expenses and fees may occur when a collector adds to the collection. These costs have increased substantially in recent years.

This chapter focuses on deductibility of the expenses of maintaining the collection, the tax treatment of gains and losses realized upon sale of the collection, and certain problems of insurance.

May the art owner deduct all, some, or a portion of such collection-related expenses and losses incurred in holding the collection as an investment, or are all those expenses nondeductible personal expenses incurred in a hobby for personal use and enjoyment?[1] Before that question can be answered, it is necessary to determine whether the person in question is a dealer, an investor, or a collector, and to examine the general statutory provisions.

The *dealer* is someone engaged in the trade or business of selling works of art primarily to customers. Although the term "trade or business" is not specifically defined in the Internal Revenue Code, the cases indicate that it is the pursuit or occupation to which one contributes a major or substantial part of one's time for the purpose of livelihood or profit.[2]

In December 1983, the United States Court of Appeals for the Second Circuit held that the determination of whether a taxpayer is engaged in a trade or business is *not* based on all the facts and circumstances.[3] Instead, the Second Circuit ruled that three specific conditions must exist for a trade or business status to be recognized, as follows:

1. The taxpayer must be regularly engaged in the activity.
2. The activity must be undertaken with the expectation of making a profit.
3. The taxpayer must hold himself or herself out to others as engaged in the selling of goods and services.

Then in 1987, in *Commissioner v. Groetzinger*,[4] the United States Supreme Court reaffirmed a "facts and circumstances" test and rejected the Second Circuit's condition that the taxpayer must hold himself or herself out to others as engaged in the selling of goods and services. The Court stated that a judicial attempt to formulate and impose a test for all situations would be counterproductive, unhelpful, and even somewhat precarious for the overall integrity of the Internal Revenue Code.

The Court stated that, in order to be engaged in a trade or business, the taxpayer must be involved in the activity with continuity and regularity, and the taxpayer's primary purpose for engaging in the activity must be for income or profit. A sporadic activity, a hobby, or an amusement diversion does not qualify. Moreover, mere investment activities do not constitute a trade or business.[5]

The *investor* is someone who buys and sells works of art primarily for investment, rather than for personal use and enjoyment or as a trade or business. The cases in the securities area that distinguish a dealer from an investor should be equally applicable to the art world.[6] The word "primarily" means of first importance.[7] The key is whether the taxpayer engaged in the investment activity with the primary objective of making a profit.

The *collector* is someone who buys and sells works of art primarily for personal pleasure and is neither a dealer nor an investor and, ordinarily, may not deduct expenses and losses.

The *statutory framework* involves the interaction of sections 67, 162, 212, 165, 183, and 262 of the Internal Revenue Code of 1986.

- Section 67 generally limits miscellaneous deductions to those that exceed 2 percent of adjusted gross income.
- Under section 162 a taxpayer may deduct from gross income all ordinary and necessary expenses incurred in a trade or business.
- Under section 212(1) and (2) a taxpayer may deduct expenses incurred in the production or collection of income.
- Section 165 permits the deduction of losses sustained in a trade or business or in a transaction entered into for profit.
- Section 183 qualifies the foregoing provisions by specifically disallowing, with certain exceptions, deductions attributable to activities not engaged in for profit.
- Section 262 denies a deduction or loss for expenses that are personal in nature.

Therefore, a taxpayer claiming a deduction for an expense under section 162 or 212, or for a loss under section 165, must be able to demonstrate an associated profit motive in order to avoid the ban of section 183 or 262.

EXPENSES

Prior Law

Before the Tax Reform Act of 1969 added section 183, collection-related expenses were deductible only by someone who is a dealer, that is, someone engaged in a trade or business, or an investor, that is, someone who holds the collection for the production of income.[8] The Court of Claims dealt with the issue of the deductibility of collection-related expenses in the *Wrightsman* case.[9]

Wrightsman was an art collector, not a dealer, who conceded that he had originally purchased some of the works of art as a hobby and that he did derive pleasure and satisfaction from keeping his collection in his residence. However, he claimed that the property was held primarily for investment and, therefore, that the expenses related to the investment were deductible. The court disallowed the deductions, ruling that the test to be applied is whether, as a factual matter from an objective view of the operative facts and circumstances, the taxpayer acquired and held the works of art primarily for investment, rather than for personal use and enjoyment.

The Court of Claims also established the following guidelines and criteria:

1. The collector must establish that the investment purpose for acquiring and holding the items in the collection was "principal" or "of first importance."[10]
2. Artworks or other items that make up a collection can be the subject matter of investment. (A number of investment funds have been started with the intention of investing only in artworks, including Sovereign American Arts, Collectors Funding, Art Fund, and Fine Arts Fund.[11])
3. It must be the intention of the collector to hold the property for investment. That intent can be shown by an analysis of the art collector's financial position, the collector's investment history, whether the collector believes that works of art are a hedge against inflation, and whether the collector has made personal declarations of investment purpose and intention that are supported by circumstances and conduct evidencing that intention.

   Other indicia of investment intent include:
   a. Consulting with experts on purchases;
   b. Reading pertinent publications;
   c. Participating in collection-related activities;
   d. Devoting time to the collection;

   e. Making an effort to display the collection publicly so as to enhance its value;
   f. Developing expertise about the collection; and
   g. Keeping businesslike records and using a businesslike method of accounting for the collection.[12]
4. Retention of a collection, without any profitable sales, is not a bar to a showing that the property is held for investment.[13]
5. Even though the collector uses part of the collection to fulfill personal needs, that use does not make the collector's overall activity a hobby.
6. The fact that pleasure is derived from investment property does not preclude deductions.[14]
7. The fact that there is no substantial relationship between the collector's principal occupation and his or her collection activities is of little significance.
8. The proportion of the collection-related expenses that is attributable to the personal use of the collection is not deductible. The proportion attributable to personal use is a close approximation based on all the facts and circumstances.[15]

On the basis of the facts presented in *Wrightsman*, the report of the Trial Commissioner of the Court of Claims recommended that the deduction for the art-related expenses be allowed.[16] There is a dissenting opinion to the decision of the full court, which adopts the conclusion of the Trial Commissioner and which we believe should have been the conclusion reached by the court.

Conclusions Under Wrightsman

The dealer who buys and sells works of art can deduct the ordinary and necessary business expenses incurred in the trade or business of being a "dealer" under section 162.

The investor who buys and holds works of art primarily for investment can deduct the ordinary and necessary expenses incurred in connection with property held for the production of income under section 212(1) or (2).

The collector *cannot* deduct art-related expenses in connection with collecting activities, since those expenses are nondeductible personal expenses under section 262.

Still, the opinion in *Wrightsman* indicates that the collector faces an extremely difficult, although not impossible, task to prove that he or she is an investor. Not many collectors are able to show that they acquired and held the works of art primarily for investment, rather than for personal use and enjoyment.

Section 183

The Tax Reform Act of 1969 introduced section 183 to the Internal Revenue Code effective January 1, 1970. Although the section is known as the "hobby loss" provision because it disallows deductions and losses from activities not engaged in for profit, it does permit the deduction of certain collection-related expenses that were not previously deductible. Section 183(a) provides:

> In the case of an activity engaged in by an individual or an S corporation, if such activity is not engaged in for profit, no deduction attributable to such activity shall be allowed under this chapter except as provided in this section.

Section 183(c) defines the term "activity not engaged in for profit" to mean:

> [A]ny activity other than one with respect to which deductions are allowable for the taxable year under section 162 or under paragraph (1) or (2) of section 212.

Therefore, for a collector to avoid the application of section 183, a collection-related expense has to be from an "activity engaged in for profit" that is otherwise deductible under section 162 or section 212(1) or (2). As previously discussed, the *Wrightsman* case makes the deduction of collection-related expenses under such sections extremely difficult because of the onerous burden of proof the taxpayer has in proving to the IRS that he or she incurred the expenses in connection with works of art held primarily for investment.

Regulation section 1.183-2 sets forth a number of factors similar to the indicia of investment activity listed in *Wrightsman* to be considered in determining whether or not an activity is engaged in for profit. These factors are as follows:

1. *The manner in which the taxpayer carries on the activity.* A businesslike manner with complete and accurate books and records is more likely than not to be profit-motivated.
2. *The expertise of the taxpayer or the taxpayer's advisers.* Preparation for the activity by an extensive study of accepted business, economic, and scientific practices or by consultations with experts may indicate a profit motive.
3. *The time and effort expended by the taxpayer in carrying on the activity.* Spending a great deal of time and effort is more likely than not to indicate a profit motive.
4. *The expectation that assets used in the activity may appreciate in value.* The term "profit" does encompass appreciation in value of the assets, but unrealized appreciation alone is not sufficient. The taxpayer must show that his or her primary purpose is ultimately to realize appreciation.
5. *The success of the taxpayer in carrying on other similar or dissimilar activities for a profit.*
6. *The taxpayer's history of income or losses with respect to the activity.* A series of realizations of income may indicate a profit motive.
7. *The amount of occasional profits, if any, that are earned.*
8. *The financial status of the taxpayer.* The fact that the taxpayer does not have substantial income or capital from sources other than the activity may indicate that the activity is engaged in for profit.

9. *Elements of personal pleasure or recreation.* The regulations indicate that, the greater the pleasure, the less likely it is that there is a profit motive. Although not required by the Internal Revenue Code or *Wrightsman*, a physical segregation of the art investment property out of the taxpayer's personal residence or office will generally help the taxpayer prove his or her profit motive.

No one of the above factors is determinative, and the determination of a profit motive is not limited to the above factors. The test is: based on "all the facts and circumstances," is a profit motive present?

The main objective of section 183, therefore, is to disallow deductions attributable to an activity not engaged in for profit. The section disallows deductions for all collectors who are not dealers or investors.

Section 183(b)

Section 183(b) does offer some help to the collector. That section allows the collector to claim deductions for expenses attributable to an activity not engaged in for profit up to the amount of the gross income derived from the activity, after first deducting those items, such as certain items of interest and taxes, that are allowable without regard to whether an activity is engaged in for profit.[17]

As discussed above, if the taxpayer can satisfy section 212(1) or (2), the collection-related expenses are deductible whether or not the taxpayer had any gross income from collection activities, since he or she is classified as an investor. If the taxpayer (as in *Wrightsman*) cannot satisfy the test of section 212 (1) or (2), the taxpayer can claim a deduction for collection-related expenses under section 183(b) up to the amount of his or her gross income from collection activities, so long as the collector is carrying on an "activity" within the meaning of section 183, and after first subtracting such items as interest and taxes that are deductible without regard to section 183. The collection-related expenses that are then deductible under section 183(b) are subject to the 2 percent rule of section 67(a) for deductions claimed on or after January 1, 1987.[18]

Example: If in *Wrightsman* there had been gross income derived from the taxpayer's collection activities, the expenses at issue in that case would have been deductible under section 183(b) up to the amount of that gross income. Under prior law, if the expenses were not deductible under section 212(1) or (2), they could not be offset against any gross income from the activity not engaged in for profit.

The regulations contain detailed provisions on how to calculate the gross income from an activity for purposes of determining the amount available to offset deduction items.[19] For example, the regulations require that capital gains and losses from the collection activity be merged with all other capital gains and losses of the collector from noncollection activity.[20] Therefore, capital gains realized from sales of items in the collection are not available to offset collection expense deductions if the collector had losses on securities transactions that reduce the gains on collection sales to zero. In addition, for capital transactions before January 1, 1987, the regulations require that the 60 percent long-term capital gains deduction of section 1202(a) be taken before arriving at the amount of capital gains gross income from collection activities that is available to offset deductions from the collection activities.[21] Although there no longer is a capital gains deduction under section 1202(a), if the distinction between capital gains and ordinary income is ever restored to the Code, the regulation will once again become operative.

Cases Under Section 183

Leonard L. Barcus[22] and *Mary L. Stanley*[23] illustrate the difficulty that a collector has in showing that he or she was engaged in an activity for profit. In *Barcus*, the court found that a married couple that bought and sold antiques was not profit-motivated. In *Stanley*, the court found that a collector of antique glass novelties and marbles had not carried the burden of proving that her collection activities were primarily for the production of income. There, however, even though the court found that there was no activity for profit, it did permit the deduction of collection-related expenses to the extent of the gross income derived from the collection activities, under section 183(b)(2). Under the law before the passage of section 183, those deductions would have been disallowed under section 262.

Maurice C. Dreicer[24] illustrates the application of section 183 and the test a taxpayer must meet to have losses allowed in an amount greater than the income received from an activity. There the taxpayer, who received a substantial income from a family trust, had traveled extensively throughout the world for many years. Twenty years before the tax years in question, his book on international dining had been published, but, because it was a commercial failure, he had received only meager royalties. Although he had written a rough draft of a book on a similar topic during the tax years in question, he had abandoned his efforts to have it published after the manuscript had been rejected by two publishers. During the years between the books, he had lectured before various travel organizations, written for a travel magazine, and participated in radio and television programs, all without compensation. The taxpayer claimed his travel and other related expenses as business expenses during the tax years in question, but the IRS disallowed the deduction on the ground that it was a hobby loss.

The Tax Court held that the taxpayer was not entitled to deduct his expenses, because he did not have a "bona fide expectation of profit" from the pursuit of his career as a writer-lecturer. However, the appellate court ruled that, although a taxpayer's expectation of profit is a factor to be considered in determining whether losses are deductible,[25] the legal standard is whether the taxpayer has engaged in the activity with the "objective of making a profit." Consequently, the court remanded the case to the Tax Court for reconsideration under the profit-objective standard.

On rehearing, the Tax Court agreed with the appellate court that the correct legal standard to be applied requires that, "[T]he facts and circumstances must indicate that the taxpayer entered into the activity, or continued the activity, with the actual and honest objective of making a profit." The court pointed out that the taxpayer's motive is the ultimate question, but the motive must be determined by a careful analysis of all the surrounding objective facts, with greater weight given to those facts than to the taxpayer's mere statement of intent.

In *Marie L. Johnson*,[26] the Tax Court seems to say that the "profit" requirement of section 183 is not to be applied with the same vigor in a sale-leaseback transaction as it is in a "hobby loss" case.

In *Dailey*,[27] the United States Court of Appeals for the Eighth Circuit affirmed a Tax Court opinion holding that a mere floating expectation of realizing a profit was not sufficient to satisfy section 183. In *Dailey*, the taxpayers intended to purchase and maintain appreciating art and antiques to provide a nest egg for their retirement. However, the court held that they could not deduct as investment expenses the costs of art and antiques magazine subscriptions, a magazine-sponsored trip to Europe, or travel within the United States, since they never took any active steps to sell any items in their collection and their expectations of realizing a profit were vague and uncertain.

LOSSES

Losses on Sale

An individual can deduct a loss on a sale incurred in a trade or business,[28] or in a transaction entered into for profit not connected with a trade or business.[29] Generally, unless a collector can come within the requirements of section 183(b), as discussed above, a loss on the sale of a collection by a collector is not deductible.

A collector is someone who is not engaged in a "trade or business" under section 165(c)(1).[30] An individual in the "trade or business" of buying and selling works of art is a dealer and realizes ordinary income on sales at a gain and has ordinary losses under section 165(c)(1) on sales at a loss.

The United States Supreme Court has held that investment activities do not constitute a trade or business.[31] Therefore, a collector can buy and sell items and not be considered a dealer engaged in a trade or business. It must then be decided if the collector is an investor, to determine whether the loss can be deducted under section 165(c)(2).

The test for deductibility under section 165(c)(2) of a loss incurred in any "transaction entered into for profit, though not connected with a trade or business" is a stricter test than that required for the deduction of expenses under section 212, under which the requirement is that an expenditure be on property "held for the production of income."[32] Therefore, satisfying section 212 does not guarantee that any loss on a sale of the collection will be deductible under section 165(c)(2). The taxpayer-collector bears the burden of proving that the "transaction was entered into for profit." Here, evidence that *at the time of purchase* the taxpayer acquired the collection with a profit motive is necessary.

In *George F. Tyler*,[33] the taxpayer showed that from the outset he undertook stamp collecting as an investment: all purchases were made in consultation with a stamp expert. The court held that the purchase of the stamps was a transaction entered into for profit, and the loss incurred on the sale of the stamps was deductible under what is now section 165(c)(2). The case is unusual in the clarity of the fact that the taxpayer was able to offer convincing evidence of investment procedures from the outset.

Reacting to the *Tyler* case, the IRS shortly thereafter issued Revenue Ruling 54-268,[34] which held that a loss sustained from the sale of a collection of stamps accumulated as a hobby does not represent a loss incurred in a trade or business or in a transaction entered into for profit within the meaning of section 165(c)(1) or (2). Accordingly, the ruling holds that such a loss is not deductible for federal income tax purposes.

An individual collector can deduct losses on sales as capital losses if it is proved that the collector is, in fact, an investor.[35] However, the allowance of such a loss would be extremely rare, since the taxpayer has the burden of proving that the loss-generating activity was a transaction entered into for profit and not merely a hobby.[36]

Section 183(b) once again offers help to the collector who cannot meet the requirement of section 165(c)(2) that he or she entered into the transaction for profit. If the collector can prove that the collection is an "activity" within the meaning of section 183, capital losses are deductible under section 183(b) up to the amount of the gross income derived from the collection during the taxable year, after first subtracting such items as interest and taxes that are otherwise deductible without regard to section 183. Therefore, capital losses from the collection activity can be used to offset capital gains from the collection activity under section 183(b). Before section 183, the gains would have been taxable, but the losses would have been nondeductible personal losses if section 165(c)(2) was not satisfied.[37]

The burden of proving that the collector is engaged in a trade or business or that purchases made by the collector were made in transactions entered into for profit or in the production or the collection of income is extremely difficult. The collector should try to satisfy as many of the factual elements of regulation section 1.183-2(b) as possible. Even if the collector cannot prove the profit motive, the collector should keep adequate records to show that he or she is engaged in an "activity," so that losses up to the amount of the gross income from that activity can be claimed as a deduction.

Losses on Inherited Property

If a collection is inherited and immediately offered for sale and is sold at a loss, the loss is capital in nature and may be deductible under section 165(c)(2).[38] However, the collection must not first be converted to personal use and thereafter offered for sale. In that situation it becomes more difficult to show that the transaction was "entered into" for profit.

Casualty Losses

A collector may desire to become a self-insurer because of the high cost of insurance for the collection. The idea behind self-insuring is that the deduction allowed for a loss from fire, theft, or other casualty may save a high-bracket taxpayer more in taxes than the cost of insurance.[39] However, the Tax Equity and Fiscal Responsibility Act of 1982 (TEFRA) raised the stakes for the self-insurer by limiting the allowable casualty loss deduction to the amount that exceeds 10 percent of adjusted gross income.[40]

Before applying the new limitation, the collector must first determine the amount of the loss. The amount of the loss from a casualty is the *lower* of (1) the fair market value of the property immediately before the casualty, reduced by the fair market value of the property immediately after the casualty (zero in the case of a theft), or (2) the property's adjusted basis.[41]

From that *lower* amount, the collector must subtract $100 for each casualty[42] and then subtract 10 percent of his or her adjusted gross income.[43] Only the amount of loss that exceeds the above limitations can be claimed as a casualty loss. The 10 percent limitation introduced by TEFRA became effective January 1, 1983.

Example: A collector purchased a painting for $10,000. Ten years later, when it had a fair market value of $50,000, it was stolen. There was no insurance, the taxpayer's adjusted gross income in the year of the theft was $100,000, and the theft took place during the year 1988. The casualty loss deduction is calculated as follows:

Amount of loss (lower of fair market value or basis) =	$10,000
Limitations: less –	100
less – 10% × 100,000 =	10,000
	$10,100
Amount deductible	-0-

If an item in a collection is purchased and later discovered to be a forgery and, hence, almost worthless, it produces a deductible loss if the transaction amounted to a "theft" under local law.[44] For it to constitute a "theft," the taxpayer must bear the burden of proving that the item was sold to him or her with an intent to defraud.

Involuntary Conversions

Of course, any amount of casualty loss is further reduced by any insurance recovery. If the collector receives insurance proceeds greater than the cost basis, the collector has a taxable gain[45] unless he or she can come within the exception of section 1033(a)(2). Under section 1033(a)(2), a gain from an involuntary conversion of property into money is not recognized if the insurance proceeds were used to purchase similar property (similar to the items collected) within two years after the close of the first taxable year in which any part of the gain on conversion was realized.[46]

In the above casualty loss example, if the collector has a $50,000 insurance recovery on the painting, he or she has a realized taxable gain of $40,000, unless he or she reinvests the insurance proceeds in similar property within the applicable time period of section 1033(a)(2).

The question of what is "similar property" for a collector was dealt with in Private Letter Ruling 8127089. A fire had caused extensive damage to a collector's lithographs and other art items. The collector had difficulty in replacing the lithographs and wanted to use part of the insurance proceeds to purchase artwork in other artistic media. The IRS ruled that artwork in one medium, destroyed in whole or in part, replaced with artwork in another medium will not be considered property similar or related in service or use. The Private Letter Ruling appears to be unduly narrow in its interpretation of the statute.

EXCHANGES

It is a common practice for collectors to exchange items, each intending to improve his or her collection. Dealers often encourage collectors to trade in works of art purchased from them in exchange for other works of art. Section 1031(a) allows certain "like kind" exchanges to be made tax-free. The statute limits such exchanges to property held for productive use in a trade or business or for investment that is exchanged solely for property of a like kind to be held for productive use in a trade or business or for investment.[47]

In the usual case, a collector is engaged in a hobby, not a business. The collector may argue that he or she is an investor and held the property for investment. The term "investment" is not defined in section 1031. Relying on *Wrightsman* and sections 162, 165, 212, and 183, the term most likely means property acquired and held primarily for profit. The burden of proof for the collector who wants to be an investor may be more difficult here because of the lack of authorities and the difference in terminology.[48] Therefore, for the collector, the difference between the fair market value of the property received and the basis of the property given up results in a taxable gain. The investor, on the other hand, may be able to avoid any taxable gain under the umbrella of section 1031(a). Note, however, that even if an individual can carry the difficult burden of proof of being an investor, there may still be a problem on the exchange as to what constitutes "like-kind" property.[49]

Whether an exchange is a taxable or nontaxable transaction for federal income tax purposes, it is treated as a sale, and a sales tax may be payable on the exchange.[50] Generally, if the exchange is between a dealer and a collector, the dealer should collect and pay over the sales tax.

RECORD-KEEPING

In planning a collector's estate, an attorney must have the collector maintain adequate records. If both a husband and a wife participate in the collecting activity, careful records should indicate who is the owner of each item, and any insurance policies should be consistent with those ownership records. If any lifetime charitable contributions are contemplated, the record-keeping requirements of the Tax Reform Act of 1984 and the Tax Reform Act of 1986 make good records imperative. These provisions are discussed in detail in chapter 12. Further, the date of purchase and the cost of each purchase are necessary to determine the gain or loss on the sale of the collection.[51]

CARRYOVER BASIS RULES UNDER THE TAX REFORM ACT OF 1976

The basis rules introduced by the Tax Reform Act of 1976 and modified by the Revenue Act of 1978 were repealed by the Crude Oil Windfall Profit Tax Bill of 1980. If those provisions are reintroduced at a later date, anyone dealing with items of tangible personal property has to give attention to those provisions.

SELF-DIRECTED RETIREMENT PLANS

Before January 1, 1982, an individual could purchase artworks or other collectibles in an individual retirement account (IRA) or qualified retirement plan. After discovering that people were purchasing collectibles in their retirement plans and making personal use of those items, the IRS urged Congress to change the law. Section 408(m) was introduced into the Internal Revenue Code by the Economic Recovery Tax Act of 1981 (ERTA). That section penalizes an individual who directs his or her IRA or any self-directed retirement plan to invest in collectibles. The term "collectibles" includes works of art.[52]

Section 408(m) treats any acquisition of a collectible by an IRA or a self-directed retirement plan as if the value of that collectible is distributed from the IRA or retirement plan to the participant. That means the participant has taxable ordinary income equal to the value of the amount treated as distributed. That interpretation has the practical effect of making it prohibitive for an IRA or a self-directed retirement plan to acquire collectibles.

The statute provides that section 408(m) is effective for property "acquired" after December 31, 1981, in taxable years ending after that date. The IRS explained, in part, the new rules pertaining to collectibles as follows:[53]

> Q. What is the effect of the new requirement on collectibles that were acquired on or before December 31, 1981?
>
> A. Since the new provision is not applicable to collectibles that were acquired on or before December 31, 1981, the retention of a collectible acquired prior to January 1, 1982 by an IRA or an individually-directed account is not treated as a distribution."

A question remains, however, as to whether a transfer or "rollover" after December 31, 1981, of works of art acquired before January 1, 1982, is an "acquisition" by the IRA after December 31, 1981, that would now be treated as a distribution.[54]

A rollover is a transfer of assets from one retirement plan to another. Generally, such a transfer is not regarded as a distribution from the plan from which the assets are transferred and is not regarded as a contribution to the plan to which the assets are transferred. That is, the distribution is tax-free and the contribution is not deductible or subject to any of the various limitations imposed on contributions to retirement plans. A rollover is merely the shifting of the pension assets from one holding vehicle to another, and, as long as the requirements of section 402(a)(5) are met, the Internal Revenue Code provides that such transfers are tax-free.

On January 23, 1984, the IRS issued proposed regulations (still not finally adopted) under section 408(m) dealing with investments in collectibles. Proposed regulation section 1.408-10(d) defines the term "acquisition" for the purpose of section 408(m) as follows:

> For purposes of this section, the term acquisition includes purchase, exchange, contribution, or any method by which an individual retirement account or individually-directed account may directly or indirectly acquire a collectible.

That is an extremely broad definition and appears to include any method by which an IRA acquired a collectible after December 31, 1981. The IRS could take the position that such a broad definition includes a rollover of a collectible acquired before January 1, 1982. However, notwithstanding the language of the regulation, IRS Notice 82-3 indicates that collectibles acquired before January 1, 1982, may be retained in an IRA. Therefore, the broad language of the regulation was probably intended to encompass in the broadest terms all acquisitions of collectibles if the collectibles were, in fact, purchased after December 31, 1981. Since a rollover is a mere shifting of assets from one retirement vehicle to another, such a transfer should not constitute an "acquisition of a collectible" after December 31, 1981, as long as the collectibles were, in fact, acquired before that date. However, there is no specific authority for the foregoing, and the IRS could take the position that a rollover is a taxable distribution.

The Tax Reform Act of 1986 amended section 408(m) to allow the purchase, after January 1, 1987, of gold and silver coins minted in the United States after October 1, 1986, as long as the coins were held in an IRA in the name of a trustee.[55]

INSURANCE

Insurance is a significant consideration for collectors, artists, and dealers. It is the insurance policy that covers the risk of loss that might occur from any number of causes. If, for example, the collector maintains the collection in his or her home, the collection should be insured against fire, theft, flood, earthquake, and all the other risks attendant to the maintenance of artwork in the home.

The insurance policy, as with any other contract, should be examined in detail to ensure that all risks that the collector wants covered are, in fact, covered. The examination would include a thorough review of the policy's exclusions. For instance, the policy might not cover mysterious disappearances or theft by dishonest employees who have been admitted to the residence.

Additionally, the policy should cover appreciation in value. This means a new appraisal for insurance purposes from time to time in order to update the policy. The collector should maintain precise inventory records, appraisals, photographs, invoices, and other documentation so that the existence and ownership of the insured items can be proved.

Further, the policy should cover what happens if the collector suffers a loss, e.g., theft of a painting, the insurance company pays the collector for the then insured value, and the painting is recovered years later when it has greatly appreciated in value. Assuming the collector is able to reclaim title and is not barred by the statute of limitations, he or she still has a problem because technically the insurance company is the true owner of the painting, having taken the collector's rights by subrogation when it paid the collector after the theft of the painting. The collector should require the insurance policy to give him or her the option to acquire title to the painting from the insurance company for the amount paid to the collector by the insurance company at the time of the loss. This is crucial because the current fair market value of the painting may be many times the amount of the insurance payment that was received by the collector. The insurance company will sometimes require an interest factor to be added before agreeing to such a provision.

If the collector is selling artwork on consignment through a dealer, he should require the dealer to insure the artwork from the time it leaves the collector's premises. The collector should make sure that the dealer's policy covers all risks and provides that the collector/consignor will be paid in full regardless of the loss that may occur. The collector should always require the dealer to furnish a copy of the insurance policy proving such coverage.

Like the collector, the artist also wants to ensure that works of art consigned for sale are fully covered by the dealer's policy. Of course, the artist should have his or her own insurance policy covering the works of art when they are on the artist's premises.

Insurance policies can be intimidating, consisting of numerous pages of fine print. It is important for an artist to engage an insurance agent who can explain the policy, the risks involved, and precisely what is being insured.

NOTES
to Chapter 11

1. I.R.C. §§ 162, 212(1), 212(2), 262, 183; Treas. Reg. § 1.212-1(c); *see* Anthoine, *The Collector of Taxes v. The Collector of Objects*, 59 TAXES 917 (1981).

2. See general definition in IRS Publication 334, *Tax Guide For Small Business* (1981). This definition has been dropped from later editions. Rev. Rul. 63-145, 1963-2 C.B. 86; *see* Boyle, *What Is a Trade or Business?*, 39 TAX LAW. 737 (1986).

3. Gajewski v. Commissioner, 723 F.2d 1062 (2d Cir. 1983), *cert. denied*, 459 U.S. 818 (1984), *rev'g* 45 T.C.M. (CCH) 967 (1983) (rejecting the facts and circumstances test in Ditunno v. Commissioner, 80 T.C. 362 (1983). *See also* Snyder v. Commissioner, 295 U.S. 134 (1935).

4. Commissioner v. Groetzinger, 107 S. Ct. 980 (1987). The *Groetzinger* case dealt with the question of whether a gambler was engaged in a "trade or business" as used in Code sections 162(a) and 62(1). The Supreme Court did limit its findings to the Code sections at issue in the case.

5. Whipple v. Commissioner, 373 U.S. 193 (1963); Higgins v. Commissioner, 312 U.S. 212 (1941); Moller v. United States, 721 F.2d 810 (Fed. Cir. 1983), *rev'g* 553 F. Supp. 1071 (Cl. Ct. 1982), *cert. denied*, 467 U.S. 1251 (1984).

6. Wood v. Commissioner, 16 T.C. 213 (1951); Kemon v. Commissioner, 16 T.C. 1026 (1951); *see* Hollis v. United States, 121 F. Supp. 191 (N.D. Ohio 1954); Seeley v. Helvering, 77 F.2d 321 (2d Cir. 1935); Nehring v. Commissioner, 16 T.C.M. (CCH) 224 (1957); Priv. Ltr. Rul. 8140015.

7. Malat v. Riddell, 383 U.S. 569 (1968); Treas. Reg. § 1.212-1(c).

8. I.R.C. § 262; Treas. Reg. § 1.212-1(c); Rev. Rul. 68-232, 1968-1 C.B. 79.

9. Wrightsman v. United States, 428 F.2d 1316 (Ct. Cl. 1970).

10. Malat v. Riddell, *supra* note 7; Treas. Reg. § 1.212-1(c).

11. *Shorting Rembrandt*, FORBES, Mar. 15, 1970, at 78; *see* Note, *Why Think Of Your Estate As A Collection?*, 117 TR. & EST. 662 (1978).

12. Tatt v. Commissioner, 166 F.2d 697 (5th Cir. 1948).

13. Higgins v. United States, 75 F. Supp. 252 (Ct. Cl. 1948); Churchman v. Commissioner, 68 T.C. 696 (1977).

14. Tyler v. Commissioner, 6 T.C.M. (CCH) 275 (1947); Dember v. Commissioner, 25 T.C.M. (CCH) 620 (1966).

15. Cohan v. Commissioner, 39 F.2d 540 (2d Cir. 1930).

16. Ct. Cl. Comm'r's Rep. No. 364-66, 69-7 Fed. Tax Rep. (CCH) ¶ 7910 (1969).

17. Treas. Reg. § 1.183-1(b).

18. I.R.C. § 67(a) limits the deduction for such expenses to amounts that exceed 2 percent of adjusted gross income. *See* Treas. Reg. § 1.67-1T(a)(iv).

19. Treas. Reg. § 1.183-1(b).

20. Treas. Reg. § 1.183-1(b)(4).

21. *Id.*

22. Barcus v. Commissioner, 32 T.C.M. (CCH) 660 (1973).

23. Stanley v. Commissioner, 40 T.C.M. (CCH) 516 (1980); *see also* Eastman v. United States, 80-2 U.S. Tax Cas. (CCH) ¶ 9742 (Ct. Cl. 1980) (No. 538-78); Allen v. Commissioner, 72 T.C. 28 (1979); Feistman v. Commissioner, 44 T.C.M. (CCH) 30 (1982) (stamp collector showed he was profit-motivated); *compare* Feistman v. Commissioner, 41 T.C.M. (CCH) 1057 (1981); Dailey v. Commissioner, 44 T.C.M. (CCH) 1352 (1982); Wilson v. Commissioner, 42 T.C.M. (CCH) 787 (1981) (foot massaging activity of the taxpayer was not profit-motivated); Steele v. Commissioner, 41 T.C.M. (CCH) 1092 (1981); Burleson v. Commissioner, 46 T.C.M. (CCH) 1394 (1983) (dog breeding expenses were profit-motivated); Estate of Elizabeth Powers v. Commissioner, 84-2 U.S. Tax Cas. (CCH) ¶ 9590 (1st Cir. June 21, 1984), *aff'g* 46 T.C.M. (CCH) 1333 (1983) (horse breeding expenses were not profit-motivated); Salzman v. Commissioner, 55 T.C.M. (CCH) 278 (1988) (licensing of ultrasonic toothbrush was not for profit); Krivitsky v. Commissioner, 54 T.C.M. (CCH) 493 (1987) (mining activities were not conducted with a profit motive); Hawkins v. Commissioner, 54 T.C.M. (CCH) 1529 (1988) (exotic animal farm was not profit motivated); Barr v. Commissioner, 56 T.C.M. (CCH) 1255 (1989) (art publishing enterprise did not have profit intention).

24. Dreicer v. Commissioner, 665 F.2d 1292 (D.C. Cir. 1981), *rev'g* 39 T.C.M. (CCH) 233 (1979), *on remand*, 78 T.C. 642 (1982).

25. *See* Treas. Reg. § 1.183-2(b) (listing factors to be considered by court in determining whether activity is engaged in for profit).

26. Johnson v. United States, 86-2 U.S. Tax Cas. (CCH) ¶ 9705 (Ct. Cl. 1986).

27. Dailey v. Commissioner, (8th Cir. 1982) (unpublished), *aff'g* 44 T.C.M. (CCH) 1352 (1982).

28. I.R.C. § 165(c)(1).

29. I.R.C. § 165(c)(2).

30. *See supra* note 2.

31. Higgins v. Commissioner, *supra* note 5.

32. Horrman v. Commissioner, 17 T.C. 903 (1951); McAuley v. Commissioner, 35 T.C.M. (CCH) 1236 (1976).

33. Tyler v. Commissioner, 6 T.C.M. (CCH) 275 (1947).

34. Rev. Rul. 54-268, 1954-2 C.B. 88.

35. Wrightsman v. United States, *supra* note 9, at 428 F.2d 1316 n.2. The loss, however, was not allowed in *Wrightsman*.

36. *See* Lee, *A Blend of Old Wines in a New Wineskin: Section 183 and Beyond*, 29 TAX L. REV. 347 (1974); Anthoine, *The Collector of Taxes vs. The Collector of Objects*, 59 TAXES 917 (1981).

37. I.R.C. § 262.

38. Reynolds v. Commissioner, 4 T.C.M. (CCH) 837 (1945), *aff'd*, 155 F.2d 620 (1st Cir. 1946) (sale of inherited jewelry); Marx v. Commissioner, 5 T.C. 173 (1945) (sale of inherited yacht); M. Assmann Estate v. Commissioner, 16 T.C. 632 (1951) (sale of inherited house); Watkins v. Commissioner, 32 T.C.M. (CCH) 809 (1973) (sale of inherited house).

39. I.R.C. § 165(c)(3), (a), (h) (effective Jan. 1, 1983); Treas. Reg. § 1.165-8.

40. I.R.C. § 165(h)(1)(B). Section 67(a)'s 2 percent limitation does not apply; *see* I.R.C. § 67(b)(3).

41. Treas. Reg. § 1.165-7(b).

42. I.R.C. § 165(h)(1)(A).

43. I.R.C. § 165(h)(1)(B).

44. I.R.C. § 165(c)(3); Treas. Reg. § 1.165-8; Gerstell v. Commissioner, 46 T.C. 161 (1966); Krahmer v. United States, 810 F.2d 1145 (Fed. Cir. 1987), *aff'g in part and rev'g in part* 85-2 U.S. Tax Cas. (CCH) ¶ 9970 (Cl. Ct. 1985).

45. I.R.C. § 1231(a); Treas. Reg. § 1.1033(c)-1(a).

46. I.R.C. § 1033(a)(2).

47. I.R.C. § 1031(a); Treas. Reg. § 1.1031(a)-1(b); *see* California Fed. Life Ins. Co. v. Commissioner, 680 F.2d 85 (9th Cir. 1982), *aff'g* 76 T.C. 107 (1981) and Rev. Rul. 76-214, 1976-1 C.B. 218; Rev. Rul. 79-143, 1979-1 C.B. 264; Rev. Rul. 82-96, 1982-1 C.B. 113; Rev. Rul. 82-166, 1982-2 C.B. 190.

48. *Compare* I.R.C. §§ 162, 165, 212, 183, *with* I.R.C. § 1031(a).

49. Priv. Ltr. Rul. 8127089.

50. *See, e.g.*, 20 N.Y. Comp. Codes R. & Regs. §§ 526.5(f), 526.7(d).

51. Franklin v. Commissioner, 77-2 U.S. Tax Cas. (CCH) ¶ 9574 (W.D.N.C. 1977); Herrald, Inc. v. Commissioner, 35 T.C.M. (CCH) 1134 (1976).

52. Treas. Reg. § 1.408-10(b)(1).

53. Notice 82-3, 1982-1 C.B. 353 (pt. III.A., Q.3).

54. I.R.C. § 402(a)(5) covers rollovers from a qualified retirement plan to an IRA account. I.R.C. § 402(a)(7) covers spousal rollovers of amounts paid to a surviving spouse from a qualified retirement plan on the death of the covered employee.

55. I.R.C. § 408(m)(3).

Tax and Estate Planning

V

12

Collectors

Most people are collectors of one thing or another, and the number of people who are serious collectors with valuable collections is growing rapidly.[1] In fact, paintings, stamps, coins, and other items of tangible personal property have increased in value at a much greater rate than have most stocks and bonds. As those collectibles increase in value, the estate planner must give them greater attention. Planning for the collector's lifetime and testamentary disposition of tangible personal property to charitable organizations was made increasingly complicated as a result of the Tax Reform Act of 1969, Tax Reform Act of 1976, Revenue Act of 1978, Economic Recovery Tax Act of 1981, Tax Equity and Fiscal Responsibility Act of 1982, Tax Reform Act of 1984, Tax Reform Act of 1986, Revenue Act of 1987, and Technical and Miscellaneous Revenue Act of 1988, each of which contained new and complex provisions. It seems that hardly a year goes by without some new and arcane legislation to confuse collectors. The problems are complicated by the fact that, in most cases, items of collectible tangible personal property (hereinafter called the "collection") are unique and difficult to value. Not knowing the value of the collection complicates the planning for its disposition.

Perhaps the most difficult problem in planning the collector's estate is knowing what he or she really wants. Most collectors have an emotional involvement to some extent with the items that make up their collections; for example a painting may have been in the collector's family for generations. Collectors may own items that they consider very valuable but that are, in fact, almost worthless, or the reverse may be true. They may be secretive about what they have and about the true worth of the collection. One moment they may want their children to have the collection, and the next moment their desires may shift to their favorite museums. Care and maintenance of the collection may be the most important part of the collector's life, taking up the greatest amount of his or her time and energy. Any encroachment or even suggestion of less involvement with the collection may be threatening to the collector. Making a decision with respect to the collection's eventual disposition may also be something that the collector wishes to avoid.

In planning a collector's estate, an attorney must know the client's particular personality traits. Gaining that knowledge requires more than a one-hour conference. It is important for the attorney to acquaint the client slowly with all the available possibilities and to give the client time to consider the alternatives. That time is crucial; the client who is devoted to and involved with his or her collection may never have thought about its disposition and may have shied away from considering the problems. Therefore, knowing the client, knowing his or her desires and needs, working together over a period of time, and developing a sense of trust are absolutely necessary in planning any collector's estate.

VALUATION

Knowing the value or approximate value of a collector's estate is of utmost importance:

- For income tax purposes if the collection is transferred during life to a charitable donee;[2]
- For gift tax purposes if the property is transferred during life to a noncharitable donee;[3]
- For estate tax purposes if the property is owned at death;[4] and
- For insurance purposes if the property is maintained dur-

ing life (since insurance companies require an appraisal in order to determine the premiums for coverage).

As important as the concept of value is, there is no simple rule or answer. Although, as discussed below, the Internal Revenue Service (IRS) has by regulation attempted to create rules of valuation, those rules are not workable in all situations and are most difficult to apply when it comes to unique items of tangible personal property.[5]

In his treatise on federal estate and gift taxation, Randolph Paul stated that value is essentially and peculiarly a difficult question of fact, with the burden of proof falling on the taxpayer.[6] The treatise pointed out, however, that valuation is more than a question of fact; it is a prophecy, a matter of opinion and judgment. In the valuation process, it is unsafe to neglect any apparent factor—the composite of all the factors involved in a single case should lead to a conclusion. Paul stated that it is wrong to assign to any particular factor a precise weight and noted that individualized treatment of each problem is essential. Paul pointed out that the courts have observed: "Market value is so dependent on times, places, conditions, and people that that which is a good rule in one case may be no rule under other circumstances."[7]

IRS Valuation Regulations

The IRS regulations for estate tax, gift tax, and income tax contain certain parallel provisions, although they are not consistent in every respect.[8]

The estate tax regulation[9] defines fair market value as "the price at which the property would change hands between a willing buyer and a willing seller, neither being under any compulsion to buy or sell and both having reasonable knowledge of relevant facts."

The gift tax and income tax regulations contain identical language.[10] The hypothetical sale must be in the market in which such property is most commonly sold to the public. When trying to place a value on a unique collection, those guidelines do not offer much help. The regulations contemplate a retail market that, when one is dealing with collectibles, may not exist. Regulation section 20.2031-1(b) gives the example of a used car to illustrate which market is to be considered retail. The regulation states that the market value is the market price at which the general public can buy the car—not the wholesale price the dealer can pay for the car. When dealing with an average automobile, there is no problem, since a market exists for its sale. However, if the automobile is a rare antique, such a market may not exist. The contemplated "retail market" rule of regulation section 20.2031-1(b) is an attempt by the IRS to formulate a simple rule where one does not fit. (The rule was injected into the estate tax regulations by T.D. 6826, 1965-2 C.B. 367. Similar language was inserted into the gift tax regulations by the same T.D. 6826, and is also contained in income tax regulation section 1.170A-1(c)(2).)

Neither the rule that value is the price at which an item can be sold at retail to the public nor the rule that value is the price that a member of the public can obtain on sale of the item is appropriate in every estate, gift, and income tax situation.

The following examples[11] show the importance of various factors, including the nature of the tax (estate tax *vis-à-vis* gift tax) involved, and how some of the mechanical rules of the IRS regulations, observed to the exclusion of relevant factors, produce an erroneous substitute for true value.

Example 1: A father buys an automobile from a dealer in order to give it to his son. Barring some unusual circumstances, the value for gift tax purposes should be the amount paid for the automobile, not the amount for which the father could sell it back to the dealer. The value for gift tax purposes should ordinarily be the same whether the father gives the cost of the automobile in cash to his son (who in turn, buys the automobile for himself), or buys the automobile and gives that to his son.

Example 2: In a variation of the facts in *Example 1*, the father buys the same automobile at the same price for the same purpose, but dies before consummating the gift. The father was heavily in debt; therefore, the executor of his estate decides that it is wise to sell the automobile, which has not been driven since its delivery to the father, to obtain cash with which to pay the father's debts and the estate's administration expenses. In that case the automobile should be valued at the sale price for estate tax purposes.

Example 3: A husband buys an expensive emerald ring as a birthday gift for his wife. He gives her the ring, but she dies a few days later in an automobile accident and by her will leaves all her jewelry to her daughter. The value of the gift for gift tax purposes, as in *Example 1* above, should usually be the amount paid for the ring. However, the value of the ring in the determinination of the estate tax liability of the donee wife may depend on several circumstances. If the deceased wife's estate was not complicated by obligations and lack of liquidity, and if neither the executor nor the daughter needs or desires to sell the ring, the value for estate tax purposes may arguably be intermediate between the amount for which the executor could sell the ring and what the executor would have to pay to buy such a ring. Under other circumstances, the estate tax value would be the realizable sales price.

In *Example 1* above, the gift tax rule set out in regulation section 25.2512-1 is proper under normal circumstances, subject to one qualification. The regulation states that "an item of property . . . which is generally obtained by the public in the retail market . . . [should be valued at] the price at which the item or a comparable item would be sold at retail." It seems that in *Example 1*, if the father bought the automobile, whether new or used, at somewhat less or more than the usual retail selling price, his actual cost should ordinarily be the value for gift tax purposes. Thus, to that extent, the detailed mechanical rule set out in the regulation seems incorrect.

In *Example 2*, the application of the mechanical estate tax rule of regulation section 20.2031-1(b) seems clearly wrong, although the general statement of valuation principles in that section is proper. The regulation states that

> the fair market value of an automobile . . . includible in the decedent's gross estate is the price for which an automobile of the same or approximately the same description, make, model, age, condition, etc., could be purchased by a member of the general public and not the price for which the particular automobile of the decedent would be purchased by a dealer in used automobiles.

But when the executor finds it advisable to sell a new car for whatever price the executor can get, as in *Example 2*, the estate tax value should normally be the actual sale price in whatever market the executor makes the sale. The difficulty with that section of the regulations is in its use of mechanical rules that in many cases do not fit the facts.

In *Example 3*, the application of the mechanical gift tax rule quoted above seems proper under most circumstances. But the application of the mechanical estate tax rule of regulation section 20.2031-1(b), which is analogous to the gift tax rule, is of questionable validity in most cases and clearly wrong in others. Again, the IRS error lies in promulgating rules that in many instances are too specific and mechanical for the determination of true value.

The presence of improper mechanical rules causes unfair valuations by the IRS. The above examples illustrate that there is no simple rule, and that value cannot always be made to depend on a retail market. If a rule exists, it should be that fair market value depends on all the facts and circumstances in each case.

IRS Valuation Procedures

Rules Prior to January 1, 1985

Two Revenue Procedures provide guidelines for the valuation of unique items of tangible personal property. Revenue Procedure 65-19, 1965-2 C.B. 1002, permits, under certain conditions, estate tax return values to be based on the bona fide sale of tangible personal property through newspaper classified ads or public auction. The Revenue Procedure equates such a sale to a retail sale at the retail price. The sale must be within a reasonable time, and there must not be any substantial change in market conditions. Therefore, if an item is sold at public auction, the IRS will generally accept the sale price as the retail fair market value.

Revenue Procedure 66-49, 1966-2 C.B. 1257, sets forth guidelines for an appraisal of tangible personal property. An appraisal of a collection, particularly in the fine arts, should include the following:

1. A complete description of the object, including the size, subject matter, medium, name or names of the artist or artists, approximate date created, and interest transferred;
2. The cost, date, and manner of acquisition;
3. A history of the item, including proof of its authenticity;
4. A photograph of a size and quality sufficient to identify the subject matter fully, preferably a 10″ x 12″ or larger print; and
5. A statement of the factors on which the appraisal was based. The statement of factors should include:
   a. The facts of sales of other works by the same artist or artists—particularly on or around the valuation date;
   b. Quoted prices in dealers' catalogs of the works by the artist or artists or of other comparable artists;
   c. The economic state of the art market at or around the time of valuation, particularly with respect to the specific property;
   d. A record of any exhibitions at which the particular art object was displayed; and
   e. A statement as to the standing of the artist in the profession and in the particular school, time, or period.

Choosing the proper appraiser is the most important consideration.[12] Revenue Procedure 66-49 refers to an appraisal by a qualified person, and requires inclusion of a summary of the appraiser's qualifications. The weight given to the appraisal by the IRS depends largely on the competence and knowledge of the appraiser with respect to the property and the market for that property. In choosing the appraiser, the attorney or the executor should inquire as to whether the appraiser is familiar with the market and whether he or she has dealt with the subject matter. For example, an appraiser who is a world authority on sixteenth century French art is probably not the best person to appraise a piece of late twentieth century sculpture.

IRS Publication 561, *Valuation of Donated Property*, sets forth additional information on preparing appraisals and choosing an appraiser. Publication 561 notes that there are many types of collections and that much written material is available to assist individuals in valuing collections. That material includes catalogs, dealers' price lists, bibliographies, textbooks, and other materials that help in determining fair market value. Publication 561 also states that "not all of these sources are always reliable indicators of fair market value" and gives this example: a dealer may sell an item for considerably less than that shown on a price list after the item has remained unsold for a long period of time. That example is consistent with the IRS policy and its Revenue Procedures, which indicate that the best measure of value is an arm's-length sale in the market. Certainly, if a dealer puts an extremely high price on an object and is unable to sell it at that price, the list price of the item should not be the measure of its fair market value. The price that the item is sold for is the fair market value that the IRS will accept.

Publication 561 indicates that a signed copy of any appraisal should accompany the tax return. The more complete the information filed with the tax return, the more unlikely it is that the IRS will question items on it. The weight given an appraisal depends upon both the qualifications of the appraiser and the completeness of the appraisal report. A satisfactory appraisal discusses all the facts on which an intelligent judgment of valuation should be based. The appraisal may not be given any weight if:

- Not all the applicable factors are considered;
- Little more than a statement of opinion is given;
- The opinion is not consistent with known factors; or
- The opinion is beyond reason and arbitrary.

In evaluating the appraiser, Publication 561 states that the weight given an appraisal depends, in addition to the completeness of the report, on the appraiser's familiarity with the property, experience, background, and knowledge of the facts at the time of the contribution. Despite the appraiser's qualifications, however, his or her opinion will not be given weight if it is clearly opposed to common sense and the existing facts. The appraiser's opinion is never more important than the facts on which it is based. An appraiser who is associated with the donor or the donee, whether the donee is an individual or an organization, may be given less weight than an appraisal by an unrelated party. In fact, as discussed below, certain related persons are now prohibited from preparing an appraisal for charitable contribution purposes.

The appraiser selected should be aware of the IRS guidelines and should be furnished a copy of Revenue Procedure 66-49, so that the appraisal will meet the guidelines contained therein.

New Appraisal Rules Effective January 1, 1985

General Rules: Section 170(a)(1) expressly declares that a charitable contribution is deductible only if it is verified in the manner required by IRS regulations. Under prior law there was no specific statutory requirement that donors obtain appraisals to verify the fair market value of their donations. Rather than amend Code section 170(a)(1) to include the substantiation requirements, section 155(a) of the Tax Reform Act of 1984 requires the Treasury Department to issue regulations under section 170 that incorporate the charitable deduction substantiation requirements of section 155(a). Therefore, effective January 1, 1985, no income tax charitable deduction is allowed for any contribution of property for which an appraisal is required under the Tax Reform Act of

1984 unless the substantiation requirements of the regulations are met.

Temporary regulations encompassing the rules contained in section 155(a) of the Tax Reform Act of 1984 were issued on December 26, 1984.[13] Hearings were held on the proposed regulations in June 1985, and final regulations were issued on May 4, 1988.

The new rules apply to any charitable contribution made after December 31, 1984, by an individual, closely held corporation, personal service corporation, partnership, or S corporation of an item of property (other than money or publicly traded securities) the claimed value of which exceeds $5,000.[14] The $5,000 amount applies to a single item of property or to the aggregate of similar items of property donated during one calendar year, such as a set or number of stamps, coins, lithographs, or books. According to the *General Explanation* of the Tax Reform Act of 1984, similar items of donated property are aggregated whether all the items are donated to one donee or the items are donated to two or more donees. For example, the substantiation requirements apply if the taxpayer claims a deduction in one year of $2,000 for rare books given to College *A*, $2,500 for rare books given to Museum *B*, and $900 for rare books given to Public Library *C*,[15] a total of $5,400, which is $400 over the approved limit.

If the $5,000 limit is reached, the taxpayer must meet the following substantiation requirements:

1. Obtain a qualified appraisal for the property contributed;
2. Attach a fully completed appraisal summary to the tax return on which the donor first claims the deduction for the contribution; and
3. Maintain records containing certain specific information about the contribution.

It is crucial to keep in mind that if a taxpayer does not conform strictly to the substantiation requirements, no deduction is allowed under section 170.[16]

Qualified Appraisal: The term "qualified appraisal" means[17] an appraisal prepared by a qualified appraiser not earlier than sixty days before the date of the contribution of the appraised property. The appraisal must be signed and dated by a qualified appraiser who charges an appraisal fee that is not based on a percentage of value and that contains the following information:

1. A detailed description of the property;
2. The physical condition of the property;
3. The date or expected date of the contribution;
4. The terms of any agreement or understanding entered into or expected to be entered into by or on behalf of the donor that relates to the use, sale, or other disposition of the property contributed;
5. The name, address, and taxpayer identification number of the appraiser;
6. A detailed description of the appraiser's background and qualifications;
7. A statement that the appraisal was prepared for income tax purposes;
8. The date on which the property was valued;
9. The appraised fair market value of the property;
10. The method of valuation used to determine the fair market value;
11. The specific basis for the valuation, such as any specific comparable sales transactions; and
12. A description of the fee arrangement between the donor and the appraiser.

Obviously, the cost to the taxpayer of having a qualified appraisal prepared is going to be high because of the detailed information required. A separate qualified appraisal is required for each item of property that is not included in a group of similar items of property. If the appraisal is for a group of similar items, the detailed information is required for each individual item other than items worth less than $100, for which a group description is allowed.

The qualified appraisal must be received by the donor before the due date (including extensions) of the taxpayer's return.[18] That deadline is extremely important, since the entire charitable deduction is lost if that provision is not complied with.

Qualified Appraiser: The term "qualified appraiser" means[19] an individual who holds himself or herself out to the public as an appraiser who is an expert as to the particular type of property being appraised; who understands that, if he or she makes a false or fraudulent overstatement of value, he or she may be subject to a civil penalty under section 6701; and who is completely independent of the donor. To be independent of the donor, the qualified appraiser cannot be the donor or the donee, a party to the transaction in which the donor acquired the property,[20] a person employed by any of the foregoing, or a person related (within the meaning of section 267(b)) to any of the foregoing.

For example, if a person acquired a painting from an art dealer and later donated the painting to a museum, the donor, the dealer who sold the painting, the museum, any person employed by the donor or the dealer or the museum, or any person related to any of the foregoing is *not* a qualified appraiser. The regulations are so broad that they appear to disqualify an auction house from being a qualified appraiser if the donor had purchased the property at auction from that auction house.

In addition to the foregoing requirements, the temporary regulations contained one additional provision that excluded certain persons from being qualified appraisers. Temporary regulation section 1.170A-13T(c)(5)(iv)(E) excluded any person whose independence might be questioned by a reasonable person because of his or her relationship to the donor, the donee, a party to the transaction in which the donor acquired the property, or any person employed by any of the foregoing. Because of its vagueness, that provision caused the most problems under the temporary regulations. The final regulations adopted on May 4, 1988, eliminated it.

The final regulations adopted on May 4, 1988, did retain the provision that disqualifies someone who regularly performs appraisals for a person who is not otherwise excluded from being a qualified appraiser and does not do a substantial number of appraisals for other persons,[21] for example, someone who performs appraisals for only one person. Also excluded as a qualified appraiser is any person who, if the donor had knowledge of the facts, would cause a reasonable person to expect that the appraiser would falsely overstate the value of the donated property. For example, the donor and the appraiser make an agreement concerning the amount at which the property will be valued, and the donor knows that the amount exceeds the fair market value of the property.

It is crucial that the appraiser selected be a "qualified appraiser," because if the donor chooses unwisely and the appraiser is later found to be disqualified, the entire charitable deduction is lost, since it is then too late to cure the defect.[22] In order to obtain the income tax deduction, a qualified appraisal prepared by a qualified appraiser must be attached to the income tax return.

Appraisal Summary: Regulation section 1.170A-13(c)(4) sets forth the required information that must be on the "appraisal summary" that must be attached to the donor's income tax return. In February 1985 the IRS issued form 8283 (Noncash Charitable Contributions—Appraisal Summary); the latest version of form 8283 was issued in August 1988. Completion of form 8283 will satisfy the appraisal summary requirements. The instructions for form 8283, revised as of August 1988, now require that for works of art with an aggregate value of $20,000 or more donated after December 31, 1987, the taxpayer must attach a complete copy of the signed appraisal and include an 8″ x 10″ color photograph (or a color transparency no smaller than 4″ x 5″). It is important to note that form 8283 must be signed and dated by *both* the appraiser and the donee charitable organization. The person signing on behalf of the donee must be an official authorized to sign the tax returns of the donee organization or a person designated by the donee organization to sign form 8283. The instructions also require that after June 6, 1988, the donor must provide the donee with a copy of the qualified appraisal.

If the taxpayer fails to attach the required appraisal summary to his or her tax return, the IRS can disallow the entire charitable deduction. However, regulation section 1.170A-13(c)(4)(iv)(H) does allow a taxpayer to submit the appraisal summary within ninety days after the IRS requests it, and the IRS will not disallow the charitable deduction if the taxpayer's failure to attach the appraisal summary was a good-faith omission.

Appraisal Fee: The fee paid to the appraiser cannot be based on a percentage of the appraised value of the donated property.[23]

Guiding Principle: The foregoing is only a brief summary of the new rules. In the future, the IRS may issue Revenue Rulings and other guidelines to clarify numerous unanswered questions. In the meantime, extreme care must be exercised in choosing the appraiser in order to make sure that he or she is an expert in the field and is not disqualified from preparing a "qualified appraisal" for the donor. It is also important to keep in mind that if the $5,000 claimed deduction amount is reached for a contribution of property, the new appraisal rules apply whether the donated property is capital-gain or ordinary-income property, whether the property has appreciated or depreciated in value since its acquisition by the donor, and whether the donee is a public charity, a private foundation, or some other donee eligible to receive contributions that may qualify for deduction under section 170.[24] See form 10 on pages 655-56.

IRS Record-Keeping Requirements

If a lifetime gift is made to a charitable organization, the income tax regulations require that the income tax return for the year in which the deduction is claimed include an attachment with information similar to that contained in Revenue Procedure 66-49. Regulation section 1.170A-13, adopted December 26, 1984, contains more detailed record-keeping requirements. The regulation retains the prior record-keeping requirements for contributions made prior to 1982 and applies new rules to contributions made on or after January 1, 1983. Even if the appraisal requirements do not apply (for example, in the case of gifts of $5,000 or less), the general rules pertaining to charitable contributions of property valued in excess of $500, other than money, will apply. The new rules contain more detailed requirements for noncash contributions than for cash contributions.[25] Donors must maintain records indicating the following:

1. The name of the donee charitable organization.
2. The date and the location of the contribution.
3. A description of the property.
4. The fair market value of the property, the method used in determining the fair market value, and a signed copy of any appraisal.
5. Factual details on section 170(e)(1) property.
6. Special rules for partial interest contributions.
7. The terms of any agreement or understanding entered into by or on behalf of the taxpayer that relates to the use, the sale, or the disposition of the property contributed.

If the value of the tangible personal property is in excess of $500, the taxpayer must also maintain records indicating the following:

8. The manner and approximate date of acquisition of the property.
9. The cost or other basis of the property. In this regard, the regulation indicates that if the property was held for more than one year, records of cost or other basis are required only if available.

Item 7 above is particularly important, and is aimed at proposed gifts that, because of certain retained rights, are not treated as completed charitable contributions eligible for the income tax charitable deduction.[26]

IRS Art Advisory Panel

A twenty-two-person advisory panel of art experts has been appointed to help the IRS determine whether realistic appraisals of fair market value have been placed on works of art.[27] The panel, which was set up in 1968, classifies the artwork valuation submitted as: clearly justified, questionable, or clearly unjustified. The panel also recommends appraisers to the IRS and reviews appraisals. Generally, if a particular item has a value of more than $20,000, it is sent by the local IRS audit office to the art panel in Washington, D.C., for consideration. The report issued by the art panel is supposed to be only advisory. However, for all practical purposes, the local IRS district offices have been considering the valuation reports to be mandatory and binding on them. Unfortunately, it often takes from six months to a year to have a request processed through the National Office, since the IRS in Washington, D.C., has a limited staff to process the huge volume of valuation cases referred. The art panel, which reviews the documentation prepared by the IRS, is also faced with an enormous volume of cases. Therefore, the taxpayer's documentation must be as complete as possible before the information is submitted to the National Office. If an attorney feels that the art panel did not review the submitted items correctly, he or she can, at an appellate conference, request a resubmission to the art panel. Additional documentation should be submitted, indicating why the art panel may have been in error. It is possible to have the art panel change the value placed on a work of art.

Following the successful format of the IRS Art Panel, and because of the recent popularity and increase in value of art prints, the IRS established an Art Print Panel on May 29, 1980. The Art Print Panel operates in the same manner as the Art Panel, but is limited to art prints.

Determining Fair Market Value

The question of the fair market value of a collection is difficult and must rest on expert appraisals. Resolving valuation disputes with the IRS, as demonstrated by the litigated cases, can be a time-consuming and expensive proposition.[28] The Tax Reform Act of 1976 recognized the plight of the taxpayer who is faced with a valuation issue and an IRS agent who supplies little or no information to support the Service's determination.

The IRS's Determination of Value

Section 7517 provides that the IRS must, on written request by a donor or executor, furnish a written statement explaining the basis on which the IRS has determined or proposes to determine a valuation of property that is different from the valuation submitted by the donor or the executor. That section applies to all valuation issues, whether the donation involves a lifetime transfer or a testamentary transfer to a charitable or a noncharitable transferee. The Conference Committee Report explains that the reason for the change is to encourage the resolution of valuation issues at the earliest possible time, and that can best be achieved if all parties have full information as to how the other arrived at the valuation. The IRS must furnish its statement within forty-five days of the date of the request or the date of its determination (or proposed determination), whichever is later. The IRS statement must (a) explain the basis on which the valuation was determined or proposed, (b) set forth any computation used, and (c) contain a copy of any expert appraisal made by or for the IRS. The statute specifically provides that the IRS statement is not intended to be a final or binding representation of the IRS position. Section 7517 is effective for transfers made after December 31, 1976.

Revenue Rulings on Valuation

The IRS has given increased attention to valuation questions in a series of recent rulings.

Revenue Ruling 79-256, 1979-2 C.B. 105: A taxpayer, who was not an art dealer, bought a substantial part of the total limited edition of a lithograph series and, after holding the prints for more than a year, contributed them to various art museums. The IRS ruled that the taxpayer's charitable deduction was limited to his cost under section 170(e)(1)(A), since the property was ordinary income property. The IRS viewed the taxpayer's activities, in terms of frequency and continuity, as equivalent to a "trade or business" for the purpose of section 170(e), even though he was not engaged in a trade or business for the purpose of any other section of the Code. The IRS deemed the taxpayer's bulk acquisition and subsequent disposal of a substantial part of the total limited edition of the prints to be substantially equivalent to the activities of a commercial art dealer. The ruling also stated that the contributions had been made before a "period of accumulation and enjoyment" of the donated property by the donor. There does not appear to be any basis in the Code to support the new tests that the IRS attempted to introduce (that is, a test of the frequency of the donor's activities and a test of the donor's period of accumulation and enjoyment) as tests in order to determine whether an individual is engaged in a trade or business in a way that would limit the deduction for the donated property to the taxpayer's cost. Note that the Tax Court recently rejected the IRS "dealer theory" in *Kenneth Sandler*, discussed at pages 564-65.

Revenue Ruling 79-419, 1979-2 C.B. 107: A donor bought art books at wholesale; the seller held them for one year before delivery, whereupon the donor contributed the books to various charitable organizations. The seller was in a country where the retail price of the books was legally fixed by law, and the donor imported them into the United States. The ruling held that the books could only have been offered at a discount to purchasers outside of the country of the seller. Again, the IRS ruled that the level of the donor's contribution activity was tantamount to the activity of a dealer selling property in the ordinary course of his trade or business. Accordingly, the donor's deduction was limited to the cost of the books or to their fair market value, whichever was less, since the books were ordinary income property under section 170(e)(1)(A). The ruling made no mention of the test of the donor's "period of accumulation and enjoyment" as stated in Revenue Ruling 79-256.

Revenue Ruling 79-432, 1979-2 C.B. 289: Revenue Ruling 79-432 specifically addressed the use of lithographs as a tax shelter. Essentially, the IRS held that the substance of the transaction did not present a situation in which the taxpayer had any property "at risk" and, therefore, denied the claimed deduction. In valuing the lithographs, the IRS returned to its longtime rule that fair market value is the value at which something changes hands between a willing buyer and a willing seller, neither under any compulsion to act.

Revenue Ruling 80-69, 1980-1 C.B. 55: A taxpayer, not a dealer, purchased assorted valuable gems from a promoter at "wholesale" and then contributed them one year later to a charitable organization that satisfied the related use rule of section 170(e)(1)(B)(i). The IRS ruled that the fair market value of the gems was the price the donor paid for them one year earlier, relying on the "willing buyer and willing seller" language of regulation section 1.170A-1(c)(2). The ruling made no mention of the level of the donor's activities being substantially equivalent to a dealer under section 170(e) or of a period of accumulation and enjoyment.

Revenue Ruling 80-233, 1980-2 C.B. 69: In a situation similar to the one presented in Revenue Ruling 80-69, a taxpayer purchased Bibles in bulk at wholesale, held them for one year, and then contributed them to various religious charities that made use of the Bibles. The IRS ruled that the fair market value was the wholesale price. In relying on the "willing buyer and willing seller" language of the regulation, the IRS said that in determining the fair market value it referred to the most active and comparable marketplace at the time of the donor's contribution. The prices at which similar quantities of Bibles are sold in arm's-length transactions are the most probative evidence of fair market value. See also Revenue Ruling 80-329, 1980-2 C.B. 70.

The most recent Revenue Rulings indicated a shift of the IRS position on fair market value away from an attack on the character of the property contributed (ordinary income property versus capital gain property) through a test of frequency of activities and period of enjoyment, back to the willing buyer and willing seller test of fair market value that is in regulation section 1.170A-1(c)(2). Those rulings indicated that the IRS will challenge any contribution scheme that does not have economic reality.

Litigation on Valuation

Evidence of IRS willingness to litigate charitable contribution schemes that have no economic reality is found in *Anselmo v. Commissioner*,[29] involving the valuation of gems donated to the Smithsonian Institution. In *Anselmo* the taxpayer purchased colored gemstones and donated them nine months later, after the long-term capital gain holding period had been satisfied. The Tax Court found that members of the public did not generally purchase unset gems; rather, the usual consumers of unset gems were manufacturing and retail jewelers who used them to create jewelry. The Tax Court looked to the regulations and the definition of "retail market" to measure fair market value. The court found that the retail market in which to find comparable values for the donated gems was the market in which the jewelry stores made their purchases and not the market in which an individual member of the public made a purchase at the jewelry store. In effect, the Tax Court said there can be more than one "retail market," and the market that is closest to the taxpayer's activities is the market the court will look to for comparable values.[30] The court further held that a separate fair market value should be determined for each unit of property donated.

More recently, in *Richard A. Skripak*,[31] the Tax Court upheld the validity of a book contribution program, but substantially lowered the value of the books contributed. In *Skripak*, the taxpayer participated in a charitable contribution tax shelter promoted by Reprints, Inc. Reprints identified libraries to receive books and contributors who would contribute the books to the libraries. The contributors bought the books from Reprints at one-third of the normal price and, after holding them for longer than six months, contributed them to libraries at their retail price. The court held that the contributions were legitimately made and were not a sham, as alleged by the IRS. However, the court further held that the books had a value of only 20 percent of the retail price, less than the amount the contributors actually paid for them.

The *Skripak* case makes it clear that a taxpayer may participate in a tax shelter that is motivated solely by the goal of obtaining a charitable deduction without having the deduction disregarded on the ground that the shelter is a sham. However, taxpayers entering into such shelters risk having the amounts of their deductions reduced if the donated properties are not properly valued, and the taxpayers could lose money, since the donated properties could be found to have a value of *less* than they paid for them. In *Skripak* the court still looked to the "retail market" for the valuation of the books, but applied a "blockage discount," since the simultaneous marketing of all the books would substantially depress the market for the books.[32] A "blockage discount" is a reduction in market value based on the theory that a large number of similar items offered for sale at one time distorts the market value and results in a reduced market value.

The *Samuel E. Hunter*[33] case involved a taxpayer who purchased a group of high quality prints by prominent artists and donated them to various charities. The story began when Marlborough Gallery sold the prints in bulk to a middleman, who was able to buy them at one-sixth Marlborough's retail list price because Marlborough was disposing of excess inventory. The art was not unsalable, and, in fact, Marlborough retained a number of the prints for sale to the public at its normal retail price. The middleman then resold the prints to the taxpayer at one-third to one-fourth of Marlborough's list price. The taxpayer claimed a charitable deduction for the Marlborough list price of each print.

The Tax Court held that the transaction was not a sham and that it was not relevant that the taxpayer never took possession of the prints. It further dismissed the IRS contention that the blockage discount applied, since the number of prints was small.

The court concluded, however, that the deduction for the taxpayer was limited to what he paid for the prints. The court reasoned that the relevant "retail market" was the market in which the middleman had sold the prints to the taxpayer, that is, the market in which the taxpayer had made his purchase. Perhaps a different result might have been arrived at if the taxpayer had made his purchases directly from Marlborough Gallery, rather than through a middleman. The case indicates that whenever a purchase and a donation are close in time the IRS will give the charitable deduction careful examination.[34]

That does not mean that if someone finds a bargain he or she cannot make a donation of the property. In *Bernard Lightman*[35] the taxpayer made an advantageous bulk purchase of a number of works of art by one artist and donated the paintings to a museum shortly after one year of their purchase. The court recognized that the taxpayer had been given a price concession on the purchase and that their cost was not indicative of the values of the individual paintings. Instead, the court used auction prices of other paintings by that artist as the measure of market value for donation purposes. For a recent case involving the advantageous purchase of a gemstone followed by its contribution, see *James H. Rhoades*.[36]

Auction prices are not the absolute measure of fair market value. In *Raymond Biagiotti*,[37] involving the valuation of pre-Columbian and Mayan art, the Tax Court observed that Sotheby's auction sales did not represent a significant portion of the sales of such art in the United States and did not accurately represent the average sale prices of that art. The court found that a better measure of value was what collectors paid private dealers, since collectors rely on dealers' guarantees of authenticity, and auction houses do not guarantee authenticity.

Buyer's Premium: When collectibles are purchased at the major auction houses a 10 percent buyer's premium is added to the final auction bid price and is paid by the buyer. (See discussion of the buyer's premium in chapter 3.) That raises the question of whether a 10 percent amount can be added to auction sales prices when auction prices are used as a measure of value for charitable contribution purposes. We believe that the buyer's premium should be viewed as one additional fact to be taken into consideration by the appraiser in the valuation process. If a decedent's estate is selling a work of art at auction and the auction price is to be the measure of value for federal estate tax purposes, then the buyer's premium should have no relevance since the decedent's estate receives no more than the final auction bid price, with the 10 percent buyer's premium going to the auction house. If, on the other hand, auction prices are used as comparable values for charitable contribution purposes, then the appraiser should consider adding the buyer's premium to the final auction bid price of the comparable work of art, since the buyer is required to pay that amount to acquire the work of art.

Penalties for Incorrect Valuations

Prior Law

Prior Code section 6659, effective January 1, 1982, through December 31, 1984, imposed a nondeductible penalty on a taxpayer for underpayments of income taxes that are attributable to overstatements of valuation made in claiming a charitable deduction. The penalty did not apply to any property that had been held by the taxpayer for more than five years as of the end of a taxable year for which there was an overstatement. The penalty was on a sliding scale that ran from 10 to 30 percent of the underpayment of tax, depending on the magnitude of the overstatement. The penalty provision did not apply to incorrect valuations for estate and gift tax purposes, and the IRS had discretionary authority to waive all or part of the penalty if the taxpayer could show that there was a reasonable basis for the valuation claimed on the return and that the claim was made in good faith.

New Penalty Rules

The Tax Reform Act of 1984 amended section 6659 by adding section 6659(f) to deal specifically with overvaluations of property contributed to charity. The new penalty provision is applicable to returns filed after 1984 and, therefore, to contributions made during 1984.[38]

The new section imposes a flat penalty equal to 30 percent of the tax liability underpayment. The 30 percent penalty is applied if works of art, real estate, and similar assets are claimed to have values for the taxpayer's income tax return of 150 percent or more of the correct values.

For example, assume that an individual collector (with a 28 percent marginal tax rate) donates a painting to a museum and claims a $200,000 deduction for the painting on his income tax return. The painting is finally determined to have a value of $100,000. The taxpayer overstated the value of the painting by more than 150 percent of its correct value (150 percent of $100,000 is only $150,000). As a result of overstating the value of the painting, the taxpayer has claimed a $200,000 charitable contribution deduction and thereby reduced his taxes by $56,000. If the taxpayer had used the correct valuation of $100,000, his taxes would have been reduced by only $28,000. Therefore, because of the valuation overstatement, the taxpayer underpaid his income taxes by $28,000. The penalty applicable to the valuation overstatement is $8,400 (that is, 30 percent of $28,000).

Section 6659 was also amended to eliminate the exception from any penalty for property held more than five years.[39]

A further amendment to section 6659 provides that the IRS may not waive any portion of the section 6659 penalty unless (1) the taxpayer shows (as required under the general section 6659 waiver provision) that there was a reasonable basis for the claimed valuation and (2) the IRS determines both that the claimed value of the property was based on a "qualified appraisal" made by a "qualified appraiser" and that, in addition to obtaining that appraisal, the taxpayer made a good-faith investigation of the value of the contributed property.[40]

There are now *two* separate requirements for obtaining the IRS waiver of the section 6659 penalty. It is not enough to obtain a "qualified appraisal" by a "qualified appraiser." The statute indicates that the taxpayer must personally make a good-faith investigation of the value of the contributed property. The regulations, when issued, may provide guidelines in that area. In the meantime, the taxpayer should double-check the information pertaining to value on the qualified appraisal and keep a personal diary as to what the taxpayer did independently to investigate the value of the property.

Since the new provision applies to returns "filed" after 1984, individuals who made charitable contributions of property in 1984 should make sure that their appraisals for 1984 contributions satisfy the new qualified appraisal rules if they want to preserve the opportunity to seek waiver of any section 6659 penalty.

Interest on the section 6659 penalty amount is also imposed to forestall intentional administrative delays by persons subject to the overvaluation penalty.[41] If a $1,000 or greater underpayment of tax is due to a valuation overstatement subject to the section 6659 penalty, the rate of interest is 120 percent of the normal interest rate under section 6621(b). Moreover, the section 6659 penalty and interest are in addition to any other penalties and interest that the IRS may impose as a result of the valuation overstatement. Those provisions raise the stakes for taxpayers who think they can inflate the value of donated artwork in order to obtain excessive income tax deductions.

Section 6661 imposes a penalty for substantial underpayment of tax liability. The Tax Reform Act of 1986 amended section 6661 to increase the penalty from 10 to 20 percent, effective January 1, 1987. The penalty is imposed on the amount of the underpayment of tax under certain conditions. The Omnibus Budget Reconciliation Act of 1986 increased the penalty to 25 percent of the underpayment. The Technical and Miscellaneous Revenue Act of 1988 clarified the matter: the 25 percent penalty rate is to apply to penalties asserted after October 21, 1986.

Section 6653(a) imposes a 5 percent negligence penalty, plus extra interest. The Tax Reform Act of 1986 amended section 6653(b) to increase the penalty for civil fraud from 50 to 75 percent.

New Disclosure Rules for Donee

The Tax Reform Act of 1984 requires a donee of any property for which an income tax charitable deduction of more than $5,000 was claimed to file an information report with the IRS if the contributed property is sold, exchanged, or otherwise disposed of within two years after the date of receipt of the contribution.[42] That provision is effective January 1, 1985. In February 1985 the IRS issued form 8282 (Donee Information Return) to be used by donees for the purpose of satisfying the filing requirement. The latest version of the form is dated August 1988. All exempt organizations have to keep records in sufficient detail to meet the filing requirements. That requirement is particularly important for charities that solicit contributions of property for the purpose of a fund-raising auction.

The regulations for new Code sections 6050L and 6050L(b), which were adopted on May 4, 1988, indicate that the information report (form 8282) must be filed by an exempt organization that disposes of donated property if the aggregate value of similar items of property equals the $5,000 amount. The donee organization must supply the following information to the IRS:

- The name, address, and employer identification number of the donee;
- A description of the property;

- The name and social security number of the donor;
- The date of the contribution to the donee;
- The amount received by the donee on any disposition;
- The date of the disposition by the donee; and
- Any other information that may be required by form 8282.

The Conference Committee Report for new section 6050L indicated that the regulations would require the donor to inform the donee of any donation of similar items made during the taxable year. At the present time, regulation sections 1.170A-13 and 1.6050L-1 do not contain such a requirement. Charities receiving property as a donation may want to consider requiring a statement from the donor that the donor will inform the charity of any contributions of similar property to other donees within the same taxable year.

Regulation of Appraisers

An appraiser may be subject to a $1,000 penalty under section 6701 if he or she aids or assists in the preparation or presentation of an appraisal in connection with the tax laws if the appraiser (1) knew that the appraisal would be used in connection with the tax laws and (2) knew that it would result in an understatement of the tax liability of another person. If the IRS proves that the appraiser had such knowledge, the appraiser is subject to the civil penalty under section 6701. In addition, the IRS can bar appraisers against whom the section 6701 penalty was assessed after July 18, 1984, from appearing before or presenting evidence to the IRS.[43] Under the IRS regulations, appraisals made before the effective date of disqualification of the appraiser are not barred from being considered qualified appraisals.

Penalties for Understatement of Estate and Gift Taxes

The Senate Finance Committee, Conference Committee, and Joint Committee on Taxation Reports for the Tax Reform Act of 1984 all refer to the extension of the section 6659 penalty provision to gift and estate taxes.[44] However, the statute as enacted does not really do that. Section 6659 clearly applies only to the income tax, that is, "an underpayment of the tax imposed by chapter 1. . . ." It does not apply to gift and estate taxes, which are imposed by chapters 11 and 12 of the Code. Therefore, section 6659, which deals with valuation overstatements, does not apply to gift and estate taxes.

The Tax Reform Act of 1984 did add section 6660 to the Code, and that section does apply to gift and estate taxes.[45] However, section 6660 applies in the case of a valuation *understatement*, not a valuation overstatement, as is penalized under section 6659. Under section 6660, penalties for a valuation understatement in the case of any underpayment of estate or gift tax are as follows:

1. If the claimed value is two-thirds or less, but not less than 50 percent, of the correct amount, the penalty imposed is equal to 10 percent of the tax underpayment attributable to the undervaluation.
2. If the claimed value is 40 percent or more but less than 50 percent, of the correct amount, the penalty imposed is equal to 20 percent of the tax underpayment attributable to the undervaluation.
3. If the claimed value is less than 40 percent of the correct amount, the penalty imposed is equal to 30 percent of the tax underpayment attributable to the undervaluation.

There is no requirement under estate or gift tax law to have a "qualified appraisal" by a "qualified appraiser." The IRS has discretionary authority to waive all or part of the section 6660 penalty if the taxpayer establishes that there was a reasonable basis for the valuation claimed and that the claim was made in good faith.

The section 6660 penalty appears to apply for estate and gift tax purposes only to a valuation understatement, not to an overstatement. Therefore, if a decedent bequeaths artwork to a museum and claims an estate tax charitable deduction, no section

6660 penalty is imposed in the event that the IRS finally determines that the work had a smaller value than that claimed on the estate tax return. In most cases there is no increase or decrease in the estate tax in case of a valuation overstatement of a charitable bequest, because the size of the gross estate increases as the charitable deduction increases, and the two cancel each other out, leaving only the remainder subject to the estate tax. Therefore, the section 6660 penalty should generally not apply to a charitable bequest that may be overstated in value. However, a valuation overstatement of a collection could increase executors' commissions and have the net effect of decreasing the estate tax. The section 6660 penalty would apply to noncharitable bequests that are understated in value.

Further, a section 6659 penalty could be applied in an estate tax situation for income tax purposes. For example, when the unlimited marital deduction applies or the estate is less than the estate tax exemption equivalent (i.e., less than $600,000), there is no estate tax. However, any artwork, as well as other tangible property of the estate, receives a step-up in basis equal to the estate tax value. If the artwork that was overvalued for estate tax purposes is later sold at a loss, the estate or the heirs have a capital loss. If the loss claimed to reduce income tax results from the overvaluation, the IRS could invoke the penalty provisions of section 6659.

Appraisal Costs

The IRS has ruled that the cost of an appraisal of property that is contributed to a charitable organization is deductible for income tax purposes under section 212(3) as an expense paid in connection with the determination of income tax liability.[46] The breadth of that section is reflected in the language of the corresponding regulation, which states that those appraisal expenses are deductible "whether the taxing authority be Federal, State, or municipal, and whether the tax be income, estate, gift, property or any other tax."[47] Accordingly, when a gift is made to a noncharitable donee, the appraisal fee incurred for the gift tax valuation is similarly an income deduction. The cost of an appraisal of property is also deductible for estate tax purposes.[48]

CHARITABLE TRANSFERS

The lifetime transfer of a collection to a charitable organization saves the donor income taxes because of the allowable income tax deduction; at the same time, the lifetime transfer relieves the donor of the expense and the worry connected with the maintenance of a valuable collection. For example, a painting that cost the collector $1,000 some years ago may have a fair market value of $10,000 today. A contribution today of the painting to charity that meets all the requirements discussed below produces an allowable charitable deduction of $10,000. For someone in the 28 percent tax bracket, such a contribution saves $2,800 in federal income taxes. Since the donor's out-of-pocket cost was only $1,000, the taxpayer has made a $1,800 tax-free economic profit and has enjoyed the painting through its years of ownership.[49] The problem for the estate planner is to make sure the contribution is correctly made, so that the tax benefit described is achieved.[50]

A testamentary transfer of a collection to a charitable organization saves the decedent's estate a great amount in estate taxes, because of the allowable estate tax deduction, and, at the same time, relieves the estate of the problem of raising the cash necessary to pay the estate tax on a potentially nonliquid asset.

Complete Inter Vivos Charitable Transfers

The Tax Reform Acts of 1969 and 1984 substantially complicated lifetime charitable transfers. Before donating a collection to a charitable organization, the donor must determine:

1. The status of the charitable organization,

2. The type of property being contributed,
3. Whether the collection satisfies the related use rule,
4. Whether there is a qualified appraisal prepared by a qualified appraiser, and
5. Whether the alternative minimum tax applies to the donor.

Each factor is considered below.

Status of the Organization

Charitable organizations are characterized as either public or private.[51] Public charities generally receive part of their support from the general public. They include churches, schools, hospitals, museums, and other publicly supported organizations; private operating foundations; and certain organizations operated in connection with another public organization. They also include those private foundations that distribute all their receipts each year. Private charities include all other exempt organizations, and include the usual kinds of private foundations.[52]

It is important to verify the status of the charitable organization as either a public or a private charity. As will be seen below, there is a different result when a taxpayer makes a contribution to a public charity as opposed to a private charity. Verification of a charity's status can be made by checking IRS Publication 78, *Cumulative List of Exempt Organizations* or by requesting the charitable organization to provide copies of letters from the IRS stating its status. It is, however, preferable to obtain copies of the letters from the IRS stating the organization's status. Note that there is a difference between the organization's exemption ruling under section 501(c)(3) and its ruling as a "public" organization under section 509(a).

Type of Property

Capital Gain Property: In most cases a collection is "capital gain property." The term includes any property the sale of which at its fair market value at the time of the contribution would have resulted in *long-term* capital gain.[53] Any appreciation in value, no matter how small, makes the property capital gain property. The property is capital gain property if:

- It has appreciated in value; and
- It has been held by the donor for more than one year for contributions made before June 22, 1984;
- It has been held for more than six months for assets acquired and contributions made between June 22, 1984, and December 31, 1987, or
- It has been held for more than one year for assets acquired and contributions made on or after January 1, 1988.

Contribution of capital gain property receives favorable tax treatment.

Even though the Tax Reform Act of 1986 removed for most taxpayers, beginning on January 1, 1988, the distinction between ordinary income and long-term capital gain for tax rate purposes, the Internal Revenue Code still retains the distinction for characterization purposes. That distinction is particularly important regarding charitable contributions, and the proper characterization of contributed property as long-term capital gain property is still crucial if the donor is to receive the full charitable deduction for appreciated tangible personal property.

Ordinary Income Property: The property is ordinary income property[54] if:

- It was created by the donor;
- It was received by the donor as a gift from the creator;
- It is held in inventory by a dealer;
- It would produce short-term capital gain if sold, that is, it is owned for one year or less before being contributed; or
- It would produce a capital loss if sold.

All works of art created by the artist will be ordinary income property, since that property, by the definition contained in section 1221(3), cannot be a capital asset. Hence, the artist may be surprised that contributions of his or her own work will not receive the favored capital gain property deduction treatment. Even more surprised may be the collector who accepted the artwork as a gift from the artist. Classification as ordinary income property greatly reduces any available charitable deduction.

A problem often encountered by a collector is the possibility of receiving a gift of a work of art from the artist who created it. In that connection, reference must be made to section 1221(3) for the definition of the term "capital asset." Section 1221(3)(C) states that the term capital asset "does not include property held by a taxpayer in whose hands the basis of such property is determined, for purposes of determining gain from a sale or exchange, in whole or in part by reference to the basis of such property in the hands" of the taxpayer whose personal efforts created the property. Under section 1015, covering the determination of basis for gifts, the basis of the property in the hands of the donee is determined by its basis in the hands of the donor. So, the collector who receives artwork as a gift from an artist has the same basis in the property as does the artist. Since artwork is ordinary income property in the artist's hands, it cannot be a capital asset in the donee collector's hands. Therefore, a taxpayer should be aware that a gift of a work of art from the creator retains its character as ordinary income property in the hands of the donee. If the property is purchased by the collector, it is converted into capital gain property, which results in an increased charitable deduction, since the collector can now claim a deduction for the fair market value of the artwork as opposed to only its basis.

The Tax Reform Act of 1976 required the basis of all property passing from a decedent to be determined by reference to the basis of the property in the hands of the decedent.[55] That was required because all inherited property was to be subject to new "carryover-basis" rules, which were postponed until January 1, 1980, by the Revenue Act of 1978, and were eventually repealed by section 401 of the Crude Oil Windfall Profit Tax Act of 1980.

The heirs of the artist would have suffered if the carryover-basis rules had been implemented. Under those rules, the artist's heirs or legatees would not have been able to realize long-term capital gain on the sale of inherited artwork, since the property would not qualify as a capital asset because of section 1221(3)(C). Before the Tax Reform Act of 1976, and under current law since the carryover-basis rules were repealed, the gain on property inherited from an artist is taxed as capital gain.[56] If the carryover-basis rules are ever restored, there may be an exception for the creative person, so that his or her estate can realize capital gains on sales after his or her death.

When advising a collector who is making a contribution, an attorney should find out how the collector acquired the property and what he or she did with it in order to determine if ordinary income property is present. For example, Revenue Ruling 79-256, 1979-2 C.B. 105, involved a man who grew plants as a hobby and contributed them to charity, and also involved a collector who purchased a substantial part of the limited edition of a particular lithograph series and later contributed the prints to various charities. In each case the IRS held that the donor's activities were substantially equivalent to the activities of a dealer selling property in the ordinary course of a trade or business; therefore, the IRS limited the charitable deduction to the donor's cost of the property. The ruling appears to be far-reaching, without any statutory or court precedent. (See discussion at pages 573-74.)

The IRS "dealer" theory was put to rest in the recent case of *Kenneth Sandler*.[57] The case involved a doctor who purchased grave sites in bulk and one year later donated them to a church. The IRS argued that the doctor's activities were substantially equivalent to those of a dealer, that the property should therefore be deemed ordinary income property, and, accordingly, that the deduction should be limited to the doctor's cost. The Tax Court held that the doctor was not engaged in the trade or business of selling grave sites and, therefore, that the property donated was not ordinary income property. However, the court looked closely at the proper marketplace to value the grave sites, holding that the proper retail market in that case was the sale to the ultimate consumer who did not hold the item for subsequent resale. Therefore, the court concluded that the proper comparable marketplace was the market in which the taxpayer-donor made his purchase and limited the taxpayer's contribution to his cost.

General Percentage Limitation: For contributions of cash and ordinary income property to a public charity, the charitable deduction is limited to 50 percent of the taxpayer's contribution base.[58] For contributions to a private charity, the limit is the lesser of (a) 30 percent of the taxpayer's contribution base; or (b) the excess of 50 percent of the taxpayer's contribution base over the amount of charitable contributions allowable to public charities, determined without regard to the 30 percent limitation (discussed below).[59] The term "contribution base" means adjusted gross income computed without regard to any net operating loss carryback to the taxable year under section 172.[60]

Ordinary Income Property Percentage Limitation: The amount of the charitable deduction for a contribution of ordinary income property is limited to the basis of the property in the hands of the donor (within the applicable general percentage limitation discussed above). That result is reached because the amount of the charitable deduction is determined by subtracting from the fair market value of the property the amount of gain that would *not* have been long-term capital gain if the property contributed had been sold by the taxpayer at its fair market value.[61] Before making a contribution, the donor must be sure the property is capital gain property and not ordinary income property, since the available income tax deduction is substantially reduced for a contribution of ordinary income property.[62]

Any excess amount over the 50 percent or 30 percent limitations for a contribution of ordinary income property to either a public or private charity may be carried forward for five years, retaining its character as ordinary income property.[63] The carryover provision was extended to contributions made to a private charity by the Tax Reform Act of 1984, effective for contributions made in taxable years ending after October 16, 1984.

Capital Gain Property Percentage Limitation: A contribution to a public charity of a collection that is capital gain property and that meets the related use rule (discussed below) is allowable as a charitable deduction to the extent of the full fair market value of the property on the date of the contribution, but not in excess of 30 percent of the taxpayer's contribution base.[64] Any amount that exceeds the 30 percent limitation may be carried forward for five years, retaining its character as capital gain property.[65] If the contributed collection satisfies the related use rule, the taxpayer may elect to increase the 30 percent limitation to 50 percent of his or her contribution base. However, if that election is made, the amount of the deduction must be reduced by 100 percent of the appreciation in value of the collection;[66] in other words, the deduction will be limited to the donor's cost.

Before December 31, 1986, the amount of reduction required if the election was made was only 40 percent of the appreciation in value. Section 301(b)(2) of the Tax Reform Act of 1986 amended Code section 170(e)(1) so that 100 percent of the appreciation in value is lost as a charitable deduction if the taxpayer elects to increase the percentage limitation for the deduction from 30 to 50 percent. That change will probably have the effect of eliminating the use of the election.

A contribution to a private charity of a collection that is capital gain property is allowable as a charitable deduction to the extent of the fair market value of the collection on the date of the contribution *reduced* (regardless of what use the charity makes of the collection) by 100 percent of the appreciation in value. After the reduction the deduction is limited to the *lesser* of (1) 20 percent of the taxpayer's contribution base or (2) the excess of 30 percent of the taxpayer's contribution base over the amount of charitable contributions allowable to public charities, determined without regard to the 30 percent limitation.[67] The amount of the charitable deduction that exceeds the applicable percentage limitation may be carried forward for five years for contributions made in taxable years ending after July 18, 1984.[68] The percentage limitations on lifetime gifts to private foundations and the loss of 100 percent of any appreciation in value as a deduction make use of a private foundation to hold a collection impractical, unless the foundation can qualify as a "private operating foundation."[69]

The Tax Reform Act of 1984 created a new limitation rule for "qualified appreciated stock" contributed to a private charity. Under section 170(e)(5), a taxpayer may claim a deduction for the full fair market value of qualified appreciated stock contributed to a private charity within the 20 percent limitation discussed above, without having to lose 100 percent of the appreciation in value as a deduction. Qualified appreciated stock is defined as any stock of a corporation for which market quotations are readily available on an established securities market and that is capital gain property.[70]

Related Use Rule

The related use rule applies to capital gain property that is "tangible personal property" contributed to a public charity. The term "tangible personal property" includes paintings and art objects not produced by the donor. The *related use rule* requires that the use of the tangible personal property by the donee organization be related to the purpose or the function constituting the basis for the donee's exemption under section 501. If the use of the collection by the donee organization is unrelated to the purpose or the function constituting the basis for the donee's exemption, the amount of the charitable deduction must be reduced by 100 percent of the appreciation in value of the collection.[71] In that instance, after the 100 percent appreciation reduction, the remainder may be deducted up to 50 percent of the taxpayer's contribution base.[72]

One of the major changes made by the Tax Reform Act of 1986 was the amendment of section 170(e)(1) so that 100 percent of the appreciation in value is lost as a charitable deduction if the related use rule is not satisfied. The new rule is effective for contributions made on or after January 1, 1987. Under the law in effect before January 1, 1987, only 40 percent of the appreciation in value was lost as a charitable deduction. Therefore, a taxpayer must be extremely careful to comply with the related use rule or else the charitable deduction for appreciated long-term capital gain property that is tangible personal property will be limited to his or her cost.

The regulations[73] provide that a taxpayer may treat a contribution of a collection as meeting the related use rule if:

1. The taxpayer establishes that the collection is not in fact put to an unrelated use by the donee; or
2. At the time of contribution it is reasonable to anticipate that the collection will not be put to an unrelated use by the donee organization.

If a collector donates a collection to a museum and the collection is of a general type normally retained by museums for museum purposes, it is reasonable for the donor to anticipate, unless he or she has actual knowledge to the contrary, that the collection will not be put to an unrelated use by the donee, whether or not the collection is later sold or exchanged by the donee. On the other hand, if an item is donated for the purpose of sale at an art auction to be run by the charity, that is an unrelated use, and 100 percent of the appreciation in value is lost as a charitable deduction.

Example 1: A painting contributed to an art museum that is a public charity and that can and, in fact, does from time to time display the painting prominently and publicly satisfies the related use rule. The contribution is deductible to the extent of the fair market value of the property within the 30 percent limitation.

Example 2: If the same painting is contributed to the Red Cross, which is a public charity and which from the outset intends to—and in fact promptly does—sell the painting, the deduction must be reduced by 100 percent of the appreciation in value, with the balance deductible within the 50 percent limitation.[74]

The regulations[75] also indicate that the related use rule is met even if the donee sells or otherwise disposes of only an "insubstantial" portion of the collection.

According to Representative Wilbur D. Mills, then chairman of the House Ways and Means Committee:

> . . . What we are trying to say is that we will allow you to give this appreciated property and take today's market value as a charitable deduction without any tax consequences to you whatsoever if you give it to a charitable organization that normally would use the property for its exempt purposes. Now, a clear case is a gift of a picture or work of sculpture, or anything of that sort, to a museum. The question does arise with respect to a college or university as to whether or not they are using this for their exempt purpose, whether it is used in their teaching. Of course, the college could have a course in art, and if the gift were to be used for that purpose it would probably qualify as such a gift.[76]

To date there have been few litigated cases on the subject of related use. However, a number of Private Letter Rulings in this area do shed some light on what the IRS considers a related use.

Private Letter Ruling 7751044: The IRS held that the related use rule was satisfied when lithographs were displayed in a camp and center devoted to handicapped and retarded children, since the lithographs were used in connection with an art appreciation program. (Private Letter Rulings 7911109 and 7934082 reach similar results in dealing with the exhibition of works of art.)

Private Letter Ruling 8009027: The IRS held that the related use rule was not satisfied when a donor gave an antique car to a university, since the university did not offer a course in antique car restoration.

Private Letter Ruling 8143029: The IRS held that the related use rule was satisfied when a donor gave his collection of porcelain art objects to a public charity operating a retirement center, since the display of the art was related to the charity's exempt purpose of creating a living environment for its residents.

Private Letter Ruling 8208059: The IRS held that the related use rule was satisfied when a donor gave his stamp collection to a college, since it would be exhibited and the college had, as part of its curriculum, the teaching of engraving skills. The donor included in the ruling request letters from the college, explaining in detail how it would use the collection.

It is important to make sure that a proper paper trail shows that it was reasonable for the taxpayer to anticipate that the property would not be put to an unrelated use by the donee.[77]

Examples

The following examples illustrate the foregoing rules.

Example 1: Ms. Collector received a painting as a gift from a little-known artist. The painting had a basis at the time of the gift of $100, representing the artist's cost for paint, canvas, and brushes. Twenty years later, after the artist had become famous, the painting has a fair market value of $10,000. If Ms. Collector now contributes the painting to an art museum, her maximum charitable deduction is $100, because the property contributed is ordinary income property. The entire $9,900 of appreciation in value is lost as a charitable deduction.

Example 2: Mr. Collector has a contribution base of $100,000. He contributes capital gain property with a fair market value of $50,000, in which he has a basis of $10,000, to a public charity. If the contribution satisfies the related use rule and there is a qualified appraisal by a qualified appraiser, Mr. Collector is allowed a deduction of $30,000 (30 percent of $100,000) and a carryover of $20,000. If the contribution does not satisfy the related use rule, Mr. Collector is allowed a deduction of $10,000 ($50,000 minus $40,000 appreciation equals $10,000), and there is no carryover. If there is not a qualified appraisal by a qualified appraiser, Mr. Collector would not be allowed any deduction.

Example 3: Mr. Collector has a contribution base of $100,000. He contributes capital gain property with a fair market value of $60,000 in which he has a basis of $40,000 to a public charity. If the contribution satisfies the related use rule and there is a qualified appraisal by a qualified appraiser, Mr. Collector is allowed a deduction of $30,000 (30 percent of $100,000) and a carryover of $30,000. If the contribution does not satisfy the related use rule or the election to increase the deduction is made, Mr. Collector is allowed a deduction of $40,000 ($60,000 minus $20,000 appreciation equals $40,000), and there is no carryover.

Alternative Minimum Tax

The Tax Reform Act of 1986 added a further complication to the process of charitable giving. Beginning in 1987 any long-term appreciation in value of property donated to a charitable organization is considered a preference item for purposes of computing the alternative minimum tax (AMT).[78] The effect of that provision is gradually to eliminate the benefits of donating appreciated long-term capital gain property. In other words, being subject to the AMT can, depending on the taxpayer's mix of income and deductions, have the economic effect of limiting the contribution to the taxpayer's cost or adjusted basis in the property.[79] However, this is only true if other items of tax preference and deductions have made the taxpayer subject to the AMT before the contribution of the appreciated property. When that happens, appreciation in value of charitable contributions produces little tax benefit, since the appreciation is subject to tax at the 21 percent rate. Moreover, in many situations, it will be the contribution of the appreciated property that moves the taxpayer into the AMT area. Nevertheless, the appreciation in value still produces a tax benefit, although it is reduced by the AMT payable.

A taxpayer with no other preferences probably can make a contribution of appreciated property up to 25 percent of his or her taxable income without being subject to the AMT. This is because the AMT tax is at 21 percent, and the maximum income tax rate is at 28 percent. Therefore, the AMT will not come into play unless the tax preferences are more than 25 percent of taxable income.

In determining whether the AMT applies in any year, it is important to understand precisely what amount is the tax preference as a result of the charitable contribution. Section 57(b)(6)(A) defines the amount of the tax preferences as "[t]he amount by which the deduction allowable under section 170 would be reduced if all capital gain property were taken into account at its adjusted basis." The statute uses the term "deduction allowable under section 170." This means that when the fair market value of the property contributed exceeds 30 percent of the taxpayer's contribution base, the amount above the 30 percent limitation is disregarded in determining the AMT. In other words, the amount of the tax preference is determined by disregarding any amount of the charitable contribution that is carried forward to another taxable year. When a portion of the charitable contribution is carried forward because it exceeds the applicable percentage limitation on contributions for the year, the portion so carried forward cannot increase the amount of the tax preference item until it is allowable as a deduction for regular tax purposes.

Example 1: Mr. Collector has a contribution base of $100,000. He contributes capital gain property with a fair market value of $50,000, in which he has a basis of $10,000, to a public charity. The related use rule is satisfied. Mr. Collector is allowed a deduction of $30,000 (30 percent of 100,000) and a carryover of $20,000. His tax preference amount is $20,000 ($30,000 minus $10,000). In the next year, assuming no other contributions, his deduction is $20,000 and his tax preference is $20,000 ($20,000 carried over minus the remaining basis of zero).

Example 2: Assume the same facts as above only the basis is now $40,000. Mr. Collector is allowed a deduction of $30,000 (30 percent of $100,000) and a carryover of $20,000. His tax preference amount is zero since the deduction allowable does not exceed his cost basis. In the next year, assuming no other contributions, his deduction is $20,000 and his tax preference is $10,000 ($20,000 carried over minus the remaining basis of $10,000).

There is no substitute for making the mathematical calculations before making any contribution. It may come as a surprise to many taxpayers to learn that the AMT will not apply to them. Our calculations indicate that the tax benefits of contributing appreciated property gradually disappear as the amount of AMT taxable income increases. Proper planning should make sure that the taxpayer does not cross over into the AMT area or, if that is unavoidable, that the amount of income subject to the AMT is at a minimum. A technique for avoiding the AMT when a large charitable contribution is made is discussed later in this chapter under "Fractional Interest" at pages 578-80.

Checklist for Collectors

To *maximize* the charitable deduction, the donor should:

- Make the contribution of appreciated tangible personal property to a public charity;
- Be sure that the contribution satisfies the related use rule;
- Make the contribution only with long-term capital gain property;
- Be sure that there is a qualified appraisal by a qualified appraiser of the contributed property; and
- Make the contribution when the AMT does not apply.

A deed of gift should be used, and formal acceptance by the charitable organization should be indicated thereon, as set forth in form 2 on page 639. In addition, the deed of gift should be drafted in such a manner that it supports the taxpayer's compliance with the related use rule, and it should also require the donee organization to sign IRS form 8283. Before the gift is made there should be discussion and correspondence with the charitable organization to make sure that the related use rule is met. The correspondence should establish the proof necessary to meet the related use rule. Consideration should be given to the special election to increase the charitable deduction from 30 to 50 percent when the appreciation in the value of the property is relatively small. After the donor dies, there is no carryover of any remaining contribution deduction to his or her estate. See forms 1, 2, and 3 on pages 637-42.

Before making the contribution, the donor should do the following:

1. Check the type of organization—public charity or private charity;
2. Check the type of property—capital gain property or ordinary income property;
3. Check compliance with the related use rule;
4. Do the mathematical calculation for application of the alternative minimum tax;
5. Consider the special election to increase the deduction from 30 to 50 percent;
6. Prepare the deed of gift and have it signed by the donor and the donee organization;
7. Obtain a qualified appraisal by a qualified appraiser;
8. Make sure IRS form 8283 is completed by the donee organization and the appraiser and that it is attached to the taxpayer's income tax return;
9. Obtain the necessary photographs for property in excess of $20,000;
10. File the gift tax return; and
11. Maintain the documentation for the income tax return required by the income tax regulations.

If the $5,000 claimed deduction amount is reached, the new appraisal rules apply whether (1) the donated property is capital gain property or not, (2) the property has appreciated or depreciated in value since its acquisition by the donor, (3) the donee is a public charity or a private foundation, and (4) the related use rule is or is not satisfied.

Partial Inter Vivos Charitable Transfers

Although a complete transfer of a collection to a charitable organization has many tax and estate planning advantages, the donor must still give up possession of the collection in order to receive the benefits from its transfer. Is it possible to obtain the tax and estate planning benefits of a complete transfer and still keep possession of the collection?

Retained Life Estate

Before 1964 a remainder interest was deductible: reserving a life interest in a collection while enjoying an immediate deduction for the present gift of the remainder to charity was a widespread practice.[80] However, the Revenue Act of 1964 added section 170(f), now section 170(a)(3), to the Code, which postpones any income tax charitable deduction for a gift of a future interest in tangible personal property until there is no intervening interest in, right of possession of, or enjoyment of the property held by the donor, the donor's spouse, or any of the donor's brothers, sisters, ancestors, or lineal descendants. That amendment was generally applicable to contributions made after December 31, 1963, and the same rule currently applies.[81]

If an individual has made a gift of a future interest in property before January 1, 1964 and has taken a charitable deduction, he can now contribute his life interest and obtain a charitable deduction based on the gift's present value and calculated in accordance with the actuarial tables of the regulations under the Code.[82] Prior to April 30, 1989, the 10 percent actuarial tables under regulation section 20.2031-7(f) were used to value such interests. New Code section 7520, effective May 1, 1989, now sets forth the tables to be used.[83]

The term "future interest" includes situations in which a donor purports to give a collection to a charitable organization, but has an understanding, arrangement, or agreement (whether written or oral) with the charitable organization that has the effect of reserving to or retaining in the donor a right to the use, possession, or enjoyment of the property.[84] In other words, there will be no present deduction allowed if a donor gives a collection away with some sort of understanding or agreement through which the donor can borrow it back when he or she desires.

The contribution of a future interest does not necessarily mean that the charitable deduction is lost; it may only be postponed. Regulation section 1.170A-5(a)(5) provides that the other provisions of section 170 are applicable to a contribution until the contribution is treated as made under section 170(a)(3).

Example 1: In 1974 Mr. Collector transferred a painting to an art museum by deed of gift, but reserved to himself the right to the use, possession, and enjoyment of the painting during his lifetime. The value of the painting in 1974 was $90,000. Since the contribution consisted of a future interest, no deduction was allowed in 1974.

Example 2: Assume the same facts as in *Example 1*, except that in 1976 Mr. Collector relinquished all his rights to the use, possession, and enjoyment of the painting and delivered it to the museum. If the value was $100,000 in 1976, Mr. Collector was entitled to a deduction of $100,000 in 1976, subject to the applicable percentage limitations.

The above examples, which are similar to those in the regulations, can be a trap for the unwary. If a charitable transfer of a remainder interest in a collection is made, the donor, as indicated above, does not receive a current charitable deduction. The danger is that he or she may incur a current gift tax liability. Under section 2522(c)(2) and regulation section 25.2522(c)-3(c)(1), there is no gift tax charitable deduction for a transfer of the remainder interest in a collection. However, since a transfer of the remainder interest has taken place, there is a transfer subject to the gift tax.[85]

Revenue Ruling 77-225, 1977-2 C.B. 73: A taxpayer claimed a charitable contribution deduction for a donation of a rare book collection. However, the taxpayer retained for his life the right of full access to the collection and the right to deny access to others. The IRS ruled that the taxpayer was not entitled to a charitable deduction, since the rights the taxpayer retained were equivalent to the retention of substantial rights to actual possession and enjoyment of the collection. Therefore, the gift was a donation of a future interest in tangible personal property, which is not deductible under section 170(a)(3). Although the ruling did not cover the gift tax question, we believe that a taxable gift was made.[86]

The future interest rule of section 170(a)(3) must be read in conjunction with the partial interest rule of section 170(f)(3)(A), which denies a deduction for a partial interest in property with certain exceptions not applicable to tangible personal property unless that interest is in the form of an annuity trust or unitrust. However, if there is no intention to avoid the application of section 170(f)(3)(A) by the conveyance, it appears that the rule does not apply.[87]

Example 3: In 1974 Mr. Collector transferred to his sons a life interest in a painting and on the same date transferred the remainder interest to charity with the intention of avoiding section 170(f)(3)(A). No deduction would be allowed to Mr. Collector for his remainder interest. If there had been no intention of avoiding section 170(f)(3)(A), section 170(a)(3) would still have prevented any current deduction, and there would have been a gift tax on the present interest and the remainder interest.

Therefore, for all practical purposes a remainder interest in a collection should never be transferred to a charitable organization.[88]

Note, however, that the foregoing discussion does not apply to transfers of a remainder interest in a collection made in trust. That type of transfer is governed by section 170(f)(2)(A) which denies any income tax charitable deduction for the value of a remainder interest in trust unless the trust is a charitable remainder annuity trust, a charitable remainder unitrust or a pooled income fund as those terms are defined in sections 664 and

642(c)(5). The practical effect of section 170(f)(2)(A) is to deny any income tax charitable deduction for the value of a remainder interest in a collection transferred in trust because such non-income producing property cannot be put in the form of a guaranteed annuity, nor can it pay out a fixed percentage yearly of its fair market value. See discussion of charitable remainder trusts at pages 588-90.

Fractional Interest

The collector who wants to give away a collection and still enjoy its possession on a part-time basis should convey an undivided fractional interest in the property to a charity. The transfer of an undivided fractional interest is *not* a transfer of a future interest that runs afoul of section 170(a)(3) or section 170(f).[89] Therefore, an immediate charitable deduction is allowable for the value of the undivided fractional interest donated. See form 4 on pages 643-44. However, the period of initial possession by the donee should not be deferred for more than one year, or the entire charitable deduction may be lost. See the case of *James L. Winokur*,[90] in which the court held that it is the right to entitlement or possession, not actual physical possession, that controls whether a purported present interest is to be regarded as a future interest.

Example: Ms. Collector transfers an undivided one-fourth present interest in a painting to an art museum by deed of gift. She is entitled to possession of the painting for nine months each year, and the museum is entitled to possession for three months each year. She can deduct one-fourth of the fair market value of the painting on the date of the gift, subject to the permissible maximum, as a charitable contribution.

The IRS position is to accept as the allowable charitable deduction the undivided percentage of the fair market value given to the charitable organization. Presumably, that is based on Revenue Ruling 57-293,[91] which gives a specific example covering that situation. The part of that ruling dealing with a gift of a future interest is no longer applicable because of section 170(f).

Of course, when the collector dies, the value of the undivided fractional interest that was kept by the collector is includable in his or her estate.[92] Because of Revenue Ruling 57-293, it would be difficult to argue that, if the retained undivided interest is bequeathed to a noncharitable beneficiary, there should be a discount for the minority undivided interest retained. There is, however, no decided case on that point. If the bequest is made to a person who does not own the other part, the taxpayer should have a fair chance of convincing the IRS to allow some discount for the fractional interest. If the bequest is made to the museum that already owns a partial interest in the painting, the estate tax charitable deduction should be the percentage owned by the decedent multiplied by the full fair market value of the painting on the decedent's date of death. Generally, before a museum will accept a fractional gift it will want assurances that it will receive the balance of the undivided interest when the collector dies. The museum does not want to be left owning a fractional interest in a work of art with the donor's heir's fighting over the remaining fractional interest. Therefore, always discuss such a gift with the museum prior to making it.

It may be possible to increase the total charitable deduction through the use of fractional gifts. In the *Example* stated above, the collector could deduct one-fourth of the fair market value of the painting on the date of the gift. A number of years later, the collector could make an additional gift of a one-fourth interest in the same painting. At that time, the painting may have increased in value not only because of the passage of time but also because it is now exhibited in a museum. Therefore, one-fourth of the fair market value on the later date may exceed the one-fourth value on the first date. If that process was carried on until the entire painting was donated, the total charitable deduction could exceed the total value of the painting on the date of the first gift. Of course, an appraiser would have to verify the increases in value each time an undivided fractional interest was donated to the museum.

The technique of making charitable contributions of undivided fractional interests has the added benefit of giving the taxpayer the ability to avoid the alternative minimum tax (AMT) that might result when appreciated property is contributed to charity. As discussed earlier in this chapter,[93] the appreciation in value of capital gain property is now a tax preference item that could result in the total or partial loss of the appreciation as a charitable deduction because of the application of the AMT. The AMT can be avoided by controlling the amount of appreciation in value (the tax preference) that is contributed to charity in any one year. This can be accomplished by calculating the maximum amount of appreciated property that can be contributed to charity in the year without incurring the AMT, and then making an undivided fractional interest gift within that limitation. Future undivided fractional interest gifts could then be made in later years to use up the full charitable deduction. At the same time, the donor can wind up over a period of years with a charitable deduction that exceeds 100 percent of the value of the work of art on the date the first part was donated to the museum.

Leaseback

A collector may donate a collection to a charity and then seek to lease it back at its fair rental value, although the rent paid is not a deductible charitable gift. In theory, that would produce a charitable deduction for the property itself at the time of the gift, and the collection should not be included as part of the donor's estate. However, if the rent is too low, the IRS may claim that the taxpayer has retained a life estate, which would make the collection includable in the gross estate. On the other hand, the fair rental value would probably be prohibitively high, and the charity would probably not participate in such an arrangement, since the rent paid might constitute "unrelated business income." Therefore, as a practical matter, the gift-leaseback technique is not workable except under unusual circumstances.[94]

Limited Present Interest

Before January 1, 1970, a transfer of a present interest in a collection to a charity for an immediate, limited period, with the remainder interest going to a noncharitable donee other than the donor, resulted in a current charitable deduction. That type of transfer was used when the taxpayer desired an immediate income tax deduction and wanted to make a gift of the collection to a member of his or her family in the future.

The Tax Reform Act of 1969 changed that result by providing that a charitable deduction is not to be allowed for contributions to a charity of less than the taxpayer's entire interest in the property, except to the extent a deduction would be allowed under the Act if the interest had been transferred in trust.[95] The effect of that amendment is to deny any charitable deduction for a contribution of the right to the present use of the collection for a period of time, since such non-income-producing property cannot be put in the form of a guaranteed annuity, nor can it pay out a fixed percentage yearly of its fair market value.[96] Therefore, the transfer of a limited present interest is an unacceptable form of contribution.

However, a deduction is allowed if the present interest is the taxpayer's entire interest and the partial interest in the collection was not created in order to avoid the restrictions under the Internal Revenue Code.[97] For example, if an individual made a contribution of a remainder interest in a collection before 1964 and now wishes to contribute the present interest that he or she retained, he or she may take a deduction for that interest.

Gift Annuities

Large charitable organizations have gift annuity plans that allow an individual to transfer a collection to charity in return for an annuity for life.[98] Briefly, a gift of a collection to a charitable organization in return for a lifetime annuity has the following features:

1. There is an income tax charitable deduction for the difference between the fair market value of the collection and the present value of the annuity.[99] All the rules discussed above that govern the amount of the deduction apply.
2. The present value of the annuity is determined by comparison with a comparable commercial contract, and the fair market value of the collection is determined by an appraisal.
3. The taxpayer has to recognize a capital gain, spread over the period of the annuity, on the difference between the basis for the collection and the present value of the annuity. The basis for the collection must be allocated between the value of the annuity and the fair market value of the collection in accordance with the bargain sale rules, discussed below.[100]

Bargain Sale

A bargain sale[101] of a collection to a charitable organization has the following features:

1. The basis of the property must be allocated between the sale portion and the gift portion.
2. The sale portion is subject to taxation—capital gain or ordinary income.
3. The gift portion is allowed as a charitable deduction to the extent of its fair market value. All the rules discussed above that govern the amount of the deduction apply.

There is a greater than usual problem of proof of fair market value on a bargain sale to a charitable organization; therefore, it may be prudent to obtain two appraisals.

Loans to Charities

The loan of a work of art to a charitable organization is treated as a transfer subject in part to federal gift tax. Section 7872(a)(1) treats an interest-free loan as a transfer of the "interest" on the loan from the lender to the borrower. The "interest" is the value of the use of the work of art. No income tax charitable deduction is allowed for such a transfer, since it is a split-interest transfer and not in the form for which a deduction is allowed. The Technical and Miscellaneous Revenue Act of 1988 amended section 2503 retroactively to July 31, 1969, by adding a new subsection to 2503 to provide that a loan of a qualified work of art to a public charity or a private operating foundation for use in carrying on its charitable purpose will not be treated as a transfer for federal gift tax purposes. For other transfer tax purposes, the work is valued as if the loan had not been made. Thus, the estate of a decedent-owner of a qualified work of art on loan at the time of his or her death will include the full value of the work of art in his or her estate for federal estate tax purposes. A qualified work of art is any archaeological, historic, or creative tangible personal property. The provision is effective for transfers occurring after July 31, 1969.

Combination of Benefits

In reviewing a client's tax situation, an attorney may be able to combine a number of the above techniques to produce a favorable tax result. For example, an elderly client with most of his or her assets tied up in a valuable collection who does not have enough income can first sell the collection to a charitable organization under the bargain sale rules. That will give him or her cash to invest to increase current income. The new 28 percent tax rate and the allowable charitable deductions combined with the bargain sale rules, will satisfy the client's need to increase current income, leave an estate to pass on to any heirs, and do so at little tax cost. There is no substitute for actually working out the mathematical calculations for each client.

Another technique is to use a charitable remainder unitrust to sell the collection during the first year of the trust. A collection may have a very low cost and be worth a great deal of money. If the collector who is in need of income sells it at auction he or she will have to pay approximately one-third of the gain in federal and state income taxes, leaving only the balance to be invested to produce income. Instead, if the collector contributes the collection to a charitable remainder unitrust and the trust is the seller, that will result in allowing the collection to be sold tax free, produce an income tax charitable deduction for the collector and preserve the one-third of the gain that would have gone in income taxes for future investment to produce a greater amount of income for the collector. The trust instrument should direct the sale in the first year of any non-income producing property to avoid any problem under section 170(f)(2)(A).

Techniques to Avoid

Three recent cases illustrate what should *not* be done with works of art.

In *J.W. Kluge*,[102] the taxpayer sold valuable works of art to a closely held corporation wholly owned by him. However, he retained the works of art in his home after the sale. The Tax Court upheld the IRS in its holding that the taxpayer received a taxable dividend equivalent to the sale prices allocated to the works of art, since he retained the beneficial use of the objects in his home. Therefore, the payment by the corporation was for his personal benefit, rather than for a valid business purpose.

In *S. Prestley Blake*,[103] the taxpayer contributed highly appreciated securities to a charity with an "understanding" that the charity would sell the securities and use the proceeds to buy the taxpayer's yacht. The Second Circuit affirmed the conclusion of the Tax Court, which was that the taxpayer, in substance, had himself sold the stock, retained the proceeds, and made a gift of the yacht to the charity. Therefore, the taxpayer had to recognize the gain on the sale of the stock by the charity. The Second Circuit based that conclusion on its finding that under state law the charitable donee was legally obligated by the terms of its understanding with the taxpayer to sell the donated stock and to buy his yacht. But the court went further and stated that it would have reached the same conclusion even if there had been no such binding legal obligation:

> [W]here there is an understanding that a contribution of appreciated property will be utilized by the donee charity for the purpose of purchasing an asset of the contributor, the transaction will be viewed as a matter of tax law as a contribution of the asset—at whatever its then value is—with the charity acting as a conduit of the proceeds from the sale of the stock.

In *Ford*,[104] the taxpayer was a limited partner in a partnership that owned one asset, an underwater research vessel with a fair market value of $600,000. After fully depreciating the vessel, the partnership transferred it to a corporation wholly owned by the partnership. The stock of the corporation was then donated to a university, and the taxpayer took a charitable contribution deduction, based on his share of the $600,000 value. The Tax Court held that the creation of the corporation was a sham, since its sole purpose was to avoid taxes. Therefore, the corporation was disregarded, resulting in a reduction of the charitable contribution to zero under section 170(e)(1)(A), which requires the amount of the contribution to be reduced by the amount of ordinary income that would have been realized on a sale of the contributed property.

Complete Testamentary Charitable Transfers

An individual may desire to keep possession of the collection during life and bequeath it to a charitable organization on death. Doing so results in an estate tax charitable deduction to the extent of the fair market value of the property at the date of death.[105] In the case of a bequest at death there is no distinction between a public charity and a private foundation. Moreover, in general, the related use rule does not apply to testamentary transfers.[106] However, section 2055(e) introduced by the Economic Recovery Tax Act of 1981 (ERTA) contains a new related use rule for a testamentary charitable transfer when there is a retained copyright interest. That provision is discussed in detail later in this chapter.

Whenever a valuable collection constitutes a substantial portion of the assets that a client wants to leave to charity on his or her death, consideration must be given to the extent of the charitable bequest. For example, a collection left to charity at the time a will is drafted may constitute only 40 percent of a testator's estate. However, by the time of the testator's death, the collection may have increased in value, and the testator's other assets may have decreased in value. That could result in the charitable bequest's constituting more than 50 percent of the testator's estate. If that situation causes a problem under local state law, provision must be made to avoid the problem by either drafting a clause with a percentage limitation or drafting the will so that it cannot be challenged.[107]

Generally, the full estate tax charitable deduction is allowable for a bequest to either a public charity or a private foundation. Private foundations include all exempt organizations other than those described in section 509(a)(1), (2), (3), or (4). However, if the bequest is to a private foundation that has *not* complied with the requirement under the Tax Reform Act of 1969 of including certain amendments in its governing instrument or that has failed to notify the IRS of its status, the entire estate tax charitable deduction will be denied.[108]

If the testator desires to bequeath a collection to a private foundation, the drafter of the will should obtain a copy of the foundation's governing instrument to ascertain whether the instrument meets the Tax Reform Act of 1969 requirement mentioned above, and should also obtain a statement from the organization that it has notified the IRS of its status.

Changes Under ERTA

ERTA amended section 2056 to provide for an unlimited estate tax marital deduction. Before January 1, 1982, it was important to integrate the marital deduction and the charitable deduction to achieve the best result.[109] For decedents dying on or after January 1, 1982, there is an unlimited marital deduction, so no charitable deduction is necessary to reduce the federal estate tax to zero if the decedent left his or her entire estate to the surviving spouse.

In fact, even if the testator wants the charitable organization to receive the collection at his or her death, the testator should *not* bequeath it to the charitable organization. Instead, the testator should leave the collection outright to the surviving spouse and have the surviving spouse make the donation to the charitable organization either during the surviving spouse's life or at death. The surviving spouse would receive an income tax charitable deduction under section 170, within the applicable percentage limitations previously discussed, for a lifetime transfer, or a charitable deduction under section 2055 for a transfer at death. There would be no federal estate tax on the estate of the deceased spouse because of the unlimited marital deduction.

Outright testamentary charitable transfers are still important for unmarried individuals. Such bequests allow the collection to be kept together as a unit and eliminate the problem of raising the money necessary to pay the estate taxes attributable to the inclusion of a valuable collection in the gross estate and eliminate any need for a forced sale of the collection in order to pay the estate taxes.

A testator who wishes to bequeath a collection to a charitable organization should make a specific bequest in his or her will. The bequest should be specific enough to identify clearly the property to be given. The testator should consider the possibility that a specific charitable organization may renounce the bequest. Therefore, the proposed gift and any conditions thereon should be discussed with the charitable organization. See forms 5 and 8 on pages 645 and 651.

The repeal of the carryover basis rules makes a consideration of the relative basis of the property making up a collection no longer necessary. Under the current rules section 1014 provides that all property takes a basis equal to the value on the date of death or six months later. Before the repeal of the carryover basis rules, estate planners working with an individual who wished to leave part of his or her collection to a charitable organization and part to family members had to consider leaving the part with the lower basis to the charity and the part with the higher basis to the family members. That is no longer necessary. However, it is still important for all collectors to maintain adequate records of their cost basis, since the concept of carryover basis may yet rear its ugly head again some time in the future.

Partial Testamentary Charitable Transfers

Before January 1, 1970, it was possible to bequeath a collection to a member of the family for life and, on that person's death, outright to a charitable organization, resulting in an estate tax charitable deduction for the value of the remainder interest. A similar deduction was obtainable for a present interest to the charitable organization with a remainder interest to a noncharitable legatee. The Tax Reform Act of 1969 eliminated those deductions.

Remainder Interest

The Tax Reform Act of 1969 denied the estate tax charitable deduction for a remainder interest in property (with certain exceptions not applicable here) unless the interest were in a trust that was a charitable remainder annuity trust, charitable remainder unitrust, or pooled income fund.[110]

The effect was to make a transfer of that type impractical, since non-income-producing property, such as a collection, cannot be put in the form of a guaranteed annuity, nor can it pay out a fixed percentage yearly of its fair market value. A charitable remainder unitrust is permitted to pay out only its income if that income is less than the stated percentage. However, if from the outset it is clear that the property put in trust will never produce any income, the charitable deduction may be denied on the ground that a valid charitable remainder unitrust was not created, since the trust cannot make an annual payment. The regulations[111] issued under section 664 indicate that a charitable remainder unitrust must make an annual payment to the noncharitable beneficiary. The regulations make no mention of a remainder interest in non-income-producing property, such as a collection. The only exceptions to the required unitrust form for a remainder interest in property given to a charity are contained in section 2055(e)(2), which concerns a remainder interest in a personal residence or farm.

Further, the regulations state that a remainder trust will not qualify under section 664 if its governing instrument contains a "provision which restricts the trustee from investing the trust assets in a manner which could result in the annual realization of a reasonable amount of income or gain from the sale or disposition of trust assets."[112]

In Revenue Ruling 73-610, 1973-2 C.B. 213, the grantor of an irrevocable trust contributed a collection of antiques, in addition to income-producing assets, to a trust. The governing instrument of the trust provided that the grantor's spouse, who was the sole income beneficiary of the trust for her life, should have the use of the antique collection for her life. At her death, the antique collection and all the remaining assets in the trust were to be distributed to a charitable exempt organization. In all other respects the trust complied with the provisions of section 664 defining charitable remainder trusts. The IRS held that the retention of a life estate in the collection of antiques for the grantor's spouse restricted the trustee from investing all the trust assets in a manner that could result in the annual realization of a reasonable amount of income or gain from the sale or disposition of trust assets. Therefore, the trust did not qualify as a charitable remainder trust. Similarly, in Revenue Ruling 76-165, 1976-1 C.B. 279, the IRS held that a remainder interest in household furnishings that were bequeathed to a surviving spouse for life and then to a charitable organization did not qualify as a deductible remainder interest.

It is our opinion that a collection cannot be put in the form of a charitable remainder trust that will qualify for the estate tax charitable deduction.[113] One way to deal with Revenue Ruling 73-610 is specifically to empower the trustee to sell all or part of the collection at his or her discretion. In such a case the trustee is not "restricted" from investing the assets. However, the problem of a yearly payout is still present, and, unless an IRS ruling is obtained, such a charitable transfer should not be made.

ERTA: As discussed above, a married individual should not, on death, leave his or her collection outright to a charitable organization, but should leave it first to the surviving spouse who can then contribute the collection to the charity and take an income tax charitable deduction for transfers made during the spouse's life and an estate tax charitable deduction for transfers made under the spouse's will. However, the testator may want assurance that the surviving spouse will, in fact, transfer the collection to the charitable organization.

Before January 1, 1982, if a testator created a trust for the surviving spouse and wanted it to qualify for the marital deduction, the surviving spouse had to have a general power of appointment over the corpus of the trust. Therefore, the first spouse to die could not be certain that the corpus of the trust would be received by the charitable organization. ERTA changed that situation in two ways.

ERTA added section 2056(b)(8), which provides that, if the surviving spouse is the only noncharitable beneficiary of an otherwise qualified charitable remainder trust, the terminable interest rule of section 2056(b)(1) does not apply, and the life interest qualifies for the marital deduction. The remainder interest qualifies for the charitable deduction under section 2055(e)(2), so there is no tax on the estate of the first spouse to die.

However, as discussed above, we believe that a collection cannot be put in the form of a charitable remainder trust. Therefore, unless a specific ruling is obtained, section 2056(b)(8) is probably not much help to the collector.

More helpful is section 2056(b)(7), which was also added by ERTA.[114] That section allows a trust that is created for the sole benefit of the surviving spouse to qualify for the marital deduction, even though the surviving spouse does *not* have a general power of appointment. That type of trust is known as a QTIP trust, that is, a trust consisting of qualified terminable interest property.

Therefore, if a collection can be left in a QTIP trust with a designated charitable organization to take the remainder after the death of the surviving spouse, there is no estate tax on the death of the first spouse to die, since the QTIP trust qualifies 100 percent for the marital deduction under section 2056(b)(7); the testator is assured that the charitable organization will receive the collection after the death of the surviving spouse; and the estate of the surviving spouse receives a charitable deduction under section 2055(a) equal to 100 percent of the then fair market value of the collection.

To reach the above result, the estate planner must see that two requirements are met. First, the QTIP trust must qualify for the marital deduction. Section 2056(b)(7)(B)(ii)(I) provides:

> (ii) QUALIFYING INCOME INTEREST FOR LIFE.—The surviving spouse has a qualifying income interest for life if—
>
> (I) the surviving spouse is entitled to all the income from the property, payable annually or at more frequent intervals, . . .

Since a collection generally does not produce any current income, is there a problem in placing a collection in a QTIP trust in light of the requirement of section 2056(b)(7)(B)(ii)(I)? Currently there is no definitive answer. However, we believe that a collection can be placed in a QTIP trust that qualifies for the marital deduction under section 2056(b)(7). Under regulation section 20.2056(b)-5(f)(4) the power to retain or invest in unproductive property is not fatal to the marital deduction under section 2056(b)(5) if the surviving spouse has the right to require that the property be productive or be converted within a reasonable time. In the case of *Estate of Robinson v. United States*[115] the trustees were authorized to invest in non-income-producing assets, but the court found that the trust, when construed in light of the overall intent of the decedent and with regard to local law, afforded the surviving spouse the degree of beneficial enjoyment necessary to satisfy the requirements of section 2056 and the applicable IRS regulations.

It is helpful to the conclusion reached above if the QTIP trust is funded not only with the collection, but also with enough other income-producing assets to provide the surviving spouse with a reasonable amount of income in light of that spouse's lifestyle. In addition, it is recommended that the trust have a provision to this effect:

> My trustee shall have no power to invest in or to retain non-income-producing property without the consent of my said [husband or wife].

Second, the remainder (including the collection) of the QTIP trust that is transferred to the charitable organization after the death of the surviving spouse must qualify for the estate tax charitable deduction in the surviving spouse's estate.[116] The Technical Corrections Act of 1982 added section 2044(c) to make it clear that property in a QTIP trust that is includable in the gross estate of the surviving spouse under section 2044(a) is treated as property passing from the surviving spouse for purposes of the charitable deduction under section 2055.[117]

Therefore, it should now be possible to place a collection in trust for a surviving spouse with the testator receiving a 100 percent marital deduction on death and the surviving spouse receiving a 100 percent charitable deduction on that spouse's death without the necessity of giving the surviving spouse a general power of appointment.

Double Deduction Denied: The Technical Corrections Act of 1982 added subsection 2056(b)(9), which provides that the value of an interest in property cannot be deducted more than once in computing a single decedent's or donor's estate or gift tax liability.[118] Apparently, that provision is intended to prevent the double deductions that could result when a transfer of property qualifies for the marital deduction and the remainder interest in the same property qualifies for the charitable deduction. However, as noted above, a split-interest bequest of a collection does not qualify for the charitable deduction.

Income Interest

The Tax Reform Act of 1969 denies the estate tax charitable deduction for an income interest in property unless that interest is in the form of a guaranteed annuity or is a fixed percentage, distributed yearly, of the fair market value of the property, to be determined yearly.[119] Therefore, a bequest to charity of a collection with the remainder to a noncharitable legatee does not result in an estate tax charitable deduction.

Fractional Interest

A bequest of an undivided fractional interest in a collection to a charitable organization does qualify for an estate tax charitable deduction.[120] For example, if the testator gave an undivided three-quarters interest to the charitable organization during his or her life, the testator could give the remaining quarter under his or her will on death. The estate tax charitable deduction would be one-quarter of the fair market value as determined for estate tax purposes.

Retained Copyright Interest

Section 423 of ERTA amended sections 2055(e) and 2522(c) to permit, under certain conditions, a charitable gift or estate tax deduction for the transfer by gift or bequest after December 31, 1981, of a work of art, but not its copyright, to a charitable organization.

On October 21, 1983, the IRS published proposed regulations pertaining to sections 2055(e) and 2522(c). On May 17, 1984, final regulations were published in the *Federal Register*.[121] Although the final regulations clarify the statute in a number of ways, they clearly point out a potential trap for the unwary artist and collector.

Tax Law Background: If a decedent or a donor transfers an interest in a property to both a charitable donee and a noncharitable donee, that is, a split interest that is less than the entire interest to each, no estate or gift tax charitable deduction is allowed unless the gift is made in certain specified forms.[122] No charitable deduction is allowed for a remainder interest unless the remainder interest qualifies as a charitable remainder annuity trust, a charitable remainder unitrust, a pooled income fund, a farm, or a personal residence. No charitable deduction is allowed for an income interest unless it is in the form of a guaranteed annuity interest or a unitrust interest.

A split-interest charitable transfer of non-income-producing property, such as a work of art, does not qualify for a charitable deduction, since it cannot be put in the form of a guaranteed annuity or pay out a fixed percentage of its fair market value yearly. To qualify as a unitrust, the trust must be able to make an annual income payment to the noncharitable beneficiary, and the trustee must not be restricted from investing the trust assets in a manner intended to realize an annual income.[123]

Under the existing IRS regulations, an original work of art and a copyright interest relating to that work of art are for tax purposes *two interests in the same property.*[124] Since a work of art cannot qualify for any of the specified forms of split-interest charitable transfers, no charitable deduction was allowable under pre-1982 law when an individual gave the original artwork to a charity and retained the copyright interest attributable to that work of art.

Copyright Law Background: The Copyright Act of 1976, which went into effect January 1, 1978, treats the original artwork and the intangible copyright as *two separate items of property.* Section 202 of the Copyright Act provides:

> Ownership of a copyright, or any of the exclusive rights under a copyright, is distinct from ownership of any material object in which the work is embodied.

A brief explanation of the Copyright Act of 1976, as it applies to the visual arts, follows.[125] The 1976 Act almost entirely eliminates common-law copyrights. All works of art are now protected by statutory copyright as soon as they are created in tangible form. The copyright is completely separate from ownership of the physical work of art. It can be transferred only in writing, and its owner or the owner's agent must sign that transfer. The term of copyright is the artist's life plus fifty years. It is possible for copyright protection to be lost if "publication" takes place without a proper copyright notice. Publication means public distribution.

The history of the Act indicates that Congress did not intend unique works of art to be considered as published when they are sold or offered for sale in such traditional ways as through an art dealer, a gallery, or an auction house. However, to be on the safe side, an artist should place the required copyright notice on a work of art before the artwork is sold or publicly displayed. The form of copyright notice is as follows: "©" or "Copr." or "Copyright" followed by the artist's name or an abbreviation by which he or she is recognized and the year of publication. The copyright notice can be placed on the front or the back of the work of art or on any backing, mounting, matting, framing, or other material to which the work is permanently attached or in which it is permanently housed.

Interaction of Tax Law and Copyright Law: The tax regulations have always treated a work of art and the copyright as two interests in the same property. The Copyright Act of 1976 treats a work of art and the copyright as two separate property interests. The inconsistency made it impossible to obtain a charitable deduction for a work of art transferred to a charity if the contributor retained the copyright interest. Section 2055(e)(4) is an attempt by Congress to allow some flexibility in that area.[126]

Section 2055(e)(4): Section 2055(e) was amended by ERTA by adding subsection (4), which provides for estate tax purposes that a work of art and its copyright are treated as separate properties *in certain cases*. The statute applies only to a "qualified contribution of a work of art"[127] and defines the term "work of art" as any tangible personal property with respect to which there is a copyright under federal law.[128] As stated above, a federal statutory copyright for a work of art comes into existence at its creation. Therefore, all works of art created after January 1, 1978, meet the definition of the statute.

The term "qualified contribution" means "any transfer of property to a qualified organization if the use of the property by the organization is related to the purpose or function constituting the basis for its exemption under Section 501."[129] (That rule is similar to the related use rule under section 170(e)(1)(B)(i).) Therefore, a contribution is a "qualified contribution" for purposes of the retained copyright provision only if the related use rule is satisfied. If the contribution is not a "qualified contribution," the old split-interest rule applies, that is, the work of art and the copyright are treated as two interests in the same property, rather than as two separate property interests.

The statute applies only to qualified contributions made to a "qualified organization."[130] The term "qualified organization" means any organization described in section 501(c)(3) other than a private foundation under section 509. For that purpose a private operating foundation under section 4942(j)(3) is not treated as a private foundation.

Therefore, section 2055(e)(4) for the first time allows a decedent to make a transfer of a work of art to a charitable organization with his or her estate retaining the copyright interest so long as the transfer satisfies the estate tax related use rule of section 2055(e)(4)(C).[131]

The Collector: Under the Copyright Act of 1976 the artist retains the ownership of the copyright in a unique work of art created on or after January 1, 1978, unless the copyright is specifically transferred in writing. Accordingly, in most cases, when the collector purchases a work of art created on or after January 1, 1978, he or she is purchasing a work of art without the copyright.

The final regulations under section 2055(e)(4) make it clear that section 2055(e)(4) does not apply to a decedent who never had the copyright interest. Section 2055(e)(4)(A) states that the work of art and the copyright are treated as separate properties for purposes of section 2055(e)(2), which applies to split-interest transfers, that is, transfers in which separate property interests in the same property pass from one person to two separate persons at the same time. If the testator never had the copyright, he or she cannot make a split-interest transfer under section 2055(e)(2). Example (2) of regulation section 20.2055-2(e)(1)(ii)(e) provides:

> B, a collector of art, purchased a work of art from an artist who retained the copyright interest. B died in 1983. Under the terms of B's will the work of art is given to Y charity. Since B did not own the copyright interest, paragraph (e)(1)(i) of this section does not apply to disallow a deduction under section 2055 for the value of the work of art, regardless of whether or not the contribution is a qualified contribution under paragraph (e)(1)(ii)(c) of this section.

Therefore, when the will of a collector transfers a work of art to a charitable organization, the collector need not worry about satisfying the related use rule of section 2055(e)(4)(C) if he or she has never owned the copyright interest. If he or she does own the copyright interest, the charitable bequest should contain specific language to the effect that the copyright is included in the transfer in order to avoid any possibility of running afoul of the related use rule of section 2055(e)(4)(C).

The Artist: The problem and the potential trap for the artist is best illustrated by a simple example: the will of an artist bequeaths a specific work of art that was created after January 1, 1978, to the artist's local church and the balance of the estate to the artist's son: "I give and bequeath my painting entitled 'xyz' to the *A* Church. All the rest of my property of any kind I give and bequeath to my son."

Since the artist owned the copyright at the time of death (federal statutory copyright comes into existence at creation) and since the *A* Church, although a public charity, probably cannot satisfy the related use rule of section 2055(e)(4)(C), will the artist's estate get the estate tax charitable deduction?

The quoted provision in the artist's will does not pass the copyright in the work of art to the charity, since the copyright is a separate property interest and must be separately bequeathed.[132] The copyright interest was not included in the charitable transfer; it was transferred as part of the residuary clause. Therefore, the transfer was a split-interest transfer that, unless the provisions of section 2055(e)(4) were satisfied, results in the loss of the charitable deduction. If the transfer to the local church did not satisfy the related use rule of section 2055(e)(4)(C), the charitable deduction is lost.

The final regulations under section 2055(e)(4) also contain an example illustrating the potential trap for the artist.[133] The example makes it clear that the IRS looks to local state law to see if the purported transfer of the work of art to the charitable organization includes the copyright. We believe that the simple will clause quoted above does not include the copyright interest in any local jurisdiction in the United States. Such a clause allows the copyright interest to become a part of the residuary estate.[134]

To avoid the problem of an inadvertent split-interest transfer that fails to satisfy the related use rule of section 2055(e)(4)(C), estate planners should examine the artist's will to make sure any charitable transfers of works of art created after January 1, 1978, are transfers that also specifically transfer the copyright interest to the same charitable organization. For example: "I give and bequeath to the *A* Charity my painting entitled 'ABC,' oil on canvas, measuring xx by xx and dated 1988, and my copyright interest in that painting." Under that provision, the copyright interest will not inadvertently fall into the residue, thereby causing a split-interest transfer that may not satisfy the related use rule. Although there is no definitive authority, a clause that merely transfers "all my right, title, and interest in and to 'ABC' painting" may not be sufficient to transfer the copyright in the work of art. The careful drafter will specifically include the copyright interest. See forms 6, 7, and 8 on pages 647, 649, and 651.

Additional Problems Under Section 2055(e)(4): The final regulations do not address the question of whether a decedent's estate receives a charitable deduction for the full fair market value of the property transferred to a charity if a copyright interest is specifically retained.

The House Committee Report on H.R. 4242 indicates that the retention of the copyright or the failure to transfer the copyright does not affect the fair market value determination.[135] The Report states that the value of a work of art and of the copyright can be determined separately from the sales of similar properties. The Report then states:

> Moreover, the use or exploitation of the artwork or copyright generally does not affect the value of the other property. Accordingly, the value of the artwork (determined from comparable sales) which is used to determine the amount of the charitable deduction should provide a high degree of correlation with the value of property received by charity.

On the basis of the foregoing, it appears that, generally, the retention of a copyright interest does not reduce the fair market value of the work of art given to a charity.

The statute speaks of a qualified contribution of a *work of art.*[136] It does not cover a contribution of a copyright interest. If a decedent transfers the copyright to a charity and retains the work of art for his or her heirs, that is not a qualified contribution of a work of art, and section 2055(e)(4) does not apply. Since such a transfer is a split-interest transfer not in unitrust form, no charitable deduction is allowed for the transfer of the copyright interest.

If the testator transfers the work of art to a public charity, satisfies section 2055(e)(4), and retains the copyright for his or her heirs, it is not clear whether the heirs can later transfer the copyright in such a manner as to receive a charitable deduction. Even if they can obtain a charitable deduction, it is a contribution of ordinary income property, since a copyright is not a capital asset under section 1221(3). Therefore, the amount of their deduction is limited to their basis in the copyright.[137]

Conclusion: Section 2055(e)(4) is a benefit for the artist who wants to bequeath works of art to a charitable organization and retain the copyright for reproduction purposes for the artist's heirs. Before January 1, 1982, that could not be done. If the artist wants to bequeath a work of art to a charitable organization, but does not intend to retain the copyright interest, care must be taken to make sure that both the work of art and the copyright are specifically transferred to the charity. Otherwise, the statute is a trap for the unwary artist, whose estate tax charitable deduction may fail because of the related use rule of section 2055(e)(4)(C).

For collectors, the new provision presents no problem as long as the collector does not own the copyright. However, in preparing a will for a collector an attorney should take care to make sure that, if the collector does own any copyright interest, it is transferred to the charitable organization, along with the work of art.

NONCHARITABLE TRANSFERS

Not all collectors want to leave their collections to charitable organizations. There may be a strong family tie to a particular item that the collector wishes to stay in the family, a younger member of the family may have developed a particular interest in the collection, or the collection may constitute a substantial portion of the collector's estate. In such cases noncharitable transfers must be considered.

Inter Vivos Transfers

Before January 1, 1977, a lifetime gift of a collection to a noncharitable beneficiary resulted in saving a large amount in estate taxes, because gift tax rates were only three-fourths as large as the estate tax rates in the corresponding bracket. The Tax Reform Act of 1976 removed some of the advantages of and the incentives for making lifetime gifts to a noncharitable beneficiary, although some do remain.

For gifts made on or after January 1, 1977, only one tax rate schedule covers both gift tax and estate tax.[138] The value of all taxable gifts made on or after January 1, 1977, is added to the taxable estate for the purpose of determining the applicable estate tax bracket. In other words, a donor can no longer take advantage of the low starting point on two separate rate schedules. To the extent that taxable gifts are made, they push the donor's estate into a higher estate tax bracket.

Advantages of Lifetime Gifts

There are still advantages in making lifetime gifts of a collection:

A married donor can take advantage of the new unlimited gift tax marital deduction, effective January 1, 1982, for gifts made on or after that date.[139] The shifting of assets to one's spouse can be an effective estate planning tool. For example, the gift can remove the value of the donated assets from the donor's estate at no cost and can increase the donee's estate to the point at which the spouse can take maximum advantage of the unified credit, so that there is no tax in the donee's estate if that spouse dies first and leaves the donee's estate to their children or in trust for the surviving spouse. However, the donee should not leave the donated property back to the donor outright.

The donor can reduce any gift tax on gifts made to someone other than the donor's spouse by having the spouse consent to those gifts and by taking advantage of the gift-splitting provisions[140] (which permit a donor to compute the gift tax as if one-half of the gifts had been made by the donor's spouse).

Property used to pay the gift tax is not included in the estate of the donor for estate tax purposes if the donor lives at least three years after the date of the gift.[141]

A gift tax is paid only on the actual amount passing to the donee. An estate tax, on the other hand, is paid not only on the amount passing to the beneficiary, but also on the money used to pay the estate tax itself.

Any appreciation in value after the date of the gift is removed from the donor's gross estate.

The amount of the gift tax can be reduced by taking advantage of the $10,000 annual exclusion.[142] ERTA increased the annual exclusion from $3,000 to $10,000 for gifts made on or after January 1, 1982. The Revenue Act of 1978 amended section 2035 to provide that, even if a donor dies within three years of a gift, if the donor was not required to file a gift tax return under section 6019, the value of the gift is not included in the gross estate.[143] Most of section 2035 was abolished under ERTA for decedents who die on or after January 1, 1982, except under certain limited circumstances.[144] That change freed from estate tax any appreciation in value of the property between the date of the gift and the date of the decedent's death.

Disadvantages of Lifetime Gifts

A lifetime gift to a noncharitable beneficiary has certain disadvantages:

First, the collector must part with dominion and control of the collection.

Moreover, on a valuable collection, the gift tax for a transfer to someone other than a spouse may be so high as to make such a transfer impractical.

Since the gift tax is payable in the year of the gift, the present loss of the gift tax money and the loss of future income on that money may be more painful than the thought of a larger estate tax that is not due until nine months after death, and then only to the extent that the estate has not decreased in value or been consumed.

A married individual who is planning to take advantage of the unlimited estate tax marital deduction on death should consider owning the collection on death, so that the surviving spouse can receive a step-up in basis for the collection under section 1014(a).[145] That will enable the surviving spouse to sell the collection and avoid the capital gains tax on any appreciation in value. If lifetime gifts are made, the advantage of a step-up in basis is lost.

Intrafamily Transfers

The lifetime gift of a collection to a noncharitable beneficiary can be outright, in trust, or a gift of a legal life estate. An intrafamily transfer, particularly if it is made to a family member living in the same household, can cause the donor a difficult burden of proof on the question of completion of the gift. A transfer of a collection to a family member must be evidenced by a deed of gift with a signed acceptance, the filing of a gift tax return, and the changing of the insurance policy, if any, to the new owner. It is also advisable to effect delivery of the collection being transferred. The foregoing is important to avoid the argument that the donor retained a lifetime use of the collection, which would make it includable in his or her estate under section 2036(a). The problem is more difficult if the donor made a lifetime gift of the collection to a family member who did not share the donor's household and the donor did not physically deliver the collection to the donee. The retention of the collection in the donor's household for the donor's lifetime probably makes it includable in the donor's estate under section 2036(a)(1), even if the donor paid a gift tax on its transfer.[146]

Basis on Transfer

As noted above, the estate of a decedent who owns a collection that has appreciated in value receives a step-up in the basis of the collection to its fair market value on the date of death or six months later. As a result of the unlimited gift tax marital deduction, transfers between spouses can be made at no gift tax cost. Therefore, one spouse can transfer a collection to the other shortly before the donee dies for the purpose of receiving a step-up in basis for the transferred collection. If the will of the donee spouse leaves the same collection to the surviving spouse, there is no estate tax, because of the unlimited estate tax marital deduction, and the surviving spouse regains the collection at a stepped up basis. To discourage such predeath transfers, section 1014(e) provides that there is no step-up in basis in the case of appreciated property acquired by a decedent by gift during the one-year period before the death if that property is then reacquired by the donor from the decedent. That provision is effective for individuals who die after December 31, 1981.

The value of a collection included in an individual's gross estate for federal estate tax purposes is generally the value on the date of the person's death. However, the executor may elect to value the collection on the alternative valuation date, which is generally six months after the decedent's death.[147] As noted above, the basis of a collection acquired from a decedent is the value of the collection on the date of death or six months later. As a result of the unlimited estate tax marital deduction, in most cases there is no estate tax on the estate of the first spouse to die. Therefore, it is advantageous to the surviving spouse to have the collection valued on the date when the value is the highest, rather than the lowest, for federal estate tax purposes. That was never the intent of section 2032 when it was enacted. The Tax Reform Act of 1984 changed the rule to provide that the alternative valuation date may be used only when both the total value of all property in the gross estate and the federal estate tax liability of the estate are reduced.[148]

Therefore, in a zero tax estate the alternative valuation date cannot be used to obtain a larger stepped-up basis for a collection in a decedent's estate.

Grantor Retained Income Trusts

Effective December 1, 1983, the IRS amended the tables in the regulations used to value income and remainder interests.[149] The basic changes were to substitute a 10 percent rate of return for the prior 6 percent rate and to substitute a single unisex table for the separate tables for males and females. The change in the valuation tables increased the value of income interests and reduced the value of remainder interests. That change permitted a donor to transfer property having a value substantially more than the amount protected from tax by the unified credit without the imposition of a gift tax.

The tables were again amended by the Technical and Miscellaneous Revenue Act of 1988, which added new section 7520 to the Code requiring the IRS to determine the value of any annuity, interest for life or a term of years, or remainder or reversionary interest under tables using an interest rate equal to 120 percent of the federal midterm rate in effect for the month in which the valuation date falls.[150] The new provision is effective for valuations made after May 1, 1989.

The foregoing is best illustrated with a simple example: a donor, aged sixty, owns a work of art with a fair market value of $1,500,000. In 1988 he makes a gift of the painting by transferring the remainder interest to his son and retaining the use of the painting (the income interest) for a ten-year period.

Under table B of regulation section 25.2512-5(f), a gift of a remainder interest for a ten-year period has a factor of 38.6. Therefore, the value of the gift is $579,000, an amount that is less than $600,000, the amount that can be donated tax-free in 1988 by making use of the maximum unified credit. The result is that the donor has the "use" of the painting for ten years, and after that period it is transferred to the donee at no further tax cost, even though the painting, which had a value of $1,500,000 on the date of the gift, may be worth $2,500,000 after the ten-year period. In effect, the donor has leveraged the use of the unified credit, since he has transferred property with a value in excess of $1,500,000 by giving only $579,000.

That result should be achieved even though the painting is not income-producing property. Regulation section 25.2512-5(c) provides that if the interest to be valued is the right of a person "to use non-income-producing property" the value is determined under table A or table B. However, no specific authority exists concerning the scope of the use concept, although it should include the use of a painting.[151]

In the above example, if the donor dies before the expiration of the ten-year period, the painting is included in his gross estate for federal estate tax purposes.[152] However, any unified credit of the donor used in connection with the gift of the painting is restored to the donor (now decedent) under section 2001(b). Therefore, there is little downside risk in making use of a leveraged gift of a painting. The one tax disadvantage is that the painting will not receive a step-up in basis on the date of the donor's death if the donor lives beyond the term of the gift. The nontax disadvantage is that the donor must give physical possession of the painting to the remainderman at the end of the term of the gift. If the donor retains possession of the painting beyond the term of the gift, the full fair market value of the painting on the date of death of the donor will be includable in his or her gross estate for federal estate tax purposes, as a transfer with a retained interest under section 2036(a)(2).

Extreme caution is advised in making use of the above leveraged gift technique. The Treasury Department proposals in a report dated November 1984 and captioned "Tax Reform for Fairness, Simplicity, and Economic Growth" include a change in the gift tax law to provide that, if a grantor makes a gift of a remainder interest and retains an income interest (use of a painting for ten years in the above example), no taxable gift occurs until the termination of the income interest, when the then fair market value of the entire property is subject to gift tax. The proposed change would be retroactive and would apply to prior transfers; however, the donor would be entitled to claim a refund of any gift tax paid and to have any unified credit used restored. That proposal would eliminate the usefulness of the leveraged gift of a collection.

The proposal described in the above paragraph was included in the Technical Corrections Bill of 1988 proposed by the House Ways and Means Committee. Fortunately, the total repeal of the leveraged gift technique was modified by the Conference Committee as it was finally adopted in the Technical and Miscellaneous Revenue Act of 1988 (TAMRA).

TAMRA added a new section 2036(c) with a cross reference to section 2501(d)(3) that under certain circumstances follows the 1984 Treasury Department proposal in treating a leveraged gift as not being a completed gift until the retained income interest expires. However, new section 2036(c)(6) creates an exception by providing that the retention of a "qualified trust income interest" in a trust is disregarded for purposes of section 2036(c). As before, the trust property is treated as retained by the transferor for the period during which the income interest continues. A "qualified trust income interest" is defined as any right to receive amounts determined solely by reference to the income from the property held in trust if (1) the retained right exists for a period not exceeding ten years, (2) the person holding the retained right is the person who transferred the property to the trust, and (3) the person is not a trustee of the trust.

Therefore, the leveraged gift techniques for a work of art will most likely still be useful if the transfer is made in trust for a period not exceeding ten years and the transferor is not the trustee. At this writing, caution is advised, since there are no proposed regulations to make it clear that non-income-producing property can be used to satisfy the requirements of being a "qualified trust income interest." Although regulation section 25.2512-

5(c) and Private Letter Ruling 8817042 do give some comfort in this regard, absolute certainty will have to await the issuance of regulations under new section 2036(c). At this time, as a further safeguard, we recommend that the trust agreement contain a provision that allows the beneficiary to require the trustee to convert the work of art to income-producing property.

Lifetime Sales

A lifetime sale of a collection generally results in a capital gain or a capital loss. A capital gain is taxable[153] and a capital loss is nondeductible[154] unless it can be shown that the collection was held as an investment property, which is discussed in detail in chapter 11. If the collection is ordinary income property, the collector will realize ordinary income on its sale.[155]

Testamentary Transfers

A collector who has not made a lifetime transfer of the collection must provide for its disposition on death. The fair market value of the collection, on the date of death or six months later, is included in the gross estate.[156] However, despite the potential tax disadvantage, the collector may prefer to enjoy possession of the collection throughout his or her lifetime.

Outright Transfer

A specific bequest in the will should be used to bequeath a collection outright to a noncharitable beneficiary or beneficiaries. See forms 6 and 7 on pages 647 and 649. The attorney should make sure that the items are sufficiently identified so that there is no confusion after the testator's death. If the beneficiary and the testator live in different cities, the problem of the cost of shipping should be considered. The cost is borne by the beneficiary unless a special clause is used in the will. See form 9 on page 653.

In *Estate of Ludwig Neugass*,[157] the decedent had a valuable art collection, some of which he wished his wife to have outright. His will provided that his wife was to have a right to take any items she chose within six months of his death. The IRS disallowed the marital deduction for the items chosen, alleging that such a right was a terminable interest, which does not qualify for the marital deduction. The Tax Court upheld the IRS, but the court of appeals reversed and held for the taxpayer.

It is safer to decide before the testator's death which items should be left to the surviving spouse and to leave those items outright. As the court in *Neugass* pointed out, the factor that determines whether the marital deduction is allowed is whether or not the action required by the surviving spouse is a mere formality, as opposed to being subject to a condition that may never be met.[158]

Transfer in Trust

A testator may wish to give the surviving spouse a life estate in a collection, with the remainder to their children on the spouse's death. The basic idea is to make one transfer cover two estates, with only one estate tax imposed. Although a legal life estate can be used, it is preferable to create a trust, because of its greater flexibility. The terms of the trust should specify who should pay for insurance, storage, and any other expenses. The life tenant may be given a special power of appointment, either inter vivos or testamentary, as to one or more or all of the items in the collection. The trustee should be given the power to cause any of the items to be sold, in which event the trust should provide how the proceeds are to be held and applied. That clause is necessary so that in the event of a family misfortune the life tenant is not left with a valuable collection and no money with which to pay bills. As always, the estate planner must be careful with the selection of the trustee and the powers given to the beneficiary, or the trust will be included in the life tenant's estate. The trust can be drafted so that it qualifies for the estate tax marital deduction.[159]

SELLING THE COLLECTION AFTER DEATH

Since a collection may constitute the bulk of a decedent's estate, the executor may have to sell all or a part of the collection in order to pay estate taxes and other administrative expenses. The sale may also be necessary to make sure that the decedent's spouse or children are financially secure and will receive income yearly. Commission expenses on the sale of a large collection can be very large. Therefore, a will must be prepared so that such commissions can be claimed as deductions on the federal estate tax return.

Section 2053(a)(2) provides:

> [T]he value of the taxable estate shall be determined by deducting from the value of the gross estate such amounts . . . for administrative expenses . . . as are allowable by the laws of the jurisdiction, whether within or without the United States, under which the estate is being administered.

Regulation section 20.2053-3(d)(2) provides:

> Expenses for selling property of the estate are deductible if the sale is necessary in order to pay the decedent's debts, expenses of administration or taxes, to preserve the estate, or to effect distribution. The phrase "expense for selling property" includes brokerage fees and other expenses attending the sale . . . .

That regulation has been in substantially similar form since 1919. The regulation imposes the requirement that the expenses be *necessary* for one of the stated purposes in order to be deductible, even though that requirement is not in the statute.

In *Sternberger's Estate*,[160] the Tax Court permitted a deduction for brokerage and legal fees incurred in connection with the sale of the decedent's residence, which the decedent's widow and daughter did not wish to occupy. The court stated that the expenses were properly allowable under New York law, and, even though the proceeds were not needed to pay the debts and expenses (and hence the residence automatically became a part of the residuary estate at the death of the decedent), a deduction was properly allowable under the predecessor of what is now section 2053(a)(2), since the executor was the one who actually made the sale.

In *Estate of Swayne*[161] the Tax Court reversed itself and disallowed similar expenses for selling a Connecticut residence because the sale was not "necessary" despite the fact that the sale was authorized by the local probate court. The court distinguished the case from *Sternberger* on the grounds that *Sternberger* involved New York law and did not raise the question of the necessity of the sale. Another distinction was that in *Swayne* the real property was specifically bequeathed, and in *Sternberger* it was part of the residue.

Estate of David Smith[162] involved a well-known artist who died owning 425 pieces of sculpture that he had created. At the time of his death, a contract with an art gallery was in existence that provided that the gallery had the exclusive right to sell the sculptures and receive commissions. That contract was renewed by his executors. The decedent's will did not specifically direct his executors to sell the sculptures but provided for his estate to go in trust for his children. The estate did sell a substantial number of the sculptures, some to satisfy claims against the estate and others to fund the trusts for his daughters. The commissions paid to the gallery were allowed by a New York surrogate's court on an intermediate accounting.

The issue in the case involved the deduction for the commissions paid to the gallery. The IRS said that the deduction for the commissions paid is limited by the "necessary" requirement of regulation section 20.2053-3(d)(2). The executor initially argued that the commissions were deductible in full because the sales were made to preserve the estate or to effect distribution of the estate or both. The executor contended that, because of the volatile nature of the art market, it was "necessary" to sell the sculptures in order to preserve the estate.

The majority opinion of the Tax Court, relying on *Swayne*, held that the commissions on the sale of the decedent's sculptures were allowable as deductions on the estate tax return only to the extent that the sales were "necessary" to pay administrative expenses, debts, and taxes. The court specifically cited the "necessary" provision of the regulations and added that the provision of the statute that deductions are permitted for expenses allowable under the applicable state law "established a threshold and not an exclusive condition; the requirement of [the] regulations must also be satisfied."

Five judges dissented from the decision of the Tax Court on the grounds that the test of the statute depends upon state law and that the "necessary" requirement of the regulations is invalid.

On appeal to the Second Circuit, the executors for the first time contested the validity of regulation section 20.2053-3(d)(2) and its "necessary" test. The Second Circuit did not pass on the legal issue of the validity of the regulation. Instead, the court said the case turns on the question of fact as to whether the gallery fees were "necessary" under section 222 of the New York Surrogate's Court Act, which required such fees to be necessary in order to be allowable. The court found that the question of the necessity of the gallery fees was not contested in the lower court (although they were approved on the accounting); therefore, the federal court could make a de novo inquiry into the factual necessity of the gallery fees. The Second Circuit then found the determination of the Tax Court in that regard was not clearly erroneous and affirmed the Tax Court decision.

One judge on the three-judge panel dissented and based his opinion on the dissent in the Tax Court and the Sixth Circuit opinion in *Estate of Park* (see page 614). The dissenting judge thought that the state surrogate's decision approving the gallery fees was binding on the federal courts and that the Tax Court had no authority to act as a surrogate Surrogate. Permission to appeal to the United States Supreme Court was denied.

The decision of the Second Circuit is questionable. Apparently, the court was saying that, if the commissions were so outrageous that they were contested at the probate court level and were allowed in whole or in part, there would not be a de novo inquiry by the Tax Court. That reasoning is incorrect, since the laws of the state are interpreted and administered by the courts of the state and not by the Tax Court.

Further, the "necessary" requirement contained in the New York statute appears to have been misinterpreted by the Second Circuit. That term has been replaced in a new statute by the term "reasonable and proper."[163] The revisers' note to the statute states that the new term is designed to incorporate the substance of its predecessor. Therefore, it is reasonable to conclude that the term "necessary" in the New York statute meant "reasonable and proper" and did not have the same meaning as the "necessary" requirement in regulation section 20.2053-3(d)(2).

In *Estate of Park*,[164] the Tax Court followed its decision in *Smith*, upholding the Commissioner's refusal to allow a deduction for the expenses of selling a residence that passed to four residuary legatees. The legatees had requested the executor to sell the house, and its sale was not "necessary" to raise cash in order to pay administrative expenses. Therefore, the Tax Court disallowed the selling expenses as an estate tax deduction.

On appeal to the Sixth Circuit, the Tax Court was reversed on the ground that the literal language of the statute permitting a deduction for expenses allowable under local law leaves the issue of deductibility to state law. The expenses involved were paid out of probate assets, were admittedly allowable under Michigan law, and hence, the Sixth Circuit held, were deductible under section 2053(a)(2). In effect, the Sixth Circuit held that the "necessary" requirement of the regulations was invalid.

The *Smith* case was followed in *Hibernia Bank*,[165] but was distinguished in *Estate of Joseph Vatter*.[166] In *Vatter* the decedent's will provided for the distribution of the residuary estate to a testamentary trust. Three parcels of rental properties, which were old and required maintenance, were part of the residuary estate. Because the trustee of the testamentary trust (a bank), would not accept the parcels as part of the trust, they were sold by the executrix. The Tax Court upheld the deductibility of the sale expenses as being necessary to "effect distribution" of the residuary estate, finding them to be allowable administration expenses both under New York law and IRS regulations, even though the entire proceeds of the sale were not needed to pay the estate's obligations for debts, expenses, and taxes. The *Vatter* case was decided by Judge Forrester, one of the dissenting Tax Court judges in *Smith*.

In Private Letter Ruling 7802006 the IRS followed *Park* in ruling that, since the selling expenses under consideration in the ruling were allowable under local Ohio law, that was enough to qualify them as deductible under section 2053(a)(2), and there was no need to establish that the expenses were "necessary," as required by the regulation. However, the ruling contained the following warning:

> The decision in the *Park* case will not be followed by the Service in disposing of similar cases outside the Sixth Circuit. In the Sixth Circuit, the Service is following *Park* for practical reasons only and may choose to litigate the issue again at some more opportune time in the future. Thus, since Ohio is in the Sixth Circuit, the deductibility of the administration expenses is determined by reference to state law alone.[167]

The case of *Estate of Vera T. Posen*,[168] decided December 10, 1980, was reviewed by the full Tax Court and contains an excellent summary of most of the recent cases. The Tax Court held that a New York estate could not deduct expenses incurred in selling a decedent's cooperative apartment, even though those expenses were allowable administration expenses under applicable New York state law, because the sale was not necessary to pay estate taxes, effect estate distribution, or preserve the estate, as required by regulation section 20.2053-3(d)(2). In so holding, the Tax Court upheld the validity of the regulation and noted that, under section 2053(a)(2), state law is not solely determinative of the deductibility of administrative expenses. The Tax Court distinguished *Vatter*, stating that in *Vatter* the sale of the real estate was necessary to "effect distribution," since the residuary trustee would not otherwise accept the property, whereas in *Posen* the sale of the cooperative apartment was made solely for the benefit of the estate's heir.

One judge dissented on the ground that the regulation was invalid because state law controlled the deduction of estate expenses. A second dissent, in which three other judges joined, agreed that the regulation was invalid, but noted that, even assuming its validity, the expenses were deductible because the sale was made in order to pay estate taxes and preserve the estate. Another dissenting judge thought that the regulation was valid, but agreed with the second dissent as to the reasons for the sale.

The Tax Court's opinion illustrates the split of opinion in the federal courts about the effect of state law on the deductibility of administrative expenses. The Fifth and Ninth Circuits follow the Tax Court in concluding that state law provides merely a threshold test for determining deductibility under section 2053(a)(2) and that the requirements of the Internal Revenue Service's regulations must also be satisfied. The Sixth and Seventh Circuits have taken the position that allowability of an expense under state law is itself determinative of deductibility as an administrative expense under section 2053(a)(2). The Second Circuit, to which *Posen* would be appealed, has not expressed an opinion as to the validity of the regulation.

In *Estate of Helen Ward DeWitt,*[169] decided in September 1987, the Tax Court once again refused to declare regulation section 20.2053-3(d)(2) and the "necessary" provision invalid. The case involved estate administration expenses that were approved by the New York state probate court as a deduction for federal estate tax purposes. The IRS had denied the deductions for executor's commissions, legal fees, accounting fees, investment counsel fees, and disbursements made by those persons. The Tax Court noted that administration expenses approved by a state court are deductible for federal estate tax purposes only if the state court's ruling is based on facts demonstrating that the expenses were actually and necessarily incurred in the administration of the estate. The Tax Court held that such proof was established for the attorney's fees, accountant's fees, and executors' commissions, but not for the fees paid to the investment adviser.

The final answer on the validity of regulation section 20.2053-3(d)(2) has not yet been given. It is clear that if the will contains a specific direction to sell, the expenses of the sale are deductible.[170] If there is no specific direction to sell, the expenses should be deductible if allowable by the local probate court, as is stated in section 2053(a). The "necessary" requirement of the regulations, which gives the Tax Court the power to question the local probate court, appears to us to be invalid.

The issue involved in *Estate of Streeter*[171] varies from the "necessary" requirement of regulation section 20.2053-3(d)(2). A collection was bequeathed in trust with a direction that it be sold by the trustees. The same persons were named as executors and trustees. The issue in the case concerned the deduction of sales commissions on the estate tax return. The executors transferred the collection to themselves in their capacity as trustees, and in that capacity signed the sales agreement with the auction house. The Tax Court held that the expenses were incurred by the trust on the sale and, therefore, were properly deductible only by the trust, not by the executors.

On appeal to the Third Circuit (first hearing), the Tax Court was reversed, and the commissions were allowed as a deduction on the estate tax return under section 2053(a)(2). The Third Circuit did not have to consider the validity of regulation section 20.2053-3(d)(2), since it held that the expenses were deductible under the regulations as written. The court found that the sole purpose of the trust was to effect distribution of the decedent's estate, and the duties imposed by the decedent on the trustees were those normally performed by executors. A dissenting opinion held that a valid trust was created and that the expenses were the expenses of the trustees, not the executors.

On rehearing before the full bench of the Third Circuit, the dissenting opinion in the first hearing was adopted, upholding the Tax Court. The majority held that a valid trust was in fact created, and that the expenses of the sale were the expenses of the trustees, not the executors. The Third Circuit noted that, had the executors been empowered and directed by the will to sell the collection, the sale expenses would have been deductible under regulation section 20.2053-3(d)(2).

The taxpayer had relied on section 2053(b) and the regulations thereunder, which pertained to expenses incurred in connection with nonprobate property. There are two categories of estate tax deductions: (1) those payable out of property subject to claims that are allowable by the law of the probate jurisdiction[172] and (2) those incurred in administering property that is included in the gross estate, but is not subject to claims.[173] Expenses of the first type are deductible under regulation section 20.2053-3(a) and expenses of the second type are deductible under regulation section 20.2053-8(a). The deductions in the second category do not include amounts pertaining to property passing through the probate estate, as was the case in *Streeter.*

The cases make it clear that, if the executor is directed to sell the collection, the expenses are allowed as a deduction under section 2053(a)(2) on the estate tax return. If no direction is included and the sale is made by the executors, the sale must run the risk of the application of the "necessary" requirement in the regulations. The estate planner must not make the mistake made in *Streeter:* leaving the collection to a trust and directing the trustee to sell the collection. Under those circumstances, the expenses would not be deductible, even if the "necessary" requirement of the regulation were finally held to be invalid.

Denial of Double Deductions

Before the Tax Reform Act of 1976, the allowability of sale expenses was important, not only for estate tax purposes but for income tax purposes, because Revenue Ruling 71-173[174] held that expenses allowable under section 2053 as a deduction on the estate tax return could also be offset against the selling price in computing the estate's taxable income. That ruling resulted in the expenses' being claimed as a deduction on the estate tax return and as a reduction of the selling price (which reduces the amount of taxable income) on the income tax return. The Tax Reform Act of 1976 changed that result by amending section 642(g) to limit the deduction for selling expenses to either the estate tax return or the income tax return. The statute eliminates the double deduction by including "an offset against the sales price of property in determining gain or loss" as the equivalent of a deduction. Revenue Ruling 71-173 no longer has any validity.[175] The new rule became effective January 1, 1977.[176]

Example: Mr. Collector died with a collection having a fair market value of $1,200,000 on the date of death. His will contained a direction to sell, and selling expenses of $200,000 were incurred.

The gross value of the collection at $1,200,000 should be included on schedule F of form 706 (the estate tax return). The executor has a choice with regard to the selling expenses. They can be claimed as a deduction on schedule J of form 706, with the result that for estate tax purposes the net amount taxable is $1,000,000 ($1,200,000 minus $200,000). For income tax purposes, the executor reports on the fiduciary income tax return (form 1041) the difference between the amount realized ($1,200,000) and the basis of the collection ($1,200,000), which was stepped-up under section 1014(a).

Alternatively, the selling expenses can be claimed as an offset on the fiduciary income tax return. For income tax purposes, the executor reports the difference between the amount realized less the selling expenses ($1,200,000 minus $200,000 equals $1,000,000) and the basis of the collection ($1,200,000). That arithmetic results in a $200,000 long-term capital loss on the sale. For estate tax purposes, the estate is taxable on the full

$1,200,000. There is no $200,000 deduction on schedule J of form 706.

The executor must compare the tax under each alternative in each case to see which alternative produces the best result. Consideration must now be given to the fact that many estates owe no federal estate tax, as a result of the unlimited marital deduction[177] introduced by ERTA.

THE MUSEUM AND RESTRICTED GIFTS

A museum's responsibility *vis-à-vis* its collection is quite different from that of the artist, collector, or dealer.[178] Museums are commonly viewed as charitable trust organizations. A trust is a fiduciary relationship whereby a party known as a trustee (in this case, the museum) holds property that must be administered for the benefit of others, known as beneficiaries. In a charitable trust the beneficiary is the public, or a broad segment of the public, and the property must be used to benefit the public.

At its core, a museum is an educational organization. Its primary purpose is to collect objects deemed worthy of preservation and to instruct the public through the presentation of exhibits and other activity generated through critical collecting. As an educational organization, a museum is obliged to promote the unfettered competition of ideas. As a charitable trust, a museum's first obligation in its collection activity is to benefit the public. Therefore, when objects are accepted for accession, that is inclusion in a museum's collection, the acceptance should be based on a good-faith judgment that such objects are appropriate for the collection.

In the past museums accepted restricted gifts as a matter of course, though not always happily. A restricted gift is one offered to a museum and accepted by it with legally binding conditions as to the gift's use or disposition. An example of such a gift would be a painting donated with the proviso that it be exhibited or retained forever. Historically, it was relatively easy for a museum to accept restricted gifts: if the object in question was of great interest to the museum, it would be pleased to acquire it; if the museum's collection was modest, it had less bargaining power than its more affluent sisters and would readily accept such a gift; if it was a prestigious organization being offered a first-rate work of art, accepting restrictions on the gift was easy to rationalize.

Over the last twenty years, however, interest has increased in the role of museums and their obligations to the public. Accordingly, the museum community, in rethinking its position on restricted gifts, has published an array of guidelines through its various interest groups, ranging from caution about to downright discouragement of the acceptance of restricted gifts. That discouragement is amply buffered by the principles of trust law: that is, as trustees, museums owe a strict duty of loyalty to their beneficiaries, the public. In the case of a restricted gift, the donor in essence is requiring the trustee to honor the donor's wishes over and above the interests of the trustee's beneficiary. Because of the museum's role as educator, that could give rise to a conflict of interest whereby, for example, in accepting a restricted gift of a collection of art from a particular period, a museum might be obligated forever to display the collection even if later scholarship might not consider the collection appropriate for exhibit, and the museum could put its space to better use.

That the museum community is taking a sterner view of restricted gifts is all the more notable because in today's market few of them can afford to buy anything worth studying. Philippe de Montebello, director of the Metropolitan Museum of Art in New York City, noted recently that he could not buy one pastel by Degas with the museum's total acquisition fund for all departments.[179]

Although most donors are aware that museums are heavily dependent upon their largess, it is nevertheless advisable for a donor to discuss with the museum the nature of any restrictions he or she intends to impose on a prospective gift to that organization. Such discussion may prevent the occurrence of a lawsuit along the lines of *Reed v. Whitney Museum of Art*,[180] in which the donor sued the museum for failure to abide by certain conditions alleged to have been accepted. The action was withdrawn when the museum agreed to relinquish the gift to another museum.

Museums have also been subject to criticism for being willing, on occasion, to accept works of art having questionable value or provenance. Such actions by a museum are in violation of its responsibilities as a charitable trust organization. Moreover, both museums and prospective donors should be aware that with respect to all gifts of artwork that leave a museum's collection (are "deaccessioned") within two years following the date of their receipt, the regulations require the filing of form 8282. That is, museums must report to the IRS the sale of any such artwork and the price at which it was sold. This is of particular importance to the donor as the IRS, cross-checking with computers, is now able to challenge the donor on his or her individual income tax return in the event of an unseemly discrepancy between the price the museum sold the work of art for and the amount of the original deduction taken by the donor.

NOTES
to Chapter 12

1. Material in this chapter has appeared in part in the following: Lerner, *Estate Planning for the Art Collector*, in P-H, SUCCESSFUL ESTATE PLANNING IDEAS AND METHODS (1988); Lerner, *Planning the Collector's Estate*, in PLI, REPRESENTING ARTISTS, COLLECTORS, AND DEALERS 19 (R. Lerner ed. 1985); Lerner, *Transferring Tangible Property to Charitable Organizations*, 114 TR. & EST. 402 (1975); Lerner, *Transfers of Tangible Personal Property to Charity*, N.Y.L.J., June 21, 1976, at 1; Lerner, *New Carryover Basis Rules*, 4 EST. PLAN. 72 (1977); Lerner, *Planning the Collector's Estate*, in PLI, ART LAW 11 (R. Lerner ed. 1988).

2. Treas. Reg. §§ 1.170A-1(a)(2)(ii), (c), 1.170A-13.

3. Treas. Reg. § 25.2512-1.

4. Treas. Reg. § 20.2031-6.

5. The discussion below encompasses the ideas presented in the proposed recommendation by the Washington subcommittee on valuation of tangible personal property of the ABA's Committee on Estate and Gift Taxes, dated June 19, 1975, and a letter from James H. Lewis, council director to the committee, dated January 4, 1975.

6. R. PAUL, FEDERAL ESTATE AND GIFT TAXATION § 18.03 (1942).

7. Chicago Ry. Equip. Co. v. Blair, 20 F.2d 10 (7th Cir. 1927).

8. Treas. Reg. §§ 20.2031-6, 25.2512-1, 1.170A-1(c)(2).

9. Treas. Reg. § 20.2031-6.

10. Treas. Reg. §§ 25.2512-1, 1.170A-1(c)(2).

11. *See supra* note 5.

12. Clark, *Fine Art: Administering this Valuable Estate Asset*, 117 TR. & EST. 132 (1978); Vencel & Whitman, *Giving Art to Museums: Special Considerations for the Estate Planner*, 122 TR. & EST. 35 (1983); Weitman, Jr., *The Changing Collectibles Market*, 128 TR. & EST. 10 (1989).

13. Treas. Reg. § 1.170A-13T.

14. Tax Reform Act of 1984, § 155(a)(2); Treas. Reg. § 1.170A-13(c)(1).

15. JOINT COMMITTEE ON TAXATION STAFF, GENERAL EXPLANATION OF THE REVENUE PROVISIONS OF THE TAX REFORM ACT OF 1984, at 506 (1984).

16. Treas. Reg. § 1.170A-13(c)(1).

17. Tax Reform Act of 1984, § 155(a)(2); Treas. Reg. § 1.170A-13(c)(3)(i).

18. Treas. Reg. § 1.170A-13(c)(3)(iv)(B).

19. Tax Reform Act of 1984, § 155(a)(2); Treas. Reg. § 1.170A-13(c)(5)(i).

20. Treas. Reg. § 1.170A-13(c)(5)(iv)(B) does allow a party to the transaction to be a qualified appraiser if the property is donated within two months of the date of acquisition and its appraised value does not exceed its acquisition price.

21. Treas. Reg. § 1.170A-13(c)(5)(iv)(F).

22. If the appraiser is not a "qualified appraiser," he or she cannot prepare a "qualified appraisal," and, therefore, the donor cannot attach a qualified appraisal to his or her return when it is due. The question of who is a qualified appraiser is raised on audit, a time after the due date of the donor's tax return. *See* Treas. Reg. § 1.170A-13(c)(3)(i)(A).

23. Treas. Reg. § 1.170A-13(c)(6)(i). There is one narrow exception for fees paid to an association that regulates appraisers.

24. GENERAL EXPLANATION, *supra* note 15, at 506.

25. Treas. Reg. §§ 1.170A-1(a)(2)(ii), 1.170A-13(b).

26. *See* Rev. Rul. 77-225, 1977-2 C.B. 73.

27. I.R.S. News Release, IR-68 (Feb. 1, 1968); *see* O'Connell, *Defending Art Valuations for Tax Purposes*, 115 TR. & EST. 604 (1976) (includes an excellent discussion of the workings of the IRS Art Panel). The Art Panel was expanded from twelve to twenty-two members in 1984 to provide expertise in pre-Columbian, Far Eastern, and Asian art. I.R.S. News Release, IR-84-7 (Jan. 16, 1984).

28. Wehausen v. Commissioner, 56 T.C.M. (CCH) 229 (1988) (involves valuation of mathematical journals); Rhoades v. Commissioner, 55 T.C.M. (CCH) 1159 (1988) (opal); Williams v. Commissioner, 54 T.C.M. (CCH) 1471 (1988) (Indian artifacts); Goldstein v. Commissioner, 89 T.C. 535 (1987); Shein v. Commissioner, 53 T.C.M. (CCH) 1292 (1987) (paintings); Frates v. Commissioner, 53 T.C.M. (CCH) 96 (1987) (paintings and sculpture); Angell v. Commissioner, 52 T.C.M. (CCH) 939 (1986) (paintings; court upheld civil fraud penalties for gross overvaluation); Biagiotti v. Commissioner, 52 T.C.M. (CCH) 588 (1986) (pre-Columbian and Mayan art objects); Koftinow, 52 T.C.M. (CCH) 261 (1986) (statue valued using French Grid system; see Action on Decision 87-023, in which IRS said it would resist such an approach); Neely v. Commissioner, 85 T.C. 934 (1985) (African art; *see* Teitell, *Deductions for African Art*, N.Y.L.J., Mar. 17, 1986, at 1); Johnson v. Commissioner, 85 T.C. 469

(1985) (Indian artifacts); Lio v. Commissioner, 85 T.C. 56 (1985) (lithographs); Harken v. Commissioner, 50 T.C.M. (CCH) 994 (1985); Skala v. Commissioner, 49 T.C.M. (CCH) 419 (1985) (vintage aircraft); Krauskopf v. Commissioner, 48 T.C.M. (CCH) 620 (1984) (racing car); Glen v. Commissioner, 79 T.C. 208 (1982) (tape recordings of interviews with noted scientists and I.R.C. § 170(e)(1)); Isbell v. Commissioner, 44 T.C.M. (CCH) 1143 (1982) (Han Dynasty ceramic jar); Hawkins v. Commissioner, 44 T.C.M. (CCH) 715 (1982) (mosaic table purchased from Vatican Studio); Peterson v. Commissioner, 44 T.C.M. (CCH) 650 (1982) (ivory carvings); Monaghan v. Commissioner, 42 T.C.M. (CCH) 27 (1981) (portrait); Reynolds v. Commissioner, 43 T.C.M. (CCH) 115 (1981) (water colors); Raznatovich v. Commissioner, 41 T.C.M. (CCH) 79 (1980) (unindexed negatives of aerial photography); Sylvester v. Commissioner, 37 T.C.M. (CCH) 1847 (1978); Vanderhook v. Commissioner, 36 T.C.M. (CCH) 1394 (1977); Furstenberg v. United States, 78-1 U.S. Tax Cas. (CCH) ¶ 9267 (Ct. Cl. 1978), 79-1 U.S. Tax Cas. (CCH) ¶ 9280 (Ct. Cl. 1979), 595 F.2d 603 (1979); Sevier v. Commissioner, 36 T.C.M. (CCH) 1392 (1977); Franklin v. Commissioner, 77-2 U.S. Tax Cas. (CCH) ¶ 9267 (W.D.N.C. 1977); Peters v. Commissioner, 36 T.C.M. (CCH) 552 (1977); Gordon v. Commissioner, 35 T.C.M. (CCH) 1227 (1976); Posner v. Commissioner, 35 T.C.M. (CCH) 943 (1976); Cupler v. Commissioner, 64 T.C. 946 (1975) (unique item of medical equipment); Jarre v. Commissioner, 64 T.C. 183 (1975); Farber v. Commissioner, 33 T.C.M. (CCH) 673 (1974), *aff'd*, 76-1 U.S. Tax Cas. (CCH) ¶ 9118 (2d Cir. 1974); Lee v. United States, 75-1 U.S. Tax Cas. (CCH) ¶ 9165 (C.D.Cal. 1975); Rupke v. Commissioner, 32 T.C.M. (CCH) 1098 (1973); Barcus v. Commissioner, 32 T.C.M. (CCH) 660 (1973); Winokur v. Commissioner, 90 T.C. 733 (1988) (paintings); Sammons v. Commissioner, 838 F.2d 330 (9th Cir. 1988) (Indian artifacts—limited to cost); Mast v. Commissioner, 56 T.C.M. (CCH) 1522 (1989) (glass stereoscopic negatives); Saltzman v. United States, 89-2 U.S. Tax Cas. (CCH) ¶ 9391 (E.D.N.Y. 1989) (videotape of Bolshoi Ballet valued at cost).

29. Anselmo v. Commissioner, 80 T.C. 872 (1983), *aff'd*, 757 F.2d 1208 (11th Cir. 1985); *see also* cases cited note 28; Ford v. Commissioner, 46 T.C.M. (CCH) No. 556 (1983); Teitell, *Charitable Donations of Art Works: The Special Considerations Involved*, 51 J. TAX'N 326 (1979); Zobel & Shore, *The IRS Crackdown on Valuation Abuses: How Far Does It Go; What Does It Portend?*, 52 J. TAX'N 276 (1980); Melvin, *Valuation of Charitable Contributions of Works of Art*, 60 TAXES 756 (1982); Anthoine, *Charitable Contributions After the 1986 Tax Act and Problems in Valuation of Appreciated Property*, 11 L. & ARTS 283 (1987).

30. Anthoine, *supra* note 29, contains an excellent discussion of recent valuation cases and the trend toward looking to the applicable retail market for comparables. *See* Dubin v. Commissioner, 52 T.C.M. (CCH) 456 (1986).

31. Skripak v. Commissioner, 84 T.C. 265 (1985).

32. *See also* Calder v. Commissioner, 85 T.C. 713 (1985).

33. Hunter v. Commissioner, 51 T.C.M. (CCH) 1533 (1986).

34. *See also* Jennings v. Commissioner, 56 T.C.M. (CCH) 595 (1988).

35. Lightman v. Commissioner, 50 T.C.M. (CCH) 266 (1985).

36. Rhoades v. Commissioner, 55 T.C.M. (CCH) 1159 (1988).

37. Biagiotti v. Commissioner, 52 T.C.M. (CCH) 588 (1986).

38. Tax Reform Act of 1984, § 155(c)(1)(B); *see* Hasson, *Foundations and Other Charities Benefit from New Law*, 61 J. TAX'N 392 (1984); GENERAL EXPLANATION, *supra* note 15, at 511 (specifically stating that the penalty provisions apply to returns filed after December 31, 1984, on which deductions are claimed for contributions made before 1985).

39. I.R.C. § 6659(c).

40. I.R.C. § 6659(f)(2).

41. Tax Reform Act of 1984, § 158(a), *amending* I.R.C. § 6601(e)(2); Tax Reform Act of 1984, § 144(a), *amending* I.R.C. § 6621(d).

42. Tax Reform Act of 1984, § 155(b), *adding* I.R.C. § 6050L. *See* Treas. Reg. § 1.6050-1T.

43. Tax Reform Act of 1984, § 156; 31 U.S.C.A. § 330 (West 1983 & Supp. 1989); 31 C.F.R. §§ 10.77-.97 (1989) (adopted at 50 Fed. Reg. 42,016 (Oct. 17, 1985)).

44. GENERAL EXPLANATION, *supra* note 15, at 510.

45. Tax Reform Act of 1984, § 155(c)(2)(A).

46. Rev. Rul. 67-461, 1967-2 C.B. 125.

47. Treas. Reg. § 1.212-1(l).

48. Treas. Reg. § 20.2053-3(d)(1).

49. The Tax Reform Act of 1986 lowered the maximum ordinary income tax rate to 38.5 percent for 1987 and 28 percent for 1988. The maximum tax rate on capital gains was increased from 20 percent for 1986 to 28 percent for 1987 and years thereafter. A 33 percent ordinary income tax rate applies in 1988 and thereafter to specified ranges of income, e.g., between $71,900 and $149,250 for married individuals filing joint returns and surviving spouses.

50. *See generally* Anthoine, *Deductions for Charitable Contributions of Appreciated Property—The Art World*, 35 TAX L. REV. 239 (1980); Speiler, *The Favored Tax Treatment of Purchasers of Art*, 80 COLUM. L. REV. 214 (1980); Feld, *Artists, Art Collectors and Income Tax*, 60 B.U.L. Rev. 625 (1980); Symposium, *Law and the Arts*, 85 DICK. L. REV. 182 (1981); Auten & Rudney, *Tax Reform and the Price of Donating Appreciated Property*, 33 TAX NOTES 285

(1986); Sanders & Toolson, *Planning for Charitable Giving After the Tax Reform Act of 1986*, TAXES (June 1987); Wittenbach & Milani, *A Flowchart Focusing on the Individual Charitable Contribution*, TAXES (Apr. 1988); Anthoine, *supra* note 29.

51. I.R.C. §§ 170(b)(1)(A)(i)-(viii), (E)(i)-(iii), 509(a); Treas. Reg. § 1.170A-9.

52. I.R.C. §§ 170(b)(1)(B), 509(a).

53. I.R.C. §§ 170(b)(1)(C)(iv), 1221; Treas. Reg. §§ 1.170A-8(d)(3), 1.170A-4(b)(2).

54. I.R.C. §§ 1221(d), 170(e)(1)(A); Treas. Reg. §§ 1.170A-8(d)(3), 1.170A-4(b)(2).

55. I.R.C. § 1023(a).

56. Fullerton v. Commissioner, 22 T.C. 372 (1954); Feber v. Commissioner, 22 T.C. 261 (1954). That assumes that the artist's estate is not deemed to be carrying on a trade or business, but is merely conducting an orderly administration of the artist's estate. *See* Strasser v. Commissioner, 52 T.C.M. (CCH) 1140 (1986).

57. Sandler v. Commissioner, 52 T.C.M. (CCH) 563 (1986); *see also* Lio v. Commissioner, 85 T.C. 61 (1986).

58. I.R.C. § 170(b)(1)(A).

59. I.R.C. § 170(b)(1)(B). The limitation was increased from 20 to 30 percent by the Tax Reform Act of 1984, effective for contributions made in taxable years ending after July 18, 1984.

60. I.R.C. § 170(b)(1)(F).

61. I.R.C. § 170(e)(1)(A); Treas. Reg. § 1.170A-4(a)(1); *see* Maniscalco v. Commissioner, 80-2 U.S. Tax Cas. (CCH) ¶ 9717 (6th Cir. 1980), 632 F.2d 6 (1980), *aff'g* 37 T.C.M. (CCH) 1174 (1978); Beghe, *The Artist, the Art Market and the Income Tax*, 29 TAX L. REV. 491 (1974); Anthoine, *supra* note 50; Bell, *Changing IRC 170(e)(1)(A): For Art's Sake*, 37 CASE W. RES. L. REV. 536 (1987).

62. *See* Orchard v. Commissioner, 34 T.C.M. (CCH) 205 (1975) (opera tapes held less than six months not capital gain property). *See also* Glen v. Commissioner, 79 T.C. 208 (1982) (valuation of tape recordings of interviews with noted scientists); Ford v. Commissioner, 46 T.C.M. (CCH) 1353 (1983).

63. I.R.C. § 170(d)(1)(A), (b)(1)(B) last sentence.

64. I.R.C. § 170(b)(1)(C)(i).

65. I.R.C. § 170(d)(1)(A), (b)(1)(C)(ii).

66. I.R.C. § 170(b)(1)(C)(iii), (e)(1).

67. I.R.C. § 170(b)(1)(C)(i), (e)(1)(B)(ii).

68. I.R.C. § 170(b)(1)(D)(ii).

69. I.R.C. § 4942(j)(3). Contributions to a private operating foundation are treated like contributions to a public charity. *See* Treas. Reg. § 53.4942(b)-1.

70. I.R.C. § 170(e)(5)(B). The rule is effective for contributions made between July 19, 1984, and December 31, 1994.

71. I.R.C. § 170(e)(1)(B)(i); Treas. Reg. § 1.170A-4(b)(3).

72. I.R.C. §§ 170(b)(1)(A), (C)(1).

73. Treas. Reg. § 1.170A-4(b)(3)(ii), (i). *See* Anthoine, *supra* notes 29 & 50.

74. *See* Isbell v. Commissioner, 44 T.C.M. (CCH) 1143 (1982).

75. Treas. Reg. § 1.170A-4(b)(3)(ii).

76. 115 Cong. Rec. H40869 (bound ed. 1969); 115 Cong. Rec. H13038 (daily ed. Dec. 23, 1969).

77. *See also* Priv. Ltr. Rul. 8536022 (condominium to charity: unrelated use); Priv. Ltr. Rul. 8439005 (manuscripts to university: related use); Priv. Ltr. Rul. 8333019 (art collection to museum: related use). *See* Coleman v. Commissioner, 56 T.C.M. (CCH) 710 (1988) (horse to American Cancer Society: unrelated use); Jennings v. Commissioner, 56 T.C.M. (CCH) 595 (1988) (paintings to cancer society, hospital, and college: unrelated use).

78. I.R.C. § 57(a)(6). A detailed description of the alternative minimum tax is beyond the scope of this book. *See generally* Kern, *The Alternative Minimum Tax for Individuals*, Taxes (May 1987).

79. *See* General Explanation, *supra* note 15, at 444; Sanders & Toolson, *supra* note 50; Auten & Rudney, *supra* note 50; Brachtl & Peller, *The Chilling Effect of the AMT on Charitable Contributions*, 128 Tr. & Est. 24 (1989).

80. Rev. Rul. 57-293, 1957-2 C.B. 153; Rev. Rul. 58-455, 1958-2 C.B. 100.

81. I.R.C. § 170(f) was renumbered I.R.C. § 170(a)(3) by Tax Reform Act of 1969, § 201(a)(1), Pub. L. No. 91-172, 83 Stat. 487, 562 (1969). *See* Treas. Reg. §§ 1.170-1(d)(2), 1.170A-5.

82. Treas. Reg. §§ 1.170A-5(b) example 5, 1.170A-7(a)(2)(i).

83. See I.R.S. Notice 89-24 (Feb. 17, 1989), which provides guidance to taxpayers in determining the present value of an annuity, an interest for life or for a term of years, or a remainder or reversionary interest pursuant to methods established under I.R.C. § 7520. The provision, added by the Technical and Miscellaneous Revenue Act of 1988, Pub. L. No. 100-647, applies to gifts made after April 30, 1989, and to the estates of decedents who die after that date.

84. Treas. Reg. § 1.170A-5(a)(4). *See also* Treas. Reg. § 1.170A-13(b)(2)(G), 1.170A-13(c)(2)(D).

85. Treas. Reg. § 25-2511-1(d). *See also* Rev. Rul. 77-300, 1977-2 C.B. 352, which deals with the gift tax question on split-interest gifts.

86. *Id.*

87. Treas. Reg. §§ 1.170A-5(b) example 1, 1.170A-5(b) example 2, 1.170A-7.

88. Tidd, *Charitable Remainder Trusts: Funding and Investment Considerations*, 57 TAXES 577 (1979) (discusses why tangible personal property should never be put in inter vivos charitable remainder trust).

89. Treas. Reg. §§ 1.170A-5(a)(2), 1.170A-7(b)(1)(i); I.R.C. § 170(f)(3)(B)(ii).

90. Winokur v. Commissioner, 90 T.C. 733 (1988). See also Priv. Ltr. Rul. 833019; Priv. Ltr. Rul. 8535019.

91. Rev. Rul. 57-293, 1957-2 C.B. 153. *See also* Priv. Ltr. Rul. 7728046; Priv. Ltr. Rul. 7934082; Note, *Contributions of Partial Interests to Charity*, 52 J. TAX'N 112 (1980).

92. I.R.C. § 2033.

93. *Supra* notes 78 and 79.

94. *See* Rev. Rul. 67-246, 1967-2 C.B. 104; I.R.C. § 512(a)(1).

95. I.R.C. § 170(f)(3)(A).

96. I.R.C. § 170(f)(2)(B); Treas. Reg. § 1.170A-6(c); *see* Note, *Denial or Charitable Deduction for the Use of Property*, 74 DICK. L. REV. 290 (1970).

97. Treas. Reg. §§ 1.170A-6(a)(2), 1.170A-7(a)(2)(i).

98. *See* Garibaldi, *Gift Annuities*, 30 N.Y.U. INST. FED. TAX'N 117 (1972); Note, *Private Annuities*, 23 VAND. L. REV. 675 (1970); Teitell, *Federal Tax Implications of Charitable Gift Annuities*, 113 TR. & EST. 642 (1974); Teitell, *Charitable Gift Annuities*, N.Y.L.J., Oct. 21, 1985, at 1; Teitell, *Technical Corrections and Miscellaneous Revenue Act of 1988*, N.Y.L.J., Nov. 21, 1988, at 3.

99. Treas. Reg. § 1.170A-1(d).

100. Rev. Rul. 69-74, 1969-1 C.B. 43; Treas. Reg. § 1.1011-2(a)(4); Note, *Private Annuities*, *supra* note 98.

101. *See* I.R.C. § 1011(b); Treas. Reg. §§ 1.1011-2, 1.170A-4(c)(2); Whittaker, *Dealing with Outright Gifts to Charity in Kind*, 30 N.Y.U. INST. FED. TAX'N 45 (1972); Ginsburg, *Bargain Sales and Charitable Gift Annuities*, in PLI, PRIVATE FOUNDATIONS TAX EXEMPTION AND CHARITABLE CONTRIBUTIONS UNDER THE TAX REFORM ACT OF 1969, at 49 (S. Weithorn ed. 1970); Moore, *Outright Charitable Giving: Sophisticated Use of Old Techniques and Development of New Techniques*, 42 N.Y.U. INST. FED. TAX'N 27 (1984); Weithorn & Leuhring, *Special Techniques for Charitable Giving: Making the Most of the Unusual*, 44 N.Y.U. INST. FED. TAX'N 37 (1986). *See also* Estate of Bullard v. Commissioner, 87 T.C. 261 (1986) (application of I.R.C. § 170(e)(1) to bargain sale).

102. Kluge v. Commissioner, 41 T.C.M. (CCH) 690 (1981).

103. Blake v. Commissioner, 42 T.C.M. (CCH) 1336 (1981), *aff'd*, 697 F.2d 473 (2d Cir. 1982).

104. Ford v. Commissioner, 46 T.C.M. (CCH) 1353 (1983).

105. I.R.C. § 2055(a).

106. I.R.C. § 170(e)(1)(B)(i); Treas. Reg. § 20.2055-1(a)(4).

107. N.Y. Est. Powers & Trusts Law § 5-3.3 (McKinney 1967); *In re* Cairo, 35 A.D.2d 76, 312 N.Y.S.2d 925 (2d Dep't 1970), *aff'd without opinion*, 29 N.Y.2d 527, 272 N.E.2d 574, 324 N.Y.S.2d 81 (1971). Section 5-3.3 was repealed, effective July 7, 1981. The memorandum in support of repeal points out that New York was one of only eight American jurisdictions that imposed restrictions on testamentary dispositions to charity and that the New York provision could be easily circumvented.

108. I.R.C. §§ 508(d)(2), (a), (e), 2055(e)(1); Treas. Reg. § 20.2055-5(b).

109. Rudick, *Bounty Twice Blessed*, 16 Tax L. Rev. 273, 304 (1961). Before January 1, 1982, the marital deduction was the greater of $250,000 or one-half the adjusted gross estate. The charitable deduction was subtracted after determining the marital deduction.

110. I.R.C. §§ 2055(e)(2)(A), 664(d); Treas. Reg. § 20.2055(e)(1).

111. Treas. Reg. § 1.664-3(a)(1).

112. Treas. Reg. § 1.664-1(a)(3). *See also* Treas. Reg. § 1.170A-6(c)(3)(iii).

113. A contrary view, with which we disagree, is expressed in Tidd, *Charitable Remainder Trusts: Funding and Investment Considerations*, 57 Taxes 577 (1979), in which Mr. Tidd expresses the opinion that

> while an individual is generally ill-advised to place tangible personal property in an inter vivos charitable remainder trust, there is no reason, generally speaking, why such property should not be placed in a testamentary charitable remainder trust.

114. A detailed analysis of section 2056(b)(7) is beyond the scope of this book. *See* Weiss, *New Estate Planning Focus*, 55 J. Tax'n 274 (1981); Garlock, *Estate Tax Unlimited Marital Deduction*, 56 J. Tax'n 236 (1982); Blattmachr, *The New Estate Tax Marital Deduction*, Tr. & Est., Jan. 1982; PLI, Planning and Drafting for the Marital Deduction (L. Hirschson ed. 1982); PLI, 19th Annual Estate Planning Institute (C. Feldman & A. Parker ed. 1988).

115. Estate of Robinson v. Commissioner, 46 A.F.T.R.2d (P-H) ¶ 6185 (E.D. Tenn. 1980).

116. Under section 2044(a) the value of the QTIP trust is includable in the gross estate of the surviving spouse.

117. That was the congressional intent. *See* STAFF OF THE JOINT COMMITTEE ON TAXATION, GENERAL EXPLANATION OF THE ECONOMIC RECOVERY TAX ACT OF 1981, at 236-37 n.4, 238 n.5 (1981).

118. *See id.* at 238 n.5.

119. I.R.C. § 2055(e)(2)(B).

120. Treas. Reg. § 20.2055-2(e)(2)(i).

121. Treas. Reg. §§ 20.2055-2(e)(1)(ii), 25.2522(c)-3(c)(1)(ii). *See generally* Lerner, *Final Regulations Under Section 2055(e)(4)*, 62 J. TAX'N 300 (1985).

122. I.R.C. §§ 2055(e)(2), 2522(c)(2).

123. Treas. Reg. § 1.664-3(a)(1), (3); *see* Rev. Rul. 73-610, 1973-2 C.B. 213.

124. Treas. Reg. §§ 1.170A-7(b)(1)(i), 20.2055-2(e)(2)(i), 25.2522(c)-3(c)(2)(i). *See generally* Stephenson, *Tax Benefits of Gifts Increased as a Result of Several Provisions in New Tax Law*, 55 J. TAX'N 218 (1981).

125. *See* T. CRAWFORD, THE VISUAL ARTIST'S GUIDE TO THE NEW COPYRIGHT LAW (1978); M. NIMMER, NIMMER ON COPYRIGHT (1988); N. BOORSTYN, COPYRIGHT LAW (1981); chapter 8.

126. The House Committee Report on H.R. 4242 (ERTA) points out at 184 the inconsistency between the copyright law and the tax law, but does not state specifically that the inconsistency is the reason for the change in the tax law.

127. I.R.C. § 2055(e)(4)(A).

128. I.R.C. § 2055(e)(4)(B).

129. I.R.C. § 2055(e)(4)(C).

130. I.R.C. § 2055(e)(4)(D).

131. The House Committee Report on H.R. 4242 (ERTA) concluded that the rule allowing a deduction in such cases should apply only for estate and gift tax purposes and not for income tax purposes.

132. *See* 3 NIMMER, *supra* note 125, at § 10.06. Section 201(d)(1) of the Copyright Act of 1976 provides that ownership of copyright "may be bequeathed by will or pass as personal property by the applicable laws of intestate succession." Section 204(a) of the Act provides that "a transfer of copyright ownership, other than by operation of law, is not valid unless an instrument of conveyance, or a note or memorandum of the transfer, is in writing and signed by the owner of the rights conveyed or such owner's duly authorized agent."

133. *See* Treas. Reg. § 20.2055-2(e)(1)(ii)(e) example (1).

134. For a discussion of copyright interests in community property states, see Bauman & Hoffman, *Estate Planning for Individuals in the Entertainment Industry*, 31 U.S.C. L. CENTER TAX INST. 875 (1979); Patry, *Copyright and Com-*

munity Property: The Question of Preemption, 28 BULL. COPYRIGHT SOC'Y 237 (1981).

135. That interpretation was confirmed in the ERTA GENERAL EXPLANATION, *supra* note 117, at 259.

136. I.R.C. § 2055(e)(4)(A).

137. I.R.C. § 170(e)(1)(A).

138. I.R.C. §§ 2001(c), 2502(a).

139. I.R.C. § 2523.

140. I.R.C. § 2513.

141. I.R.C. § 2035(c).

142. I.R.C. § 2503(b)

143. I.R.C. § 2035(b)(2).

144. I.R.C. § 2035(d).

145. *See also* I.R.C. § 1014(b)(10), added by the Technical Corrections Act of 1982.

146. *See* Roemer v. Commissioner, 46 T.C.M. (CCH) 1176 (1983); Neuwirth, *How to Protect Lifetime Transfers from Being Included in the Estate of the Transferor*, TAX'N FOR LAWS. (May-June 1982).

147. I.R.C. § 2032(a).

148. I.R.C. § 2032(c) (effective for decedents who die after July 18, 1984).

149. Treas. Reg. §§ 20.2031-7(f) table A, 20.2031-7(f) table B, 25.2512-5(f).

150. I.R.S. Notice 89-24 (Feb. 17, 1989).

151. On the topic of leveraged gifts, *see generally* U.S. TRUST CO., PRACTICAL DRAFTING, 403 (Apr. 1984); *id.* at 1071 (Jan. 1987); *id.* at 1307 (Oct. 1987); *id.* at 1388 (Jan. 1988). *See* Rev. Rul. 79-280, 1979-2 C.B. 340; Priv. Ltr. Rul. 8717051; Priv. Ltr. Rul. 8642028; Priv. Ltr. Rul. 8817042.

152. I.R.C. § 2036(a)(1).

153. I.R.C. §§ 1001, 1002.

154. I.R.C. § 262.

155. I.R.C. § 1221(3).

156. I.R.C. § 2033.

157. Neugass v. Commissioner, 77-1 U.S. Tax Cas. (CCH) ¶ 13192 (2d Cir. 1977), *rev'g and remanding* 65 T.C. 188 (1976).

158. *See* Rev. Rul. 82-184, 1982-2 C.B. 215.

159. *See* I.R.C. § 2056(b)(7). See also the discussion of QTIP trusts below.

160. Sternberger's Estate v. Commissioner, 18 T.C. 836 (1952), *aff'd*, 207 F.2d 600 (2d Cir. 1953), *rev'd on other issue*, 348 U.S. 187 (1955).

161. Estate of Swayne v. Commissioner, 43 T.C. 190 (1964); *see* Estate of Carson v. Commissioner, 35 T.C.M. (CCH) 330 (1976).

162. Estate of David Smith v. Commissioner, 57 T.C. 650 (1972), *aff'd*, 510 F.2d 479 (2d Cir.), *cert. denied*, 423 U.S. 827 (1975).

163. New York Surrogate's Court Act section 222 was in effect in the *Smith* case. That section was succeeded as of September 1, 1967 by what is now N.Y. Est. Powers & Trusts Law § 11-1.1(b)(22) (McKinney Supp. 1989).

164. Estate of Park v. Commissioner, 475 F.2d 673 (6th Cir. 1973), *rev'g* 57 T.C. 705 (1972). *See* Estate of Joslyn v. Commissioner, 78-1 U.S. Tax Cas. (CCH) ¶ 13,227 (9th Cir. 1978).

165. Hibernia Bank v. Commissioner, 75-2 U.S. Tax Cas. (CCH) ¶ 13,102 (N.D. Cal. 1975), *aff'd*, 78-2 U.S. Tax Cas. (CCH) ¶ 13,261 (9th Cir. 1978).

166. Estate of Joseph Vatter v. Commissioner, 65 T.C. 633 (1975), *aff'd*, 77-1 U.S. Tax Cas. (CCH) ¶ 13,169 (2d Cir. 1977); *see* Spragens, *Current Appellate Cases Create Conflict in Deductibility of Selling Costs as Administration Expenses Under Section 2053(a)(2)*, Taxes (July 1976).

167. Priv. Ltr. Rul. 7802006. *See* Priv. Ltr. Rul. 7912006.

168. Estate of Vera T. Poser v. Commissioner, 75 T.C. 355 (1980). *See also* Marcus v. United States, 83-1 U.S. Tax Cas. (CCH) ¶ 13,521 (11th Cir. 1983), *rev'g and remanding* 81-2 U.S. Tax Cas. (CCH) ¶ 13,431 (D. Fla. 1981); Ferguson v. United States, 81-1 U.S. Tax Cas. (CCH) ¶ 13,409 (D. Ariz. 1981).

169. Estate of DeWitt v. Commissioner, 54 T.C.M. (CCH) 759 (1987).

170. See Priv. Ltr. Rul. 8119002, in which an auctioneer's commissions that were incurred in selling the decedent's property, and that were allowable administrative expenses under applicable (New York) state law, were deductible by the estate because the decedent's will directed that his property be sold and the proceeds distributed to the estate's beneficiaries. The commissions were, therefore, necessary "to effect distribution" of the estate.

171. Estate of Streeter v. Commissioner, 74-1 U.S. Tax Cas. (CCH) ¶ 12,970 (3d Cir. 1974), *aff'g* 30 T.C.M. (CCH) 1118 (1971).

172. Treas. Reg. § 20.2053-1(a)(1).

173. Treas. Reg. § 20.2053-1(a)(2).

174. Rev. Rul. 71-173, 1971-1 C.B. 204.

175. The statute also changes the holding in Estate of Bray v. Commissioner, 46 T.C. 557 (1966), *aff'd*, 396 F.2d 452 (6th Cir. 1968).

176. I.R.C. § 642(g).

177. I.R.C. § 2056(a).

178. For an excellent, in-depth treatment of the subject, see Malaro, *Restricted Gifts and Museum Responsibilities*, 18 J. Arts Mgmt. & L. 41 (1986).

179. Cosmopolitan at 144 (Mar. 1989).

180. *See* J. Merryman & A. Elson, Law, Ethics and the Visual Arts 619 (1987).

FORMS

FORM 1

INFORMATION REQUIRED BEFORE CONTRIBUTION

XYZ Charity

Address

Gentlemen:

I am considering making a contribution to you of a work of art [described briefly]. Before doing so, I wish to have your counsel's opinion as to: (1) Whether your operations qualify you as a "public-type organization" within the meaning of Section 170(b)(1)(A)(i) through (viii) of the Internal Revenue Code; and (2) whether the use to which that work of art will be put by your organization is related to the purpose or function constituting the basis for your exemption under Section 501 of the Internal Revenue Code. I would also like to know the grounds for your counsel's opinion.

Very truly yours,

Art Collector Donor

FORM 2

DEED OF GIFT OF ENTIRE INTEREST

I, ... , residing at . . . . , being the absolute owner of the original oil painting called ". . . . . ," painted by the artist . . . . , and dated . . . . , do hereby give, assign, and transfer over to the . . . . Museum of the City of . . . . and State of . . . . all of my right, title, and interest in and to said painting, including any copyright interest therein, if any, absolutely and forever. It is my intention that this transfer of the above-described painting shall constitute a gift of the same by me to said . . . . Museum, and that the oil painting called ". . . . ." shall be displayed, from time to time, as part of the . . . . Museum's regular collection.

IN WITNESS WHEREOF, I have hereunto set my hand and seal this . . . . day of . . . . , 19 _____.

____________________ ss.
Donor

____
Notary Public

The above described gift is accepted by me on behalf of the .... Museum, of .... City and .... State, this .... day of .... 19 _____, and we agree to acknowledge our acceptance of the gift on IRS Form 8283.

____
President

____
Notary Public

FORM 3

DEED OF GIFT OF ENTIRE INTEREST

WHEREAS, ... is the owner of the following paintings:

	Title	*Description*	*Artist*
1.			
2.			

and

WHEREAS, ... is desirous of giving said paintings to . . . . University upon the terms and conditions hereinafter set forth;

NOW, THEREFORE, the undersigned does give, grant, convey, and confirm unto the . . . . University all of his right, title, and interest in and to said paintings, including any copyright interest therein, if any, upon the condition that said paintings be made generally available by the . . . . University for inspection by the general public at such time and under such regulations and upon such conditions as the . . . . University may reasonably impose and be utilized by the . . . . University as a part of its program for educating its students and upon the further condition that each painting be identified as being a part of the . . . . Collection by a suitable inscription or plaque.

IN WITNESS WHEREOF, the undersigned has hereunto set his hand and seal this . . . . day of . . . . , 19 _____.

____________________ ss.
Donor

____
Notary Public

The above described gift is accepted by me on behalf of the . . . . University this . . . . day of . . . . , 19 ____, and we agree to acknowledge our acceptance of the gift on IRS Form 8283.

____
President

____
Notary Public

FORM 4

DEED OF GIFT OF ONE-FOURTH INTEREST

I, ... , of . . . . City, ... State, am the owner of the painting hereinafter described and I desire to give to the . . . . Museum, of . . . . City, ... State, an undivided one-fourth interest in said painting. To carry out my purpose and vest immediately in said . . . . Museum the title and ownership in an undivided one-fourth interest in said painting, I do hereby give, assign, transfer, and deliver to said . . . . Museum an undivided one-fourth interest in said painting, including any copyright interest therein, if any, which is described as follows ". . . . ." by . . . . dated . . . .

It is my purpose to vest in said . . . . Museum the absolute ownership of an undivided one-fourth interest in said painting at this time, it being understood that said . . . . Museum shall have rights of possession, dominion, and control of said painting for the number of months during and twelve-month period after the date hereof that the interest of said . . . . Museum bears to the entire interest, said . . . . Museum to have the sole discretion to decide the months during which it will exercise such rights.

IN WITNESS WHEREOF, I have hereunto set my hand and seal this . . . . day of . . . . , 19 _____.

____________________ ss.
Donor

____
Notary Public

The above-described gift is accepted by me on behalf of the .... Museum, of .... City and .... State, this .... day of ...., 19 ____, and we agree to acknowledge our acceptance of the gift on IRS Form 8283.

____
President

____
Notary Public

FORM 5

SPECIFIC BEQUEST OF A WORK OF ART

TENTH: I give and bequeath to the . . . . Museum in the City of . . . . and the State of . . . . , the items described below, including any copyright interest therein, if any:

1. Oil painting entitled ". . . . ." by . . . . dated . . . .
2. Etc.

PROVIDED, HOWEVER, if at the time of my death the . . . . Museum is not an organization described in section 2055(a) of the Internal Revenue Code of 1986, or corresponding provisions of any subsequent Federal tax laws, I give and bequeath said items to such other organization as is described in said section 2055(a) and is designated by my Executor.

FORM 6

SPECIFIC ITEMS TO NAMED INDIVIDUALS

TENTH: I give and bequeath the following articles of tangible personal property, including any copyright interest therein, if any, to such of the following persons as shall survive me:

(a) To my son, ... , the oil painting entitled ". . . . ." by . . . . dated . . . .

(b) To my friend, ... , the sculpture entitled ". . . . ." by . . . . dated . . . .

(c) Etc.

(d) I give and bequeath all of my tangible personal property not hereinbefore effectually disposed of in this Clause TENTH, subdivisions (a) through (c) to . . . .

FORM 7

ITEMS TO CLASS A INDIVIDUALS

TENTH: To my son, ... , and my daughters, ... and . . . . , or such of them as shall survive me, I give and bequeath all paintings and sculpture, including any copyright interest therein, if any, that are not in the preceding paragraphs of my Will otherwise specifically disposed of. In the event my son or daughters surviving me do not agree between them as to the division of such property, my son, ... , shall have the right of first selection, and my daughter, ... , shall have the right to second selection, and my daughter, ... , shall have the right to third selection, and so on thereafter, my said son and daughters in such order each having the right of further selection until all articles of tangible personal property covered by this Clause TENTH have been selected.

FORM 8

SPECIFIC ITEMS TO UNNAMED CHARITIES

TENTH: I give and bequeath the following described items:

1. Oil painting entitled ". . . . ." by . . . . dated . . . ., including any copyright interest therein, if any;

2. [Etc.] to such organization or organizations as my Executors, in their sole and absolute discretion, shall select, designate, and appoint. The words "organization or organizations" as hereinabove used in this Clause TENTH shall be deemed to mean and include only such organization or organizations to which a transfer is deductible for Federal estate tax purposes and is described in Section 2055(a) of the Internal Revenue Code of 1986, or corresponding provision of any subsequent Federal tax laws.

FORM 9

EXPENSES FOR TANGIBLES

TENTH: . . . .

I direct that all expenses of insuring, storing, transporting, and otherwise caring for any property bequeathed in this [Subdivision No. ____, Clause No. ____] shall be paid by my Executor as an expense of administration out of my general estate until actual delivery of each article of property to the legatee at the place designated by him or her.

FORM 10
INFORMATION REQUIRED TO BE CONTAINED IN AN APPRAISAL OF TANGIBLE PERSONAL PROPERTY BEING CONTRIBUTED TO CHARITY FOR WHICH A DEDUCTION WILL BE CLAIMED FOR FEDERAL INCOME TAX PURPOSES

QUALIFIED APPRAISAL

The following information is required pursuant to Treas. Reg. Section 1.170A-13(b)(2)(ii). Donors of tangible personal property to charity should require the appraiser to include the following information in the appraisal.

1. DESCRIPTION OF THE PROPERTY—in sufficient detail for a person who is not generally familiar with the type of property to ascertain that the property that was appraised is the property that was—or will be—contributed.

   Description should include dimensions, color, materials used, and, if known, date of creation, maker, location of origin and whatever other factual details would be helpful.
2. PHYSICAL CONDITION of the property—the appraisal should note any repairs, defects, worn elements, fading, etc.
3. DATE—OR EXPECTED DATE—OF CONTRIBUTION TO Charity.
4. DATE OR DATES ON WHICH THE PROPERTY WAS VALUED by the appraiser—note that the appraisal can not be prepared more than 60 days prior to the actual date of contribution of the appraised property.
5. METHOD OF VALUATION used to determine the fair market value—such as comparable sales approach or replacement cost-less-depreciation approach.
6. SPECIFIC BASIS FOR VALUATION, if any, such as specific comparable sales transactions.
7. TERMS OF ANY AGREEMENT—or understanding between the donor and the donee charity relating to the use, sale or other disposition of the property. If none, the appraisal should so state, or if there are, the appraisal should explain.
8. FEE ARRANGEMENT between donor and appraiser—fees based on a percentage of the value will render the appraisal invalid for income tax contribution purposes.
9. QUALIFICATIONS of the APPRAISER including background, experience, education and membership, if any, in professional

appraiser associations. There should be included, in addition, specific examples of qualifications by way of experience or background to appraise the particular items which are the subject of the appraisal.

10. FAIR MARKET VALUE—the appraised value of the property which is the subject of the appraisal as of the date (or expected date) of contribution.
11. PURPOSE OF APPRAISAL—a statement that the appraisal was prepared for federal income tax purposes.
12. SIGNATURE of appraiser on the appraisal. The name, address and taxpayer identification number of the appraiser must be on the appraisal.

Form **8282**
(Rev August 1988)
Department of the Treasury
Internal Revenue Service

Donee Information Return

(Sale, Exchange, or Other Disposition of Donated Property)

▶ **See instructions on back.**

OMB No 1545-0908
Expires 3-31-90

Give Copy to Donor

Please Print or Type	
Charitable organization (donee) name	Employer identification number
Number and street	
City or town, state, and ZIP code	

Note: *If you are the original donee, **DO NOT** complete Part II, or column (c) of Part III*

Part I **Information on ORIGINAL DONOR, and DONEE YOU GAVE THE PROPERTY TO**

1(a) **Name of the original donor** of (first person to give) the property | (b) Identification number

Complete 2(a)–2(d) only if you gave this property to another charitable organization (successor donee):

2(a) **Name of charitable organization** | (b) Identification number (EIN)

(c) Address (number and street)

(d) City or town, state, and ZIP code

Part II **Information on PREVIOUS DONEES—Complete this part only if you were not the first donee to receive the property.** If you were the second donee, leave item 4 blank. If you were a third or later donee, then complete both items 3 and 4. In item 4 give information on the preceding donee (the one who gave you the gift).

3(a) **Name of original donee** | (b) Identification number (EIN)

(c) Address (number and street)

(d) City or town, state, and ZIP code

4(a) **Name of preceding donee** | (b) Identification number (EIN)

(c) Address (number and street)

(d) City or town, state, and ZIP code

Part III **Information on DONATED PROPERTY**

(a) Description of donated property sold, exchanged, or otherwise disposed of (attach a separate sheet if more space is needed)	(b) Date you received the item(s)	(c) Date the first donee received the item(s) (if you weren't the first)	(d) Date item(s) sold, exchanged, or otherwise disposed of	(e) Amount received upon disposition

For Paperwork Reduction Act Notice, see instructions on back.

Form **8282** (Rev 8-88)

General Instructions

Paperwork Reduction Act Notice

We ask for this information to carry out the Internal Revenue laws of the United States. We need it to ensure that taxpayers are complying with these laws and to allow us to figure and collect the right amount of tax. You are required to give us this information.

The time needed to complete this form will vary depending on individual circumstances. The estimated average time is:

Recordkeeping . . . 3 hrs. and 7 min.
Learning about the law or the form . . . . 30 min.
Preparing and sending the form to IRS . . . . 34 min.

If you have comments concerning the accuracy of these time estimates or suggestions for making this form more simple, we would be happy to hear from you. You can write to the **Internal Revenue Service,** Washington, DC 20224, Attention: IRS Reports Clearance Officer, TR:FP; or the **Office of Management and Budget,** Paperwork Reduction Project, Washington DC 20503.

Purpose

Donee organizations use Form 8282 to report information to the Internal Revenue Service about dispositions of certain charitable deduction property made within two years after the donor contributed the property.

Definitions

Note: *For purposes of Form 8282 and instructions, the term "donee" includes all donees, unless specific reference is made to "original" or "successor" donees.*

Original Donee–The first donee to or for which the donor gave the property. The original donee is required to sign an appraisal summary presented by the donor for charitable deduction property.

Appraisal Summary–Section B of **Form 8283,** Noncash Charitable Contributions.

Successor Donee–Any donee of property other than the original donee.

Charitable Deduction Property–Property (other than money or certain publicly traded securities) contributed after December 31, 1984, for which the original donee signed, or was presented with for signature, an appraisal summary on Form 8283.

Generally, only items or groups of similar items for which the donor claimed a deduction of more than $5,000 are included on an appraisal summary. There is an exception if a donor gives similar items to more than one donee organization and the total deducted for these similar items exceeds $5,000. For example, if a donor deducts $2,000 for books given to a donee organization and $4,000 for books to another donee organization, the donor must present a separate appraisal summary to both organizations. For more information, see the Instructions for Form 8283.

Who Must File

Form 8282 must be filed by original donees and successor donees. File Form 8282 if you are a donee organization who sells, exchanges, consumes, or otherwise disposes of (with or without consideration) charitable deduction property within two years after the date the original donee received the property. For successor donees, the form must be filed only for property transferred by the original donee after July 5, 1988.

Exceptions.—There are two situations where Form 8282 does not have to be filed.

1. Items valued at $500 or less.—You do not have to file if, at the time the original donee signed the appraisal summary, the donor had signed a statement on Form 8283 that the appraised value of the specific item was not more than $500. If Form 8283 contains more than one similar item, this rule applies only to those items that are clearly identified as having a value of $500 or less. However, for purposes of the donor's determination of whether the appraised value of the item exceeds $500, all shares of nonpublicly traded stock, or items that form a set, are considered one item. For example, a collection of books written by the same author, components of a stereo system, or six place settings of a pattern of silverware, are considered one item.

If by January 31, 1986, the original donee received a Form 8283 for signature and the form did **not** have the required donor statement, you will not be required to file Form 8282 for items valued at $500 or less if the original donee obtained the required statement by March 31, 1986. The statement may be on either an amended Form 8283 or an attachment to the original Form 8283. However, if the original donee received the Form 8283 after January 31, 1986, the form must have contained the required donor statement at the time the original donee signed it. If not, you will have to file Form 8282.

2. Items consumed or distributed for charitable purpose.—You do not have to file Form 8282 if an item is consumed or distributed without consideration. The consumption or distribution must be in furtherance of your purpose or function as a tax-exempt organization. For example, no reporting is required for medical supplies consumed or distributed by a tax-exempt relief organization in aiding disaster victims.

When To File

If you dispose of charitable deduction property within two years of the date the original donee received it and you do not meet exception **1** or **2** above, you must file Form 8282 within 125 days after the date of disposition.

Exception: *If you did not file because you had no reason to believe the substantiation requirements applied to the donor, but you later become aware that they did apply, file Form 8282 within 60 days after the date you become aware you are liable.*

The above exception would apply if you were never given an appraisal summary, and it was reasonable to believe that the property you received was worth $5,000 or less.

If Information Is Not Available

You must complete at least Part III, item (a). You are not required to complete the remaining items if the information is not available. For example, you may not have the information necessary to complete all entries if the donor's appraisal summary is not available to you.

Where To File

File this form with the Internal Revenue Service Center in Cincinnati, OH 45944.

Penalties

There is a $50 penalty for each failure to file this form.

If you file Form 8282 but fail to include all of the correct information required by the form, there is a penalty of $5 for each failure.

For more information on penalties, see sections 6676, 6721, and 6723 of the Internal Revenue Code.

Other Requirements

Information You Must Furnish a Successor Donee.—You must provide the following to your successor donee (if the property is transferred to another charitable organization within the 2-year period discussed earlier):

1. The name, address, and EIN of your organization;

2. A copy of the appraisal summary (the Form 8283 that you received from the donor or a preceding donee); and

3. A copy of this Form 8282 within 15 days after you file it.

You must furnish items 1 and 2 within 15 days after the latest of:

- The date you transferred the property;
- The date the original donee signed the appraisal summary; or
- In the case where you are also a successor donee, the date you received the appraisal summary from the preceding donee.

Note: *The successor donee organization to whom you transferred this property is required to give you their organization's name, address, and EIN within 15 days after the later of the date you:*

- *transferred the property, or*
- *furnished them a copy of the appraisal summary.*

Information You Must Furnish the Donor.—You must furnish a copy of your Form 8282 to the donor of the property.

Appraisal Summary.—You must keep a copy of the appraisal summary in your records.

*U.S. Government Printing Office: 1988-242-473/80005

Form **8283** (Rev. August 1988)

Department of the Treasury
Internal Revenue Service

Noncash Charitable Contributions

► Attach to your Federal income tax return if the total claimed deduction for all property contributed exceeds $500.

► See separate Instructions.

OMB No. 1545-0908
Expires 3-31-90

Attachment Sequence No. 55

Name(s) as shown on your income tax return

Identification number

Note: *Compute the amount of your contribution deduction before completing Form 8283. (See your tax return instructions.)*

Section A Include in Section A **only** items (or groups of similar items) for which you claimed a deduction of $5,000 or less per item or group, and certain publicly traded securities (see Instructions).

Part I **Information on Donated Property**

1	(a) Name and address of the donee organization	(b) Description of donated property (attach a separate sheet if more space is needed)
A		
B		
C		
D		
E		

Note: *Columns (d), (e), and (f) do not have to be completed if the amount you claimed as a deduction for the item is $500 or less.*

	(c) Date of the contribution	(d) Date acquired by donor (mo., yr.)	(e) How acquired by donor	(f) Donor's cost or adjusted basis	(g) Fair market value	(h) Method used to determine the fair market value
A						
B						
C						
D						
E						

Part II **Other Information**—Complete question 2 if you gave less than an entire interest in property listed in Part I. Complete question 3 if restrictions were attached to a contribution listed in Part I.

2 If less than the entire interest in the property is contributed during the year, complete the following:

(a) Enter letter from Part I which identifies the property ________. (Attach a separate statement if Part II applies to more than one property.)

(b) Total amount claimed as a deduction for the property listed in Part I for this tax year ____________;
for any prior tax year(s) ________________.

(c) Name and address of each organization to which any such contribution was made in a prior year (complete only if different from the donee organization above).

Charitable organization (donee) name

Number and street

City or town, state, and ZIP code

(d) The place where any tangible property is located or kept. ________________

(e) Name of any person, other than the donee organization, having actual possession of the property. ________________

3 If conditions were attached to any contribution listed in Part I, answer the following questions:

	Yes	No
(a) Is there a restriction either temporarily or permanently on the donee's right to use or dispose of the donated property?		
(b) Did you give to anyone (other than the donee organization or another organization participating with the donee organization in cooperative fundraising) the right to the income from the donated property or to the possession of the property, including the right to vote donated securities, to acquire the property by purchase or otherwise, or to designate the person having such income, possession, or right to acquire?		
(c) Is there a restriction limiting the donated property for a particular use?		

For Paperwork Reduction Act Notice, see separate Instructions.

Form **8283** (Rev. 8-88)

Form 8283 (Rev. 8-88) Page 2

Name(s) as shown on your income tax return | **Identification number**

Section B **Appraisal Summary**—Include in Section B only items (or groups of similar items) for which you claimed deduction of more than $5,000 per item or group. *(Report contributions of certain publicly traded securities on[ly] in Section A.)*

If you donated art, you may have to attach the complete appraisal. See the **Note** in Part II below.

Part I **Donee Acknowledgment** *(To be completed by the charitable organization.)*

1 This charitable organization acknowledges that it is a qualified organization under section 170(c) and that it received the donated property as described in Part II on ______________________ (Date)

Furthermore, this organization affirms that in the event it sells, exchanges, or otherwise disposes of the property (or any portion thereof) within two years after the date of receipt, it will file an information return (**Form 8282,** Donee Information Return) with the IRS and furnish the donor a copy of that return. This acknowledgment does not represent concurrence in the claimed fair market value.

Charitable organization (donee) name	Employer identification number
Number and street	City or town, state, and ZIP code
Authorized signature	Title Date

Part II **Information on Donated Property** *(To be completed by the taxpayer and/or appraiser.)*

2 Check type of property:

☐ Art* (contribution of $20,000 or more) ☐ Real Estate ☐ Gems/Jewelry ☐ Stamp Collections
☐ Art* (contribution of less than $20,000) ☐ Coin Collections ☐ Books ☐ Other

*Art includes paintings, sculptures, watercolors, prints, drawings, ceramics, antique furniture, decorative arts, textiles, carpets, silver, rare manuscript[s], historical memorabilia, and other similar objects. **Note:** *If you donated art after December 31, 1987, and your total art contribution deduction was $20,00[0] or more, you must attach a complete copy of the signed appraisal and include an 8 × 10 inch color photograph (or a color transparency, no smaller than 4 × 5 inches).*

3	(a) Description of donated property (attach a separate sheet if more space is needed)	(b) If tangible property was donated, give a brief summary of the overall physical condition at the time of the gift	(c) Appraised fair market value
A			
B			
C			
D			

	(d) Date acquired by donor (mo., yr.)	(e) How acquired by donor	(f) Donor's cost or adjusted basis	(g) For bargain sales after 6/6/88, enter amount received	See instructions (h) Amount claimed as a deduction	See instructions (i) Average trading price of securities
A						
B						
C						
D						

Part III **Taxpayer (Donor) Statement**—List any item(s) included in Section B, Part II, that is (are) separately identified i[n] the appraisal as having a value of $500 or less. See instructions.

I declare that the following item(s) included in Part II above has (have) to the best of my knowledge and belief an appraised value of not more than $500 (pe[r] item). *(Enter identifying letter from Part II and describe the specific item)*: ______________________

Signature of taxpayer (donor) ► Date ►

Part IV **Certification of Appraiser** *(To be completed by the appraiser of the above donated property.)*

I declare that I am not the donor, the donee, a party to the transaction in which the donor acquired the property, employed by, married to, or related to any o[f] the foregoing persons, or an appraiser regularly used by any of the foregoing persons and who does not perform a majority of appraisals during the taxabl[e] year for other persons.

Also, I declare that I hold myself out to the public as an appraiser or perform appraisals on a regular basis; and that because of my qualifications as describe[d] in the appraisal, I am qualified to make appraisals of the type of property being valued. I certify the appraisal fees were not based upon a percentage of th[e] appraised property value. Furthermore, I understand that a false or fraudulent overstatement of the property value as described in the qualified appraisal o[r] this appraisal summary may subject me to the civil penalty under section 6701(a) (aiding and abetting the understatement of tax liability). I affirm that [I] have not been barred from presenting evidence or testimony by the Director of Practice.

Please Sign Here Signature ► Title ► Date of appraisal ►

Business address | Identification number

City or town, state, and ZIP code

* U.S. GPO 1988 — 205-32

Department of the Treasury
Internal Revenue Service

Instructions for Form 8283

(Revised August 1988)

Noncash Charitable Contributions

(Section references are to the Internal Revenue Code, unless otherwise noted.)

General Instructions

Paperwork Reduction Act Notice

We ask for this information to carry out the Internal Revenue laws of the United States. We need it to ensure that taxpayers are complying with these laws and to allow us to figure and collect the right amount of tax. You are required to give us this information.

The time needed to complete and file this form will vary depending on individual circumstances. The estimated average time is:

Recordkeeping	20 minutes
Learning about the law or the form	25 minutes
Preparing the form	35 minutes
Copying, assembling, and sending the form to IRS	35 minutes

If you have comments concerning the accuracy of these time estimates or suggestions for making this form more simple, we would be happy to hear from you. You can write to either IRS or the Office of Management and Budget at the address listed in the instructions of the tax return with which this form is filed.

Purpose

Use Form 8283 to report certain required information about noncash charitable contributions. Do not report on Form 8283 out-of-pocket expenses for volunteer work or amounts you gave by check or credit card. Treat these items as cash contributions.

Additional Information

Do not use this form to figure your charitable deduction. For information on computing the amount of the charitable deduction, see your tax return instructions. You may also want to get **Pub. 526,** Charitable Contributions (for individuals), and **Pub. 561,** Determining the Value of Donated Property. If you contribute depreciable property, get **Pub. 544,** Sales and Other Dispositions of Assets.

Who Must File

You must file Form 8283 if the amount of your deduction for all noncash gifts is more than $500. (For this purpose, "amount of your deduction" means your deduction BEFORE applying any income limitations that could result in a carryover. The carryover rules are explained in Pub. 526.)

If you must complete Form 8283, you may need to complete Section A, Section B, or both, depending on the type of property and the amount claimed as a deduction. See **Which Sections To Complete.**

Form 8283 is filed only by:

- Individuals
- Partnerships
- S corporations
- Closely held corporations
- Personal service corporations
- Other C corporations

Note: *C corporations, other than personal service corporations and closely held corporations, must file Form 8283 only if the amount claimed as a deduction is over $5,000 and donated after June 6, 1988.*

Reductions to Fair Market Value (FMV).—Make any required reductions to FMV before you determine if you must file Form 8283. Attach a computation to your tax return showing the reduction. The amount of the reduction (if any) depends on whether the property is ordinary income property or capital gain property. See the FMV discussion below.

When To File

File Form 8283 with your tax return for the tax year you contribute the property and first claim a deduction.

Fair Market Value (FMV)

Although it is the amount of your deduction that may cause you to file Form 8283, you also need to have information about the value of your contribution to complete the form.

Fair market value (FMV) is the price a willing buyer would pay a willing seller when neither has to buy or sell, and both are aware of the sale conditions.

You may not always be able to deduct the FMV of your contribution. Depending on the type of property donated, you may have to reduce the FMV to get to the deductible amount, as explained below.

Ordinary income property is property that would result in ordinary income or short-term capital gain if it were sold on the date it was contributed. Examples of ordinary income property are inventory, works of art created by the donor, and capital assets held for 6 months or less (1 year or less if acquired after December 31, 1987). The deduction for a gift of ordinary income property is limited to the FMV less the amount that would be ordinary income if the property were sold at its FMV.

Capital gain property is property that would result in long-term capital gain if it were sold at its FMV on the date of contribution. It includes certain real property and depreciable property used in your trade or business, and generally held for more than 6 months (more than 1 year if acquired after December 31, 1987). You usually may deduct gifts of capital gain property at their FMV. However, you must reduce the FMV by the amount of the appreciation if:

- the capital gain property is contributed to certain private nonoperating foundations;
- you choose the 50% limit instead of the special 30% limit; or
- the contributed property is tangible personal property that is put to an unrelated use by the charity.

Qualified Conservation Contribution.—If your donation qualifies as a "qualified conservation contribution" under section 170(h), attach a statement that shows the claimed FMV of the underlying property before and after the gift and the conservation purpose furthered by the gift.

Which Sections To Complete

Section A

Include in Section A only items (or groups of similar items) for which you claimed a deduction of $5,000 or less per item (or group of similar items). Also include certain publicly traded securities even if the deduction exceeds $5,000.

The publicly traded securities you should report in Section A even if the deduction claimed exceeds $5,000 are:

1. Securities listed on an exchange in which quotations are published daily;

2. Securities regularly traded in national or regional over-the-counter markets for which published quotations are available; or

3. Securities that are shares of a mutual fund for which quotations are published on a daily basis in a newspaper of general circulation throughout the United States.

Section B

Include in Section B only items (or **groups of similar items**) for which you claimed a deduction of more than $5,000 (except for certain publicly traded securities reportable in Section A).

Similar items of property are items of the same generic category or type, such as stamp collections, coin collections, lithographs, paintings, books, nonpublicly traded stock, land, or buildings.

Example. *You claimed a deduction of $400 for clothing, $7,000 for publicly traded securities (quotations published daily), and $6,000 for a collection of 15 books ($400 for each book). Report the clothing and the securities in Section A and the books (a group of similar items) in Section B.*

With certain exceptions, items reported in Section B will require information based on a written appraisal by a qualified appraiser.

Special Rule for Contributions of Inventory and Scientific Equipment by Certain C Corporations

A special rule applies for deductions taken by certain C corporations under section 170(e)(3) or (4) for contributions of inventory or scientific equipment. To determine if you must file Form 8283, or which section to complete, take into account only the amount claimed as a deduction in excess of the amount you would have deducted as cost of goods sold (COGS) had you sold the property instead. This rule is only for purposes of Form 8283. It does not change the amount or method of computing your contribution deduction.

You must attach a statement to your tax return (similar to the one in the example below) if the rule causes you not to have to file Form 8283. Also attach it if it causes you to be able to complete Section A instead of Section B.

Example. *You donated clothing from your inventory for the care of the needy. The clothing cost you $5,000 and your claimed charitable deduction is $8,000. Complete Section A instead of Section B since the excess of the deduction over what would have been your COGS deduction is $3,000 ($8,000 − $5,000). Attach a statement to Form 8283 similar to the following:*

Form 8283—Inventory

$8,000	contribution deduction
−$5,000	COGS (if sold, not donated)
=$3,000	for Form 8283 filing purposes.

Specific Instructions

Identification Number

Donors who are individuals must enter their social security number. All other donors should enter their employer identification number.

Partnerships and S Corporations

A partnership (S corporation) that claims a contribution deduction of over $500 must file Form 8283 with Form 1065 (1120S). If the total deduction of any item or group of similar items exceeds $5,000, the partnership (S corporation) must complete Section B of Form 8283 even if the amount allocated to each partner (shareholder) does not exceed $5,000.

The partnership (S corporation) must give a completed copy of Form 8283 to each partner (shareholder) who receives an allocation of the contribution deduction shown on the partnership's (S corporation's) Section B.

Partners and Shareholders

The partnership (S corporation) will provide information about your share of the contribution on your Schedule K-1 (Form 1065 or Form 1120S).

In some cases, the partnership (S corporation) must give you a copy of the partnership's (S corporation's) Form 8283. In these cases, attach a copy of the Form 8283 you received to your tax return. Deduct the amount shown on your Schedule K-1, not the amount shown on the Form 8283.

If the partnership is not required to give you Form 8283, combine the amount of noncash contributions shown on Schedule K-1 with your noncash contributions to see if you must file. If you need to file Form 8283, you do not have to complete all the information requested in Section A for your share of the partnership (S corporation) contributions. Do not complete line 1, columns (a)–(f) and (h). Instead, write "From Schedule K-1 (Form 1065 or 1120S)" across columns (c)–(f). Enter your share of the contribution on line 1, column (g).

Section A

Part I, Information on Donated Property

Line 1

Column (b).—Describe the property in sufficient detail. The greater the value, the more detail is needed. For example, a car should be described in more detail than pots and pans.

For securities, include the following:

- name of the issuer,
- kind of security,
- whether it is regularly traded on a stock exchange or in an over-the-counter market, and
- whether it is a share of a mutual fund.

Note: *Columns (d), (e), and (f) do not have to be completed if the amount you claimed as a deduction for the item is $500 or less.*

Column (d).—Enter the approximate date you acquired the property. If it was created, produced, or manufactured by or for you, enter the date it was substantially completed.

Column (e).—State how you acquired the property, i.e., by purchase, gift, inheritance, or exchange.

Column (f).—Do not complete for:

- Publicly traded securities; or
- Property held 12 months or more (6 months or more if donated in tax years beginning after December 31, 1982, and before June 7, 1988).

Keep records on cost or other basis.

Note: *If you have reasonable cause for not providing the acquisition date in column (d), or the cost basis when required in column (f), attach an explanation.*

Column (g).—Enter the fair market value (FMV) of property on the date you gave it. If you were required to reduce the FMV of your deduction, or if you gave a qualified conservation contribution, you must attach a statement. FMV, reductions to FMV, and the type of statement you may have to attach are explained on page 1.

Column (h).—Enter the method(s) used to determine the FMV of your donation. FMV of used household goods and clothing is usually much lower than when new. For this reason, standard formulas or methods to value this kind of property are generally not appropriate.

A good measure of value might be the price that buyers of these used items actually pay in consignment or thrift shops.

Examples of entries to make include "Appraisal," "Thrift shop value" (for clothing or household goods), "Catalog" (for stamp or coin collections), or "Comparable sales" (for real estate and other kinds of assets). See Pub. 561.

Part II, Other Information

Attach a separate statement if Part II applies to more than one property. Give the required information for each property separately. Identify which property listed in Part I the information relates to.

Line 2

Complete lines 2(a)–2(e) only if you contributed less than the entire interest in the donated property during the tax year. Enter on line 2(b) the amount claimed as a deduction for this year and in any earlier tax years for gifts of a partial interest in the same property. If the organization that received the prior interest in the property is the same as the one listed on line 1, column (a), do not complete line 2(c).

Line 3

Complete lines 3(a)–3(c) only if you attached restrictions to the right to the income, use, or disposition of the donated property. Attach a statement explaining:

- The terms of any agreement or understanding regarding the restriction; and
- Whether the property is designated for a particular use.

An example of a "restricted use" is furniture that you gave only to be used in the reading room of an organization's library.

Section B

Part I, Donee Acknowledgment

The donee organization must complete Part I. Before submitting page 2 of Form 8283 to the donee for acknowledgment, complete at least your name, identification number, and description of the donated property (line 3, column (a)). If tangible property is donated, also describe its physical condition (line 3, column (b)) at the time of the gift. Complete the Taxpayer (Donor) Statement in Part III, if applicable, before submitting the form to the donee. See the instructions for Part III.

The person acknowledging the gift must be an official authorized to sign the tax returns of the organization, or a person specifically designated to sign Form 8283. After completing Part I, the organization must return Form 8283 to you, the donor. A copy of Section B of this form must be provided to the donee organization. You may then complete any remaining information required in Part II. Also, Part IV may be completed at this time by the qualified appraiser.

In rare and unusual circumstances, it may be impossible to get the donee's signature on the appraisal summary. The deduction will not be disallowed for that reason if you attach a detailed explanation why it was impossible.

Note: *If the donee (or a successor donee) organization disposes of the property within 2 years after the date the original donee received it, the organization must file* ***Form 8282****, Donee Information Return, with IRS and send a copy to the donor. An exception applies to items having a value of $500 or less if the donor identified the items and signed the statement in Part III (Section B) of Form 8283. See the instructions for Part III.*

Part II, Information on Donated Property

You must have a written appraisal from a qualified appraiser that supports the information in Part II. **Exception:** You do not need a written appraisal if the property is:

1. Nonpublicly traded stock of $10,000 or less;
2. Securities for which market quotations are readily available. See Regulations section 1.170A-13(c)(7)(xi); or
3. Property donated by C corporations (other than closely held corporations and personal service corporations) after June 6, 1988.

Use Part II to summarize your appraisal(s). Generally, you do not need to attach the appraisals, but you should keep them for your records. **Exception:** *If your total deduction for art is $20,000 or more, attach a complete copy of the signed appraisal and include an 8 x 10 inch color photograph (or a color transparency, no smaller than 4 x 5 inches).*

Appraisal Requirements

The appraisal must be made not earlier than 60 days before the date you contribute the property. You must receive it before the due date (including extensions) of the return on which you first claim it as a deduction. For a deduction first claimed on an amended return, the appraisal must be received before the date the amended return was filed.

A separate qualified appraisal and a separate Form 8283 are required for each item of property except for an item which is part of a group of similar items. Only one appraisal is required for a group of similar items contributed in the same tax year, if it includes all the required information for each item.

The appraiser may select any items whose aggregate value is appraised at $100 or less for which a group description rather than a specific description of each item will suffice.

If you gave similar items to more than one donee for which you claimed a deduction of more than $5,000, you must attach a separate form for each donee.

Example. *You claimed a deduction of $2,000 for books given to College A, $2,500 for books given to College B, and $900 for books given to a public library. You must attach a separate Form 8283 for each donee.*

See Regulations section 1.170A-13(c)(3)(i)–(ii) for the definition of a "qualified appraisal" and information to be included in the appraisal.

Line 3

Note: *You must complete at least column (a) of line 3 (also column (b) if applicable) before submitting Form 8283 to the donee. You may then complete the remaining columns.*

Column (a).—Describe the property in enough detail so that a person not familiar with it could tell that the property appraised is the property that was contributed.

Column (c).—Include the FMV from the appraisal. If one was not required, include the FMV you determine to be correct.

Columns (d–f).—If you have reasonable cause for not providing the information for any of these columns, attach an explanation so that your deduction won't be automatically disallowed.

Column (g).—A bargain sale is a transfer of property which is in part a sale or exchange, and in part a contribution. Enter the amount received ("consideration") for bargain sales after June 6, 1988.

Column (h).—Complete column (h) only if you were not required to get an appraisal, as explained earlier.

Column (i).—Complete column (i) only if you donated securities for which market quotations are considered to be readily available because the issue satisfies the 5 requirements described in Regulations section 1.170A-13(c)(7)(xi)(B).

Part III, Taxpayer (Donor) Statement

If you (the donor) complete Part III, the donee is relieved of filing Form 8282 for items valued at $500 or less. (See the **Note** in Part I instructions of this section for more information on the filing of Form 8282 by the donee.)

Complete Part III only for items included in Part II that have an appraised value of $500 or less per item. Be sure to clearly identify these items in Part III. This is necessary because the donee may not know the value of the donated property, since you are not required to show it in Part II on the donee's copy of Form 8283.

The amount of information you give in Part III depends on the description of the donated property you enter in Part II. If you separately show a single item as "Property A" in Part II, and that item is appraised at $500 or less, then the entry "Property A" in Part III is enough. However, if "Property A" consists of several items and the total appraised value is over $500, list in Part III any item(s) you gave that is (are) valued at $500 or less.

All shares of nonpublicly traded stock, or items in a set, are considered one item. For example, a book collection by the same author, components of a stereo system, or six place settings of a pattern of silverware are one item for the $500 test.

Example. *You donated books valued at $6,000. The appraisal states that one of the items, a collection of books by author "X" is worth $400. On the Form 8283 that you are required to give the donee, you decide not to show the appraised value of all of the books. But you also don't want the donee to have to file Form 8282 if the collection of books is sold. If on line 3 of Part II your description of Property A includes all the books, then specify in Part III the "collection of books by X included in Property A." But if in Part II your Property A description is "collection of books by X," the only required entry in Part III is "Property A."*

In the above example you may have instead chosen to give a completed copy of Form 8283 to the donee. The donee would then be aware of the value. If in Part II you include all the books as Property A, and thus enter $6,000 in column (c), you may still want to describe the specific collection in Part III so the donee can sell it without filing Form 8282.

Part IV, Certification of Appraiser

If you had to get an appraisal, the appraiser MUST complete Part IV to be considered qualified. See Regulations section 1.170A-13(c)(5) for a definition of a qualified appraiser.

Persons who cannot be qualified appraisers are listed in the Certification of Appraiser (Part IV) of Form 8283. Usually, a party to the transaction will not qualify to sign the certification. But a person who sold, exchanged, or gave the property to the donor may sign the certification if the property is donated within 2 months of the date the donor acquired it and the property's appraised value does not exceed its acquisition price.

An appraiser may not be considered qualified if the donor had knowledge of facts that would cause a reasonable person to expect the appraiser falsely to overstate the value of the property. An example of this is an agreement between you and the appraiser about the property value when you know that the agreed amount exceeds the actual FMV.

Usually, appraisal fees cannot be based on a percentage of the appraised value unless the fees were paid to certain not-for-profit associations. See Regulations section 1.170A-13(c)(6)(ii).

Failure To File Form 8283, Section B

If you donate property required to be reported in Section B and you fail to attach the form to your return, the deduction will be disallowed unless your failure was due to a good faith omission. If IRS asks you to submit the form, you have 90 days to send a completed Section B of Form 8283 before your deduction is disallowed.

★U.S.GPO:1988-0-205-329

13

Artists

Tax and estate planning for an artist involves many unique problems. For one, often the artist is not accustomed to coping with sophisticated tax problems and is more concerned with the present state of his art and his career than with what may happen in the future. Moreover, making decisions with respect to the eventual disposition of the art may be something the artist wishes to avoid; the artist may be emotionally involved with the work and unsure of how he or she wants to dispose of it. The artist may also believe that his or her art is very valuable when in reality, it is not, or the reverse may be true. Additionally, the value of the art may vary radically between the time an artist's estate plan is drawn up and the time of death.

Constant changes in the tax law, including the Tax Reform Act of 1969, Tax Reform Act of 1976, Revenue Act of 1978, Economic Recovery Tax Act of 1981, Tax Equity and Fiscal Responsibility Act of 1982, Tax Reform Act of 1984, Tax Reform Act of 1986, Revenue Act of 1987, and Technical and Miscellaneous Revenue Act of 1988, have radically altered the tax treatment of artists' estates over the years. The tax laws treat charitable contributions by artists, as the artist may see it, unfairly. All those problems are further complicated when the artist is distrustful of lawyers and accountants. Obviously, the first and most important function in planning an artist's estate is to gain the artist's confidence and learn what he or she really wants. Knowing and working with the artist over a period of time and developing a sense of trust is absolutely essential in planning any artist's estate.

VALUATION

Knowing the value or approximate value of an artist's estate is necessary for estate planning. Determining the value of an artist's works is extremely difficult because of the unique qualities inherent in each piece of artwork, the uncertainties of the art market, the variations in quality, and the effect when a large number of items by the same artist are put on the market for sale. In fact, the death of the artist may influence the value of the art.

As important as the concept of value is, there is no simple rule or answer. The estate tax regulation[1] defines fair market value as

> the price at which the property would change hands between a willing buyer and a willing seller, neither being under any compulsion to buy or sell and both having reasonable knowledge of relevant facts.

The gift tax and income tax regulations contain identical language.[2] The general concept and basic rules regarding valuation are discussed in chapter 12 on the collector's estate at pages 532-60, and are not repeated here. Those concepts and rules are equally applicable to artists. The following discussion emphasizes the valuation problems unique to artists' estates.[3]

As is the case in planning the collector's estate, the most important consideration is the choice of the proper appraiser. The appraiser must be familiar with the market for the particular artist and one who has dealt with the artist's works in the past.[4] It is also a good idea in a large estate to have a second appraisal. Appraisals that are unrealistic will in the long run cause problems.[5]

Appraisals of artists' estates are difficult. It is not simply a matter of determining the price at which the last pieces sold and multiplying that amount by the number of pieces left in the artist's estate. Sometimes artwork has a greater value when the artist is alive than when the artist is dead. Sometimes the price of an artist's work is adversely affected after death because of the great number of pieces that come on the market. Marketing and selling artwork often involves a great deal of patience and selective selling, with intermittent shows. In other words, there may be a limited market for an artist at a certain price, and, once that market is exhausted, there may be no willing buyers. The regulations[6] specifically state that "all relevant facts and elements of value as of the applicable valuation date shall be considered in every case." The appraiser must be familiar with all those factors and try to document them to the extent possible.

Estate of David Smith

The case of the *Estate of David Smith*[7] illustrates many of the problems involved in valuing an artist's estate, although it does not provide many answers. David Smith was a sculptor who died owning 525 pieces of his work. He had sold fewer than 100 pieces during the twenty-five years before his death. Although he had great artistic success, only in the last few years before his death did his works have great financial success. The pieces were unusual in that most were very large: half were more than seven feet tall and many weighed several tons. The pieces were located at his studio in Bolton Landing, New York. The executors valued the works at their highest hypothetical retail sale price, that is, the price each would bring if it were the only item offered for sale, then subtracted 75 percent for a blockage discount and 33⅓ percent of the remainder for selling commissions that were contracted for, to reach a value of $714,000. The Internal Revenue Service (IRS) first had a figure of $5,250,418 and, before trial, reduced that figure to $4,284,000, which was the executors' figure for the highest value on an item-by-item basis. The court decided that the value was $1,700,000, not far from the midway point between the IRS value and the executors' value.[8]

The Principle of Blockage

The courts and the IRS concede a discount from the fair market value of an individual item when a large number of items must be absorbed by the market.[9] No specific percentage is applicable in all cases. The amount of discount should be based on an art dealer's opinion of the effect on the market of offering a large number of works by the same artist at the same time, with consideration given to the number of works on hand, the number previously sold, the size of the potential market, and the necessity of price reductions and concessions to make sales. The market for a seven-foot sculpture weighing five tons is smaller than the market for a three-foot-by-two-foot oil painting. Relative price also enters into the determination, that is, the market for oil paintings selling for more than $100,000 is probably smaller than the market for those selling for between $1,000 and $10,000. The *Smith* case holds that "the impact of such simultaneous availability of an extremely large number of items of the same category is a significant circumstance which should be taken into account." The blockage principle is also illustrated below in the discussion of the estate of Alexander Calder. The following points should be considered in valuing an artist's estate:[10]

1. The state of the artist's reputation at death (Has the artist's reputation fully blossomed?);
2. Marketplace acceptance of works of such size and character;
3. The relationship of the works to all the artist's other works, including relative size, the period in the artist's life when they were created, and their quality when compared with other works by the artist;
4. Whether the works are part of a complete series owned by the artist;
5. The number and the prices of sales during the artist's life and the prices at which sales were made during the period immediately before and after death (In *Smith* the court

noted that in considering the sales after death, sales too far removed from the date of death should not be considered, and little weight was given to sales more than two years after the artist's death.[11]); and

6. The accessibility of the works of art. Large transportation or other expenses involved in getting the works of art to the market may be taken into consideration in determining value.[12]

Although the Tax Court in *Smith* considered the above factors, the case is inconclusive, since it never discussed the weight and the importance of each factor. The decision is made more vague by the Tax Court's statement, in referring to the above factors, that "we do not mean to imply that we have set forth every consideration which has influenced our decision herein."[13] Therefore, we are left to guess as to what other factors influenced the court in reaching its "Solomon-like pronouncement" of value.

In addition to the above factors, a court should consider the following factors in the valuation of an artist's works at death.

1. The nature of the art market and how it functions, including the influence of art critics, museum shows, and gallery shows;[14]
2. The possibility that the works on hand are unsold because they are the less desirable works by the artist and, therefore, not worth so much as those sold before the artist's death; and
3. The impact of the artist's death on the market value of his or her works. The difficult question of that impact was not resolved by *Smith*. Obviously, once an artist dies, he or she can produce no more works. But that does not necessarily mean that the value of the artist's works will automatically increase. Often, after an artist dies, the executors must sell many of the works to raise cash for the administration of the estate, and that can have an adverse effect on prices. The fact of the artist's death should

> be one of many facts taken into consideration, but it should be given little weight. The IRS regulations require a valuation at the date of death, not two or three years after death.

The other major issue in *Smith* dealt with the deductibility of the selling commissions from the value of the works of art. That issue is discussed in detail in chapter 12 at pages 611-19. Generally, commission expenses are not a factor affecting value.[15] For such expenses to be deductible as administrative expense under section 2053, the will should direct the sale of the works. Such a direction prevents the IRS from raising the question of the "necessity" of the sale, which is the test required by the regulations, but on which the courts have reached differing opinions.[16] It is often difficult to determine at the time of the drafting of the artist's will which, if any, items he or she may want sold after death. One solution is to direct the executor to sell such items at such times and under such conditions as the executor in his or her discretion may determine to be necessary in order to raise sufficient funds for the payment of estate taxes and administrative expenses. The timing of such sales can stretch out over years, and an estimate of the net amount realized after expenses of the sales is a factor in determining value.

Louisa J. Calder

The case of *Louisa J. Calder*,[17] dealing with the blockage discount in a gift tax context, disclosed facts pertaining to the blockage discount in Alexander Calder's estate. Louisa J. Calder, the widow of Alexander Calder, inherited 1,226 Calder gouaches from the estate. At the audit of the federal estate tax return, the IRS agent valued the gouaches at a fair market value approximately three times greater than the value placed on the works by Calder's estate. However, the IRS did acknowledge that, because of the large number of works of art by Calder in the estate, a blockage discount was appropriate. The IRS allowed a blockage discount of 60 percent of the separate retail values of the 1,226 items, and that discount made the value reported on the estate tax return acceptable to the IRS.

Less than two months after Alexander Calder's death, his widow made, through trusts, gifts of the 1,226 items inherited from her husband to six separate persons. Mrs. Calder attempted to claim that the gifts of the works of art were subject to the same blockage discount (60 percent) that was allowed in her husband's estate. The Tax Court held that the blockage discount must be applied against each separate gift, rather than against the combined total block (all the gifts combined), and that it was not realistic to apply the total sales figure for all the gouaches sold during the year to each gift separately in determining the liquidation period.

The Tax Court characterized the IRS's approach, i.e., treating the gouaches as a large number of liquid assets whose worth could be realized only through liquidation over a period of time at a uniform rate yielding an assumed amount of dollars each year over the period, as being valid only to the extent that the underlying assumptions regarding the number of paintings that could be liquidated each year were valid.[18] The IRS approach proved wrong in practice. Its prediction of the number of gouaches to be sold each year far exceeded the annual sales. The Tax Court, therefore, recalculated the blockage discount, using actual sales figures for each of the six gifts, rather than arbitrary estimates applied by the IRS. The result was that, in view of fewer sales, the Tax Court determined that it would take a significantly longer period of time to liquidate each gift, resulting in a larger blockage discount and a gift tax value almost half that calculated by the IRS.

Smith and *Calder* illustrate the vagaries of the application of the blockage discount. The executor of an artist's estate must exercise care not to claim a discount that is unrealistic; otherwise penalties could be imposed on the estate.

Penalties

The Tax Reform Act of 1984 added section 6660 to the Internal Revenue Code. Under section 6660, penalties for a valuation understatement in the case of any underpayment of estate tax are as follows:

1. If the claimed value is two-thirds or less, but not less than 50 percent, of the correct amount, the penalty imposed is equal to 10 percent of the tax underpayment attributable to the undervaluation.
2. If the claimed value is 40 percent or more, but less than 50 percent of the correct amount, the penalty imposed is equal to 20 percent of the tax underpayment attributable to the undervaluation.
3. If the claimed value is less than 40 percent of the correct amount, the penalty imposed is equal to 30 percent of the tax underpayment attributable to the undervaluation.

The above penalties also apply to an underpayment of the gift tax.

There is no requirement under estate tax law or gift tax law to have a qualified appraisal by a qualified appraiser. Those technical terms apply to charitable contributions for income tax purposes. The IRS has the discretionary authority to waive all or part of the section 6660 penalty if the taxpayer establishes that there was a reasonable basis for the valuation claimed and that the claim was made in good faith.

CHARITABLE TRANSFERS

Inter Vivos Transfers

Artists want to have their work owned and exhibited at museums, which, of course, enhances an artist's reputation and increases the value of the work. Before the Tax Reform Act of 1969, museums found it easy to solicit contributions of artwork from artists. Then, the artist realized no income on the contribution and received a charitable deduction from income equal to the market value of the artwork donated; any costs to produce the work taken as deductions in previous years did not have to be recaptured and offset against the amount of the charitable deduction.[19]

Effective January 1, 1970, any artist who contributes his or her work to a charitable organization is entitled to a charitable deduction only to the extent of the cost of the materials used in the creation of the work of art, since, in the artist's hands, artwork is ordinary income property, i.e., property whose sale would not result in long-term capital gain.[20] Works created by artists are not capital assets.[21]

The amount of a charitable deduction for a contribution of ordinary income property is limited to the basis of that property in the hands of the donor within the applicable percentage limitation. That result is reached because the amount of the charitable deduction is determined by subtracting from the fair market value of the property the amount of gain that would not have been long-term capital gain if the donated property had been sold by the taxpayer at its fair market value.[22] In *J. Maniscalco*[23] the court held that a professional artist was not entitled to a charitable contribution deduction for the market value of three portraits donated to charitable organizations because the allowable charitable contributions deduction for an artist's own works was limited to the cost basis and no amount was allowable for the value of the artist's own labor. The artist's constitutional objection to section 170(e) also was held to be without merit.

Example: An artist created a work that cost him $100 for paint and canvas. A number of years later he contributed the work to a museum when the work had a fair market value of $5,000. The artist is limited to a charitable deduction of $100.

If the artist gives the work as a gift to a collector and the collector contributes it to a museum, the collector's charitable deduction is the same as it was for the artist, that is, the cost.[24] Therefore, an artist should *sell* work to the collector if the collector ever intends to contribute it to a museum. If the work is purchased by the collector and then contributed to a public (50 percent-type) charitable organization, such as a museum supported by the public, the donor can claim the full fair market value of the donated work as a charitable deduction within the applicable percentage limitations, assuming that the "related use" rule is satisfied. The charitable contribution rules pertaining to the collector are discussed in detail in chapter 12 herein.

The above limitations, which became effective January 1, 1970, drastically reduced the number of artworks donated by artists to museums.[25] Several bills have been introduced in Congress to give artists some increased tax benefits on the contribution of artwork to museums.[26] To date, none has become law.

Testamentary Transfers

Since at the present time artists receive very limited tax benefits from lifetime gifts to museums, they make few contributions. However, on an artist's death, the income tax restrictions do not apply.

The estate of an artist may claim a deduction on its estate tax return for the full fair market value on the artist's date of death for the works of art bequeathed to charitable organizations.[27] The deduction is not limited to the artist's cost of materials, as it is for income tax purposes. The amount of the deduction is unlimited and is not subject to any percentage limitations. The full estate tax deduction is available, whether the bequest is to a public charity or a private foundation. Private foundations include all tax-exempt organizations other than those described in section 590(a)(1), (2), (3), or (4). However, if the bequest is to a "private foundation" that has not complied with the requirement of the Internal Revenue Code to include certain amendments in its governing instrument, or that has failed to notify the IRS of its status, the entire estate tax charitable deduction will be denied.[28]

If the artist desires to bequeath his or her works to a private foundation, the drafter of the will should obtain a copy of the governing instrument of the private foundation to ascertain whether the instrument meets the IRS requirements mentioned above. The drafter should also obtain a statement from the organization that it has notified the IRS of its status.

The artist may wish to create a private foundation. If so, the foundation should be created during the life of the artist, rather than under the artist's will, with initial funding of $100. The foundation can then apply for tax-exempt status under section 501(c)(3), and the artist's will can bequeath the artist's work to the then existing IRS-approved foundation. The foundation should have powers broad enough to dispose of the artwork to other charitable organizations and to sell artwork to meet expenses.

Whether works of art are bequeathed to a public charity or to a private foundation, the will should be prepared in a manner that clearly identifies the artworks. Doing so is often a problem in an artist's will because the work the artist wants to leave to a charitable organization may vary from the time the will is drafted to the time of the artist's death. The drafter of the will must be careful of incorporation by reference problems, and should consider the possibility that a specific charitable organization may renounce the bequest. Any proposed gift and any condition imposed should be discussed with the charitable organization before the will is signed by the artist.

Generally, a testator making a testamentary charitable transfer under his or her will is not concerned with the "related use" rule (the artwork must be related to the exempt purpose of the charity) that applies to an income tax charitable transfer. However, section 2055(e)(4)(C) does contain a "related use" rule that applies to certain split-interest testamentary charitable transfers.

The problem and the potential trap for the artist is best illustrated by a simple example: the will of an artist bequeaths a specific work of art that he created after January 1, 1978, to his local church and the balance of his estate to his son: "I give and bequeath my painting entitled 'xyz' to the *A* Church. All the rest of my property of any kind I give and bequeath to my son."

Since the artist owned the copyright at the time of his death (federal statutory copyright comes into existence at creation), and since the *A* Church, although a public charity, probably cannot satisfy the new "related use" rule of section 2055(e)(4)(C), will the artist's estate get the estate tax charitable deduction?[29]

The quoted provision in the artist's will does not pass the copyright in the work of art to the charity, since the copyright is a separate property interest and must be separately bequeathed. Since the copyright interest was not included in the charitable transfer, it was transferred as part of the residuary clause. Therefore, the transfer was a split-interest transfer that, unless the requirements of section 2055(e)(4) were satisfied, results in the loss of the charitable deduction. So, if the transfer to the local church does not satisfy the "related use" rule of section 2055(e)(4)(c), the charitable deduction is lost.

Example (1) of the final regulations under section 2055(e)(4)[30] makes it clear that the IRS looks to local state law to see if the purported transfer of the work of art to the charitable organization includes the copyright. We believe that the simple will clause quoted above does not include the copyright interest in any local jurisdiction in the United States. Such a clause allows the copyright interest to become a part of the residuary estate.

To avoid the problem of an inadvertent split-interest transfer that fails to satisfy the "related use" rule of section 2055(e)(4)(c), estate planners should examine the wills of artists to make sure that any charitable transfers of works of art created after January 1, 1978, are transfers that also specifically transfer the copyright interest to the same charitable organization. For example: "I give and bequeath to the *XYZ* Charity my painting entitled 'ABC,' oil on canvas, measuring xx by xx and dated 1988, and my copyright interest in that painting." Under that will provision, the copyright interest will not inadvertently fall into the residue, thereby causing a split-interest transfer that may not satisfy the "related use" rule.

Although there is no definitive authority, a clause that merely transfers "all my right, title, and interest in and to 'ABC' painting" may not be sufficient to transfer the copyright in the work of art. The careful drafter should specifically include the copyright interest.

A testamentary charitable transfer by an artist is very beneficial to the artist's estate. As described above, the value of the artwork is deductible in full, thereby reducing the taxable estate and, hence, the tax assessed against the estate. That helps prevent a forced sale of the artist's works to raise the necessary cash to pay taxes and administrative expenses. Although a testamentary charitable transfer reduces the potential size of the allowable marital deduction (the marital deduction is now unlimited), a planned bequest to the proper museum may in the long run enhance the value of the remaining works of art for the artist's heirs.

As an alternative, the artist could leave the works of art to his or her surviving spouse free of estate tax because of the unlimited marital deduction. Then the surviving spouse could make a lifetime contribution of the works of art to charity. Since on the death of the artist the character of the works of art is changed from ordinary income property to capital gain property, the surviving spouse would be able to obtain an income tax charitable deduction for the full fair market value of the artwork contributed, within the applicable percentage limitations.

The drafter must also consider the size and the content of any charitable bequest. If the artist wishes to leave more than 50 percent of his or her estate to charity, there may be a problem. Local state law may require a clause with a percentage limitation or a drafting of the will so it cannot be challenged.[31]

NONCHARITABLE TRANSFERS

Most artists do not want to leave all their works to charitable organizations. Since the works of art often constitute the bulk of the assets in the artists' estate, they are the artists' means of providing financial security for their families.

Inter Vivos Transfers

Generally

Before January 1, 1977, a lifetime gift by an artist of his or her work to a noncharitable donee resulted in a saving in estate taxes because gift tax rates were only three-fourths of estate tax rates in the corresponding bracket. For gifts on or after January 1, 1977, the same tax rate schedule covers both the gift tax and the estate tax.[32] The advantages and the disadvantages are summarized in general terms in chapter 12.

One important reason for an artist to make lifetime gifts is to remove his or her work from the estate at a low value and to avoid the tax on the appreciation in value over the years. If a gift is made to family members, the artist should adhere to certain formalities, such as

- Using a deed of gift with signed acceptance
- Filing a gift tax return
- Changing the physical location of the work
- Procuring new insurance[33]

Following such formalities prevents questions after the artist's death about whether the property is includable in the artist's estate as a transfer with a retained life estate.[34]

Assignment of Income

The artist may want to make gifts of works of art in order to shift the income tax burden to other family members in lower tax brackets.[35] The donee takes the artist's basis in the work and any gain on its sale is ordinary income.[36] That assumes that the artist realizes no income on the donative transfer[37] and that the income realized on the donee's subsequent sale of the work is attributed to the donee, rather than to the artist.[38] When the property is the product of the donor's personal efforts, rather than personal services rendered to another, the creator is not taxed on the income realized when the donee subsequently sells the property.[39]

Mark Tobey[40] is the most significant case bearing on the issue whether proceeds of sales of artwork constitute earned income of the artist. Mark Tobey, an artist, was a United States citizen living in Switzerland. During the years in question, he sold certain paintings through galleries in the United States and received the net proceeds. The issue in the case was whether the proceeds constituted foreign earned income within the meaning of section 911, eligible for the $25,000 exclusion.

The IRS took the view that the receipts could not be earned income, since they were not receipts for Tobey's services but receipts from the sale of his paintings. The income resulted from the sale of personal property, so it was not earned income.[41] The taxpayer argued that the income from the sale of his paintings was compensation for personal service actually rendered.[42] The Tax Court held that "if the taxpayer's personal efforts result in the creation of personal property, the gain derived from the sale of that property is properly categorized as 'earned income.'" The court concluded:

> The concept of the artist as not "earning" his income for the purposes of section 911 would place him in an unfavorable light. For the most part, the present-day artist is a hard-working, trained, career-oriented individual. His education, whether acquired formally or through personal practice, growth and experience, is often costly and exacting. He has keen competition from many other artists who must create and sell their works to survive. To avoid discriminatory treatment, we perceive no sound reasons for treating income earned by the personal efforts, skill and creativity of a Tobey or a Picasso any differently from the income earned by a confidence man, a brain surgeon, a movie star or, for that matter, a tax attorney.

The question raised by the *Tobey* case is this: if an artist makes a gift of his or her work to a family member, has the artist effectively shifted the income, that is, the proceeds of the sale, to the donee, or has the artist run afoul of the assignment-of-income rules?[43]

The decision in *Tobey* should not require that the artist's income be equated with personal service income for all tax purposes in which an issue may turn on the presence or absence of "property."[44] A gift of created property is unlike the assignment of the right to income from future services, in which the donor retains control, or of rights to income from past services, in which the donor's disposition of the right to receive the income is deemed to result in an economic benefit to the donor.[45] In the absence of any prearranged sale, the artist-donor does not have any definite right to income on the transfer of property that the donor created. By making the gift, the artist parts with the ability to control whether and when the income from the sale of the artwork will be realized. The lack of the accrual of any "right to income" is the reason there should be no income taxation to the artist at the time of the gift and no income taxation to the artist at the time of sale by the donee. Therefore, gifts to family members are effective devices to shift income to members of the artist's family who are in lower tax brackets.

The later case of *Robert H. Cook*[46] followed *Tobey* in holding that an American sculptor living in Italy and selling noncommissioned sculptures made in Italy through his United States dealers did not have United States source income. The court held that for section 911 purposes, the artist is entitled to treat the sales as from his "labor or personal services," to be sourced as earned abroad under sections 861(a)(3) and 862(a)(3) and not from the sale of personal property to be sourced in the United States under section 863.

The Tax Reform Act of 1986 greatly reduced the ability of the artist-taxpayer to shift income to a minor child in a lower tax bracket. Effective January 1, 1987, the net unearned income of a child under the age of fourteen in excess of $1,000 ($500 plus the applicable standard deduction) is subject to tax at the top marginal rate of the parents. The applicable standard deduction for unearned income was $500 in 1987 and is adjusted for inflation every year beginning in 1988.[47]

Right of Termination Under the Copyright Act

The interaction of the tax law and the copyright law can produce odd results, as was shown in the discussion of section 2055(e)(4) in this chapter. In discussing inter vivos gifts by an artist, we must consider the "right of termination" under the copyright law and its possible effects on the gift tax and the estate tax.

The Copyright Act of 1976 created a right of termination that permits an artist to terminate any inter vivos (but not testamentary) transfer or license of a copyright or of any of the separate rights therein with respect to a work of art created on or after January 1, 1978.[48] This means that even if an artist transferred the copyright to a work of art he can terminate the transfer and get back his or her copyright so long as the right is exercised within certain narrow time periods. The right of termination is exercisable by the artist during his lifetime. After the artist's death, the right of termination is exercisable by a majority in interest of his spouse and children. The right of termination passes only by operation of law. Special timing rules govern the narrow time periods during which a right of termination may be exercised.[49]

Therefore, the tax issues arise: can the donor-artist (the copyright owner) make a gift of a copyright, or does the right of termination make the gift incomplete for gift tax purposes? To make a completed gift, the donor must relinquish dominion and control over the property given.[50] If a gift is subject to a right of termination, the IRS might argue that the gift is incomplete, that is, the donor-artist has not parted with complete dominion and control, even though the right of termination is conferred by statute and might never be exercisable. The better interpretation is that copyrights can be effectively transferred by gift and that the right of termination is, at best, a claim that may under certain circumstances be exercised against the transferred property. A transferred copyright may also be interpreted as a completed gift for a term of years.[51] In any event, the right of termination does not enable the artist's heirs to reclaim possession of the work of art transferred by gift. The property subject to the right of termination is the copyright interest and in most cases is of little or no value as it applies to a work of art. Although there is no authority, the right of termination should not make an otherwise validly transferred copyright includable in a deceased artist's estate under section 2038, since the right of termination was not retained by the artist, but was reserved to the artist by statute. Remember, the right of termination only applies to works of art created on or after January 1, 1978.

Testamentary Transfers

Generally

An artist must provide for the disposition of his or her unsold works after death. The fair market value of the artwork on the date of death or six months later is included in the artist's gross estate and the estate tax is calculated by including in the tax base the artist's taxable gifts made after December 31, 1976.[52]

A specific bequest in the will should be used to leave the artwork outright to the beneficiary. The bequest should include any copyright interest that may exist in the artwork. The item must be sufficiently identified to prevent confusion and law suits after the artist's death. When an artist leaves a great many works, identification often presents a problem, so identification should be as precise as possible. If the beneficiary lives in a different city from the testator, the cost of shipping must be considered. That cost is borne by the beneficiary unless a special clause is used in the will.

If the artist leaves artwork in trust, it is advisable to include a clause pertaining to unproductive property. This should be done when a credit shelter or nonmarital trust is part of the artist's estate plan. (See form at end of chapter.) If the trust is to qualify for the marital deduction then a provision giving the surviving spouse the power to make the trust productive of income must be included in the trust clause.

Will-Bumping

The interaction of the tax law and the copyright law can produce another unforeseen problem with regard to works of art created before January 1, 1978, as to which there is a dual term of copyright protection. For works of art created after January 1, 1978, the term of copyright protection is generally fifty years after the artist's death.[53] Under the old copyright law, the period of protection was unrelated to the artist's death. Instead, it was for a term of twenty-eight years that could be renewed in the final year for another twenty-eight years.[54] The renewal right could be exercised by the artist or his or her successors. Therefore, under the old copyright law, for a work of art in its initial term when the artist died, the artist's will could only dispose of what was left of the initial term, since the right to renew the copyright, and consequently the copyright ownership during the renewal term, were governed by the Copyright Act, which established priorities among family members with regard to the right to renew. This means that the artist may think he has disposed of the copyright in one manner under his or her will when in fact the will is "bumped" and the copyright is disposed of under the copyright law.[55] Although this will not be a problem in cases when the copyright is disposed of to family members in the same manner as the copyright law provides or when the copyright is of no value, the careful estate planner must nevertheless be aware of the potential problem.

Selling Expenses

The deductibility of selling expenses is discussed in detail in chapter 12. If the artist's will directs the sale of his or her works, the gallery commissions and other selling expenses are allowable as estate tax deductions.[56] The rules governing deduction of selling expenses from the artist's estate are the same as those with respect to the collector's estate and are discussed in detail in chapter 12 at pages 611-19.

Post Mortem Sales

Under current law when an artist dies, his or her works of art receive for income tax purposes for sales after his or her death, a stepped up basis equal to the fair market value at the date of death.[57] As a practical matter, the six-month alternative valuation is the same as the valuation on the date of death. The full amount of the predeath appreciation is not subject to the income tax. Equally important, the character of the works of art for income tax purposes changes from ordinary income property to capital gain property, and any post mortem appreciation realized on sales by the estate or the heirs is treated as capital gain.[58] That assumes that the artist's estate is not deemed to be in the trade or business of selling paintings. Ordinarily, if the executor merely conducts an orderly administration of the artist's estate in collecting and protecting assets and maximizing their value, even over a long period of time, the executor is not deemed to be carrying on a trade or business.

The difference in character between ordinary income and capital gain income is less critical now than before the 1988 revisions of the Internal Revenue Code went into effect. Under the Tax Reform Act of 1986, the distinction between capital gain and ordinary income is eliminated for tax rate purposes, beginning in 1988. However, the distinction is still important, since it is likely that the tax rates on ordinary income will increase, and, as shown above, a charitable contribution of ordinary income property produces a vastly different result from a contribution of capital gain property.

The *Tobey* case, discussed at pages 679-80, held that an artist's income from the sale of his or her work was "earned income" for the purpose of the foreign income exclusion under section

911. That finding will cause problems if it is extended beyond its application to section 911. Income earned before death is characterized as "income in respect of a decedent," as that term is defined in section 691, when it is received.[59] Therefore, the IRS might argue that under the *Tobey* rationale the proceeds of sales of the artist's work after death constitute income in respect of a decedent,[60] that there is no step-up in basis on the artist's death,[61] and that the sales proceeds are ordinary income.[62] Obviously, that result would not be nearly so favorable to the taxpayer as a step-up in basis and capital gain treatment.

Notwithstanding *Tobey*, post mortem sales should not be treated as income in respect of a decedent.[63] The proper test of whether an item is income in respect of a decedent is whether the decedent had a right to the proceeds at the time of death.[64] The courts have rejected the "economic activities" test of the IRS. Under that theory, post mortem income derived from a disposition of a creative person's works and copyrights was treated as income in respect of a decedent on the premise that such income was "earned" by the deceased artist during his or her lifetime and is tantamount to deferred compensation. The preferred test is this: if further negotiations or activities are necessary to realize the proceeds on sale, the post mortem proceeds are not income in respect of a decedent.[65]

Generally, four elements must be present for an item to be income in respect of a decedent:[66]

1. The decedent must have entered into a legally significant arrangement for the disposition of the property to elevate the legal right beyond a mere expectancy;
2. The decedent must have performed the substantive acts required as conditions to the sale, so that the property was in a deliverable state at the date of the decedent's death;
3. There must be no economically material contingencies in existence at the date of the decedent's death that might disrupt the sale; and

4. The decedent would have eventually received the proceeds if he or she had lived.

Therefore, under current law the post mortem sales in an artist's estate are not treated as income in respect of a decedent.

The above result would have been changed under the carryover basis rules that were scheduled to come into effect on January 1, 1980, but that were repealed by the Crude Oil Windfall Profits Tax Bill of 1980. Under what was to have been section 1023(a), the basis of all "carryover basis property" that passes from a decedent was to be determined by reference to the basis of the property in the hands of the decedent. Section 1221(3)(C) stated that the term "capital asset" does not include property held by a taxpayer "in whose hands the basis of such property is determined, for purposes of determining gain from a sale or exchange, in whole or in part by reference to the basis of such property in the hands" of the taxpayer whose personal efforts created the property. Therefore, under the proposed carryover basis rules, the creator could not leave artwork under a will to an individual who could realize capital gains on their sale, since the property could not qualify as a capital asset. If those provisions are ever reintroduced into the Internal Revenue Code, it would be extremely important to check their effects on an artist's estate.

PAYING THE TAX

The federal estate tax is due nine months after the death of the artist.[67] If the assets in the estate consist of valuable works of art, there may be insufficient funds available to pay the estate tax.

The IRS may grant an extension of time to pay the estate tax for a reasonable period up to twelve months. Section 6161 gives the IRS the sole discretion to grant an extension on the basis of a showing of reasonable cause. The extension may be for a period up to ten years if the proper application is made and the IRS determines that there is sufficient reasonable cause. Reasonable cause may include:

1. Insufficient liquid assets to pay the tax;
2. Substantial estate assets consisting of rights to receive payments in the future;
3. Assets subject to litigation claims; and
4. Insufficient funds to pay family allowances and creditors' claims.[68]

The executor of the artist's estate may also elect to pay the estate tax in installments. Under section 6166, the estate tax may be paid in installments over a fourteen-year period, with the first four annual payments consisting of interest only. For the estate to be eligible for installment payments, the artist must have been actively engaged in the trade or business of being an artist and producing the works of art that are a part of the estate. Although the term "trade or business" is not specifically defined, the United States Supreme Court in *Commissioner v. Groetzinger*[69] does offer some help. In *Groetzinger* the Court stated that, in order to be engaged in a trade or business, the taxpayer must be involved in the activity with continuity and regularity, and the taxpayer's primary purpose for engaging in the activity must be for income or profit. A sporadic activity, a hobby, or an amusement diversion does not qualify. The Court reaffirmed the "facts and circumstances" test and thereby rejected the test that a trade or business involves holding oneself out to others as being engaged in the selling of goods and services. The Court stated that a judicial attempt to formulate and impose a test for all situations would be counterproductive, unhelpful, even somewhat precarious for the overall integrity of the Internal Revenue Code.

To be eligible for installment payments the artist's estate must also consist of works of art created by the artist whose value exceeds 35 percent of the artist's adjusted gross estate (the gross estate less all deductions other than marital and charitable deductions).

If the artist's estate is eligible for installment payments, interest only at a preferred rate is payable on the first four installments.

The interest on the first $345,800 of tax liability ($1 million worth of assets) less the unified credit of $192,800 is limited to a 4 percent rate. Generally, that rate applies only to $153,000 of tax liability ($345,800 minus $192,800). The regular interest rate (which changes every six months) will apply on all amounts in excess of $153,000 of tax liability. The maximum payment period is fourteen rather than fifteen years because the due date for the last payment of interest coincides with the due date for the first installment of tax.

Disposition of the works of art by the estate may accelerate the payment of the deferred tax liability to the year of disposition.[70] The artist's estate may also claim an estate tax deduction for the interest payable on the deferred payment of the estate tax.

FIDUCIARY RESPONSIBILITY

No discussion of an artist's estate is complete without mentioning *In re Rothko*.[71] Mark Rothko, an abstract expressionist painter, died on February 25, 1970. His will was admitted to probate on April 27, 1970, and letters testamentary were issued to his executors. On May 21, 1970, less than one month after their appointment, the executors signed contracts selling 798 works of art by Rothko to corporations controlled by one of the executors.

The executors of Rothko's estate were Bernard J. Reis of Marlborough Gallery, his dealer; Theodoros Stamos, a friend and struggling artist; and Morton Levine, a friend and professor. Reis also drafted Rothko's will, even though he was not licensed to practice law in New York. The case, because of Rothko's fame and the enormous dollar amounts involved, received a great deal of publicity, but really did no more than reaffirm existing New York law.

An executor must not be involved in self-dealing of any kind or nature, must avoid all conflicts of interest, and must not violate the duty of loyalty to the estate.[72] An executor must use such diligence and prudence in the care and management of the estate assets and affairs as would prudent persons of discretion and intelligence, accented by "not honesty alone, but the punctillio of an honor the most sensitive."[73] Alleged good faith on the part of a fiduciary who is forgetful of his or her duty is not enough.

Reis and Stamos each had an obvious conflict of interest; both were fined and removed as executors. Levine had no conflict of interest, had objected orally to the proposed sales to the corporations controlled by Reis, and had sought independent legal counsel. That was not enough—in fining Levine over $6 million and removing him as an executor, the court stated:

> [H]e could not close his eyes, remain passive or move with unconcern in the face of the obvious loss to be visited upon the estate by participation in those business arrangements and then shelter himself behind the claimed counsel of an attorney.[74]

It should be clear that selection of an executor of an artist's estate should be done with care and in such a manner to avoid the problems that arose in the *Rothko* case. The *Rothko* decision should be read and reread each year by every attorney who represents artists.

THE ARTIST'S INCOME TAX

An artist completes schedule C of form 1040—the federal income tax return—reporting income from sales and deducting the ordinary and necessary expenses in creating the works of art. The Tax Reform Act of 1986 attempted to change the manner in which an artist claimed deductions for expenses. New section 263A, effective January 1, 1987, provided uniform capitalization rules to govern the treatment of costs incurred in the production of property for resale. The section was enacted to prevent the inappropriate mismatching of income and expenses that results from allowing the current deduction of the costs of producing the property. Section 263A vastly complicated the record-keeping burden for artists by requiring them to capitalize expenses and allocate the expenses among the various works of art.

Partial relief from those rules was granted by Internal Revenue News Release IR-88-81 of May 13, 1988, which created a simplified method for deducting the business expenses of artists. Under the new method, the artist can generally deduct 50 percent of his or her business expenses in the year in which they were incurred and 25 percent in each of the two succeeding years.

Further relief was granted by the Technical and Miscellaneous Revenue Act of 1988. That Act adds new section 263A(h), which provides that the uniform capitalization rules of section 263A do not apply to any otherwise deductible expense paid by an individual engaged in the business of being an artist. An artist is defined as any individual whose personal efforts create or may reasonably be expected to create a picture, painting, sculpture, statue, etching, drawing, cartoon, graphic design, or original print edition. Expenses paid or incurred by a personal service corporation that directly relate to the activities of a qualified employee-owner may also qualify for the exemption to the extent that the expenses would qualify if paid or incurred directly by the employee-owner (the artist).

In determining whether an expense is paid or incurred in the business of being an artist, the originality and the uniqueness of the item created (or to be created) and the predominance of the aesthetic value over the utilitarian value of the item created are to be taken into account. The House Committee Report gives this as an example: any expense paid or incurred in producing jewelry, silverware, pottery, furniture, and similar household items is generally not considered as being paid or incurred in the business of being an artist.

MISCELLANEOUS ISSUES AFFECTING ARTISTS

The Artist and Merchandising Rights

Those artists who become well known to the public should be aware of the cluster of prerogatives known as merchandising rights. Generally, they include the right to authorize the use of the name, likeness, or other attribute of an artist or artistic work on or in connection with the products of another party.[75] Thus the creator of a work of "pop art," for example, might not be averse to licensing the right to reproduce his or her work on, for instance, tote bags or coffee mugs—and to receive royalties from their sale. The contract granting merchandising rights to another party, that is the licensee, should include, among other items, the following provisions:

Grant

The artist would grant the licensee the exclusive rights to produce and distribute specified attributes of the artist or an artistic work on or in connection with the specified goods. The grant should include a reservation of all other rights to the artist. The goods in connection with the license should be as narrowly described as possible to permit the artist to license many different parties to manufacture and sell many different kinds of goods. For example, an artist might wish to license one party to reproduce and sell an artistic work on a poster and another party to reproduce and sell the same artistic work on paper plates. Therefore, neither license should be for "paper goods," but rather for the specific category or categories of goods involved.

Ownership

The artist is the sole and exclusive owner of all merchandising rights in the artistic work subject only to the specific rights licensed to the licensee, and all permitted uses of the artistic work will inure to the benefit of the artist.

Consideration

The artist should be paid a percentage of all moneys received by the licensee arising from that party's exercise of any rights granted under the contract.

Term

The duration of the license agreement should be specified. The licensee should generally be permitted a nonexclusive right to sell off inventory for a specific period of time, often six months.

Territory

The territory covered by the grant of rights should be specified.

Quality Control

A sample of each category of licensed goods, as well as a sample of each item of packaging, advertising, and promotional material relating to the goods, should be submitted to the artist for written approval prior to distribution. Approval should not be unreasonably withheld. No item disapproved by the artist should be distributed.

Indemnity

The licensee should indemnify and hold harmless the artist from any loss or liability incurred by the artist from any defect or violation of third-party rights relating to the licensed goods or any of the packaging, advertising, or promotional material relating to the goods when the artist's work is used in connection with the merchandising agreement.

Definition of Artist as It Applies to Real Estate

A few states, such as New York, have passed special legislation addressing the living and working space of artists—either exceptions to zoning laws or special provisions for artists.

Who qualifies as an artist under statutes of this nature has posed problems. The New York City ordinance defines "artist" to mean a person who is regularly engaged in the fine arts, such as painting and sculpture, or in the performing and creative arts, including choreography and film-making, or in the composition of music on a professional basis, and who is certified by the City

Department of Cultural Affairs, the State Council on the Arts, or both.[76] The question of who can be so certified raises complex questions that could easily lead to litigation.

Photography

The photograph as a work of art is becoming more important, and prices for older photographs have risen dramatically. The photographer as an artist has a number of problems. Most important, he or she must convince the buyer that the photograph is a unique, original work that exists in no other copy or in no more than a given number of copies. Obviously, an unlimited number of duplicates could be produced from a photographic negative, each of which would be an original, lessening the value of the first copy.

One solution would be to have the artist sign the back of the first photograph, indicating the number of copies made and warranting that no further copies will be made, perhaps indicating that the negative will be destroyed.

Computer technology has caused new problems for the photographer. Photographs can now be changed by deleting parts of the image, adding new parts, or simply moving the image around. Questions as to what is the original, who owns the copyright, and whether a new work of art is being created are new potential problems for the photographer.

Video Art

With the advent of hand-held cameras, the ability to make video recordings on videocassettes with extensive special effects has become available to more and more individuals. Artists have been experimenting with videotape as art. The artist who creates a work of art on videotape may use multiple tapes or may create the tape in conjunction with other art forms. The video artist would want to make sure that when his or her work of art is exhibited, it is shown in the manner in which it was created. The most difficult problem for the video artist is the ease of video reproduction, which means that copyright protection for the video artist is most important. The artist selling a video artwork should use an agreement that protects the copyright, and if the artist sells the video artwork through a gallery, the gallery should be required to protect the artist's copyright. This can be done by written agreement requiring any individual who purchases or rents a video artwork not to make further copies, reproduce it in any manner, or show it in any manner not consistent with the manner in which it was created.[77]

Artistic Materials

Questions can arise concerning the durability of a work of art over a period of time. In other words, is there some implied warranty of fitness that an artist or his or her gallery makes to a buyer with respect to the quality or durability of the materials used in the work of art? A collector who purchases an expensive work would not be happy if it began to fade or fall apart after a period of time and might seek redress against the artist, the gallery, or both.

NOTES
to Chapter 13

1. Treas. Reg. § 20.2031-6.

2. Treas. Reg. §§ 25.2512-1, 1.170A-1(c)(2).

3. *See* Sloane, *Valuing Artists' Estates: What is Fair?*, ARTNEWS, Apr. 1976, *reprinted in* 2 ART & L. No. 5 (Summer 1976); Echter, *Equitable Treatment for the Artist's Estate*, 114 TR. & EST. 394 (1975); Cutrow, *Estate Planning for the Artist*, in PLI, ART LAW 413 (R. Lerner ed. 1988).

4. Rev. Proc. 66-49, 1966-2 C.B. 1257.

5. *Compare* Maudlin v. Commissioner, 60 T.C. 749 (1973); *with* Rebay v. Commissioner, 22 T.C.M. (CCH) 181 (1963).

6. Treas. Reg. § 20.2031-l(b).

7. Estate of David Smith v. Commissioner, 57 T.C. 650 (1972), *aff'd*, 510 F.2d 479 (2d Cir.), *cert. denied*, 523 U.S. 827 (1975). See further discussion of *Smith* in chapter 12 at pages 611-12.

8. Hoffman, *Artists May Have Unexpectedly Large Estates*, CPA J., June, 1972.

9. Treas. Reg. § 20.2031-2(e); Rev. Rul. 59-60, 1959-1 C.B. 237.

10. Cutrow, *supra* note 3; Smith, *supra* note 7, at 658.

11. *See* Smith, *supra* note 7, at 659.

12. *See* Smith, *supra* note 7, at 659; Treas. Reg. § 20.2031-1(b).

13. *See* Smith, *supra* note 7, at 658.

14. *See* Echter, *Equitable Treatment for the Artist's Estate*, 114 TR. & EST. 394 (1975).

15. *See* Smith, *supra* note 7, at 659; Publicker v. Commissioner, 206 F.2d 250 (3d Cir. 1953).

16. Treas. Reg. § 20.2053-3(d)(2). See discussion and cases in chapter 12 at pages 611-17.

17. Calder v. Commissioner, 85 T.C. 713 (1985).

18. The IRS attempted to guess how many works from each of the six gifts would be sold each year and multiplied the annual estimated sales by each of the six persons by the agreed-on value of each work. The IRS then applied a present-value factor and treated the sale as if it were an annuity.

19. Berghe, *The Artist, the Art Market and the Income Tax*, 29 Tax L. Rev. 491, 514 (1974); Feld, *Artists, Art Collectors and Income Tax*, 60 B.U.L. Rev. 625 (1980).

20. I.R.C. § 170(e)(1)(A); Treas. Reg. § 1.170A-4(a)(1).

21. I.R.C. § 1221(3)(C).

22. I.R.C. § 170(e)(1)(A); Treas. Reg. § 1.170A-4(a)(1).

23. Maniscalco v. Commissioner, 632 F.2d 6 (6th Cir. 1980), *aff'g* 37 T.C.M. (CCH) 1174 (1978).

24. I.R.C. §§ 1221(3)(C), 1015.

25. R. Duffy, Art Law: Representing Artists, Dealers, and Collectors 234 (1977).

26. Berghe, *supra* note 19.

27. I.R.C. § 2055(a).

28. I.R.C. §§ 508(d)(2), (a), (e), 2055(e)(1); Treas. Reg. § 20.2055-5(b).

29. This provision is discussed in greater detail in chapter 12 at pages 567-71.

30. See Treas. Reg. § 20.2055-2(e)(i)(ii)(e) example (1).

31. N.Y. Est. Powers & Trusts Law § 5-3.3 (repealed 1981 N.Y. Laws ch. 461, effective July 7, 1981); *In re* Cairo, 35 A.D.2d 76, 321 N.Y.S.2d 925 (2d Dep't 1970), *aff'd without opinion*, 29 N.Y.2d 527, 272 N.E.2d 574, 324 N.Y.S.2d 81 (1971).

32. I.R.C. §§ 2001(c), 2502(a).

33. Duffy, *supra* note 25, at 237; Cutrow, *supra* note 3.

34. I.R.C. § 2036; Treas. Reg. § 25.2511-2.

35. *See* Duffy *supra* note 25, at 200; Berghe, *supra* note 19, at 505.

36. I.R.C. §§ 1221(3)(C), 1015.

37. Estate of W.G. Farrier v. Commissioner, 15 T.C. 277 (1950) (*acq.*); SoRelle v. Commissioner, 22 T.C. 459 (1954).

38. S. Rep. No. 2375, 81st Cong., 2d Sess. 43-44 (1950); *see* Wodehouse v. Commissioner, 177 F.2d 881 (2d Cir. 1949); Wodehouse v. Commissioner, 178 F.2d 987 (4th Cir. 1949).

39. Heim v. Fitzpatrick, 262 F.2d 887 (2d Cir. 1959); Commissioner v. Reece, 233 F.2d 30 (lst Cir. 1956).

40. Tobey v. Commissioner, 60 T.C. 227 (1973). *See* Gen. Couns. Mem. 36, 492 (Nov. 17, 1975).

41. *Id.* at 230.

42. *Id.*

43. Lucas v. Earl, 281 U.S. 111 (1930). The theory in the assignment of income cases is that the one who earns the right to income has retained sufficient control over that income so that it is not properly taxed to anyone else.

44. Berghe, *supra* note 19, at 499; DUFFY, *supra* note 25, at 202.

45. Berghe, *supra* note 19, at 506.

46. Cook v. United States, 599 F.2d 400 (Ct. Cl. 1979).

47. I.R.C. §§ 63(c)(5), 1(i).

48. 17 U.S.C. § 203(a) (1988), as amended by 1988 Act; *see generally* Schaaf, *Estate Planning for Authors and Artists.*, 423 Tax. Mgmt. (BNA).

49. *See* Schaaf, *supra* note 48; Cutrow, *supra* note 3.

50. Treas. Reg. § 25.2511-2.

51. Schaaf, *supra* note 48.

52. I.R.C. §§ 2033, 2001(b)(1).

53. 17 U.S.C. § 302 (1988), as amended by 1988 Act. *See* chapter 8.

54. Copyright Act of 1909, § 23, 35 Stat. 1075 (1909). *See* chapter 8.

55. For an excellent discussion of the problem, see Nevins, *The Magic Kingdom of Will-Bumping: Where Estates Law and Copyright Law Collide*, 35 J. COPYRIGHT SOC'Y 77 (1988).

56. I.R.C. § 2053(a)(2); Treas. Reg. § 20.2053-3(d)(2). *Compare* Estate of David Smith v. Commissioner, 57 T.C. 650 (1972).

57. I.R.C. § 1014.

58. Estate of Jacques Ferber v. Commissioner, 22 T.C. 261 (1954); Garrett v. United States, 120 F. Supp. 193 (Ct. Cl. 1954); Fullerton v. Commissioner, 22 T.C. 372 (1954).

59. I.R.C. § 691; *see* Ferguson, *Income and Deduction in Respect of Decedents and Related Problems*, 25 TAX L. REV. 5 (1969).

60. I.R.C. § 691(a)(3).

61. I.R.C. § 1014(c).

62. I.R.C. §§ 691(a)(3), 1221(3)(C).

63. *See* Berghe, *supra* note 19.

64. Trust Co. v. Ross, 392 F.2d 694 (5th Cir. 1967), *aff'g per curiam* 262 F. Supp. 900 (N.D. Ga. 1966).

65. Keck v. Commissioner, 415 F.2d 531 (6th Cir. 1969), *rev'g* 49 T.C. 313 (1968). *See* Treas. Reg. § 1.691(a)-2(b) example 5(2); Schaaf, *supra* note 48; Biblin & Klinger, *Selected Problems in Estate Planning for Artists and Athletes*, 8 ANN. UCLA-CEB EST. PLAN. INST. 81 (May 1988).

66. Estate of Peterson v. Commissioner, 74 T.C. 630(1980); Note, *Tax Court Enunciates Four Requirements for Determining Whether a Decedent Possessed the Requisite Right to Sale Proceeds at the Time of Death for Purposes of Section 691*, 7 EST. PLAN. 362 (1980).

67. I.R.C. §§ 6018, 6075.

68. Treas. Reg. § 20.6161-1(a).

69. Commissioner v. Groetzinger, 107 S. Ct. 980 (1987); *see* Boyle, *What Is a Trade or Business?*, 39 TAX LAW. 737 (1986): Barcal, *IRS Active Trade or Business Requirement for Estate Tax Deferral: An Analysis*, 54 J. TAX'N 52 (Jan. 1981).

70. I.R.C. § 6166(g).

71. *In re* Rothko, 84 Misc. 2d 830, 379 N.Y.S.2d 923 (Sur. Ct. 1975), *modified*, 56 A.D.2d 499, 392 N.Y.S.2d 870 (1st Dep't), *aff'd*, 43 N.Y.2d 305, 372 N.E.2d 291, 401 N.Y.S.2d 449 (1977).

72. *In re* Scarborough Properties Corp., 25 N.Y.2d 553, 255 N.E.2d 641, 307 N.Y.S.2d 641 (1969); Renz v. Beeman, 589 F.2d 735 (2d Cir. 1978), *cert. denied*, 444 U.S. 834 (1979); RESTATEMENT (SECOND) OF TRUSTS § 170 (1959).

73. Meinhard v. Salmon, 249 N.Y. 458, 464, 164 N.E.2d 545, 550 (1928).

74. Rothko, *supra* note 71, at 320, 372 N.E.2d at 297, 401 N.Y.S.2d at 455.

75. For further reading on this topic, see Borchard & Hart, *Solving Common Problems Arising from Use of Trademarks in the Arts*, 10 COLUM.-VLA J. L. & ARTS 171 (1986).

76. N.Y. MULT. DWELL. LAW art. 7-B, § 276 (McKinney 1986).

77. *See* T. CRAWFORD, LEGAL GUIDE FOR THE VISUAL ARTIST 142 (1986).

FORMS

FORM

CREDIT SHELTER NONMARITAL TRUST FOR ARTIST'S WORKS OF ART

The property bequeathed to the Trustees of the Trust created under this Paragraph B. of Clause FOURTH may consist substantially or entirely of works of art, and it is my intention in creating this trust that my Trustees retain such works of art as investment assets of the trust estate. Notwithstanding the provisions of Clause FOURTH requiring current distribution of the income of the trust, my Trustees shall be under no obligation to sell any work of art or any other non-income-producing asset of the trust estate or to make the trust estate productive of income, except as my Trustees shall in their sole discretion determine, and, for that purpose, I expressly intend that any provisions of the laws of the State of ______________ regarding underproductive property shall not apply to such trust. My Trustees shall not be subject to surcharge for any decline in value of any original assets of such trust.

My Trustees shall be authorized to pay out of the income or out of the principal of the trust created by Clause FOURTH hereof such sums as they shall in their sole discretion determine for insurance, storage, or other care or maintenance of any works of art and to retain out of the income of the trust such sums as they may consider necessary as a reserve for future expenditures for such care and maintenance. I direct that the determination of my Trustees to pay such sums or to retain such income and the determination of my Trustees as to what assets of such trust are properly included in the expression "works of art" shall be conclusive and binding upon all persons interested in such trust.

Tables of Authorities

Cases

References are to chapter (in italic) and footnote.

A

B

C

D

E

F

G

H

I

J

K

L

M

N

O

P

R

S

T

U

V

W

Y

Z

Code of Federal Regulations

Internal Revenue Code

SECTION

Private Letter Rulings

Revenue Proceedings

Revenue Rulings

Treasury Regulations

Uniform Commercial Code

United States Code

28 U.S.C. § 1346(a)(2) . . . *4*: n. 9
28 U.S.C. § 1498(b) . . . *4*: n. 10
31 U.S.C. § 330 . . . *12*: n. 43
41 U.S.C. §§ 601–13 . . . *4*: n. 9

State Statutes

Ala. Code § 13A-9-10 (Supp. 1987) . . . *2*: n. 217
Ala. Code § 41-9-45(4) (1982) . . . *7*: n. 82
Alaska Stat. § 11.46.530 (Supp. 1987) . . . *2*: n. 217
Alaska Stat. § 44.27.050(4) (Supp. 1988) . . . *7*: n. 82
Alaska Stat. § 45.0.326 (Supp. 1986) . . . *1*: n. 38
Ariz. Rev. Stat. Ann. § 13-2004 (Supp. 1987) . . . *2*: n. 217
Ariz. Rev. Stat. Ann. § 41-982(B)(4) (1985) . . . *7*: n. 82
Ariz. Rev. Stat. Ann. §§ 44-351–44-356 (1987) . . . *5*: n. 114
Ariz. Rev. Stat. Ann. § 44-1231.01 (West 1987) . . . *2*: n. 227
Ariz. Rev. Stat. Ann. §§ 44-1771–44-1778 (Supp. 1988) . . . *1*: n. 38
Ark. Code § 5-37-213 (Supp. 1987) . . . *2*: n. 217
Ark. Stat. Ann. §§ 4-73-301–4-73-305 (1987) . . . *2*: n. 230
Ark. Stat. Ann. §§ 68-1806–68-1811 (Supp. 1985) . . . *1*: n. 38
Cal. Civ. Code § 970(h) (1988) . . . *7*: n. 135
Cal. Civ. Code § 970(n)(3) (1988) . . . *7*: n. 137
Cal. Civ. Code § 982 (West Supp. 1976) . . . *8*: n. 9
Cal. Civ. Code § 986 (1988) . . . *10*: ns. 2, 13
Cal. Civ. Code § 986(a) (1988) . . . *10*: ns. 16, 20, 22, 29
Cal. Civ. Code § 986(a)(1) (1988) . . . *10*: n. 23
Cal. Civ. Code § 986(a)(3) (1988) . . . *10*: n. 26
Cal. Civ. Code § 986(a)(7) (1988) . . . *10*: n. 28
Cal. Civ. Code § 986(b) (1988) . . . *10*: n. 19
Cal. Civ. Code § 986(b)(1) (1988) . . . *10*: n. 18
Cal. Civ. Code § 986(b)(2) (1988) . . . *10*: n. 24
Cal. Civ. Code § 986(b)(3) (1988) . . . *10*: n. 27
Cal. Civ. Code § 986(b)(4) (1988) . . . *10*: n. 25
Cal. Civ. Code § 986(c)(1) (1988) . . . *10*: n. 21
Cal. Civ. Code § 986(c)(2) (1988) . . . *10*: n. 17
Cal. Civ. Code § 987 (West Supp. 1988) . . . *9*: n. 34
Cal. Civ. Code § 989 (West Supp. 1988) . . . *9*: n. 35
Cal. Civ. Code § 990 (1988) . . . *7*: n. 134
Cal. Civ. Code § 1738 (1988) . . . *1*: ns. 38, 39, 42
Cal. Civ. Code § 1738.5–1738.9 (1988) . . . *1*: ns. 38, 39, 42
Cal. Civ. Code §§ 1740–1745.5 (West Supp. 1988) . . . *2*: n. 230
Cal. Civ. Code §§ 1790 *et seq.* (West Supp. 1988) . . . *2*: n. 90
Cal. Civ. Code §§ 1899–1899.11 (West Supp. 1988) . . . *5*: n. 114
Cal. Civ. Code § 3344 (1988) . . . *7*: n. 124
Cal. Civ. Proc. Code § 338.3 (West Supp. 1985) . . . *2*: n. 186

Colo. Rev. Stat. §§ 6-15-101–6-15-104 (Supp. 1986) . . . *1*: n. 38
Colo. Rev. Stat. §§ 12-44.5-101–12-44.5-108 (1986) . . . *2*: n. 227
Colo. Rev. Stat. § 18-5-110 (Supp. 1986) . . . *2*: n. 217
Colo. Rev. Stat. § 18-7-104(a) (Supp. 1985) . . . *7*: n. 81
Colo. Rev. Stat. § 18-7-104(b) (Supp. 1985) . . . *7*: n. 81
Conn. Gen. Stat. Ann. § 10-370 (West Supp. 1989) . . . *7*: n. 82
Conn. Gen. Stat. Ann. §§ 42-116k–42-116m (West Supp. 1987) . . . *1*: n. 38
Conn. Gen. Stat. Ann. § 53a-140 (West Supp. 1988) . . . *2*: n. 216
Conn. Gen. Stat. Ann. § 53a-141 (West Supp. 1987) . . . *2*: n. 217
Fla. Stat. Ann. § 540.08 (West 1972) . . . *7*: ns. 139, 140
Fla. Stat. Ann. §§ 686.501–686.503 (West 1989) . . . *1*: n. 38
Ga. Code Ann. § 16-12-80(b)(2) (1984) . . . *7*: n. 81
Ga. Code Ann. § 50-12-23(4) (1986) . . . *7*: n. 82
Ga. Code Ann. §§ 106-2001–106-2008 (Supp. 1986) . . . *2*: n. 230
Hawaii Rev. Stat. §§ 481F-1–481F-9 (Supp. 1987) . . . *2*: n. 230
Idaho Code §§ 28-11-101–28-11-106 . . . *1*: n. 38
Ill. Rev. Stat. Ann. ch. 121½, ¶¶ 361–369 (West Supp. 1987) . . . *2*: n. 230
Ill. Rev. Stat. Ann. ch. 121½, ¶¶ 1401–1407 (West Supp. 1988) . . . *1*: n. 38
Ind. Code Ann. § 4-23-2-2(d) (Burns 1986) . . . *7*: n. 82
Iowa Code Ann. § 728.7 (1979) . . . *7*: n. 81
Iowa Code Ann. §§ 556D.1–556D.5 (West 1989) . . . *1*: n. 38
Ky. Rev. Stat. § 391.170 (1984) . . . *7*: ns. 131, 139
Ky. Rev. Stat. § 516.110 (Supp. 1986) . . . *2*: n. 217
Ky. Rev. Stat. Ann. § 365.850–365.990 (Michie Co. 1987) . . . *1*: n. 38
La. Rev. Stat. Ann. § 25.345 (West Supp. 1988) . . . *5*: n. 114
La. Rev. Stat. Ann. § 51:2151 (1987) . . . *1*: n. 38
Mass. Ann. Laws ch. 104A, §§ 1–6 (Law. Co-op. Supp. 1987) . . . *1*: n. 38
Mass. Ann. Laws ch. 231, § 85S; ch. 260, § 2c (1984) . . . *9*: n. 39
Mass. Gen. Laws Ann. ch. 106, § 2-316A (West Supp. 1988) . . . *2*: n. 90
Md. Com. Law Code Ann. § 2-316.1 (Supp. 1987) . . . *2*: n. 90
Md. Com. Law Code Ann. § 11-8A-01–11-8A-04 (1983) . . . *1*: n. 38
Md. Com. Law Code Ann. §§ 14-501–14-505(1987) . . . *2*: n. 230
Me. Rev. Stat. Ann. tit. 11, § 2-316(5) (West Supp. 1987) . . . *2*: n. 90
Me. Rev. Stat. Ann. tit. 27, § 601 (Supp. 1988) . . . *5*: n. 114
Me. Rev. Stat. Ann. tit. 27, § 303 (Supp. 1987) . . . *9*: n. 38
Mich. Comp. Laws Ann. §§ 442.311–442.315 (West Supp. 1987) . . . *1*: n. 38
Mich. Comp. Laws Ann. §§ 442.321–442.325 (West Supp. 1987) . . . *2*: ns. 22, 222
Mich. Comp. Laws Ann. § 442.323 (West Supp. 1987) . . . *2*: n. 51
Mich. Comp. Laws Ann. § 442.324 (West Supp. 1987) . . . *2*: n. 223

N.Y. Arts & Cult. Aff. Law § 13.01(4) (McKinney 1984 & Supp. 1988) . . . *2*: n. 50

N.Y. Arts & Cult. Aff. Law § 14.03 (McKinney 1988) . . . *4*: n. 12, *9*: n. 36

N.Y. City Admin. Code tit. 10, ch. 1, § 10-117 (McKinney 1988) . . . *7*: ns. 2, 70

N.Y. City Admin. Code tit. 15, ch. 5, subch. 2, §§ 20-707–20-711 (1988) . . . *2*: n. 254

N.Y. City Admin. Code tit. A, ch. 64, reg. 206 (1988) . . . *2*: n. 233

N.Y. Civ. Prac. L.&R. 213(6) (McKinney 1972 & Supp. 1989) . . . *2*: n. 195

N.Y. Civ. Prac. L.&R. 302(a) (McKinney 1972 & Supp. 1988) . . . *3*: n. 47

N.Y. Civ. Rights Law § 50 (McKinney 1976 & Supp. 1988) . . . *7*: ns. 124, 127

N.Y. Civ. Rights Law § 50-a (McKinney 1976 & Supp. 1988) . . . *7*: ns. 124, 127

N.Y. Civ. Rights Law § 50-b (McKinney 1976 & Supp. 1988) . . . *7*: ns. 124, 127

N.Y. Civ. Rights Law § 51 (McKinney 1976 & Supp. 1988) . . . *7*: ns. 124, 127

N.Y. Est. Powers & Trusts Law § 5-3.3 (McKinney 1967) (repealed 1981 N.Y. Laws ch. 461, effective July 7, 1981) . . . *12*: n. 107, *13*: n. 31

N.Y. Est. Powers & Trusts Law § 11-1.1(b)(22) (McKinney Supp. 1989) . . . *12*: n. 163

N.Y. Exec. Law § 63(12) (McKinney 1982) . . . *3*: n. 17

N.Y. Gen. Bus. Law art. 12-E (McKinney 1966) . . . *8*: n. 8

N.Y. Gen. Bus. Law § 24 (McKinney 1988) . . . *3*: n. 31

N.Y. Gen. Bus. Law § 136 (McKinney 1988) . . . *7*: ns. 26, 28

N.Y. Gen. Bus. Law § 137 (McKinney 1988) . . . *7*: n. 69

N.Y. Gen. Bus. Law § 349 (McKinney 1988) . . . *3*: n. 17

N.Y. Gen. Oblig. Law § 5-701 (McKinney 1989) . . . *1*: n. 20

N.Y. Gen. Oblig. Law § 5-701(a)(1) (McKinney 1989) . . . *1*: n. 22

N.Y. Gen. Oblig. Law § 5-701(a)(6) (McKinney 1989) . . . *3*: ns. 13, 14

N.Y. Mult. Dwell. Law art. 7-B, § 276 (McKinney 1986) . . . *13*: n. 76

N.Y. Penal Law § 155.05 (McKinney 1975 & Supp. 1989) . . . *1*: n. 15

N.Y. Penal Law § 170.05 (McKinney 1975 & Supp. 1988) . . . *2*: n. 214

N.Y. Penal Law § 170.45 (McKinney 1975 & Supp. 1988) . . . *2*: n. 218

N.Y. Penal Law § 235.21 (McKinney 1980 & Supp. 1989) . . . *7*: n. 122

N.C. Gen. Stat. §§ 25C-1–25C-5 (Supp. 1986) . . . *1*: n. 38

N.C. Gen. Stat. § 121-2 (Supp. 1988) . . . *5*: n. 114

N.C. Gen. Stat. § 121-7 (Supp. 1988) . . . *5*: n. 114

N.D. Cent. Code § 47-07-14 (1987) . . . *5*: n. 114

N.D. Cent. Code § 54-54-05.4 (1982) . . . *7*: n. 82

Ohio Rev. Code Ann. §§ 1339.71–1339.78 (Page Supp. 1986) . . . *1*: n. 38

Ohio Rev. Code Ann. § 2913.31 (Baldwin Supp. 1987) . . . *2*: ns. 213, 219, 220

Ohio Rev. Code Ann. § 2913.32 (Baldwin Supp. 1987) . . . *2*: n. 217

Okla. Stat. Ann. tit. 21, § 1021.1 (West 1983) . . . *7*: n. 81

VA. CODE § 18.2-383(2) (1988) . . . *7*: n. 81
WASH. REV. CODE ANN. § 2-316(A) (West Supp. 1988) . . . *2*: n. 90
WASH. REV. CODE ANN. §§ 18.110.010–18.110.905 (Supp. 1987) . . . *1*: n. 38
WASH. REV. CODE ANN. § 27.40.034 (1988) . . . *5*: n. 113
W. VA. CODE § 61-8A-1(7)(c) (1989) . . . *7*: n. 81
WIS. STAT. ANN. §§ 129.01–129.08 (West Supp. 1986) . . . *1*: n. 38
WIS. STAT. ANN. § 943.38(3)(a) (West Supp. 1987) . . . *2*: n. 217
WYO. STAT. § 9-2-903(a)(v) (1987) . . . *7*: n. 82

Index

B

C

D

E

G

H

J

K

L

M

Q

R

U

V

Y

Z